FEB   1997

FRIENDSWOOD PUBLIC LIBRARY

3 3093 00111 0010

261.08
ENC

Encyclopedia of
  Mormonism.
  Selections.
The church and society
  : selections from

Friendswood Public Library
416 So. Friendswood Drive
Friendswood, TX 77546-3952

DEMCO

Friendswood Public Library
416 So. Friendswood Drive
Frienc   952

D1472875

THE CHURCH AND SOCIETY

BOARD OF EDITORS

EDITOR IN CHIEF

Daniel H. Ludlow
Brigham Young University

SENIOR EDITORS

Robert J. Matthews
Brigham Young University

Charles D. Tate, Jr.
Brigham Young University

Robert K. Thomas
Brigham Young University

EDITORS

Stan L. Albrecht
Brigham Young University

S. Kent Brown
Brigham Young University

Richard L. Bushman
Columbia University

Ronald K. Esplin
Brigham Young University

Addie Fuhriman
University of Utah

Jeanne B. Inouye
Provo, Utah

Truman G. Madsen
Brigham Young University

Terrance D. Olson
Brigham Young University

Larry C. Porter
Brigham Young University

Noel B. Reynolds
Brigham Young University

John W. Welch
Brigham Young University

PROJECT COORDINATOR

Doris Bayly Brower

THE CHURCH AND SOCIETY

SELECTIONS FROM THE
ENCYCLOPEDIA OF MORMONISM

EDITED BY
DANIEL H. LUDLOW

Friendswood Public Library
416 So. Friendswood Drive
Friendswood, TX 77546-3952

DESERET BOOK COMPANY
SALT LAKE CITY, UTAH

© 1992 by Macmillan Publishing Company, a division of Macmillan, Inc.

This collection of articles from the *Encyclopedia of Mormonism* is published by Deseret Book Company under license from Macmillan Publishing Company.

© 1995 by Deseret Book Company

All rights reserved. No part of this book may be reproduced or transmitted in any form or by any means, electronic or mechanical, including photocopying, recording, or by any information storage and retrieval system, without permission in writing from Macmillan Publishing Company, 866 Third Avenue, New York, NY 10022 or Maxwell Macmillan Canada, Inc., 1200 Eglinton Avenue East, Suite 200, Don Mills, Ontario M3C 3N1.

Deseret Book is a registered trademark of Deseret Book Company.

Library of Congress Cataloging-in-Publication Data

Encyclopedia of Mormonism. Selections.
   The church and society : selections from the Encyclopedia of
Mormonism / edited by Daniel H. Ludlow.
     p.   cm.
   Includes bibliographical references and index.
   ISBN 0-87579-925-6 (pbk.)
    1. Church of Jesus Christ of Latter-day Saints—Encyclopedias.
   2. Mormon Church—Encyclopedias. 3. Mormons—Encyclopedias.
   I. Ludlow, Daniel H. II. Title.
BX8605.5.E623   1995
261'.08'8283—dc20   95-31445
                                                        CIP

Printed in the United States of America

10 9 8 7 6 5 4 3 2 1

CONTENTS

LIST OF ARTICLES

LIST OF CONTRIBUTORS

Frank D. Allan
George Washington Medical School
Autopsy

Darl Anderson
Businessman, Mesa, AZ
Non-Mormons, Social Relations with

Gerald S. Argetsinger
Rochester Institute of Technology, Rochester, NY
Cumorah Pageant

Stephen J. Bahr
Brigham Young University
Social Characteristics

Margaret P. Baker
Brigham Young University—Hawaii
Humor

Steven W. Baldridge
Brigham Young University
Granite Mountain Record Vault

Brent A. Barlow
Brigham Young University
Procreation

Roger M. Barrus
Hamden-Sydney College, VA
Politics: Political History

Mary K. Beard
Physician, Salt Lake City
Abortion

Martha Nibley Beck
Writer, Provo, UT
Women, Roles of: Historical and Sociological Development

Kenneth H. Beesley
LDS Business College, Salt Lake City
LDS Business College

Terrell H. Bell
Former U.S. Commissioner of Education
Education: Educational Attainment

Alfred Benney
Fairfield College, Fairfield, CT
Catholicism and Mormonism

Allen E. Bergin
Brigham Young University
Mental Health

William E. Berrett
Brigham Young University
Church Educational System (CES)

Robert W. Blair
Brigham Young University
Vocabulary, Latter-day Saint

Reed H. Blake
Brigham Young University
Calamities and Disasters

V. Ben Bloxham
Brigham Young University
Family History Centers

Reed H. Bradford
Brigham Young University
Family: Teachings About the Family

Martha Sonntag Bradley
Brigham Young University
Folk Art

Merrill Bradshaw
Brigham Young University
Mormon Youth Symphony and Chorus

F. Neil Brady
San Diego State University
Ethics

Rodney H. Brady
Bonneville International Corp., Salt Lake City
Bonneville International Corporation
Business: Church Participation in Business

Carlfred Broderick
University of Southern California
Suffering in the World

Doris Bayly Brower
Brigham Young University
World Conferences on Records

Victor L. Brown, Jr.
Church Welfare Services, Citrus Heights, CA
Fathers' Blessings
Homosexuality

Gary C. Bryner
Brigham Young University
Politics: Political Teachings

Gary L. Bunker
Brigham Young University
Stereotyping of Latter-day Saints

Eliot A. Butler
Brigham Young University
Brigham Young University: Provo, Utah, Campus

L. Reynolds Cahoon
Church Family History Dept., Salt Lake City
FamilySearch™

Tad R. Callister
Attorney, Glendale, CA
Dedications

Elaine Anderson Cannon
Author, St. George, UT
LDS Student Associations

Janath Russell Cannon
Church Temple Matron, Frankfurt, Germany
Sisterhood

Mark W. Cannon
Consultant, Washington, DC
Civic Duties

K. Codell Carter
Brigham Young University
Epistemology

David J. Cherrington
Brigham Young University
Poverty, Attitudes Toward
Work, Role of

Alan Cherry
Oral History Researcher, Provo, UT
Blacks

C. Richard Chidester
Church Educational System, Salt Lake City
Worldly, Worldliness

Bruce L. Christensen
Public Broadcasting System, Alexandria, VA
Broadcasting
Satellite Communications System

Bryce J. Christensen
Rockford Institute Center on the Family in America, Rockford, IL
Adultery

Joe J. Christensen
General Authority, Salt Lake City
Seminaries

Carol L. Clark
Church General Relief Society Office, Salt Lake City
Mormon Handicraft

Victor B. Cline
University of Utah
Pornography

Robert A. Cloward
Church Educational System, Cedar City, UT
Dead Sea Scrolls: LDS Perspective

John Cobb, Jr.
Claremont College
Theodicy

Rex E. Cooper
Church Correlation Dept., Salt Lake City
Symbols, Cultural and Artistic

Soren F. Cox
Brigham Young University
Interfaith Relationships: Other Faiths

Richard H. Cracroft
Brigham Young University
Literature, Mormon Writers of: Novels

Frank Moore Cross, Jr.
Harvard University
Dead Sea Scrolls: Overview

James V. D'Arc
Brigham Young University
Mormons, Image of: Film

Karen Lynn Davidson
Writer, Pasadena, CA
Hymns and Hymnody

Virgie D. Day
Brigham Young University
Mormons, Image of: The Visual Arts

K. Newell Dayley
Brigham Young University
Mormon Tabernacle Choir

Genevieve DeHoyos
Brigham Young University
Indian Student Placement Services

Jill Mulvay Derr
Brigham Young University
Sisterhood

John Dillenberger
Graduate Theological Union
Protestantism
Restorationism, Protestant

Donald B. Doty
Physician, Bountiful, UT
Prolonging Life

Josiah W. Douglas
Church Curriculum Dept., Salt Lake City
Blind, Materials for the

James T. Duke
Brigham Young University
Marriage: Eternal Marriage

W. Cole Durham, Jr.
Brigham Young University
Church and State
Murder

George D. Durrant
Brigham Young University
Genealogical Society of Utah

William G. Dyer
Brigham Young University
Occupational Status

Jaroldeen Edwards
Author, Los Angeles
Lifestyle

Homer S. Ellsworth
Physician, Lehi, UT
Birth Control

Jessie L. Embry
Brigham Young University
Blacks

Max J. Evans
Utah State Historical Society, Salt Lake City
Libraries and Archives

Paul H. Evans
Church Public Communications, Salt Lake City
Mormon Tabernacle Choir Broadcast ("The Spoken Word")

William E. Evenson
Brigham Young University
  Evolution

Franklin T. Ferguson
Architect, Salt Lake City
  Architecture

Isaac C. Ferguson
Church Welfare Services, Salt Lake City
  Humanitarian Service

William L. Fillmore
Attorney, Provo, UT
  Light-Mindedness

Enoc Q. Flores
Brigham Young University
  Race, Racism

Rita de Cassia Flores
Writer, Provo, UT
  Race, Racism

Charles Jay Fox
Brigham Young University
  Polynesian Cultural Center

David B. Galbraith
Brigham Young University
  Brigham Young University: Jerusalem
  Center for Near Eastern Studies

David P. Gardner
University of California, Berkeley, CA
  Education: Attitudes Toward
  Education

Arnold K. Garr
Brigham Young University
  Brigham Young College

Gary P. Gillum
Brigham Young University
  Christology
  Creeds

H. Wallace Goddard
Utah State University, Logan, UT
  Dating and Courtship

Kenneth W. Godfrey
Church Educational System, Logan, UT
  Freemasonry and the Temple
  Freemasonry in Nauvoo

Kristen L. Goodman
Church Correlation Dept., Salt Lake City
  Divorce

David M. Grant
University of Utah
  Matter

Arnold H. Green
Brigham Young University
  World Religions (Non-Christian) and
  Mormonism: Islam
  World Religions (Non-Christian) and
  Mormonism: Judaism

Elizabeth M. Haglund
University of Utah
  Public Relations

Ralph C. Hancock
Brigham Young University
  Constitution of the United States of
  America

H. Reese Hansen
Brigham Young University
  Premarital Sex

Louise G. Hanson
Brigham Young University
  Columbus, Christopher

Charles R. Harrell
Brigham Young University
  Theogony

Grant Von Harrison
Brigham Young University
  Profanity

Gerald M. Haslam
Brigham Young University
  International Genealogical Index™
  (IGI)

Tim B. Heaton
Brigham Young University
  Vital Statistics

Martin B. Hickman [deceased]
Brigham Young University
Diplomatic Relations

Michael D. Hicks
Brigham Young University
Music

Stuart W. Hinckley
Attorney, Salt Lake City
Capital Punishment

Douglas L. Hind
Church Curriculum Dept., Salt Lake City
Deaf, Materials for the

Patricia Terry Holland
Author, Salt Lake City
Motherhood

Thomas B. Holman
Brigham Young University
Marriage: Social and Behavioral Perspectives

Darlene Chidester Hutchison
Church Public Communications, Salt Lake City
Sex Education

Dillon K. Inouye
Brigham Young University
Celibacy

Jeanne B. Inouye
Attorney, Provo, UT
Abuse, Spouse and Child
Stillborn Children

Richard H. Jackson
Brigham Young University
Community

Florence Smith Jacobsen
Formerly with Church Arts and Sites, Salt Lake City
Christus Statue
Museums, LDS

Phyllis C. Jacobson
Brigham Young University
Dance

Mary Ellen Stewart Jamison
Writer, Glendale, CA
Christmas
Easter

John C. Jarman
Church Family History Dept., Salt Lake City
Family Registry™

Donald K. Jarvis
Brigham Young University
Mormonism, Mormons

Clayne R. Jensen
Brigham Young University
Sports

De Lamar Jensen
Brigham Young University
Protestant Reformation

Darwin A. John
Church Information Systems, Salt Lake City
Computer Systems

David J. Johnson
Brigham Young University
Archaeology

Peter N. Johnson
Brigham Young University
Motion Pictures, LDS Productions

Eleanor Park Jones
Writer, Salt Lake City
Non-Mormons, Social Relations with

Bruce W. Jorgensen
Brigham Young University
Literature, Mormon Writers of: Short Stories

Roger R. Keller
Brigham Young University
Catholicism and Mormonism
Christians and Christianity
Clergy
Cross
Protestantism
Restorationism, Protestant

Wm. Clayton Kimball
Bentley College, Waltham, MA
  Politics: Political Culture

Eleanor Knowles
Deseret Book Co., Salt Lake City
  Deseret Book Company

Phillip R. Kunz
Brigham Young University
  Family Organizations

Connie Lamb
Brigham Young University
  Immaculate Conception

Neal E. Lambert
Brigham Young University
  Brigham Young University: Provo,
    Utah, Campus
  Mormons, Image of: Fiction

Harold R. Laycock
Brigham Young University
  Academies

Robert L. Leake
Church Melchizedek Priesthood Dept.,
Salt Lake City
  AIDS

Rex E. Lee
Brigham Young University
  Constitutional Law

Richard P. Lindsay
General Authority, Salt Lake City
  Interfaith Relationships: Christian

Joanne Linnabary
Editor, Provo, UT
  Journals

Wayne B. Lynn
Church Curriculum Dept., Salt Lake
City
  Curriculum

James K. Lyon
University of California, San Diego
  Saints

Joseph Lynn Lyon
University of Utah Medical School, Salt
Lake City
  Alcoholic Beverages and Alcoholism
  Coffee
  Tea
  Tobacco
  Word of Wisdom

Val Dan MacMurray
Thruler Foundation, Salt Lake City
  Self-Sufficiency (Self-Reliance)

Arch L. Madsen
Bonneville International Corp., Salt
Lake City
  KSL Radio
  Public Communications

Carol Cornwall Madsen
Brigham Young University
  Woman Suffrage

Truman G. Madsen
Brigham Young University Center for
Near Eastern Studies, Jerusalem, Israel
  Religious Experience
  Theodicy

David B. Magleby
Brigham Young University
  Politics: Contemporary American
    Politics

Richard J. Marshall
Evans Communications, Inc., Salt Lake
City
  Exhibitions and World's Fairs

James O. Mason
U.S. Health Education and Welfare
Dept., Washington, DC
  Health, Attitudes Toward

Dean L. May
University of Utah
  Agriculture
  Social and Cultural History

Frank O. May, Jr.
Church Curriculum Dept., Salt Lake City
Artificial Insemination

David M. Mayfield
Family History Dept., Salt Lake City
Ancestral File™
Personal Ancestral File®

Kahlile Mehr
Church Family History Dept., Salt Lake City
Name Extraction Program

Charles L. Metten
Brigham Young University
Drama

Brent C. Miller
Utah State University, Logan, UT
Dating and Courtship

Robert L. Miller
University of Utah
Science and Scientists

Wayne A. Mineer
Physician, Orem, UT
Organ Transplants and Donations

James P. Mitchell
Church Educational System, Logan, UT
Family Home Evening

Terri Tanner Mitchell
Writer, Hyde Park, UT
Family Home Evening

Michael F. Moody
Church Music Committee, Salt Lake City
Musicians

Stephen D. Nadauld
General Authority, Salt Lake City
Business: LDS Attitudes Toward Business

Robert A. Nelson
Brigham Young University
Literature, Mormon Writers of: Drama

Robert E. Nelson, Jr.
U.S. Army
Chaplains

William O. Nelson
Church Correlation Dept., Salt Lake City
Anti-Mormon Publications

Richard A. Nimer
Physician, Pleasant Grove, UT
Blood Transfusions

Keith E. Norman
Employee Development, BP America, Solon, OH
Deification, Early Christian

Leslie Norris
Brigham Young University
Literature, Mormon Writers of: Poetry

Don E. Norton
Brigham Young University
Journals

Gen. Robert C. Oaks
U.S. Air Force
Military and the Church

Bruce L. Olsen
Church Public Communications Dept., Salt Lake City
Cremation
Family Prayer

Steven L. Olsen
Museum of Church History and Art, Salt Lake City
Celebrations
Centennial Observances

Terrance D. Olson
Brigham Young University
Sexuality

Richard G. Oman
Museum of Church History and Art, Salt Lake City
Artists, Visual
Sculptors

Sandra Bradford Packard
Brigham Young University
Animals

Spencer J. Palmer
Brigham Young University
World Religions (Non-Christian) and
Mormonism: Overview
World Religions (Non-Christian) and
Mormonism: Buddhism
World Religions (Non-Christian) and
Mormonism: Confucianism
World Religions (Non-Christian) and
Mormonism: Hinduism
World Religions (Non-Christian) and
Mormonism: Shinto

Erich Robert Paul
Dickinson College, Carlisle, PA
Science and Religion

Martha Moffitt Peacock
Brigham Young University
Art in Mormonism

Morris S. Petersen
Brigham Young University
Earth

Evan T. Peterson
Brigham Young University
Senior Citizens

Grethe Ballif Peterson
University of Utah
University of Deseret

Stanley A. Peterson
Church Educational System, Salt Lake City
Institutes of Religion

Roger B. Porter
White House, Washington, DC
United States of America

David H. Pratt
Brigham Young University
Family History, Genealogy

Paul Alfred Pratte
Brigham Young University
Press, News Media, and the Church

Dennis Rasmussen
Brigham Young University
Metaphysics

Mary Stovall Richards
Brigham Young University
Feminism

Frank D. Richardson
Church Welfare Services, Salt Lake City
Emergency Preparedness

Chauncey C. Riddle
Brigham Young University
Philosophy

Robert E. Riggs
Brigham Young University
Civil Rights

R. Thayne Robson
University of Utah
Wealth, Attitudes Toward

George Romney
Former Governor of Michigan
Tolerance

Joseph Rosenblatt
Businessman, Salt Lake City
Interfaith Relationships: Jewish

Lorry E. Rytting [deceased]
*Church Public Communications Dept.,
Salt Lake City*
Sterilization

Scott Samuelson
Ricks College, Rexburg, ID
Ricks College

Ray G. Schwartz
Daily Herald, Provo, UT
Drugs, Abuse of

A. Lynn Scoresby
Brigham Young University
Fatherhood

Gareth W. Seastrand
Alpine School District, American Fork, UT
Visitors Centers

Jan Shipps
Indiana University—Purdue University at Indianapolis
Mormonism, an Independent Interpretation

Eric B. Shumway
Brigham Young University—Hawaii
Polynesians

Barbara B. Smith
Former General President, Church Relief Society, Salt Lake City
Women, Roles of: Gospel Principles and the Roles of Women

Lowell M. Snow
Attorney, Salt Lake City
Scouting

A. D. Sorensen
Brigham Young University
Equality

Clyde E. Sullivan
Brigham Young University
Suicide

Charles D. Tate, Jr.
Brigham Young University
Burial
Conscientious Objection
Gambling

Stanley A. Taylor
Brigham Young University
Economic Aid

Elaine Thatcher
Consultant, Salt Lake City
Material Culture

Donlu DeWitt Thayer
Brigham Young University
Literature, Mormon Writers of: Personal Essays

Darwin L. Thomas
Brigham Young University
Family: Family Life
Socialization

Janet Thomas
Church Magazines, Salt Lake City
Magic
Satanism

Robert K. Thomas
Brigham Young University
Abuse, Spouse and Child

Ryan L. Thomas
Brigham Young University
Adoption of Children

Shirley W. Thomas
Former Counselor in General Presidency, Church Relief Society, Salt Lake City
Women, Roles of: Gospel Principles and the Roles of Women

Brent C. Thompson
Church Historical Dept., Salt Lake City
Prohibition

Michele Thompson-Holbrook
Writer, Cape Elizabeth, ME
Modesty in Dress

Clark T. Thorstenson
Brigham Young University
Physical Fitness and Recreation

David K. Udall
Attorney, Mesa, AZ
Non-Mormons, Social Relations with

Alton L. Wade
Brigham Young University—Hawaii
Brigham Young University—Hawaii Campus

David A. Wanamaker
LDS Foundation, Orem, UT
LDS Foundation

Stan E. Weed
Institute for Research and Evaluation, Salt Lake City
Values, Transmission of

Gerald R. Williams
Brigham Young University
Lawsuits

William A. Wilson
Brigham Young University
  Folklore

Robert S. Wood
Naval War College, Newport, RI
  War and Peace

Lael J. Woodbury
Brigham Young University
  Pageants

Raymond S. Wright III
Brigham Young University
  Family History Library

Lawrence A. Young
Brigham Young University
  Cult
  Sect

PREFACE

This preface appears in volume 1 of the Encyclopedia of Mormonism. *Its spirit applies to all the volumes containing selections from the* Encyclopedia.

According to a standard definition, an encyclopedia is to "treat comprehensively all the various branches of knowledge" pertaining to a particular subject. The subject of this *Encyclopedia* is The Church of Jesus Christ of Latter-day Saints, widely known as the Mormon church. This is the first major encyclopedia published about the Mormons. It presents the work of hundreds of Latter-day Saint (LDS) lay scholars and others from throughout the world and provides a comprehensive reporting of Mormon history, scripture, doctrines, life, and knowledge, intended for both the non-Mormon and the LDS reader. Readers will find an article on almost any topic conceivably related to the general topic of Mormonism, and yet no article is exhaustive because of space limitations. Most articles include bibliographic references; cross-references to other articles in the *Encyclopedia* are indicated by small capital letters.

When Macmillan Publishing Company asked authorities at Brigham Young University whether they would be interested in developing an encyclopedia about The Church of Jesus Christ of Latter-day Saints, President Jeffrey R. Holland took the query to his Board of Trustees. They instructed him to proceed. Working closely with Church authorities and Macmillan, President Holland chose an editor in chief and a board of editors. Discussion of possible titles concluded that the work should be called the *Encyclopedia of Mormonism* since that is the term by which the Church is most widely known, though unofficially.

The contract called for a work of one million words in about 1,500 articles in four volumes including pictures, maps, charts, appendices, indices, and a glossary. It soon became apparent that references to what the Church calls the standard works—the Bible, the Book of Mormon, the Doctrine and Covenants, and the Pearl of Great Price—would be so frequent that readers who did not have ready access to those works would be at a serious disadvantage in using the *Encyclopedia*. A fifth volume was decided upon to include all the LDS standard works except the Bible, which is readily available everywhere.

The Church does not have a paid clergy or a battery of theologians to write the articles. It functions with a lay ministry, and all members are encouraged to become scholars of the gospel. Over 730 men and women were asked to write articles on topics assigned because of previous interest and study.

Six major articles unfold the history of the Church: (1) the background and founding period in New York; (2) the Ohio, Missouri, and Illinois period ending with the martyrdom of Joseph Smith; (3) the exodus west and the early pioneer period under Brigham Young; (4) the late pioneer Utah period ending at the turn of the century and statehood; (5) a transitional period during the early twentieth century; and (6) the post–World War II period of international growth. The history of the Church has been dramatic and moving, considering its brief span of just over 160 years. Compared to Catholicism, Judaism, ancient Far East religions, and many Protestant churches, the Church has a very short history. Nearly 250 articles explain the doctrines of the Church, with special emphasis on basic principles and ordinances of the gospel of Jesus Christ. Twenty-four articles are clustered under the title "Jesus Christ," and another sixteen include his name in the title or relate directly to his divine mission and atonement.

Over 150 articles relate the details on such topics as the First Vision, Zion's Camp, Handcart Companies, Plural Marriage, the Salt Lake Temple, Temple Square, and the Church throughout the world. Biographies cover men and women contemporary in the life of Joseph Smith, Presidents of the Church, and auxiliary founders and past presidents. The only biography of a person living at the time of publication is on the present prophet and President of the Church, Ezra Taft Benson. [Since the publication of the *Encyclopedia of Mormonism*, Howard W. Hunter was sustained as President of the Church.]

And finally, there are over a hundred articles primarily concerned with how Latter-day Saints relate to their families, the Church, and to society in general. It is said there is a "Mormon culture," and several articles explore Mormon lifestyle, folklore, folk art, artists, literature, and other facets that distinguish Latter-day Saints.

It may be that the growth of the Church in the last decades has mandated the encyclopedic account that is presented here. Yet, even as the most recent programs were set down and the latest figures listed, there is an acute awareness that the basic tenet of the Church is that its canon is open-ended. The contemporary President of the Church is sustained as a "prophet, seer, and revelator." While this makes some theological discussion moot, the basic beliefs of the Latter-day Saints, summarized in the Articles of Faith, do not change.

In several areas, the Church shares beliefs held by other Christians, and a number of scholars from other faiths were asked to present articles. However, the most distinctive tenets of the Church—those regarding the premortal and postmortal life, living prophets who receive continuous and current revelation from God, sacred ordinances for deceased ancestors, moral and health codes that provide increasingly well-documented benefits, and the potential within man for progression into an infinite future—are all treated primarily by writers selected from among Latter-day Saints.

Lest the role of the *Encyclopedia* be given more weight than it deserves, the editors make it clear that those who have written and edited have only tried to explain their understanding of Church history, doctrines, and procedures; their statements and opinions remain their own. The *Encyclopedia of Mormonism* is a joint product of Brigham Young University and Macmillan Publishing Company, and the contents do not necessarily represent the official position of The Church of Jesus Christ of Latter-day Saints. In no sense does the *Encyclopedia* have the force and authority of scripture.

ACKNOWLEDGMENTS*

The support and assistance of many persons and groups are necessary to produce a work as extensive as an encyclopedia. Special thanks are extended to the executives of Macmillan Publishing Company who introduced the idea of the the *Encyclopedia of Mormonism* to Brigham Young University. Charles E. Smith made initial contacts on the project, while Philip Friedman, President and Publisher of Macmillan Reference Division, and Elly Dickason, Editor in Chief of Macmillan Reference Division, have followed through on the multitudinous details, demonstrating skill and patience in working with us in the preparation of this five-volume work.

The editors also wish to thank the General Authorities of the Church for designating Brigham Young University as the contractual Author of the *Encyclopedia*. Two members of the Board of Trustees of the university, who are also members of the Quorum of the Twelve Apostles, were appointed by the First Presidency to serve as advisers to the project: Elder Neal A. Maxwell and Elder Dallin H. Oaks. Other General Authorities who accepted special assignments related to the project include four members of the Quorum of Seventy: Elders Dean L. Larsen, Carlos E. Asay, Marlin K. Jensen, and Jeffrey R. Holland.

Special support also came from the Administration of BYU. Jeffrey R. Holland, president of BYU at the time the project was initiated, was instrumental in appointing the Board of Editors and in developing early guidelines. Rex E. Lee, current president of BYU, has continued this support.

* The major parts of the acknowledgments appear in volume 1 of the *Encyclopedia of Mormonism*. The statement has been modified here by (1) deleting credits to individuals and institutions providing general help, illustrations, and photographs for the *Encyclopedia* and (2) adding the names of those giving special assistance to the preparation of this particular publication.

xxx ⚘ ACKNOWLEDGMENTS

The efforts of the Board of Editors and the Project Coordinator, whose names are listed at the front of each volume, have shaped and fashioned every aspect of the project. We offer special thanks to them, and to companions and family members for graciously supporting our efforts over many months. Others who shared in final editing include Bruce B. Clark, Soren F. Cox, Marshall R. Craig, and Ellis T. Rasmussen.

Many others have provided assistance in specialized areas, including Larry E. Dahl, Michelle Eckersley, Gary R. Gillespie, Devan Jensen, Luene Ludlow, Jack M. Lyon, Robert J. Matthews, Frank O. May, Charlotte McDermott, Robert L. Millet, Don E. Norton, Monte S. Nyman, Patricia J. Parkinson, Charlotte A. Pollard, Larry C. Porter, Merle Romer, Evelyn E. Schiess, Judith Skousen, Charles D. Tate, Jr., Jay M. Todd, and John Sutton Welch. Special thanks also to Ronald Millett and Sheri Dew at Deseret Book Company for their help with this volume.

Finally, we express appreciation to the 738 authors who contributed their knowledge and insights. The hopes of all who were involved with this project will be realized if the *Encyclopedia* assists readers to come to a greater understanding and appreciation of the history, scriptures, doctrines, practices, and procedures of The Church of Jesus Christ of Latter-day Saints.

TOPICAL OUTLINE

The topical outline is designed to help the reader discover all the articles in this volume related to a particular subject. The title of every article in this volume is listed in the topical outline at least once.

This volume contains the major articles from the *Encyclopedia of Mormonism* on activities, problems, morals, and other sensitive issues faced by members of the Church and society.

A. **Church members as they perceive themselves and relate to other members of the Church.**

1. *Emphasis on the importance and the eternal nature of the family and on family history (genealogy):* Adoption of Children; Ancestral File™; Dating and Courtship; Family*; Family History Centers; Family History, Genealogy; Family History Library; Family Home Evening; Family Organizations; Family Prayer; Family Registry™; FamilySearch™; Fatherhood; Fathers' Blessings; Feminism; Genealogical Society of Utah; Genealogy; Granite Mountain Record Vault; Home; International Genealogical Index™ (IGI); Journals; Marriage*; Name Extraction Program; Personal Ancestral File®; Procreation; Sisterhood; Stillborn Children; Woman Suffrage; Women, Roles of*; Women's Topics; World Conferences on Records.

2. *Emphasis on the importance of education:* Academies; Brigham Young College; Brigham Young University*; Church Educational System (CES); Curriculum; Education*; Institutes of Religion; LDS Business College; LDS Foundation; LDS Student Association; Libraries

---

* Indicates additional related articles are clustered under that entry title.

and Archives; Ricks College; Schools; Seminaries; University of Deseret; Values, Transmission of.

3. *Emphasis on the development of the arts and letters:* Architecture; Art in Mormonism; Artists, Visual; Dance; Drama; Fine Arts; Folk Art; Folklore; Humor; Hymns and Hymnody; Literature, Mormon Writers of*; Mormon Handicraft; Mormon Tabernacle Choir; Mormon Youth Symphony and Chorus; Mormons, Image of*; Motion Pictures, LDS Productions; Museums, LDS; Music; Musicians; Pageants; Sculptors; Symbols, Cultural and Artistic.

4. *Emphasis on the importance of good physical and mental health:* Alcoholic Beverages and Alcoholism; Coffee; Health, Attitudes Toward; Mental Health; Physical Fitness and Recreation; Tea; Tobacco; Word of Wisdom.

5. *Utilization of media and other means of communication:* Bonneville International Corporation; Broadcasting; Christus Statue; Exhibitions and World's Fairs; KSL Radio; Mormon Tabernacle Choir; Mormon Tabernacle Choir Broadcast ("The Spoken Word"); Motion Pictures, LDS Productions; Pageants; Polynesian Cultural Center; Press, News Media, and the Church; Public Communications; Public Relations; Satellite Communications System; Visitors Centers.

6. *Programs and materials for special groups and needs:* Blind, Materials for the; Calamities and Disasters; Deaf, Materials for the; Economic Aid; Emergency Preparedness; Indian Student Placement Services; Self-Sufficiency (Self-Reliance); Senior Citizens.

7. *Symbols, celebrations, observances, pageants, and dedications:* Burial; Celebrations; Centennial Observances; Christmas; Christus Statue; Cumorah Pageant; Dedications; Easter; Symbols, Cultural and Artistic; Vocabulary, Latter-day Saint.

8. *Other areas in which the LDS Church has special interest:*
Agriculture; Columbus, Christopher; Dead Sea Scrolls*;
Earth; Material Culture; Polynesians; Suffering in the
World.

B. **Church members as they are perceived by others and
as they relate to other churches and groups.**

1. *Anti-LDS beliefs and publications:* Anti-Mormon
Publications; Cult; Stereotyping of Latter-day Saints.

2. *Beliefs and practices in selected areas shared with other
groups in society:* Animals; Archaeology; Blacks;
Catholicism and Mormonism; Chaplains; Church and
State; Civic Duties; Civil Rights; Community; Constitu-
tional Law; Constitution of the United States of America;
Diplomatic Relations; Economic Aid; Education*;
Emergency Preparedness; Equality; Ethics; Family
History, Genealogy; Family Organizations; Fatherhood;
Freemasonry in Nauvoo; Freemasonry and the Temple;
Home; Humanitarian Service; Interfaith Relationships*;
Lawsuits; Light-mindedness; Lifestyle; Matter; Military
and the Church; Minorities; Mormonism, An Independent
Interpretation; Mormonism, Mormons; Motherhood;
Music; Non-Mormons, Social Relations with; Philosophy;
Politics*; Poverty, Attitudes Toward; Protestant
Reformation; Protestantism; Race, Racism; Religious
Experience; Religious Freedom; Restorationism,
Protestant; Science and Religion; Science and Scientists;
Scouting; Sect; Socialization; Society; Sports; Tolerance;
United States of America; Values, Transmission of; War
and Peace; Wealth, Attitudes Toward; Woman Suffrage;
Women, Roles of*; Women's Topics; Word of Wisdom;
Work, Role of; Worldly, Worldliness; World Religions*.

3. *The position of the Church on some of the traditional
teachings of Christianity:* Christians and Christianity;
Christology; Clergy; Creeds; Cross; Cult; Deification,
Early Christian; Divorce; Epistemology; Immaculate

KEY TO ABBREVIATIONS

AF	Talmage, James E. *Articles of Faith*. Salt Lake City, 1890. (All references are to pagination in printings before 1960.)
BOM	The Book of Mormon: Another Testament of Jesus Christ. Salt Lake City, 1981.
CHC	*Comprehensive History of the Church*, 6 vols., ed. B. H. Roberts. Salt Lake City, 1930.
CR	*Conference Reports*. Salt Lake City, 1898–.
CWHN	*Collected Works of Hugh Nibley*, ed. S. Ricks, J. Welch, et al. Salt Lake City, 1985–.
Dialogue	*Dialogue: A Journal of Mormon Thought*, 1965–.
D&C	The Doctrine and Covenants of The Church of Jesus Christ of Latter-day Saints. Salt Lake City, 1981.
DS	Smith, Joseph Fielding. *Doctrines of Salvation*, 3 vols. Salt Lake City, 1954–1956.
ER	*Encyclopedia of Religion*, 16 vols., ed. M. Eliade. New York, 1987.
F.A.R.M.S.	Foundation for Ancient Research and Mormon Studies. Provo, Utah.
HC	*History of the Church*, 7 vols., ed. B. H. Roberts. Salt Lake City, 1st ed., 1902; 2nd ed., 1950. (All references are to pagination in the 2nd edition.)
HDC	Historical Department of the Church, Salt Lake City.
IE	*Improvement Era*, 1897–1970.
JC	Talmage, James E. *Jesus the Christ*. Salt Lake City, 1915.
JD	*Journal of Discourses*, 26 vols., ed. J. Watt. Liverpool, 1854–1886.
JST	*Joseph Smith Translation of the Bible*.
MD	McConkie, Bruce R. *Mormon Doctrine*, 2nd ed. Salt Lake City, 1966.
MFP	*Messages of the First Presidency*, 6 vols., ed. J. Clark. Salt Lake City, 1965–1975.
PGP	The Pearl of Great Price. Salt Lake City, 1981.
PJS	*Papers of Joseph Smith*, ed. D. Jessee. Salt Lake City, 1989.
PWJS	*The Personal Writings of Joseph Smith*, ed. D. Jessee. Salt Lake City, 1984.
T&S	*Times and Seasons*, 1839–1846.
TPJS	*Teachings of the Prophet Joseph Smith*, comp. Joseph Fielding Smith. Salt Lake City, 1938.
WJS	*Words of Joseph Smith*, ed. A. Ehat and L. Cook. Provo, Utah, 1980.

A

ABORTION

The Church of Jesus Christ of Latter-day Saints considers the elective termination of pregnancy "one of the most . . . sinful practices of this day" (*General Handbook of Instructions*, 11-4), although not necessarily MURDER. The Lord has said, "Thou shalt not . . . kill, nor do *anything* like unto it" (D&C 59:6; emphasis added in Packer, p. 85).

Members of the Church must not "submit to, be a party to, or perform an abortion" (*General Handbook*, 11-4). The only exceptions are where "incest or rape was involved, or where competent medical authorities certify that the life of the mother is in jeopardy, or that a severely defective fetus cannot survive birth" (Packer, p. 85). Even these exceptions do not justify abortion automatically. Church members are counseled that they should consider abortion in such cases only after consulting with their bishop and receiving divine confirmation through prayer.

"Church members who encourage, perform, or submit to an abortion are subject to Church discipline as appropriate" to help them repent (*General Handbook*, 11-4). As far as has been revealed, the sin of abortion is one for which a person may repent and gain forgiveness (*General Handbook*, 11-4; Packer, p. 86).

BIBLIOGRAPHY

General Handbook of Instructions. Salt Lake City, 1989.

Packer, Boyd K. "Covenants." *Ensign* 20 (Nov. 90):84–86.

MARY K. BEARD

ABUSE, SPOUSE AND CHILD

Abuse is behavior that deliberately threatens or injures another person. It may be physical, emotional, or sexual. Some forms of physical and emotional abuse include beatings, neglect, and threats of abandonment. While it also may take varied forms, sexual abuse of another adult usually involves the use of force or intimidation to coerce sexual activity. Sexual abuse of a child, on the other hand, includes any sexual behavior between the child and someone in a position of power, trust, or control (see *Child Abuse: Helps for Ecclesiastical Leaders*, Salt Lake City, 1985).

Individuals who abuse their spouses or children violate the laws of both God and society. Church leaders have counseled that even more subtle forms of abuse are evil—among them, shouting at or otherwise demeaning family members and demanding offensive intimate relations from one's spouse (Gordon B. Hinckley, "Keeping the Temple Holy," *Ensign* 20 [May 1990]:52). Church members guilty of abusing others are directed to seek the counsel of their bishops and, where necessary, professional help. Church disciplinary procedures may need to be instituted to help abusers repent and to protect innocent persons.

While the causes of abuse are myriad and complex, all forms of abusive behavior are antithetical to the spirit of service and sacrifice exemplified in the life of the Savior Jesus Christ. Because it is often designed to control another person, abuse is inconsistent with agency, which is central to God's plan of salvation. In a revelation given in 1839, the Lord said, "No power or influence can or ought to be maintained by virtue of the priesthood, only by persuasion, by long-suffering, by gentleness and meekness, and by love unfeigned" (D&C 121:41). Abuse is a serious sin and cannot be ignored, but abusers can be forgiven when they truly repent.

BIBLIOGRAPHY
Hinckley, Gordon B. "To Please Our Heavenly Father." *Ensign* 15 (May 1985):48–51.
Monson, Thomas S. "A Little Child Shall Lead Them." *Ensign* 20 (May 1990):53–60.
Peterson, H. Burke. "Unrighteous Dominion." *Ensign* 19 (July 1989):6–11.

JEANNE B. INOUYE
ROBERT K. THOMAS

ACADEMIES

Between 1875 and 1910, the LDS Church sponsored thirty-three academies for secondary education in seven western states, Canada, and Mexico. Factors contributing to the development of the academy system were (1) the lack of public educational facilities in Utah before 1900; (2) the influx of a non-Mormon population with the accompanying establishment of academies by other denominations, schools that attracted many LDS youth; and (3) the need to provide schools in areas newly settled under the colonization program that the Church carried out in the western United States, Mexico, and Canada.

A typical academy experienced three phases of curricular development. Until about 1900, elementary subjects predominated, with some piecemeal additions of secondary and normal (teacher-training) courses. The curriculum provided basic academic subjects with an emphasis on vocational and cultural fields, including mechanical and agricultural skills, gymnastics, homemaking, vocal music, and art.

From 1900 to 1910 the academies offered more diversified secondary courses leading to terminal diplomas in preparation for vocations and missionary service. They featured enlarged academic departments and a broader offering including, dramatics, choirs, bands, orchestras, music clubs, debate societies, athletics, and sports. Normal courses were expanded to three and four years, and college-level classes made their appearance in a number of the schools.

After 1910 specialized courses were consolidated into standard four-year high school curricula, including much more extensive music and other cultural offerings than were found in the public high schools of the day. All of the schools served as cultural centers in their communities, sponsoring performances and sports involving much of the adult populace and importing artists, lecturers, and dramatic companies.

Some of these schools succumbed to the widespread economic depression following the Panic of 1893 and to the rise of public schools in Utah Territory after the free school act of 1890. Twenty-two of the academies, however, continued to thrive during the early twentieth century, constituting the only secondary schools in many LDS communities until after 1911.

By 1927 the Church had closed or turned over to the states all but eight of the academies. Six remained as accredited normal schools or two-year colleges, one as a university, and one as a secondary school. By 1934 only three—BRIGHAM YOUNG UNIVERSITY, RICKS COLLEGE, and Juárez Academy—continued under Church sponsorship. All three are presently operating (1991).

Factors leading to closing or transferring the academies to state education systems included the burden of financing two competing systems as public high schools emerged and the success of church-sponsored SEMINARIES and INSTITUTES in supplementing secular education with religious training.

During the mid-twentieth century, schools similar in purpose and scope to the earlier academies were established in the South Pacific and elsewhere administered by the CHURCH EDUCATIONAL SYSTEM.

In 1953 legislation was passed in Utah as part of a cost-reduction effort to return Weber, Snow, and Dixie Colleges to the Church, but in a statewide referendum Utah voters rejected the proposal and the colleges remained with the state.

A list of some of the principal academies with their founding dates, locations, name changes, and 1991 status follows:

• Brigham Young Academy, 1875, Provo, Utah; became Brigham Young University in 1903; continues to the present.

• Brigham Young College, 1877, Logan, Utah; a four-year college briefly in 1903, but closed as a junior college in 1926.

• Salt Lake Stake Academy, 1886, Salt Lake City, Utah; a high school, known at various times as LDS High School, LDS University, and LDS College; closed in 1931 and transformed into LDS Business College, which continues today.

• St. George Stake Academy, 1888, St. George, Utah; Dixie Normal College, 1917; Dixie Junior College, 1923; state-operated Dixie College, 1933 to the present.

• Bannock Stake Academy, 1888, Rexburg, Idaho; Fremont Stake Academy, 1898; Ricks Academy, 1902; Ricks Normal College, 1917; Ricks College, 1918; made a four-year college, 1948; a junior college, 1956 to the present.

- Sanpete Stake Academy, 1888, Ephraim, Utah; Snow Academy, 1900; Snow Normal College, 1917; Snow Junior College, 1923; Snow College, a state junior college, 1932 to the present.

- Weber Stake Academy, 1888, Ogden, Utah; Weber Academy, 1908; Weber Normal College, 1918; Weber College, 1922; a state junior college, 1922; a four-year college 1962; Weber State College, 1963; Weber State University, 1991.

- St. Joseph Stake Academy, 1891, Thatcher, Arizona; LDS Academy, 1898; Gila Academy, 1911; Gila Normal College, 1920; Gila Junior College, 1923; Eastern Arizona Junior College, 1932 to the present time.

- Juárez Stake Academy, 1897, Colonia Juárez, Mexico; Academia Juárez, 1963 to the present.

BIBLIOGRAPHY

Bennion, Milton Lynn. *Mormonism and Education.* Salt Lake City, 1939.

Jenson, Andrew. *Encyclopedic History of the Church of Jesus Christ of Latter-day Saints.* Salt Lake City, 1941. (Academies listed under latest titles.)

Laycock, Harold R. "A History of Music in the Academies of the Latter-day Saints Church, 1876–1926." D.M.A. diss., University of Southern California, 1961.

HAROLD R. LAYCOCK

ADOPTION OF CHILDREN

The adoption of children is common among members of the Church. This is no doubt in part a concomitant of the Church's opposition to ABORTION and its emphasis on the central importance of the FAMILY. President Ezra Taft Benson, commenting on adoption, stated that many "have prayerfully chosen to adopt children, and . . . [you] wonderful couples we salute . . . for the sacrifices and love you have given to those children you have chosen to be your own" (Benson, p. 11).

There are no doctrinal limitations on the legal adoption of children by members of the Church. Under most circumstances, adopted children may be sealed to the adoptive parents in an LDS temple. However, living children born in the covenant, that is, born to parents who have been sealed to each other in an LDS temple, cannot be sealed to any other parents although they can be adopted for life; and children who have been previously sealed to another couple may not be sealed to adoptive parents without cancellation of the former sealing. The temple sealing of a living adopted child into an eternal family relationship is performed only after legal adoption is finalized in accordance with local law (*General Handbook of Instructions*, Salt Lake City, 1989, 6-6).

Adopted children who have been sealed to adoptive parents are considered as natural children for all doctrinal purposes, including tracing genealogical lineage. All sealed children are entitled to all the blessings promised to children born in the covenant.

The desire to adopt children is strong among Church members, but Church leaders have cautioned them never to become involved in adoption practices that are legally questionable. In a letter dated April 20, 1982, the First Presidency urged members to "observe strictly all legal requirements of the country or countries involved in the adoption." It was also stated that "the needs of the child must be a paramount concern in adoption." Members considering adoption are counseled to work through the Church's Social Services agency or through others with the "specialized professional knowledge" necessary to ensure that the child's needs are met.

BIBLIOGRAPHY

Benson, Ezra Taft. Annual Parents Fireside, Feb. 22, 1987. *Church News* (Feb. 28, 1987):3, 10.

RYAN L. THOMAS

ADULTERY

Adultery constitutes a grievous violation of the law of chastity. For Latter-day Saints it is defined as sexual intercourse between a married person and someone other than his or her legal and lawful spouse, while fornication involves two unmarried parties. Both transgressions fall under condemnation in scripture and in the teachings of The Church of Jesus Christ of Latter-day Saints.

The Lord forbids adultery in the ten commandments and elsewhere in the law of Moses (see, e.g., Ex. 20:14; Lev. 20:10; Deut.

22:22). Both in Israel and in the Western Hemisphere, Christ commanded his followers not to commit adultery in thought or deed (Matt. 5:27–28; 3 Ne. 12:27–28). In this dispensation, the Lord has again prohibited adultery, and "anything like unto it" (D&C 59:6), while reproving even adulterous thoughts as an offense against the Spirit (D&C 42:23–26). In an official pronouncement in 1942, the First Presidency of the Church decried sexual sin—including adultery, fornication, and prostitution—as an offense "in its enormity, next to murder" (*IE* 45 [Nov. 1942]:758; *MFP* 6:176).

Because adultery or fornication breaks baptismal covenants and temple vows and may involve other members of the Church, penitent offenders are to confess the sin to their bishop or other Church authority, who may convene a disciplinary council. After prayerful deliberation, the council may excommunicate or disfellowship an adulterer, or implement some type of probation to help the offender repent. The excommunication of an adulterous priesthood leader is almost certain. A disciplinary council usually requires the adulterer to seek forgiveness from the betrayed spouse and from anyone drawn into the sin. By demonstrating an abhorrence for past sin and a commitment to righteousness, the repentant adulterer may, after an adequate period of probation, become fully reconciled to Christ, rebaptized, and reinstated in the Church and find forgiveness from God (D&C 58:47–48).

BIBLIOGRAPHY
Kimball, Spencer W. "The Sin Next to Murder." In *The Miracle of Forgiveness*, pp. 61–75. Salt Lake City, 1969.

BRYCE J. CHRISTENSEN

AGRICULTURE

The Latter-day Saints were pioneers in developing techniques and institutions of irrigated agriculture and dry farming in the Far West, probably because of a particular juxtaposition of modern attitudes toward farming and farm life, skills gained in early industrial Britain and the United States, and the pressing need to increase production on Utah's hardscrabble farms.

Most American-born Latter-day Saints, even if trained in a trade, had some experience with farming in more humid areas before moving into the desert wilderness in 1847. They were joined by a major influx of converts from the British Isles, most from the industrialized regions of England and Wales and therefore with little farming experience. In Utah, virtually all the pioneers had to become farmers to survive. Until the transcontinental railroad was completed in 1869, they had to raise enough food for themselves and for the immigrants who would arrive too late to grow anything. Finding Utah's annual rainfall insufficient to raise most crops, they had to irrigate the crops with water diverted from canyon streams. Also, only a small amount of land was situated so that canals could be built above the fields to irrigate the crops below. All of these circumstances—and the LDS ethic of community action—combined to shape the role of Mormons in the agricultural history of the United States.

Unlike many traditional farmers, the Latter-day Saints had a modern view of their lands and farming. Land was necessary for making a living, but it was not imbued with mystical qualities that gave superior virtue, independence, or permanence to farm life. President Brigham Young, himself a craftsman, supported manufacturing and artisan crafts as well as farming and did not impute moral superiority to one over the others. Farming for the Saints was not "a way of life" but a way of making a living, and this attitude freed them from undue reverence for traditional farming practices and from any reluctance to leave the land to take up ranching, manufacturing, trade, professions, and other pursuits that might assure a better standard of living. Moreover, the paucity of irrigable land kept most farms small, limiting production to barely more than a household subsistence level, in spite of a willingness, even eagerness, to engage in commercial agriculture.

The need to irrigate crops impelled LDS farmers to become innovators in western irrigation. Paradoxically, the high number of people previously skilled in manufacturing may have helped them to do so. The artisan-farmers applied the hydraulic engineering techniques they had learned in factories and workshops powered by water to the task of bringing water to fields. Necessity forced them to do so quickly, if sometimes clumsily. But they demonstrated that irrigated agriculture on a regional scale was possible.

A whole set of cooperative management techniques for building and maintaining dams and canal systems, distributing water to individual farmers, and applying it to the fields evolved into a model for later settlers in the arid West. It was appropriate that the first National Irrigation Congress be held in Salt Lake City in 1891, for many considered Utah a model of what was being accomplished in the West through irrigation. Ordinary farmers from Utah, skilled in irrigation techniques, have been well represented among those who have opened land in Canada and in federally sponsored irrigation projects in Idaho, Arizona, New Mexico, Wyoming, California, Oregon, and Washington, spreading both their farming techniques and their faith throughout the West.

The urgent need to maximize production on Utah's small farms led many Latter-day Saints to study scientific agriculture. Perhaps chief among them was John A. Widtsoe, later an apostle, who, after a Harvard education in physical chemistry, concentrated on expanding agricultural production. Directing the Utah Agricultural Experiment Station, he encouraged studies on soils, climate, fertilizers, and soil-working techniques, which led to publication of his *Principles of Irrigation Practice* (1914). He directed dry-farming experiments for nonirrigable lands, which culminated in *Dry Farming: A System of Agriculture for Countries Under a Low Rainfall* (1910).

Other Latter-day Saints who improved farming practices were Edgar B. Brossard in the economics of farm production; William M. Jardine (secretary of agriculture under President Calvin Coolidge) in agronomy; Phillip V. Cardon (administrator of the Agricultural Research Administration and director general of the United Nations Food and Agriculture Organization) in forage crops and diseases; Franklin S. Harris in agronomy and sugar beet culture; Lowry Nelson in rural sociology; Thomas L. Martin in agronomy; and Willard Gardner in soil physics.

Church President Ezra Taft Benson (secretary of agriculture under President Dwight D. Eisenhower) devoted much of his life to founding farmer cooperatives. The Ezra Taft Benson Agriculture and Food Institute at Brigham Young University (1975) fosters cooperative agricultural techniques in developing countries.

Latter-day Saints continue as individuals and under Church auspices to work at improving crop yields throughout the world and applying cooperative principles to improving the standard of living in developing regions. Since the early 1970s some Latter-day Saints have been called by the Church as "additional assignment" missionaries to encourage practical self-help programs and better farming techniques in regions of Africa, Asia, and the Americas. Gordon Wagner, a Latter-day Saint with a doctorate in economics from Cornell, worked on his own during the 1970s and 1980s to apply LDS cooperative principles to agricultural development problems in impoverished regions of Africa.

BIBLIOGRAPHY

Arrington, Leonard J., and Davis Bitton. *The Mormon Experience: A History of the Latter-day Saints*, pp. 310–19. New York, 1979.

Arrington, Leonard J., and Dean May. "'A Different Mode of Life': Irrigation and Society in Nineteenth-Century Utah." *Agricultural History* 49 (Jan. 1975):3–20.

Mead, Elwood, et al. *Report of Irrigation Investigations in Utah.* Washington, D.C., 1903.

DEAN L. MAY

AIDS

The First Presidency statement on AIDS (acquired immune deficiency syndrome) released May 27, 1988, admonishes Church members to become informed about AIDS and to avoid all actions that place themselves or others at risk. Members are also encouraged to become informed about AIDS-related laws and policies in the country where they live and to join in wise and constructive efforts to stem the spread of AIDS.

The statement calls for Church members to extend Christlike sympathy and compassion to all who are infected or ill with AIDS. Particular concern and sympathy are expressed for those having received the virus through blood transfusions, babies infected by their mothers, and marriage partners infected by a spouse. Leaders and members are encouraged to reach out with kindness and comfort to the afflicted, ministering to their needs and assisting them with their problems.

While hope is expressed that medical discoveries will make it possible both to prevent and cure AIDS, the observance of clearly understandable and divinely given guidance regardless of such potential discoveries will do more than all else to check a potential AIDS epidemic: "That guidance is chastity before marriage, total fidelity in marriage, abstinence from all homosexual relations, avoidance of illegal drugs, and reverence and care for the body, which is the temple of God."

The First Presidency statement includes remarks given about AIDS by Gordon B. Hinckley, First Counselor in the First Presidency, in the April 1987 general priesthood meeting: "Prophets of God have repeatedly taught through the ages that practices of homosexual relations, fornication, and adultery are grievous sins. Sexual relations outside the bonds of marriage are forbidden by the Lord. We reaffirm those teachings. . . . Each of us has a choice between right and wrong. But with that choice there inevitably will follow consequences. Those who choose to violate the commandments of God put themselves at great spiritual and physical jeopardy."

In January 1989 a special bulletin on AIDS was sent to Church leaders throughout the world to provide (1) scientific and medical information about AIDS; (2) counsel reaffirming the blessings and protection that come from living God's commandments; and (3) guidelines and policies dealing with interviewing and assisting those infected with the AIDS virus. Some items treated in the four-page special bulletin are:

- Church teachers and activity leaders who on occasion may be involved in cleaning up blood or rendering first aid should become aware of, and follow, local health department recommendations regarding the prevention of AIDS infection.

- AIDS-infected individuals who may be contemplating marriage are to be encouraged by local Church leaders to be honest with potential marriage partners and to disclose their AIDS infection. For a person to do less would be deceitful, and in violation of one's covenants with God.

- Where transgression of God's laws has resulted in infection, the Church advocates the example of Jesus Christ, who condemned the sin but loved the sinner.

• AIDS victims who seek membership in the Church, temple recommends, or other blessings are treated as all others who express faith in God, repent, request baptism, and are living the teachings of Jesus Christ.

BIBLIOGRAPHY
Public Communications Department. "First Presidency Statement on AIDS." Salt Lake City, May 27, 1988; cf. "News of the Church," *Ensign* 18 (July 1988):79.
Questions and Answers for Priesthood Leaders Regarding AIDS (special bulletin). Salt Lake City, Jan. 1989.

ROBERT L. LEAKE

ALCOHOLIC BEVERAGES AND ALCOHOLISM

Active members of The Church of Jesus Christ of Latter-day Saints abstain from drinking alcoholic beverages. This practice of abstinence derives from an 1833 revelation known as the WORD OF WISDOM, which states "that inasmuch as any man drinketh wine or strong drink among you, behold it is not good, neither meet in the sight of your Father" (D&C 89:5). The harmful effects of ethyl alcohol (the active ingredient in all alcoholic beverages) on human health are also noted in the Bible (Prov. 31:4–5; Isa. 5:11). Although the Word of Wisdom was given originally to show the will of God and not as a commandment, abstinence from alcohol was expected of fully participating Church members by the early twentieth century and faithful observance is virtually prerequisite to temple work and leadership callings in the church.

Ethyl alcohol is produced by yeast fermentation in grains and fibers containing sugar. The amount of alcohol in wine and beer is normally less than 10 percent because fermentation stops when the ethyl alcohol concentration reaches this level. In modern times, however, the amount in alcoholic beverages has been increased by distillation.

The availability of beverages with higher concentrations of alcohol has increased the number of social and medical problems associated with ingesting it. Some conditions that are increased among those who use alcohol include cancers of the oral cavity, larynx, and esophagus; cirrhosis of the liver; degenerative diseases of the central nervous system; and higher accidental death rates (both automobile and pedestrian accidents).

The proscription on alcohol ingestion has reduced the incidence of all of these conditions among Latter-day Saints. The number of alcoholics in any population is usually estimated from the number of deaths caused by cirrhosis of the liver. An unpublished study conducted at the University of Utah in 1978 found that the number of deaths from alcoholic cirrhosis of the liver among LDS people was about half that of the non-LDS in Utah and other areas of the United States. This suggests that while the Word of Wisdom does not prevent alcoholism entirely, it has been effective in reducing its incidence.

BIBLIOGRAPHY

Gilman, A. G., L. S. Goodman, and A. Gilman, eds. *Goodman and Gilman's The Pharmacological Basis of Therapeutics*, 6th ed., pp. 376–86. New York, 1980.

Hawks, Ricky D. "Alcohol Use Trends Among LDS High School Seniors in America from 1982–1986." *AMCAP Journal* 15, 1 (1989):43–51.

———. "Alcohol Use Among LDS and Other Groups Teaching Abstinence." In *Drug and Alcohol Abuse Reviews*, R. R. Watson, ed., pp. 133–49. Clifton, N.J., 1990.

JOSEPH LYNN LYON

ANCESTRAL FILE™

Ancestral File™ is a large genealogical database published on compact disks (CD-ROM) for use in personal computers. Its purpose is to preserve genealogies of families throughout the world, make these genealogies available to researchers of all faiths and nationalities, and help them avoid unnecessary effort and expense. The file is produced and maintained by the FAMILY HISTORY LIBRARY of The Church of Jesus Christ of Latter-day Saints located in Salt Lake City.

By January 1990 Ancestral File contained approximately 7 million lineage-linked names; it is expected that millions more will be added each year. The distinguishing features of this file are that it:

1. displays and prints ancestors' individual records, pedigrees, family groups, and descendancy charts;

2. uses standardized spelling of names, locality cross-references, and other convenient retrieval techniques;

3. facilitates correcting and updating the data;
4. gives a reference number for a microfilm copy of the original information;
5. contains the names and addresses of persons who contributed the information;
6. enables users to copy family-linked data onto diskettes to be matched and merged with their own files.

Open participation in Ancestral File is essential to its purposes. All researchers can contribute their genealogies by providing additional information on entire families, and by using PERSONAL ANCESTRAL FILE® or other genealogical software that accommodates the GED-COM (Genealogical Data Communication) format. Ancestral File is available at the Family History Library in Salt Lake City and at hundreds of its affiliated FAMILY HISTORY CENTERS in outlying stake centers of the Church. Mail-order printouts may be obtained by correspondence.

Ancestral File and Personal Ancestral File are trademarks of the Corporation of the President of The Church of Jesus Christ of Latter-day Saints.

BIBLIOGRAPHY
Mayfield, David M., and A. Gregory Brown. "Family Search." *Genealogical Computing* (July 1990).

DAVID M. MAYFIELD

ANIMALS

Latter-day Saints believe that animals, like humans, have spirits, in the form of their bodies (D&C 77:2). Like humans and plants, animals were created first as spirits in heaven and then physically on the earth (Moses 3:5). Mortal and subject to death, animals will be saved through the atonement of Christ (*TPJS*, pp. 291–92). Humans and animals will eventually live in peace on this earth (Isa. 11:6–9; 2 Ne. 30:12–15; D&C 101:24–26). The Prophet Joseph Smith taught that animals will be found in heaven, in myriad forms, from myriad worlds, enjoying eternal felicity, and praising God in languages God understands (*TPJS*, pp. 291–92).

Animals, like other "good things which come of the earth . . . are made for the benefit and the use of man," but are "to be used, with judgment, not to excess, neither by extortion" (D&C 59:16–20). God gave Adam and Eve dominion over the animals (Gen. 1:28), but legitimate dominion is neither coercive nor exploitive (D&C 121:34–46). He sanctions the eating of animal flesh but forbids its waste (Gen. 9:2–5; D&C 49:18–21). The Joseph Smith Translation of the Bible (JST) cautions, "Surely, blood shall not be shed, only for meat, to save your lives; and the blood of every beast will I require at your hands" (JST Gen. 9:11).

Destroying animal life merely for sport has been strongly criticized by several Latter-day Saint leaders, including Lorenzo Snow, Joseph F. Smith, Joseph Fielding Smith, and Spencer W. Kimball. Lorenzo Snow called it a "murderous amusement."

When the Prophet Joseph Smith saw his associates about to kill three rattlesnakes at their campsite, he said, "Let them alone—don't hurt them! How will the serpent ever lose its venom, while the servants of God possess the same disposition, and continue to make war upon it? Men must become harmless before the brute creation, and when men lose their vicious dispositions and cease to destroy the animal race, the lion and the lamb can dwell together, and the sucking child can play with the serpent in safety" (*TPJS*, p. 71).

Heber C. Kimball criticized the use of spurs and whips, saying, "[Horses] have the same life in them that you have, and we should not hurt them" (*JD* 5:137). Brigham Young called neglect of livestock a "great sin" (*JD* 12:218). So far, no authoritative Church statement on the use of animals in medical research and product testing is available.

BIBLIOGRAPHY

Jones, Gerald E. "The Gospel and Animals." *Ensign* 2 (Aug. 1972):62–65.
Kimball, Spencer W. "Fundamental Principles to Ponder and Live." *Ensign* 8 (Nov. 1978):43–46.
Smith, Joseph Fielding. *Answers to Gospel Questions*, Vol. 4, pp. 42–47. Salt Lake City, 1963.
Snow, Lorenzo. *Teachings of Lorenzo Snow*, Williams, Clyde J., comp., pp. 188–89. Salt Lake City, 1984.

SANDRA BRADFORD PACKARD

ANTI-MORMON PUBLICATIONS

Anti-Mormonism includes any hostile or polemic opposition to Mormonism or to the Latter-day Saints, such as maligning the founding prophet, his successors, or the doctrines or practices of the Church. Though sometimes well intended, anti-Mormon publications have often taken the form of invective, falsehood, demeaning caricature, prejudice, and legal harassment, leading to both verbal and physical assault. From its beginnings, The Church of Jesus Christ of Latter-day Saints and its members have been targets of anti-Mormon publications. Apart from collecting them for historical purposes and in response to divine direction, the Church has largely ignored these materials, for they strike most members as irresponsible misrepresentations.

Few other religious groups in the United States have been subjected to such sustained, vitriolic criticism and hostility. From the organization of the Church in 1830 to 1989, at least 1,931 anti-Mormon books, novels, pamphlets, tracts, and flyers have been published in English. Numerous other newsletters, articles, and letters have been circulated. Since 1960 these publications have increased dramatically.

A major reason for hostility against the Church has been its belief in extrabiblical revelation. The theological foundation of the Church rests on the claim by the Prophet Joseph Smith that God the Father, Jesus Christ, and angels appeared to him and instructed him to restore a dispensation of the gospel.

Initial skepticism toward Joseph Smith's testimony was understandable because others had made similar claims to receiving revelation from God. Moreover, Joseph Smith had brought forth the Book of Mormon, giving tangible evidence of his claim to revelation, and this invited testing. His testimony that the book originated from an ancient record engraved on metal plates that he translated by the gift and power of God was considered preposterous by disbelievers. Hostile anti-Mormon writing and other abuses grew largely out of the perceived need to supply an alternative explanation for the origin of the Book of Mormon. The early critics focused initially on discrediting the Smith family, particularly Joseph Smith, Jr., and attempted to show that the Book of Mormon was entirely of nineteenth-century origin. Later critics have focused more on points of doctrine, individual leaders, and Church operation.

EARLY CRITICISMS (1829–1846). Joseph Smith's disclosure that heavenly messengers had visited him was met with derision, particularly by some local clergymen. When efforts to dissuade him failed, he became the object of ridicule. From the time of the First Vision (1820) to the first visit by the angel Moroni (1823), Joseph "suffered every kind of opposition and persecution from the different orders of religionists" (Lucy Mack Smith, *History of Joseph Smith*, p. 74).

The first serious attempt to discredit Joseph Smith and the Book of Mormon was by Abner Cole, editor of the *Reflector*, a local paper in Palmyra, New York. Writing under the pseudonym Obadiah Dogberry, Cole published in his paper extracts from two pirated chapters of the 1830 edition of the Book of Mormon, but was compelled to desist because he was violating copyright law. Cole resorted to satire. He attempted to malign Joseph Smith by associating him with money digging, and he claimed that Joseph was influenced by a magician named Walters.

Alexander Campbell, founder of the Disciples of Christ, wrote the first published anti-Mormon pamphlet. The text appeared first as articles in his own paper, the *Millennial Harbinger* (1831), and then in a pamphlet entitled *Delusions* (1832). Campbell concluded, "I cannot doubt for a single moment that [Joseph Smith] is the sole author and proprietor of [the Book of Mormon]." Two years later he recanted this conclusion and accepted a new theory for the origin of the Book of Mormon, namely that Joseph Smith had somehow collaborated with Sidney Rigdon to produce the Book of Mormon from the Spaulding Manuscript.

The most notable anti-Mormon work of this period, *Mormonism Unvailed* (sic), was published by Eber D. Howe in 1834. Howe collaborated with apostate Philastus Hurlbut, twice excommunicated from the Church for immorality. Hurlbut was hired by an anti-Mormon committee to find those who would attest to Smith's dishonesty. He "collected" affidavits from seventy-two contemporaries who professed to know Joseph Smith and were willing to speak against him. *Mormonism Unvailed* attempted to discredit Joseph Smith and his family by assembling these affidavits and nine letters written by Ezra Booth, also an apostate from the Church. These documents allege that the Smiths were money diggers and irresponsible people. Howe advanced the theory that Sidney Rigdon obtained a manuscript written by Solomon Spaulding, rewrote it into the Book of Mormon, and then convinced Joseph Smith to tell the public that he had translated the book from plates received from an angel. This theory served as an alternative to Joseph Smith's account until the Spaulding Manuscript was discovered in 1884 and was found to be unrelated to the Book of Mormon.

The Hurlbut-Howe collection and Campbell's *Delusions* were the major sources for nearly all other nineteenth- and some twentieth-century anti-Mormon writings, notably the works of Henry Caswall, John C. Bennett, Pomeroy Tucker, Thomas Gregg, William Linn, and George Arbaugh. Most of these writers drew routinely from the same body of anti-Mormon lore (see H. Nibley, "How to Write an Anti-Mormon Book," *Brigham Young University Extension Publications*, Feb. 17, 1962, p. 30).

Perhaps the most infamous manifestation of anti-Mormonism came in the Missouri conflict, during which Governor Lilburn W. Boggs issued an Extermination Order. "The Mormons," he wrote, "must be treated as enemies and must be exterminated or driven from the state, if necessary for the public good" (*HC* 3:175). This order led to the expulsion of the Mormons from Missouri and their resettlement in Illinois.

While incarcerated in Liberty Jail in 1839, Joseph Smith wrote to the Saints and instructed them not to respond polemically but to "gather up the libelous publications that are afloat; and all that are in the magazines, and in the encyclopedias, and all the libelous histories that are published, and are writing, and by whom" so that they could bring to light all misleading and untruthful reports about the Church (D&C 123:4–5, 12–13). This procedure has been followed by Latter-day Saints over the years.

After the Saints moved to Nauvoo, Illinois, a principal antagonist was Thomas C. Sharp, editor of the *Warsaw Signal*. Alarmed over the Church's secular power, he used his paper to oppose it. In 1841 he published *Mormonism Portrayed*, by William Harris.

Six notable anti-Mormon books were published in 1842. The first was *The History of the Saints*; or, *An Exposé of Joe Smith and Mormonism*, by John C. Bennett, who had served as Joseph Smith's counselor in the First Presidency and was also the first mayor of Nauvoo. After he was excommunicated from the Church for immorality, he turned against the Mormons and published a series of letters in a Springfield, Missouri, newspaper. He charged that Joseph Smith was "one of the grossest and most infamous impostors that ever appeared upon the face of the earth." Bennett's history borrowed heavily from *Mormonism Portrayed.*

That same year, Joshua V. Himes published *Mormon Delusions and Monstrosities,* which incorporated much of Alexander Campbell's *Delusions.* The Reverend John A. Clark published *Gleanings by the Way,* and Jonathan B. Turner, *Mormonism in All Ages.* Both books relied heavily on Howe and Hurlbut's *Mormonism Unvailed.* Daniel P. Kidder's *Mormonism and the Mormons* expanded the Spaulding theory of Book of Mormon origins to include Oliver Cowdery in addition to Joseph Smith and Sidney Rigdon.

Called the "Anti-Mormon Extraordinaire," the Reverend Henry Caswall published *The City of the Mormons,* or *Three Days at Nauvoo.* He claimed that he gave Joseph Smith a copy of a Greek manuscript of the Psalms and that Smith identified it as a dictionary of Egyptian hieroglyphics. Caswall invented dialogue between himself and Smith to portray Joseph Smith as ignorant, uncouth, and deceptive. In 1843 Caswall published *The Prophet of the Nineteenth Century* in London, borrowing most of his material from Clark and Turner.

By 1844 Joseph Smith also faced serious dissension within the Church. Several of his closest associates disagreed with him over the plural marriage revelation and other doctrines. Among the principal dissenters were William and Wilson Law, Austin Cowles, Charles Foster, Francis and Chauncey Higbee, Charles Ivins, and Robert Foster. They became allied with local anti-Mormon elements and published one issue of a newspaper, the *Nauvoo Expositor.* In it they charged that Joseph Smith was a fallen prophet, guilty of whoredoms, and dishonest in financial matters.

The Nauvoo City Council and Mayor Joseph Smith declared the newspaper an illegal "nuisance" and directed the town marshal to destroy the press. This destruction inflamed the hostile anti-Mormons around Nauvoo. On June 12, 1844, Thomas Sharp's newspaper, the *Warsaw Signal,* called for the extermination of the Latter-day Saints:

"War and extermination is inevitable! Citizens arise, one and all!!! Can you *stand* by, and suffer such infernal devils! to rob men of their property and rights, without avenging them. . . . Let [your comment] be made with powder and ball!!!" Two weeks later Joseph Smith and his brother Hyrum were assassinated in Carthage Jail while awaiting trial on charges of treason.

Sharp defended the killing on the grounds that "the most respectable citizens" had called for it. Sharp and four others eventually were tried for the murders, but were acquitted for lack of evidence.

Many felt that the Church would die with its founders. When the members united under the leadership of the Twelve Apostles, anti-Mormon attacks began with new vigor. Sharp renewed his call for the removal of the Mormons from Illinois. By September 1845, more than 200 Church members' homes were burned in the outlying areas of Nauvoo. In February 1846, the Saints crossed the Mississippi and began the exodus to the West.

Revenge was possibly a motive of some anti-Mormons, especially apostates. Philastus Hurlbut, Simonds Ryder, Ezra Booth, and John C. Bennett sought revenge because the Church had disciplined them. Alexander Campbell was angered because he lost many of his Campbellite followers when they joined the Latter-day Saints. Mark Aldrich had invested in a real-estate development that failed because Mormon immigrants did not support it, and Thomas Sharp had lost many of his general business prospects.

MORMON STEREOTYPING AND THE CRUSADE AGAINST POLYGAMY (1847–1896). Settlement in the West provided welcome isolation for the Church, but public disclosure of the practice of polygamy in 1852 brought a new barrage of ridicule and a confrontation with the federal government.

The years from 1850 to 1890 were turbulent ones for the Church because reformers, ministers, and the press openly attacked the practice of polygamy. Opponents founded antipolygamy societies, and Congress passed antipolygamy legislation. Mormons were stereotyped as people who defied the law and were immoral. The clear aim of the judicial and political crusade against the Mormons was to destroy the Church. Only the 1890 Manifesto, a statement by Church President Wilford Woodruff that abolished polygamy officially, pacified the government, allowing the return of confiscated Church property. Voluminous anti-Mormon writings, lectures, and cartoons at this time stereotyped the Church as a theocracy that defied the laws of conventional society; many portrayed its members as deluded and fanatical; and they alleged that polygamy, secret rituals, and blood atonement were the theological underpinnings of the Church. The main motives were to discredit LDS belief, morally to reform a perceived evil, or to exploit the controversy for financial and political profit. The maligning tactics that were used included verbal attacks against Church leaders; caricatures in periodicals, magazines, and lectures; fictional inventions; and outright falsehoods.

Probably the most influential anti-Mormon work in this period was Pomeroy Tucker's *Origin, Rise, and Progress of Mormonism* (1867). A printer employed by E. B. Grandin, publisher of the *Wayne Sentinel* and printer of the first edition of the Book of Mormon, Tucker claimed to have been associated closely with Joseph Smith. He supported the Hurlbut-Howe charge that the Smiths were dishonest and alleged that they stole from their neighbors. However, he acknowledged that his insinuations were not "sustained by judicial investigation."

The Reverend M. T. Lamb's *The Golden Bible or the Book of Mormon: Is It from God?* (1887) ridiculed the Book of Mormon as "verbose, blundering, stupid, . . . improbable, . . . impossible, . . . [and] a foolish guess." He described the book as unnecessary and far inferior to the Bible, and he characterized those who believe the Book of Mormon as being misinformed.

Of fifty-six anti-Mormon novels published during the nineteenth century, four established a pattern for all of the others. The four were sensational, erotic novels focusing on the supposed plight of women in the Church. Alfreda Eva Bell's *Boadicea, the Mormon Wife* (1855) depicted Church members as "murderers, forgers, swindlers, gamblers, thieves, and adulterers!" Orvilla S. Belisle's *Mormonism Unveiled* (1855) had the heroine hopelessly trapped in a Mormon harem. Metta Victoria Fuller Victor's *Mormon Wives* (1856) characterized Mormons as a "horrid" and deluded people. Maria Ward (a pseudonym) depicted Mormon torture of women in *Female Life Among the Mormons* (1855). Authors wrote lurid passages designed to sell the publications. Excommunicated members tried to capitalize on their former membership in the Church to sell their stories. Fanny Stenhouse's *Tell It All* (1874) and Ann Eliza Young's *Wife No. 19* (1876) sensationalized the polygamy theme. William Hickman sold his story to John H. Beadle, who exaggerated the Danite myth in *Brigham's Destroying Angel* (1872) to caricature Mormons as a violent people.

Church leaders responded to these attacks and adverse publicity only through sermons and admonitions. They defended the Church's fundamental doctrine of revelation and authority from God. During the period of federal prosecution, the First Presidency condemned the acts against the Church by the U.S. Congress and Supreme Court as violations of the United States Constitution.

THE SEARCH FOR A PSYCHOLOGICAL EXPLANATION (1897–1945). After the Church officially discontinued polygamy in 1890, the public image of Mormonism improved and became moderately favorable. However, in 1898 Utah elected to the U.S. Congress B. H. Roberts, who had entered into plural marriages before the Manifesto. His election revived polygamy charges and further exposés by magazine muckrakers, and Congress refused to seat him. During the congressional debate, the Order of Presbytery in Utah issued a publication, *Ten Reasons Why Christians Cannot Fellowship the Mormon Church*, mainly objecting to the doctrine of modern revelation.

The election of Reed Smoot to the U.S. Senate (January 20, 1903) prompted additional controversy. Although he was not a polygamist, Smoot was a member of the Quorum of the Twelve Apostles. Ten months after he had been sworn in as a senator, his case was reviewed by the Senate Committee on Privileges and Elections. The Smoot hearings lasted from January 1904 to February 1907. Finally, in 1907 the Senate voted to allow him to take his seat. The First Presidency then published *An Address to the World*, explaining the Church's doctrines and answering charges. The Salt Lake Ministerial Association rebutted that address in the *Salt Lake Tribune* on June 4, 1907.

During 1910 and 1911, *Pearson's, Collier's, Cosmopolitan, McClure's*, and *Everybody's* magazines published vicious anti-Mormon articles. *McClure's* charged that the Mormons still practiced polygamy. *Cosmopolitan* compared Mormonism to a viper with tentacles reaching for wealth and power. The editors called the Church a "loathsome institution" whose "slimy grip" had served political and economic power in a dozen western states. These articles are classified by Church historians as the "magazine crusade."

The advent of the motion picture brought a repetition of the anti-Mormon stereotype. From 1905 to 1936, at least twenty-one anti-Mormon films were produced. The most sordid of them were *A Mormon Maid* (1917) and *Trapped by the Mormons* (1922). The films depicted polygamous leaders seeking women converts to satisfy their lusts, and Mormons murdering innocent travelers in secret rites. Some of the most virulent anti-Mormon writings at this time came from Britain. Winifred Graham (Mrs. Theodore Cory), a professional anti-Mormon novelist, charged that Mormon missionaries were taking advantage of World War I by proselytizing women whose husbands were away to war. The film *Trapped by the Mormons* was based on one of her novels.

When the Spaulding theory of Book of Mormon origins was discredited, anti-Mormon proponents turned to psychology to explain Joseph Smith's visions and revelations. Walter F. Prince and Theodore Schroeder offered explanations for Book of Mormon names by way of imaginative but remote psychological associations. I. Woodbridge Riley claimed in *The Founder of Mormonism* (New York, 1903) that "Joseph Smith, Junior was an epileptic." He was the first to suggest that Ethan Smith's *View of the Hebrews* (1823) and Josiah Priest's *The Wonders of Nature and Providence, Displayed* (1825) were the sources for the Book of Mormon.

At the time the Church commemorated its centennial in 1930, American historian Bernard De Voto asserted in the *American Mercury*, "Unquestionably, Joseph Smith was a paranoid." He later admitted that the *Mercury* article was a "dishonest attack" (*IE* 49 [Mar. 1946]:154).

Harry M. Beardsley, in *Joseph Smith and His Mormon Empire* (1931), advanced the theory that Joseph Smith's visions, revelations, and the Book of Mormon were by-products of his subconscious mind. Vardis Fisher, a popular novelist with Mormon roots in Idaho, published *Children of God: An American Epic* (1939). The work is somewhat sympathetic to the Mormon heritage, while offering a naturalistic origin for the Mormon practice of polygamy, and describes Joseph Smith in terms of "neurotic impulses."

In 1945 Fawn Brodie published *No Man Knows My History,* a psychobiographical account of Joseph Smith. She portrayed him as a "prodigious mythmaker" who absorbed his theological ideas from his New York environment. The book repudiated the Rigdon-Spaulding theory, revived the Alexander Campbell thesis that Joseph Smith alone was the author of the book, and postulated that *View of the Hebrews* (following Riley, 1903) provided the basic source material for the Book of Mormon. Brodie's interpretations have been followed by several other writers.

Church scholars have criticized Brodie's methods for several reasons. First, she ignored valuable manuscript material in the Church archives that was accessible to her. Second, her sources were mainly biased anti-Mormon documents collected primarily in the New York Public Library, Yale Library, and Chicago Historical Library. Third, she began with a predetermined conclusion that shaped her work: "I was convinced," she wrote, "before I ever began writing that Joseph Smith was not a true prophet," and felt compelled to supply an alternative explanation for his works (quoted in Newell G. Bringhurst, "Applause, Attack, and Ambivalence—Varied Responses to Fawn M. Brodie's *No Man Knows My History,*" *Utah Historical Quarterly* 57 [Winter 1989]:47–48). Fourth, by using a psychobiographical approach, she imputed thoughts and motives to Joseph Smith. Even Vardis Fisher criticized her book, writing that it was "almost more a novel than a biography because she rarely hesitates to give the content of a mind or to explain motives which at best can only be surmised" (p. 57).

REVIVAL OF OLD THEORIES AND ALLEGATIONS (1946–1990). Anti-Mormon writers were most prolific during the post-Brodie era. Despite a generally favorable press toward the Church during many of these years, of all anti-Mormon books, novels, pamphlets, tracts, and flyers published in English before 1990, more than half were published between 1960 and 1990 and a third of them between 1970 and 1990.

Networks of anti-Mormon organizations operate in the United States. The *1987 Directory of Cult Research Organizations* contains more than a hundred anti-Mormon listings. These networks distribute anti-Mormon literature, provide lectures that attack the Church publicly, and proselytize Mormons. Pacific Publishing House in California lists more than a hundred anti-Mormon publications.

A broad spectrum of anti-Mormon authors has produced the invective literature of this period. Evangelicals and some apostate Mormons assert that Latter-day Saints are not Christians. The main basis for this judgment is that the Mormon belief in the Christian Godhead is different from the traditional Christian doctrine of the Trinity. They contend that Latter-day Saints worship a "different Jesus" and that their scriptures are contrary to the Bible. Another common tactic is to attempt to show how statements by past Church leaders contradict those by current leaders on such points as Adam as God, blood atonement, and plural marriage.

A current example of ridicule and distortion of Latter-day Saint beliefs comes from Edward Decker, an excommunicated Mormon and cofounder of Ex-Mormons for Jesus, now known as Saints Alive in Jesus. Professing love for the Saints, Decker has waged an attack on their beliefs. Latter-day Saints see his film and book, both entitled *The Godmakers*, as a gross misrepresentation of their beliefs, especially the temple ordinances. A regional director of the Anti-Defamation League of B'nai B'rith and the Arizona Regional Board of the National Conference of Christians and Jews are among those who have condemned the film.

Though anti-Mormon criticisms, misrepresentations, and falsehoods are offensive to Church members, the First Presidency has counseled members not to react to or debate those who sponsor them and has urged them to keep their responses "in the form of a positive explanation of the doctrines and practices of the Church" (*Church News*, Dec. 18, 1983, p. 2).

Two prolific anti-Mormon researchers are Jerald and Sandra Tanner. They commenced writing in 1959 and now offer more than 200 publications. Their main approach is to demonstrate discrepancies, many of which Latter-day Saints consider contrived or trivial, between current and past Church teachings. They operate and publish under the name of the Utah Lighthouse Ministry, Inc. Their most notable work, *Mormonism—Shadow or Reality?* (1964, revised 1972, 1987), contains the essence of their claims against the Church.

During the 1950s, 1960s, and early 1970s, the Church had a

generally favorable public image as reflected in the news media. That image became more negative in the later 1970s and the early 1980s. Church opposition to the equal rights amendment and the excommunication of Sonia Johnson for apostasy, the Church's position with respect to priesthood and BLACKS (changed in 1978), a First Presidency statement opposing the MX missile, the John Singer episode including the bombing of an LDS meetinghouse, tensions between some historians and Church leaders, the forged "Salamander" letter, and the other Mark Hofmann forgeries and murders have provided grist for negative press and television commentary. The political leverage of the Church and its financial holdings have also been subjects of articles with a strong negative orientation.

A widely circulated anti-Mormon book, *The Mormon Murders*, by Steven Naifeh and Gregory White Smith (1988), employs several strategies reminiscent of old-style anti-Semitism. The authors use the Hofmann forgeries and murders as a springboard and follow the stock anti-Mormon themes and methods found in earlier works. They explain Mormonism in terms of wealth, power, deception, and fear of the past.

Church leaders have consistently appealed to the fairness of readers and urged them to examine the Book of Mormon and other latter-day scriptures and records for themselves rather than to prejudge the Church based on anti-Mormon publications. In 1972 the Church established the Public Communications Department, headquartered in Salt Lake City, to release public information about the Church.

BIBLIOGRAPHY

No definitive history of anti-Mormon activities has been written. A sample of LDS sources on anti-Mormonism follows:

Allen, James B., and Leonard J. Arrington. "Mormon Origins in New York: An Introductory Analysis." *BYU Studies* 9 (1969):241–74. Analyzes pro-Mormon and anti-Mormon approaches.

Anderson, Richard Lloyd. "Joseph Smith's New York Reputation Reappraised." *BYU Studies* 10 (1970):283–314. Analyzes the Hurlbut-Howe affidavits published in *Mormonism Unvailed*.

Bunker, Gary L., and Davis Bitton. *The Mormon Graphic Image 1834–1914*. Salt Lake City, 1983. Traces the history of anti-Mormon caricature.

Bushman, Richard L. *Joseph Smith and the Beginnings of Mormonism*. Urbana, Ill., 1984. Discusses the early anti-Mormonism writings of Campbell, Howe, and Hurlbut.

Kirkham, Francis W. *A New Witness for Christ in America*, 2 vols. Independence,

Mo., 1942, and Salt Lake City, 1952. Examines the early newspaper articles and anti-Mormon explanations for the origin of the Book of Mormon.
Nibley, Hugh W. *The Mythmakers*. Salt Lake City, 1961. Surveys the anti-Mormon writers during the Joseph Smith period.
———. "Censoring the Joseph Smith Story," *IE* 64 (July, Aug., Oct., Nov. 1961). Serialized articles examining how fifty anti-Mormon works treat the Joseph Smith story.
———. *Sounding Brass*. Salt Lake City, 1963. Surveys the anti-Mormon writers during the Brigham Young period.
———. *The Prophetic Book of Mormon*, CWHN 8 chaps. 4–8, 10–12, examines anti-Mormon arguments.
Scharffs, Gilbert W. *The Truth About the Godmakers*. Salt Lake City, 1986. Treats the film *The Godmakers*.

WILLIAM O. NELSON

ARCHAEOLOGY

Archaeology is the study and interpretation of past human cultures based on known material remains. Biblical and Mesoamerican archaeological research is of special interest to Latter-day Saints.

Archaeological data from the ancient Near East and the Americas have been used both to support and to discredit the Book of Mormon. Many scholars see no support for the Book of Mormon in the archaeological records, since no one has found any inscriptional evidence for, or material remains that can be tied directly to, any of the persons, places, or things mentioned in the book (Smithsonian Institution).

Several types of indirect archaeological evidence, however, have been used in support of the Book of Mormon. For example, John L. Sorenson and M. Wells Jakeman tentatively identified the Olmec (2000–600 B.C.) and Late Pre-Classic Maya (300 B.C.–A.D. 250) cultures in Central America with the Jaredite and Nephite cultures, based on correspondences between periods of cultural development in these areas and the pattern of cultural change in the Book of Mormon.

Likewise, parallels between cultural traits of the ancient Near East and Mesoamerica perhaps indicate transoceanic contacts between the two regions. Among these are such minor secondary traits as horned incense burners, models of house types, wheel-made pottery, cement, the true arch, and the use of stone boxes. All of these may, however, represent independent inventions. Stronger evidence for contacts may be found in the Tree of Life motif, a common religious theme, on Stela 5 from Izapa in Chiapas, Mexico. Jakeman, in 1959, studied Stela 5 in detail and concluded that it represented the sons of a legendary ancestral couple absorbing and perhaps recording their knowledge of a munificent Tree of Life. This can be compared favorably to the account of Lehi's vision in the Book of Mormon (1 Ne. 8).

The presence of a bearded white deity, Quetzalcoatl or Kukulcan, in the pantheon of the Aztec, Toltec, and Maya has also been advanced as indirect evidence of Christ's visit to the New World. The deity is represented as a feathered serpent, and elements of his worship may have similarities to those associated with Christ's Atonement.

Recent work by LDS professional archaeologists such as Ray Matheny at El Mirador and by the New World Archaeological Foundation in Chiapas has been directed toward an understanding of the factors that led to the development of complex societies in Mesoamerica in general. Under C. Wilfred Griggs, a team of Brigham Young University scholars has sponsored excavations in Egypt, and other LDS archaeologists have been involved in projects in Israel and Jordan.

Another area of archaeological investigation is in LDS history. Dale Berge's excavations at Nauvoo; the Whitmer farm in New York; the early Mormon settlement of Goshen (Utah); the Utah mining town of Mercur; and, most recently, Camp Floyd, the headquarters of Johnston's army in Utah, have provided information about the economic and social interactions between early Mormon and non-Mormon communities.

BIBLIOGRAPHY

Griggs, C. Wilfred, ed. *Excavations at Seila, Egypt*. Provo, Utah, 1988.

Jakeman, M. Wells. "The Main Challenge of the Book of Mormon to Archaeology; and a Summary of Archaeological Research to Date Giving a Preliminary Test of Book-of-Mormon Claims." In *Progress in Archaeology, An Anthology*, ed. R. Christensen, pp. 99–103. Provo, Utah, 1963.

———. "Stela 5, Izapa, as 'The Lehi Tree-of-Life Stone.'" In *The Tree of Life in Ancient America*, ed. R. Christensen. Provo, Utah, 1968.

Matheny, Ray T. "An Early Maya Metropolis Uncovered, Elmirador." *National Geographic* 172, no. 3 (1987):316–39.

Smithsonian Institution. "Statement Regarding the Book of Mormon." Department of Anthropology, National Museum of Natural History, SIL-76, 1982.

Sorenson, John L. "An Evaluation of the Smithsonian Institution's 'Statement' Regarding the Book of Mormon" *F.A.R.M.S. Paper*. Provo, Utah, 1982.

———. *An Ancient American Setting for the Book of Mormon*. Salt Lake City, 1985.

DAVID J. JOHNSON

ARCHITECTURE

In the first generation the architecture of The Church of Jesus Christ of Latter-day Saints bore the stamp of individuality and originality. With a membership of less than fifteen thousand, Latter-day Saints undertook three daring projects: the Kirtland Temple in Ohio, the master plan for the city of Nauvoo, Illinois, and the Nauvoo Temple.

The Kirtland Temple, designed by the Prophet Joseph Smith and Artemis Millett, has a pristine exterior free of extraneous detail and a well-planned interior bathed in natural light. The master plan for Nauvoo, created by Joseph Smith and others, was similar in concept to Smith's "plat for the City of Zion." It consisted of a grid of streets with gardens adjoining each dwelling. The highest hill was reserved for the temple, which rose above all other structures and made Nauvoo, as originally planned, a clear visual statement of the religious and social priorities of Mormon life. The Nauvoo Temple, designed by William Weeks, was similar to the Kirtland Temple but larger and more ornate.

After the westward migration to the Great Basin, other demanding projects were undertaken. City planning for Salt Lake City was similar to the master plan for Nauvoo, with the temple as the dominant feature. Four temples were commissioned to be built in four Utah cities: in Salt Lake City, St. George, and Logan under architect Truman O. Angell, and in Manti under architect William H. Folsom. The block and bulwark form of the earlier temples was retained but, except for St. George, the facades were elaborate. The tower scheme of the Salt Lake Temple became the symbol of the new dispensation and embodied the growing proclivity of the Church to prefer complexity rather than simplicity in its architecture.

In addition to temples, the Church continued to produce other important buildings that were architecturally impressive, notably its tabernacles. Among the most distinguished were the Coalville, Logan, and Brigham City tabernacles. The Salt Lake Tabernacle, designed by Truman O. Angell assisted by William H. Folsom and Henry Grow, remains the ideal of architectural integrity and is the zenith of Mormon architecture.

After 1900 the rapidly growing Church continued to produce a wide variety of religious structures, including temples, meetinghouses, and educational buildings, especially at Brigham Young University. Meetinghouses typically incorporated an axially organized chapel with pews arranged before an elevated central pulpit and an off-center sacrament table. Works of art and natural light were used sparingly. Early buildings in Salt Lake City included the classically detailed Church headquarters building, whose architect was Joseph Don Carlos Young, and the adjacent Hotel Utah. These structures, with the temple and tabernacle, became the architectural center of the Latter-day Saints and of Salt Lake City.

In the early decades of the twentieth century the Church commissioned temples in the western United States, Canada, Europe, and the South Pacific. The form of these structures differed from the earlier temples. Most were designed by Edward O. Anderson, and each featured a large, rectangular, flat-roofed assembly hall surmounted by a tower and enclosed by a lower mass of ancillary spaces. Natural light was admitted to the interior sparingly. The opaque character became the hallmark of future temples, including the Alberta Temple in Cardston, designed by Harold W. Burton. Its design received architectural commendation from outside the Church.

In response to worldwide growth and changes in organization, new buildings were added to the Church headquarters enclave. On Temple Square an annex was added to the temple, altering its symmetry. A 28–story office tower and plaza were constructed, designed by architect George Cannon Young. Restoration of the Lion and Beehive houses, originally Brigham Young's residences, was completed.

Burgeoning growth led to a centralized Church Building Committee. Standard plans were developed, first for meetinghouses or chapels and then for temples. The meetinghouses, categorized by size, phases, and configuration, were uniformly designed for wards and stakes regardless of location. The standard-plan temples, initially the work of architect Emil Fetzer, and first built in Ogden and Provo, were designed to accommodate up to 100 endowment sessions a day with maximum mobility. These single-towered edifices, of which more than a dozen have been built, all followed the same basic plan but employed changes and decoration in an attempt to capture a sense of individuality. After 1980 a second generation of standard-plan temples, credited to the Church architectural staff, was commissioned. These small, slightly differentiated structures, built in large urban centers worldwide, typically featured a broad, low roof with various tower arrangements which, by replicating the most obvious elements of the Salt Lake Temple, announced the Church's presence.

Throughout its history Mormon architecture has been more functional than experimental, more temperate than ornate, more restrained than innovative. There is a marked tendency to avoid any distraction from direct and personal spirituality. Latter-day Saints' concern for uniting heavenly principles with earthly practices has been adequately expressed in practical, durable, and extraordinarily well-maintained buildings and grounds.

FRANKLIN T. FERGUSON

ARTIFICIAL INSEMINATION

Artificial insemination is defined as placing semen into the uterus or oviduct by artificial rather than natural means. The Church does not approve of artificial insemination of single women. It also discourages artificial insemination of married women using semen from anyone but the husband. "However, this is a personal matter that ultimately must be left to the husband and wife, with the responsibility for the decision resting solely upon them" (*General Handbook of Instructions*, 11-4). Children conceived by artificial insemination have the same family ties as children who are conceived naturally. The *General Handbook of Instructions* (1989) states: "A child conceived by artificial insemination and born after the parents are sealed in the temple is born in the covenant. A child conceived by artificial insemination before the parents are sealed may be sealed to them after they are sealed."

BIBLIOGRAPHY
General Handbook of Instructions, 11-4. Salt Lake City, 1989.

FRANK O. MAY, JR.

ARTISTS, VISUAL

While the work of LDS artists encompasses many historical and cultural styles, its unity derives from their shared religious beliefs and from recurring LDS religious themes in their works. The absence of an official liturgical art has kept the Church from directing its artists into specified stylistic traditions. This has been especially conducive to variety in art as the Church has expanded into many different cultures, with differing artistic styles and traditions. Some of the aesthetic constants of LDS artists are the narrative tradition in painting, a reverence for nature, absence of nihilism, support of traditional societal values, respect for the human body, a strong sense of aesthetic structure, and rigorous craftsmanship.

The history of LDS painters begins in Nauvoo in the 1840s, in the second decade following the establishment of the LDS Church (1830). Two factors especially influenced the early development of an artistic tradition within this small, new church on the American frontier: missionary work abroad and the desire of new converts to join the main body of the members.

The first two LDS painters, both English converts, were Sutcliffe Maudsley (1809–1881), from Lancashire, and William W. Major (1804–1854), from Bristol. Maudsley painted the earliest portraits among the Latter-day Saints—primitive but accurate profiles of members of the Smith family in Nauvoo. Major, who crossed the plains in 1848, was the earliest painter in the Utah Territory. His most famous painting, begun in Winter Quarters and completed in the Salt Lake Valley, depicts Brigham Young and his family in the stagelike interior of an imaginary English mansion, an attempt to transplant to the American frontier a British art tradition that goes back to Gainsborough.

In 1853 another English convert painter, Frederick H. Piercy (1830–1891), journeyed to Utah, making detailed sketches and watercolor drawings along the way to illustrate an LDS emigrant guide book, *Route from Liverpool to Great Salt Lake Valley*. This visual record is the earliest extant series showing the Mormon route. Many of its original paintings and drawings are in the Boston Museum of Fine Arts.

Over the next quarter of a century, many more British converts who were artists, most with limited formal education and modest art training in England, migrated to Utah. Almost all of them painted the mountains and the Great Salt Lake in the exaggerated and romantic styles then popular in England. Romantic landscapes were linked to their religious faith. They saw the face of the Lord in nature and Zion in the purity of the western wilderness. Very few of these early works by British converts depict genre or historical subjects. A major exception is the huge painting of Joseph Smith preaching to the Indians done for the Salt Lake Temple by London-born William Armitage (1817–1890).

Other prominent English convert painters from this period were Alfred Lambourne (1850–1926) and Henry Lavender Adolphus Culmer (1854–1914). Culmer received the most national recognition, primarily through his large paintings of the canyons and deserts of southern Utah published in the March 1907 issue of the *National Geographic Magazine*.

Contemporaneous Scandinavian convert painters included C. C. A. (Carl Christian Anton) Christensen (1831–1912), from Denmark, and Danquart A. Weggeland (1827–1918), from Norway. Both were trained at the Royal Academy of Art in Copenhagen and favored historical and genre paintings. Christensen's *Mormon Panorama* is the most significant series of LDS historical paintings from the nineteenth century. It includes twenty-three tempera paintings, each six feet by ten feet, recounting the pre-Utah history of the Church in epic dimensions. These paintings have been widely published (*Art in America* 58 [May–June 1970]:52–65) and exhibited (Whitney Museum of American Art, 1970).

An American-born painter in this early period was George M. Ottinger (1833–1917), from Philadelphia. His art includes both historical and landscape painting.

In 1890 the Church called some of the most skilled younger LDS painters to study in Paris. These "art missionaries," John Hafen (1856–1910), Lorus Pratt (1855–1923), John B. Fairbanks (1855–1940), Edwin Evans (1860–1946), and Herman H. Haag (1871–1895), studied art to prepare to paint the murals in the Salt Lake Temple. They studied academic figure drawing formally and impressionism informally. Other artists who also studied in Paris in this early period were James T. Harwood (1860–1940) and John W. Clawson (1858–1936), a grandson of Brigham Young.

These artists returned to Utah to paint and teach, and then sent their best students to Paris to study. This second wave included Mahonri M. Young (1877–1957), also a grandson of Brigham Young, and Donald Beauregard (1884–1914). Young returned to Utah and then went to New York City, where he taught at the Art Students League. In his lifetime he developed a national reputation as a sculptor and graphic artist. Beauregard spent most of his short artistic life in New Mexico, contributing to the early Santa Fe art tradition.

With the coming of World War I, the center of training for Utah painters shifted from Paris to New York City. The two most significant LDS artists of this period were Minerva K. Teichert (1888–1976) and LeConte Stewart (1891–1990). Both sought to celebrate their faith and tradition artistically, but in different ways. Teichert painted historical and genre scenes from LDS and western history and religious scenes from the Book of Mormon, while Stewart celebrated the pioneer landscape of Utah.

The next major leaders in LDS painting were Arnold Friberg (b. 1913) from Illinois, and Alvin Gittens (1921–1981), a convert from England. Both taught at the University of Utah. Friberg's most significant commissions included work for Cecil B. DeMille's *Ten Commandments* (for which he was nominated for an Academy Award), a series of scenes from the Book of Mormon, and portraits of Great Britain's Prince Charles and Queen Elizabeth II. Gittens was best known as a portrait painter and a teacher. He put his students through rigorous courses in anatomy and perspective when other art schools were emphasizing expressionism. Gittens was the region's preeminent portrait painter until his death.

In the early 1970s a new group of LDS painters began to form around Brigham Young University. These artists were particularly interested in exploring the interface between their religious faith and their art. The leading artists of the group were Gary E. Smith (b. 1942), a convert from Oregon; Dennis Smith (b. 1942) and William F. Whitaker, Jr. (b. 1943) from Utah; James Christensen (b. 1943) from California; and Trevor Southey (b. 1940), a convert from Zimbabwe. The Mormon Arts Festival, held annually at BYU from 1969 to 1984, served as a showplace for some of their best religious work.

Utah continues to attract LDS convert artists from outside the United States, and BYU has become a focus for this artistic immigration. Two of the most recent immigrant faculty are Wulf Barsch (b. 1943) from Germany and Soren Edsberg (b. 1945) from Denmark. Barsch, a winner of the 1975–1976 Prix de Rome, has built a national reputation from his strong semiabstract paintings, which often include LDS themes. Edsberg, the son of Knud Edsberg (b. 1911), a prominent Danish portrait and genre painter, has built a European reputation for his geometric paintings.

There are many other LDS painters who have not come to Utah. Giovanna Lacerti (b. 1935) and Pino Drago (b. 1947) from Italy and Johan Bentin (b. 1936) from Copenhagen are notable European LDS artists. Some of the most prominent Latin American and Caribbean LDS painters are Jorge Cocco (b. 1936) of Mexico, Antonio Madrid (b. 1949) of Panama, and Henri-Robert Bresil (b. 1952) from Haiti. They have produced important LDS paintings using artistic approaches totally different from their fellow LDS artists in Utah. Cocco and Madrid look to Spain for stylistic models. Bresil draws on the bright and exuberant folk tradition of Haiti.

In the South Pacific, Rei Hamon (b. around 1915), a part-Maori member of the Church from New Zealand, is an environmental artist. His tight stipple drawings celebrate his profoundly religious attachment to the land, plants, and animals of New Zealand.

In the American Southwest, many Native Americans have joined the Church as a result of missionary work going back to the 1850s. Some of the finest Hopi artists are LDS. Among the most prominent are Fannie Nampeyo Polacca (c. 1900–1987), her son Thomas (b. 1935), and Helen Naha (b. 1922), potters; Lowell Talishoma (b. 1950) and Emil Pooley (1908–1980), kachina carvers; and Wayne Sekaquaptewa (1923–1979) and Michael Sockyma (b. 1942), silversmiths. Among the Navajo, Lucy McKelvey (b. 1946) has a national reputation as a potter. Ida Redbird (1888–1971) is perhaps the most famous Maricopa potter. Among the Santa Clara, Christina (1892–1980) and Terrisita Naranjo (b. 1919) have national and international reputations as potters.

In Indonesia, where batik is the preeminent art form, Hadi Pranoto (b. 1937), from Java, is a respected batik artist. In Guatemala, where textile weaving is the main national art form, Juan Zarate (b. 1930), is an accomplished weaver.

Many Latter-day Saint women are fine quilters. Those with national reputations include Charlotte Anderson (b. 1952), from Kearns, Utah; Joyce Stewart (b. 1940), from Rexburg, Idaho; and Marva Dalebout (b. 1928), from St. George, Utah.

In the mountain West many LDS painters are known for their western and wildlife art. The rise of this art is part of a new self-confidence in a growing region of the country that is beginning to come of age. Jackson Hole, Wyoming; Santa Fe, New Mexico; and Scottsdale, Arizona, are significant centers of the American art market. The West, with its landscape, people, and animals, has become the wellspring of American mythology, and because many LDS people live in the West and have experienced much of the western heroic experience, western art has been a natural area of interest for them. Some of the leading LDS artists in this genre are Michael Coleman (b. 1946), Robert Duncan (b. 1941), Valoy Eaton (b. 1938), and Jim Norton (b. 1953), from Utah; Nancy Glazier (b. 1947) and Gary Carter (b. 1939), living in Montana; and Jim Wilcox (b. 1941), Harold Hopkinson (b. 1918), and Mel Fillerup (b. 1924), from Wyoming. Most paint in either a realist or an impressionist manner. In theme and intention, they are philosophical descendants of the early British and Scandinavian LDS immigrant artists who came west and were awed by the land but held to the epic tradition of which they were a part.

The geographical and cultural diversity of the LDS people has brought aesthetic variety to the LDS art tradition. The artists' shared religious faith and values have constantly infused that tradition with meaning.

Many works by LDS artists are displayed in the Museum of Church History and Art in Salt Lake City, which plays an important role in sharing LDS art with the world.

[*See also* Art in Mormonism; Musicians; Sculptors.]

BIBLIOGRAPHY

Gibbs, Linda Jones. *Masterworks*. Salt Lake City, 1984.

——. *Harvesting the Light: The Paris Art Mission and Beginnings of Utah Impressionism*. Salt Lake City, 1987.

Haseltine, James L. *100 Years of Utah Painting*. Salt Lake City, 1965.

Horne, Alice Merrill. *Devotees and Their Shrines: A Hand Book of Utah Art*. Salt Lake City, 1914.

Olpin, Robert S. *Dictionary of Utah Art*. Salt Lake City, 1980.

Oman, Richard G. "LDS Southwest Indian Art." *Ensign* 12 (Sept. 1982):33–48.

——, and Richard L. Jensen. *C. C. A. Christensen, 1831-1912: Mormon Immigrant Artist*. Salt Lake City, 1984.

Piercy, Frederick H. *Route from Liverpool to Great Salt Lake Valley*. Liverpool, 1855.

RICHARD G. OMAN

ART IN MORMONISM

From the earliest days of the Church, its leaders have recognized the significant role art plays in enlightening and inspiring Church members. For this reason, the First Presidency encouraged a group of young artists to study in France in the 1880s. They brought back both new artistic skills and an enthusiasm for the art they had seen in Europe. The many temple murals and other paintings done by these artists continue to educate, encourage, and inspire generations of Latter-day Saints. Because Mormon art has been primarily oriented toward service in the Church, much of it has been didactic. Artworks have been used to help teach gospel principles. Images illustrating Book of Mormon and Church history events have become familiar reminders of them. Artworks are also used to teach non-Mormons about Church history and doctrine.

The Church has supported the production of art vocally by pronouncement from the pulpit and financially by purchasing artwork for most of its buildings other than meetinghouses. It has established a Church art museum, which provides exhibition space for past and present LDS artists. Additionally, it sponsors an annual art competition. Many of its leaders, especially President Spencer W. Kimball (1972–1985), have challenged Church members to develop their artistic talents so that they can tell the story of the Church in art. Many LDS artists have accepted the challenge and are trying to create art that is both instructive and spiritually inspiring. Consequently, much LDS art has to do with things peculiar to the heritage of the Church and the LDS experience.

The purposes of inspiration and encouragement are equally important to the purpose of instruction in LDS art. Whether it is conveyed through a painted landscape or a sculpted human figure in solitary prayer, the spirit of LDS art is essentially the same: it evokes a sense of the goodness of God and of a belief in his eternal plan for mankind. It is this overarching philosophy, this spiritual perspective, that binds LDS artists together.

Even though LDS artists have been aware of contemporary trends in art, they have generally chosen not to follow the current avant-garde fashion. They have tried to relate their art in a pervasive, eternal sense to concerns that continually affect mankind. Their quest consists of the attempt to translate their religious ideals into their various mediums. Their search thus takes them on a different path from that of many other artists and attempts to lead them to the spiritual sources of their beliefs. Feeling that they will reach their goals only through direct access to this spiritual source, LDS artists seek inspiration as a means of attaining this quality in their art. For them, painting or sculpting is a private activity imbued with purpose that affects more than their artistic lives. By conducting their lives with a sense of truth and integrity, they hope to be brought closer to this spiritual core.

Much discussion about a "Mormon aesthetic" has taken place in recent years, but it seems that the very personal nature of this spiritual artistic quest prevents the attainment of a prevalent aesthetic. LDS artists are now found in many parts of the world, and their diverse cultures are providing the input of a wide variety of heritages. While LDS art is characterized by stylistic diversity, it also shows certain common features because of the shared faith of the artists.

BIBLIOGRAPHY
Bradshaw, Merrill K. "Toward a Mormon Aesthetic." *BYU Studies* 21 (Winter 1981):91–99.
Carmer, Carl. "A Panorama of Mormon Life." *Art in America* 58 (May–June 1970):52–65.
Packer, Boyd K. "The Arts and the Spirit of the Lord." *BYU Studies* 16 (Summer 1976):575–88.
"A Portfolio of Mormon Painters." *Ensign* 7 (July 1977):39–57.
Wheelwright, Lorin F., and Lael J. Woodbury, eds. *Mormon Arts*. Provo, Utah, 1972.

Young, Mahonri Sharp. "Mormon Art and Architecture." *Art in America* 58 (May–June 1970):66–69.

MARTHA MOFFITT PEACOCK

AUTOPSY

The Church of Jesus Christ of Latter-day Saints holds that an autopsy may be performed if the family of the deceased gives consent and if the autopsy complies with the law of the community. The purpose of an autopsy is, where possible, to examine the results of trauma or disease recorded in the vital organs of the body so as to define the specific cause of death for the family, the community, and the professionals who attended the deceased. It also permits the training and instruction of those who continue the search for better ways of coping with disease. It is one of the methods whereby both those who die and those who examine them contribute to improving the quality of life and health of their fellow human beings.

FRANK D. ALLAN

B

BIRTH CONTROL

The *General Handbook of Instructions* for Church leaders has the following instructions concerning birth control: "Husbands must be considerate of their wives, who have a great responsibility not only for bearing children but also for caring for them through childhood. . . . Married couples should seek inspiration from the Lord in meeting their marital challenges and rearing their children according to the teachings of the gospel" (*General Handbook*, 11-4).

Interpretation of these general instructions is left to the agency of Church members. One of the basic teachings of the Church, however, is that spirit children of God come to earth to obtain a physical body, to grow, and to be tested. In that process, adults should marry and provide temporal bodies for those spirit children. For Latter-day Saints, it is a blessing, a joy, and also an obligation to bear children and to raise a family.

One of the cornerstones of the gospel is agency or choice. Latter-day Saints believe that everyone will be held responsible for the choices they make. Many decisions involve the application of principles where precise instructions are not given in the *General Handbook of Instructions* or in the scriptures. The exercise of individual agency is therefore required, and Latter-day Saints believe that personal growth results from weighing the alternatives, studying matters carefully, counseling with appropriate Church leaders, and then seeking inspiration from the Lord before making a decision.

Church members are taught to study the question of family planning, including such important aspects as the physical and mental health of the mother and father and their capacity to provide the basic necessities of life. If, for personal reasons, a couple prayerfully decides that having another child immediately is unwise, birth control may be appropriate. Abstinence, of course, is a form of contraception. Like any other method, however, it has its side effects, some of which may be harmful to the marriage relationship.

Prophets past and present have never stipulated that bearing children was the sole function of the marriage relationship. They have taught that physical intimacy is a strong force in expressing and strengthening the love bond in marriage, enhancing and reinforcing marital unity.

Decisions regarding the number and spacing of children are to be made by husband and wife together, in righteousness, and through empathetic communication, and with prayer for the Lord's inspiration. Latter-day Saints believe that persons are accountable not only for what they do but for why they do it. Thus, regarding family size and attendant questions, members should desire to multiply and replenish the earth as the Lord has commanded. In that process, God intends that his children use the agency that he has given them in charting a wise course for themselves and their families.

BIBLIOGRAPHY
The Church of Jesus Christ of Latter-day Saints. *General Handbook of Instructions*, 11-4. Salt Lake City, 1989.
"I Have a Question." *Ensign* 9 (Aug. 1979):23–24.

HOMER S. ELLSWORTH

BLACKS

The history of black membership in The Church of Jesus Christ of Latter-day Saints can be divided between the era from 1830 to June 1978 and the period since then.

HISTORY.   Though few in number, blacks have been attracted to the

Church since its organization. Early converts (such as Elijah Abel) joined during the 1830s; others (such as Jane Manning James) joined after the Saints moved to Illinois. Among those who came to Utah as pioneers were Green Flake, who drove Brigham Young's wagon into the Salt Lake Valley, and Samuel Chambers, who joined in Virginia as a slave and went west after being freed. Throughout the twentieth century, small numbers of blacks continued to join the Church, such as the Sargent family of Carolina County, Virginia, who joined in 1906; Len and Mary Hope, who joined in Alabama during the 1920s; Ruffin Bridgeforth, a railroad worker in Utah, converted in 1953; and Helvécio Martins, a black Brazilian businessman, baptized in 1972 (he became a General Authority in 1990). These members remained committed to their testimonies and Church activities even though during this period prior to 1978 black members could not hold the priesthood or participate in temple ordinances.

The reasons for these restrictions have not been revealed. Church leaders and members have explained them in different ways over time. Although several blacks were ordained to the priesthood in the 1830s, there is no evidence that Joseph Smith authorized new ordinations in the 1840s, and between 1847 and 1852 Church leaders maintained that blacks should be denied the priesthood because of their lineage. According to the book of Abraham (now part of the Pearl of Great Price), the descendants of Cain were to be denied the priesthood of God (Abr. 1:23–26). Some Latter-day Saints theorized that blacks would be restricted throughout mortality. As early as 1852, however, Brigham Young said that the "time will come when they will have the privilege of all we have the privilege of and more" (Brigham Young Papers, Church Archives, Feb. 5, 1852), and increasingly in the 1960s, Presidents of the Church taught that denial of entry to the priesthood was a current commandment of God, but would not prevent blacks from eventually possessing all eternal blessings.

Missionaries avoided proselytizing blacks, and General Authorities decided not to send missionaries to Africa, much of the Caribbean, or other regions inhabited by large populations of blacks. Before World War II, only German-speaking missionaries were sent to Brazil, where they sought out German immigrants. When government war regulations curtailed proselytizing among Germans, missionary work was expanded to include Portuguese-speaking Brazilians. Determining genealogically who was to be granted and who denied the priesthood became increasingly a sensitive and complex issue.

During the civil rights era in the United States, denial of the priesthood to blacks drew increasing criticism, culminating in athletic boycotts of Brigham Young University, threatened lawsuits, and public condemnation of the Church in the late 1960s. When questioned about the Church and blacks, Church officials stated that removal of the priesthood restriction would require revelation from God—not policy changes by men.

RECENT DEVELOPMENTS.   On June 9, 1978, President Spencer W. Kimball announced the revelation that all worthy males could hold the priesthood. Following this official revelation, proselytizing was expanded worldwide to include people of African descent. Between 1977 and 1987, Church membership grew from 3,969,000 to 6,440,000, an increase of 62 percent. Because LDS membership records do not identify race, it is impossible to measure accurately the growth of black membership, except in areas where people are largely or exclusively of African descent. In the Caribbean, excepting Puerto Rico, membership grew from 836 to 18,614 and in Brazil from 51,000 to 250,000 during that decade.

In other areas of Latin America, such as Colombia and Venezuela, increasing numbers of blacks also joined the Church. In Europe, blacks, including African immigrants to Portugal, joined the Church. Moreover, in Ghana, Nigeria, and throughout west and central Africa, missionary work expanded at a phenomenal rate. Excluding South Africa, where the membership was predominantly white, membership grew from 136 in 1977 to 14,347 in 1988, almost all in west Africa.

The LDS Afro-American Oral History Project, conducted by the Charles Redd Center for Western Studies at Brigham Young University, demonstrated the increasing number of black members in the United States. Through interviews with black Latter-day Saints throughout the country, a symposium on LDS Afro-Americans held at Brigham Young University, and responses to a mailed survey, a more reliable flow of data was generated about the thoughts, feelings, convictions, and experiences of LDS Afro-Americans. The study found that within the Church Afro-Americans experience both high acceptance and, paradoxically, cultural miscommunications. For example, in response to the survey, 81 percent felt their future as blacks in the Church was hopeful. They explained that they experienced more social interactions and more meaningful relationships with Church members of all races, especially whites. At the same time, however, 46 percent said white members were not aware of the "needs and problems of black members." Some felt a lack of fellowship as well as economic and racial prejudice from white members.

Black Latter-day Saints are a nonhomogeneous mix of various "kindreds, tongues, and peoples" emerging from thousands of years of unprecedented religious and cultural exclusions. As with LDS Afro-Americans, many black members outside the United States encounter contrasting circumstances of full ecclesiastical involvement, on the one hand, and general Church ignorance of their respective cultures, on the other hand. Local leaders and members (primarily white Latter-day Saints) often lack a good working knowledge of black members' needs, concerns, and circumstances. Despite the 1978 priesthood revelation and expanded missionary work among blacks, unexplored challenges to their growth and retention remain in counterpoint to their happiness with priesthood inclusion.

Despite the cultural miscommunications that remain, black Latter-day Saints enjoy opportunities in all phases of Church activity, including missionary work, quorum leadership, bishoprics, and stake presidencies, along with other members. The first entirely black African stake was organized in 1988. Indeed, black Latter-day Saints may be an LDS historical enigma that has emerged as a prime example of success in LDS brotherhood and sisterhood.

BIBLIOGRAPHY

Bringhurst, Newell G. *Saints, Slaves, and Blacks*. Westport, Conn., 1981.

Carter, Kate B. "The Negro Pioneer." In *Our Pioneer Heritage*, Vol. 8, pp. 497–580. Salt Lake City, 1965.

Embry, Jessie L. "Separate but Equal? Black Branches, Genesis Groups, or Integrated Wards?" *Dialogue* 23 (Spring 1990):11–37.

LDS Afro-American Oral History Project. Brigham Young University, Provo, Utah, 1985–1988.

ALAN CHERRY
JESSIE L. EMBRY

BLIND, MATERIALS FOR THE

During his earthly ministry, Jesus was always sensitive to individuals and their personal needs. He paid particular attention to those with handicaps and healed many of their infirmities (e.g., Matt. 11:5). Today, The Church of Jesus Christ of Latter-day Saints teaches similar sensitivity to people with special needs.

Since 1904, the Church has produced gospel materials for the blind and the visually impaired, and now all such people may obtain these materials in a wide variety of helpful formats.

Access to printed material is often inadequate for the visually impaired. To help overcome this lack, the Church produces materials on audiocassettes, in Braille, and in large-print versions. Audiocassettes are available at both standard and half-speed. Half-speed cassettes require the type of slow-speed cassette player that the Library of Congress lends to visually impaired persons in the United States.

The Church provides the scriptures on audiocassettes, in large type, in Braille and it also produces courses of study and selected Church books in Braille and on audiocassettes. The words to Church hymns are available in Braille and on recordings.

The *Ensign* magazine and selections from the *New Era* and *Friend* magazines are recorded on half-speed, four-track audiocassettes each month and mailed as the *Ensign Talking Book* to several thousand subscribers worldwide. The First Presidency Message and the *Friend* are also produced in Braille each month.

JOSIAH W. DOUGLAS

BLOOD TRANSFUSIONS

Although there are references in scripture to the sacredness of blood, the Church does not hold that any scripture or revelation prohibits giving or receiving blood or blood products, such as gamma globulin, the antihemophilic factor, and antibodies through transfusion or injection, and it is therefore not opposed to its members engaging in such practices. In fact, individual wards sometimes have blood drives to increase a supply on hand when a ward member might need a transfusion. The Church, however, leaves the decision of whether to be a donor or a recipient of a blood transfusion or blood products to the individual member or family concerned.

The Church recognizes that the use of blood transfusions and blood products often saves lives by replacing blood serum volume, red and white cells, platelets, and other substances that may have been lost or damaged by disease, accident, or surgical operation. It is also aware that many operative procedures, such as open-heart surgery and organ transplantation, could not be as safely performed and that many diseases, such as leukemia, aplastic anemia, and certain types of cancers, could not be adequately treated without blood and blood-product transfusions.

Blood transfusions can carry very harmful and life-threatening diseases, such as acquired immunodeficiency syndrome (AIDS), hepatitis, and other infectious diseases, and therefore may be a hazard. However, these hazards may be completely eliminated in non-emergency operations by the process of autotransfusion, whereby a patient's own blood is donated, stored, and given back when needed. This practice is feasible because blood can be stored for a number of months. However, the Church leaves all decisions about the use or nonuse of blood to the member or family concerned in consultation with their physician.

RICHARD A. NIMER

BONNEVILLE INTERNATIONAL CORPORATION

In 1964 KSL and other Church-owned commercial broadcasting stations and operations were consolidated into Bonneville International Corporation (BIC), headquartered in Salt Lake City. The founding president of BIC was Arch L. Madsen. He was succeeded by Rodney H. Brady in 1985. Historically, its board of directors has included a member of the First Presidency.

In addition to KSL Radio and Television, Bonneville has acquired and founded several other units: (1) a television station in Seattle, (2) radio stations in Seattle, New York City, Kansas City, Los Angeles, Chicago, San Francisco, Dallas, and Phoenix; (3) Bonneville Media Communications, a full-service production and advertising company located in Salt Lake City; (4) Bonneville Washington News Bureau, in the nation's capital; (5) Bonneville Broadcasting System (BBS), a music programming service in Northbrook, Illinois, that provides "easy listening" and "soft adult contemporary" music programming to radio stations throughout the United States and abroad; (6) Bonneville Satellite Corporation, which was formed in Salt Lake City in 1980 and much of which was sold in 1987, with BIC retaining interest as a limited partner; and (7) Bonneville Entertainment Company, incorporated in 1981.

Bonneville programming reaches an international audience through placement of programs, public service messages, and other services on stations throughout the world, with emphasis on values-oriented programming. Bonneville stations do not proselytize for the Church, and religious programming (generally confined to Sunday morning) includes representation from all major religions. Neither BIC nor its divisions use their facilities to solicit funds for the Church. Bonneville and its divisions are taxpaying, commercial enterprises.

The philosophy of BIC is summarized in this excerpt from the company's statement of "Mission and Commitments": "We are a values-driven company composed of values-driven people. We are committed to serving and improving individuals, communities, and society through providing quality broadcast entertainment, information, news, and values-oriented programming."

BIBLIOGRAPHY

"Bonneville International Corporation." Brochure, Salt Lake City, 1989.
Wolsey, Heber G. "The History of Radio Station KSL from 1922 to Television." Ph.D. diss., Michigan State University, 1967.

RODNEY H. BRADY

BRIGHAM YOUNG COLLEGE

President Brigham Young founded Brigham Young College (BYC) in Logan, Utah, on July 24, 1877, just two years after he founded Brigham Young Academy (Brigham Young University from 1903) in Provo, Utah. Established to train the youth of the Church in northern Utah, southern Idaho, and western Wyoming, BYC had nearly

40,000 students in its forty-nine years of operation (1877–1926). At first a normal school primarily preparing elementary teachers (1877–1894), it then inaugurated college courses and for fifteen years granted bachelors' degrees (1894–1909). During its final period (1910–1926), the school operated as a high school and junior college. With the Church Board of Education decision to discontinue its schools except Brigham Young University, Brigham Young College closed its doors in May 1926; gave its library to Utah State Agricultural College, also in Logan; and sold its buildings and land to Logan City to be used as a high school. The old BYC buildings were demolished in the 1960s, and the new Logan High School was built on the site.

Four alumni of Brigham Young College became members of the Quorum of the Twelve Apostles: Richard R. Lyman, Melvin J. Ballard, John A. Widtsoe, and Albert E. Bowen.

BIBLIOGRAPHY

Garr, Arnold Kent. "A History of Brigham Young College, Logan, Utah." Master's thesis, Utah State University, 1973.

Sorensen, A. N. "Brigham Young College." In *The History of a Valley: Cache Valley, Utah-Idaho*, ed. Joel E. Ricks, pp. 349–69. Logan, Utah, 1956.

ARNOLD K. GARR

BRIGHAM YOUNG UNIVERSITY

PROVO, UTAH, CAMPUS

Brigham Young University (BYU) is a four-year private institution located in Provo, Utah, owned and operated by The Church of Jesus Christ of Latter-day Saints as part of the Church Educational System. Twenty-seven thousand students from all fifty states and many other countries study under the direction of approximately 1,500 full-time faculty in the ten colleges and two professional schools. Approximately 80 percent of the students are enrolled in one of the 130 different undergraduate programs. Along with these extensive undergraduate programs, BYU offers master's and doctoral degrees in a variety of disciplines through fifty-seven graduate departments as well as the Law School and the Graduate School of Management. BYU awarded 6,421 degrees in the 1989–1990 school year. With its close ties to the sponsoring Church, BYU has been committed to providing the best possible postsecondary education for the youth of the Church in an atmosphere that emphasizes both teaching and scholarly research—both reasoned and revealed learning.

BYU functions under the direction of the Church through a board of trustees that includes the First Presidency, the general presidents of the women's auxiliary organizations, and selected General Authorities. The university operates on a budget provided by the Church, one-third of which is derived from student tuition.

STUDENTS. About 9,000 of BYU's 27,000 students are from Utah, 16,000 from other states, and 2,000 from countries outside the United States. Approximately 49 percent of the students are women, and 51 percent, men. About 25 percent of the students are married. Approximately 40 percent have served as missionaries for the Church. Most students live in apartments or dormitories on or near campus, and many work to support themselves while at school; about one-third of the students are employed part-time by the university.

In 1989, entering freshmen had an average American College Test (ACT) composite score of 24.7 (of a possible 36; the national average for all freshmen that year was 18.6) and an average high school grade point average (GPA) of 3.43 (of a possible 4.0). At that time BYU was fifth among the nation's private universities in the number of undergraduates who went on to earn doctoral degrees and eighteenth among all universities in the United States in the number of entering National Merit scholars.

Most students at BYU are members of The Church of Jesus Christ of Latter-day Saints; members of other faiths who will accept and observe its standards of conduct are welcome.

FACULTY. The 1,500 faculty members at Brigham Young University have degrees from most of the major universities of the United States, and most are members of the Church. This is the natural result of an expectation that the faculty member should be involved fully in the work of the university and should be able to exert influence on students in the full breadth of the mission of BYU, including teaching of religious education courses. Realizing that students are influenced religiously in all their classes, the university officers have sought to attract the best-qualified members of the Church to faculty positions;

however, well-qualified persons of other faiths are also employed on the faculty.

MISSION OF THE UNIVERSITY. The religious focus of BYU is evident in its *Bulletin's* declaration of purpose: "The mission of Brigham Young University—founded, supported, and guided by The Church of Jesus Christ of Latter-day Saints—is to assist individuals in their quest for perfection and eternal life. That assistance should provide a period of intensive learning in a stimulating setting where a commitment to excellence is expected and the full realization of human potential is pursued" (p. 1).

Latter-day Saints believe that the study of all truth is especially important for those who have received the saving truths of the gospel of Jesus Christ. The Lord has instructed, "Teach ye diligently and my grace shall attend you, that you may be instructed more perfectly in . . . things both in heaven and in the earth, and under the earth; things which have been, things which are, things which must shortly come to pass; . . . a knowledge also of countries and of kingdoms. . . . Seek ye out of the best books words of wisdom; . . . seek learning, even by study and also by faith" (D&C 88:78–79, 118).

On the occasion of his inauguration, Dallin H. Oaks, eighth president of BYU, said, "Our reason for *being* is to be a university. But our reason for *being a university* is to encourage and prepare young men and women to rise to their full spiritual potential as sons and daughters of God" (Inauguration Response of President Dallin H. Oaks, Nov. 1971, p. 18).

HISTORY. By the 1870s the economic state of the Church and its members was tenuous at best as they struggled to establish themselves in the Great Basin. A deep-rooted determination to learn had led them to establish community schools almost as soon as townsites were chosen (*see* ACADEMIES). The vision was higher than the performance, and although attendance was poor in some of the community elementary schools, President Brigham Young and others were planning more consequential and more influential schools, for, as he said, "all science and art belong to the Saints" (*JD* 10:224). "It is the business of the Elders of this Church," President Young said at another time, "to gather up all the truths in the world pertaining to life and salvation, to the Gospel we preach, to mechanism[s] of every kind, to the sciences, and to philosophy, wherever [they] may be found in every nation, kindred, tongue, and people, and bring it to Zion" (*JD* 7:283–84).

Consequently, late in 1875, Brigham Young donated a building and established the Brigham Young Academy in Provo. A preliminary term of instruction was held, beginning in January 1876; and in April of that year, Karl G. Maeser, a young, well-educated German immigrant, was appointed to lead the school. Maeser was instructed that "neither the alphabet nor the multiplication tables were to be taught without the Spirit of God" (Wilkinson and Skousen, p. 67). The school began with twenty-nine pupils in the elementary program and one teacher, Karl Maeser. In the words of Ernest L. Wilkinson, seventh president of BYU,

> The school was born in poverty, nurtured in conflict, orphaned by the death of Brigham Young, . . . left homeless when its uninsured building was completely destroyed by fire, threatened with faculty and administrative resignations because of irregular or missed salary payments, and nearly abandoned on many occasions because of lack of funds. . . . [At first the academy] was a private school without a sponsor or means of support. . . . It survived only because of the financial sacrifices made by its faculty and Board of Trustees and voluntary gifts from its friends and from The Church of Jesus Christ of Latter-day Saints. [Finally, after 21 years of struggling existence,] the school was incorporated as an educational subsidiary of the LDS Church, which assumed responsibility for its survival [Wilkinson and Skousen, p. xi].

In 1903 the board of trustees changed the name of the school from Brigham Young Academy to Brigham Young University. Nine years later, the board set enrollment limits at 1,300 for the high school and 250 for the college, with a maximum of fifteen paid teachers for the latter. Forty years after its founding, BYU awarded its first four-year college degree.

The university grew from 1,500 students in 1945 to 25,000 by 1970. Since 1970, by decision of the board of trustees, enrollment has been limited to between 25,000 and 27,000 students. Growth has continued, but in less visible ways, with improving facilities, students, and faculty and with the university taking a respected place among other institutions in the state, region, and nation. It continues to struggle with significant problems of growth. With the continuing expansion of Church membership, BYU feels pressure to admit more students than it can adequately accommodate.

The following men have led the institution for the past 115 years: Brigham Young Academy was directed initially by Warren N. Dusenberry (1875–1876) and then for a longer period by Karl G. Maeser (1876–1892), whose character and high educational standards had a permanent impact on the fledgling institution. The presidents of the university thereafter have been Benjamin Cluff, Jr. (1892–1903), George H. Brimhall (1904–1921), Franklin S. Harris (1921–1945), Howard S. McDonald (1945–1949), Ernest L. Wilkinson (1949–1971), Dallin H. Oaks (1971–1980), Jeffrey R. Holland (1980–1989), and Rex E. Lee (from 1989).

RELIGION AND RELIGIOUS EDUCATION.   LDS students at BYU are assigned to student wards, which hold their Sunday services in the academic buildings on campus. About 200 students belong to each ward. In these wards, many of the pastoral functions, including sermons, instruction, friendship, and support, are provided by the students themselves. Weekday social activities for students are organized around Church wards. BYU encourages students of other faiths to be actively associated with wards or with their congregations in the community.

Religious instruction represents the university's commitment to a wide spectrum of learning and is a direct response to such divine declarations as "it is impossible for a man to be saved in ignorance" (D&C 131:6) and "the glory of God is intelligence, or, in other words, light and truth" (D&C 93:36). Religious Education has fifty full-time and eighty part-time faculty who teach over 400 classes daily to approximately 22,000 students. It offers courses in scripture study (including the Old Testament, New Testament, Book of Mormon, Doctrine and Covenants, and Pearl of Great Price), Christian history, LDS Church history, family history (genealogy), comparative religion, biblical languages, and other topics.

GENERAL AND HONORS EDUCATION.   Honors and general education are emphasized at BYU. General education both underpins and complements fields of major study. The general education curriculum is designed to inform students of how fields of study have come to the present state of knowledge and to enhance their awareness of the methodological and cognitive constraints on the pursuit of truth. In addition, given BYU's concern that the development of individuals be eternal, general education entails continued inquiry into the gospel of Jesus Christ and its implications for knowledge, society, and truth. General-education courses undergo continuing faculty review and evaluation to consider the integration of material and rigorousness of method for each course.

The university's honors education program links a broad university perspective with the specific concentration of a major. It is open to all students, whether or not they choose to complete all the requirements for the designation "University Honors" at graduation.

COLLEGES AND PROGRAMS (1991).   The College of Biology and Agriculture has 100 faculty members and offers degrees in the following areas: agronomy and horticulture, animal science, biology, botany and range science, food science and nutrition, microbiology, and zoology. In addition, the college manages research and student training on an 800-acre farm and a 6,200-acre livestock ranch. The college oversees the Ezra Taft Benson Agriculture and Food Institute, which emphasizes training and research in small-plot agriculture and family nutrition for developing areas of the world. The college also manages a 460-acre wildlife preserve in southern Utah and the M. L. Bean Life Science Museum, which houses the university's extensive botanical and zoological collections.

The College of Education, with ninety-five faculty members, offers degree programs in education leadership, educational psychology, elementary education, and secondary education. In addition to an extensive program in the preparation of public school teachers and administrators on both the elementary and secondary levels, the college offers study in early childhood teaching, special-education teaching (for students who will work with those who have intellectual or emotional handicaps or learning disabilities), and communication sciences and disorders (speech and language pathology and audiology).

The College of Engineering and Technology has ninety-eight faculty in six departments: chemical engineering, civil engineering, electrical and computer engineering, mechanical engineering, industrial education, and technology. Research programs include the

Advanced Combustion Engineering Research Center, the CAM (computer-aided manufacturing) Software Research Center, the Catalysis Laboratory, the Engineering Computer Graphics Laboratory, and the Digital Signal Processing program.

The College of Family, Home, and Social Sciences has 200 faculty in fifteen academic departments and centers, including anthropology, clothing and textiles, economics, family sciences, geography, history, home economics, political science, psychology, social work, and sociology. The college supervises several centers and institutes, including the Center for Studies of the Family; the Charles Redd Center for Western Studies, which promotes research and publishing regarding the American West and maintains a large oral history program; the Joseph Fielding Smith Institute for Church History, which is primarily engaged in research and writing of history about The Church of Jesus Christ of Latter-day Saints, for both a professional and a general audience; the Center for Family and Community History, which supervises genealogy, family, community, and public history programs; and the David M. Kennedy Center for International Studies, which sponsors and supervises interdisciplinary programs in American, Asian, Canadian, European, Latin American, and Near Eastern studies.

The College of Fine Arts and Communications, with 135 faculty, offers thirty-seven areas of emphasis in art, communications, design, music, and theatre and film. The college has for its use five speech and drama theaters; two concert halls; two art galleries; a major art museum; and journalism, advertising, and broadcast laboratories, including a campus daily newspaper, and the university radio (KBYU-FM) and television (KBYU-TV) stations. The BYU Motion Picture Studio became part of the Church Audiovisual Department in 1991. In addition, musical ensembles and performing groups from the college tour each summer throughout the United States, Europe, and Asia.

The College of Humanities has 230 full-time faculty and offers majors in Asian, Classical, English, French, Germanic, Near Eastern, Portuguese, Slavic, and Spanish languages and literatures; humanities; comparative literature; library and information sciences; linguistics; and philosophy. As a result of their two-year mission experience in a foreign country, many students at BYU elect to continue language study in addition to their major emphasis, resulting in an unusually high number of students speaking foreign languages at BYU. The college also oversees the work of the Humanities Research Center, with a main emphasis on computer-assisted language and literature research; *BYU Studies*, a quarterly journal for the community of LDS scholars; the Center for the Study of Christian Values in Literature; and almost a dozen different foreign-language houses where students live in residence and carry on daily activities with native teachers.

The College of Nursing has forty faculty. It accepts approximately 120 baccalaureate students and fifteen master's students into its NLN-accredited program annually (National League for Nursing). Its programs offer emphases in family, medical-surgical, child, and psychological nursing.

The College of Physical and Mathematical Sciences, with 155 faculty, has departments of chemistry, computer science, geology, mathematics, physics and astronomy, and statistics. The college has established a number of special facilities and programs, including four State Centers of Excellence: X-ray imagery, chemical separations, computer-aided education, and supercritical fluid-separation technologies. The college also oversees the Center for Thermodynamics, the Center for Statistical and Computing Research, and research programs and special facilities for solid-state physics, astrophysics and astronomy, calorimetry, environmental chemistry, molecular structure studies, chemical separations, earth sciences, and fission-track dating.

The College of Physical Education has ninety faculty members and offers degrees in health sciences; physical education—dance; physical education—sports; recreation management and youth leadership. In intercollegiate athletics, BYU is a member of the Western Athletic Conference and participates in most intercollegiate sports for both men and women. The college oversees, in addition to its own degree programs, a campuswide intramural program consisting of more than sixty events involving thousands of women and men. The university's athletic facilities include not only large intercollegiate facilities for basketball, football, and track but also indoor and outdoor tracks, pools, courts, and playing fields that accommodate the intramural programs and other recreational exercise for students and faculty members.

The J. Willard and Alice S. Marriott School of Management has approximately 110 faculty in its six academic departments, including accountancy, business management, information management, managerial economics, public management, and organizational behavior. The Graduate School of Management offers the master of accountancy, the master of business administration, the executive MBA, the master of organizational behavior, the master of public administration, and the executive MPA programs. In addition, the School of Management coordinates university programs in Air Force and Army ROTC with their sixteen military faculty.

The J. Reuben Clark Law School, with its twenty-eight faculty members, offers a six-semester course of graduate professional study leading to the doctor of jurisprudence degree. The Law School also offers a master of comparative law program.

BYU offers several Study-Abroad programs, including semesters in several European and Asian countries, Mexico, and Israel (*see* BRIGHAM YOUNG UNIVERSITY: JERUSALEM CENTER FOR NEAR EASTERN STUDIES).

The Division of Continuing Education at BYU enrolls more than 390,000 students yearly in evening classes, independent study, conferences and workshops, travel study, study abroad, and other courses at centers in California; Ogden, Utah; Salt Lake City; and Rexburg, Idaho.

ACCREDITATION. BYU is fully accredited by the Northwest Association of Schools and Colleges. In addition, most professional programs of the university are reviewed, evaluated, and accredited by national and state associations and boards.

BIBLIOGRAPHY

Bergera, Gary James, and Ronald Priddis. *Brigham Young University: A House of Faith*. Salt Lake City, 1985.

Brigham Young University Bulletin (annual catalog). Provo, Utah, 1990.

Butterworth, Edwin. *Brigham Young University: 1,000 Views of 100 Years*. Provo, Utah, 1975.

Clark, Marden J. "On the Mormon Commitment to Education." *Dialogue* 7 (Winter 1972):11–19.

Holland, Jeffrey R. *A School in Zion*. Provo, Utah, 1988.

Kimball, Spencer W. "Second Century Address." *BYU Studies* 16 (Summer 1976):445–57.

King, Arthur H. "The Idea of a Mormon University." *BYU Studies* 13 (Winter 1973):115–25.

Pardoe, T. Earl. *The Sons of Brigham*. Provo, Utah, 1969.

Poll, Richard Douglas. *The Honors Program at Brigham Young University, 1960–1985*. Provo, Utah, 1985.

Waterstradt, Jean Anne, ed. *They Gladly Taught: Ten BYU Professors*. Provo, Utah, 1986.

Wilkinson, Ernest L., et al. *Brigham Young University: The First One Hundred Years*, 4 vols. Provo, Utah, 1975–1976.

———, and W. Cleon Skousen. *Brigham Young University: A School of Destiny*. Provo, Utah, 1976.

ELIOT A. BUTLER

NEAL E. LAMBERT

JERUSALEM CENTER FOR NEAR EASTERN STUDIES

The Jerusalem Center for Near Eastern Studies grew out of a Jerusalem "semester abroad" educational program for undergraduates instituted by Brigham Young University (BYU) in 1968. It became popular among Latter-day Saint students because of their commitment to the religious traditions of the Bible. The academic offerings at the Center focus on biblical and contemporary studies, correlated with a study of archaeology, biblical geography, Near Eastern history, Judaism, Islam, Near Eastern languages, and international relations and politics. Studies are enhanced with weekly field trips to biblical and historical sites in Israel and extended study tours to Jordan and Egypt.

Several academic programs, varying in content and covering periods ranging from a few weeks to six months, are offered at the Center for undergraduates and graduates. Research scholars from Brigham Young University also use these facilities, often in association with scholars and universities in the Middle East. In addition, the Center hosts a variety of continuing education programs or "travel study tours" for youths and adults.

The Center provides students a period of intensive learning in a stimulating setting in which a commitment to excellence is expected. Ideally, students conclude their studies in the Holy Land with deepened spiritual and intellectual appreciation of its history, peoples, and cultures.

The Jerusalem Center facilities are located on the northern half of the Mount of Olives, adjacent to the Mt. Scopus campus of Hebrew University. The eight-floor study center is terraced into the hillside. It is constructed of white Jerusalem limestone and designed with an architectural blend of domes, arches, and straight lines, complemented by flower gardens that feature several species of trees and bushes referred to in the Bible. The interior of the Center, with its cupolas, arches, galleries, and vaulted ceilings, is also congenial to its Near Eastern setting. Large windows and spacious patios offer a magnificent panorama of old and modern Jerusalem.

In the early 1980s the construction of the Center faced resolute opposition from certain religious circles and Israeli nationalist groups who feared that the Center might become a base for Mormon proselytizing of Jews. In the spirit of accommodation and out of a desire for peaceful INTERFAITH RELATIONS, BYU agreed with the government of Israel that the Center would be used exclusively for educational and cultural activities.

The Center also helps to serve the spiritual needs of Latter-day Saints, visiting or residing, in the Holy Land. An ecclesiastical organization consisting of a district and several branches has been established to provide worship services each sabbath.

BIBLIOGRAPHY
"BYU's Jerusalem Center Opens." *Ensign* 17 (June 1987):77.
"David Galbraith Heads BYU Jerusalem Center." *Ensign* 17 (Aug. 1987):79.

DAVID B. GALBRAITH

BRIGHAM YOUNG UNIVERSITY—HAWAII CAMPUS

BYU—Hawaii is a four-year, liberal arts institution located on northeastern Oahu, thirty-seven miles from Honolulu. Its multiracial student body of 2,000 comes from over fifty countries: 60 percent from Hawaii and the U.S. mainland, and 40 percent from the South Pacific and the Asian rim.

In 1865 the Church purchased 6,000 acres of land at Laie, where missionaries had conducted a primary school for many years. In 1921 David O. McKay, a member of the Quorum of the Twelve Apostles, visited the islands and became convinced that Church-sponsored higher education in Hawaii was essential to serve the Pacific basin. It was not until the late 1940s, however, that Church leaders of Oahu seriously began to investigate educational needs. In 1954 David O. McKay, then President of the Church, took definite steps to establish a school by appointing Dr. Reuben D. Law to head a proposed junior college in Laie.

In 1955, with a student body of 153—nearly all from Hawaii—and a faculty of 20, the Church College of Hawaii (CCH) was established as a two-year college and began classes in six war-surplus buildings while labor missionaries built a permanent campus. The school quickly expanded into a four-year teacher-training institution for Church schools in the South Pacific, which it remained for its first two decades. Midway through this period, following several years of effort to find a way to provide employment opportunities for the student body, the Church opened the POLYNESIAN CULTURAL CENTER in October 1963, which currently provides employment for nearly half the students.

In the early 1970s, CCH temporarily underwent a change of direction toward becoming a vocational school. A significant drop in enrollment resulted, however, and after careful study and reconsideration—both in Hawaii and in Utah—a decision was made to reestablish the college as a liberal-arts institution.

Major restructuring was initiated in 1974, when Church College of Hawaii was renamed Brigham Young University—Hawaii Campus and came under the direction of the president of BRIGHAM YOUNG UNIVERSITY in Provo, Utah. Since that time, enrollment has increased to 2,000 students.

Accredited by the Western Association of Schools and Colleges, the school is organized into seven academic divisions. Although there is no religious requirement for admission, all students and faculty are expected to follow the dress, grooming, and moral standards of the school's honor code. Since the late 1960s, BYU—Hawaii has excelled in various athletic competitions and has won national championships in rugby and men's and women's volleyball.

BIBLIOGRAPHY
Britsch, R. Lanier. *Moramona: The Mormons in Hawaii.* Laie, Hawaii, 1989.
Law, Reuben D. *The Founding and Early Development of The Church College of Hawaii.* St. George, Utah, 1972.

ALTON L. WADE

BROADCASTING

The Church of Jesus Christ of Latter-day Saints is a broadcasting entity. Its involvement in radio and television parallels the rapid expansion of those technologies that began during the early 1900s. In 1921 the Latter-day Saints University in Salt Lake City, Utah, received the first U.S. broadcast license issued to an educational institution. Radio in America developed primarily as a commercial rather than an educational service, as did the Church's broadcasting activities. On May 6, 1922, radio station KZN went on the air in Salt Lake City, and the Church began a long and complex involvement in broadcast and programming innovation.

In 1925 the call letters were changed to KSL when the Church assumed majority ownership of the station and hired Earl J. Glade, one of broadcasting's early pioneers, to manage its operation (*see* KSL RADIO).

KSL affiliated with the National Broadcasting Company (NBC) in 1929, which immediately began carrying broadcasts of the MORMON TABERNACLE CHOIR. These broadcasts continued until 1933, when KSL became a Columbia Broadcasting System (CBS) affiliate station. In 1936 the Tabernacle Choir Broadcast program took its present format as "Music and the Spoken Word" with Richard L. Evans as host. This Sunday morning radio program originating from the Mormon Tabernacle on Temple Square continues today as the longest continuously broadcast network program in America. "Music and the Spoken Word" has been translated for radio distribution into several languages. The format and style of this radio program set the pattern for much of the Church's subsequent programming efforts.

Technical innovation designed to improve signal quality and increase geographic coverage enhanced the Church's broadcast facilities. By 1933 KSL-AM was a Federal Communications Commission (FCC) Class 1-A clear-channel station transmitting at 50,000 watts, the maximum allowable power. During the 1940s and 1950s, FM radio and television stations were added, and the Church also acquired minority interest in two Idaho broadcast properties. FM radio, black-and-white and later color television, stereo sound, cable television, and satellite transmissions have become a major part of the Church's wide-ranging broadcast capabilities.

KSL-AM and its sister FM radio and television stations emerged as the equivalent of a graduate school in broadcast management, programming, engineering, journalism, and advertising. Many, like Arch L. Madsen, who had worked with Glade during KSL's early years, became leaders of international stature and reputation. Under Madsen's leadership in the late 1950s the regional intermountain broadcast activities of the Church were transformed into their present international scope.

In 1961 the Church expanded its international activities with the purchase of WNYW, call letters for five shortwave radio transmitters near Boston. Daily broadcasts to Europe and Latin America, most of them non–Church-related, were made in English, Spanish, Portuguese, French, and German. Church broadcasts included programs on Church news, values, and culture. The Tabernacle Choir broadcast and sessions of general conference were also programmed. In 1974, when the newer technologies of satellites, cable, and videotape were developed, the Church sold WNYW.

Bonneville International Corporation was formed in 1964 as the holding company for the Church's broadcast properties. Bonneville acquired radio and television stations in Seattle, Washington, and additional radio facilities throughout the United States, giving it commercial licenses for seven FM, five AM, and two television stations in 1990.

Three more FCC noncommercial, educational licenses are held by the Church's educational institutions in Utah and Idaho. Brigham Young University operates KBYU-FM and TV. RICKS COLLEGE operates KRIC-FM, primarily for student training. The production capacity of these stations also allows them to serve Church educational objectives that are unfeasible for commercial broadcast activities.

The Church also holds interests in satellite communications and cable television distribution systems. The first intercontinental satellite transmission between North America and Europe included a performance by the Tabernacle Choir.

Early commercial network affiliation with NBC and CBS led to a basic broadcast philosophy grounded in a belief that FCC licenses are held as a public trust and not as preaching tools. The Church has avoided an evangelistic style of radio and television broadcasting and has limited the religious content of its programming. It is felt that the value and contribution of these facilities would diminish if the stations were used exclusively for religious purposes.

Most of the Church's programming efforts in both radio and television have been keyed to creating a favorable image for the Church rather than presenting its doctrine and making converts. "Music and the Spoken Word," public service announcements, BYU basketball and football games, and an assortment of public affairs and cultural programs have dominated the Church's primary programming content.

The Church's semiannual general conference broadcasts are a significant exception to this rule. The first general conference was broadcast by KSL in 1924. Since then the broadcast reach of general conference has been expanded to cover much of the world. Through broadcast, cable, satellite, and videotape distribution, the conferences are translated into several languages and distributed to stations in many countries through Bonneville International productions.

During the 1970s the Church experimented with a more direct approach to broadcasting a doctrinal message through a prime-time special, "A Christmas Child." Since this broadcast, a number of Church-produced programs have focused on specific doctrinal messages. The production of programs that teach gospel principles directly to the audience has moved higher on the list of Church broadcast priorities.

BIBLIOGRAPHY

Emery, Walter B. *Broadcasting and Government: Responsibilities and Regulations*, pp. 37–38. East Lansing, Mich., 1961.

Kahn, Frank J., ed. *Documents of American Broadcasting*, 3rd ed., pp. xvii, 72–73, 426–27. Englewood Cliffs, N.J., 1978.

Witherspoon, John, and Roselle Kovitz. "The History of Public Broadcasting," pp. 7, 81. Washington, D.C., 1987.

BRUCE L. CHRISTENSEN

BURIAL

The Church of Jesus Christ of Latter-day Saints counsels its members to bury their dead in the earth to return dust to dust, unless the law of the country requires CREMATION. However, the decision whether to bury or cremate the body is left to the family of the deceased, taking into account any laws governing the matter. Burial of the body usually follows a funeral or graveside service. The body of a deceased member of the Church who has received the temple endowment should be dressed in temple clothing. Relief Society sisters dress deceased women, and priesthood brethren the men. When it is not possible to clothe the body, temple clothing may be laid over it.

A member of the bishopric typically presides at the burial, where a simple, earnest prayer is offered to dedicate the grave, with blessings promised as the Spirit dictates. This prayer may include a dedication of the grave as a sacred resting place until the resurrection if the person giving the prayer holds the Melchizedek Priesthood and has been asked to give such a dedication. The grave site often becomes a sacred spot for the family of the deceased to visit and care for.

CHARLES D. TATE, JR.

BUSINESS

[*This is a two-part entry:*

LDS Attitudes Toward Business
Church Participation in Business

The first article explains the Church position toward business in general, and the second article describes the nature of the Church's participation in business activities through recently affiliated corporations. For historical information, see Community.]

LDS ATTITUDES TOWARD BUSINESS

Business endeavors hold no mandated interest for the Church or its members. Church members involve themselves in all avenues of life in much the same proportion as the general population of the region or country in which they live (*see* OCCUPATIONAL STATUS). Church members are urged to be honest in all their dealings with their fellow men, including business and professional activities. Elements of history, theology, and practice combine to form a positive LDS attitude toward honest business endeavors.

Many LDS attitudes toward business are rooted in the Church's frontier heritage. As the Church developed settlements in Ohio, Missouri, Illinois, and the Great Basin, it became necessary and desirable to be involved in business activities. Cooperative business efforts were necessary for success, independence, and survival.

In addition to its spiritual and cultural roles, the Church sponsored economic initiatives that could not be mounted by individual entrepreneurs. For example, when it was determined that sugar would be expensive and difficult to obtain in the Great Basin, the Church in the 1850s sponsored a business venture to cultivate and process sugar beets. Converts brought capital and equipment from Europe, and factories were constructed. After extended difficulties, a thriving sugar beet industry resulted in the 1890s. Similarly, to provide banking services, a Church-sponsored bank was incorporated. A general store—Zion's Cooperative Mercantile Institution (ZCMI)—was begun, as were a newspaper, the *Deseret News,* and several hospitals; later, radio and television stations were acquired by the Church (*see* BROADCASTING). As the capital needed for these businesses became available from private sources, the Church divested itself of nearly all business activities unrelated to its ecclesiastical mission.

Thus, historically, members of the Church have been integrally involved in business activities. In their pioneer environment, Latter-day Saints developed, out of necessity, traits of self-sufficiency, pragmatism, and resourcefulness. This heritage is reflected in an entrepreneurial spirit and penchant for hard work that lend themselves very well to business endeavors.

The theology of the Church is also supportive of honest business. Church doctrines emphasize individual agency and self-determination, which provide fertile conceptual soil for fostering business attitudes of free enterprise. The Church teaches that property and wealth are stewardships and that all people will be held accountable to God for what they have done with the time and resources entrusted to them (Young, p. 301). Church leaders continue to encourage members to live within their means, to save and be frugal, and to remain economically independent by avoiding debt. Such principles are harmonious with business success and help prepare Church members to perform well in a business environment.

In addition, the Church's organizational practices provide an opportunity for developing skills that are useful in business. Each member, young and old, is called upon to serve in some calling. Young boys and girls give talks in Church and develop public-speaking skills. Church youth are given leadership opportunities, and adult men and women fill numerous leadership and teaching positions in every local congregation. Budgeting, counseling, organizing, and performing administrative tasks are carried out on a regular basis. From these experiences, members develop business-related skills that are useful in many business contexts.

Over the years, Church leaders have spoken forthrightly about maintaining high standards of business ethics and have warned against becoming carried away by business endeavors: "Material blessings are a part of the gospel if they are achieved in the proper way and for the right purpose" (N. Eldon Tanner, *Ensign* 9 [Nov. 1979]:80). Fair business dealing, giving value for value received, is scripturally required (Lev. 19:11, 35–36; 25:14; Deut. 24:14–15). Thus, President Spencer W. Kimball distinguished clean money from filthy lucre or compromise money: Clean money is "compensation received for a full day's honest work, . . . reasonable pay for faithful service, . . . fair profit from the sale of goods, commodities, or service; . . . income received from transactions where all parties profit" (Kimball, p. 948), and he counseled against conducting business unnecessarily on the Sabbath.

Employers are admonished to be generous and kind; employees, to be loyal and diligent. President Brigham Young encouraged "every man who has capital [to] create business and give employment and means into the hands of laborers"; he saw economic strength in "the bone and sinew of workingmen and women," and encouraged all to be industrious: "If we all labor a few hours a day, we could then spend the remainder of our time in rest and the improvement of our minds" (Young, pp. 300–302). "Let every man and woman be industrious, prudent, and economical in their acts and feelings, and while gathering to themselves, let each one strive to identify his or her interests with . . . those of their neighbor and neighborhood, let them seek their happiness and welfare in that of all" (Young, p. 303).

[*See also* Wealth, Attitudes Toward.]

BIBLIOGRAPHY
Kimball, Spencer W. "Keep Your Money Clean." *IE* 56 (Dec. 1953):948–50.
Young, Brigham. *Discourses of Brigham Young*, comp. J. Widtsoe. Salt Lake City, 1954.
On the business experiences and philosophies of a prominent LDS entrepreneur in the 1930s, see Dean L. May, "Sources of Marriner S. Eccles's Economic Thought," *Journal of Mormon History* 3 (1976):85–99.

STEPHEN D. NADAULD

CHURCH PARTICIPATION IN BUSINESS

Historically, two purposes have characterized Church participation in business: to provide important services to the community that might not otherwise be available, and to provide a reasonable return on the resources of the Church. During the first half century of settlement in Utah, the Church started or helped to start many businesses. Some continue to operate; but as communities became self-sufficient, the Church withdrew from such business activities as banking, health care, commercial printing, sugar processing, and the Hotel Utah.

Most of the business assets of the Church originated in the pioneer era when its people were isolated from other business and commercial centers. When a newspaper was needed to help keep people of Utah informed, the Church established the *Deseret News* in 1850. In the 1920s, federal officials urged newspapers to develop broadcast operations. In 1922 the *Deseret News* did as requested, and that was the beginning of KSL and BONNEVILLE INTERNATIONAL CORPORATION. To help Utah farmers develop a cash crop that they could sell beyond the borders of the state, the Church helped pioneer the sugar beet industry. ZCMI department stores were the outgrowth of a cooperative movement among the early pioneers. When hotel accommodations were insufficient to provide housing for a growing number of visitors to Temple Square and other points of interest in Salt Lake City shortly after the turn of the century, the Church joined with other community interests to construct Hotel Utah. Over a period of years, the Church bought out other investors to become the sole owner of Hotel Utah. The Church became more involved in Salt Lake City real estate primarily to preserve the beauty and the integrity of the downtown area, especially around Temple Square. That purpose guided Church officials when they decided in the late 1960s to lease to Salt Lake County, for one dollar per year, the property on which

Symphony Hall and the Salt Palace Convention Center are now located.

At the beginning of 1990, major commercial businesses owned by the Church included Beneficial Development Company, Beneficial Life Insurance Company, Bonneville International Corporation, Deseret Book Company, Deseret News Publishing Company, Deseret Trust Company, Farm Management Companies, Temple Square Hotel Corporation, Utah Home Fire Insurance Company, and Zions Securities Corporation. The Church also owns Laie Resorts, Inc., a small motel, restaurant, and service station located adjacent to the POLYNESIAN CULTURAL CENTER in Hawaii. These businesses come under the umbrella of Deseret Management Company, a holding company that receives and distributes profits, performs internal audits, generates consolidated financial statements, files consolidated income tax returns for the group, coordinates activities, and reviews business operations and plans.

The Church of Jesus Christ of Latter-day Saints Foundation receives from Church businesses contributions from their pretax earnings, which in turn are given to the community as contributions to the arts, education, and charitable groups, and other beneficiaries. The LDS FOUNDATION coordinates the distribution of major portions of the charitable contributions designated by Church-owned businesses. In recent years, the Foundation has been a significant contributor to the new LDS Hospital wing, the new Primary Children's Medical Center, the new Holy Cross Hospital, the Salvation Army, Saint Vincent De Paul Center soup kitchen for the homeless, the Salt Lake City Homeless Shelter, the Utah Symphony, Ballet West, the United Way, and related organizations. Income from Church business operations permits participation in local community causes without using the tithing of members from around the world. Those tithes are dedicated to continuing the primary work of the Church, which includes teaching the gospel to the world, building faith and testimony and promoting activity among the membership, and helping members to complete sacred temple ordinances in proxy for the deceased.

Other business activities are under the aegis of the Investment Properties Division of the Church. For example, it oversees Church-owned farmland in several states and Canada, although many of the agricultural activities on the land are managed by Farm Management Companies.

The Church does not publish financial data regarding its privately owned businesses. However, Church officials have indicated that profits from business operations are used to provide living allowances for the General Authorities of the Church. While business profits are not disclosed, President Gordon B. Hinckley, a member of the First Presidency, said in 1985 that the combined income from all these business interests would not keep the work of the Church going for longer than a very brief period (Hinckley, 1985, p. 50).

In addition to its wholly owned businesses, the Church has controlling interest in the chain of ZCMI department stores. Also, the Church once owned U and I Sugar Company, but many assets of that company have been sold. The company name was changed to U and I, Inc., and, more recently, to AgriNorthwest Company. Its remaining assets are held by Deseret Management Company. The Church also has a significant but noncontrolling interest in Heber J. Grant and Company, a holding company. Other investments include a varied portfolio of stocks and bonds.

Each of the businesses owned by the Church operates in a competitive environment and must succeed or fail according to standard business operating principles. These companies pay taxes to federal, state, and local governments. (The Church is the fourth largest payer of real estate taxes in Salt Lake County.) Church businesses have boards of directors that set policies for the individual companies. In most cases, Church leadership is represented on the boards of directors, but many boards include persons of other faiths.

Operating management is in the hands of professional managers, who need not be Church members. The Church requires them to operate the businesses in harmony with its principles and values of honesty, integrity, sensitivity, and service.

The Church expects its businesses to return something back to the communities from which they derive their revenues, and it encourages managers to participate actively in community activities and in business and professional associations. The Church expects them to set standards of excellence, to be leaders in their particular industries, and always to be conscious of the values of the ownership that they represent.

The major commercial businesses owned by the Church engage in the following activities:

Beneficial Development Company is a property development company dealing primarily with real estate holdings in and around Salt Lake City. In a very few instances, the company has installed roads, water systems, and other amenities for residential developments.

Beneficial Life Insurance Company offers the full range of life insurance protection. The company operates subsidiary insurance companies in Des Moines, Iowa, and Portland, Oregon.

Bonneville International Corporation is a commercial radio and television broadcast company with stations in Salt Lake City, Seattle, San Francisco, Los Angeles, Kansas City, Phoenix, Dallas, Chicago, and New York. A division, Bonneville Communications, provides promotional services, and produces and distributes the weekly MORMON TABERNACLE CHOIR BROADCAST, the general conferences of the Church, the Homefront Series public service announcements, items for the Missionary Department, and various seasonal programs. The company also provides commercial advertising and promotional services for national businesses and organizations.

DESERET BOOK COMPANY operates retail book stores in Utah, Idaho, California, Oregon, and Arizona. The company also serves as a publishing arm of the Church to publish books and other materials for and about the Church. In addition, the company operates the Mormon Handicraft outlet in Salt Lake City.

Deseret News Publishing Company publishes Salt Lake City's afternoon daily, the *Deseret News*, and is a partner in the Newspaper Agency Corporation, which handles printing, advertising, and circulation for the two Salt Lake City dailies.

Deseret Trust Company receives and administers trust funds and trust properties given to the Church.

Farm Management Company manages commercial farms and other agricultural properties owned or leased by the Church, including Deseret Ranches of Florida (Orlando), Deseret Land and Livestock (Rich County, Utah), Deseret Farms of California

(Sacramento), Rolling Hills (Emmett, Idaho), West Hills Orchards (Elberta, Utah), and Cactus Lane Ranch (Phoenix, Arizona).

Temple Square Hotel Corporation operates The Inn at Temple Square, a small European-style hotel across from Temple Square; and The Lion House, a historic building in downtown Salt Lake City that is used for luncheons, dinners, wedding receptions, and other social events.

Zions Securities Corporation manages properties owned by the Church, primarily in the downtown area of Salt Lake City, including the ZCMI Mall, the Eagle Gate Plaza office tower, the Eagle Gate Apartments, the Gateway Condominiums, several other apartment buildings, and a number of parking facilities.

BIBLIOGRAPHY

Hinckley, Gordon B. "Questions and Answers." *Ensign* 15 (Nov. 1985):49–52.

———. Untitled address to the Governor's Conference on Utah's Future, Sept. 7, 1988. (Available upon request from the Church's Public Communications Department.)

Lindsey, Robert. "The Mormons—Growth, Prosperity and Controversy." *New York Times Magazine*, Jan. 12, 1986.

Parrish, Michael. "The Saints Among Us." *Rocky Mountain Magazine* 2 (Jan.–Feb. 1980):17–32.

Turner, Judd. "The Church in Business." *This People* 10 (Summer 1989):50–55.

See also the following series of articles on Church and business:

"*Arizona Republic* Explores LDS Financial Holdings." *Deseret News*, June 30, 1991, pp. A1, A4.

"LDS Revenues Come Primarily from Tithing." *Deseret News*, July 1, 1991, pp. A1, A4.

"LDS Church Real Estate Holdings Include Farms, Ranches, Buildings. *Deseret News*, July 2, 1991, pp. A1, A4, A5.

"LDS Church Uses Media Empire to Set Example in Communities." *Deseret News*, July 3, 1991, pp. A1, A5.

RODNEY H. BRADY

C

CALAMITIES AND DISASTERS

Calamities and disasters are sudden, unexpected events that cause extensive destruction, death, or injury and result in widespread community disruption and individual trauma. From its beginnings, The Church of Jesus Christ of Latter-day Saints has sought to be prepared against natural disasters following admonitions such as "if ye are prepared, ye shall not fear" (D&C 38:30). Preparedness is carried out on both individual and institutional levels.

In their homes, members are encouraged to have food storage sufficient for a year and other essentials of EMERGENCY PREPAREDNESS: clothing, bedding, fuel (where possible), and the like. Church members are also advised to have sufficient supplies to enable them to be completely self-sustaining for at least fourteen days without the benefit of electricity and clean running water.

On the organizational level, the Church response to disasters is administered by the Presiding Bishopric at Church headquarters, by the stake president, and by the ward bishop. Each ward and stake has lay specialists called to assist in welfare and emergency preparedness. Meetinghouses are equipped to shelter people displaced by disasters, and regional storehouses can be drawn on for basic supplies. Large-scale disasters are responded to through the office of the Presiding Bishop.

Historically, Latter-day Saints organized to cope with the handcart crises in 1856, the flu epidemic of 1918, postwar crises in western Europe after both world wars, the Teton Dam disaster in southeast Idaho, mudslides and flooding in many places, and hurricane destruction in the South Pacific. The Church attempts to be in constant readiness to handle such immediate needs as search and rescue, food distribution, and shelter management. In addition, it addresses itself to individual members' needs such as vocational training and emotional therapy, through the Welfare Services and LDS Social Services Departments of the Church.

REED H. BLAKE

CAPITAL PUNISHMENT

Ancient scriptures indicate that capital punishment is an appropriate penalty for murder. God said to Noah, "And whoso sheddeth man's blood, by man shall his blood be shed; for man shall not shed the blood of man" (JST Gen. 9:12). And to Moses the Lord said: "He that killeth any man shall surely be put to death" (Lev. 24:17). Thus it is clear that when the civil and religious authorities were combined, as in the days of the Old Testament prophets, capital punishment was the directed result.

In modern times with the separation of church and state, the power to take physical life is reserved to the state. Modern revelations do not oppose capital punishment, but they do not direct its imposition to civil government. In the same revelation where the Lord instructed the Prophet Joseph Smith, "And again, I say, thou shall not kill; but he that killeth shall die," the Lord made the application of capital punishment contingent on the laws of civil government: "And it shall come to pass, that if any persons among you shall kill they shall be delivered up and dealt with according to the laws of the land . . . and it shall be proved according to the laws of the land" (D&C 42:19, 79). In a headnote to the published account of this revelation, the Prophet specified the revelation embraced "the law of the Church," which might indicate that even when capital punishment does not result from murder the murderer dies as to things pertaining to the Spirit.

The First Presidency and the Quorum of the Twelve Apostles

affirmed this position against murder in an official declaration dated December 12, 1889, written in response to rumors perpetrated by enemies of the Church that it taught its members that they were not bound by the laws of the United States. Included in that official declaration is the proclamation "this Church views the shedding of human blood with the utmost abhorrence" (*MFP* 3:183).

Church leaders have frequently made statements consistent with the scriptures and declarations quoted above. Elder Orson F. Whitney said in the October 1910 general conference, "To execute a criminal is not murder" (*CR*, Oct. 1910, p. 51). Elder Bruce R. McConkie wrote, "Mortal man is not authorized, except in imposing the requisite death penalties for crimes, to take the blood of his fellow beings under any circumstances" (McConkie, p. 257).

In summary, capital punishment is viewed in the doctrines of the Church to be an appropriate penalty for murder, but that penalty is proper only after the offender has been found guilty in a lawful public trial by constitutionally authorized civil authorities.

BIBLIOGRAPHY

Clark, James R., ed. *Messages of the First Presidency*, Vol. 3. Salt Lake City, 1966.

Doxey, Roy W. "The Law of Moral Conduct." *Relief Society Magazine* 47 (Aug. 1960):539–46.

McConkie, Bruce R. *The Promised Messiah*. Salt Lake City, 1978.

STUART W. HINCKLEY

CATHOLICISM AND MORMONISM

Roman Catholicism and Eastern Orthodoxy are grounded in the same theological tradition. They are similar to each other doctrinally and hold teachings that differ from Mormonism.

GOD. Both Catholicism and Orthodoxy believe God to be the Creator of the universe, and that God's being is trinitarian—that the persons of Father, Son, and Holy Spirit exist simultaneously in one divine nature. LDS doctrine is, on the other hand, tritheistic; it is subordinationist. The Son is subordinate to the Father, and the Holy Spirit is "sent forth by the will of the Father through Jesus Christ, his son." Both Catholic traditions teach that God is a self-revealing mystery whose perfect manifestation is in Jesus Christ, who is present to the world in the Church. Latter-day Saints affirm that Jesus Christ has a separate nature and is a separate entity from the Father, and that as Jesus Christ was and is visible, embodied, and glorified, so is the Father.

CHRIST.   According to Catholic belief, Jesus was born of a virgin, and is the "Incarnate Son of God." As both God and man, he is the "Savior of the World." For Latter-day Saints Christ was not, is not now, and never will be united in nature or substance with the Father. His oneness with the Father is spiritual in spirit, purpose, and mind. Jesus, in LDS belief, is the Only Begotten Son of the Father in the flesh. He entered mortality, subject to growth as well as being, and fulfilled the will of the Father as exemplar, savior, and mediator. He was not given all power on earth and in heaven until he received the fulness of the glory of the Father.

ATONEMENT.   In both Catholic traditions Christ's atonement provides access to salvific grace. Christ's death-resurrection is the saving event and the cross, the symbol of salvation. For Latter-day Saints the atonement of Jesus Christ was a descending below all things in order to rise above all. He suffered "according to the flesh" because in no other way could he know the anguish of sin and sinfulness, exemplify redemptive love, and reconcile justice and mercy. The Atonement reunites man with God both through sanctification and resurrection. All that Christ received from the Father may be received by man from the Father through Christ. This transformation is akin to the Eastern Orthodox view of theosis. The goal of discipleship is to become, through Christ, the image and likeness of God (*see* DEIFICATION).

AUTHORITY.   Catholics believe that Jesus bestowed his pastoral authority on Peter, who thus became the first "Vicar of Christ" and head of the church, and that this authority to teach and to sanctify has been passed on in unbroken succession in the institution of the Papacy. Eastern Orthodoxy holds that Peter was first among equals, therefore patriarchs have equal authority. They also ascribe a special authority to the first seven ecumenical councils. Latter-day Saints believe that Peter held the keys of apostolic authority, which were also conferred upon the twelve apostles. Priesthood powers are not indelible but inseparably connected to righteousness. The loss of the full keys of the priesthood was a failure to transmit. Their modern reconferral was under the hands of Peter, James, and John. Every worthy male in the Church is to receive ordination to the priesthood with authority to perform saving ordinances, and every father is to function as a patriarch to his own family.

SCRIPTURE.   For Catholics and Orthodox, the Old and New Testament is the "inexhaustible source of Christian belief." The canon is closed. For Latter-day Saints the canon remains open. Scripture is the record of prophetic utterance given under inspiration. There is no final revelation. Revelation in on-going. Neither written scripture, nor natural theology, supersedes the "living oracles" (*see* RELIGIOUS EXPERIENCE).

CHURCH.   Catholicism and Orthodoxy understand the Church as a "communion of saints." The Holy Spirit enlivens the Church with grace empowering it to carry on the work of Christ in history. It is a community of salvation where the gospel is preached and the sacraments received. Latter-day Saints believe that with the restoration of the higher priesthood came three elements lost from the New Testament Church: (1) organizational patterns and their related offices, including a quorum of twelve apostles; (2) the spirit of prophecy, and all the spiritual gifts; and (3) the temple with its essential ordinances and practices. Catholics affirm that grace centers in God's free gift offered through Christ in the sacraments and is infused to the soul. Baptism is essential for salvation. All sacraments are the necessary means of the grace needed for salvation. Mormon rites or ordinances are processes of spiritual rebirth in which the powers of godliness are manifest. They are received by all, and all the ordinances are essential to salvation, from baptism to the higher ordinances of the temple. Their efficacy requires proper forms, ordained priesthood authority, and the faith and repentance of the person. There are degrees of salvation and the fulness of salvation or exaltation requires the fulness of the ordinances.

EUCHARIST.   For both Catholic traditions, the Eucharist is a sacrament in which the true body and blood of Jesus is physically present, that is, the actual saving reality of the Lord. The liturgical act of consecration is a true sacrifice in which, through transubstantiation, the elements of bread and wine become the body and blood of Christ. The Orthodox associates the act of the priest in this liturgy with veneration for icons, which represent their prototype who is Christ. Latter-day Saints understand the sacrament as a remembrance of the body and blood of Christ. Sanctification is from the Spirit and takes place in the recipients who bring a broken heart and contrite spirit to the prayer and the partaking.

MARRIAGE AND FAMILY.   Although Catholicism and Orthodoxy understand celibacy to be a spiritual ideal, marriage is a grace-giving sacrament that symbolizes the bond between Christ and the Church. Catholics hold that this is a life-long contract and do not permit divorce. Latter-day Saints teach that the eternal glorification of the family, and of the community of families within the Church, is the highest spiritual possibility. As the high priest who officiated in the ancient temple was married; and as the apostles were married, so today marriage is a high ordinance, to which others are preparatory. The nurture and love of the family of man, which is ultimately the family of God, is the proper work and glory of the saintly life. When sealed and sanctified by the authority of the priesthood, the covenants and relationships and duties of parenthood continue into the next world (*see* CELIBACY; MARRIAGE: ETERNAL).

While honoring Mary, Latter-day Saints have no equivalent of the doctrines of the immaculate conception, perpetual virginity, and bodily assumption of Mary, nor of the Orthodox veneration of icons. Other LDS teachings differ significantly from traditional Catholic teaching: modification of classical readings of the omnipotence and omnipresence of God; the premortal existence of the spirits of all mankind; the affirmation that spirit is refined matter; the Fall as planned, voluntary, and essential to the growth of the soul amid contrast and opposition; the denial of original sin and of pedobaptism; the inclusive nature of the Abrahamic covenant; and the replacement of heaven-hell distinction with the teaching of degrees of glory in the resurrection.

BIBLIOGRAPHY
Florovsky, Georges. *Bible, Church, Tradition: An Eastern Orthodox View*. Belmont, Mass., 1972.
McBrien, Richard P. *Catholicism*, Study Edition. San Francisco, 1981.

McManners, John, ed. *The Oxford Illustrated History of Christianity*. New York, 1990.

Patrinacos, Rev. Nicon D. *A Dictionary of Greek Orthodoxy*. Pleasantville, N.Y., 1984.

Rahner, Karl, and Herbert Vorgrimler. *Dictionary of Theology*. New York, 1981.

ALFRED BENNEY
ROGER R. KELLER

CELEBRATIONS

Through their religious and community celebrations, members of The Church of Jesus Christ of Latter-day Saints express some of their spiritual and social values and expectations. Although events and traditions in families and localities are celebrated often by members throughout the Church, the major celebrations help to define and express the unique religious identity and heritage of Latter-day Saints.

The mortal life cycle of individual Church members is typically marked by the performance of a series of formal priesthood ordinances. The most prominent are naming and blessing children, baptism and confirmation, endowment, and sealing (temple marriage). These ceremonies, usually witnessed or participated in by the person's family and friends, consist of making sacred covenants, and receiving priesthood blessings, and inspired counsel that provide guidance through mortality and prepare the recipient for eternity. These ordinances are often marked by informal celebrations with family and friends.

The family as a unit of both religious worship and eternal association is celebrated by many Latter-day Saints in daily activities and weekly FAMILY HOME EVENINGS. The daily activities may consist of scripture study, gospel discussion, prayers, or singing activities held usually at the beginning or ending of the day. Family home evening generally occupies one night a week. It is designed to strengthen the bonds of family members through a wide variety of spiritual, social, educational, and recreational activities, and thus it augments involvement in traditional holidays such as Christmas, Easter, Thanksgiving, and Mother's Day. Extended LDS families often participate on a larger scale with periodic family reunions.

The identity of Latter-day Saints as "modern Israel" finds its most exuberant expression in Pioneer Day. This annual celebration commemorates the entrance of the first LDS pioneers into the Salt Lake Valley on July 24, 1847. For Latter-day Saints, this commemoration has come to symbolize the establishment of a divinely ordained "promised land" in the American West.

Since 1849, Pioneer Day has given Latter-day Saints an excellent opportunity to express their identity as a covenant people. In the context of devotionals, parades, dances, sporting events, banquets, and a host of other activities, Mormons review the manifestation of God's hand in the course of their history, the creation and sustaining of their mode of life, and the religious dimension of their continuing associations. Although the focus of Pioneer Day is Salt Lake City and the Mormon West, Latter-day Saints throughout the Church memorialize their religious heritage on July 24 with celebrations appropriate to their particular settings and circumstances.

The LDS identification of the Church as the living kingdom of God on earth finds its greatest cultural and religious expression at general conferences. These semiannual gatherings in April and October have been observed by Church leaders and members alike almost since the organization of the Church on April 6, 1830. The conferences are currently held on the first Sunday of April and October, plus the preceding Saturday. The months symbolically mark the changing of the seasons between winter and summer, and April is also usually the month when Easter comes, commemorating the resurrection of Jesus Christ.

General conference unites the divine authority, organization, doctrine, and spiritual resources of the Church. The salient symbols include the architecture of Temple Square; the hierarchical seating of Church leadership from the First Presidency through the Quorum of the Twelve Apostles, the quorums of the Seventy, and the leading men and women of the auxiliary organizations; the use of the scriptures and revelation in the addresses given; the expression of both diversity and solidarity by the gathered Church membership representing many nations in their sustaining the leadership; and reports heralding significant growth in the rapidly expanding Church membership.

The general conferences also serve as major occasions of personal pilgrimages for thousands of Latter-day Saints to travel to Salt Lake City in April or October. It is likewise an occasion of vicarious involvement for millions of others who follow the conference sessions through various telecommunications media. In addition, the conference proceedings are later printed and distributed. As a result, the general conferences have become an extremely important collective spiritual experience for Latter-day Saints throughout the world.

Through general conferences, and on a smaller scale through the weekly congregational worship services of individual wards and stakes, Latter-day Saints renew and celebrate their membership in the organization that they recognize as the kingdom of God on earth.

BIBLIOGRAPHY
Olsen, Steven L. "Community Celebrations and Cultural Identity: Pioneer Day in Nineteenth Century Mormonism." Unpublished paper, 1987.
Shipps, Jan. *Mormonism: The Story of a New Religious Tradition*, pp. 131–49. Urbana, Ill., 1985.

STEVEN L. OLSEN

CELIBACY

Celibacy, the deliberate renunciation of marriage, is foreign to LDS life. Like other forms of ascetic withdrawal, it may deprive the participant of crucial life experiences. Spiritual maturity and exaltation in the highest degree of the celestial kingdom require marriage (D&C 131:2–3).

The norm of Latter-day Saint teaching and practice is for individuals to marry, procreate, and foster righteous living in their families as indicated in the scriptures: "Be fruitful, and multiply, and replenish the earth" (Gen. 1:28). "Marriage is honourable in all" (Heb. 13:4). "Whoso forbiddeth to marry is not ordained of God, for marriage is ordained of God unto man" (D&C 49:15). Those who are unable to marry in a temple in mortality through no fault of their own will receive compensatory blessings later (D&C 137:5–8).

The practice of celibacy was not widespread among the Christian clergy until centuries after the death of the apostles. "Forbidding to marry" was, for Paul, a sign of apostasy (1 Tim. 4:3). Because ancient and modern revelation endorses marriage and because most religious leaders in the Old and New Testaments were married, Latter-day Saints reject attempts to interpret the Bible as advocating celibacy.

BIBLIOGRAPHY
Lea, Henry C. *History of Sacerdotal Celibacy in the Christian Church*, 4th ed. London, 1932.

DILLON K. INOUYE

CENTENNIAL OBSERVANCES

The historical consciousness of Latter-day Saints in the twentieth century has been richly expressed in the celebration of centennial anniversaries of important foundational events. Building on the elaborate jubilee (fifty-year) celebrations in 1880 of the organization of the Church and in 1897 of the beginnings of the LDS colonization in the American West, the Church ushered in the twentieth century in 1905 with the centenary of the birth of the Prophet Joseph Smith. For this occasion, President Joseph F. Smith led a group of Church leaders and Smith family members to Sharon, Vermont, Joseph Smith's birthplace, and dedicated a memorial cottage and large granite obelisk to his memory. Many LDS congregations held local observances.

The Joseph Smith Memorial became one of the first historical sites of the Church. Following its dedication, the Smith company visited a number of other Mormon historic sites. This tour confirmed a growing interest by Latter-day Saints in preserving their past through the restoration of such historical sites in later commemorations.

Another major centenary was celebrated on September 22, 1927, when President Heber J. Grant conducted a devotional on the hill Cumorah at the approximate location where Joseph Smith received the gold plates of the Book of Mormon from the angel Moroni one hundred years earlier. On September 25, congregations throughout the Church held commemorative programs as part of their Sunday worship services.

The 1930 centenary of the organization of the Church saw a much more ambitious memorial. The major celebration centered on the week of April 6. Church leaders arranged for participation in the festivities to extend beyond the 100,000 who gathered in Salt Lake City by installing radio receivers in more than a thousand meeting-houses within the broadcasting range of KSL radio. For the opening session of general conference, congregations assembled in these chapels and many others not so equipped. At an appointed time, Latter-day Saints throughout the Church stood and gave the sacred Hosanna Shout, normally reserved for the dedication of temples. As the general conference continued on the following Monday and Tuesday, many speakers reviewed the Church's hundred-year legacy. Each evening of the week of April 6–12, the Salt Lake Tabernacle was filled to overflowing for the pageant "Message of the Ages," an ambitious stage production by a thousand actors, singers, and musi-cians that chronicled a sacred history of the gospel. The Church's seven temples were also dramatically illuminated for the centennial. For Pioneer Day (July 24) that year, Saints from the eastern United States and Canada and missionaries serving in the area gathered to the hill Cumorah to witness "Footprints on the Sands of Time," the first of the PAGEANTS at that historic site.

The 1947 centennial of the arrival of the first company of Mormon pioneers into the Salt Lake Valley was the largest LDS cel-ebration to date. The entire year was one of observances throughout the Church, but it centered on July 24. That day included all the tra-ditional Pioneer Day activities—devotionals, concerts, banquets, parades, rodeos, sports contests, and dances—but on a grander scale. Particularly memorable was the reenactment of the Mormon exodus from Nauvoo. This modern "pioneer trek" included many Church leaders and other dignitaries who drove the Mormon pioneer trail in automobiles decorated as covered wagons and who rehearsed pioneer activities along the way. At the mouth of Emigration Canyon, east of Salt Lake City, President George Albert Smith dedicated the "This Is the Place" Monument, a series of sculptures created by Mahonri M. Young, grandson of Brigham Young.

The 1980 sesquicentennial of the founding of the Church brought another year-long celebration with a variety of observances by Latter-day Saints worldwide. The highlight of this commemora-tion came April 6 in conjunction with general conference. President Spencer W. Kimball dedicated the reconstructed Peter Whitmer, Sr., log home on the original site, in the township of Fayette, New York, where the Church had been organized in 1830. Millions witnessed the occasion via the Church's first satellite broadcast (*see* SATELLITE COMMUNICATIONS SYSTEM).

Featured in an expanded Pioneer Day parade that year was the display of hundreds of banners made by the Young Women from throughout the Church expressing their basic values through an artistic tradition dating back to Pioneer Day parades of the nineteenth century.

A number of smaller-scale sesquicentennials have since commemorated both the historical roots of the Church and its early geographical spread beyond the borders of the United States. The most memorable of these were the sesquicentennial anniversaries of the first Latter-day Saint mission to Great Britain (1987)—the first outside North America—and the founding of Nauvoo, Illinois (1989).

BIBLIOGRAPHY
Anderson, Paul. "Heroic Nostalgia: Enshrining the Mormon Past." *Sunstone* 5 (July–Aug. 1980):47–55.
Belding, Patricia. "A Monumental Race with Winter: The Dedication of the Joseph Smith Birthplace." *Vermont Life* 38 (Fall 1983):45–48.
Bitton, Davis. "The Ritualization of Mormon History." *Utah Historical Quarterly* 43 (1975):67–85.

STEVEN L. OLSEN

CHAPLAINS

The Church of Jesus Christ of Latter-day Saints endorses a corps of chaplains who serve in the U.S. armed forces. The history of LDS chaplains began in the Spanish-American War. Then Elder B. H. Roberts of the Seventy, at age sixty, and two others were appointed to the U.S. Army chaplaincy in 1917. The first LDS Naval chaplains served in World War II, and the first LDS Air Force chaplain was appointed in 1948.

By the beginning of the Vietnam War in Southeast Asia, most LDS chaplains who served during the Korean War had been released and new eligibility requirements precluded the appointment of most lay ministers, including Latter-day Saints. In 1965, however, the requirements were altered to allow for the lay ministry background of many LDS applicants. As with other religious groups, a person must be endorsed by a church before applying to the government for appointment as a chaplain. Prerequisites for an LDS chaplain include the Melchizedek Priesthood, an honorable mission, temple MARRIAGE, and a master's degree in counseling.

LDS chaplains have contributed to the development of military chaplaincy policy. For example, an LDS chaplain played a significant research role in the constitutional defense of the U.S. chaplaincy in federal court in 1979 and 1985.

LDS chaplains conduct religious services comparable to those led by chaplains of the Protestant faiths, and they provide counseling, classroom instruction, and other support activities to military personnel and their families. They provide such services through coordination with other chaplains or ministers. LDS chaplains are approved and supervised by the Church's Military Relations Committee.

BIBLIOGRAPHY
Boone, Joseph F. *The Roles of The Church of Jesus Christ of Latter-day Saints in Relation to the United States Military 1900–1975*. Ph.D. diss., Brigham Young University, 1975.
Maher, Richard T. *For God and Country: Memorable Stories from the Lives of Mormon Chaplains*. Bountiful, Utah, 1975.

ROBERT E. NELSON, JR.

CHRISTIANS AND CHRISTIANITY

The Old World origin of the word "Christian" is obscure. Possibly it was first used by pagans in Antioch to identify those who followed Christ. However, by the end of the first century A.D., it was an accepted self-designation among Church members as reflected in the writings of Ignatius (c. 35–c. 107 A.D.). The word is used three times in the New Testament (Acts 11:26; 26:28; 1 Pet. 4:16).

In the new world (Book of Mormon world), there was a similar designation for Church members (Mosiah 18:12–17; Alma 46:13–16; 48:10). "Christian" designated those who were "true believers in Christ" and who "took upon them, gladly, the name of Christ, or Christians as they were called, because of their belief in Christ who should come" (Alma 46:15). Here the term "Christian" referred to those who believed Christ *would* come, and not only, as in the New Testament, to those who believed he *had* come.

Perhaps the term first used by Old World Christians for themselves was the Greek word *hagioi*, meaning "holy ones" or "saints." Latter-day Saints have taken upon themselves this New Testament designation (Acts 9:13; 32, 41; Rom. 1:7; 1 Cor. 1:2; Phil. 1:1). Such terminology is seen in the Book of Mormon (1 Ne. 13:5, 9; 14:12, 14; 2 Ne. 9:18–19; Morm. 8:23; Moro. 8:26), the Doctrine and Covenants (1:36; 84:2; 88:114; 104:15), and the Pearl of Great Price (Moses 7:56).

The Church of Jesus Christ of Latter-day Saints does not see itself as one Christian denomination among many, but rather as God's latter-day restoration of the fulness of Christian faith and practice. Thus, from its earliest days LDS Christians sought to distinguish themselves from Christians of other traditions. Other forms of Christianity, while bearing much truth and doing much good under the guidance of the Holy Spirit, are viewed as incomplete, lacking the authority of the priesthood of God, the temple ordinances, the comprehensive understanding of the plan of salvation, and the non-paradoxical understanding of the Godhead. Therefore, the designation "saint" reflects attachment to the New Testament church, and also designates a difference from Catholic, Eastern Orthodox, and Protestant Christianity in the current dispensation.

In response, and for a variety of other reasons, some Catholic, Orthodox, and Protestant Christians have been reticent to apply the term "Christian" to Latter-day Saints. One reason is that the Latter-day Saints claim the only divinely established line of authority is within the Church. If that divine authority was not transmitted after the death of the first Apostles, then the sacrament, ordinations, credal formulations, and ecclesiastical structures of other Christian groups lack divine sanction. Many traditional Christians see this stance as placing Latter-day Saints outside the Christian family as defined by some confessions of faith and accepted ordinances.

Further, Latter-day Saints claim that God spoke and manifested himself not only to persons of biblical times, but also to the people in the Book of Mormon, and that he continues to speak to his people through revelation today. Thus, Latter-day Saints are not always viewed as "biblical Christians," when that term requires the belief that the canon of scripture is complete in the Bible. To the Mormons, God is still a God of continuing revelation, which means that credal and confessional statements are not final. No one confession, or even all of them together, can fully comprehend the dynamism of God. He is to be heard and his words are to be recorded as he gives continuing divine guidance through revelation. Hence, the LDS canon is open; the Doctrine and Covenants becomes an official, open-ended locus for revelations that affect the whole Church; and revelations continue to come to the living prophets, seers, and revelators of the Church, to be communicated to the members.

Latter-day Saints hold that Christians in the broadest sense are those who base their beliefs on the teachings of Jesus and who have a personal relationship with him. Within that definition they recognize Catholic, Eastern Orthodox, Protestant, and Latter-day Saint Christians, with the understanding that Latter-day Saint Christianity is the restored fulness of Christ's gospel. The lives of Latter-day Saints are their affirmations of their Christian faith. As President Brigham Young stated, "If we are not Christlike we are not Christian" (Watson).

Traditional Christianity often defines Christian affiliation as the acceptance of certain beliefs and dogmas. Because Latter-day Saints do not accept certain extrascriptural dogmas—especially those bearing the philosophical overlay of much post–New Testament Christian teaching—some in other churches feel that Latter-day Saints cannot be Christian. They are not "orthodox" in this sense. But for the Mormon, right beliefs (orthodoxy) and right behaviors (orthopraxy) are those congruent with the revealed mind and will of the Lord. Some of the misunderstandings between traditional communities and the Latter-day Saints arise from this issue: whether Christians must first believe traditional, especially credal, dogmas in order to live "correct Christian lives."

An inclusive definition of Latter-day Saint Christianity is in the Book of Mormon: "And we talk of Christ, we rejoice in Christ, we preach of Christ, we prophesy of Christ, and we write according to our prophecies, that our children may know to what source they may look for a remission of their sins" (2 Ne. 25:26). Christ and his atoning sacrifice have been the undergirding message of The Church of

Jesus Christ of Latter-day Saints from its inception. Christ has been the central message of all the latter-day prophets and apostles. They understand that Old Testament prophets anticipated him, New Testament apostles preached and testified of him, Book of Mormon prophets heralded him, and the Doctrine and Covenants presents his word to this generation. Jesus Christ is the living Lord of the Church. Apart from him there is no salvation.

President Spencer W. Kimball said, "There can be no real and true Christianity, even with good works, unless we are deeply and personally committed to the reality of Jesus Christ as the Only Begotten Son of the Father who bought us, who purchased us in the great act of Atonement" (Kimball, p. 68). He also expressed the hope that all would come to realize that every LDS prayer, hymn, and sermon is centered in the Lord Jesus Christ. "We are true followers of Jesus Christ; and we hope the world will finally come to the conclusion that we are Christians, if there are any in the world" (Kimball, p. 434).

BIBLIOGRAPHY

Gealy, F. D. "Christian." In *The Interpreter's Dictionary of the Bible*, Vol. 1, pp. 571–72. Nashville, Tenn., 1962.

Grundmann, Walter. "Chiro." *Theological Dictionary of the New Testament*, Vol. 9, pp. 27–580. Grand Rapids, Mich., 1964–1974.

Kimball, Edward L., ed. *The Teachings of Spencer W. Kimball*. Salt Lake City, 1982.

Watson, Eldon J., comp. *Brigham Young Addresses*, Vol. 4, p. 5 for July 14, 1861. Unpublished, March 1980.

ROGER R. KELLER

CHRISTMAS

Christmas is the holiday when Latter-day Saints and other Christians celebrate the birth of Jesus Christ. This epochal event, seen in vision by ancient prophets, heralded the entry into mortality of the Son of God, the Jehovah of the Old Testament, and the promised Messiah. Even though Latter-day Saints believe that the birth of Jesus actually occurred in the spring of the year (D&C 20:1), they observe the December celebration when, more than at any other time of year, the

Christian world unites in remembering Christ's birth and practicing his teachings of love, charity, self-sacrifice, and tolerance.

Most Latter-day Saints include some of the traditions, games, decorations, music, and food associated with the Christmas customs of their homelands in their family celebrations. Such items as Christmas trees, stockings, gifts, and greeting cards add to the beauty of the holiday and are not discouraged. But the recommended focus is religious. The Church encourages family closeness, concern for neighbors, thoughtfulness for fellow workers, renewal of friendships, and acts of Christlike love, giving, and celebration. Appropriate sermons, lessons, songs, and programs are presented in Sabbath services during the Christmas season. Latter-day Saints are cautioned that holiday shopping, decorating, and festivities should not obscure the remembrance of Christ nor hinder the quest for peace on earth.

BIBLIOGRAPHY
Packer, Boyd K. "Keeping Christmas." In *BYU Speeches of the Year, 1966–1967*. Provo, Utah, 1967.

MARY ELLEN STEWART JAMISON

CHRISTOLOGY

Christology is the theological study of the human and divine natures and roles of Jesus Christ.

It developed soon after the death of the apostles in the first century, as conflicting teachings arose over the proper understanding of Christ. Christology served both as a response to heresies and as a development of a systematic theology that orthodox Christians could accept. Eventually these teachings were discussed in councils and formulated into CREEDS, for instance, at Nicaea (A.D. 325), Constantinople (A.D. 381), and Chalcedon (A.D. 451). These creeds insisted upon a full communion of Christ's divine and human natures, as opposed to the teaching that he was either divine or human, or part one and part the other. In every sense, the councils concluded, Christ is God and of the same substance (*homoousios*).

Various Christologies competed in the early Christian church. Docetists taught that Jesus Christ only seemed to suffer on the cross, since he only appeared to have a body. Modalists taught that there is only one God in three modes; Arianism, that there are three persons united in purpose. Nestorianism insisted upon two separate wills in a dyadic unity, while Apollonarianism taught that Jesus' human body was inhabited by a divine soul.

Over the years, others have insisted that Jesus Christ is merely the ideal man for humanity, since Jesus often called himself "the Son of man." They have felt that he seldom drew attention to his divinity, as Albert Schweitzer argues in his famous *Quest of the Historical Jesus* (1911).

Some modern Lutheran theologians believe that Jesus was not simultaneously on the earth as a human and in heaven as God. Under this view, Jesus was divine in the preexistence but gave up his godly status and divine properties, except moral attributes, and took upon himself flesh and became a man. This is called the "kenotic" theory.

John Hick, a British philosopher-theologian, feels that Christianity should return to the earliest Christology, the "grace" theory, which teaches that Christ was transformed into a being sharing the divine properties by being infused with his Father's grace.

Although the term "Christology" is not frequently used by Latter-day Saints, the doctrine of the Church can be described in the following manner: Jesus Christ descended from his high pre-existent station as a God when he came to earth to die for mankind's sins. He was Jehovah come to earth in a physical body as the Only Begotten of the Father in the flesh. While on earth he was still God, but he received from his Father "grace for grace," as do God's other children (D&C 93:12). The Book of Mormon and Doctrine and Covenants speak forcefully of the divine sonship of Christ and also of his humanity (Mosiah 15:2–3; Alma 6:8; 11:38; 13:16; 34:2; 3 Ne. 11:7; 28:10; D&C 93).

Like Jesus Christ, all mortals live in a state of humiliation, but through the mediation of the Christ they may progress to a state of exaltation (*see* DEIFICATION). There is no ultimate disparity between the divine and human natures; Joseph Smith asserted that mankind is of the same species as God, having been made in God's image (theomorphism) and being eternal, with unlimited capacity (*TPJS*, pp. 345–46). One early LDS leader proclaimed, "As man now is, God once was. As God now is, man may be" (Lorenzo Snow). Latter-day

Saints speak of man as a god in embryo and of Jesus Christ as mankind's elder brother. A favorite LDS children's hymn is titled "I Am a Child of God."

Latter-day Saint doctrine can be understood to have appreciation for Christ and applications for man that go beyond traditional Christology. It is LDS teaching that all the Father's children possess the potential to strive toward the same godhood that the Godhead already has; because in their humanity there is a divinity that is progressing and growing according to the faith, intelligence, and love that abound in their souls. Like the attribute of perfection, divinity is not a static absolute but a dynamic progression.

BIBLIOGRAPHY

Brown, Raymond E. "Christology." In *The New Jerome Biblical Commentary*, ed. R. Brown, J. Fitzmyer, and R. Murphy. Englewood Cliffs, N.J., 1990.
Hick, John. "An Inspiration Christology for a Religiously Plural World." In *Encountering Jesus: A Debate on Christology*, ed. Stephen T. Davis, pp. 5–22. Atlanta, 1988.
O'Collins, Gerald. "Jesus." *ER* 8:19–23.

GARY P. GILLUM

CHRISTUS STATUE

Replicas of the Christus statue by Danish sculptor Bertel Thorvaldsen (1768–1844) are located in several LDS VISITORS CENTERS. These white carrara marble statues of Christ, with his hands outstretched, inviting all to come to him, help present the central doctrine of the Church: that Jesus of Nazareth is the Son of God and the Savior and Redeemer of the world.

The first such statue acquired by the Church was a gift of Stephen L Richards, First Counselor to President David O. McKay (1951–1959). In 1966 this heroic-size (11 feet, 1 inch) Christus was placed in the North Visitors Center on Temple Square in Salt Lake City.

The second Christus was commissioned for display in the Church's pavilion at the New York World's Fair (1964–1965) and was sculpted by Aldo Rebachi of Florence, Italy. It was intended to help visitors understand that Latter-day Saints (or Mormons) are

Christians. This statue was later placed in the Visitors Center on the grounds of the Los Angeles Temple.

Additional Christus statues are currently located at visitors centers adjacent to temples in New Zealand; Hawaii; Mexico City; Washington, D.C.; and Mesa, Arizona.

BIBLIOGRAPHY

Marshall, Richard J. "Mormon Pavilion at the New York World's Fair . . . A Progress Report." *IE* 68 (Apr. 1965):290–97, 334–35.

Sheridan, Luise. "Bertel Thorvaldsen: Creator of Christus." *IE* 67 (Apr. 1964):272–75, 307.

Top, Brent L. "Legacy of the Mormon Pavilion New York World's Fair." *Ensign* 19 (Oct. 1989):22–28.

FLORENCE SMITH JACOBSEN

CHURCH AND STATE

Latter-day Saints believe that the separation of church and state is essential in modern societies prior to the Millennium. LDS scriptures teach that civic laws should not interfere with religious practices, nor should religious institutions manipulate governments to their advantage. Many LDS teachings emphasize the role of governments in preserving individual freedom of conscience. The Church is active in countries with various types of governments and encourages its members to be involved in civic affairs and to honor the laws of the land (*see* CIVIC DUTIES). LDS practice tended to be more integrationist and theocratic in the isolated early Utah period and has been more separationist in the twentieth century.

Discourse within the Church on issues of church and state proceeds on at least two planes: (1) in discussions of historical and contemporary church-state relations, and (2) in discussions of ideal settings, such as will exist in the Millennium, when "Christ will reign personally upon the earth" (A of F 10), or in the celestial kingdom.

The principles of free agency and freedom of conscience, which are fundamental to LDS church-state theory, are consistent on both planes of discourse. However, the institutional implications of these principles are different in the two settings. In the present world, where believers are subject to the imperfections of human government, separation of church and state is vital to the protection of religious liberty. On the ideal plane, in contrast, Latter-day Saints anticipate more integrated theocratic, or what Joseph Smith called "theodemocratic" institutions (*T&S* 5 [Apr. 15, 1844]:510), both because of the inherent legitimacy of divine rule and because the participants in millennial or celestial societies willingly accept such rule. Nevertheless, LDS prophets have consistently taught that even in the millennial society freedom of conscience will be respected. For example, Brigham Young stated, "In the Millennium men will have the privilege of their own belief" (*JD* 12:274; cf. *DS* 3:63–64). The Church does not advocate theocracy for the premillennial world. It instructs members to "be subject to the powers that be, until he reigns whose right it is to reign" (D&C 58:22)—that is, until Christ comes.

In the meantime, several principles apply. As noted above, the fundamental assumption is that human beings have free agency and a number of inherent human rights, most notably "the free exercise of conscience" (D&C 134:2). The Church declares, "We believe that religion is instituted of God; and that men are amenable . . . to him only, for the exercise of it, unless their religious opinions prompt them to infringe upon the rights and liberties of others; . . . that the civil magistrate should restrain crime, but never control conscience; should punish guilt, but never suppress the freedom of the soul" (D&C 134:4). This recognition of freedom of conscience includes a commitment to toleration, as is emphasized in the Church's eleventh Article of Faith: "We claim the privilege of worshiping Almighty God according to the dictates of our own conscience, and allow all men the same privilege, let them worship how, where, or what they may."

A corollary of freedom of conscience is that human law does not have the right "to interfere in prescribing rules of worship to bind the consciences of men, nor dictate forms for public or private devotion" (D&C 134:4). This principle of nonintervention by the state in religious affairs is understood to proscribe not only interference with individual practice but also interference with the autonomy of the Church as an institution pursuing its religious mission. The position of the Church in this regard was vindicated in the U.S. Supreme Court in *Corporation of The Presiding Bishop of the Church of Jesus Christ of Latter-day Saints et al. v. Amos et al.* (483 U.S. 327 [1987]) and is consistent with international understanding of religious liberty (e.g., Principle 16 of the Concluding Document of the Vienna Meeting of the Conference on Security and Co-operation in Europe [1989]). Consistent with this position, the Church believes in maintaining strict independence for itself and affiliated institutions, such as Church-sponsored schools and universities, and accordingly does not accept direct aid or subsidies from governmental sources because of the actual or potential regulatory interference this might entail.

The Church is also committed to separation of church and state from the religious side. "We do not believe it just to mingle religious influence with civil government, whereby one religious society is fostered and another proscribed in its spiritual privileges, and the individual rights of its members, as citizens, denied" (D&C 134:9). This does not mean that the Church is precluded from taking a stand on moral or other issues when it is religiously motivated to do so or that religious values must be pushed to the margin of public life; nor does it mean that the Church cannot have indirect influence on the state as a result of the Church's efforts to teach religious principles and to make positive contributions in its members' lives. It does mean that it is inappropriate for a religious organization to manipulate the machinery of secular power to procure advantages for itself or disadvantages for others.

The Church is not viewed as a worldly organization. It avails itself of legal structures, such as corporate or other organizational entities available to it in various countries, to arrange its temporal affairs, and it complies with all legal requirements this may entail, but it is not dependent for its spiritual authority on any worldly institution. Latter-day Saints believe that their Church is established and guided by God through a prophet and apostles who hold the keys and priesthood authority needed to teach gospel truths and to officiate in the ordinances necessary for salvation and exaltation.

The Church teaches the importance of government and encourages its members to obey the law of the land wherever they live. Human governments and laws are admittedly imperfect, but they play an important role in preserving order and providing stable contexts within which individuals can seek truth and strive to live in accordance with the dictates of conscience. Governmental leaders are accountable to God "for their acts . . . both in making laws and administering them, for the good and safety of society" (D&C 134:1; cf. 124:49–50).

Implementation of the foregoing principles in history has moved through a number of phases. In the earliest phase, the Church was essentially a small, persecuted religious group seeking religious liberty and a place to settle, first in western New York and then in Ohio, Missouri, and Illinois. During much of this period, the Church relied heavily on its own organization to manage its social structure. The Nauvoo Charter permitted some overlap of church and state. Toward the end of the Nauvoo period, Joseph Smith organized the Council of Fifty, which was intended to provide a potential framework within which Christ's millennial reign could be organized.

During the mid-nineteenth-century exodus from Nauvoo to the Great Basin, social, political, and economic organization was managed by the Church, since no other effective organization was available. Church leaders worked to establish separate governmental institutions, first in the form of a state of Deseret, then in the Territory of Utah, and in continuing efforts to secure Utah's statehood. During much of the nineteenth century, however, the federal government in particular was a hostile rather than a neutral force in the community. This reinforced the tendency for the Church to manage society through its own channels. Dreams of building Zion also contributed to tendencies to work through the Church.

After the Manifesto officially ended plural marriage in 1890 and Utah attained statehood in 1896, tension between the Church and state institutions gradually abated and reciprocal trust grew. During the twentieth century, therefore, the Church has pursued a more consistently separationist policy and has been free to emphasize its primarily spiritual mission. The Church is now established in well over 100 countries, and this internationalization has further reinforced the idea that the essential mission of the Church can be accomplished within a wide range of legal and political systems as long as there is sufficient separation of church and state to afford effective protection for religious liberty. Church teachings reinforce a constellation of values in its members that most governments welcome: family stability, honesty, hard work, avoidance of drug dependency, loyalty to country, and obedience to law. The result is that while the Church contributes to religious pluralism wherever it is found, it simultaneously contributes to social stability and the improvement of diverse societies.

[*See also* Civic Duties; Constitutional Law; Politics: Political History; Politics: Political Teachings.]

BIBLIOGRAPHY

Firmage, Edwin Brown, and Richard Collin Mangrum. *Zion in the Courts: A Legal History of the Church of Jesus Christ of Latter-day Saints, 1830-1900.* Urbana, Ill., 1988.

Jensen, Therald N. "Mormon Theory of Church and State." Ph.D. diss., University of Chicago, 1938.

Mangrum, Richard Collin. "Mormonism, Philosophical Liberalism, and the Constitution." *BYU Studies* 27 (Summer 1987):119–37.

Melville, J. Keith. "Theory and Practice of Church and State During the Brigham Young Era." *BYU Studies* 3 (Autumn 1960):33–55.

Taylor, John. *The Government of God.* Liverpool, 1852.

W. COLE DURHAM, JR.

CHURCH EDUCATIONAL SYSTEM (CES)

The Church of Jesus Christ of Latter-day Saints has established educational programs throughout the United States and in some ninety other countries to provide an effective combination of religious and secular education to its members. The primary aim shared by these programs is to assist students in gaining an understanding and personal witness of the restored gospel of Jesus Christ at the same time as they pursue their secular studies. Latter-day Saints are taught by their leaders and their scriptures to seek after truth in every sphere.

CES comprises the various educational programs of the Church. BRIGHAM YOUNG UNIVERSITY, BRIGHAM YOUNG UNIVERSITY—HAWAII CAMPUS, RICKS COLLEGE, and LDS BUSINESS COLLEGE provide higher education balanced with religious instruction for students attending these Church-owned institutions. SEMINARIES offer weekday religious instruction for high school students, and INSTITUTES offer similar instruction for college students attending non-LDS colleges and universities. Extensive adult and continuing education programs with headquarters at BYU provide educational opportunities for those not officially enrolled in the formal institutions. In addition, the Church maintains a few elementary and secondary schools in less developed nations.

EDUCATIONAL PHILOSOPHY.   Since the early days of the Church, leaders have placed a strong emphasis on education. The Prophet Joseph Smith, in discussing the purpose of earth life, consistently stressed learning. He said that one of the fundamental principles of Mormonism is to "receive truth let it come from where it may" (*WJS*, p. 229). Revelations given to Joseph Smith state that "the glory of God is intelligence" (D&C 93:36) and that "whatever principle of intelligence we attain unto in this life, it will rise with us in the resurrection" (D&C 130:18). Other revelations further emphasize the importance of both religious and secular learning:

> Teach ye diligently and my grace shall attend you, that you may be instructed more perfectly . . . in all things that pertain unto the kingdom of God, that are expedient for you to understand; of things both in heaven and in the earth, and under the earth; things which have been, things which are, things which must shortly come to pass; things which are at home, things which are abroad; the wars and the perplexities of the nations, and the judgments which are on the land; and a knowledge also of countries and of kingdoms [D&C 88:78–79].

Brigham Young, the second president of the Church, advanced the same concept, teaching that "all wisdom, and all the arts and sciences in the world are from God, and are designed for the good of His people" (*JD* 12:147). These ideas and scriptures have become the foundation of the educational philosophy of the Church (*see* EDUCATION: ATTITUDES TOWARD EDUCATION).

HISTORY OF EARLY EDUCATIONAL INSTITUTIONS.   As the Saints moved to Ohio, Missouri, and Illinois, they established elementary and secondary schools in each settlement. Schools of the Prophets were organized for adult leaders beginning in Kirtland, Ohio, in 1833. In 1840, a university was established in Nauvoo. During their trek to the Rocky Mountains the Saints conducted elementary classes in the temporary camps. In the fall of 1847, just three months after the first company of pioneers arrived in the Salt Lake Valley, schools were organized. Three years following, in 1850, the UNIVERSITY OF DESERET was founded. (In 1892 the territorial legislature changed the name to the University of Utah.)

Beginning in 1875, the Church established ACADEMIES throughout the intermountain United States and some in Canada and Mexico to provide elementary and secondary secular and religious education. To coordinate the programs and growth of the academies, a General Church Board of Education was organized in 1888, consisting of selected Church leaders. Karl G. Maeser was named the first superintendent of Church schools, a position that later became the Commissioner of Church Education. By 1907 the Church Board of Education was responsible for the administration of some thirty-five academies.

About 1890, with the increased availability of free public high schools, attendance at Church academies declined. Some closed their doors, and others were reorganized as junior colleges. By 1931 only Juárez Academy in Mexico remained as an academy. At that time the Church began transferring its junior colleges to state governments. However, it retained Ricks College in Rexburg, Idaho, and Brigham Young Academy in Provo, Utah, which developed into Brigham Young University.

As an increasing number of LDS youth began to attend public secondary schools, Church leaders recognized the need to provide a religious curriculum to complement regular secular studies. In 1912 the Church began building seminaries on Church-owned property adjacent to public high schools, where students could take a daily class in religion. Some public districts released students for an hour for this purpose; other students attended early morning classes before school started. To facilitate the religious training of students attending non-LDS colleges and universities, the Church established institutes of religion adjacent to college campuses beginning in 1926. The success of seminaries and institutes resulted in the spread of these programs to many parts of the world.

ORGANIZATION. In 1989 the Church Board of Education decided to decentralize the administration of all CES programs and the position of commissioner was abolished. Direct administration of Brigham Young University, Brigham Young University—Hawaii Campus, Ricks College, and LDS Business College was taken over by the boards of trustees legally established for each institution. These boards all have the same membership as the Church Board of Education. They are comprised of the First Presidency and other General Authorities and officers of the Church as assigned, including specifically the presidents of the two women's auxiliary organizations. By virtue of their assignments to each of these boards, these officers serve each institution concurrently. Also, the operation of seminaries, institutes of religion, religious education in adult and continuing education programs, and the operation of elementary and secondary schools of the Church is guided by the general Church Board of Education.

CHURCH SCHOOLS, SEMINARIES, AND INSTITUTES. Members of the Church are encouraged to take full advantage of public education opportunities where available. However, in some areas where there is a high concentration of members and few public education opportunities, the Church Board of Education has established elementary, middle, or secondary schools in which both secular and religious instruction is offered. Some 9,300 students attend Church schools located in Mexico, Kiribati, Fiji, Tonga, Western Samoa, and New Zealand. While serving as Commissioner of Church Education, Neal A. Maxwell explained the objectives of these schools: "Literacy and basic education are gospel needs. Without literacy individuals are handicapped—spiritually, intellectually, physically, socially and economically. Education is often not only the key to the individual member's economic future, but also to his opportunities for self-realization, for full Church service and for contributing to the world around him— spiritually, politically, culturally and socially" (*Annual Report*, 1971).

Where public education is readily available, CES offers seminary and institute programs to supplement secular education with religious teachings. During the 1988–1989 school year, 255,361 high school students participated in seminary, constituting 55 percent of all eligible LDS youth. Institute enrollment was 125,534—54 percent of those eligible. Courses in seminaries and institutes center around the reading and study of the Old Testament, New Testament, Book of Mormon, Doctrine and Covenants and Church history, and Pearl of Great Price. The teachings of these courses emphasize the reality of a living God, the resurrected Christ, the visitation of heavenly beings in restoring the gospel and Church of Jesus Christ to Joseph Smith, the continuing nature of revelation, the teachings of living prophets, and the gifts of the spirit. Students in seminary and institute are taught that personal religious knowledge can be obtained by seeking individual revelation, living the principles taught by Christ, and witnessing the results of doing the will of God.

The CES Salt Lake office is responsible for maintaining the quality of the curriculum and teaching staff of seminaries and institutes. Full-time teachers within the United States and Canada are required to have a bachelor's degree and to participate in an intensive training course at BYU or at one of the approved institutes. The training procedure varies somewhat in areas outside the United States and Canada where there are fewer Church members.

BIBLIOGRAPHY

Arrington, Leonard J. "The Founding of the L.D.S. Institutes of Religion." *Dialogue* 2 (Summer 1967):137–47.

Backman, Milton V., Jr. *The Heavens Resound*, pp. 264–75. Salt Lake City, 1983.

Bennion, M. Lynn. *Mormonism and Education*. Salt Lake City, 1939.

Berrett, William E. *A Miracle in Weekday Religious Education*. Salt Lake City, 1988.

Buchanan, Frederick S. "Education Among the Mormons: Brigham Young and the Schools of Utah." *History of Education Quarterly* 22 (Winter 1982):435–59.

Chamberlin, Ralph V. *The University of Utah, A History of Its First Hundred Years 1850 to 1950*. Salt Lake City, 1960.

French, Calvin V. "Organization and Administration of the Latter-day Saint School System of Free Education, Common School Through University at Nauvoo, Illinois, 1840–1845." Master's thesis, Temple University, 1965.

Monnett, John Daniel. "The Mormon Church and Its Private School System in Utah: The Emergence of the Academies, 1880–1892." Ph.D. diss., University of Utah, 1984.

Quinn, D. Michael. "Utah's Educational Innovation: LDS Religion Classes, 1890–1929." *Utah Historical Quarterly* 43 (Fall 1975):379–89.

Tuttle, A. Theodore. "Released Time Religious Education Program of the Church of Jesus Christ of Latter-day Saints." Master's thesis, Stanford University, 1949.

WILLIAM E. BERRETT

CIVIC DUTIES

Latter-day Saint teachings emphasize many aspects of civic duty, including responsible self-government; an informed, public-spirited citizenry; and obedience to law. LDS scriptures and leaders also encourage activity in organizations that build and maintain COMMUNITY life, making oneself available for public and military service, and avoidance of government welfare dependency. LDS teaching stresses EDUCATION and a healthy lifestyle, both of which contribute to a strong citizenry (*see* WORD OF WISDOM).

In September 1968 the First Presidency urged members "to do their civic duty and to assume their responsibilities as individual citizens in seeking solutions to the problems which beset our cities and communities." Members are obligated to respect governmental authority. The twelfth Article of Faith states, "We believe in being subject to kings, presidents, rulers, and magistrates, in obeying, honoring, and sustaining the law." This commitment to good citizenship is further elucidated in scripture: "We believe that all men are bound to sustain and uphold the respective governments in which they reside, while protected in their inherent and inalienable rights by the laws of such governments; and that sedition and rebellion are unbecoming every citizen thus protected" (D&C 134:5).

LDS emphasis on civic duty stems from Christian commitment to community service and individual freedom. The CONSTITUTION OF THE UNITED STATES, which also promotes these values, was established by God through "wise men" for the "protection of all flesh" (D&C 101:77–80). Latter-day Saints are to strive to elect "honest" and "wise" leaders who will support constitutional freedoms, particularly freedom of religion (D&C 98:10). The Christian tradition of civic virtue that underlay the American founding has been documented by LDS scholars (Vetterli and Bryner). Latter-day Saints tend to take seriously their responsibility to participate in the political process. Since World War II, Utah has been the state with the highest percentage of eligible voters who do in fact vote in presidential elections (72 percent). Latter-day Saints are also strongly encouraged to be patriotic and share in the responsibility of defending their homelands through military service, if necessary, wherever they might live ("First Presidency Statement," *Church News*, May 24, 1969, p. 12).

Latter-day Saint women were involved in public life long before women in other parts of the United States. They have always voted in Church congregations. The University of Deseret, founded in Salt Lake City in 1850, was the first coeducational university west of the Mississippi. H. H. Bancroft's *History of Utah* reported that women voted in the provisional government before territorial status in 1850 (p. 272, San Francisco, 1890). The first documented women voters in modern times were in Salt Lake City on February 14, 1870. Mary

W. Chamberlain was elected mayor of Kanab, Utah, with an all-female town board, in 1912. The first woman state senator elected in the United States (Dr. Mattie Hughes Paul Cannon, 1896) and the first woman elected to the U.S. Senate who was neither the wife nor the daughter of a politician (Paula Hawkins, Florida, 1980) were Latter-day Saints.

The Church encourages its members to make themselves available for public office, and many have responded. Latter-day Saints have served as governors of such states as California (Culbert Olson and Goodwin Knight) and Michigan (George Romney). In 1952 two Latter-day Saints were serving in the U.S. House of Representatives and two in the U.S. Senate. In 1991 there were nine LDS representatives and one nonvoting territorial delegate in the House and three Latter-day Saints in the Senate. There have been five LDS cabinet members (Ezra Taft Benson, Agriculture; Stewart L. Udall, Interior; George W. Romney, Housing and Urban Development; David M. Kennedy, Treasury; and Terrell H. Bell, Education). Latter-day Saints have served as both domestic and national security advisers in the Bush administration. Prior to 1952, no Latter-day Saint had served as a federal judge. Since then, eleven have been appointed to federal district courts and four to appeals courts.

Church members are encouraged to help their communities through volunteerism. The LDS Church is one of the most active sponsors of the SCOUTING movement in the United States. Concern for the international community was evident when members fasted in 1985 and contributed nearly $11 million for Ethiopian and other famine relief and agricultural development for distribution largely through other agencies (see HUMANITARIAN SERVICE).

In times of increasing dependence on government programs and assistance, Latter-day Saints as a group consciously try to live in such a way as to reduce their burden on government. Their lifestyle, teachings, and youth programs are often cited as explanations for low rates of crime, drug abuse, alcoholism, illness, and unemployment in the areas where they live. Through these and other means, they invest in, and promote, education, moral behavior, and leadership—and with some success. For example, medical studies now document the healthiness of the Mormon lifestyle (*USA Today*, Dec. 6, 1989, p. 1), which presumably contributes to a stronger and less dependent citizenry. LDS social services and employment and welfare programs save governments millions of dollars annually. The predominantly LDS state of Utah regularly ranks first in the proportion of high school graduates who take advanced placement courses. *Fortune* magazine ranked metropolitan Salt Lake City first in the availability of intelligent, enthusiastic, and loyal workers (Oct. 22, 1990, p. 49), and *Financial World* ranked Utah the second best-governed state (Apr. 17, 1990, p. 31).

[*See also* Politics: Political Teachings; Politics: Contemporary; United States of America.]

BIBLIOGRAPHY
Vetterli, Richard, and Gary Bryner. *In Search of the Republic: Public Virtue and the Roots of American Government.* Totowa, N.J., 1987.

MARK W. CANNON

CIVIL RIGHTS

Civil rights are legal guarantees designed to protect persons from arbitrary or discriminatory treatment. Common examples are those protecting freedom of speech, freedom of worship, freedom of assembly, the right to due process of law, the right to vote, the right to equal protection of the law, and safeguards for persons accused of crime, such as the right against self-incrimination, the right to confront one's accuser, the right to a jury trial, the right to counsel, and the right to a speedy trial. These and other rights are declared in the Constitution of the United States of America and in the constitutions of many other countries (*see* CONSTITUTIONAL LAW). Civil rights are found in statutes as well as in constitutions and may provide, for example, detailed guarantees against public and private discrimination on the basis of such characteristics as race, gender, age, and religion. Civil rights issues arise when people disagree about the rights that are, or ought to be, guaranteed by law.

The Church of Jesus Christ of Latter-day Saints and its members have an obvious interest in securing their own rights. Beyond this, several strands of doctrine and belief—sometimes competing— shape the views of members and leaders regarding civil rights in general. The principle of free agency seems most compatible with a legal system guaranteeing wide latitude for individual choice and decision. With respect to religious liberties, agency is reinforced by individual and institutional interests in freedom from governmental restraint. In the UNITED STATES OF AMERICA, commitment to individual rights is further reinforced by allegiance to the personal liberties guaranteed by the U.S. Constitution, which Latter-day Saints regard as an inspired document. On the other hand, the Church teaches its members to obey properly constituted governmental authority (D&C 134:5; 98:6; A of F 12), which may lead to accommodation and submission when core religious interests are not threatened. In addition, Church teachings on moral questions sometimes predispose members, as well as the institutional Church, to take positions on political issues (ABORTION, for example) that run counter to the rights claimed by others. As a result, the position of the Church and its members toward current civil rights issues is complex.

A Church statement of belief regarding government, adopted in 1835, singled out "free exercise of conscience, the right and control of property, and the protection of life" as rights essential to the peace of society (D&C 134:2; *see* POLITICS: POLITICAL TEACHINGS). This 1835 statement repeatedly stressed the importance of religious freedom, and the Church and its members have sometimes found it necessary to take legal action to vindicate free exercise rights. In *Corporation of the Presiding Bishop of The Church of Jesus Christ of Latter-day Saints et al. v. Amos et al.* (483 U.S. 327 [1987]), for example, the Church successfully defended its right to impose a religious test for employment in certain Church-owned establishments. The Church as an institution has avoided legal action where possible, but has been willing to defend its rights in court when necessary.

Apart from its special legal interests, the Church is publicly committed to a broad range of civil rights for all. An oft-cited 1963 statement by a member of the Church First Presidency, Hugh B. Brown, called for "full civil equality for all of God's children," saying "it is a moral evil . . . to deny any human being the right to gainful employment, to full educational opportunity, and to every privilege of citizenship, just as it is a moral evil to deny him the right to worship" (p. 1058).

In the political arena, where competing claims to civil rights are frequently debated, the Church participates indirectly by encouraging members to vote and to foster a society congenial to Christian teaching and righteous living. Occasionally, when public issues implicate important matters of doctrine and morals, the Church publishes recommended positions on disputed issues and encourages members and others to follow their counsel. Thus, the Church has urged restrictions on the sale of alcoholic beverages, opposed the legalization of gambling and lotteries, favored right-to-work legislation (no closed or union shop), advocated the defeat of the equal rights amendment (ERA), and spoken out against pornography, abortion, and child abuse.

Within the Church, individual rights play a muted role as compared with secular society. Love and duty are stressed far more than individual claims of right. Moreover, the Church is a voluntary organization whose sanctions extend only to rights of membership and participation within the group, so fewer safeguards are necessary. Thus, Church disciplinary proceedings do not provide the full set of procedural protections the accused would receive in secular courts. Although due process notices and appeal rights are given, service of process is not strictly enforced and there is no right to confront one's accuser, no jury trial, and no right to counsel. Indeed, confession of sin by the repentant sinner may be at odds with the right against self-incrimination. Free speech is another illustration of the contrast with secular society. Members are free to say or publish what they wish. Yet, Church etiquette and policies, obligations of confidentiality, respect for divine and holy things, and the need to avoid offending others impose restraints upon freedom of expression. Likewise, voting within the Church involves the concept of common consent, but has none of the trappings of democratic elections and in most instances amounts to ratification of leadership callings and decisions. As for gender equality and children's rights, the relationships of men, women, and children are governed by religious principles, freely adopted by members, which teach EQUALITY but emphasize differences in roles. These principles are taught as eternal patterns, not derived from prevailing attitudes toward civil rights in any secular society, past or present.

BIBLIOGRAPHY
Allen, James B., and Glen M. Leonard. *The Story of the Latter-day Saints*. Salt Lake City, 1976.

Brown, Hugh B. *IE* 66 (Dec. 1963):1058.

Cowan, Richard O. *The Church in the Twentieth Century*. Salt Lake City, 1985.

Firmage, Edwin Brown, and Richard Collin Mangrum. *Zion in the Courts: A Legal History of the Church of Jesus Christ of Latter-day Saints, 1830–1900*. Urbana, Ill., 1988.

Mangrum, R. Collin. "Mormonism, Philosophical Liberalism, and the Constitution." *BYU Studies* 27 (Summer 1987):119–37.

McAffee, Thomas B. "Constitutional Interpretation and the American Tradition of Individual Rights." *BYU Studies* 27 (Summer 1987):139–69.

Melville, J. Keith. "Joseph Smith, the Constitution, and Individual Liberties." *BYU Studies* 28 (Spring 1988):65–74.

ROBERT E. RIGGS

CLERGY

The word "clergy" generally designates those who are priests or ministers within the Catholic, Eastern Orthodox, or Protestant traditions. Since the term refers to full-time paid professionals, it is not used by Latter-day Saints. They refer to their Church officers as branch presidents, bishops, or stake presidents. These individuals are laypersons who, without professional training in theology, are called to these positions for limited periods of time by those having authority.

Some Latter-day Saints have ambivalent feelings about the clergy of other Christian traditions, in part because some professional ministers participated in the early persecution of the Saints and others in current times continue to produce ANTI-MORMON PUBLICATIONS. Also, because Latter-day Saints believe that the Lord has revealed the fulness of the gospel through his modern prophets, the professional clergy have been viewed as teaching only part of the truth. However, The Church of Jesus Christ of Latter-day Saints readily acknowledges the extensive contributions of Jewish, Catholic, Eastern Orthodox, Protestant, and other clergy to the spiritual and moral well-being of their communities and their parishioners.

BIBLIOGRAPHY

Bangerter, William Grant. "'Tis a Two-Way Street." *Ensign* 10 (July 1986):66–71.

ROGER R. KELLER

COFFEE

Active Latter-day Saints abstain from drinking coffee. This practice derives from an 1833 revelation known as the WORD OF WISDOM, which states that "hot drinks are not for the body or the belly" (D&C 89:9). Hyrum Smith, Assistant President of the Church, later defined "hot drinks" as coffee and TEA (*T&S* 3 [June 1, 1842]:800), establishing the official interpretation for subsequent generations. The Word of Wisdom was given originally to show the will of God, though not as a commandment. Abstinence from coffee has been expected of fully participating members since the early twentieth century.

The main chemical in coffee that has caused health concerns is caffeine, a cerebral and cardiovascular stimulant. A large number of other substances are also found in coffee, and their effects on health are not yet well understood.

BIBLIOGRAPHY
Gilman, A. G.; L. S. Goodman; and A. Gilman, eds. *Goodman and Gilman's The Pharmacological Basis of Therapeutics*, 6th ed., pp. 592–604. New York, 1980.
Stratton, Clifford J. "The Xanthines: Coffee, Cola, Cocoa, and Tea." *BYU Studies* 20 (Summer 1980):371–88.

JOSEPH LYNN LYON

COLUMBUS, CHRISTOPHER

Latter-day Saints generally regard Columbus as having fulfilled a prophecy contained early in the Book of Mormon. Nephi₁ recorded a vision of the future of his father's descendants. After foreseeing the destruction of his own seed, Nephi beheld a Gentile "separated from the seed of my brethren by the many waters," and saw that the Spirit of God "came down and wrought upon the man; and he went forth upon the many waters, even unto the seed of my brethren, who were in the promised land" (1 Ne. 13:12).

Nephi appears to give an accurate account of Columbus's motives. Even though he was well-acquainted with the sciences of his day and his voyages have been viewed by some historians as primarily an economic triumph of Spain over Portugal, Columbus apparently had bigger motives for his voyage and felt himself spiritually driven to discover new lands. Newly acknowledged documents show that medieval eschatology, the scriptures, and divine inspiration were the main forces compelling him to sail. His notes in the works of Pierre d'Ailly and his own unfinished *Book of Prophecies* substantiate his apocalyptic view of the world and his feelings about his own prophetic role.

Among the themes of this book was the conversion of the heathen. Columbus quoted Seneca, "The years will come . . . when the Ocean will loose the bonds by which we have been confined, when an immense land shall lie revealed" (Watts, p. 94). He believed himself chosen by God to find that land and deliver the light of Christianity to the natives there. He was called *Christoferens* (the Christ-bearer). A map contemporaneous with his voyages depicts him bearing the Christ child on his shoulders across the waters. He believed that he was to help usher in the age of "one fold, and one shepherd," citing John 10:16 (cf. 3 Ne. 15:21), and spoke of finding "the new heaven and new earth."

Writing to King Ferdinand and Queen Isabella to gain financial support, Columbus testified that a voice had told him he had been watched over from infancy to prepare him for discovering the Indies. He felt that he was given divine keys to ocean barriers that only he could unlock (Merrill, p. 135). In a second letter, he emphasized his prophetic role: "Reason, mathematics, and maps of the world were of no use to me in the execution of the enterprise of the Indies. What Isaiah said [e.g., Isa. 24:15] was completely fulfilled" (Watts, p. 96). Unknowingly, Columbus also fulfilled Nephi's prophecy.

BIBLIOGRAPHY

Merrill, Hyde M. "Christopher Columbus and the Book of Mormon." *IE* 69 (1966):97–98, 135–36.

Nibley, Hugh W. "Columbus and Revelation." *Instructor* 88 (1953):319–20; reprinted in *CWHN* 8:49–53.

Watts, Pauline Moffitt. "Prophecy and Discovery: On the Spiritual Origins of Christopher Columbus's 'Enterprise of the Indies.'" *American Historical Review* 90 (1985):73–102.

LOUISE G. HANSON

COMMUNITY

For Latter-day Saints, community is an essential and eternal part of life in this world and in the world to come. From the time the Church was established (1830), its teachings have placed emphasis on principles of unity, cooperation, mutual assistance, and beautification of one's surroundings. The community of believers envisioned by the Prophet Joseph Smith continues today, based essentially on the principles he established. Changes, however, occurred as the Church moved to the Intermountain West, where Mormon towns and cities rose, and later as the Church spread to many parts of the world. As the Church has grown, the community embodied in the ward has become a special focus of spiritual and social life among Church members, however small or isolated the congregation. Wherever Latter-day Saints find themselves, they form a community of believers based on human relationships that are expected to endure forever.

TEACHINGS OF JOSEPH SMITH AND BRIGHAM YOUNG.   The advantages of village life described by Joseph Smith are an extension of life in a New England town. The Smiths brought to the frontier their New England background, emphasizing the importance of the community in providing education, mutual assistance, and political and economic organization. Joseph Smith's ideas about the importance of community life were an application of a revelation received in February 1831 on the law of consecration and stewardship (D&C 42). This revelation encouraged the members of the Church to band together and live a communitarian life in which the wealthy would voluntarily share their surplus with the poor. These ideas about community were partially implemented in Kirtland, Ohio, in 1831. Participants soon moved to Jackson County, Missouri, to be involved with Joseph Smith's City of Zion plan, through which he envisioned many social, educational, intellectual, economic, and professional advantages to the Saints from living together in communities, each containing 15,000 to 20,000 people, rather than being scattered on farms, as was the custom on the frontier at that time (*CHC* 1:311–12).

However, persecution drove the Saints from Missouri in 1838–1839, and some 12,000 of them fled to the Nauvoo area in

Illinois. Based on a modified plan of the City of Zion, Nauvoo became a general model for community development later used by the Latter-day Saints in settling the Intermountain West.

An essential element of the organization of the communities established by the Latter-day Saints between 1830 and 1846 was the division of the larger communities into wards and stakes, each with its own leaders. The bishop of each ward was a major figure in this organization. Nauvoo was eventually divided into a number of wards, each representing a geographic area of the city and the countryside beyond it. The bishop, with his counselors, was involved in supervising both the temporal and the spiritual affairs of the families within his ward's boundaries.

The guidelines left by Joseph Smith and fifteen years of experience in community building in Ohio, Missouri, and Illinois provided the basis for the principles that President Brigham Young followed during the migration to Utah and the establishment and development of the LDS settlements of the Intermountain West.

The first principle was based on Joseph Smith's belief that the Latter-day Saints should live in a village and commute to rural farming areas around the community.

Second, property rights of residents of LDS communities were to be held under the principle of stewardship, which suggested that the interest of the group was more important than that of the individual. This principle was later implemented by Brigham Young, who tried for thirty years to incorporate these communitarian teachings into the settlement of the Intermountain West.

Third, the duty of the Saints was to care for, and beautify, the earth (Nibley, pp. 3–29). The belief that the earth could be improved through the efforts of an industrious and dedicated community of Saints was of particular importance as the Church migrated to the arid Great Basin.

The fourth principle advocated frugality and the economic independence of the Saints.

The fifth principle emphasized the importance of unity and cooperation among Church members. Community cooperation allowed them to establish hundreds of settlements in the arid West, based on principles of faith, love, charity, kindness, service, and sharing one another's burdens.

SETTLEMENT OF THE INTERMOUNTAIN WEST. The communitarian principles established and developed during the formative years of the Church were institutionalized in the settlement of the Great Basin. One of the distinguishing characteristics of the Intermountain West is the presence of LDS communities based on these principles. Historically, these settlements ranged through southern Idaho, southwestern Wyoming, Utah, Nevada, California, Arizona, northwestern New Mexico, and southern Colorado. The role of religion was unique in their establishment.

The ward became the main base for organizing cooperation, economic development, spiritual and temporal welfare, and even the administration of justice in the new settlements. Salt Lake City, for example, was divided geographically into wards, with the bishop of each responsible for the well-being of the members within his jurisdiction. In each ward unit, believers unified their efforts in such prosaic activities as building a fence to protect the ward's newly sown crops, digging irrigation ditches to provide water for the land within the ward's boundary, caring for widows or the families of men who were absent on missions for the Church, assisting with births, burying the dead, and being involved in every other aspect of life within the ward. Disputes over water or land also were handled by the priesthood within the ward boundaries.

The importance of concerted efforts in LDS communities is still obvious to any observer of these small western towns. Many have only one ward. Thus, the Meadow Utah Ward is also the town of Meadow, Utah. The activities of the ward are the focus of the social, political, and economic life of the community, involving even the few non-Mormons who reside there. In larger cities and in places where there are fewer Latter-day Saints, the ward remains the focus of activity for believers.

THE TWENTIETH CENTURY. The modern LDS community operates in basically the same manner as the earliest communities founded under the direction of Joseph Smith. The fundamental principles of cooperation, equality, beautifying the earth, frugality and independence, unity and cooperation, and stewardship of material possessions are modified only in emphasis, not in principle. The continued reliance on an unpaid leadership allows the majority of ward members to be involved in providing services for the local congregation.

From the bishop to the home teachers and visiting teachers who regularly visit each LDS home, all members are invited to become actively involved with the well-being of the entire community. The ward provides not only worship services but friends, economic assistance, and a support group that can be relied upon to provide the assistance any family might need, particularly in a society in which extended family members may not be nearby to provide such assistance. In this way, for many the ward becomes a surrogate family, and the common practice of addressing fellow Saints as "Brother" and "Sister" takes on enhanced and spiritually literal meaning. One belongs in the community of Saints regardless of one's other affiliations or lack of them; one is welcome in the ward however outcast one may feel elsewhere.

The effectiveness of the individual ward varies from place to place as a function of the ability and commitment of the leaders and members. The extent of unity among ward members and their commitment to the principles of mutual assistance and concern for one another also affect the effectiveness of the individual ward; yet, in general, the wards function as an instant community for the Latter-day Saint wherever he or she may move.

Membership in the LDS community is not restricted to those who have been longtime members of the Church. The Church is actively involved in proselytizing, with nearly 50,000 missionaries throughout the world who introduce prospective members to the ward or branch community, where they are encouraged to attend and become involved. The Church organizations are the structures used to fellowship them into the community.

The ward community strives to operate on what Joseph Smith said was the basis of governance in the Church: teach the members correct principles and let them govern themselves (*JD* 10:57–58). While the principle of equality of resources is not now practiced as it was in the 1830s or 1870s, members of the Church still dedicate their time and talents to the welfare of the community as a whole and are encouraged to tithe and to contribute to the assistance of the poor.

LIFE IN THE MORMON COMMUNITY. The importance of the Church in the lives of its members cannot be overstated. Not only are its principles and practices a part of everyday life in such matters as dress, food, personal habits, and financial and time management, but the involvement of the entire ward in helping one another also creates a strong bond among ward members. The Church emphasizes the integrity of the family and teaches that a fundamental purpose of the Church is to strengthen the family. In addition to formal and informal family religious observances, Church meetings consist (as of 1990) of a three-hour block of time on Sundays, the focus of which is an hour-long general meeting in which members of the congregation deliver talks on gospel principles and partake of the sacrament of the Lord's Supper; following the sacrament meeting, sessions for Sunday School, priesthood, Relief Society, Young Women, and Primary are held. In earlier decades various auxiliary meetings, youth activities, and ward events were held during the week, and the meetinghouse was a bustling center of ward and stake activities and classes nearly every day.

Members also have contact with one another through the home teaching and visiting teaching programs, through assisting one another as needs arise, and through the other meetings and activities associated with the various Church auxiliary organizations. Members of wards and stakes may participate in sports activities. The ward sponsors periodic socials, Scouting activities, and cultural events that involve the members of the community, both LDS and others. The cooperation of members of the ward in helping widows, the poor, the ill, the aged, and others with special needs provides additional opportunities for interaction. In combination, the activities and opportunities for service among members of the ward strengthen the ties of the LDS community and enhance their commitment to "love one another," as Christ commanded (John 13:34–35).

ETERNAL PERSPECTIVES. The attitudes of Latter-day Saints regarding community are influenced by the belief that human relationships are eternal. People are by nature social beings whose lives and feelings are eternally intertwined with those of others. In premortal life, all human beings were born as spirit children in the family of God and therefore became members of an eternal and divine society. In the present life, people can become members of the Church by entering into the new and everlasting covenant of baptism, which binds people together as members of the kingdom of God. The Latter-day

Saint view of the kingdoms of glory yet to come anticipates immortal beings living together forever. In other words, heaven includes life with other people and with God. In the highest degree of the celestial glory, a fulness of joy is found in eternal marriage and familial relationships. Indeed, the nature of godhood itself and the composition of the Godhead as three personages eternally united in a common cause demonstrate the divine prototype for personal relationships.

Latter-day Saints have faith that all people will come forth at the day of judgment and continue at various levels thereafter. This expectation gives a permanent and sensitive dimension to friendships, companionships, and virtually all contacts with other people in local and worldwide communities, both religious and civic. The ideal of human existence looks toward the creation of a people of Zion modeled after the city of Enoch and the establishment of a perfected community, a New Jerusalem, under the personal governance of Jesus Christ.

[*See also* Society.]

BIBLIOGRAPHY

Alder, Douglas D. "The Mormon Ward: Congregation or Community?" *Journal of Mormon History* 5 (1978):61–78.

Arrington, Leonard J. *Great Basin Kingdom*. Cambridge, Mass., 1958.

———. *Brigham Young: American Moses*. New York, 1985.

Arrington, Leonard J., et al. *Building the City of God*. Salt Lake City, 1976.

Embry, Jessie L., and Howard A. Christy, eds. *Community Development in the American West: Past and Present, Nineteenth- and Twentieth-Century Frontiers*. Provo, Utah, 1985.

Hine, Robert V. *Community on the American Frontier*. Norman, Okla., 1980.

Hunter, Milton R. *Brigham Young the Colonizer*. Salt Lake City, 1940.

Jackson, Richard H., ed. *The Mormon Role in the Settlement of the West*. Provo, Utah, 1978.

Nibley, Hugh. "Brigham Young on the Environment." In *To the Glory of God*, ed. T. Madsen and C. Tate, pp. 3–29. Salt Lake City, 1972.

O'Dea, Thomas F. *The Mormons*. Chicago, 1957.

Peterson, Charles S. "A Mormon Town: One Man's West." *Journal of Mormon History* 3 (1976):3–12.

Poll, Richard D., et al., eds. *Utah's History*, rev. ed., pp. 133–52, 275–335. Logan, Utah, 1989.

RICHARD H. JACKSON

COMPUTER SYSTEMS

For many years The Church of Jesus Christ of Latter-day Saints used mechanical punched-card systems for accounting and other administrative purposes. These were replaced by modern computers. In 1962 the Church's computer systems were expanded to help provide names for temple work. They also were applied to managing the large and rapidly expanding genealogical information base. Church computer resources now serve every level, from general Church administration to the individual member.

In Church temples, computer systems are used to record biographical information of individuals, living and dead, who have received temple ordinances. Family history computer systems maintain growing catalogs of worldwide genealogical records, a lineage-linked ANCESTRAL FILE, and an index of completed ordinances and other lists to help interested persons pursue family history work.

Computers also aid in the administration of various Church programs, including the international missionary program, where computers are used to track all missionaries and route individual requests for missionary visits. Financial contributions are recorded on computers by clerks at the ward level, making possible regular reports to contributors and to the Church. All central budgeting and financial transactions are managed by computer. The Church maintains detailed membership records which are created on computers in the wards and are regularly updated and forwarded to central computers at Church headquarters or region/area offices.

The Church uses computers to prepare, print, and distribute a wide range of materials through its distribution centers in various parts of the world. Scriptures, lesson manuals, handbooks, forms, and Church magazines are prepared with the use of computers. These materials are printed in as many as eighty-one languages, and computers are used extensively in the translation process.

PUBLIC COMMUNICATIONS uses computers to monitor public response to Church media. Computer systems also manage information in areas such as Church welfare, historical records, physical facilities, magazine subscriptions, and purchasing. The SEMINARIES and INSTITUTES track potential and enrolled students throughout the world by computer.

Large numbers of Latter-day Saints use personal computers in their homes to facilitate religious activities. Many use disk versions of the scriptures to enhance individual scripture research and study. Personal genealogical research has moved to a personal computer format that will allow exchanges of information with the large genealogical data bases in Salt Lake City.

DARWIN A. JOHN

CONSCIENTIOUS OBJECTION

While any member of the Church is free to object to military combat service because of conscience, simply holding membership in the Church in and of itself is not a justification. Church leaders have discouraged conscientious objection in every conflict of the twentieth century. Although it is opposed to war and recognizes that going to war is a very poor alternative means of resolving conflicts, the Church considers it the loyal duty of citizenship for members to answer the call of their various countries for military service.

At the same time, it recognizes the right of individual members to determine for themselves whether their deep, spiritual consciences will allow them to serve in combat or require them to request assignment to alternate service. The Church will not support a member in that request until he or she has consulted with the appropriate bishop and stake president and has spiritual confirmation that the way decided upon by the member concerned is acceptable to the Lord.

BIBLIOGRAPHY

Boone, Joseph F. "The Roles of The Church of Jesus Christ of Latter-day Saints in Relation to the United States Military, 1900–1975." Ph.D. diss., Brigham Young University, 1975.

CHARLES D. TATE, JR.

CONSTITUTIONAL LAW

As a people, the Latter-day Saints are committed to sustaining constitutional government as the best instrument for maintaining peace, individual freedom, and community life in modern society. This commitment is reinforced by their scriptures, which affirm that constitutional law "supporting that principle of freedom in maintaining rights and privileges, belongs to all mankind, and is justifiable before [the Lord]" (D&C 98:5). The scripture cited further explains that not only has God made people free by giving them agency, but "the law also maketh you free" (verse 8). Furthermore, any standard other than constitutional law "cometh of evil" (verse 10). This principle applies not only in the UNITED STATES OF AMERICA, but wherever Latter-day Saints might live throughout the world. However, Latter-day Saints everywhere believe also "in being subject to kings, presidents, rulers, and magistrates, in obeying, honoring, and sustaining the law" (A of F 12).

Latter-day Saints have both contributed to, and benefited from, laws and American constitutional law. The Constitution of the United States of America made the restoration of the gospel possible because it limits governmental power, protects individual rights, and sets a moral tone tolerating controversial religious views and rights of expression and assembly. LDS belief in the divine origin of the Constitution contributes to respect for the document.

The majority of the main events associated with the restoration of the Church occurred in the United States. Its message was controversial and provocative, and without the protections of the United States Constitution, the Church likely would not have survived. President Wilford Woodruff taught that at that time the United States of America was the only place where the Lord could have established his Church and kingdom (*JD* 25:211). President David O. McKay, in the dedicatory prayer for the Los Angeles Temple, expressed gratitude for the Constitution and for the fact that it made the establishment of the Church possible (*IE* 59 [Apr. 1956]:226). This idea is expressed frequently by Latter-day Saints and is more than patriotic rhetoric; a brief examination of the U.S. Constitution shows why.

The United States was especially hospitable to the restoration of the Church because its Constitution limits governments, both state and federal, thereby protecting individual rights. It limits governmental power in two ways: through two structural features commonly referred to as the separation of powers and federalism and through a series of express prohibitions.

The separation of powers refers to the division of governmental power on a horizontal plane among the three distinct branches of the federal government—legislative, executive, and judicial. Federalism divides governmental power on a vertical plane between the national government and the state governments. The separation of powers and federalism, by allocating governmental powers among several entities and by making each of these entities a competitor with the others, minimize the likelihood that government will trample individual rights.

The most famous of the express prohibitions against governmental action are contained in the first eight of the ten amendments to the Constitution that make up the Bill of Rights. By themselves, these provisions had been interpreted to apply only to the federal government, but the Fourteenth Amendment has now been held by the U.S. Supreme Court to make most of those Bill of Rights guarantees binding on state governments as well (*see* CIVIL RIGHTS). Because the Bill of Rights and the structural provisions of the Constitution protect individual rights against government intrusions, Latter-day Saints and other religious groups have been its distinct and identifiable beneficiaries.

Beyond its limitations on government, the Constitution sets a moral tone tolerating controversial religious views and rights of expression in general. This tone extends beyond its immediate impact on government. Without it, the public opposition to the Church, combined with the zeal of its adherents, might have brought about its demise. That Joseph Smith was born soon after the adoption and ratification of the Constitution is no coincidence in the LDS view.

Latter-day Saints have participated significantly in the development of American law dealing with constitutional protections of civil rights. The starting point for modern constitutional analysis of First Amendment freedoms—including not only the free exercise of religion but all First Amendment rights—is provided by *Reynolds v. United States* (98 U.S. 145 [1879]), which involved the prosecution of a nineteenth-century Church leader for practicing polygamy. *Reynolds* was the first Supreme Court interpretation of the First Amendment. It draws a distinction between beliefs, which it holds are absolutely protected by the First Amendment, and conduct, which it says enjoys no protection.

That distinction between belief and conduct is still the cornerstone of First Amendment analysis. The first half of it (absolute protection for belief) is still good law, though the second half (no protection for conduct) is not. The present rule for religiously motivated conduct, which was not clearly developed until almost a century after the *Reynolds* decision was handed down, is that government actions adversely affecting religious behavior are prohibited by the First Amendment's free exercise clause unless government can show that its actions are based on a compelling state interest and that its regulation or other infringement is narrowly tailored to the achievement of that objective (*Wisconsin v. Yoder et al.*, 406 U.S. 205 [1972]). The test strongly favors individual rights over government interests and is therefore conducive to RELIGIOUS FREEDOM. It is also a test from which the Church has benefited.

As a group, Latter-day Saints in the United States are deeply patriotic. They sustained the Constitution even when, in times of severe persecution, some of its protections were denied them. Partly because of the Church's history and partly because of their unique understanding of the nation's origins, most Latter-day Saints in the United States accept the responsibility to study and understand their Constitution as being rooted not only in patriotism but in religion as well. The devotion of the Church and its leaders to the Constitution can be traced to early times. Doctrine and Covenants 134, "A Declaration of Belief Regarding Governments and Laws," adopted by unanimous vote at a general assembly of the Church held at Kirtland, Ohio, on August 17, 1835, is a vigorous statement on the importance of preserving individual rights, particularly those relating to religious and other expressive freedoms. As expressed by one Church President, Latter-day Saints "have a tremendous obligation to be good citizens, to uphold the Constitution of this land, to adhere to its basic concepts" (Benson, pp. 615–16; *see also* POLITICS: POLITICAL TEACHINGS).

Another aspect of the LDS understanding of the Constitution is the belief gained from scripture concerning its divine origins, which enhances Latter-day Saints' respect and even reverence for the document, particularly in the United States. The Lord revealed to Joseph

Smith, "And for this purpose have I established the Constitution of this land, by the hands of wise men whom I raised up unto this very purpose" (D&C 101:80; cf. 3 Ne. 21:4). Some Church members espouse a view which goes beyond this scriptural language, esteeming the Constitution beyond criticism and as near scriptural. What the scripture in fact says is simple, informative, and understandable: this remarkably successful document did not emerge by chance or human wisdom alone. God had a hand in its creation—not in the same, direct, revelatory way that he creates scripture, but by assembling and inspiring, at the one crucial point in American history when it was sorely needed, probably the most talented collection of statesmen with which any nation has ever been blessed.

BIBLIOGRAPHY
Benson, Ezra Taft. *Teachings of Ezra Taft Benson*. Salt Lake City, 1988.
Lee, Rex E. *A Lawyer Looks at the Constitution*. Provo, Utah, 1980.
Mangrum, R. Collin. "Mormonism, Philosophical Liberalism, and the Constitution." *BYU Studies* 27 (Summer 1987):119–37.
Reynolds, Noel B. "The Doctrine of an Inspired Constitution." *BYU Studies* 16 (Spring 1976):315–40.

REX E. LEE

CONSTITUTION OF THE UNITED STATES OF AMERICA

While LDS scripture reinforces the traditional Christian duty of "respect and deference" to civil laws and governments in general as "instituted of God for the benefit of man" (D&C 134:1, 6), Latter-day Saints attach special significance to the Constitution of the UNITED STATES OF AMERICA. They believe that the Lord "established the Constitution of this land, by the hands of wise men whom [he] raised up unto this very purpose" (D&C 101:80). The Prophet Joseph Smith once described himself as "the greatest advocate of the Constitution of the United States there is on the earth" (*HC* 6:56–57). All of his successors as President of the Church have reaffirmed the doctrine of an inspired Constitution. This consistent endorsement is notable, for basic LDS teachings are far removed from the premises of American liberalism, and largely as a result of these differences,

Latter-day Saints suffered considerable persecution before achieving an accommodation with mainstream America.

The idea of an inspired Constitution is rare in contemporary public discourse and wholly absent from contemporary constitutional and historical scholarship. Seeking to discern the hand of divinity in America's beginnings, however, was once common not only in popular rhetoric but also among eminent nineteenth-century historians such as George Bancroft. Perhaps even more important is the repeated acknowledgment of divine aid by America's founding fathers. Notably, George Washington frequently expressed gratitude to God for felicitous circumstances surrounding the rise of the United States and chose the occasion of his first inaugural address to recognize the providential character of the framing of the Constitution:

> No people can be bound to acknowledge and adore the invisible hand which conducts the affairs of men, more than the People of the United States. Every step by which they have advanced to the character of an independent nation seems to have been distinguished by some token of providential agency. And in the important revolution just accomplished in the system of their united government, the tranquil deliberations and voluntary consent of so many distinct communities, from which the event has resulted, cannot be compared with the means by which most governments have been established, without some return of pious gratitude, along with an humble anticipation of the future blessings which the past [blessings] seem to presage [W. Allen, ed., *George Washington: A Collection*, p. 461. Indianapolis, Ind., 1988].

LDS teaching and revelation are in harmony with this self-understanding of the founding generation. Latter-day Saints believe that the Lord established the Constitution, not by communicating specific measures through oracles, but by raising up and inspiring wise men to this purpose (see D&C 101:80). This emphasis on the extraordinary character of the American founders—and perhaps, more generally, on the founding generation as a whole—accords with assessments by contemporaries, as well as by later students of the period. Thomas Jefferson, then U.S. ambassador to France, described the Constitutional Convention of 1787 as "an assembly of demigods." More than forty years later, Alexis de Tocqueville, the noted French observer of American society, included the American people as a whole in his praise of the founding:

> That which is new in the history of societies is to see a great people, warned by its lawgivers that the wheels of government are stopping, turn its attention on itself without haste or fear, sound the depth of the ill, and then wait for two years to find the remedy at leisure, and then finally, when the remedy has been indicated, submit to it voluntarily without its costing humanity a single tear or drop of blood [Vol. 1, p. 113].

This understanding of the divine inspiration of the Constitution as mediated through the human wisdom of the founders and the founding generation invites the inference that new needs and circumstances might require the continued exercise of inspired human wisdom by statesmen and citizens alike. LDS leaders have taught that the Constitution is not to be considered perfect and complete in every detail (as evidenced most clearly by its accommodation with slavery, contrary to modern scripture; e.g., D&C 101:79) but as subject to development and adaptation. It was part of the wisdom of the founders to forbear from attempting to decide too much; they therefore provided constitutional means for constitutional amendment. President Brigham Young explained that the Constitution "is a progressive—a gradual work"; the founders "laid the foundation, and it was for after generations to rear the superstructure upon it" (*JD* 7:13–15).

If the wisdom embodied in the Constitution is considered open to future development, so must it be understood as rooted in the past. J. Reuben Clark, Jr., perhaps the most thorough expositor of the Constitution among past LDS Church leaders, emphasized the dependence of the founders' wisdom on "the wisdom of the long generations that had gone before and which had been transmitted to them through tradition and the pages of history" (1962, p. 3). He saw the Constitution as the product of Englishmen's centuries-long struggle for self-government. This historical perspective fits well with the account of the Book of Mormon, according to which the Lord guided the discovery, colonization, and struggle for independence of America (1 Ne. 13:12–13), in order to establish it as a "land of liberty" (2 Ne. 10:11). Latter-day Saint teaching differs from the traditional providential view of the founding chiefly in holding this liberty not only a blessing in itself but also a condition for the restoration of the fulness of the gospel of Jesus Christ.

LDS teaching about the wisdom of the founders readily acknowledges that it was both conditioned by the past and open to the future. But there can be no question of completely reducing the Constitution to its historical conditions. If the document framed in 1787 remains a touchstone today, this is because, in some admittedly imperfect way, it aims at "the rights and protection of all flesh, according to just and holy principles" (D&C 101:77). Church President David O. McKay affirmed that "there are some fundamental principles of this republic which, like eternal truths, never get out of date. . . . Such are the underlying principles of the Constitution" (p. 319).

The scriptural reference to "just and holy principles" appears to locate these fundamentals in certain "rights." Section 98 of the Doctrine and Covenants recommends friendship to constitutional law based on the harmony between freedom under its law and freedom under God (D&C 98:6, 8). Similarly, revelation links human "rights" with the opportunity to "act in doctrine and principle pertaining to futurity, according to the moral agency which I have given unto him, that every man may be accountable for his own sins in the day of judgment" (D&C 101:78). In this way, the reverence of Latter-day Saints for the Constitution is anchored in the fundamental doctrine of free agency, or the idea that God makes possible people's progress toward eternal life in part by exposing them to the consequences, good or bad, of their choices. LDS scholars who have examined the Constitution from the standpoint of this fundamental interest in moral freedom have exhibited its connection with the basic principles of the rule of law (Reynolds, in Hillam) and of the separation of powers (Hickman, in Hillam), both of which concepts are connected with the ideal of limited government.

If "moral agency" stands at the core of the doctrine of an inspired Constitution, then one might say that whereas LDS teaching in the nineteenth century emphasized the agency, Church leaders in the twentieth century have increasingly stressed the moral foundations of the Constitution, echoing the prophet Mosiah₂ in the Book of Mormon: "If the time comes that the voice of the people doth choose iniquity, then is the time that the judgments of God will come upon you"

(Mosiah 29:26–7; cf. Ether 2:8–12). Their praise of the Constitution has often been paired with warnings against the evils of Marxist communism, a system opposed to the Constitution and moral freedom.

LDS attachment to the Constitution has been further encouraged by an important oral tradition deriving from a statement attributed to Joseph Smith, according to which the Constitution would "hang by a thread" and be rescued, if at all, only with the help of the Saints. Church President John Taylor seemed to go further when he prophesied, "When the people shall have torn to shreds the Constitution of the United States the Elders of Israel will be found holding it up to the nations of the earth and proclaiming liberty and equal rights to all men" (*JD* 21:8). To defend the principles of the Constitution under circumstances where the "iniquity," or moral decay, of the people has torn it to shreds might well require wisdom at least equal to that of the men raised up to found it. In particular, it would require great insight into the relationship between freedom and virtue in a political embodiment of moral agency.

BIBLIOGRAPHY

Benson, Ezra Taft. *The Constitution: A Heavenly Banner*. Salt Lake City, 1986.
———. *The Teachings of Ezra Taft Benson*. Salt Lake City, 1988. Part 5, "Country," collects many statements relative to the Constitution by a Mormon apostle and Church President and former U.S. secretary of agriculture.
Cannon, Donald Q. *Latter-day Prophets and the United States Constitution*. Provo, Utah, 1991.
Clark, J. Reuben, Jr. *Stand Fast by Our Constitution*. Salt Lake City, 1962.
Hillam, Ray C., ed. *"By the Hands of Wise Men": Essays on the U.S. Constitution*. Provo, Utah, 1979. See in particular Richard L. Bushman, "Virtue and the Constitution," pp. 29–38; Martin B. Hickman, "J. Reuben Clark, Jr.: The Constitution and the Great Fundamentals," pp. 39–57, reprinted from *BYU Studies* 13 (Spring 1973):255–72; and Noel B. Reynolds, "The Doctrine of an Inspired Constitution," pp. 1–28, reprinted from *BYU Studies* 16 (Spring 1976):315–40.
Lee, Rex E. *A Lawyer Looks at the Constitution*. Provo, Utah, 1980.
Mangrum, R. Collin. "Mormonism, Philosophical Liberalism, and the Constitution." *BYU Studies* 27 (Summer 1987):119–37. Seeks a justification for Mormon celebration of the Constitution in a compatibility between Mormon theology and the liberal idea that "each individual is entitled to pursue whatever his or her individual *nomos* requires, subject to the equal right of others to do the same."
Vetterli, Richard. *The Constitution by a Thread*. Salt Lake City, 1967. Advocates an interpretation of the U.S. Constitution as consistent with the fundamentals of "Mormon political and religious philosophy" and opposed to the philosophies of Marx, Freud, and the "new liberal intellectual."

RALPH C. HANCOCK

CREEDS

The Church of Jesus Christ of Latter-day Saints has no creed, as that term is understood in traditional theology. Truth and the things of God are comprehended by study, faith, reason, science, experience, personal revelation, and revelation received through the prophets of God. Creeds, on the other hand, tend to delimit this process.

From the beginning of the Church until the present, its view has always been that such formulas are incompatible with the gospel's inclusive commitment to truth and continual revelation. The Doctrine and Covenants states, "He that receiveth light, and continueth in God, receiveth more light and that light groweth brighter and brighter until the perfect day" (D&C 50:24). In his first vision in 1820, the young Prophet Joseph Smith was told that the creeds of the competing churches around him "were an abomination in [God's] sight" (HC 1:19). These sweeping words were clarified in his Wentworth Letter (1842): "all were teaching incorrect doctrines." During the April 1843 conference of the Church, the Prophet said: "It does not prove that a man is not a good man because he errs in doctrine" (HC 5:340), and later he elaborated: "I cannot believe in any of the creeds of the different denominations, though all of them have some truth. I want to come up into the presence of God, and learn all things, but the creeds set up stakes, and say, 'Hitherto shalt thou come, and no further,' which I cannot subscribe to" (HC 6:67).

Since Joseph Smith's day, the Christian world has moved in this direction by acknowledging that creeds are "historically conditioned," and that confessions of faith are to be seen as "guidelines" rather than as final pronouncements.

Authoritative statements found in LDS literature are not viewed as elements in a creed. For example, although its thirteen Articles of Faith are scriptural, they are open-ended. One of them says, "We believe all that God has revealed, all that He does now reveal, and we believe that He will yet reveal many great and important things pertaining to the Kingdom of God" (A of F 9). During fast and testimony meetings, usually on the first Sunday of each month, the conviction is often expressed by members that they know that God lives, that Jesus is the Christ, the Son of the Living God, and that Joseph Smith and the living prophets are true prophets of God. These words in some respects parallel the Islamic confession of faith, or Shahadah, which is also not considered a creed.

BIBLIOGRAPHY

Gerrish, B. A. "Creeds." In *Encyclopedia of Religion*, ed. Mircea Eliade. New York, 1987.

McConkie, Bruce R. *MD*, pp. 170–72. Salt Lake City, 1966.

GARY P. GILLUM

CREMATION

Since the organization of the Church in 1830, Latter-day Saints have been encouraged by their leaders to avoid cremation, unless it is required by law, and, wherever possible, to consign the body to burial in the earth and leave the dissolution of the body to nature, "for dust thou art, and unto dust shalt thou return" (Gen. 3:19). President Spencer W. Kimball wrote, "The meaning of death has not changed. It releases a spirit for growth and development and places a body in . . . Mother Earth" (p. 45). In due time the mortal body returns to native element, and whether it is laid away in a family-selected site or buried in the depths of the sea, every essential part will be restored in the Resurrection: "Every limb and joint shall be restored to its body; yea, even a hair of the head shall not be lost; but all things shall be restored to their proper and perfect frame" (Alma 40:23).

To understand the LDS feeling about cremation, it is essential to understand the doctrine of the Church regarding the body. In a general conference Elder James E. Talmage, an apostle, stated, "It is peculiar to the theology of the Latter-day Saints that we regard the body as an essential part of the soul. Read your dictionaries, the lexicons, and encyclopedias, and you will find that nowhere, outside of The Church of Jesus Christ, is the solemn and eternal truth taught that the soul of man is the body and the spirit combined" (*CR*, Oct. 1913, p. 117).

BIBLIOGRAPHY
Kimball, Edward L., ed. *The Teachings of Spencer W. Kimball*, p. 45. Salt Lake City, 1982.
Lockhart, Barbara. "The Body: A Burden or a Blessing?" *Ensign* 15 (Feb. 1985):57–60.
Nelson, Russell M. "The Magnificence of Man." *Ensign* 18 (Jan. 1988):64–69.

BRUCE L. OLSEN

CROSS

The cross, a traditional symbol of Christianity, is displayed extensively in Catholicism, Eastern Orthodoxy, and Protestantism. In each tradition, the symbol of the cross focuses the worshiper's attention on central elements of the Christian faith. However, different theological points may be emphasized. For example, in Catholicism the crucifix (the cross with the dead Christ hanging on it) symbolizes the crucifixion of Christ and invites meditation on the Atonement. In contrast, the plain cross used by Protestants symbolizes not only the crucifixion but also the resurrection of Christ, for the cross is empty. The Eastern Orthodox crucifix is a symbolic concept somewhere between those of Catholicism and Protestantism: Christ hangs on the cross, but as the living Lord, his head not bowed in death but raised in triumph. Thus, the crucifixion, the atonement, the resurrection, and the Lordship of Christ are all graphically presented in the Orthodox crucifix.

Latter-day Saints do not use the symbol of the cross in their ARCHITECTURE or in their chapels. They, like the earliest Christians, are reluctant to display the cross because they view the "good news" of the gospel as Christ's resurrection more than his crucifixion.

The LDS conception of the plan of salvation is comprehensive. It encompasses a Council in Heaven; Jehovah's (Jesus') acceptance of his role as Savior; the virgin birth; Jesus' life and ministry; his saving suffering, beginning in Gethsemane and ending with his death at Golgotha; his burial; his preaching to the spirits of the righteous dead; his physical resurrection; and his exaltation to the right hand of the Father. No one symbol is sufficient to convey all this. Moreover, the cross, with its focus on the death of Christ, does not symbolize the message of a living, risen, exalted Lord who changes the lives of his followers. Thus, President Gordon B. Hinckley, counselor in the First Presidency, stated that the lives of people must become a "meaningful expression of our faith and, in fact, therefore, the symbol of our worship" (p. 92).

While the symbol of the cross is not visually displayed among the Latter-day Saints, the centrality of the Atonement is ever present in their observance of baptism, the sacrament of the Lord's Supper, and the temple ordinances, and in their hymns and testimonies. Without the atonement of Jesus Christ, there is no hope for the human family. Scripture is replete with the admonition that disciples of Christ must "take up their cross," yielding themselves in humility to their Heavenly Father (D&C 56:2, 14–16; 112:14–15), releasing themselves from the ties of WORLDLINESS (3 Ne. 12:20), and submitting themselves to persecution and even martyrdom for the gospel of Jesus Christ (2 Ne. 9:18; Jacob 1:8).

BIBLIOGRAPHY
Hinckley, Gordon B. "The Symbol of Christ." *Ensign* 5 (May 1975):92–94.
Pocknee, Cyril E. *Cross and Crucifix*. London, 1962.

ROGER R. KELLER

CULT

The word "cult" has usages that range from neutral to pejorative. It derives from the Latin *cultus*, meaning "care" or "adoration." A neutral usage of the word refers to the system of beliefs and rituals connected to the worship of a deity. By this definition, virtually all religions, including The Church of Jesus Christ of Latter-day Saints, exhibit some cultic aspects.

However, the term "cult" more commonly refers to a minority religion that is regarded as unorthodox or spurious and that requires great or even excessive devotion. While the term is commonly used by the mass media and anticult movement in the late twentieth century as a negative label for such recently formed groups as the Unification Church and the International Society for Krishna Consciousness (the Hare Krishna movement), it has also been used to describe Pauline Christianity, Islam during the life of Muhammad, and MORMONISM in the nineteenth century.

The most common social-scientific definition identifies a cult as the beginning phase of an entirely new religion. As defined by this approach, a cult's central characteristic is that it provides a radical break from existing religious traditions (Roberts). The LDS Church's self-understanding of being a restoration movement that restored divine truths, rather than a reformation movement that purified existing truths, is consistent with the social-scientific understanding that nineteenth-century Mormonism was a cult due to its break from the existing religious traditions.

References to cult and other organizational classifications describe the characteristics of religious groups at particular moments in their history. Social scientists use these classifications to describe the normal process of religious evolution. Most groups that start as cults fail to survive more than a single generation; very few evolve into a developed new religion recognized by nonadherents as legitimate or conventional. Obviously, both Christianity and Islam successfully survived the transition from cult to new religion. Social scientists generally agree that The Church of Jesus Christ of Latter-day Saints is no longer properly classified as a cult and should instead be viewed as a new religion. For example, sociologist Rodney Stark identified the LDS Church as the single most important case on the agenda of the scientific study of religion because it demonstrates how a successful new religious movement differs from the thousands of cults that fail to survive or develop into new religions.

[*See also* Sect.]

BIBLIOGRAPHY

Roberts, Keith A. *Religion in Sociological Perspective*, 2nd ed. Belmont, Calif., 1990.
Stark, Rodney. "The Rise of a New World Faith." *Review of Religious Research* 26, no. 1 (1984):18–27.
———. "How New Religions Succeed: A Theoretical Model." In *The Future of New Religious Movements*, ed. D. Bromley and P. Hammond, pp. 11–29. Macon, Ga., 1987.

LAWRENCE A. YOUNG

CUMORAH PAGEANT

America's Witness for Christ has been presented at the hill Cumorah in upstate New York nearly every summer since 1937. Recognized as one of America's largest and most spectacular outdoor theatrical events, it attracts an annual audience of almost 100,000 visitors to its seven performances.

This tradition dates back to 1917, when B. H. Roberts and a group of missionaries went to the Joseph Smith farm outside Palmyra, New York, to celebrate Pioneer Day. Commencing in 1922, the "Palmyra Celebration" became an annual missionary conference for the Eastern States Mission. In July 1935, as part of the dedicatory exercises for the Angel Moroni Monument, trumpeters at the crest of the hill heralded the commencement of the first production at Cumorah. The next year a pageant, "Truth from the Earth," was presented, and plans were announced to make a pageant at the hill Cumorah an annual event.

Two pageants were presented in 1937: a play about the Mormon pioneer handcart companies, *The Builders* by Oliver R. Smith, on July 24, and *America's Witness for Christ* by H. Wayne Driggs on July 23 and 25. The latter script, with occasional revisions, was then presented annually for fifty years (excluding 1943–47). Harold I. Hansen, a missionary with theatrical training, was named codirector and thereafter continued as director for forty years, overseeing the installation of a sound system built by stereophonic sound pioneer Harvey Fletcher, the expansion of the all-volunteer cast and crew to almost six hundred participants, and the run extended to seven performances. In 1957 the pageant was recorded with original music by Crawford Gates.

On July 22, 1988, a new *America's Witness for Christ*, written by Orson Scott Card with music again by Crawford Gates, premiered. Its major theme—the reality of Christ's Atonement, resurrection, and ministry to the Nephites—is boldly portrayed through events recorded in the Book of Mormon. The visual aspects of the pageant were also updated, with new stages, seating, properties, costumes, and special effects, and a recontoured and landscaped hill.

BIBLIOGRAPHY

Argetsinger, Gerald S. "Palmyra: A Look at 40 Years of Pageant." *Ensign* 7 (Dec. 1977):70–71.

Armstrong, Richard N., and Gerald S. Argetsinger. "The Hill Cumorah Pageant: Religious Pageantry as Suasive Form." *Text and Performance Quarterly* 2 (1989):153–64.

Whitman, Charles W. "A History of the Hill Cumorah Pageant, 1937–1964." Ph.D. diss., University of Minnesota, 1967.

GERALD S. ARGETSINGER

CURRICULUM

The Church provides a standard set of curricular materials to all of its units throughout the world. Some matters of basic curriculum had been formatted and distributed to the Church membership since the early days of the Church, but as the auxiliary organizations were formed, such as the Sunday School, Primary, Relief Society, and the Young Men and Young Women, each developed its own curriculum to help teach members. Eventually it became desirable to coordinate curriculum materials among these auxiliary organizations to avoid undesirable duplication and to ensure the coverage of important topics at all age levels.

At present, over 200 topics are considered annually in the lesson manuals prepared for the courses included in the Church curriculum. These topics are in the general areas of gospel principles and doctrines, home and family relationships, priesthood and Church government, historical study of the scriptures and the Church, development of individual talents and abilities, community relations, development of leadership abilities, teaching skills and talents, recreational and social activities, and fellowshipping and service activities (Table 1).

TABLE 1

1. HOME AND FAMILY RELATIONSHIPS
   1.1 Maintaining a spiritual atmosphere in the home
      1.1.1 Having regular family and individual prayers
      1.1.2 Keeping the Sabbath Day holy
      1.1.3 Establishing the home as the center for gospel study

      1.1.4   Seeking the inspiration of the Holy Ghost in all family affairs

1.2   Building right relationships with other family members

1.3   Building confidence and trust in the lives of members of the family

1.4   Developing and fostering individual talents and abilities within the family circle

1.5   Settling family problems harmoniously

1.6   Managing family finances according to gospel principles

1.7   Developing self-discipline and proper conduct in the home

1.8   Promoting respect for the property of other family members

1.9   Learning about human maturation and the process of procreation in the family circle

1.10 Conducting an eternal courtship

1.11 Honoring the priesthood and the patriarchal order in the home

1.12 Honoring womanhood and the distinctive role of girls and women

1.13 Honoring manhood and the distinctive role of men and boys

1.14 Developing modesty and virtue in the home

1.15 Playing together and having fun as a family

1.16 Sharing in the family work schedule

1.17 Appreciating and loving relatives

1.18 Developing parental skills

1.19 Learning to use time wisely

1.20 Being responsible for the temporal well-being of family members

2. GOSPEL PRINCIPLES AND DOCTRINES

    2.1   Developing an understanding of and a love for the members of the Godhead

        2.1.1   The Father

        2.1.2   The Son

        2.1.3   The Holy Ghost

    2.2   Learning the true nature of man and his relationship to the Godhead

        2.1.1   As an intelligence

        2.2.2   As a spirit child of Heavenly Father

        2.2.3   As spirit brothers and sisters of Jesus Christ

        2.2.4   The potential to become like Heavenly Father

             2.2.4.1   Understanding oneself and developing self-esteem

    2.3   Gaining an understanding and testimony of the plan of salvation

        2.3.1   The premortal existence of man

             2.3.1.1   The grand council in heaven

             2.3.1.2   The principle of agency in the pre-existence

3.3 Understanding general priesthood responsibilities
    3.3.1 Home teaching
    3.3.2 Welfare
    3.3.3 Genealogy
    3.3.4 Missionary work
    3.3.5 Family home evenings
    3.3.6 Fellowshipping and service

3.4 Understanding priesthood organization
    3.4.1 The family
    3.4.2 Priesthood quorums
    3.4.3 Wards and branches
    3.4.4 Stakes and mission membership districts
    3.4.5 Missions
    3.4.6 Regions
    3.4.7 General offices
    3.4.8 Priesthood departments and programs
    3.4.9 Auxiliaries
    3.4.10 Church Education System
    3.4.11 Calling and sustaining of Church officers
    3.4.12 Record keeping

3.5 Knowing the priesthood offices and their duties

3.6 Gaining an understanding of the distinctive role of women in the priesthood structure of the Church
    3.6.1 How women share in priesthood blessings and opportunities

3.7 Financial contributions and how they are used

3.8 Church meetings and their purpose

3.9 The Church judicial system

4. HISTORICAL STUDY OF THE SCRIPTURES AND THE CHURCH
  4.1 Learning of God's commandments and his dealings with men through a historical study of the scriptures
  4.2 Obtaining an overview of the scriptures, how we received them, and what they contain
  4.3 An overview of the Old Testament and Pearl of Great Price
    4.3.1 A study of the creation of the earth and man's beginnings upon the earth (Genesis, Abraham, Moses)
    4.3.2 Ancient Israel and the prophets (Old Testament)
  4.4 An overview of the New Testament
    4.4.1 The life and mission of Jesus Christ (The four Gospels)
    4.4.2 The Early Church (Acts, the Epistles, and Revelation)
  4.5 The Apostasy

4.5.1 The Reformation period

4.6 An overview of the Book of Mormon

    4.6.1 God establishes a covenant people in the New World (1 Nephi through Omni)

    4.6.2 God's dealings with the ancient Americans before Christ (Words of Mormon through Helaman)

    4.6.3 The Church of Jesus Christ in ancient America (3 Nephi through Moroni)

4.7 The Restoration, an overview of early modern Church history and the Doctrine and Covenants

    4.7.1 Organization and establishment of the Latter-day Church (Doctrine and Covenants, Joseph Smith, Documentary History of the Church)

4.8 Modern prophets and Church growth

    4.8.1 A study of later modern Church history and Church expansion (Conference Reports and other official documents)

5. DEVELOPMENT OF INDIVIDUAL TALENTS AND ABILITIES

    5.1 Understanding and applying the simple social graces

    5.2 Appreciating and participating in things of cultural value

        5.2.1 Drama

        5.2.2 Music

        5.2.3 Literature

        5.2.4 Dance

        5.2.5 Art and handicraft

        5.2.6 Speech

    5.3 Continuing with formal or informal education in secular and religious fields

    5.4 Improving employment and career planning skills

    5.5 Improving homemaking and household maintenance skills

    5.6 Keeping physically fit and active

    5.7 Gaining an appreciation for nature and the creations of God

    5.8 Knowing the skills of outdoor living and survival

    5.9 Knowing the values of good health care

    5.10 Knowing the values of work and of being self-sustaining

    5.11 Knowing how to handle health emergencies

6. COMMUNITY RELATIONS

    6.1 Fulfilling our responsibilities in civil government and community affairs

    6.2 Maintaining high community standards

    6.3 Making appropriate use of community facilities and institutions

6.4 Taking appropriate part in community social and service organizations

6.5 Building a positive community image for the Church and Church members

6.6 Balancing involvement in community and Church activity

6.7 Being obedient to civil laws

6.8 Being a good friend and neighbor

7. DEVELOPMENT OF LEADERSHIP ABILITIES

7.1 Developing effective communication skills

7.2 Delegating responsibility

7.3 Following up on delegated responsibility

7.4 Learning the duties of our callings

7.5 Utilizing problem-solving techniques

7.6 Using inspiration in decision making

7.7 Conducting effective meetings

7.8 Setting and achieving goals

7.9 Keeping and using adequate minutes and records

7.10 Following line and staff organizational patterns

7.11 Recognizing and developing the leadership potential in others

7.12 Sustaining and using the help and counsel of those who preside over us

7.13 Working with committees and groups

7.14 Keeping an eye single to the glory of God

7.15 Observing the stewardship principle

7.16 Motivating ourselves and others

7.17 Evaluating progress and recovering from temporary setbacks

7.18 Accepting responsibility and being personally accountable

7.19 Using Church organizations and programs to accomplish objectives

7.20 Effective planning

8. DEVELOPMENT OF TEACHING SKILLS AND TALENTS

8.1 Identifying student needs and interests

8.2 Teaching for understanding of ideas and concepts

8.3 Teaching for reinforcement of or change in behavior

8.4 Reaching individual needs of class members

8.5 Making proper preparation to teach

8.6 Seeking qualified help to improve teaching skills

8.7 Practicing in a teaching situation

8.8 Teaching with testimony and with the power and influence of the Holy Spirit

8.9 Using a variety of methods and techniques

8.10 Maintaining order and reverence in the classroom

8.11 Setting a proper example for those whom we teach

8.12 Evaluating the progress of students

8.13 Establishing effective communication with and among students

9. RECREATION AND SOCIAL ACTIVITIES
   9.1 Participating in sports and competitive athletics on ward, stake, region, and multi-region levels
   9.2 Participating in camping and nature study activities
   9.3 Participating in dancing, parties, outings, and other social activities

10. FELLOWSHIPPING AND SERVICE ACTIVITIES
    10.1 Orienting new members to Church programs and activities
    10.2 Using Church programs, resources, and activities to fellowship members and nonmembers
    10.3 Fellowshipping those from varying racial, national, cultural, and language backgrounds
    10.4 Participating in service activities and projects
       10.4.1 In families
       10.4.2 In priesthood quorums
       10.4.3 In girls' and women's groups
       10.4.4 In ward, stake, and regional groups
    10.5 Sharing individual resources with those in need
       10.5.1 Material goods
       10.5.2 Skills and talents
    10.6 Brotherhood and sisterhood

The gospel of Jesus Christ, as expounded in the scriptures and supplemented and interpreted by living prophets, forms the basis of LDS curriculum. The purpose of the curriculum was defined by the Prophet Joseph Smith: "The fundamental principles of our religion are the testimony of the Apostles and Prophets concerning Jesus Christ, that He died, was buried, and rose again the third day, and ascended into heaven; and all other things which pertain to our religion are only appendages to it" (*TPJS*, p. 121). In support of this purpose, LDS curriculum centers on the scriptures, and focuses on the nature of the Godhead, the nature and purpose of mortal life, the commandments God has given to his children, and the virtues they should develop. A master plan provides the necessary coordination to assure that all members are taught these principles several times throughout their lives at different levels of understanding and experience.

Although the curriculum is highly coordinated, there are still variations in content and its application. Local units and teachers adapt the materials sent from Church headquarters to meet the local needs and fit the local culture. In areas where literacy is limited or members have had little prior instruction in gospel principles, a simplified curriculum may be used at the discretion of local leaders. Materials for the use of members with disabilities are also provided.

In addition to the lesson materials, the Church has supportive materials to aid both teachers and members. Libraries in most meetinghouses contain illustrations, audio recordings, video presentations, motion pictures, maps, and other aids for both teacher and member use. Satellite broadcasts are also periodically available. The Church also produces three monthly magazines for English-speaking children, youth, and adults, and an international magazine in several different languages to supplement the curriculum of the Church for teachers and to support scripture study by members.

In 1961, Elder Harold B. Lee, then of the Quorum of the Twelve, described the objective of the Church curriculum as "building up a knowledge of the gospel, a power to promulgate the same, a promotion of the growth, faith, and stronger testimony of the principles of the gospel" (Lee, p. 79). He also announced a new emphasis on correlation, citing a need for better coordination among the courses of study and for a reduction in new courses of study each year. The outcome of this charge was an all-Church coordinating council, three coordinating committees (one each for children, youth, and adults), and an extensive curricular planning guide.

In 1972, the Church formed the Internal Communications Department and gave it the responsibility for curriculum planning and writing. All the curricular materials were examined, and from that assessment developed Curriculum Planning Charts. The purposes of the charts were twofold: to measure existing materials, and from the measurement to plan a well-balanced future offering. The actions resulted in the formation of an Instructional Development Department and the establishment of numerous writing committees, whose responsibility is to plan lesson content and methodology for courses in all age groups within the priesthood and auxiliary organizations. Once again, the primary curricular resources are the scriptures, supplemented by quotations from modern prophets. Computer technology discloses the extent of the distribution of the topics throughout the curriculum. The planning charts track not only the number of times a topic is considered, but where the topic has a primary or secondary focus. Instrumental in the development of the present overall curricular plan, the planning charts continue to guide instructional decision making and to produce a unified, balanced, and standardized curriculum, marked by stability and expansiveness.

BIBLIOGRAPHY
Lee, Harold B. *CR* (Oct. 1961):79.

WAYNE B. LYNN

D

DANCE

In 1830 when the Church was organized, many Christian denominations were hostile toward recreation and play, particularly dance. However, the Prophet Joseph Smith and his successors advocated dance and participated in recreational dancing. Joseph Smith was a skillful dancer and enjoyed hosting dances in his home (Holbrook, p. 122). Brigham Young and the Quorum of the Twelve "danced before the Lord" to the music of a small orchestra in the Nauvoo Temple after long days of joyous participation in temple ordinances (*HC* 7:557, 566; Holbrook, p. 123).

The revealed doctrine that the body and spirit together comprise the soul tends to encourage physical activity (D&C 88:15). Early Latter-day Saints commended dancing as healthful to body and mind, but only when conducted in accordance with Church principles. Emphasis was on propriety, good company, and the spirit of praising the Lord. During their difficult trek west, the pioneers danced as "camps of Israel." President Brigham Young said "I want you to sing and dance and forget your troubles. . . . Let's have some music and all of you dance" (Holbrook, p. 125). Around the campfires they danced polkas, Scotch reels, quadrilles, French fours, and other figures.

In the West, the Saints continued to enjoy dancing. Brigham Young emphasized that fiddling and dancing were not to be part of formal worship (Holbrook, p. 131), and he counseled that those who cannot serve God with a pure heart in the dance should not dance. Under these guidelines, dance continued as an integral part of Mormon culture.

The Deseret Musical and Dramatic Society was organized in 1862, and theatrical dance soon became a favorite attraction. Worship services and social activities were usually held in the same place, although at separate times. This practice, which prevailed in the frontier "brush bowery," continues today in LDS meetinghouses, which typically feature a cultural-recreation hall, complete with stage, adjacent to the chapel.

In the early and mid-twentieth century, the Mutual Improvement Association sponsored recreational and theatrical dance training and exhibitions. Gold and Green Balls were annual social events in each ward and stake. All-Church dance festivals held in Salt Lake City from 1922 to 1973 gained national recognition. After 8,000 dancers in bright costumes participated at the festival in 1959, a national news magazine described the Church as the "dancingest denomination" (Arrington, p. 31). In 1985, 13,000 dancers performed in the Southern California Regional Dance Festival with more than 100,000 viewing the two performances. Dance festivals continued at local levels from 1973 to 1990, when they were finally discontinued as major performances.

Dancing, however, continues as an integral part of youth and adult activities in the Church. It permeates many facets of campus life, entertainment, and performing arts programs at Church-sponsored schools. For example, more than 12,000 BRIGHAM YOUNG UNIVERSITY students enroll annually for academic credit in ballet, ballroom, folk, modern, jazz, tap, aerobic, and precision dance courses. Student performing companies in ballet, ballroom, folk, and modern dance have gained national and international recognition.

BIBLIOGRAPHY

Arrington, Georganne Ballif. "Dance in Mormonism." In *Focus on Dance X: Religion and Dance*, ed. Dennis J. Fallon and Mary Jane Wolbers. Reston, Va., 1982.

Holbrook, Leona. "Dancing as an Aspect of Early Mormon and Utah Culture." *BYU Studies* 16 (Autumn 1975):117–38.

PHYLLIS C. JACOBSON

DATING AND COURTSHIP

Members of the Church are somewhat distinctive in their dating and courtship practices, but they are also influenced by broader cultural patterns. In some cultures, parents still closely supervise courtship and arrange children's marriages, but youth worldwide have increasing choices in dating and mate selection. For most young people in the United States outside the Church, dating begins at an early age (about age thirteen during the 1980s); it has no set pattern of progression, and is often informal and unsupervised. These contemporary dating patterns form a social context that influences somewhat the majority of LDS youth.

However, although courtship patterns change and vary across cultures, there is quite a conservative pattern for dating and courtship among Latter-day Saints in Western nations. It is expected that LDS youth will not begin dating until the age of sixteen. Serious, steady dating and marriage-oriented courtship are expected to be delayed longer, perhaps until after a mission for males and after completing high school for females. A chaste courtship is expected to lead to a temple MARRIAGE, in which a couple make binding commitments to each other for all time and eternity.

Two doctrinally based principles guide the dating and courtship of LDS youth: first, because of the religious significance of marriage, virtually everyone who can is expected to marry; second, because of the spiritual and social importance of chastity, sexual relations must wait until after marriage.

Latter-day Saints place an unusually strong emphasis on marriage, believing that marriage is ordained of God (D&C 49:15) and is a prerequisite for obtaining the highest heavenly state after mortality (D&C 131:1–4). Because of the belief that people should be married and the doctrine that they can maintain marital ties throughout eternity, Latter-day Saints take dating and courtship more seriously than those for whom marriage has less religious significance.

Latter-day Saints believe that premarital chastity is a scriptural commandment reaffirmed by current revelation. From the New Testament: "Flee fornication. . . . He that committeth fornication sinneth against his own body" (1 Cor. 6:18). From a modern Church leader: "Chastity should be the dominant virtue among young

people" (McKay, p. 458). LDS youth are also taught that they should
not participate in sexual activities that often precede sexual intercourse: "Among the most common sexual sins our young people commit are necking and petting. Not only do these improper relations
often lead to fornication, pregnancy, and abortions—all ugly sins—
but in and of themselves they are pernicious evils, and it is often difficult for youth to distinguish where one ends and another begins"
(Kimball, 1969, p. 65). Although Latter-day Saints consider sexual
relationships outside of marriage to be sinful, sexual relations within
marriage are not only right and proper but are considered sacred and
beautiful (*see* SEXUALITY).

Like most of their non-Mormon peers in dating cultures, LDS
youth date to have fun as they participate in social activities with
other boys and girls. As plainly stated by prominent leaders of the
Church, "It is natural to date. Every right-thinking young person has
a native desire to become acquainted with the opposite sex, looking
eventually to pairing off in honorable marriage" (Petersen, p. 37).
"Dating has become the accepted form of social recreation for the
purpose of getting acquainted before young people can safely have a
serious interest in each other. Because the selection of a mate in life
is so extremely important, we should intelligently seek the experiences which will help us to make that great decision" (Hunter, pp.
101–102). Typical of the advice given to LDS youth is the following
counsel about dating:

> Who? Only those whose standards are high, like your own.
>
> Where? Clean places, decent places, proper places where you can
> be proud to be.
>
> Why? Associating with others under wholesome circumstances
> helps develop friendships and permits you to learn about qualities and
> characteristics in others, to get to know them, to have fun together, to
> widen areas of choice, to achieve a wider and wiser vision of what one
> may seek in an eternal companion.
>
> When? Not too young, not too often, not on school nights as a rule,
> not too expensively.
>
> What? Fun things, wholesome things, good and useful things—. . .
> things pleasing to you, to parents, to God.
>
> How? With others, in groups, chaperoned when proper, appropri-
> ately dressed, cheerfully, courteously, modestly, wisely, prayerfully.

And let parents know where you are, with whom, doing what, and when you will return. Have a happy time! [Hanks, pp. 134–35]

While dating and courtship patterns among LDS reflect broader societal patterns, there are several age-graded characteristics of dating and courtship in the Church that are special.

Age twelve is a line of demarcation in the life of a young member of the Church. At this age LDS boys and girls leave Primary, the Church's organization for children, and enter the Young Women and Young Men organizations. Here, young people participate, usually once a week, in gender-segregated activities designed with an adult adviser for their particular age group. Occasionally, joint activities are planned that include boys and girls together. These are structured and well-supervised social and religious activities that bring teenage boys and girls together to help them develop appropriate social relationships.

While the Church sponsors joint social activities, its leaders have strongly discouraged early dating. "Young men and women, not yet ready for marriage, should be friends with many others, but they should not engage in courting. . . . Friendship, not courtship, should be the relationship of teenagers. . . . The change of this one pattern of social activities of our youth would immediately eliminate a majority of the sins of our young folks" (Kimball, 1986, pp. 287–88). Steady dating is further discouraged until youth are ready for courtship.

In the past, LDS youth were basically counseled not to begin dating, especially steady dating, until they were "old enough and mature enough" to consider marriage. During the 1970s the age of sixteen took on special significance in this regard when Spencer W. Kimball, as President of the Church, said: "When you get in the teen years, your social associations should still be a general acquaintance with both boys and girls. Any dating or pairing off in social contacts should be postponed until at least the age of 16 or older, and even then there should be much judgment used in the selections and in the seriousness" (Kimball, 1975, p. 4). As a consequence of this teaching, the age of sixteen has become the acceptable age when dating can begin.

Nineteen is an especially pivotal age in the social and religious life of late adolescent LDS youth. The males are expected to leave home for a two-year Church mission. Many young women upon reaching twenty-one will serve missions. Missionaries leave romantic relationships behind and are counseled not to worry about or telephone girlfriends or boyfriends. They are restricted from all dating activities during their missionary service. Although many boyfriend-girlfriend relationships do not last through the mission separation, the mission experience frequently brings a maturity that better prepares young men and women for eventual marriage.

Despite the postponing effect of missions on dating activities, LDS men tend to marry at an age younger than national averages, while LDS women marry at about the norm. Presumably, the value placed on marriage makes LDS youth less likely to postpone marriage for education and career advancement; they are certainly less likely to cohabit instead of marrying, and the customary pattern is to continue courting until the time of marriage. LDS prophets have consistently instructed young Mormon men that it is wrong to delay marriage unnecessarily (Benson; Kimball, 1975).

Because marrying a person of the same faith is important to Latter-day Saints, families that live away from the concentrations of Church population often encourage the children to attend BRIGHAM YOUNG UNIVERSITY or RICKS COLLEGE or to participate in the programs of the INSTITUTES OF RELIGION at other colleges or universities, where they are more likely to find a suitable partner of their own faith. Also, units of the Church specifically for young adults are organized throughout the world, where numbers allow, to facilitate social opportunities. Because of the religious significance of mate selection to Latter-day Saints, a variety of common practices has developed. Couples seriously considering marriage are likely to pray for heavenly confirmation in their marriage decision. The choice of a partner is usually discussed with parents, and young couples planning to marry often go together to seek the advice of their Church leaders.

BIBLIOGRAPHY
Benson, Ezra Taft. "To the Single Adult Brethren of the Church." *Ensign* 18 (May 1988):51–53.
Hanks, Marion D. "The Six." *IE* 70 (June 1967):134–35.
Hunter, Howard W. *Youth of the Noble Birthright*, pp. 101–109. Salt Lake City, 1960.
Kimball, Spencer W. "Marriage and Divorce." In *1976 Speeches of the Year*. Provo, Utah, 1977.

———. "The Marriage Decision." *Ensign* 5 (Feb. 1975):2–6.

———. *The Miracle of Forgiveness.* Salt Lake City, 1969.

———. *The Teachings of Spencer W. Kimball,* ed. Edward L. Kimball. Salt Lake City, 1986.

McKay, David O. *Gospel Ideals.* pp. 458–64. Salt Lake City, 1953.

Petersen, Mark E. *Live It Up!* Salt Lake City, 1971.

BRENT C. MILLER
H. WALLACE GODDARD

DEAD SEA SCROLLS

[*This entry has two parts:*

Overview
LDS Perspective.]

OVERVIEW

The major corpus of the Dead Sea scrolls, about 600 manuscripts, dates from c. 250 B.C.E. to 68 C.E. Other works from the Southern Jordan Rift, Nahal Hever and Nahal Seelim chiefly, date from 131 to 135 C.E. Masada produced materials from the first century B.C. to A.D. 73.

The manuscripts include segments of all the Hebrew scriptures (except Esther), and more than one variant of many. For example, the three Samuel manuscripts from Qumran are much fuller texts than those of the Masoretic Bible (the traditional text). Also found were fragments of apocryphal and pseudepigraphical books, as well as manuscripts of previously unknown religious works, including a Temple Scroll, a Manual of Discipline, and a Thanksgiving Scroll.

The scrolls have required reappraisal of understanding in three categories: (1) the development of Hebrew scriptures before the formation of the canon; (2) the dating and pervasive influence of apocalyptic thinking; and (3) the religious milieu of the New Testament.

1. The "biblical" library of Qumran represents a fluid stage of the biblical text. Those documents show no influence of the rabbinic recension of the canon, the direct ancestor of the traditional Hebrew Bible. The scrolls help to place both the Pharisaic text and the canon in the era of Hillel, roughly the time of Jesus. In their selection of canonical books, the rabbis excluded those

attributed to prophets or patriarchs before Moses (e.g., the Enoch literature, works written in the name of Abraham and other patriarchs). They traced the succession of prophets from Moses to figures of the Persian period. Late works were excluded, with the exception of Daniel, which, the rabbis presumably, attributed to the Persian period.

2. The literature of Qumran includes apocalypses and works colored by apocalyptic. The writers saw world history in the grip of a final war between the Spirit of truth and the Spirit of evil; this conflict is at once cosmic and earthly. They considered themselves proper heirs of Israel and placed themselves under a new covenant as Sons of Light to contend with Sons of Darkness. They had a strict reading of the law, lived in daily self-denial, practiced ablutions, and had ceremonial meals. Their Manual of Discipline reflects the expectation of the immediate coming of the heavenly kingdom. A "Teacher of Righteousness" was apparently the priestly head of the earthly community of God; the forces of good were also led by a cosmic power or Holy Spirit called the "Prince of Light." The writers saw their own age as the age of consummation. The Messiah was about to appear, "bringing the sword." Collapse of other social structures was imminent before the new age. The people at Qumran, probably Essenes, expected that the Davidic or royal Messiah would appear to defeat the earthly and cosmic powers of wickedness. Commentaries on the biblical materials, found in the same area, treat traditional prophecies in this eschatological setting. Theirs was a church of anticipation.

The Temple Scroll shows that these Jewish priests were separatists, maintaining that the Temple cultus was defunct. They replaced the lunar with a solar calendar for the festivals and introduced feasts of oil and wine mentioned nowhere in the Pentateuch. Considering themselves warriors in the last holy war, fighting alongside holy angels, they forbade all uncleanness (which in their view included the lame, blind, or diseased) both in the anticipated temple and in the temple city. At least for the duration of the war they were celibate.

Apocalypticism is now to be seen as a major element in the complex matrix that formed the background for the development of both Tannaitic Judaism and early Christianity. Gershom

Scholem shocked scholars of this generation by demonstrating the existence and importance of apocalyptic mysticism in the era of Rabbi Akiba. It is now necessary to place apocalyptic thinking as beginning earlier than scholars had previously supposed, perhaps as early as the fourth century B.C.E. and lasting half a millennium.

3. The New Testament reflects these apocalyptic theological tendencies that scholars heretofore passed over lightly. For example, it now appears that the thought and teachings of John the Baptist and Jesus of Nazareth are more apocalyptic than prophetic in their essential character. The dualistic, apocalyptic, and eschatological framework marks John as the most Jewish of the four Gospels. In John's Gospel the spirit of truth is called the Paraclete or Advocate. He is the Holy Spirit, but as at Qumran he is not precisely identical with God's own spirit, which explains why he does not speak on his own authority (John 16:13). The emphasis on light and darkness, unity, community, and love is reiterated and expanded. The theme of religious knowing in an eschatological sense is comparable to statements in the epistles of Paul and the Gospel of Matthew. The Gospel of Luke quotes almost verbatim a pre-Christian apocalypse of Daniel, found in Cave 4, which refers to an eschatological king, whom we take to be the royal Messiah, from the titles "Son of God" and "Son of the Most High." In the parable of the banquet in Luke 14:15–24, Jesus condemns those who seek places of rank in his kingdom, perhaps in polemic response to the Essene exclusion from their banquet of all except the elite of the desert who shared their goods and were "men of renown."

For the Essenes, the New Age was still anticipated. For early Christians, Jesus had been resurrected as the Messiah who brought the New Age. Both communities lived in anticipation of the full coming of redemption or the consummation of the kingdom of God. The Essenes formed a community of priestly apocalyptists. The early Christian movement was made up largely of lay apocalyptists, much like the Pharisaic party. Both searched the prophets for allusions to the events of their times, which they understood to be the "last times," and both spoke in language pervaded by the terminology of Jewish apocalyptic.

FRANK MOORE CROSS, JR.

LDS PERSPECTIVE

Like many Jews and like other Christians, Latter-day Saints were deeply interested in the announcement that ancient manuscripts from New Testament times were discovered in Palestine in 1947. Initial zeal led to some superficial treatments, sensationalism, and misunderstandings. But in the decades since the initial finds, Latter-day Saints who have followed the more careful analyses have come to appreciate several contributions of the Dead Sea Scrolls, including insights into the literary and sectarian diversity of Judaism at the time of Jesus, new evidence relating to the history and preservation of the biblical text, advances in the science of dating Hebrew and Aramaic documents based on changing styles of script, and valuable additions to the corpus of Jewish texts and text genres.

Certain aspects of the scrolls have particularly interested Latter-day Saints. For example, the Essenes of Qumran accepted the concepts of continuing revelation and open canon much as Latter-day Saints do, in contrast to the current teaching of most Christians and Jews. Qumran commentaries on the books of Habakkuk, Nahum, and other prophets from the Old Testament contain new Essene prophetic interpretations of world events of the last days, and the Qumran Temple Scroll claims to be a direct revelation to Moses. Similarly, Latter-day Saints believe that the Bible does not contain all of God's word, but that he has revealed his will to prophets in the Book of Mormon and to Joseph Smith, and he continues to reveal new truths to modern prophets.

Latter-day Saints point out that the Bible does not require or demand its own uniqueness. Now the Qumran library has shown that some of the most pious and observant Jews around the time of Christ consulted not only extrabiblical texts but also a variety of differing texts of the biblical books. For the Essenes, the sacredness of scripture did not impose a fixed or standard text. For example, their library contains several versions of the book of Isaiah, with minor differences in wording. They used both long and short versions of Jeremiah. They had varying collections of the Psalms. This open-mindedness about scriptural words and editions is similar to LDS views (see, for example, various LDS accounts of the Creation). The Dead Sea Scrolls provide evidence that the successive theological concepts of (1) an authoritative text, (2) a fixed text, and ultimately (3) an inerrant text originated with Pharisaic or rabbinic Judaism.

Some people have made much of comparisons between Essene practices and those of the New Testament church, or between both of these and elements of Mormonism. For example, Essene cleansing rituals are in some ways similar to New Testament baptisms, and Essene ritual meals can be interpreted as sacramental. Some see the Christian idea of conversion in the Essene doctrine that an individual is elected to the community by deliberate choice and initiation rather than by birth and infant circumcision. Some relate the Essene communal council, with its twelve men and three priests, to Jesus' calling of twelve apostles and favoring among them Peter, James, and John, or to the Latter-day Saint organization with twelve apostles and a three-member First Presidency. The role of New Testament or modern LDS bishops seems to correspond to many of the functions of the Qumranic *maskil*, or "guardian."

For Latter-day Saints, the emergence of such parallels is not surprising. The covenants of the Old and New Testaments are more alike than different. They proceed from the same God. However, the similarities are counterbalanced by radical differences between Essene practices and the teachings of Jesus Christ, of Paul, or of the Church in modern times. Notably, the Essenes taught their adherents to hate their enemies. Their sect was strict and exclusive. Their ideas of ritual cleanness effectively barred women from the temple and from the temple city of Jerusalem. Such Essene doctrines are opposite to later Christian and LDS teachings. Similarities between Essenism and Christian or LDS concepts should therefore be explained as a dispersion of ideas among groups that share ancient connections rather than as evidences of more intrinsic relationships.

Much is still to be learned from the Dead Sea Scrolls. Many fragments and some scrolls remain unpublished or are not yet fully understood. Much light may yet be shed on ancient Jewish worship patterns, apocalyptic literature, angelology, and sectarianism beyond what is available in biblical accounts.

BIBLIOGRAPHY

For a more ample general statement, see S. Kent Brown, "The Dead Sea Scrolls: A Mormon Perspective," *BYU Studies* 23 (Winter 1983):49–66. Hugh Nibley discusses broad patterns in *An Approach to the Book of Mormon*, *Since Cumorah*, and *The Prophetic Book of Mormon*, in *CWHN*, Vols. 6–8. For a listing of editions of the scrolls, see Robert A. Cloward, *The Old Testament Apocrypha and Pseudepigrapha and the Dead Sea Scrolls: A Selected Bibliography of Text Editions and English Translations*, Provo, Utah, 1988.

ROBERT A. CLOWARD

DEAF, MATERIALS FOR THE

The Church makes a serious effort to serve the hearing impaired with gospel materials in formats they can understand. These formats include simplified versions, signed inserts (interpreters superimposed on film who sign conversations and sounds), closed captions (words that show on the screen only when decoded), printed signs, productions with all-deaf casts, and Church manuals translated into signing for the deaf on videocassettes. Each Church film is signed or closed-captioned. All satellite broadcasts and special programs are closed-captioned. To use closed-captioned videos requires a decoder, which the Church provides to units serving the hearing impaired.

All general conference sessions are signed and closed-captioned. The deaf and hearing impaired who attend general conference in Salt Lake City, Utah, are invited to the Church Office's auditorium to view the proceedings with an interpreter. Those who do not attend in person may participate via closed captions on the Church's satellite network at their local meetinghouses. The sessions are also recorded on videos, with sign language inserts, and made available on loan. Temple ordinances are also presented in formats understandable by the hearing impaired.

A handbook for interpreters and a dictionary of words and phrases peculiar to the Church are available in print and on videocassettes. The Book of Mormon is being translated into American Sign Language (ASL) on videocassette targeted for completion in 1994. A current list of all materials, including their costs and how to order, is available on request from the Special Curriculum Department of the Church.

In a meetinghouse serving the hearing impaired, the Church provides a Com Tek System which amplifies the spoken language. The

Church participates in supplying TTY/TDDs (telecommunication devices) for the deaf and hearing-impaired members to carry on Church functions.

DOUGLAS L. HIND

DEDICATIONS

Dedication is the act of devoting or consecrating something to the Lord, or "setting apart" something for a specific purpose in building the kingdom of God. It is a priesthood function performed through an official and formal act of prayer.

For members of The Church of Jesus Christ of Latter-day Saints, dedications serve at least two clear functions. First, they call down the powers of heaven to establish a sacred space or time in the furthering of the desired purpose. Second, they consecrate the participants, focusing their souls upon the meaning of the dedicated object or act. In this way the secular is brought into sacred relationships, and the blessings of God are invoked so that the powers of heaven and earth are joined to bring about works of righteousness.

LDS church buildings are always dedicated to the Lord, usually after all indebtedness is removed. In the Bible the first recorded dedicatory prayer is that of the Temple of Solomon (1 Kgs. 8:22–53), at which time the glory of the Lord filled the temple, in divine approval. The first temple dedication in this dispensation was on March 27, 1836, when the Prophet Joseph Smith dedicated the Kirtland Temple as "a house of prayer, a house of fasting, a house of faith, a house of learning, a house of glory, a house of order, a house of God" (D&C 109:8). Since then many LDS temples and thousands of meetinghouses around the world have been similarly dedicated to the Lord. Church buildings such as schools, VISITORS CENTERS, storehouses, office buildings, and historical sites are also dedicated to the Lord for their intended uses. Schools may be dedicated as institutions of learning and character development, while bishops' storehouses are dedicated to provide welfare and physical supplies for the needy.

Lands and countries may be dedicated, sometimes more than once, for divinely appointed purposes. On October 24, 1841, Elder Orson Hyde ascended the Mount of Olives and dedicated the land of

Palestine for the return of the Jews and the rearing of a temple. It was rededicated on several other occasions. More than thirty-two countries and entire continents have been dedicated for the preaching of the gospel.

Homes of the SAINTS, whether or not they are free of debt, may be dedicated "as sacred edifices where the Holy Spirit can reside, and as sanctuaries where family members can worship, find safety from the world, grow spiritually, and prepare for eternal family relationships" (*General Handbook of Instructions*, 11-2, 1989). On some occasions it has been deemed appropriate to dedicate business places or enterprises to accomplish righteous and divine purposes. It is customary in the Church to dedicate graves as the final resting place for the deceased, asking that the ground be hallowed and protected until the day of resurrection.

Olive oil is also consecrated by a dedicatory prayer. It is thus set apart by the power of the priesthood for the divinely prescribed purposes of blessing the sick and anointing in the temple (James 5:14; D&C 109:35; 124:39).

TAD R. CALLISTER

DEIFICATION, EARLY CHRISTIAN

From the second to eighth centuries, the standard Christian term for salvation was *theopoiesis* or *theosis*, literally, "being made God," or deification. Such language survived sporadically in the mystical tradition of the West and is still used in Eastern Orthodoxy. LDS doctrines on eternal progression and exaltation to godhood reflect a similar view of salvation.

In its classical form, particularly in the works of Athanasius (fourth-century bishop of Alexandria), deification was built upon the concept of the incarnation of Christ. The Council of Nicaea (A.D. 325) defined the Son as *homoousios* (of the same substance) with the Father, and thus fully God. By taking upon himself our flesh through birth, Jesus as God united the essence of humanity to the divine nature. Eventually Christ's divinity overcame the limits of the flesh through resurrection and glorification, transforming and raising his body to the full level of godhood. As Athanasius summarized, "God was made man that we might be made God" (*On the Incarnation of the Logos* 54).

Although the doctrine has been dismissed by later scholars as a mere "physical theory of redemption" focused on the Resurrection, deification is more than a synonym for immortality. Church Fathers argued that deification not only restores the image of God that was lost in the Fall, but also enables mankind to transcend human nature so as to possess the attributes of God. "I may become God as far as he became man," declared Gregory of Nazianzus in the late fourth century (*Orations* 29.19). Descriptions of deification included physical incorruptibility, immunity from suffering, perfect virtue, purity, fullness of knowledge and joy, eternal progression, communion with God, inheritance of divine glory, and joint rulership with Christ in the kingdom of God in heaven forever.

The roots of the Christian doctrine of deification are primarily biblical. Beginning with the creation of humanity in the image of God (Gen. 1:26–27), the church fathers developed aspects of deification from such concepts as the command to moral perfection and holiness (e.g., Lev. 19:1–2; Matt. 5:48; 1 Jn. 3:2; 1 Cor. 11:1; 2 Pet. 1:3–7), adoption as heirs of God (Rom. 8:15–17; Gal. 4:4–7), unification with God in Christ (John 17:11–23), and partaking in Christ's sufferings in order to be elevated with him in glory (e.g., Rom. 8:16–18; 2 Cor. 3:18; 4:16–18; Philip. 3:20–21; 2 Tim. 2:10–12). They also pointed to examples of humans described as "gods" in scripture (Ex. 4:16; 7:1; Ps. 82:6; John 10:34–36).

Jewish thought, particularly in response to developing CHRISTOLOGY and its perceived threat to monotheism, was more reticent to speak of humans attaining divinity. Nevertheless, Jews shared some of the crucial biblical texts underlying deification. Talmudic Judaism tended to stress humanity's obligation to imitate God's holiness in consequence of being created in the divine image. Moses and other prophets were spoken of as sharing God's glory and becoming "secondary gods" in relation to other mortals (Meeks, pp. 234–35). Philo described Moses' glorification as "a prototype . . . of the ascent to heaven which every disciple hoped to be granted" (Meeks, p. 244).

Due to its incongruity with the doctrine of God in Western Christianity, deification fell out of favor as the preferred way of describing salvation. Catholic theology increasingly stressed the transcendence of God, who alone was self-existent and eternal. All other beings were created ex nihilo, "out of nothing," having only contingent being. This theological development culminated in Augustine. For him, God's absolute oneness and otherness was so different from humanity's created status and dependence on divine grace that salvation could not bridge the gap between the eternal Creator and the creatures contingent upon him. Ever since, talk of deification has been suspect or heretical in Western Christianity and has formed a major point of objection among traditional Christians to the teachings of Latter-day Saints on the subject.

BIBLIOGRAPHY

Barlow, Philip L. "Unorthodox Orthodoxy: The Idea of Deification in Christian History." *Sunstone* 8 (Sept.–Oct. 1983):13–18.

Benz, Ernst W. "Imago Dei: Man in the Image of God." In *Reflections on Mormonism*, ed. T. Madsen, pp. 201–219. Provo, Utah, 1978.

Gross, Jules. *La divinisation du chrétien d'après les pères grecs*. Paris, 1938.

Meeks, Wayne A. *The Prophet-King: Moses Tradition and the Johannine Christology*. Leiden, 1967.

Norman, Keith E. "Deification: The Content of Athanasian Soteriology." Ph.D. diss. Duke University, 1980.

———. "Divinization: The Forgotten Teaching of Early Christianity." *Sunstone* 1 (1975):15–19.

Pelikan, Jaroslav. *The Christian Tradition*, Vols. 1 and 2. Chicago, 1971–1974.

KEITH E. NORMAN

DESERET BOOK COMPANY

The Deseret Book Company had its beginnings in George Q. Cannon and Sons, a retail bookstore and publishing company established in Salt Lake City in 1866. Cannon was an apostle and a counselor in the First Presidency of The Church of Jesus Christ of Latter-day Saints. After his death in 1901, the company was purchased by the Church's *Deseret News* and renamed the Deseret News Bookstore. Meanwhile, the Church Sunday School organization began publishing its own lesson manuals and supplementary instructional materials in the early 1870s and later included book publishing and a retail bookstore. The two companies were merged in 1919 and subsequently named the Deseret Book Company.

A subsidiary of the Church's Deseret Management Corporation, the Deseret Book Company has three divisions: retail, publishing, and wholesale. The retail division operates stores in several states in the western United States: Mormon Handicraft, which is a Salt Lake City consignment shop for handmade goods; a book club; and a mail- and telephone-order shopping service. The publishing division pro- duces books related to family life, history, biography, LDS doctrine and theology, fiction, and inspiration for both children and adults. It also produces audio- and videotapes and compact discs. The whole- sale division distributes Deseret Book titles and books from other publishers to retailers throughout the world.

ELEANOR KNOWLES

DIPLOMATIC RELATIONS

Joseph Smith undertook his first diplomatic mission for the Church when he journeyed to Washington, D.C., in 1839 and met with President Martin Van Buren to seek federal intervention on behalf of Church members who had lost their lives or property during the Missouri persecutions. Since then, the diplomatic contacts of the Church with the governments of the world have been aimed mostly at securing legal recognition for the Church and freedom for its mem- bers to preach the gospel to others, meet together for religious wor- ship, and live according to their religious precepts.

For a century and a half the Church had no formal diplomatic office; mission presidents or General Authorities on special assign- ment were responsible for creating a favorable climate for the Church's missionary effort and for resolving problems with host gov- ernments. In 1842, Lorenzo Snow, an apostle, sought to establish a favorable impression of Latter-day Saints by presenting a handsome bound copy of the first British edition of the Book of Mormon to Queen Victoria and Albert, the Prince Consort. As the Church began practicing plural marriage, the task of maintaining a favorable public image became more difficult. That effort was not helped by a note sent by the U.S. government in 1887 to the governments of Great Britain and Scandinavia asking them to curtail immigration of Latter- day Saints to the United States—a move intended to stem the growth of polygamy. Since the Scandinavian countries did little and the note was ridiculed by the British press, the Church found it unnecessary to take any diplomatic initiative.

Fifty years later, a statute adopted by the legislature of Tonga barring entry of LDS missionaries was the subject of a diplomatic protest by the Church to the British government. The matter landed on the desk of Winston Churchill, who was then colonial secretary. He took no action because the British government could not veto a Tongan statute, and the Foreign Office informed him that the U.S. government would not protest if the statute did not apply retroactively to missionaries in the country but only to those subsequently applying for entry. The Church took no further action, since the mission president was able to convince the Tongan legislature to repeal the measure.

The rather limited extent of the Church's diplomatic relations with the governments of northern Europe, where the Church's missionary effort was concentrated in the nineteenth century, gave way in the twentieth to more extensive contacts as the Church became more ambitious in the reach of its missionary program. In many countries the right to proselytize was limited not only by statute but also by informal practice and tradition, stemming in part from the influence of an established state church with a special legal status. Moreover, the spread of communism had raised ideological barriers to missionary work in general. Still the Church maintained its policy of leaving the conduct of any needed diplomatic relations in the hands of mission presidents or General Authorities either permanently or temporarily in the country. That policy changed after 1975 when Spencer W. Kimball became President of the Church. He was determined to increase the Church's missionary effort, including gaining legal recognition in the countries where such recognition had been denied either as a matter of government policy or through the opposition of the established state church. The decision resulted in a policy that required organizational changes at Church headquarters. Such changes had been discussed during the tenure of President Harold B. Lee, but no steps had been taken before his death. N. Eldon Tanner, who served as first counselor to both President Lee and President Kimball, reviewed with President Kimball those previous discussions. They decided to appoint a special representative responsible to the First Presidency who would negotiate with governments outside the United States for removal of restrictive visa policies and for legal recognition of the Church where it had been denied. The special representative would also serve as liaison between the Church and U.S. embassies in foreign countries.

President Kimball appointed David M. Kennedy as the special representative of the First Presidency. Kennedy had extensive experience working with international governments and leaders as an international banker, as U.S. secretary of the treasury under U.S. President Richard M. Nixon, as ambassador-at-large, and as ambassador to the North Atlantic Treaty Organization (NATO).

Since the Church wanted to gain legal recognition as rapidly as possible, the First Presidency and its special representative examined countries one by one, exploring the possibilities each offered. Barriers existed in each country. Some had statutes limiting freedom of religion. There were long-standing religious and cultural barriers in others. In some, legal recognition was possible, but statutes severely limited the right to proselytize. When President Kimball decided that legal recognition should be the first goal, he sent Kennedy to Greece, where recognition had long been withheld despite the vigorous efforts of Church leaders. Kennedy learned from his contacts in the Greek government and the U.S. embassy there that the key to recognition as "a house of prayer" required the approval of the Archbishop of Athens and All Greece, His Beatitude Seraphim. In a crucial interview, Kennedy pointed out that the Greek Orthodox Church enjoyed full freedom of religion in the United States, that the Greek government had honored President David O. McKay for the aid the Church had sent to Greece after the devastating earthquake of 1953, and that the Church was fully recognized by most of the other countries of Western Europe. Greece eventually gave legal recognition to the Church. Other countries where recognition would be sought and eventually granted included Yugoslavia, Portugal, and Poland.

When it became known that the Church was seeking recognition from communist countries, representatives of the media began asking how such action could be reconciled with the Church's ideological opposition to communism. Kennedy responded to those queries by referring to the Church's belief in "being subject to kings, presidents, rulers, and magistrates, in obeying, honoring, and sustaining the law" (A of F 12). The essential reality, Kennedy emphasized, is that the Church could enter, and prosper in, any country that would "permit us to offer our sacraments, . . . permit us in our homes to have our family organization and live within our religious patterns" (Hickman, p. 340). These minimal freedoms were all Latter-day Saints needed to live consistently with their general beliefs. Kennedy also drew a distinction between the economic and political systems that Church members preferred as private citizens and those restrictions on individual freedoms that would make it impossible for the Church to exist as an institution or prevent its members from following its fundamental precepts. Through Kennedy, the Church reemphasized that its mission was to preach the restored gospel to all the world and to help its members' lives to be marked by moral and spiritual growth—not to import the American political and economic systems.

In every country visited, the Church's first goal was to gain recognition that included the right to open a mission, entry rights for missionaries, the right to proselytize openly, and the right to hold public worship meetings. The most notable success in reaching these goals was achieved in Portugal, where the 1974 revolution had resulted in the adoption of a statute granting freedom of religion. In other countries, notably Poland, the Church was successful in gaining legal recognition permitting it to own property, to hold religious meetings, and to send Church representatives to the country, but the right to proselytize was refused. Despite that limitation, Church leaders believed that legal recognition was a significant step forward and that the Polish government's offer should be accepted even though it did not contain the right to proselytize. The Church was granted legal recognition in Yugoslavia on essentially the same terms. In each country where the Church undertook negotiations, Kennedy, as special representative of the First Presidency, emphasized that the Church was recognized in many countries of the world and that in the United States members held important positions in government, education, and business. He also stressed that Church members were recognized in the United States for their honesty, reliability, and work ethic.

In recent years there have occurred several changes that have improved the diplomatic relations of the Church. Changes in Eastern

Europe have made it easier for the Church to gain recognition than it was in 1975, and restrictions on proselytizing are also being removed. The revelation announced by President Kimball in 1978 granting the priesthood to every worthy male member of the Church has been followed by the establishment of more missions in Africa. Because of these changes, the First Presidency decided that the task assigned to its special representative had been achieved; hence, in 1990, Kennedy was released from that calling, and no replacement was named. The responsibilities of the special representative were assumed by the Area Presidencies and mission presidents.

BIBLIOGRAPHY

Hickman, Martin B. *David Matthew Kennedy: Banker, Statesman, Churchman*, pp. 334–65. Salt Lake City, 1987.

Kimball, Edward L., and Andrew E. Kimball. *Spencer W. Kimball*. Salt Lake City, 1977.

Palmer, Spencer J., ed. *The Expanding Church*. Salt Lake City, 1978.

MARTIN B. HICKMAN

DIVORCE

The Church of Jesus Christ of Latter-day Saints officially disapproves of divorce but does permit both divorce (the legal dissolution of a marriage bond) and annulment (a decree that a marriage was illegal or invalid) in civil marriages and "cancellation of sealing" in temple marriages.

Latter-day Saints believe that God intended marriage to be an eternal union when he commanded that a man and woman "shall be one flesh" (Gen. 2:24). However, under Jewish interpretation of the law of Moses, a man had the right to divorce his wife if she found disfavor in his eyes or for "uncleanness" (adultery or other reasons). The man was required to give his wife a written bill of divorcement, which freed her to remarry (Deut. 24:1–2), although in some cases he was not allowed to "put away" his wife (Deut. 22:29).

Jesus Christ condemned divorce under most circumstances, saying, "What therefore God hath joined together, let not man put asunder" (Matt. 19:6). He explained that Moses had permitted divorce only "because of the hardness of your hearts" and because the people could not live the higher law of eternal marriage, "but from the beginning it was not so" (Matt. 19:8). To this he added, speaking in the Sermon on the Mount to those who would strive to be the light of the world and the children of God, "Whosoever putteth away his wife, and marrieth another, committeth adultery: and whosoever marrieth her that is put away from her husband committeth adultery" (Luke 16:18; Matt. 5:31–32; 3 Ne. 12:31–32).

The Doctrine and Covenants reiterates the teaching that marriage is ordained of God (D&C 49:15–16). The Church distinguishes between (1) civil marriages, which are valid for "time" (until divorce or the death of one spouse), and (2) temple marriages, or sealings, solemnized by proper ecclesiastical authority, which are binding for "time and all eternity" if the participants are obedient to the gospel (see MARRIAGE: ETERNAL). Legal annulments and divorces free the individuals married civilly for remarriage. Only the President of the Church can authorize a "cancellation of sealing" in temple marriages to free a worthy member to remarry in the temple. Without a cancellation of sealing, divorced members may remarry for time only.

For nineteenth-century Latter-day Saints, feelings about divorce were mixed. President Brigham Young did not approve of men divorcing their wives, but women were relatively free to dissolve an unhappy marriage, especially a polygamous union. Such divorces were handled in ecclesiastical courts because polygamous marriages were not considered legal by the government. Records of the number of divorces granted between 1847 and 1877 show a relatively high rate of divorce for polygamous marriages. This rate was high, not so much because polygamy was difficult, but because LDS society had not developed clear rules and expectations for the practice or the participants (Campbell and Campbell, p. 22).

Early Utah laws reflected general LDS beliefs and may have influenced the incidence of divorce. An 1851 territorial divorce law had lenient residency requirements and allowed divorce when it was clear "that the parties cannot live in peace and union together, and that their welfare requires a separation" (First Legislative Assembly of the Territory of Utah, 1851, p. 83).

Current Church statistics on divorces among Latter-day Saints show somewhat fewer divorces among U.S. Mormons than among the general U.S. population. Data from a 1981 Church membership survey in the United States show that 16 percent of members (as compared to 23 percent of U.S. whites, statistically the most comparable group) had been divorced (Goodman and Heaton, p. 93). Latter-day Saints in Canada, Great Britain, Mexico, and Japan were more likely than their respective national populations to be divorced. However, converts who had divorced before joining the Church contributed to the relatively high proportion of divorced members outside the United States.

Recent U.S. data from the National Survey of Families and Households indicate that about 26 percent of both Latter-day Saints and non-LDS have experienced a divorce (Heaton et al., Table 2). If these trends continue, researchers project that about one-third of recent U.S. LDS marriages may end in divorce (Goodman and Heaton, p. 92). Nationally, experts predict that 50–60 percent of recent marriages will end in divorce or separation (Cherlin, p. 148).

Societal pressures and individual characteristics affect the likelihood of divorce. There will be a higher incidence of divorce among Latter-day Saints if they marry younger than age twenty or older than age thirty, have less than a college education, or marry outside the faith. These factors correlate with factors influencing divorce among U.S. citizens generally. In addition, divorce is more common when Latter-day Saints marry within the faith but do not have the marriage sealed in the temple. Goodman and Heaton found that such marriages are five times more likely to end in divorce than are temple marriages (p. 94). Those who choose a temple marriage usually are more committed to the Church and are required to comply with strict behavioral standards of chastity and fidelity to qualify for the temple marriage.

Severe personal and economic consequences usually accompany divorce among Latter-day Saints. LDS women are often not well prepared to support themselves and their children, and men may pay little in child support or alimony. About one-third of female-headed LDS households, a majority of which were the result of divorce, are living in poverty, despite a high rate of employment among single mothers (Goodman and Heaton, pp. 101, 104).

Divorced Latter-day Saints have lower religious participation than married members. They attend Church less often, and they pray, pay tithing, and hold Church callings less frequently than married members. These may be symptomatic of both the causes and the consequences of divorce.

Divorced Latter-day Saints are also more likely to remarry than the general divorced U.S. population. More than three-fourths of divorced Mormons probably will remarry (Goodman and Heaton).

After the divorce of their parents, most LDS children live with their mothers. They attend Church less frequently than children in two-parent households, even when the custodial parent attends regularly. Church researchers estimate that one-third of LDS children in the United States will live with a single or remarried parent.

Twentieth-century Church leaders speak of divorce as a threat to the family. In the April 1969 general conference, President David O. McKay declared, "Christ's ideal pertaining to marriage is the unbroken home, and conditions that cause divorce are violations of his divine teachings. Except in cases of infidelity or other extreme conditions, the Church frowns upon divorce" (*IE* 72 [June 1969]:2–5). President Spencer W. Kimball said that relatively few divorces are justifiable. He also told members that divorce frequently results from selfishness and other sins of one or both spouses (Kimball, 1975, p. 6). Other Church leaders also emphasize selfishness and mention additional causes of divorce, such as poor choice of a marriage partner, infidelity, lack of understanding of the divine nature of marriage, poor financial management, and lack of continued marital enrichment. "The current philosophy—get a divorce if it doesn't work out—handicaps a marriage from the beginning" (Haight, p. 12).

Church leaders urge members to prepare for marriage, marry within the faith, marry in the temple, live righteously and nurture their marriage relationships, pray for guidance, and counsel with each other and with priesthood leaders to resolve differences and deter divorce. Priesthood leaders are advised to help members strengthen their marriages but, when necessary, to permit divorce and to determine whether disciplinary action should be taken against any spouse guilty of moral transgression, such as infidelity or abuse. Priesthood leaders are to "cast out" (i.e., excommunicate) unrepentant adulterers from among the SAINTS, but to accept the victims of divorce (D&C 42:74–77).

Church members who are divorced and the children of divorced parents sometimes report feelings of isolation or lack of acceptance because of the strong orientation toward two-parent families in the Church (Hulse, p. 17). Church leaders admonish all members to be sensitive to the needs of people in difficult circumstances and to offer help and appropriate encouragement and compassionate service wherever possible.

BIBLIOGRAPHY

Campbell, Eugene E., and Bruce L. Campbell. "Divorce Among Mormon Polygamists: Extent and Explanations." *Utah Historical Quarterly* 46 (Winter 1978):4–23.

Cherlin, Andrew. "Recent Changes in American Fertility, Marriage and Divorce." *ANNALS, AAPSS* 510 [July 1990]:148.

Foster, Lawrence. "A Little-Known Defense of Polygamy from the Mormon Press in 1842." *Dialogue* 9 (Winter 1974):21–34.

———. *Religion and Sexuality: Three American Communal Experiments of the Nineteenth Century.* New York, 1981.

Goodman, Kristen L., and Tim B. Heaton. "LDS Church Members in the U.S. and Canada: A Demographic Profile." *AMCAP Journal* 12 (1986):88–107.

Haight, David B. "Marriage and Divorce." *Ensign* 14 (May 1984):12.

Heaton, Tim B., and Kristen L. Goodman. "Religion and Family Formation." *Review of Religious Research* 26 (June 1985):343–59.

Heaton, Tim B., et al. "In Search of a Peculiar People: Are Mormon Families Really Different?" Meeting of the Society for the Scientific Study of Religion, October 1989, Table 2.

Hulse, Cathy. "On Being Divorced." *Ensign* 16 (Mar. 1986):17.

Kimball, Spencer W. "The Time to Labor is Now." *Ensign* 5 (Nov. 1975):6.

———. *Marriage.* Salt Lake City, 1978.

KRISTEN L. GOODMAN

DRAMA

Latter-day Saints have supported and participated in theatrical activities throughout their history. Members of the Church established one of the first community theaters in America at Nauvoo, Illinois, in the 1840s. The Prophet Joseph Smith directed that a home dramatic company be established. He taught the Saints to seek after all things "virtuous, lovely, or of good report, or praiseworthy" (A of F 13). These included theater, drama, and the related arts—music, dance, painting, singing, acting, and writing. Theatrical activity in Nauvoo did not cease until 1846, when the city was besieged and the Saints were driven out.

Soon after arriving in Salt Lake Valley in 1847, the Latter-day Saints erected what they called a bowery (a temporary shelter made from placing tree boughs on a frame structure) on the southeast corner of what became Temple Square. Three successively larger boweries replaced the first. Concerts, plays, and dances were performed there. President Brigham Young observed, "If I were placed on a cannibal island and given a task of civilizing its people, I should straightway build a theatre" (Skidmore, p. 47).

Social Hall in Salt Lake City was formally dedicated in 1853, scarcely more than five years after the arrival of the Mormon pioneers in the valley. In *Utah and the Mormons*, Benjamin G. Ferris described the presentations held there: "During the winter they keep up theatrical exhibitions in Social Hall, and generally the performances are better sustained in all their parts than in theatres of Atlantic cities" (quoted in Maughan, p. 5).

The Salt Lake Theatre, one of the finest theater buildings of its time, was dedicated in 1862. Brigham Young believed that it had been created for an ennobling purpose. During the dedicatory service, he said, "On the stage of a theatre can be represented in character evil and its consequences, good and its happy results and rewards, the weaknesses and follies of man and the magnanimity of the virtuous life" (quoted in Maughan, p. 84).

The tradition of theater continues in the Church today. Latter-day Saints write and produce plays, musicals, and roadshows. Roadshows are original mini-musicals, locally created and produced under the sponsorship of ward and stake activities committees. The Church also sponsors religious pageants, including those presented annually in Palmyra-Manchester, New York; Nauvoo, Illinois; Independence, Missouri; Temple View, New Zealand; Calgary, Canada; Oakland, California; Mesa, Arizona; and Manti and Clarkston, Utah (*see* PAGEANTS).

BRIGHAM YOUNG UNIVERSITY in Utah and RICKS COLLEGE in Idaho have theater departments that train playwrights, actors, directors, and designers. The Promised Valley Playhouse in Salt Lake City is owned and operated by the Church. It stages its own productions, and its facilities are also available for stake and ward performances.

BIBLIOGRAPHY

Clinger, Morris M. "A History of Theatre in Mormon Colleges and Universities." Ph.D. diss., University of Minnesota, 1963.

Gledhill, Preston R. "Mormon Dramatic Activities." Ph.D. diss., University of Wisconsin, 1950.

Maughan, Ila Fisher. *Pioneer Theatre in the Desert*. Salt Lake City, 1961.

Skidmore, Rex A. "Mormon Recreation in Theory and Practice: A Study of Social Change." Ph.D. diss., University of Pennsylvania, 1941.

CHARLES L. METTEN

DRUGS, ABUSE OF

The abuse of drugs is contrary to the teachings of the Church. Leaders have frequently cautioned members against using narcotics such as marijuana, heroin, LSD, and crack-cocaine, as well as misusing prescription medication or over-the-counter drugs. In the October 1974 general conference, President Spencer W. Kimball stated, "We hope our people will eliminate from their lives all kinds of drugs so far as possible. Too many depend upon drugs as tranquilizers and sleep helps, which is not always necessary. Certainly numerous young people have been damaged or destroyed by the use of marijuana and other deadly drugs. We deplore such" (*Ensign* 4 [Nov. 1974]:6).

Latter-day Saints view drug abuse as harmful to both the physical and spiritual health of the individual. Drug abuse frequently results in substance addiction, which severely limits personal freedom. That agency is vital and has eternal consequences is reason enough to avoid abuse and addiction. Furthermore, the impact on one's health and general well-being is often severe. Though not explicitly mentioned in the WORD OF WISDOM, the Church's health code revealed in 1833, drug abuse is nonetheless viewed as contrary to its precepts. President Joseph Fielding Smith explained that additional revelation in regard to drugs was unnecessary because if members "sincerely follow what is written with the aid of the Spirit of the Lord, [they] need no further counsel" (*IE* 59 [Feb. 1956]:78).

Bishops counsel drug addicts to seek professional treatment to

DRUGS, ABUSE OF

help them overcome their addiction, and offer assistance as appropriate through LDS Social Services.

Swinyard, Ewart A. "Wisdom in All Things." *New Era* 4 (Sept. 1974):44–49.

RAY G. SCHWARTZ

E

EARTH

Latter-day Saints believe that God created this earth to provide his children, the human race, with the opportunity to receive physical bodies and to hear and accept his gospel that they might be prepared for life with him on a celestialized earth hereafter. They also believe that this earth eventually will become a celestial, glorified world. Jesus Christ, under direction of God the Father, was the creator of the earth and all things in it (John 1:1–3). Creation was first a spirit creation followed by a physical creation of the planet and life on it. One LDS scholar observed, "The Latter-day Saints are the only Bible-oriented people who have always been taught that things were happening long, long before Adam appeared on the scene" (*CWHN* 1:49). Because God created the earth for these eternal purposes, Latter-day Saints view its natural resources and life forms as a sacred stewardship to be used in ways that will ensure their availability for all succeeding generations. Latter-day scriptures also teach of a plurality of worlds. In itself this is not a unique concept among the religions of the world, but the LDS doctrine is distinctive (Crowe, pp. 241–46).

THE AGE OF THE EARTH.   The scriptures do not say how old the earth is, and the Church has taken no official stand on this question (*Old Testament*, pp. 28–29). Nor does the Church consider it to be a central issue for salvation.

Discussions of the age of the earth feature separate and distinct interpretations of the word "day" in the creation accounts. Very few Latter-day Saints hold to the theory that the days of creation were twenty-four hours long. Some have attempted to accommodate scientific theories to scriptural accounts of creation by extending creation day lengths to one thousand years each. Support for this view has been found in scriptures suggesting "one day is with the Lord as a thousand years" (2 Pet. 3:8; cf. Abr. 3:2–4; 5:13; Facsimile No. 2).

But because even seven thousand years fails to approximate the billions of years suggested by contemporary scientific accounts, many Latter-day Saints have emphasized the possibility that the scriptural days of creation may have been vastly greater time periods. They point to the fact that "the Hebrew word for *day* . . . can also be used in the sense of an indeterminate length of time," and to Abraham's account of creation in which he "says that the Gods *called* the creation periods days" (*Old Testament*, pp. 28–29; see Eyring; Abr. 4:5, 8).

THE ORIGIN AND DESTINY OF THE EARTH.   Joseph Smith wrote, "We believe . . . that the earth will be renewed and receive its paradisiacal glory" (A of F 10). LDS revelation declares that the earth is destined to become a celestial body fit for the abode of the most exalted or celestial beings (D&C 88:18–20, 25–26). This is a unique departure from the traditional Christian beliefs that heaven is the dwelling place for all saved beings, and that after fulfilling its useful role the earth will become uninhabited, or be destroyed. Doctrine and Covenants 130:9 teaches that finally the earth will become sanctified and immortalized, and be made crystal-like. The "sea of glass" spoken of in Revelation 4:6 "is the earth, in its sanctified, immortal, and eternal state" (D&C 77:1). Elder James E. Talmage wrote of this earthly regeneration: "In regard to the revealed word concerning the regeneration of earth, and the acquirement of a celestial glory by our planet, science has nothing to offer either by way of support or contradiction" (*AF*, p. 381).

Latter-day Saints understand the entire history of the earth to be directly linked to its role in God's plan of salvation for his children, his work and glory, "to bring to pass the immortality and eternal life of man" (Moses 1:39). The earth was created as a paradise. Because of the fall of Adam and Eve, it was transformed to a telestial state, or the present mortal earth. This interval will end with the return of the

Savior, after which the earth will be changed to a terrestrial state and prepared during the Millennium for its final transformation into a celestial sphere after the Millennium (D&C 88:18–19). The ancient Nephite concept derived from Christ's teachings to them includes the idea that before the final judgment the earth will be "rolled together as a scroll, and the elements [will] melt with fervent heat" (Morm. 9:2), "and the heavens and the earth [shall] pass away" (3 Ne. 26:3). This historical account is linear, marked by unique, important events that link the theological and physical history of the earth, that is, creation, fall, renewal at the second coming of Christ, and final glory.

Against the backdrop of this progressive history is the constancy of spiritual and physical law immanently affecting succeeding generations of God's children on earth. In this context President John Taylor said, "Change succeeds change in human affairs, but the laws of God in everything are correct and true; in every stage and phase of nature, everything on the earth, in the waters and in the atmosphere is governed by unchangeable, eternal laws" (*Gospel Kingdom*, p. 70, Salt Lake City, 1987).

THE GREAT FLOOD.   The Old Testament records a flood that was just over fifteen cubits (sometimes assumed to be about twenty-six feet) deep and covered the entire landscape: "And all the high hills, that were under the whole heaven, were covered" (Gen. 7:19). Scientifically this account leaves many questions unanswered, especially how a measurable depth could cover mountains. Elder John A. Widtsoe, writing in 1943, offered this perspective:

> The fact remains that the exact nature of the flood is not known. We set up assumptions, based upon our best knowledge, but can go no further. We should remember that when inspired writers deal with historical incidents they relate that which they have seen or that which may have been told them, unless indeed the past is opened to them by revelation.

> The details in the story of the flood are undoubtedly drawn from the experiences of the writer. Under a downpour of rain, likened to the opening of the heavens, a destructive torrent twenty-six feet deep or deeper would easily be formed. The writer of Genesis made a faithful report of the facts known to him concerning the flood. In other localities the depth of the water might have been more or less. In fact, the details of the flood are not known to us [Widtsoe, p. 127].

SPECIAL CONCERNS OF LATTER-DAY SAINTS.   President Brigham Young taught: "The whole object of the creation of this world is to exalt the intelligences that are placed upon it, that they may live, endure, and increase for ever and ever. We are not here to quarrel and contend about the things of this world, but we are here to subdue and beautify it" (*JD* 7:290). Viewing themselves as tenants upon the earth, Latter-day Saints regard its resources as a sacred trust from God for the use of all while upon the earth: "I, the Lord . . . make every man accountable, as a steward over earthly blessings, which I have made and prepared for my creatures" (D&C 104:13). The earth was created by Christ for specific purposes: "We will take of these materials, and we will make an earth whereon these may dwell; and we will prove them herewith, to see if they will do all things whatsoever the Lord their God shall command them" (Abr. 3:24–25). President Brigham Young taught that the dominion God gives human beings is designed to test them, enabling them to show to themselves, to their fellow beings, and to God just how they would act if entrusted with God's power (Nibley, 1978, p. 90).

Brigham Young supervised the relocation of the Church to the American West, which in the late 1840s was sparsely inhabited. His strong commitment to preservation of the environment and wise use of all natural resources influenced early Church colonizing efforts. Such prudence and wisdom in the use of land, water, air, and living things are still encouraged throughout the Church. In modern days of widespread concern for preserving the fragile relationships between the earth and its biosphere, Brigham Young's counsel remains vital:

> There is a great work for the Saints to do. Progress, and improve upon, and make beautiful everything around you. Cultivate the earth and cultivate your minds. Build cities, adorn your habitations, make gardens, orchards, and vineyards, and render the earth so pleasant that when you look upon your labours you may do so with pleasure, and that angels may delight to come and visit your beautiful locations [*JD* 8:83].

BIBLIOGRAPHY

Cracroft, Paul. "How Old Is the Earth?" *IE* 67 (Oct. 1964):827–30, 852.

Crowe, M. J. *Extraterrestrial Life Debate 1750–1900*. Cambridge, U.K., 1986.

Eyring, Henry. "The Gospel and the Age of the Earth." *IE* 68 (July 1965):608–609, 626, 628.

Jeffery, Duane E. "Seers, Savants and Evolution: The Uncomfortable Interface." *Dialogue* 8, nos. 3/4 (1973):41–75.

Jones, Albert. "Is Mother Earth Growing Old?" *IE* 13 (May 1910):639–43.

Nibley, Hugh W. "Before Adam." In *CWHN* 1:49–85.

———. "Brigham Young on the Environment." In *To the Glory of God*, ed. T. Madsen and C. Tate, pp. 3–29. Salt Lake City, 1972.

———. "Man's Dominion." *New Era* 2 (Oct. 1972):24–31.

———. "Subduing the Earth." In *Nibley on the Timely and the Timeless*, ed. T. Madsen, pp. 85–99. Provo, Utah, 1978.

———. "Treasures in the Heavens." In *CWHN* 1:171–214.

Old Testament: Genesis–2 Samuel [Religion 301] Student Manual, 2nd ed., rev. Salt Lake City, 1981.

Pratt, Orson. *JD* 16:324–25.

Smith, Joseph Fielding. *Man: His Origin and Destiny*. Salt Lake City, 1954.

Talmage, James E. "Prophecy as the Forerunner of Science—An Instance." *IE* 7 (May 1904):481–88.

Widtsoe, John A. *Evidences and Reconciliations*. Salt Lake City, 1987.

MORRIS S. PETERSEN

EASTER

Easter is the Christian holiday celebrating the resurrection of Jesus Christ. After Christ died on the cross, his body was placed in a sepulcher, where it remained, separated from his spirit, until his resurrection, when his spirit and his body were reunited. Latter-day Saints affirm and testify that Jesus Christ was resurrected and lives today with a glorified and perfected body of flesh and bone. Following his resurrection, Jesus appeared first to Mary Magdalene and then to other disciples. Some were not convinced of his resurrection, believing that his appearances were those of an unembodied spirit. Jesus assured them, "Behold my hands and my feet, that it is I myself: handle me, and see; for a spirit hath not flesh and bones, as ye see me have" (Luke 24:39). He then ate fish and honey in their presence, further dispelling their doubt.

Easter is a celebration not only of the resurrection of Christ but also of the universal resurrection. Because of the atonement of Jesus Christ, all people will be resurrected. Their bodies and spirits will be reunited, never to be separated again. Latter-day Saints know the truth of Paul's statement, "But now is Christ risen from the dead, and become the firstfruits of them that slept. . . . For as in Adam all die, even so in Christ shall all be made alive" (1 Cor. 15:20; cf. Alma 11:42–45).

Latter-day Saints conduct Easter Sunday services but do not follow the religious observances of Ash Wednesday, Lent, or Holy Week. LDS Easter services traditionally review New Testament and Book of Mormon accounts of Christ's crucifixion, his resurrection, and surrounding events. For these services, chapels are often decorated with white lilies and other symbols of life. Ward choirs frequently present Easter cantatas, and congregations sing Easter hymns. As at services on other Sundays, the emblems of the sacrament are passed to the congregation.

Some LDS families include Easter bunnies and eggs in their family festivities for the delight of children. Such traditions are not officially discouraged, though they have no religious significance to Latter-day Saints. The focus of the holiday is religious. For Latter-day Saints, Easter is a celebration of the promise of eternal life through Christ. They share the conviction of Job, "For I know that my redeemer liveth, and that he shall stand at the latter day upon the earth: And though after my skin worms destroy this body, yet in my flesh shall I see God" (Job 19:25–26).

BIBLIOGRAPHY

Kimball, Spencer W. "The Real Meaning of Easter." *Instructor* 93 (Apr. 1958):100–101.

MARY ELLEN STEWART JAMISON

ECONOMIC AID

Economic aid offered by the Church to needy people in various countries is intended to promote the well-being of individuals and families. In addition to temporary welfare assistance given by the Church to its members and to a variety of emergency and HUMANITARIAN SERVICES, the Church has rendered longer-term economic aid to many groups in a variety of nations. Church members are taught that family well-being depends upon, among other things, the means to provide food, clothing, and shelter. Just as individual members are taught to acquire skills necessary for this economic well-being (*see*

EMERGENCY PREPAREDNESS; SELF-SUFFICIENCY), the Church encourages nations to provide economic opportunity for their citizens and to establish an economic atmosphere wherein individual skills can be used for the benefit of families and the nation.

The Church has not established political criteria for selecting recipients of its economic aid. Joseph Smith echoed the counsel of the Savior to feed the hungry and clothe the naked (Matt. 25:35–40; T&S 3 [Mar. 1842]:732).

Many of the humanitarian projects supported by the Church have had a monetary component to them. In addition to the food and blankets sent to many peoples in Europe after World War II, money was sent to purchase land and buildings to be used for longer-term relief. In 1983, the Church sent emergency food and clothing to both Colombia (earthquake) and Tahiti (hurricane), and Church funds also were used to provide building materials for those whose homes had been devastated ("News of the Church," Ensign 13 [June 1983]:77). Similarly, aid to both Armenia and Africa included funds for economic development in addition to monies used for more immediate relief. As part of the 1989 aid to Armenia following earthquakes in the region, materials and tools were donated by the Church to allow craftsmen to rebuild homes and businesses (The Daily Universe, Dec. 6, 1989, Provo, Utah, p. 2). And in the $10 million aid to Africa in 1985 and 1986, approximately one-third of the funds were used to support long-term economic development projects (Ferguson, pp. 10–15). For example, in concert with Africare, some of the funds were used to construct dams, develop irrigation and other water projects, and train farmers in Ethiopia. Economic aid from the Church also supported vocational school development and marketing cooperatives in the Sudan, and agricultural rehabilitation in Chad, Niger, and Cameroon ("News of the Church," Ensign 15 [Nov. 1985]:109). Special funds also have been used to support local self-sufficiency enterprises, literacy and health services, and agricultural development in Kenya, Zimbabwe, Mozambique, Zaire, Ghana, Mali, Nigeria, Chad, and in Central and South America.

One of the more extensive and systematic resources to provide Church economic aid has been the Ezra Taft Benson Agriculture and Food Institute located at BRIGHAM YOUNG UNIVERSITY. This institute, founded in 1975, was commissioned to raise the quality of life through improved nutrition and introduction of more effective agricultural practices. The institute conducts research, teaches, and carries out agricultural projects in countries around the world. It is well known for its development and promotion of small-scale food-growing projects that have been effective particularly in Bolivia, Ecuador, Guatemala, and Mexico. The Benson Institute conducts nutrition assessments and training; has developed, for small-scale farms, appropriate technology in developing countries (tractors, solar-powered water pumps and grain grinders, and wind-driven water pumps); trains students from developing countries; and has entered into several agreements with governments of developing countries to assist them in their agricultural development efforts. The institute collects and sends abroad medical and agricultural equipment and coordinates volunteers who wish to live in a country for varying periods of time to help with health, nutrition, and agricultural development (see various issues of the semiannual *Benson Institute Review*).

In 1977, E. W. Thrasher donated $14 million as an endowment to the Church to be used to benefit the health of children throughout the world. A member of the Presiding Bishopric of the Church is chairman of the executive committee of the Thrasher Research Fund. The fund has expended millions of dollars since 1977 to support research in nutrition and infectious diseases and to promote the health of children, primarily in developing countries. In one instance, the fund ran a project in a small village in Nigeria to demonstrate that low-cost appropriate health care technology and knowledge can be transferred to local residents (see *Annual Reports* of the Thrasher Research Fund, Salt Lake City, Utah).

BIBLIOGRAPHY

Benson Institute. *Benson Institute Review*. Provo, Utah, 1984.

Ferguson, Isaac C. "Freely Given." *Ensign* 18 (Aug. 1988): 10–15.

"News of the Church." *Ensign* 13 (June 1983):77.

"News of the Church." *Ensign* 15 (Nov. 1985):109.

STANLEY A. TAYLOR

EDUCATION

[*This entry discusses:*

Attitudes Toward Education
Educational Attainment

See also Academies; Brigham Young University; Church Educational System; Schools; Social and Cultural History.]

ATTITUDES TOWARD EDUCATION

The Articles of Faith underscore the deep and fundamental role that knowledge plays in the teachings of The Church of Jesus Christ of Latter-day Saints: "If there is anything virtuous, lovely, or of good report or praiseworthy, we seek after these things" (A of F 13). Speaking of the LDS commitment to learning and education, M. Lynn Bennion wrote: "It is doubtful if there is an organization in existence that more completely directs the educational development of its people than does the Mormon Church. The educational program of the Church today is a consistent expansion of the theories promulgated by its founders" (Bennion, p. 2).

The educational ideas and practices of the Church grew directly out of certain revelations received by Joseph Smith that emphasize the eternal nature of knowledge and the vital role learning plays in the spiritual, moral, and intellectual development of mankind. For example: "It is impossible for a man to be saved in ignorance" (D&C 131:6) of his eternal nature and role. "The glory of God is intelligence, or, in other words, light and truth" (D&C 93:36). "Whatever principle of intelligence we attain unto in this life, it will rise with us in the resurrection. And if a person gains more knowledge and intelligence in this life through his diligence and obedience than another, he will have so much the advantage in the world to come" (D&C 130:18–19). "Knowledge saves a man, and in the world of spirits a man cannot be exalted but by knowledge" (*TPJS*, p. 357). An often-quoted statement from the Book of Mormon reads: "To be learned is good if they hearken unto the counsels of God" (2 Ne. 9:29). In June 1831 Joseph Smith received a revelation concerning "selecting and writing books for schools in this church" (D&C 55:4), and another on December 27, 1832, establishing the broad missions of education in the Church:

And I give unto you a commandment that you shall teach one another the doctrine of the kingdom. Teach ye diligently and my grace shall attend you, that you may be instructed more perfectly in theory, in principle, in doctrine, in the law of the gospel, in all things that pertain unto the kingdom of God, that are expedient for you to understand; of things both in heaven and in the earth, and under the earth; things which have been, things which are, things which must shortly come to pass; things which are at home, things which are abroad; the wars and the perplexities of the nations, and the judgments which are on the land; and a knowledge also of countries and of kingdoms—that ye may be prepared in all things [D&C 88:77–80].

The Church has been built on the conviction that eternal progress depends upon righteous living and growth in knowledge, religious and secular. "Indeed, the necessity of learning is probably the most frequently-repeated theme of modern-day revelations" (L. Arrington, "The Founding of the L.D.S. Institutes of Religion," *Dialogue* 2 [Summer 1967]:137).

Joseph Smith and many of the early Mormon pioneers came from a New England Puritan background, with its reverence for knowledge and learning (Salisbury, p. 258). The LDS outlook assumes the perfectibility of man and his ability to progress to ever-higher moral, spiritual, and intellectual levels. In this philosophy, moreover, knowledge of every kind is useful in man's attempt to realize himself in this world and the next. "It is the application of knowledge for the spiritual welfare of man that constitutes the Mormon ideal of education" (Bennion, p. 125). The early leaders of the Church, therefore, saw little ultimate division between correct secular and religious learning. Broad in scope and spiritual in intent, LDS educational philosophy tends to fuse the secular with the religious because, in the LDS context, the two are part of one seamless web (Bennion, pp. 120–23).

In 1833, Joseph Smith founded the Church's first educational effort, the School of the Prophets, in Kirtland, Ohio. That school was devoted to the study of history, political science, languages (including Hebrew), literature, and theology. Its main purpose was to prepare Church leaders to magnify their callings as missionaries to warn all people and testify of the gospel (D&C 88:80–81). It also set an example of adult learning that was followed "in Missouri, Illinois, and Utah, where parents joined their children in the pursuit of knowledge" (Bennion, p. 10).

In 1840, Joseph Smith sought the incorporation of the City of Nauvoo, Illinois, and along with it authority to establish a university. The Nauvoo Charter included authority to "establish and organize an institution of learning within the limits of the city, for the teaching of the arts, sciences and learned professions, to be called the 'University of the City of Nauvoo'" (quoted in Salisbury, p. 269).

The first academic year in Nauvoo was that of 1841–42. The university probably was among the first municipal universities in the United States (Rich, p. 10); it was certainly an optimistic and ambitious undertaking. The curriculum included languages (German, French, Latin, Greek, and Hebrew), mathematics, chemistry and geology, literature, and history; but "the data are too scant to reveal the scholastic rating of the instruction given. It was probably superior to the average secondary work of the time. The faculty represented considerable scholarship and indeed was a rather remarkable group to be found in a frontier city" (Bennion, p. 25).

The murder of Joseph Smith in 1844 abruptly ended the dream of the University of the City of Nauvoo and set in motion the difficult journey to the Great Basin. Despite the hardships, education was not forgotten. Brigham Young instructed the migrating Saints to bring with them

> at least a copy of every valuable treatise on education—every book, map, chart, or diagram that may contain interesting, useful, and attractive matter, to gain the attention of children, and cause them to love to learn to read; and, also every historical, mathematical, philosophical, geographical, geological, astronomical, scientific, practical, and all other variety of useful and interesting writings, maps, etc., to present to the General Church Recorder, when they shall arrive at their destination, from which important and interesting matter may be gleaned to compile the most valuable works, on every science and subject, for the benefit of the rising generation [*MS* 10 (1848):85].

The charter of the University of the City of Nauvoo served as the foundation for the UNIVERSITY OF DESERET (now the University of Utah), established by Brigham Young in Salt Lake City in 1850. "Education," he once told this school's Board of Regents, "is the power to think clearly, the power to act well in the world's work, and the power to appreciate life" (Bennion, p. 115). He advised: "A good school teacher is one of the most essential members in society" (*JD* 10:225).

In 1851 the territorial legislature granted a charter providing for "establishment and regulation of schools" (Bennion, p. 40), but for some years the struggle for survival eclipsed the effort to establish a formal system of education. Utah's first schools were private, paid for by parents or by adult students, and classes took place during either the day or the evening, depending on local needs, interests, and resources (Rich, pp. 13, 17–18). Attendance rose and fell with the seasons and the demands of an agricultural society in which human labor was scarce and precious. Curricula varied as well, often depending on the academic strengths or interests of the teacher; some schools offered traditional subjects, others more practical pursuits such as carpentry or masonry. The existence of these frontier schools was always precarious and their operation intermittent (Rich, p. 18), but they were an eloquent and often moving testimony to the commitment of early Mormon pioneers to education, demanding as they did considerable sacrifice of scarce time and resources.

Brigham Young's philosophy of education was practical and pragmatic, but he was not opposed, as has sometimes been assumed, to liberal education; he simply felt it was overstressed in the educational environment of his day (Bennion, p. 107). "Will education feed and clothe you, keep you warm on a cold day, or enable you to build a house? Not at all. Should we cry down education on this account? No. What is it for? The improvement of the mind; to instruct us in all arts and sciences, in the history of the world, in the laws of nations; to enable us to understand the laws and principles of life, and how to be useful while we live" (*JD* 14:83). He believed that "every art and science known and studied by the children of men is comprised within the Gospel" (*JD* 12:257).

President Young's educational philosophy was further enhanced by Karl G. Maeser, a German educator who joined the Church and immigrated to Salt Lake City in 1860. In 1876 Brigham Young appointed Maeser the principal of the Brigham Young Academy in Provo (*see* ACADEMIES). "The development of the Academy movement and the direction of Church policies in education were largely determined by this German educator" (Bennion, p. 117). His approach to education included a belief that "knowledge should be supported by corresponding moral qualities. The formation of character depends upon the nature of the moral training which accompanies intellectual advancement" (Maeser, p. 43). He maintained that religion was "the fundamental principle of education" and was its "most effective motive power" (Maeser, p. 56). His influential and widely circulated syllabus, *School and Fireside* (1898), clearly identified the critical functions of education as preparing people for practical life in the family and in the nation and inculcating fundamental principles of spiritual development.

In the early pioneer days, most schools in Utah Territory were LDS Church schools, and religion was an integral part of the curriculum. With the increasing diversification of Utah's population and the passage of the Edmunds-Tucker Act in 1887, which had the effect of prohibiting the teaching of religion in public schools, the Church looked for other means of assuring spiritual instruction for its young people. Between 1890 and 1929, the Church sponsored special religion classes conducted in ward meetinghouses for children in the first to the ninth grades in a movement that was "the first effort of the Mormons to supplement (but not to replace) secular education"; it was "America's first experiment in providing separate weekday religious training for public school children" (Quinn, p. 379).

This endeavor grew into the CHURCH EDUCATIONAL SYSTEM, which consists of several levels. First is SEMINARY, a daily religious education program held in a seminary building near the school for grades nine through twelve that provides for the study of the Book of Mormon, Old Testament, New Testament, and Doctrine and Covenants/Church History. Second, INSTITUTES OF RELIGION adjacent to campuses serve students enrolled in postsecondary programs by offering religion classes, usually scheduled twice a week to fit in with college schedules. Third, the Church sponsors four institutions of higher education: BRIGHAM YOUNG UNIVERSITY in Provo, Utah; BRIGHAM YOUNG UNIVERSITY—HAWAII in Laie, Hawaii; RICKS COLLEGE in Rexburg, Idaho; and LDS BUSINESS COLLEGE in Salt Lake City. In addition, in Mexico and the Pacific, the Church sponsors seven elementary schools, thirteen middle schools, and nine secondary schools that provide both secular and religious training.

In 1988–1989, the Church's educational system extended to 90 countries or territories and served about 250,000 seminary students, 124,500 institute students, 37,600 students in Church colleges and universities, and 9,300 students in other Church schools. The system employs over 4,100 full- and part-time employees, in addition to 15,000 members who are called to teach in the seminary and institute programs.

In sum, the attitude of the Church toward education is unusual in several respects. First, the Church is distinctive in the degree to which its members, child and adult alike, participate in the many educational activities of the Church: "As a people we believe in education—the gathering of knowledge and the training of the mind. The Church itself is really an educational institution. Traditionally, we are an education-loving people" (Widtsoe, 1944, p. 666). Second, its commitment is to education as an essential component of religious life: "Every life coheres around certain fundamental core ideas. . . . The fact that [God] has promised further revelation is to me a challenge to keep an open mind and be prepared to follow wherever my search for truth may lead" (Brown, 1969, p. 11). Third, it holds a deep conviction that knowledge has an eternal dimension because it advances man's agency and progress here and in the world to come: "Both creative science and revealed religion find their fullest and truest expression in the climate of freedom. . . . Be unafraid of new ideas for they are as steppingstones to progress. You will, of course, respect the opinions of others but be unafraid to dissent—if you are informed" (Brown, 1958, p. 2–3). Fourth, it is insistent that secular and spiritual learning are not at odds but in harmony with each other: Latter-day Saints do not emphasize "the spiritual education of man to the neglect of his intellectual and physical education. . . . It is not a case of esteeming intellectual and physical education less, but of esteeming spiritual education more" (Roberts, pp. 122–23). "Secular knowledge is to be *desired*" as a tool in the hands of the righteous, but "spiritual knowledge is a *necessity*" (S. Kimball, *Faith Precedes the Miracle*, p. 280).

BIBLIOGRAPHY
Bennion, Milton Lynn. *Mormonism and Education.* Salt Lake City, 1939.
Brown, Hugh B. "An Eternal Quest—Freedom of the Mind." *BYU Speeches of the Year*, May 13, 1969.
———. "What Is Man and What He May Become." *BYU Speeches of the Year*, March 25, 1958.

Clark, J. Reuben, Jr. "The Charted Course of the Church in Education." Provo, Utah, 1936.

Clark, Marden J. "On the Mormon Commitment to Education." *Dialogue* 7 (Winter 1972):11–19.

Gardner, David P., and Jeffrey R. Holland. "Education in Zion: Intellectual Inquiry and Revealed Truth." *Sunstone* 6 (Jan.–Feb. 1981):59–61.

Kimball, Spencer W. "Second Century Address." *BYU Studies* 16 (Summer 1976):445–57.

Maeser, Karl G. *School and Fireside*. Utah, 1898.

Nibley, Hugh W. "Educating the Saints," and "Zeal without Knowledge." In *Nibley on the Timely and the Timeless*, ed. T. Madsen, pp. 229–77. Provo, Utah, 1978.

Quinn, D. Michael. "Utah's Educational Innovation: LDS Religion Classes, 1890–1929." *Utah Historical Quarterly* 43 (1975):379–89.

Rich, Wendell O. *Distinctive Teachings of the Restoration*, pp. 7–34, 161–88. Salt Lake City, 1962.

Roberts, B. H. "The Mormon Point of View in Education." *IE* 2 (Dec. 1898):119–26.

Salisbury, H. S. "History of Education in the Church of Jesus Christ of Latter Day Saints." *Journal of History* 15 (July 1922):257–81.

Widtsoe, John A. "The Returning Soldier." *IE* 47 (Nov. 1944):666, 701–702.

Young, Brigham. *Discourses of Brigham Young*, comp. John A. Widtsoe, pp. 245–63. Salt Lake City, 1978.

DAVID P. GARDNER

EDUCATIONAL ATTAINMENT

Latter-day Saints have a significantly higher level of educational attainment than does the population of the United States as a whole. Contrary to the norm for other religious denominations, members of The Church of Jesus Christ of Latter-day Saints who have earned advanced academic degrees are more likely to be deeply involved in religious practices and activity in the Church, both from a personal standpoint and in rendering service in their Church.

These phenomena may be the result of the doctrinal emphasis on learning and education that is so prevalent in the Church. Latter-day Saints are taught from early childhood that they must read and ponder the scriptures. The high priority given education in the lives of most Latter-day Saints has its roots in specific scriptures in the Bible, the Book of Mormon, the Doctrine and Covenants, and the Pearl of Great Price, which assure the Saints that "to be learned is good if they hearken unto the counsels of God" (2 Ne. 9:29).

Latter-day Saints are taught that what they learn in this life will go with them into eternity (D&C 130:18–19), that all truth and knowledge are available to each individual to acquire. They are gifts from God, but each individual must be worthy of them through diligent effort to learn. From birth to death, Church members hear from the pulpit, learn in Church meetings, and read in the scriptures that each individual must learn and grow in talent and ability. A quick rejoinder to a Mormon youth who might complain of finding nothing interesting or challenging to do is to read the scriptures, study from the great books, and follow the commandment to better oneself. This should be done not only for today and tomorrow but for eternity, since what one learns is a possession that never leaves. Latter-day Saints are taught that, although they cannot take their wealth or earthly goods with them into the next life, all of what they learn will be an everlasting possession.

The establishment of schools and colleges has been a priority since the founding of the Church. Only three years after the organization of the Church in 1830, the Prophet Joseph Smith established the School of the Prophets in Kirtland, Ohio. Only seven months after the arrival of the pioneers in the Great Salt Lake Valley, a university was established (see UNIVERSITY OF DESERET). Throughout the history of the Church, schools were established in Ohio, Missouri, Illinois, and Utah and in virtually every other location where the Saints have settled.

In Utah, where a large majority of the population are members of the Church, youth respond to scriptural precepts that stress the importance of learning by enrolling in high numbers in high school advanced placement courses that offer college-level credit. According to the annual report published in 1989 by the U.S. Department of Education, Utah ranked first among all the fifty states in the percentage of its high school seniors who took advanced placement courses (U.S. Department of Education State Education Performance Chart, 1989), in spite of the fact that Utah ranks among the lowest states in average expenditure per pupil.

Another factor motivating LDS youth to qualify for college credit while still in high school is the strong expectation in most of their families that they will serve as missionaries for the Church. With college being interrupted for missionary service, some of the time lost from pursuing a college degree can be recovered through heavy participation in advanced placement programs offered in high school.

Motivation to reach higher levels of education extends beyond the family and the scriptures. Outstanding accomplishments and milestone events in educational attainment are recognized from the pulpit in Church meetings where local leaders highlight distinguished academic accomplishments. The *Deseret News*, the daily newspaper published by the Church, adds to this momentum by sponsoring an annual "Sterling Scholars" program, which highlights outstanding student accomplishments in public high schools. This program features the best scholars in various fields of study at the high school level, culminating with photographs and biographical stories on semifinalists and finalists.

Because of their commitment to education, Latter-day Saints complete more schooling than the United States population as a whole (Albrecht and Heaton, p. 49). While 53.5 percent of Mormon males and 44.3 percent of Mormon females have at least some education beyond high school, only 36.5 percent of the males and 27.7 percent of the females in the U.S. population as a whole have any college-level education after high school.

Albrecht and Heaton also found that this traditionally high level of educational attainment among Latter-day Saints has not resulted in a decrease in their religious commitment. National survey data published by the Princeton Religious Research Center (1982) indicate the opposite result concerning the impact of higher education for the nation as a whole: the higher the level of educational attainment, the lower the level of religious zeal. The Princeton Center data suggest that it is generally quite difficult for academically preoccupied individuals to hold a view of the world that is at the same time both religious and scholarly. But, according to the research of Albrecht and Heaton (1984, pp. 43–57), LDS intellectuals have less often been caught in this dilemma. In these studies religiosity was measured in terms of making financial contributions, rendering services, and attending Church meetings.

BIBLIOGRAPHY

Albrecht, Stan L., and Tim B. Heaton. "Secularization, Higher Education, and Religiosity." *Review of Religious Research* 26 (Sept. 1984):43–58.

Princeton Religious Research Center. *Religion in America*. Princeton, N.J., 1982.

United States Department of Education. State Education Statistics: Student Performance Chart. Washington, D.C., 1989.

TERRELL H. BELL

EMERGENCY PREPAREDNESS

Latter-day Saints are taught to prepare for potential problems. Since the gospel is concerned with mankind's temporal as well as spiritual welfare, the Church considers any potential emergency that would adversely affect the quality of life or produce suffering to be a cause for advance preparation. This includes natural disasters, unemployment, disease, injuries, and other circumstances that could threaten life or personal well-being. The Church teaches its members to prepare for such emergencies.

The rationale for emergency preparedness is that by living providently and by acquiring in advance the skills and resources necessary to cope effectively with difficulties, Latter-day Saints can minimize or avoid the suffering that accompanies the unexpected. They can also have the sense of security and peace of mind (D&C 38:30) that are essential to spiritual development. They are also taught to work toward SELF-SUFFICIENCY—to provide adequately for themselves, to assist those in need, and to avoid unnecessary dependence upon the efforts or resources of others. They are told to put aside something when times are good so that they can care for themselves and others when times are bad. For Latter-day Saints, preparing for emergencies is more akin to saving for a "rainy day" than surviving "doomsday" (Kimball, p. 78).

For more than a hundred years, Church leaders have taught the members to store grain and other essentials that would sustain life in times of drought or famine (*Essentials of Home Production and Storage*, p. 17). The current guidelines for home storage are intended to apply internationally. They include having a supply of food, clothing, and, where possible, the fuel necessary to sustain life for one year (Benson, p. 33). Church guidance states, "We have never laid down an exact formula for what anybody should store. Perhaps if we think not in terms of a year's supply of what we ordinarily would use, and think more in terms of what it would take to keep us alive in case we didn't have anything else to eat, that last would be very easy to put in storage for a year" (*Essentials*, p. 6).

Home gardens, canning, and sewing have long been encouraged among the women by the Relief Society through homemaking lessons and workdays. Latter-day Saints are counseled to seek education and training opportunities that prepare them to adapt to changes in the working world, to avoid personal indebtedness, to maintain good health by eating and exercising properly, to learn first aid, and to know how to protect their lives and possessions against fire, flood, and theft. They are counseled to obtain life, medical, and property insurance where it is available. They are also urged to avoid panic buying, purchasing emergency resources on credit, pursuing fads, and giving official endorsement to specific brands, suppliers, or techniques.

Institutionally, the Church practices the principles of preparedness. Under the aegis of its Welfare Services, the Church's welfare farms, canneries, and bishops' storehouses grow, process, and distribute commodities for consumption by those in need in the Church. These facilities maintain approximately a year's supply of inventory, in both production supplies and finished goods. Church-owned grain reserves are stored to help provide needs from harvest to harvest, with a suitable margin for some who may come into need during more prolonged economic downturns. The Church does not attempt, however, to maintain emergency storage for its entire membership. Long-term security against catastrophic emergencies depends upon the faithful preparation of individual members and families throughout the world.

Consistent preparedness has enabled the Church to participate in humanitarian projects to relieve suffering resulting from such catastrophes as World War II, the rupture of the Teton Dam in Idaho in 1976, food shortages in Poland in 1982, flooding in Brazil in 1983, earthquakes in Mexico City in 1985, hurricanes in the Caribbean and South Carolina in 1989, and other natural and man-made disasters.

Ecclesiastical units of the Church (wards, stakes, regions, and areas) are directed to prepare and maintain a written emergency response plan. The scope and level of detail contained in the plans vary, depending upon the nature and severity of emergencies likely to occur in each area. Emergency response plans generally address leadership and communication issues, reporting procedures, the location and extent of resources available for emergency response efforts, guidelines for the use of Church buildings as shelters, and the names and addresses of emergency-response specialists.

The presiding officers of all Church units are encouraged to coordinate emergency planning and response efforts with appropriate community agencies. The importance of good citizenship by all Church members in times of need is axiomatic.

BIBLIOGRAPHY

Benson, Ezra Taft. "Prepare for the Days of Tribulation." *Ensign* 10 (Nov. 1980):32–34.

Essentials of Home Production and Storage. Salt Lake City, 1979.

Kimball, Spencer W. "Welfare Services: The Gospel in Action." *Ensign* 7 (Nov. 1977):76–79.

FRANK D. RICHARDSON

EPISTEMOLOGY

Epistemology is the branch of philosophy dealing with the nature and scope of knowledge. The Church of Jesus Christ of Latter-day Saints has no uniform position on the classical issues of epistemology, such as the relationship of the sources of knowledge, theories of truth, and modes of verification, but the superiority of knowing by revelation from God is commonly cited from the scriptures.

The word "knowledge" is used in different ways and has different meanings in different cultures. Different kinds of knowledge may be independent of each other.

The Western philosophical tradition, like Western thought generally, emphasizes knowledge in the sense of knowing facts. But this emphasis may not be appropriate, especially from a gospel perspective. Some scriptures teach that other kinds of knowledge may be more important. Thus, Jesus prays, "This is life eternal, that they might know thee the only true God, and Jesus Christ, whom thou hast sent" (John 17:3). This is knowledge by acquaintance more than "knowledge about" (cf. JST Matt. 7:32–33). There are also indications that factual knowledge alone is not sufficient for salvation: "But be ye doers of the word, and not hearers only" (James 1:22). At the request of President Spencer W. Kimball, a prophet, the words in an LDS children's hymn were changed from "Teach me all that I must know" to "Teach me all that I must do," because it is not enough just to know; one must do the will of the Lord.

A related gospel theme is that knowing comes from doing. "If any man will do his will, he shall know of the doctrine, whether it be of God, or whether I speak of myself" (John 7:17). The Prophet Joseph Smith taught, "We cannot keep all the commandments without first knowing them, and we cannot expect to know all, or more than we now know unless we comply with or keep those we have already received" (*TPJS*, p. 256).

In formal philosophy, "knowing," in the sense of knowing facts, is often defined to mean true belief together with good reasons. In other words, a person knows some statement X if and only if that person believes X, and if X is true, and if the person has good reasons for believing X. The European-American philosophical tradition recognizes two kinds of reasons that support the claim to know: rational argument and empirical evidence. Within the Church these are tacitly accepted as sources of knowledge, sometimes even of religious knowledge. For example, after reviewing the traditional arguments for the existence of God, James E. Talmage observed that some were "at least strongly corroborative" of God's existence (*AF*, p. 29).

However, there is a continuing tradition, based on the scriptures and reinforced by modern Church leaders, that specifically religious knowledge requires a different and distinctively spiritual source. "We believe that no man can know that Jesus is the Christ, but by the Holy Ghost. We believe in [the gift of the Holy Ghost] in all its fulness, and power, and greatness, and glory" (*TPJS*, p. 243; D&C 76:114–16). It is widely accepted by Latter-day Saints that gospel knowledge must ultimately be obtained by spiritual rather than exclusively rational or empirical means (e.g., 1 Cor. 12:3). Thus, in The Church of Jesus Christ of Latter-day Saints, there is no clear counterpart to the Roman Catholic tradition of natural theology.

One of the most suggestive and frequently cited scriptures in LDS teaching makes the point: "And by the power of the Holy Ghost ye may know the truth of all things" (Moro. 10:4–5). This scripture is usually taken to apply to all knowledge. This suggests that both rational argument and empirical evidence, the two traditional approaches to knowledge, can be either supplanted by or encompassed within spiritual knowledge. Of course, the scripture does not say that knowledge comes only by the Holy Ghost. Yet, within the Church, it is often held that what might be thought of as secular learning, for example, modern scientific knowledge, is directly associated with the restoration of the gospel and is rooted in divine inspiration throughout the world.

[*See also* Science and Religion.]

K. CODELL CARTER

EQUALITY

Equality among persons is understood by Latter-day Saints as essential to divine love, which explains and justifies all other ethical virtues and principles (Matt. 22:37–40). All persons are of equal value in the sight of God. Each person (of every nation and every race) is as precious to him as another (2 Ne. 26:33; Alma 26:37). From God all people will receive equivalent opportunities through Jesus Christ to attain eternal life, his greatest blessing (1 Ne. 17:33–35; Hel. 14:17; D&C 18:10–12). All who are worthy to become heirs of Christ will enjoy equality with him and with each other in the celestial kingdom (D&C 88:106–107).

Latter-day Saints believe that when people love as God requires them to love (John 15:9–12), having full and equal regard for one another, they can form a Zion society as directed by the Lord and enjoy in this world the type of equality that defines relations between persons in the celestial world (D&C 78:4–8; 105:4–5). References to equality in latter-day scriptures primarily concern the building of Zion and living according to celestial law. In Zion the people have "all things common among them" (3 Ne. 26:19; 4 Ne. 1:3; cf. D&C 82:17–18; 104:70). They have equal chances to develop their abilities and equal opportunity to realize them in the work of Zion, all contributing according to their individual strengths and talents (D&C 82:17–18; Alma 1:26). A Zion people labor together as equals by organizing themselves according to the principle of "equal power" (D&C 76:94–95; 78:5–7; 105:4–6). For example, on the local level "all things" are done according to the "counsel" and "consent" of the community (D&C 104:21). Each member has an equal role in giving counsel and an equal vote in giving consent. But equality of power also defines the relations between members so that each is the center of decision and action in performing an individual stewardship within the community (D&C 82:17; 104:70–76).

Celestial law also requires that persons receive as equals that which is essential to survival and contributes to well-being. Consequently, in Zion there are "no poor among them" (Moses 7:18; 4 Ne. 1:3). This does not mean that every person receives the same amount. The "needs," "wants," and "circumstances" of individuals vary so that treatment of them must also vary to be equal in effect (D&C 51:3, 8; 42:33). Still, it is "not given that one should possess that which is above another." When such inequality exists, "the world lieth in sin" (D&C 49:20; cf. Alma 5:53–54), and "the abundance of the manifestations of the Spirit [are] withheld" (D&C 70:14).

A. D. SORENSEN

ETHICS

The Church of Jesus Christ of Latter-day Saints is typically involved in three levels of ethical concern: the theory of values; the foundations of moral decision; and the integration of personal and professional codes of ethics, such as those relating to medical, military, or governmental service. The inner dynamism of the Church and its increasing involvement with a confluence of cultures point beyond closed ethical systems. Latter-day Saints espouse an ethic of divine approbation; to discern the will of God and receive assurance that one is acting under God's approval are the ceaseless quest of discipleship. This may be called Spirit-guided morality.

The scriptures affirm that questions of the good and the right are intertwined with questions of the holy and with the primal Jewish-Christian imperative "Be ye holy for I am holy" (1 Pet. 1:16; cf. Lev. 11:44). Daily tensions between the sacred and the secular are part of the ethical dilemma, and Latter-day Saints seek help from the scriptures and classical sources.

Philosophers often distinguish two approaches to ethics: teleology and deontology. The teleological approach appraises the morality of an act by its relation to an end or purpose, while the deontological approach understands morality primarily in terms of duty or response to law. In Christian ethics, these views have proved difficult to reconcile. For Latter-day Saints, however, both obedience to divine imperatives and pursuit of ultimate happiness are correlative elements in the maturation of human beings. The conflict between duty and desire is overcome as one grows closer to God through faith and service and finds joy in upholding divine counsels and commandments.

Ethicists likewise contrast performance and motive in the religious life. Rabbinical tradition, for example, emphasizes the continuous study and scrupulous observance of Torah, while Reformation Protestantism stresses motive. Again, Latter-day Saints reject this perennial division; both are crucial in the religious life. "Ye shall know them by their fruits" (Matt. 7:16). Grace transforms men toward a Christlike nature. But purity of heart is manifest in scripture study and vigorous service; thus, mastery of law and inner change go hand in hand as components of discipleship and joyful living.

Classical Christian thought encourages the cultivation of habits and dispositions tied to both intellectual and moral virtues. Both ancient and modern revelations advocate such virtues as "knowledge, temperance, patience, brotherly kindness, godliness, charity, humility, diligence" (2 Pet. 1:5–7; cf. D&C 4:5), and all the Christlike attributes of the Sermon on the Mount. There are correlative warnings against besetting vices: pride, unrighteous dominion, lust, anger, unforgiveness, covetousness, idleness, halfheartedness. The Saints are constantly reminded to "seek not the things of this world but seek ye first to build up the kingdom of God and to establish his righteousness" (JST Matt. 6:38). Nephi$_1$ and Moroni$_2$, both prophets of the Book of Mormon, teach, as does the apostle Paul, the importance of faith, hope, and charity, which is defined as "the pure love of Christ" (1 Cor. 13:1–13; 2 Ne. 31:20; Moro. 7:21–48).

Much ethical discussion today revolves around whether there are any external and binding sanctions for ethics and morality. In the theological context, there is the classical dilemma of whether God's will is right because he wills it or whether he wills it because it is right. Latter-day Saints are not committed to certain theories of natural law. Modern scriptures suggest that ethical laws and "bounds" and conditions exist independent of God (D&C 88:3–40). They also teach that God both institutes laws and adapts them (*TPJS*, p. 320). Both the meaning and the application of law in changing circumstances require revelation of the present will of God.

LDS ethics are neither extremely atomistic nor social-communitarian but recognize the importance of both the individual and social aspects of human existence. "And that same sociality which exists among us here will exist among us there [the eternal world], only it will be coupled with eternal glory, which glory we do not now enjoy" (D&C 130:2).

Ethical discussion often focuses on how one comes to know what is good or right. Appeals to intuition or conscience are opposed by radical conventionalism, which presumes that values are reducible to custom and that the mores of a given group or individual are not known (discovered) but simply preferred. Latter-day Saints respect conscience, and the scriptures reiterate that conscience must be refined and directed by the Holy Ghost. They consider ethical maturity to derive from experience; including religious experience; from rational and practical deliberation; and from the mandates, both general and specific, that recur in scripture and the counsels of the prophets.

BIBLIOGRAPHY
Hill, Donald G., Jr., ed. *Perspectives in Mormon Ethics*. Salt Lake City, 1983.

F. NEIL BRADY

EVOLUTION

The position of the Church on the origin of man was published by the First Presidency in 1909 and stated again by a different First Presidency in 1925:

> The Church of Jesus Christ of Latter-day Saints, basing its belief on divine revelation, ancient and modern, declares man to be the direct and lineal offspring of Deity. . . . Man is the child of God, formed in the divine image and endowed with divine attributes.

The scriptures tell why man was created, but they do not tell how, though the Lord has promised that he will tell that when he comes again (D&C 101:32–33). In 1931, when there was intense discussion on the issue of organic evolution, the First Presidency of the Church, then consisting of Presidents Heber J. Grant, Anthony W. Ivins, and Charles W. Nibley, addressed all of the General Authorities of the Church on the matter, and concluded:

> Upon the fundamental doctrines of the Church we are all agreed. Our mission is to bear the message of the restored gospel to the world. Leave geology, biology, archaeology, and anthropology, no one of which has to do with the salvation of the souls of mankind, to scientific research, while we magnify our calling in the realm of the Church. . . .
>
> Upon one thing we should all be able to agree, namely, that Presidents Joseph F. Smith, John R. Winder, and Anthon H. Lund were right when they said: "Adam is the primal parent of our race" [First Presidency Minutes, Apr. 7, 1931].

WILLIAM E. EVENSON

EXHIBITIONS AND WORLD'S FAIRS

From its beginnings, the Church has characteristically presented its message through personal contact or in small groups: Faith and testimony are interpersonal. The Church has placed extensive emphasis on the mass media, and in participating in exhibits such as world's fairs. In addition, in recent years these activities have provided the Church an opportunity to present the message of the gospel amid milestone presentations of the arts, the sciences, and industry. The witness of the living and revealed Jesus Christ has been implicit in all Church exhibits, with two related themes given prominence: life's greatest questions—Where did I come from? Why am I here? What follows death?—and family values.

The first Church participation in a world's fair on a truly international scale was at the World's Columbian Exposition in Chicago in 1893, where the Mormon Tabernacle Choir won high honors in the choral competition. The Church later sponsored booths in several expositions and fairs, including the International Hygiene Exposition at Dresden, Germany, in 1930, and the Century of Progress Exposition in Chicago in 1933–1934. Exhibits were also mounted at international expositions held in San Diego in 1935–1936 and San Francisco in 1939–1940.

The Church's participation in the New York World's Fair in 1964 was a major effort. Its pavilion was a full-size replica of the three east towers of the Salt Lake Temple. Original paintings, the presentation of the film *Man's Search for Happiness*, and a replica of the Thorvaldsen CHRISTUS STATUE were featured. A large staff of trained volunteer guides conducted tours and question-and-answer sessions for the more than six million visitors who came to the pavilion.

Exhibits have since been presented at fair pavilions in Montreal, Canada; Osaka, Japan; San Antonio, Texas; and Seattle, Washington. Some of the exhibit artifacts have since been placed in VISITORS CENTERS throughout the world.

RICHARD J. MARSHALL

F

FAMILY

[*This entry consists of two articles:*

Teachings about the Family
Family Life

The first article presents the major teachings about the family that tend to set Latter-day Saints apart from other people and focuses on latter-day scriptures and teachings of Church leaders. The second article provides a substantial explanation of the way in which families experience Church membership together, including the fact that the standard orientation of Church programs is toward families. The family is central to LDS theology, religion, society, and culture. In addition to the articles appearing below, see Fatherhood; Marriage; *and* Motherhood. *Regarding specific Church policies and practices concerning the family, see* Abuse, Spouse and Child; Adoption of Children; Birth Control; Divorce; Family Home Evening; *and* Family Prayer.]

TEACHINGS ABOUT THE FAMILY

The basic unit of The Church of Jesus Christ of Latter-day Saints is the family: "The home is the basis of a righteous life, and no other instrumentality can take its place nor fulfill its essential functions" (McKay, Preface). Within the family, people experience most of life's greatest joys and greatest sorrows. The family relationships of every person on earth are of cardinal importance, and of all the social organizations created for human beings, only the family is intended to continue into the next life.

FAMILIES ON EARTH ARE AN EXTENSION OF THE FAMILY OF GOD. According to the LDS concept of the family, every person is a child of heavenly parents as well as mortal parents. Each individual was created spiritually and physically in the image of God and Christ (Moses 2:27; 3:5). The First Presidency has declared, "All men and women are in the similitude of the universal Father and Mother, and are literally the sons and daughters of Deity" (*MFP* 4:203). Everyone, before coming to this earth, lived with Heavenly Father and Heavenly Mother, and each was loved and taught by them as a member of their eternal family. Birth unites the spirit with a physical body so that together they can "receive a fulness of joy" (D&C 93:33; cf. 2 Ne. 2:25).

MARRIAGE IS ORDAINED OF GOD. "Whoso forbiddeth to marry is not ordained of God, for marriage is ordained of God unto man" (D&C 49:15). The marriage sanctioned by God provides men and women with the opportunity to fulfill their divine potentials. "Neither is the man without the woman, neither the woman without the man, in the Lord" (1 Cor. 11:11). Husbands and wives are unique in some ways and free to develop their eternal gifts, yet as coequals in the sight of their heavenly parents they are one in the divine goals they pursue, in their devotion to eternal principles and ordinances, in their obedience to the Lord, and in their divine love for each other. When a man and woman who have been sealed together in a temple are united spiritually, mentally, emotionally, and physically, taking full responsibility for nurturing each other, they are truly married. Together they strive to emulate the prototype of the heavenly home from which they came. The Church teaches them to complement, support, and enrich one another.

THE FAMILY CAN BECOME AN ETERNAL UNIT. Worthy members can be sealed by the power of the priesthood in holy temples for time and eternity either in or after marriage. At the time of their temple sealing, both husband and wife enter "an order of the priesthood [called] the new and everlasting covenant of marriage" (D&C 131:1–4). Without worthiness and authority, a marriage cannot endure eternally and is "of no efficacy, virtue, or force in and after the resurrection from the dead" (D&C 132:7). If a husband and wife are faithful to their temple marriage, they will continue as co-creators in God's celestial kingdom through the eternities. They will administer the affairs of their family in unity with the guidance of the Holy Spirit. Regarding members of the Church not born into such homes or not married in this life through no fault of their own, President Spencer W. Kimball taught that those "who would have responded if they had [had] an appropriate opportunity—will receive all those blessings in the world to come" (Kimball, p. 295).

THE POWER TO CREATE LIFE IS A GIFT FROM GOD. Because the procreative powers come from God, sexual purity is spiritual and mental, as well as physical and emotional (*see* SEXUALITY). Jesus said, "Whosoever looketh on a woman, to lust after her, hath committed adultery already in his heart. Behold, I give unto you a commandment, that ye suffer none of these things to enter into your heart" (3 Ne. 12:28–29). Chastity is sacred (cf. Jacob 2:28).

PROCREATION IS A COMMANDMENT OF GOD. Through the sexual experience, husbands and wives enrich their marriage and create physical bodies for spirits to come to earth to achieve divine purposes. Latter-day Saints strive to create a home life dedicated to fulfilling these purposes. It is both a joy and a responsibility for parents to bring heavenly spirits into this world. Adam and Eve were commanded to "be fruitful, and multiply" (Gen. 1:22). Latter-day revelation has given the same instructions. Church members are taught not to postpone or refuse to have children for selfish or materialistic reasons. On questions such as how many children a couple will have, the spacing of children, and BIRTH CONTROL, Latter-day Saints are instructed to use their agency, selecting a course as husband and wife in accordance with divine principles and seeking confirmation from the Holy Spirit.

PARENTS ARE RESPONSIBLE FOR TEACHING THEIR CHILDREN THE GOSPEL OF JESUS CHRIST. "Inasmuch as parents have children . . . that teach them not to understand the doctrine of repentance, faith in Christ the Son of the living God, and of baptism and the gift of the Holy Ghost . . . the sin be upon the heads of the parents. . . . And they shall also teach their children to pray, and to walk uprightly before the Lord" (D&C 68:25, 28). Parents are admonished to be examples to their children, realizing that their children are also their spirit brothers and sisters.

AN ENVIRONMENT OF LOVE IS NECESSARY FOR REARING CHILDREN. The spirit of a righteous home is love. The Lord said, "Thou shalt live together in love" (D&C 42:45)—love of heavenly parents, the Lord Jesus Christ, and the Holy Ghost; of husband and wife; and of parents for children, children for parents, and siblings for each other.

MAKING ONE'S HOME A PLACE OF PEACE AND JOY TAKES EFFORT. The effort that goes into making a peaceful home requires consistent planning, prayer, and cooperation. The Church encourages families to hold weekly FAMILY HOME EVENINGS, in which all members of the family study eternal gospel principles and ordinances and do things together that bring them joy. Two Church Presidents have stated, "The most important of the Lord's work [you] will ever do will be the work you do within the walls of your own homes" (Lee, p. 7), and "No other success can compensate for failure in the home" (McKay, p. iii).

WORTHY FAMILY MEMBERS LOOK FORWARD WITH FAITH AND HOPE TO ETERNAL FAMILY RELATIONSHIPS. Earthly families expect to live again as extended families with ancestors and descendants who have died. They become those "who received the testimony of Jesus, and believed on his name, . . . and are sealed by the Holy Spirit of promise, which the Father sheds forth upon all those who are just and true" (D&C 76:51, 53).

THE RIGHTEOUS ARE BLESSED. All righteous individuals, who maintain personal worthiness, love, and faithfulness, are promised the riches of eternity, which include the eventual blessings of being sealed to other family members who also qualify for celestial blessings.

BIBLIOGRAPHY

Benson, Ezra Taft. *God, Family, Country: Our Three Great Loyalties*, pp. 167–273. Salt Lake City, 1974.

Kimball, Spencer W. *The Teachings of Spencer W. Kimball*, ed. Edward L. Kimball. Salt Lake City, 1982.

Lee, Harold B. *Strengthening the Home* (pamphlet). Salt Lake City, 1973.

McConkie, Oscar W., Jr. "LDS Concept of the Family." *Journal of the Collegium Aesculapium* 2 (July 1984):46–51.

McKay, David O. *Family Home Evening Manual*. Salt Lake City, 1965.

White, O. Kendall, Jr. "Ideology of the Family in Nineteenth-Century Mormonism." *Sociological Spectrum* 6 (1986):289–306.

REED H. BRADFORD

FAMILY LIFE

FAMILY DEMOGRAPHICS.   The inherent emphasis on family in Latter-day Saint theology is expressed in demographic patterns that are different for Mormons compared to the general population. First, Mormon fertility rates have consistently been higher than national averages. Utah has traditionally had the highest fertility rate of any state in the Union due to the high percentage of Latter-day Saints in the state (approximately 70 percent).

Research shows that the larger than average family size among Latter-day Saints is not due to their reluctance to use various methods of birth control. Heaton and Calkins' research (1983) shows that in a national sample they are just as likely to use modern birth control methods as are the rest of the nation. But for Latter-day Saints, contraceptives often are not used until after child rearing has occurred and is used less frequently so that the desired larger family size can be obtained. Heaton concludes that the larger family size for Latter-day Saints is associated with beliefs of LDS parents regarding the value of having children, involvement with an LDS reference group, and socialization in a context which favors having children (1988, p. 112).

In the general population, as family size increases, so does coercive discipline. Affectional family relationships decrease. But research among Latter-day Saints shows an opposite pattern, with larger families reporting increased affectional relations (Thomas, 1983, p. 274).

Latter-day Saints consistently report lower than national average rates of premarital sexual experience, teenage pregnancy, and extramarital sexual experience (Heaton, 1988). Yet, research reported by Smith (1976) shows that inactive Mormons were changing toward more liberal sexual attitudes and behavior during the 1970s, even while active Latter-day Saints showed no movement toward more liberal attitudes or behavior. The percentages reporting no present premarital sexual activity by active Latter-day Saints actually increased between 1950 and 1972, from 95 percent to 98 percent for men and from 96 percent to 98 percent for women (pp. 79–81).

Current data show that a higher percent of Latter-day Saints will marry than does the general population. They will also marry younger, have a lower divorce rate, and remarry after divorce at a higher rate than is found in the general population (Heaton, 1988, pp. 110–11).

With respect to divorce, it is clear that the most religiously committed Latter-day Saints have divorce rates considerably lower than the inactive or noncommitted Church members, even though Utah is one of the mountain and western states which have generally had higher than national average divorce rates (Thomas, 1983, p. 277). Heaton and Goodman's research (1985) shows that of Latter-day Saints attending church regularly, 10 percent of men and 15 percent of women report divorce, compared to 21 percent of men and 26 percent of women who do not attend regularly. Also, among men with temple marriages, 5.4 percent reported divorce compared to 27.8 percent of the nontemple group. For women with temple marriages, 6.5 were divorced while 32.7 percent were divorced in nontemple marriages.

FAMILY ROLES AND THE CHURCH.   With the emphasis upon family found within all of the organizations of the Church, from Primary to priesthood quorums, the husband and wife become the main points of contact between family and Church. The wife's involvement with the Church will most likely emerge through Primary and Relief Society activities. The husband's contact with the Church can emerge through almost any organization with the exception of the Relief Society, which is limited to women.

Since the Church is organized around a lay male priesthood, more positions of leadership are occupied by husbands than by wives. In addition, the reorganization of Church procedures and functions begun under the general heading of "priesthood correlation" reemphasized the role of the father in conducting family councils, which were seen as part of the councils designed to govern the Church extending all the way to the council of the First Presidency. The family is seen as the most basic unit of the Church, and all Church programs are designed to strengthen the family.

Given the role of the priesthood in LDS Church government, as well as the teachings about the family, Latter-day Saints have been seen generally as encouraging traditional division of labor along gender lines within families, while at the same time emphasizing the authority of the father through priesthood lines. When researchers have asked about who should perform various functions within the family, Latter-day Saints have tended to score high on measures of traditional beliefs regarding who *ought* to do what in a family (Brinkerhoff and MacKie, 1988). However, in research that asks husbands and wives what they actually do in decision making within the family or how they carry out various duties (that traditionally were seen as belonging to either the husband or the wife), Latter-day Saints have consistently emerged as high on egalitarian measures (Thomas, 1983; Brinkerhoff and MacKie, 1983, 1988). These somewhat paradoxical patterns have not been adequately explained. A common explanation, namely that egalitarian pressures from the larger society is changing the behavior of LDS husbands and wives, is not a convincing one, in light of these recent research findings. Wuthnow advises those who study religious influence to keep a healthy skepticism toward any description of religion "as a force in the service of social conservatism" (1973, p. 128). His advice seems especially relevant to this issue with LDS attitudes and beliefs.

In addition, while the Latter-day Saint father is given responsibility to lead the family, he is expected to do so in a manner which helps every family member grow and develop. LDS beliefs also emphasize the egalitarian nature of men-women relationships. LDS doctrine teaches that there is a Mother in Heaven as well as a Father, that Eve's eating of the forbidden fruit furthered God's plan of salvation, that women must perform certain essential priesthood ordinances in the temple, and that the highest order of the priesthood and the complete blessings of exaltation are available only to the married couple; neither can enter exaltation without the other.

This egalitarian relationship between men and women is symbolized in the LDS portrayal of relationships between Adam and Eve after their expulsion from the Garden of Eden. The two must earn their bread by the sweat of their brows and "Eve did labor with him" (Moses 5:1). They are both commanded to offer sacrifices, and they teach their children all these things (Moses 5:5, 12). Eve along with Adam mourns for the wickedness of their children, and they seek the Lord in prayer together (Moses 5:13–16). After receiving information from God, Eve in turn instructs Adam about some basic points of the gospel (Moses 5:11).

Another egalitarian emphasis emerges in temple ceremonies and ordinances. Without women performing sacred priesthood ordinances in the temple, the highest saving ordinances performed on earth by men and women could not be completed. This is symbolic of men-women relationships generally. Alone they remain incomplete while united man and woman develop their highest divine potential.

PARENTAL BELIEFS AND FAMILY BEHAVIOR. Family commitment is deemed crucial for both husbands and wives, although the wife typically bears the greater responsibility for management of the home and the nurturing of the children. Thomas (1988) studied a sample of LDS parents and documented that the degree to which husbands and wives shared in their child-rearing duties was the second strongest influence on marital satisfaction. More recent research (Thomas and Cornwall, 1990) has documented that it is the wife's marital satisfaction that is highly correlated with shared child-rearing, while the husband's marital satisfaction is unrelated to shared child rearing. This finding corroborates a long-standing general pattern in family research which shows that what happens in family life is more central to a wife's definition of satisfaction than a husband's. It also points to the need for LDS husbands to realize that their increased involvement in child care will be one of the best contributions they can make to their wife's marital satisfaction. Also, those families that score high on the measure of home religious observance (FAMILY PRAYER, scripture reading, and family council) also report the highest amount of shared child-rearing.

In related findings, whether the couple had been married in the temple was the best indicator of whether the family would carry out their home religious observance. These data support the conclusion that temple marriage is related to family behaviors which include more home religious activities, increased husband involvement in shared child-rearing activities, and thus increased marital satisfaction.

The emphasis among Latter-day Saints on family often can lead to greater involvement with members of the extended family. The Church encourages families to organize across generations to foster FAMILY HISTORY and genealogical work deemed essential to the family's well-being in eternity. Such work is often discussed at family reunions. However, there is not good comparative research available to know to what degree LDS families are different from or similar to other families on extended family interaction.

THE CHURCH AND FAMILY FUNCTIONING.   These demographic realities mean that generally LDS families are larger, are more likely to avoid divorce, are characterized by religious commitment and activities centered around child-rearing, and require great financial resources. In addition to providing financially for the family, running the household, and rearing children, adults usually have one or more Church callings that may involve extensive time in service to others. And, since the number of LDS women who are employed outside the home is virtually equal to the national average in the United States (see Mason, p. 103; Heaton, 1986, p. 184, 190), making home a first priority is a genuine challenge. As children grow, parents are encouraged to include them in doing household tasks, with the goal that the resulting skills and attitudes which they develop can contribute to the quality of family life, as well as prepare them for confidence and competence in the world external to the family. Church leaders are encouraged to minimize the time they and other members spend in their callings and to safeguard family time from constant intruding influences.

Sometimes the focus of Church activities on the two-parent family belies the truth that not all members are in a stage of life where they can rear children with a committed mate. Those who never married, are divorced, are widowed, are single parents, or are married to non-Latter-day Saints are always in LDS wards and, ideally, they are included in the community of Saints. Priesthood quorums and the Relief Society are charged both to integrate such families into ward activities as well as provide for special needs. And, when members of any family become involved in such activities as drug abuse, divorce, or family violence, the Church intends that leaders provide a network of emotional support, prevention, and rehabilitation.

BIBLIOGRAPHY

Bahr, Howard M.; S. J. Condie; and K. L. Goodman. *Life in Large Families.* Washington, D.C., 1982.

Brinkerhoff, Merlin B., and Marlene MacKie. "Religious Sources of Gender Traditionalism." In *The Religion and Family Connection: Social Science Perspectives*, ed. D. Thomas, pp. 232–57. Provo, Utah, 1988.

Heaton, Tim B. "The Demography of Utah Mormons." In *Utah in Demographic Perspective*, ed. T. Martin; T. Heaton; and S. Bahr, pp. 181–93. Salt Lake City, 1986.

———. "Four C's of the Mormon Family: Chastity, Conjugality, Children, and

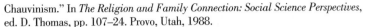

Chauvinism." In *The Religion and Family Connection: Social Science Perspectives*, ed. D. Thomas, pp. 107–24. Provo, Utah, 1988.

———, and S. Calkins. "Family Size and Contraceptive Use among Mormons: 1965–75." *Review of Religious Research* 25, no. 2 (1983):103–14.

———, and Kristen L. Goodman. "Religions and Family Formation." *Review of Religious Research* 26, no. 4 (1985):343–59.

Lee, Harold B. *Strengthening the Home*. Salt Lake City, 1973, (pamphlet).

Mason, Jerry. "Family Economics." In *Utah in Demographic Perspective*, ed. T. Martin; T. Heaton; and S. Bahr, pp. 91–109. Salt Lake City, Utah, 1986.

Smith, W. E. "Mormon Sex Standards on College Campuses, or Deal Us Out of the Sexual Revolution." *Dialogue* 10, no. 2 (1976):76–81.

Thomas, Darwin L. "Future Prospects for Religion and Family Studies: the Mormon Case." In *The Religion and Family Connection: Social Science Perspectives*, ed. D. Thomas, pp. 357–82. Provo, Utah, 1988.

———. "Family in the Mormon Experience." In *Families and Religions: Conflict and Change in Modern Society*, ed. W. D'Antonio, and J. Aldous, pp. 267–88. Beverly Hills, Calif., 1983.

———, and Marie Cornwall. "The Religion and Family Interface: Theoretical and Empirical Explorations." Paper presented at the XII World Congress of Sociology, International Sociological Assn., Madrid, Spain, July, 13, 1990.

Wuthnow, R. "Religious Commitment and Conservatism: In Search of an Elusive Relationship." In *Religion in Sociological Perspective*, ed. C. Glock. Belmont, Calif., 1973.

DARWIN L. THOMAS

FAMILY HISTORY CENTERS

Family History Centers are extensions of the FAMILY HISTORY LIBRARY in Salt Lake City, Utah. The first center opened in 1964. Originally, they were known as branch genealogical libraries. When the Genealogical Library became the Family History Library in 1987, the branches became Family History Centers. In 1990 there were over 1,500 such centers in 49 countries.

Located most often in LDS stake centers, Family History Centers are open to the public, generally twenty hours per week, staffed entirely by volunteers. There is no charge, but space is often limited. At a Family History Center, researchers have access to the Family History Library's microfilm copies of family history records, which can be lent to the center for a specified time. Many local centers also have significant collections of genealogical source material on microfiche, and some have their own collections of research materials specific to their area.

At a Family History Center, patrons find many of the same research tools that are available at the central Family History Library, including microfiche editions of the Family History Library Catalog, the INTERNATIONAL GENEALOGICAL INDEX™ (IGI), the FAMILY REGISTRY™, and a series of instructional handouts that describe how to do research in the United States and many other countries. Many centers also provide access to FAMILYSEARCH™, a computer system that organizes data and simplifies the task of family history research.

Addresses of worldwide Family History Centers are available from the Family History Library.

V. BEN BLOXHAM

FAMILY HISTORY, GENEALOGY

The terms "family history" and "genealogy" are synonymous for Latter-day Saints. Dallin H. Oaks, a member of the Quorum of Twelve Apostles, said, "The process by which we identify our place in our eternal family is called genealogy. Genealogy is family history" (Regional Representatives Seminar, April 3, 1987). To emphasize the family nature of genealogy, the First Presidency in 1987 changed the name of the Genealogical Department to the Family History Department and the name of the Genealogical Library to the FAMILY HISTORY LIBRARY.

LDS interest in family history is based on the fundamental doctrines of salvation, agency, and exaltation. It is the plan of God that all persons shall have the opportunity to hear the gospel of Jesus Christ and receive the saving ordinances, regardless of when they lived on earth. If they do not hear the gospel preached through the Lord's authorized servants in this life, they will hear it in the spirit world after death. Latter-day Saints identify their ancestors and arrange for baptism and other ordinances to be performed by proxy— that is, with a living person standing in for the deceased person—in a temple. This is not an optional function of LDS belief; it is, rather, a commandment of God. As Elder Oaks further explained, "We are not hobbyists in genealogy work. We do family history work in order to provide the ordinances of salvation for the living and the dead" (1989, p. 6).

Members of the Church were instructed in the sacred role of family history work in 1894, when President Wilford Woodruff declared, "We want the Latter day Saints from this time to trace their genealogies as far as they can, and to be sealed to their fathers and mothers. Have children sealed to their parents, and run this chain through as far as you can get it. . . . This is the will of the Lord to this people" (p. 543). The purpose of family history, President Woodruff explained, is to obtain names and statistical data so that temple ordinances can be performed in behalf of deceased ancestors who did not have the opportunity to hear the restored gospel during mortal life. He taught on another occasion that "we have got to enter into those temples and redeem our dead—not only the dead of our own family, but the dead of the whole spirit world" (*JD* 21:192).

Fundamental to the doctrine of the salvation of the dead is the exercise of agency. When persons die, their spirits continue living in the postmortal spirit world and are capable of making choices. Latter-day Saints perform baptisms for the dead so that those who live as spirits may choose whether or not to accept baptism in the true Church of Jesus Christ in the spirit world. If they do not accept the baptism, it is of no effect. The same is true of the other saving ordinances that members perform in the temples in behalf of the dead.

Love is the central motivation for family history work. Identifying ancestors and performing saving ordinances for them are an expression of love. It is the spirit and power of Elijah, who gave the keys of this power to Joseph Smith in the Kirtland Temple in 1836, to "turn the hearts of the fathers to the children, and the children to the fathers" (D&C 110:15; see also Mal. 4:5–6; JS—H 1:39; D&C 2:2). The desire to discover one's ancestors and complete temple ordinances for them is sometimes referred to as the Spirit of Elijah. President Joseph Fielding Smith associated family history and temple work with love for mankind, declaring that laboring on behalf of the dead is "a work that enlarges the soul of man, broadens his views regarding the welfare of his fellowman, and plants in his heart a love for all the children of our Heavenly Father. There is no work equal to that in the temple for the dead in teaching a man to love his neighbor as himself" (p. 3).

In response to President Woodruff's teaching regarding family history responsibilities, Latter-day Saints organized the GENEALOGICAL

SOCIETY OF UTAH in Salt Lake City in 1894. Over the years, the society, through the Family History Library and its worldwide network of more than 1,500 family history centers, has become a major support of the Church's efforts to provide instruction in family history through research information (first in book form and later in microfilm and then in compact disc) and through making available a skilled staff to assist researchers to identify their ancestors.

Interest in family history is not limited to Latter-day Saints. There has been remarkable growth of interest in genealogy and family history dating from about 1836, when Elijah committed the keys to the Prophet Joseph Smith. In many countries, thousands of people have joined genealogical and historical societies, and more than half of the patrons of the Family History Library and its associated Family History Centers are members of other faiths. The Church has joined in cooperative efforts with hundreds of genealogical and family history societies, archives, and libraries in identifying family history records and preserving the information found in them (*see* WORLD CONFERENCES ON RECORDS).

Modern technology has played a significant role in the advance of family history in the second half of the twentieth century. The Church has developed an extensive worldwide microfilming program. Since 1938, it has done microfilming in more than a hundred countries, and has accumulated more than 1.3 billion exposures with approximately 8 billion names. Microfilm records have provided the basis for dramatic expansion of family history research. They have enabled rapid growth of the collections of the Family History Library and has made possible both the distribution of family history information to the Church's Family History Centers and the NAME EXTRACTION PROGRAMS that have allowed the extensive automation of family history information contained in the FAMILYSEARCH™ computer system.

As a result, doing family history research has never been easier than it now is. Through FamilySearch, patrons of the Family History Library and Family History Centers have access to the 147 million names in the INTERNATIONAL GENEALOGICAL INDEX™ and the growing 9.67–million-name lineage-linked ANCESTRAL FILE™. As name extraction programs convert information from paper records (such as the 1880 U.S. Federal Census and the 1881 British Census) and as people from around the world contribute information to the Ancestral File, the computer resources associated with FamilySearch will make identifying one's ancestors a much simpler task.

The Church teaches that members' family history duties are threefold. First, they must develop a desire to help redeem the dead. As members gain a testimony of the principle of salvation of the dead, they feel a personal responsibility to help. They also care about those in the spirit world who are waiting for temple ordinances to be performed.

Second, they must determine what to do. Every Latter-day Saint can do something to further the family history work. Dallin H. Oaks counseled, "Our effort is not to compel everyone to do everything, but to encourage everyone to do something" (1989, p. 6). Accordingly, Latter-day Saints are encouraged to participate in activities relating to the salvation of the dead. What and how much a member does depend on personal circumstances and abilities, what one's family may have already accomplished, individual guidance from the Spirit, and direction from Church leaders. Activities include identifying one's ancestors and performing temple ordinances for them, participating in family organizations, serving in the Name Extraction Program, keeping a personal journal, preparing personal and family histories, and accepting Church callings in temple and family history service. Identifying ancestors of the first few generations usually does not require extensive library research or sophisticated research tools. The beginning of family history research usually involves checking known family records (*see* JOURNALS), consulting family members either orally or by letter, and looking at readily available public records, such as birth certificates. Identifying ancestors beyond the first few generations usually requires the resources of libraries, computer tools available with systems like FamilySearch, and expert help. Family organizations enable members to pool information and resources to further the family history work. The Name Extraction Program enables persons to convert information found on microfilm copies of paper records—parish registers, census rolls, and so forth—to a computer format to become part of FamilySearch files or to supply needed names to the temples.

Third, members must continue to serve. The work of the Family

History Department will not be complete until every name is recorded and every ordinance performed.

BIBLIOGRAPHY

Come unto Christ Through Temple Ordinances and Covenants, 2nd ed. Salt Lake City, 1988.

Greenwood, Val D. *The Researcher's Guide to American Genealogy*, 2nd ed. Baltimore, 1990.

Instructions for Priesthood Leaders on Temple and Family History Work. Salt Lake City, 1990.

Oaks, Dallin H. "Family History: 'In Wisdom and Order'." *Ensign* 19 (June 1989):6–8.

Smith, Joseph Fielding. *Church News* (Oct. 24, 1970):3.

Woodruff, Wilford. *Deseret Weekly* (April 21, 1894):543.

DAVID H. PRATT

FAMILY HISTORY LIBRARY

The Family History Library in Salt Lake City supports the LDS practice of family history research that identifies forebears and makes possible the temple work leading to salvation of the dead. It provides services and resources that enable Latter-day Saints and others to identify and learn more about their ancestors. It is also a developmental center where new resources and programs are perfected and made available to Church members worldwide through FAMILY HISTORY CENTERS.

On November 13, 1894, the GENEALOGICAL SOCIETY OF UTAH was organized. One of its purposes was the "establishing and maintaining [of] a genealogical library for the use and benefit of its members and others" (Minutes of the Genealogical Society of Utah, Nov. 13, 1894). From its modest beginnings in an upstairs room of the Church Historian's Office with about 300 books, the collection has grown and its facilities have changed commensurately, so that in 1990 the library occupied a modern five-story building which housed 200,000 books, 300,000 microfiches, and more than 1.6 million rolls of microfilm, making it the largest library of its kind in the world.

During its first fifty years, the library was open only to dues-paying members. In 1944 it was incorporated under the administration of the Church, and its resources were made available to the pub-

lic. In 1989, the library had 813,000 visitors. Genealogists, historians, demographers, geneticists, and other researchers from many
countries travel to Salt Lake City to utilize the wealth of information
available in the library. They are attracted by its collections, the
expertise of the staff, and the nearly 700 classes offered annually in
research sources and methodology.

The biggest attraction is the microfilm collection. Since 1938,
the Genealogical Society of Utah and its successor organization, the
LDS Church Family History Department, have been preserving
copies of original documents on microfilm. In 1990 the library sponsored approximately 200 microfilming projects in various parts of the
world. These efforts have added microfilmed copies of more than 5
million manuscripts to the library's collections. The microfilms show
the original records of births, marriages, and deaths; military records;
censuses; wills; notaries' records; cemetery records; and other kinds
of documents that describe people and families from the past. Other
resources include compiled genealogies, local histories, old maps,
city directories, and name indexes. The largest collections are from
countries in North America and Europe, with substantial collections
from Latin America. The library has also acquired written and oral
materials from Asia, Africa, Australia, and the islands of the Pacific
Ocean.

Computer terminals give patrons access to the FAMILYSEARCH™
system, which guides researchers into the Family History Library
Catalog, the INTERNATIONAL GENEALOGICAL INDEX™ (IGI), and ANCES-
TRAL FILE™. These computer files of family history information are
stored on compact discs. The compact-disc edition of the catalog provides access to books and microfilms that contain original records,
reference sources, and family histories and genealogies.

Library visitors can also learn how to use PERSONAL ANCESTRAL
FILE®. This computer program enables families to manage family history records on their personal computers. In addition, users can easily exchange genealogical information with others who have
compatible computer programs or with Ancestral File.

Another resource is the FAMILY REGISTRY™. This service helps
both individuals and family organizations to share with others information they may have about deceased individuals and to ask for
information about an ancestor who is currently the subject of their

research. Library visitors have access to microfiche records listing the ancestors and family organizations that have been registered. This file eases coordination of research with others who may share the same family lines.

At the Family History Library professional genealogical reference consultants, library attendants, and hundreds of volunteers serve library visitors. They are trained to guide patrons to sources identifying their families and to help them interpret the information in these books and documents. Staff members are multilingual and can read handwriting from many countries and time periods.

BIBLIOGRAPHY

Cerny, Johni, and Wendy Elliott, eds., *The Library: A Guide to the LDS Family History Library.* Salt Lake City, 1988.

Mayfield, David M. "The Genealogical Library of The Church of Jesus Christ of Latter-day Saints." *Library Trends* 32 (Summer 1983):111–27.

RAYMOND S. WRIGHT III

FAMILY HOME EVENING

Family home evening is a weekly observance of Latter-day Saints for spiritual training and social activity, usually held on Monday evenings. In 1915, the First Presidency of the Church wrote: "We advise and urge the inauguration of a 'Home Evening' throughout the Church, at which time fathers and mothers may gather their boys and girls about them in the home and teach them the word of the Lord. . . . This 'Home Evening' should be devoted to prayer, singing hymns, songs, instrumental music, scripture-reading, family topics and specific instruction on the principles of the Gospel, and on the ethical problems of life, as well as the duties and obligation of children to parents, the home, the Church, society, and the Nation" (*IE* 18 [June 1915]:733). To assist parents in their stewardship, the first home evening manual was prepared that same year and distributed to members of the Church.

This emphasis on home gospel instruction echoes the call of prophets throughout the ages who have instructed parents to teach their children diligently of love and to bring them up in the nurture and admonition of the Lord (Deut. 6:5–7; Eph. 6:4). The Prophet

Joseph Smith received revelations that admonish parents to "bring up your children in light and truth" (D&C 93:40) and to teach them "to understand the doctrine of repentance, faith in Christ the Son of the living God, and of baptism and the gift of the Holy Ghost" (D&C 68:25) and "to pray, and to walk uprightly before the Lord" (D&C 68:28). President Brigham Young urged parents to take time to "call their families together . . . and teach them the principles of the gospel" (*MFP* 2:288).

Between 1915 and the 1960s, a large proportion of Church membership shifted from a family-centered rural population to an urban one. With that change came renewed emphasis from the First Presidency on the importance of the family. In general conference, April 1964, President David O. McKay reminded parents that "No other success can compensate for failure in the home" (*IE* 67 [June 1964]:445). In 1965, the weekly family home evening program was more fully implemented, and a lesson manual was given each family to aid parents in teaching their children. Families were encouraged to participate in a home night once each week, which could consist of scripture reading, singing, and activities suited to the ages of the children. In 1966, stakes were urged to set aside a regular night for family home evening and to avoid scheduling Church activities on that night. In 1970, Monday evening was designated as family home evening, Churchwide, with no competing ecclesiastical functions to be held. Revised home evening manuals, with suggested weekly lessons and activities, were provided from 1965 to 1984.

In 1985, a *Family Home Evening Resource Book*, designed to be used for a decade, was introduced. It provided broader resource material for gospel instruction and additional ideas for family activities, and was designed to be adapted for use by single adults, couples, single-parent families, and families with children of all ages. In 1987, a family home evening video supplement was made available. Nineteen video vignettes were included, treating important educational and moral topics.

A typical family home evening might proceed as follows: A parent or older child, whose turn it is to plan the lesson, selects a lesson, such as "Heavenly Father Provided Us a Savior," from the *Family Home Evening Resource Book*. After an opening hymn and prayer, the lesson material, adapted to the needs and interest level of the family members, is presented. After the lesson the family discusses family schedules, family business, and special concerns. A family activity follows that helps strengthen bonds of love among family members. This could be any activity that the family enjoys doing together, such as playing a game, helping the needy, gardening, or attending a cultural event. Following the activity, the family kneels together in family prayer and then often enjoys refreshments. Single adults or others who live alone may join as a group to participate in family home evening activities, or they may observe appropriately modified weekly activities individually. Home evening activities allow for considerable variation in the desires and needs of each family or group. Always, however, the emphasis is spiritual enrichment.

Family home evening is intended to be a regular event that helps parents teach, protect, and prepare children for responsible living. Family councils, personal parent interviews, scripture reading, serving or playing together, family prayer, and meaningful family home evenings all help to build quality family relationships. Families who do these things are promised that "love at home and obedience to parents will increase, and faith will develop in the hearts of the youth of Israel, and they will gain power to combat [the] evil influences and temptations" that beset them (*Family Home Evening Manual*, 1965, p. v).

BIBLIOGRAPHY

Johnson, Sherrie. "Using the New Family Home Evening Resource Book." *Ensign* 14 (Jan. 1984):6–9.

Kimball, Spencer W. "Home: The Place to Save Society." *Ensign* 5 (Jan. 1975):3–10.

Lee, Harold B. "Priesthood Correlation and the Home Evening." *IE* 67 (Dec. 1964):1077–81.

———. "The Home Evening." *IE* 70 (Jan. 1967):22–23.

Lynn, Wayne B. "Better Home Evenings." *Ensign* 20 (June 1990):22–25.

JAMES P. MITCHELL
TERRI TANNER MITCHELL

FAMILY ORGANIZATIONS

Latter-day Saints think of families with respect to both this life and the next. They strive to organize family groups at the individual family level and in extended family relationships and organizations. Family organizations provide social and familial support, historical awareness, instruction, and genealogical information necessary to bind generations together by temple ordinances (*see* FAMILY HISTORY).

From the early days of the Church, LDS families have regularly established family organizations, held reunions, and worked to make strong family identity. In 1978 the Church asked all families to organize themselves at three levels: immediate families, grandparent families, and ancestral families.

The immediate family consists of husband and wife, and begins when they are married. Later, if a couple is blessed with children, the size and concerns of this unit grow. When the children marry and have children of their own, the grandparent organization is initiated. Beyond that, each family is ideally involved in an ancestral organization, which consists of all the descendants of an earlier common progenitor couple.

The immediate family holds FAMILY HOME EVENINGS and family councils, encourages and assists in missionary work, family preparedness, family history, temple work, and teaching the gospel, and provides cultural and social activities for its members. The grandparent organization is involved in similar activities, but is also concerned with family reunions, which include the grandparents' children and grandchildren. The purpose of the ancestral organization is to coordinate genealogical activity on common lines. Such organizations frequently raise money for family history research, publish family histories, and generally direct the activities of the larger family.

Many families use the ancestral organization as a repository of photographs, journals, family histories, and other materials that might be used by family members or general researchers as they prepare their own histories. Some families occasionally have an ancestral family reunion, but more usually they have representatives who meet to coordinate family history and genealogical activities. Some may be organized as nonprofit corporations or trusts that may be recognized as charitable organizations if their purposes are limited to religious activities.

The benefits of a family organization can be significant. One benefit is that involvement with family organizations increases one's sense of identity and heritage. For example, in a recent survey of university students who were LDS, Catholic, Protestant, or of no particular religion, the number of ancestors' names and origins known by the LDS students was significantly higher than for the other groups.

BIBLIOGRAPHY

Benson, Ezra Taft. "Worthy of All Acceptation." *Ensign* 8 (Nov. 1978):30–32.

Jacobson, Cardell K.; Phillip R. Kunz; and Melanie W. Conlin. "Extended Family Ties: Genealogical Researchers." In S. Bahr and E. Peterson, eds., *Aging and the Family*. Lexington, Mass., 1989.

PHILLIP R. KUNZ

FAMILY PRAYER

It is considered a duty and privilege by Latter-day Saint parents to lead their children in regular family prayer. The scriptural basis for this practice is seen in the Book of Mormon. As the Savior was teaching the Nephites, he said, "Pray in your families unto the Father, always in my name, that your wives and your children may be blessed" (3 Ne. 18:21). President Ezra Taft Benson has said, "Family prayer is . . . the means to acknowledge appreciation for blessings and to humbly recognize dependence on Almighty God for strength, sustenance, and support" (*CR* [April 1984] p. 7).

Ideal circumstances find the LDS family kneeling in prayer twice daily, morning and evening. As family members grow older and engage in an increasing variety of activities, finding a convenient time for all members to be present for group prayer is often difficult. Some never meet the challenge, whereas others hold prayer and scripture study early in the morning when they are less likely to be interrupted. Another common time for group prayer is just before breakfast and dinner.

Family prayer affords the opportunity for both children and parents to lead in prayer, one at one family prayer and another at the next. Most prayers thank the Lord for blessings received and on behalf of the family petition for desired blessings. Challenges facing family members and friends are often placed before Father in Heaven in united supplication. Specific concerns for the well-being of each family member can be enumerated. Sometimes the family fasts and joins in family prayer on behalf of family members, friends, neighbors, or others who are ill or in special need of the Lord's blessings.

Family prayer allows individuals and families to focus attention and affection on God. It builds faith and loyalty within the family and epitomizes Christ-centered family worship. Family prayer affords the opportunity to offer praise to God and gratitude for daily blessings as well as for the Savior's mission, example, and love. Church members believe that the benefits of daily family prayer include family unity, strength in the Lord, freeing the heart of evil inclinations, tender moments of divine communication, and an understanding of God's relationship to his children.

Many members who live alone participate in a family prayer experience by choosing to pray aloud for family members and others. They may also join family home evening groups or other friends and associates for regular group prayer.

BIBLIOGRAPHY

Groberg, John H. "The Power of Family Prayer." *Ensign* 12 (May 1982):50–52.
Hinckley, Gordon B. "The Force of Family Prayer." *IE* 66 (June 1963):528–32.
Kimball, Spencer W. "Family Prayer." In *Prayer*, pp. 84–87. Salt Lake City, 1977.
Perry, L. Tom. "Our Father Which Art in Heaven." *Ensign* 13 (Nov. 1983):11–13.

BRUCE L. OLSEN

FAMILY REGISTRY™

Family Registry is a service provided by the Family History Department of The Church of Jesus Christ of Latter-day Saints to help people who are doing research on the same family lines to cooperate with one another and share results, thus avoiding unnecessary duplication of effort and expense. This service provides a way for individuals and family organizations to ask for information about an ancestor who is currently the subject of their research or to share with others information they may have about deceased individuals.

The Family Registry has an alphabetical list of the surnames being researched, together with the names and addresses of persons who have registered. The index is updated periodically and published on microfiche. The January 1990 edition contained 287,000 names. Those who register are expected to respond to others who wish to coordinate research efforts. The Family Registry index can be personally searched by anyone at the FAMILY HISTORY LIBRARY in Salt Lake City, Utah, or at more than 1,500 FAMILY HISTORY CENTERS or other libraries that participate in offering this service. There is no charge for registration or for searching the index.

BIBLIOGRAPHY

"A New Tool for Genealogists." *Church News* (Dec. 18, 1983):12.

Nichols, Elizabeth L. "The Family Registry." *Genealogy Digest* 16 (Summer 1985):26–31.

JOHN C. JARMAN

FAMILYSEARCH™

FamilySearch™ is an automated computer system that simplifies the task of family history research. The FamilySearch system includes search-and-retrieval programs designed to work on personal computers and computer files of family history information. FamilySearch was developed by the Family History Department of The Church of Jesus Christ of Latter-day Saints.

The information in each file is distributed on compact discs, each capable of storing the equivalent of about 320,000 pages of text. They are read by computers equipped with a compact-disc player and with the FamilySearch software.

FamilySearch is available to the public at the FAMILY HISTORY LIBRARY in Salt Lake City and over time will be distributed to FAMILY HISTORY CENTERS affiliated with the library.

FamilySearch's primary purpose is to help members of the Church identify their ancestors and complete temple ordinances for them. The power of the program, together with the large files available to it, make FamilySearch a valuable research tool.

When the system was introduced in 1990, it included the following files:

1. The Family History Library Catalog, which has been available for many years in a microfiche edition in the Family History Library in Salt Lake City and in family history centers, describes the

collection of the library and provides help in locating the book, microfilm, or other research tool a patron may need. The automated edition simplifies use of the catalog.

2. The INTERNATIONAL GENEALOGICAL INDEX™ (IGI), which has been available for many years in a microfiche edition. The automated edition gives information about deceased persons for whom temple ordinances have been performed. It also lists birth, christening, and marriage dates and temple ordinance information.

3. Ancestral File™ is a family-linked file containing genealogies contributed by members of the Church since 1979. Many other genealogies have also been included, and additional contributions of family history information are welcomed.

Other files will be added to FamilySearch as they become available.

BIBLIOGRAPHY
"FamilySearch™ Software," Attachment, First Presidency Letter, April 2, 1990.
Mayfield, David M., and A. Gregory Brown. "FamilySearch." *Genealogical Computing* 10 (1990):1.

L. REYNOLDS CAHOON

FATHERHOOD

LDS fathers have primary responsibility for providing spiritual and physical support for all other family members (D&C 68:25, 28; 75:28). Giving Christlike service as a husband and father is the most important work a man can perform during mortality. Far more than mere procreation, fatherhood entails the lifelong care of children and loving support of their mother. Elder Theodore Tuttle wrote that for husbands to be effective fathers they should strive to learn and express those attributes they understand Heavenly Father to possess (pp. 66–68).

Latter-day Saints view parenthood as the highest and most sacred calling from God to his children on earth. Mothers and fathers are taught to labor together in faith and love to bring children into the world, to care for them, and to teach them the gospel of Jesus Christ so that they may receive eternal life, thus as parents following the example of their Father and Mother in Heaven (D&C 93:40). Through sacred covenants with God and with each other, men and women establish in this life families that have the potential to endure forever.

Fatherhood is best represented in men who unselfishly cherish and befriend their wives and promote their children's happiness and righteousness. This includes nurturing and expressing love, establishing obedience of their children through firmness and warmth, and teaching the gospel in home and Church settings. Fathers are also encouraged to lead by example (Benson, 1985).

Boys and men are taught the characteristics that exemplify loving and responsible fathers. As part of the Primary organization curricula, songs and lessons teach children to admire their fathers and to associate manhood and fatherhood with the characteristics of Christ. As members of a priesthood quorum, young men are taught self-reliance, self-mastery, achievement, honor and respect for women, and chastity. Youth activities, Church sermons, and family programs also emphasize the importance of service to and sacrifice for others as part of fatherhood. Adult men are exposed to continuing emphasis on fatherhood. Formal instruction in Melchizedek Priesthood quorums is often aimed at motivating and inspiring men to esteem women as fellow children of the Father of all human beings, to observe strict marital fidelity, to give appropriate emphasis to the needs of children, and to learn skills that promote happy and successful lives for all family members.

Men in leadership positions are admonished not to neglect their family duties. When necessary, men may be released from demanding Church positions in order to give appropriate time to their families. Fathers are taught to spend time with their families; to bring the family together in frequent prayer, scripture study, and family meetings; and to teach children to keep God's commandments, to work, and to respect others (Mosiah 4:14–15; 3 Ne. 18:21).

[*See also* Fathers' Blessings; Lifestyle; Marriage; Motherhood.]

BIBLIOGRAPHY
Benson, Ezra Taft. "Worthy Fathers, Worthy Sons." *Ensign* 15 (Nov. 1985):35–37.
Father, Consider Your Ways (pamphlet). Salt Lake City, 1978.
Perry, L. Tom. "Train Up a Child." *Ensign* 18 (Nov. 1988):73–75.
"The Role of the Father in the Home." In *Seek to Obtain My Word: Melchizedek Priesthood Personal Study Guide 1989*, pp. 199–204. Salt Lake City, 1988.
Tanner, N. Eldon. "Fatherhood." *Ensign* 7 (June 1977):2–5.
Tuttle, A. Theodore. "The Role of Fathers." *Ensign* 4 (Jan. 1974):66–68.

A. LYNN SCORESBY

FATHERS' BLESSINGS

Fathers' blessings are given by the power of the Melchizedek Priesthood following the pattern of the ancient patriarchs, such as Adam, Noah, Abraham, Isaac, Jacob, Lehi, Mosiah, Alma$_2$, and Mormon. All gave blessings to their children. Adam's final blessing upon several of his descendants is described in Doctrine and Covenants 107:53–57. So significant was the ordinance on that occasion that "the Lord appeared unto them, and they rose up and blessed Adam" (*TPJS*, p. 38).

For the earthly blessing to be honored in heaven, it is necessary that a father has been baptized, has received the Holy Ghost, and bears the Melchizedek Priesthood. Through these ordinances and covenants, the father may claim the powers of heaven to guide his thoughts and ratify his words. To give such a blessing, the father places his hands upon the head of his child, and assures the child by word and spirit that the blessing, spoken by a loving parent, comes with divine approval and inspiration.

The father may give blessings when requested by his wife or children or when he feels their need. He does not force a blessing on anyone, for that would conflict both with the law of agency and the spirit of love. There is no ideal frequency for such blessings, only as the needs of the person and the whisperings of the Spirit suggest. A father will find performing this sacred ordinance easier if his relationships with his children are gentle and kind. If there is a conflict between father and child, it may be necessary to reconcile it before attempting the blessing.

A father's blessing is both an ordinance authorized by God and an action that draws father and child together even as it reassures a mother, who sees her husband spiritually minister to their child. It is a symbolic and official godlike act of pure love.

BIBLIOGRAPHY

"Fathers Blessings and Patriarchal Blessings." *Melchizedek Priesthood Personal Study Guide*, p. 43. Salt Lake City, 1988.

VICTOR L. BROWN, JR.

FEMINISM

Feminism is the philosophical belief that advocates the equality of women and men and seeks to remove inequities and to redress injustices against women. Far from a monolithic ideology, feminist theory embraces a variety of views on the nature of women and argues for a pluralistic vision of the world that regards as equally important the experiences of women of all races and classes.

In the United States, "feminism" has been an umbrella term encompassing a coalition of those women and men who share a devotion to the cause of women's rights but who often differ on specific goals and tactics. Personal, religious, and political values all influence which reforms and measures a specific feminist will support.

The doctrine of The Church of Jesus Christ of Latter-day Saints converges in some areas with the ideals of feminism and diverges in others. It insists on the absolute spiritual equality of women and men, proclaiming that "all are alike unto God," both "black and white, bond and free, male and female" (2 Ne. 26:33; Gal. 3:28). Gifts of the Spirit are given equally to men and women: "And now, he imparteth his word by angels unto men, yea, not only men but women also" (Alma 32:23). LDS principles argue unequivocally for the development of the full potential of each person, regardless of gender.

So central is the equality of all humankind to Christ's message that during his earthly ministry Christ openly rejected cultural proscriptions that relegated women to an inferior spiritual and political status. He recognized women's spirits and intellects; he taught them directly (Luke 10:38–42); he identified himself as the Messiah to a woman, the first such affirmation recorded in the New Testament (John 4:26); he healed women (Matt. 15:22–28) and raised a woman from the dead (Luke 8:49–56). After his resurrection, he appeared first to a woman, whom he asked to tell his apostles of the glorious event (John 20:11–18), although according to Jewish law women were not considered competent as legal witnesses.

Such equality of women and men is based on the celestial model of heavenly parents, both Father and Mother, who share "all power" and have "all things . . . subject unto them" (D&C 132:20) and who invite their children to emulate their example of perfect love and unity and become as they are. Mormons are taught that righteous power, held by heavenly parents and shared with their children, is never coercive but is characterized "by persuasion, by long-suffering, by gentleness and meekness, and by love unfeigned" (D&C 121:41). While the implications of these expansive beliefs are always subject to individual implementation, Mormon women and men have found in these doctrines sources of spiritual strength, including the desire to know more about Mother in Heaven.

LDS doctrine is, however, at odds with several versions of feminism, including those that emphasize female sufficiency apart from men. Because Church doctrine stresses the necessity of overcoming differences and forging a celestial unity between husband and wife in order to achieve exaltation (cf. 1 Cor. 11:11), the radical feminist critique of the family as an institution of repression for women and the call for its replacement find little support among Latter-day Saints. While individual families may be repressive and dysfunctional, most Latter-day Saints believe that the defect is not inherent in the structure. Indeed, the family is viewed as the source of both men's and women's greatest work and joy, not only on earth but also in eternity.

BIBLIOGRAPHY

Beecher, Maureen Ursenbach, and Lavina Fielding Anderson, eds. *Sisters in Spirit: Mormon Women in Historical and Cultural Perspective.* Urbana, Ill., 1987.

Dialogue 6 (Summer 1971) and 14 (Winter 1981). Both issues have a number of essays on women in the Church.

Donovan, Josephine. *Feminist Theory: The Intellectual Traditions of American Feminism.* New York, 1985.

MARY STOVALL RICHARDS

FINE ARTS

[*Historically, the fine arts have been important to Latter-day Saints, who have encouraged participation in, and provided support for, art, dance, drama, literature, music, and public speaking. For articles about LDS fine arts, see* Architecture; Art; Artists, Visual; Christus Statue; Folk Art; Material Culture; Sculptors; *and* Symbols. *On dance, see* Dance. *On drama, see* Cumorah Pageant; Drama;

Pageants; *and* Polynesian Cultural Center. *On literature, see the entry* Literature *with articles on* Drama, Novels, Personal Essays, Poetry, *and* Short Stories. *On music, see* Hymns and Hymnody; Mormon Tabernacle Choir; *and* Mormon Youth Symphony and Chorus.]

FOLK ART

Through a combination of religious and western American metaphors and images, the whole saga of the Church has been artistically represented, from its origins in 1820 in a grove near Palmyra, New York, to the present. Songs and stories about the migration to Utah and the colonization of the Great Basin, anecdotal biographies of Church leaders, folklore incidents of faith, and the miraculous and sometimes comical struggles of the pioneer Saints form integral parts of LDS culture (*see* ART IN MORMONISM). Mormon folk art perpetuates a sense of inclusiveness and serves to bind Latter-day Saints together and help define who they are. Overwhelmingly, Mormon folk art has been the work of a faithful, pragmatic people.

For Latter-day Saint artists, the migration west was "the worst of times and the best of times." Driven from Nauvoo, they faced the prospect of building a new Zion, a home in the mountains. Their folk art is richly expressive of connections to their past and of their unique experience on the frontier. When one pioneer woman, Bathsheba Smith, packed her trunk for the journey into western territory, she carefully selected what to take and what to leave behind. Deep in the corner of her single trunk she placed her paints, paper, and brushes wrapped in cloth. She added her lace-making tools and fibers to make the beautiful delicate lace for which she was famous. These tools of art she placed beneath the folds of a quilt made by her mother for her wedding day.

In a concrete sense, Bathsheba Smith was blending the old and the new by preserving the past and welcoming the future. When she once again took up her paints, this time in Utah, she would paint the story of the journey. Pioneer artist C. C. A. Christensen would do likewise, chronicling a story that would figure prominently in the folk art of the Mormon people. William Clayton would immortalize the faith of the pioneers in the words of a hymn: "Come, come, ye Saints, no toil nor labor fear; but with joy wend your way."

Mormon folk art was practical—functional, yet often beautiful and decorative. The imagery of the LDS pioneer quilt reflected a western preoccupation with the natural environment. Pine trees, oaks, and mountain laurels had always been favored quilt motifs, but new images, notably the sego lily and the beehive, told of the work of the Mormon pioneers in Deseret.

The beehive appears in every genre of Mormon folk art—quilts, paintings, sculptures, architecture, and gravestones. The stonework of nineteenth-century Mormon culture is a rich statement of popular values, legends, and religion. A strong visual connection exists between pioneer gravestone imagery and New England tombstone art. But the cemeteries of small towns throughout Utah speak also of the unique LDS belief system and pioneer heritage. In addition to traditional motifs, religious emblems associated with the outside of temples flourished in this lively local art form.

One need not travel far into rural Utah to notice the distinctive folk architecture that existed among the Saints. The most common design was the "I" house, or old "Nauvoo style" house. It was a tall two-story house with a chimney at each gable end and usually a symmetrical arrangement of doors and windows at the front. Larger homes were constructed by connecting two or three I houses together to create a "T," "L," or "H" house. The most common indigenous building material was adobe, a local unfired brick produced by a mixture of mud and straw.

Distinct Mormon folklore also reflected the Latter-day Saint belief system. Stories of visits from the Three Nephites often served as spiritual landmarks for the teller, and Elder J. Golden Kimball became a sort of folk hero through stories about his experiences and wit. Like quilts, Mormon folklore had a very specific function: usually it sought to enhance the faith and the sense of spirit of its audience. The story of the migration of the Mormon pioneers and the building of Zion became almost a kind of modern-day scripture.

Early twentieth-century LDS women continued the pioneer tradition of their mothers. Their Relief Society "workdays" became the institutional means for preserving folk art traditions. The emphasis on homemaking reflected a respect for traditional art forms that were displayed in quilting, fine sewing, and other household arts and crafts. Homemaking day became a monthly social event as Relief Society sisters met in a group for home crafts, homemaking lessons, and supper. The result was sometimes a somewhat modern-day version of Mormon folk art, different from the more personal expression of nineteenth-century women.

In the mid-twentieth century the Church often adopted an institutional method of preserving past art forms. The Church-wide dance festivals held into the 1970s brought young people together from across the world to share in an evening of the celebration of folk dance forms. Similarly, roadshows gave expression to local members' talents in miniplays that often depicted pioneer heritage values and customs (*see* DRAMA). Musicals like *My Turn on Earth* and *Saturday's Warrior* in much the same way as nineteenth-century folklore perpetuated folk traditions about premortal existence and the significance of life on earth (*see* MUSIC).

Twentieth-century Mormon folk art also reflects a faithful people as the story of the founding events and of the pioneers continues to figure prominently in every type of folk art. In general, it features respect for traditional art forms and mass participation. Folk art forms now flourishing in many different cultures have been welcomed as personal expressions of the testimony and love of Church members around the world.

[*See also* Folklore; Material Culture.]

BIBLIOGRAPHY

Brunvand, Jan Harold. *A Guide for Collectors of Folklore in Utah*. Salt Lake City, 1971.

Cannon, Hal. *The Grand Beehive*. Salt Lake City, 1980.

Fox, Sandi. *Quilts in Utah*. Salt Lake City, 1987.

MARTHA SONNTAG BRADLEY

FOLKLORE

Mormon folklore comprises that part of the Church's cultural heritage which Latter-day Saints pass on from person to person and from generation to generation, not through written documents or formal instruction but through the spoken word or customary example. That is, someone will listen to tales told at home or at a Church meeting about the sufferings of the Mormon pioneers and then will repeat these accounts to others; or a young girl will watch and then assist her grandmother make "temple quilts" (quilts on which the form of the Mormon temple in which a couple is married is stitched) for the marriages of each grandchild, and in the process will eventually learn to make her own quilts; or each evening children will be gathered by their parents into family prayer and then one day will continue the practice in their own families.

The materials of Mormon folklore fall roughly into three broad categories. First are things people make with words (from songs and stories of grandparents struggling to establish a New Zion in the harsh Great Basin Kingdom, to contemporary accounts of God's providential hand guiding "the affairs of the saints" and directing the efforts of missionaries in an ever-expanding church, to humorous tales that caricature Mormon foibles and ease the pressures of "being in the world but not of it"). Second are things people make with their hands (from traditional implements, such as the Mormon hay derrick, to homemade "quiet books" designed to keep small children constructively occupied during Church meetings, to home preserves and special holiday foods, to a decorative family Book of Remembrance [see MATERIAL CULTURE]). And third are things people make with their actions (from "creative dating" practices of youth, to special family celebrations of birth and baptismal dates, to family genealogical meetings, to church and community celebrations of traditional holidays from Thanksgiving to Pioneer Day).

This listing of examples focuses very consciously on the word "make," because the categories of Mormon folklore are dynamic rather than static. Each recounting of a miraculous healing, each quilting of a familiar log-cabin pattern, each performance of a family birthday game is in every instance a new act of creation that speaks from both the past and the present. They speak from the past because the forms are traditional and recurring, having been developed by the LDS community over decades. They speak from the present because the forms are constantly reshaped to fit the needs of contemporary Latter-day Saints and to reflect contemporary values and concerns.

Because of this constant regeneration and reshaping of older forms, Mormon folklore lies not at the periphery but at the center of LDS culture. It is not, as is sometimes thought, simply a survival from the past kept alive primarily by older, less educated, and agrarian Church members; rather, it is a vital, functioning force in the lives of all Latter-day Saints. Further, as the Church continues to grow and change, new forms of folklore that speak more directly to present needs will sometimes replace the old. For just as Latter-day Saints in the pioneer era generated and transmitted folklore in response to the circumstances of their lives, so, too, contemporary Latter-day Saints will create and pass along folklore as they react to the strains and stresses, the joys and the sorrows of their lives. For example, converts to the Church living in the mission fields, away from Church centers in the mountain West, may be little moved by tales of pioneer suffering and may know little of earlier stories of the providential saving of the pioneers' crops from swarms of locusts or of the legends of the three Nephites; but they will know and tell stories of their own miraculous conversions and of the ridicule and suffering they endure, with the help of God, as they struggle to survive as the only Latter-day Saints in sometimes unfriendly and often hostile communities.

Properly to understand the Latter-day Saints, one must know their folklore—must see how it bolsters their faith, builds a sense of community, ties them to the past, and provides them an escape through humor from pressures that might otherwise be their undoing. Especially, one must understand Mormon folklore in order to understand the Mormon ethos. This is so because people tell stories about those events that interest them most or participate in customary practices that are most important to them. Because these stories and practices depend on the spoken word or on voluntary participation for their survival, those that fail to appeal broadly to a Mormon value center, a common body of LDS attitudes and beliefs, will simply cease to exist. Those that persist, therefore, serve as an excellent barometer for prevailing Mormon cultural and religious values.

In a number of Utah and western towns a Mormon temple, usually built on a hill or in the center of the valley, dominates the landscape, symbolizing for all who pass by the religious values that originally brought LDS settlers to the region. In towns and valleys

surrounding the temples, in Sunday School classes, in family gatherings, among friends, the descendants and converts of these settlers
relate stories that tell of the price paid for blessings now enjoyed, that
give evidence of the providential hand of God in the lives of the faithful, that lift sagging spirits, bolster courage, promote obedience and
give hope for the eventual and ultimate victory of Zion. The stories
give a glimpse of this rich and ever-growing body of narratives, the
lore of faith.

The question remains whether narratives embodying these values are really "true"—and, concomitantly, if they are not true, what
is their ultimate value? Although the stories frequently are based on
actual events, their details clearly change as they are passed along
by word of mouth. These changes, however, do not occur randomly;
they are dictated by cultural determinants. As stories are transmitted from person to person, they are often changed, usually uncon-
sciously, to express the new tellers' beliefs and to meet their needs.
Because folk narratives mirror and reinforce these beliefs, and
because the beliefs are themselves historical facts, moving people to
action more handily than the realities on which they are based, they
can yield valuable historical data. But it is more profitable to turn to
them for other reasons, to view them not as history but as literature,
and to discover in them not the ledger-book truths of actual events
but expression of the people's heart and mind. To a greater or lesser
degree, Mormon folk stories may or may not be factually accurate.
But as keys to understanding the Latter-day Saints and their church,
they are always true.

BIBLIOGRAPHY

For studies in Mormon folklore see Austin Fife and Alta Fife, *Saints of Sage and
Saddle: Folklore Among the Mormons* (Bloomington, Ind., 1956); and William A.
Wilson, "The Study of Mormon Folklore: An Uncertain Mirror for Truth," *Dialogue*
22 (Winter 1989):95–110.

For bibliographic references see Jill Terry, "Exploring Belief and Custom: The Study
of Mormon Folklore," *Utah Folklife Newsletter* 23 (Winter 1989):1–4; and William
A. Wilson, "A Bibliography of Studies in Mormon Folklore," *Utah Historical
Quarterly* 44 (1976):389–94.

WILLIAM A. WILSON

FREEMASONRY IN NAUVOO

The introduction of Freemasonry in Nauvoo had both political and religious implications. When Illinois Grand Master Abraham Jonas visited Nauvoo on March 15, 1842, to install the Nauvoo Masonic Lodge, he inaugurated an era of difficulty with other Illinois Masons and introduced to Nauvoo ancient ritual bearing some similarity to the LDS temple ordinances (*see* FREEMASONRY AND THE TEMPLE).

Regular Masonic procedure calls for an existing lodge to sponsor each new proposed lodge. Early in the summer of 1841, several Latter-day Saints who were Masons, including Lucius N. Scovil, a key figure in Nauvoo Freemasonry, asked Bodley Lodge No. 1, in Quincy, Illinois, to request that the Illinois Grand Lodge appoint certain individuals as officers of a Nauvoo lodge. Indicating that the persons named were unknown in Quincy as Masons, the lodge returned the letter with instructions for further action.

Less than a year later, Nauvoo had a lodge without the normal sponsorship. Grand Master Jonas apparently waived the rule and granted Nauvoo a "special dispensation" to organize. He also made Joseph Smith and his counselor, Sidney Rigdon, "Masons at sight." Some believe that Jonas was willing to follow this course because he envisioned the growing Mormon vote supporting his own political ambitions. Although the action may have endeared him to some Latter-day Saints, it antagonized other Masons. Joseph Smith had reason to expect that the Saints might benefit from the network of friendship and support normally associated with the fraternal organization, but instead, the Nauvoo Lodge only produced friction.

Jonas published an account of the March 15 installation of the Nauvoo Lodge in his newspaper, *Columbia Advocate.* "Never in my life did I witness a better dressed or more orderly and well-behaved assemblage," he wrote (*HC* 4:565–66). During the installation ceremonies, held in the grove near the temple site, Joseph Smith officiated as Grand Chaplain. That evening, with the Masons assembled in his office, the Prophet received the first degree of Freemasonry. Nauvoo Masons then commenced weekly early morning meetings.

In August 1842, Bodley Lodge No. 1 protested the granting of a dispensation to the Nauvoo Lodge, resulting in a temporary suspension of activities. An investigation found that approximately three hundred Latter-day Saints had become Masons during the brief existence of the lodge, but found no irregularities warranting dissolution. The Grand Lodge not only authorized reinstatement of the Nauvoo Lodge but subsequently granted dispensations for other lodges nearby made up principally of Latter-day Saints. Eventually nearly 1,500 LDS men became associated with Illinois Freemasonry, including many members of the Church's governing priesthood bodies—this at a time when the total number of non-LDS Masons in Illinois lodges barely reached 150.

As long-time rivals of Nauvoo for political and economic ascendancy, neighboring Masons feared and resisted Mormon domination of Freemasonry. Charging the Nauvoo Lodge with balloting for more than one applicant at a time, receiving applicants into the fraternity on the basis that they reform in the future, and making Joseph Smith a Master Mason on sight, enemies forced an investigation in October 1843. The Grand Lodge summoned Nauvoo officials to Jacksonville, Illinois. Armed with pertinent books and papers, Lucius Scovil and Henry G. Sherwood answered the allegations. Though the examining committee reported that everything appeared to be in order, it expressed fear that there *might* be something wrong, and recommended a year's suspension. At this point, Grand Master Jonas, in an impassioned speech, declared that the books of the Nauvoo Lodge were the best-kept he had seen and stated his conviction that but for the fact that the Nauvoo Lodge was composed of Mormons, it would stand as the highest lodge in the state. A committee was appointed to make a thorough investigation in Nauvoo. Though the committee reported no wrongdoing, the Nauvoo Lodge was again suspended. The injunction was later removed, but the Nauvoo Lodge continued to lack the support of its fellow Masons.

In April 1844, the Nauvoo Lodge dedicated a new Masonic hall. By this time, the lodge had been severed from the Grand Lodge and one Illinois Mason had been expelled from his lodge for attending the dedication. The Nauvoo Lodge continued its activities in the newly built hall until April 10, 1845, when Brigham Young advised Lucius Scovil to suspend the work of the Masons in Nauvoo. Only a few additional meetings were held prior to the Latter-day Saints' departure for the Great Basin in 1846.

Joseph Smith participated minimally in Freemasonry and, as far as is known, attended the Nauvoo Masonic Lodge on only three occasions. Nonetheless, LDS Masons commented on his mastery of its orders, tenets, and principles and of his understanding of the allegorical symbolism of its instructions.

Most scholars who have looked carefully at the Nauvoo Masonic Lodge agree that it was more victim than villain. All agree that widespread anti-Mormon feelings and the extensive hatred of Latter-day Saints by local rivals, and not irregularities or misconduct, caused the controversy with regard to the Masonic Lodge in Nauvoo.

BIBLIOGRAPHY

Hogan, Mervin B. "Mormonism and Freemasonry: The Illinois Episode." In *Little Masonic Library*, ed. Silas H. Shepherd, Lionel Vibert, and Roscoe Pound, Vol. 2, pp. 267–326. Richmond, Va., 1977.

Ivins, Anthony W. *The Relationship of "Mormonism" and Freemasonry*. Salt Lake City, 1934.

McGavin, E. Cecil. *Mormonism and Masonry*. Salt Lake City, 1954.

KENNETH W. GODFREY

FREEMASONRY AND THE TEMPLE

Students of both Mormonism and Freemasonry have pondered possible relationships between Masonic rites and the LDS temple ceremony. Although some argue that Joseph Smith borrowed elements of Freemasonry in developing the temple ceremony, the endowment is more congruous with LDS scriptures (especially the book of Abraham and the book of Moses) and ancient ritual than with Freemasonry. Latter-day Saints view the ordinances as a revealed restoration of ancient temple ceremony and only incidentally related to Freemasonry. The two are not antithetical, however, nor do they threaten each other, and neither institution discourages research regarding the ancient origins of their two ceremonies.

Many sacred ceremonies existed in the ancient world. Modified over centuries, these rituals existed in some form among ancient Egyptians, Coptic Christians, Israelites, and Masons, and in the Catholic and Protestant liturgies. Common elements include the wearing of special clothing, ritualistic speech, the dramatization of archetypal themes, instruction, and the use of symbolic gestures. One theme common to many—found in the Egyptian Book of the Dead, the Egyptian pyramid texts, and Coptic prayer circles, for example— is man's journey through life and his quest, following death, to successfully pass the sentinels guarding the entrance to eternal bliss with the gods. Though these ceremonies vary greatly, significant common points raise the possibility of a common remote source.

The Egyptian pyramid texts, for example, feature six main themes: (1) emphasis on a primordial written document behind the rites; (2) purification (including anointing, lustration, and clothing); (3) the Creation (resurrection and awakening texts); (4) the garden (including tree and ritual meal motifs); (5) travel (protection, a ferryman, and Osirian texts); and (6) ascension (including victory, coronation, admission to heavenly company, and Horus texts). Like such ancient ceremonies, the LDS temple endowment presents aspects of these themes in figurative terms. It, too, presents, not a picture of immediate reality, but a model setting forth the pattern of human life on earth and the divine plan of which it is part.

Masonic ceremonies are also allegorical, depicting life's states— youth, manhood, and old age—each with its associated burdens and challenges, followed by death and hoped-for immortality. There is no universal agreement concerning when Freemasonry began. Some historians trace the order's origin to Solomon, Enoch, or even Adam. Others argue that while some Masonic symbolism may be ancient, as an institution it began in the Middle Ages or later.

Though in this dispensation the LDS endowment dates from Kirtland and Nauvoo, Latter-day Saints believe that temple ordinances are as old as man and that the essentials of the gospel of Jesus Christ, including its necessary ritual and teachings, were first revealed to Adam. These saving principles and ordinances were subsequently revealed to Seth; Noah; Melchizedek; Abraham, and each prophet to whom the priesthood was given, including Peter. Latter-day Saints believe that the ordinances performed in LDS temples today replicate rituals that were part of God's teachings from the beginning.

The Prophet Joseph Smith suggested that the endowment and Freemasonry in part emanated from the same ancient spring. Thus, some Nauvoo Masons thought of the endowment as a restoration of a ritual only imperfectly preserved in Freemasonry and viewed Joseph

Smith as a master of the underlying principles and allegorical symbolism (Heber C. Kimball to Parley P. Pratt, June 17, 1842, Church Archives). The philosophy and major tenets of Freemasonry are not fundamentally incompatible with the teaching, theology, and doctrines of the Latter-day Saints. Both emphasize morality, sacrifice, consecration, and service, and both condemn selfishness, sin, and greed. Furthermore, the aim of Masonic ritual is to instruct—to make truth available so that man can follow it.

Resemblances between the two rituals are limited to a small proportion of actions and words; indeed, some find that the LDS endowment has more similarities with the Pyramid texts and the Coptic documents than with Freemasonry. Even where the two rituals share symbolism, the fabric of meanings is different. In addition to creation and life themes, one similarity is that both call for the participants to make covenants. Yet, the endowment alone ties covenants to eternal blessings and to Jesus Christ. The Masonic ceremony does not emphasize priesthood or the need to be commissioned by God to represent him. The active participation of God in the world and in men's lives is a distinctly LDS temple motif. While Masons believe in an undefined, impersonal God, everything in the LDS endowment emanates from, or is directed to, God who is a personage and man's eternal Father. The endowment looks to the eternities and to eternal lives, but Freemasonry is earthbound, pervaded by human legend and hope for something better.

Freemasonry is a fraternal society, and in its ritual all promises, oaths, and agreements are made between members. In the temple endowment all covenants are between the individual and God. In Freemasonry, testing, grading, penalizing, or sentencing accords with the rules of the fraternity or membership votes. In the endowment, God alone is the judge. Within Freemasonry, rank and promotions are of great importance, while in the LDS temple rites there are no distinctions: all participants stand equal before God. The clash between good and evil, including Satan's role, is essential to, and vividly depicted in, the endowment, but is largely absent from Masonic rites. Temple ceremonies emphasize salvation for the dead through vicarious ordinance work, such as baptism for the dead; nothing in Masonic ritual allows for proxies acting on behalf of the dead. Women participate in all aspects of LDS temple rites; though

Freemasonry has women's auxiliaries, Masonic ritual excludes them. The endowment's inclusion of females underscores perhaps the most fundamental difference between the two rites: LDS temple rites unite husbands and wives, and their children, in eternal families (*see* MAR-RIAGE). Latter-day Saint sealings would be completely out of place in the context of Masonic ceremonies.

Thus, Latter-day Saints see their temple ordinances as fundamentally different from Masonic and other rituals and think of similarities as remnants from an ancient original.

BIBLIOGRAPHY

Ivins, Anthony W. *The Relationship of "Mormonism" and Freemasonry.* Salt Lake City, 1934.

Madsen, Truman G., ed. *The Temple in Antiquity.* Provo, Utah, 1984.

Nibley, Hugh W. *The Message of the Joseph Smith Papyri: An Egyptian Endowment.* Salt Lake City, 1975.

Packer, Boyd K. *The Holy Temple.* Salt Lake City, 1980.

Shepherd, Silas H.; Lionel Vibert; and Roscoe Pound, eds. *Little Masonic Library,* 5 vols. Richmond, Va., 1977, esp. Mervin B. Hogan, "Mormonism and Freemasonry: The Illinois Episode," Vol. 2, pp. 267–326.

KENNETH W. GODFREY

G

GAMBLING

The Church of Jesus Christ of Latter-day Saints condemns gambling, games of chance, and lotteries as moral evils and admonishes its members not to participate in them in any form. Gambling is based on the morally wrong philosophy of getting something for nothing, of taking money without giving fair value in exchange. Not only is gambling morally wrong, but it is also bad economics for customers. The lavish gambling centers around the world stand as ample evidence that the chances of winning are weighted heavily in favor of the establishment and against the bettor. This same remoteness of winning is part of state-run lotteries. The chance of purchasing a winning ticket in one 1990 state lottery was noted by the news media as 1 in 14 million. The Church considers lotteries as gambling, and the First Presidency has asked Latter-day Saints not to participate in them and to oppose establishing them in their states:

> There can be no question about the moral ramifications of gambling, including government-sponsored lotteries. Public lotteries are advocated as a means of relieving the burden of taxation. It has been demonstrated, however, that all too often lotteries only add to the problems of the financially disadvantaged by taking money from them and giving nothing of value in return. The poor and the elderly become victims of the inducements that are held out to purchase lottery tickets on the remote chance of winning a substantial prize. It is sad to see governments now promot-

ing what they once enacted laws to forbid. We urge members of the Church to join with others with similar concerns in opposing the legalization of gambling and government-sponsorship of lotteries [*Church News*, Oct. 5, 1986, p. 4].

BIBLIOGRAPHY

Oaks, Dallin H. "Gambling—Morally Wrong and Politically Unwise." *Ensign* 17 (June 1987):69–75.

CHARLES D. TATE, JR.

GENEALOGICAL SOCIETY OF UTAH

The Genealogical Society of Utah, organized in 1894, became The Genealogical Society of The Church of Jesus Christ of Latter-day Saints in 1944. In 1976 it became The Genealogical Department, and in 1987 the name was changed to The Family History Department. Each name change brought renewed emphasis and expanded resources to further the search for ancestors. The name Genealogical Society still continues as the microfilm section of the Family History Department of the Church.

The central purpose of the organization is expressed in a statement by Elder Joseph Fielding Smith: "Salvation for the dead is the system whereunder those who would have accepted the gospel in this life, had they been permitted to hear it, will have the chance to accept it in the spirit world, and will then be entitled to all the blessings which passed them by in mortality" (*DS* 2:100–196). Provisions have been made, therefore, for the living to provide, vicariously, ordinances of salvation for their deceased family forebears and friends. This cannot be done without information about the dead.

In April 1894, President Wilford Woodruff said, "We want the Latter-day Saints from this time to trace their genealogies as far as they can, and to be sealed to their fathers and mothers . . . and run this chain as far as you can get it" (Durham, p. 157). On November 13, 1894, the First Presidency of the Church authorized the organization of the Genealogical Society of Utah as an aid to genealogical research, and appointed Franklin D. Richards president. Of this beginning Archibald F. Bennett, a later executive secretary, gave the following historical summary: "It was to be benevolent, educational, and religious in purpose—benevolent in gathering together into a library books that would help the people trace their ancestry; educational in teaching the people how to trace their ancestry . . . ; religious in that they would do all in their power to encourage the people to perform in the temples all the necessary ordinances" (Genealogical Society of Utah, minutes, Nov. 13, 1894, Genealogical Department of the Church).

Some of the widely known facilities and resources that have been established over the past century to facilitate these purposes are: (1) the FAMILY HISTORY LIBRARY at Salt Lake City; (2) the extensive collection of microfilmed and microfiche records of family history; and (3) THE INTERNATIONAL GENEALOGICAL INDEX™ (IGI).

1. The Family History Library is the largest of its kind in the world. Patrons come from all over the globe to search for information about past generations. More than 1,000 branches of this library have been established in forty-three countries to make these records available to all who are interested.

2. The microfilm and microfiche collection is continually expanding. From 1938 to the present, irreplaceable records have been preserved on microfilms. Some 1.5 million rolls of microfilm and approximately 200,000 microfiche containing the names of an estimated 1.5 billion deceased people are now available to researchers.

3. The IGI includes names and vital statistics of millions of people who lived between the early 1500s and 1875 in some ninety countries, alphabetized by surname and arranged geographically. Millions of names are added each year. This index is accessible on microfiche and is computerized.

These and other resources have aided millions of researchers in finding their "roots," and have made possible the performance of temple ordinances for millions who lived and died without that opportunity.

The continued commitment to identify ancestors and provide temple ordinances for them which began in this dispensation with divine revelations to the Prophet Joseph Smith, and was furthered by the organization of the Genealogical Society of Utah, and has enabled millions of genealogists throughout the world to develop a strong association between family history and The Church of Jesus Christ of Latter-day Saints.

BIBLIOGRAPHY

Durham, G. Homer, ed. *Discourses of Wilford Woodruff*, p. 157. Salt Lake City, 1946.

GEORGE D. DURRANT

GENEALOGY

[*Genealogy is a record of lineage showing the descent of a person or family from an ancestor or ancestors. Searching for and compiling genealogical information are sacred responsibilities to Latter-day Saints. Therefore, extensive activity is conducted by the Church and by members to obtain and record vital statistical information, to compile family histories, and to strengthen family ties both on earth and in the hereafter. In LDS doctrine the family is of eternal significance. Thus, three major purposes of compiling genealogical records are to identify one's roots, to perform saving ordinances in a temple for persons who did not receive them in mortal life, and to seal individuals together for eternity as families.*

Articles relating to this subject are Ancestral File™; Family; Family History; Family History Centers; Family History Library; Family Organizations; Family Registry™; FamilySearch™; Genealogical Society of Utah; Granite Mountain Record Vault; International Genealogical Index™ (IGI); Name Extraction Program; Personal Ancestral File®; World Conferences on Records.]

GRANITE MOUNTAIN RECORD VAULT

Since 1938, the GENEALOGICAL SOCIETY OF UTAH has been collecting genealogical and historical information on rolls of microfilm. The Granite Mountain Record Vault is the permanent repository for these microfilms. It is located about one mile from the mouth of Little Cottonwood Canyon in Utah's Wasatch Range, twenty miles southeast of downtown Salt Lake City.

The Vault, as it is commonly known, is a massive excavation

reaching 600 feet into the north side of the canyon. Constructed between 1958 and 1963 at a cost of $2 million, it consists of two main areas. The office and laboratory section sits beneath an overhang of about 300 feet of granite and houses shipping and receiving docks, microfilm processing and evaluation stations, and administrative offices. Under 700 feet of stone, the Vault proper is situated farther back in the mountain behind the laboratory section and consists of six chambers (each 190 feet long, 25 feet wide, and 25 feet high), which are accessed by one main entrance and two smaller passageways. Specially constructed Mosler doors weighing fourteen tons (at the main entrance) and nine tons (guarding the two smaller entrances) are designed to withstand a nuclear blast. In the six chambers, nature maintains constant humidity and temperature readings optimum for microfilm storage.

Each chamber contains banks of steel cabinets ten feet high. As of February 1991, approximately 1.7 million rolls of microfilm, in 16mm and 35mm formats, were housed in two of the six chambers. The collection increases by 40,000 rolls per year. Alternate media, such as optical disks with greater capacity for storage than microfilm, are being considered for use and may make further expansion of the Vault unnecessary.

The genealogical information contained on these microfilms is collected from churches, libraries, and governmental agencies and consists primarily of birth, marriage, and death registers; wills and probates; census reports; and other documents that can be used to establish individual identities. Latter-day Saints use such information to assemble family group charts and pedigrees for the purpose of binding together ancestral lines of kinship through sealing ordinances performed by proxy in temples. Such ordinances are considered essential for the salvation of the dead—that is, those who died without hearing the full message of the gospel of Jesus Christ.

BIBLIOGRAPHY
Schueler, Donald G. "Our Family Trees Have Roots in Utah's Mountain Vaults." *Smithsonian* 12 (Dec. 1981):86–95.
Shoumatoff, Alex. *The Mountain of Names: A History of the Human Family*. New York, 1985.

STEVEN W. BALDRIDGE

H

HEALTH, ATTITUDES TOWARD

In light of modern revelation, Latter-day Saints believe that the physical body and its health and well-being are an essential part of the gospel of Jesus Christ. One purpose of mortality is to acquire and care for a physical body that is united with a spirit in a temporary union. The body is the house or tabernacle of each person's unique eternal spirit. At death, the body and the spirit are temporarily separated. One cannot fulfill his or her eternal potential, however, when the spirit and body are apart. In the resurrection the spirit and the then-immortal body will become eternally reunited and inseparable.

The physical body is a gift from God. No mortal body is perfect; some persons are born with handicaps or serious disabilities. Nevertheless, in premortal life spirits looked forward with great anticipation to receiving a physical body. Latter-day Saints look upon the body as an essential component in the progress to become perfect, even as the Heavenly Father is perfect.

The health laws or commandments given in the scriptures are to teach mankind how to care for their bodies. Such laws have spiritual consequence. Obedience to health laws can enhance physical, mental, and spiritual well-being.

Latter-day Saints are counseled not to take harmful and habit-forming things into their bodies. Tobacco, alcoholic beverages, coffee, tea, and drugs are to be avoided. Fruits, vegetables, herbs, grains, and fish are good for the body; meats, however, should be used sparingly (*see* WORD OF WISDOM).

In addition, the Lord counseled, "Cease to be idle; cease to be unclean; . . . retire to thy bed early, . . . arise early, that your bodies and your minds may be invigorated" (D&C 88:124). Modern prophets have stressed that people should keep their bodies healthy.

Other principles, such as love, kindness, compassion, forgiveness, and charity, foster a healthy and positive mental perspective. A God-given moral code promotes good health and enduring family life by requiring chastity before marriage and total fidelity within marriage.

Without a solid foundation of ethical values, including integrity, responsibility, self-esteem, and self-discipline, children and adults are in danger of being drawn to high-risk behaviors that impair both the body and the spirit. Mortality is a time for the spirit to constrain and discipline the body's appetites. The choices made on a day-to-day basis determine whether one is incapacitated by addictive substances, suffers from sexually transmitted diseases (including AIDS), dies prematurely from degenerative diseases, or suffers traumatic injury.

Thus, Latter-day Saints believe that God has mandated striving to achieve and maintain optimal health. A central purpose of mankind's creation is negated when one trivializes, through wrong choices, the sacredness of one's own body or the body of another. The apostle Paul declared, "What? Know ye not that your body is the temple of the Holy Ghost which is in you, which ye have of God, and ye are not your own?" (1 Cor. 6:19).

BIBLIOGRAPHY
McKay, David O. "The 'Whole' Man." *IE* 55 (Apr. 1953):221–22.
Smith, Barbara B. "Good Health—A Key to Joyous Living." *Ensign* 8 (Nov. 1978):77–78.

JAMES O. MASON

HOME

["Home" refers to more than a dwelling for a family. Latter-day Saints consider the ideal home a sacred place where holiness can be lived and

taught. It is where civilization is created, one family at a time, and where God's plan of salvation is taught to the next generation, by both example and precept. Home and family relationships can be eternal. Children are to be nurtured in an atmosphere of love. Homes are to be characterized by service, cooperation, and even sacrifice by and for each other. The ideal home can become a haven from worldliness, materialism, and selfishness. While living in a relationship of fidelity, parents are to make home commitments their first priority.

Articles on the home environment are Abuse, Spouse and Child; Divorce; Family: Family Life; Fatherhood; Marriage; Motherhood; *and* Women, Roles of. *Articles related to children and adolescents in the home are* Adoption of Children; Dating and Courtship; *and* Sex Education. *Articles on parental responsibilities and home organization are* Birth Control; Emergency Preparedness; Family History; Family Home Evening; Family Organizations; Family Prayer; Fathers' Blessings; Procreation; Sexuality; *and* Values, Transmission of.]

HOMOSEXUALITY

God's teachings about human sexuality are clear, unambiguous, and consistent from Adam to the present. "God created man in his own image . . . male and female created he them" (Gen. 1:27). "And the Gods said: Let us make an help meet for the man, for it is not good that the man should be alone, therefore we will form an help meet for him. . . . Therefore shall a man . . . cleave unto his wife, and they shall be one flesh" (Abr. 5:14–18). "Neither is the man without the woman, neither the woman without the man, in the Lord" (1 Cor. 11:11).

When two people of the same sex join in using their bodies for erotic purposes, this conduct is considered homosexual and sinful by The Church of Jesus Christ of Latter-day Saints, comparable to sexual relations between any unmarried persons. Masturbation is not condoned but is not considered homosexual.

People who persist in committing acts that violate divine law are subject to Church disciplinary councils to help them understand the damage they are doing to their eternal well-being. Particularly offensive is any conduct that harms others, especially those who because of their youth are vulnerable to seduction or coercion. The eternal laws that pertain to chastity before marriage and personal purity within marriage apply to *all* sexual behavior. However, "marriage is not doctrinal therapy for homosexual relations" (Oaks, p. 10). The restored gospel of Jesus Christ exalts the relationship of husband and wife, as particularly illustrated in the temple ordinances. From these doctrines, covenants, and ordinances, it is clear that any sexual relationship other than that between a legally wedded heterosexual husband and wife is sinful. The divine mandate of marriage between man and woman puts in perspective why homosexual acts are offensive to God. They repudiate the gift and the Giver of eternal life.

Recognizing that failure to keep the covenants of the gospel of Jesus Christ deprives a person of God's blessings, the Church offers counseling to help those who are troubled by homosexual thoughts or actions to learn to use their agency to live in accord with divine laws and thereby enjoy the rich blessings a benevolent Father offers to all his children, whatever their temptation or thoughts. "That has been the message of the Jewish and Christian prophets in all ages: repent. Abandon your sins; confess them; forsake them. And become acceptable to God" (Oaks, p. 7).

BIBLIOGRAPHY
Oaks, Dallin H. CBS-TV interview, Dec. 30, 1986, unpublished transcript.
Packer, Boyd K. "Covenants." *Ensign* 20 (Nov. 1990):84–86.

VICTOR L. BROWN, JR.

HUMANITARIAN SERVICE

The Church of Jesus Christ of Latter-day Saints has a continuing commitment to relieve human suffering, to help eliminate life-threatening conditions, and to promote self-reliance among all people. Assistance is to be provided as Christian service, without regard to race, nationality, or religion. This obligation is an expression of scriptural counsel such as is found in the Book of Mormon:

> They did not send away any who were naked, or . . . hungry, or that were athirst, or that were sick, or that had not been nourished; and they did not set their hearts upon riches; therefore they were liberal to all, both

old and young, both bond and free, both male and female, whether out of the church or in the church, having no respect to persons as to those who stood in need [Alma 1:30].

Church giving is possible because of donations by individual members, who honor the counsel of Joseph Smith regarding one's temporal obligation to others:

Respecting how much a man . . . shall give annually we have no special instructions to give; he is to feed the hungry, to clothe the naked, to provide for the widow, to dry up the tear of the orphan, to comfort the afflicted, whether in this church or in any other, or in no church at all, wherever he finds them [*T&S* 3:732].

The Church has always felt a responsibility to "take care of its own," but traditionally it has also reached out to the general population in times of need, both in North America and throughout the world. As early as 1851, just four years after reaching the Salt Lake Valley, Brigham Young instituted a program of teaching Indians to farm by appointing three men as "farmers to the Indians." By 1857 more than 700 acres were under cultivation among the Indians (L. J. Arrington, *Brigham Young: American Moses*, New York, 1985, pp. 217–18).

The Church has responded to major world calamities according to its ability to give. In 1918 the U.S. House of Representatives formally expressed its appreciation to the Relief Society women of the Church "for . . . contributions of wheat to the Government for the use of the starving women and children of the allies, and for the use of our soldiers and sailors in the army and navy of the United States" (*IE* 21:917). The Relief Society had provided from its storage granaries more than 200,000 bushels of "first-class milling wheat" to the United States for the cause of human liberty and to save the lives of thousands who might have suffered for the lack of bread.

Even more extensive assistance to Europe during and after World War II was made possible in part because of a Church Welfare Services plan implemented in 1936. The plan taught members frugality and provident living and encouraged donations for the needy, which then would be available for emergencies and calamities.

President David O. McKay summarized the Church's actions during World War II: "We have given to the national Red Cross in Washington very large sums, and expect to add to these from time to time. Insofar as contributions toward foreign sufferers in war-ridden countries is concerned, we have sent considerable sums . . . to those countries to help our needy Church membership there and have made available for charitable purposes considerable local funds in those countries" (*MFP* 6:163–64).

Post–World War II humanitarian aid included ninety-two railway carloads of welfare supplies (about two thousand tons) sent to Europe from the Church in Salt Lake City. Ezra Taft Benson, then a member of the Quorum of the Twelve Apostles, spent 1946 in Europe supervising the distribution of this aid, consisting mainly of food, clothing, utensils, and medical supplies. These goods were supplemented by a program in which Church members in North America sent tens of thousands of individual food and clothing parcels. While a primary objective of the Church's efforts was to assist Church members in Europe, generous amounts of food and clothing were given to local child-care and feeding programs (Babbel, pp.168–69).

In 1953, a cooperative movement on the part of all Utah denominations collected relief supplies for Greece to relieve suffering caused by earthquakes. The United Churches Ionian Relief Committee was formed with Dr. J. Frank Robinson, president of Westminster College in Salt Lake City, as chairman. Among the denominations represented were the Greek Orthodox and Roman Catholic churches, the Jewish synagogues, and the Latter-day Saints. Expressing thanks to the Church for its efforts, Mr. John Tzounis, Greek consul in San Francisco, stated: "It is no secret, and I am thankful for this opportunity to stress the fact publicly, that the contribution of the Mormon Church was the greatest single contribution to the relief fund, not only in the United States, but the whole world over" ("President McKay Given Royal Award by King of Greece," *Deseret News*, Dec. 4, 1954, p. 2).

The Welfare Services Missionary Program was created in 1971, allowing service beyond emergency circumstances. Health professionals called as missionaries to various lands have provided training in hospitals, clinics, and community health organizations, as well as health education for the general population through seminars and workshops. Agricultural missionaries were added to the welfare missionary ranks in 1973, giving technical assistance to farmers in Central and South America, in the South Pacific, and on Indian reservations in the United States and Canada.

The Church's humanitarian response to the proliferation of refugees coming from Vietnam, Cambodia, and Laos in the 1970s began, through an agreement with the United Nations High Commission for Refugees (UNHCR), with a team of Welfare Services missionaries at the Phenot Nikom Refugee Camp in Thailand. From 1978 to the present, missionary teams have provided continuous training in English language and American culture for refugees bound for the United States at camps in Thailand, the Philippines, and Hong Kong.

By 1980, some 768 welfare missionaries (volunteers to give humanitarian aid) were serving in more than forty Church mission areas throughout the world. By 1990, more than 350 missionaries with specific professional backgrounds (nurses, doctors, educators, agricultural specialists) also were providing temporal assistance in many nations (including countries in eastern Europe), primarily in health, agriculture, and leadership development.

A severe drought and civil war in northeast Africa resulted in famine during 1984 and 1985. The First Presidency and the Quorum of the Twelve "determined that Sunday, January 25, 1985, should be designated as the special fast day when our people will be invited to refrain from partaking two meals and contribute the equivalent value, or more, to the Church to assist those in need. All fast offering funds contributed on this day will be dedicated for the use of the victims of famine and other causes resulting in hunger and privation among people of Africa, and possibly in some other areas, . . . regardless of Church membership" (The First Presidency Letter to General and Local Priesthood Authorities, Jan. 11, 1985). This special fast day in the United States and Canada produced contributions from the Latter-day Saints of $6.4 million (Welfare Services Department, unpublished document).

The Church immediately collaborated with reputable organizations in providing temporal assistance to the famine-stricken populations of northeast Africa. Specific contributions of grain, tents, and trucks for transporting the needed goods were made to the

International Committee of the Red Cross (ICRC) and Catholic Relief Services, valued at more than $3.5 million. Additional donations were made to Catholic Relief Services, CARE, and Africare for projects relating to longer-term relief in the same geographic region (*see* ECONOMIC AID).

Additional monies were later contributed to the ICRC and Catholic Relief Services for airlifting needed food to isolated populations in Ethiopia and the Sudan, where civil strife made trucking the goods impossible. The entire $6.4 million contributed during the first fast, as well as the accumulated interest, had been spent for assistance to Africa by the end of 1986. A second fast, also undertaken in 1985 in concert with a resolution by the U.S. Congress (The First Presidency Letter to General and Local Priesthood Authorities, Jan. 11, 1985), produced an additional $4 million to assist the needy. Special events such as these supplement regular, ongoing humanitarian efforts in the Church. Surpluses from the Welfare Services system are regularly contributed to charitable organizations in the form of food, clothing, and other in-kind household goods throughout the United States and internationally.

Most recently, more than twenty development projects have been sponsored by the Church in Africa (e.g., Kenya, Zimbabwe, Mozambique, Zaire, Chad, Mali, Nigeria, Ghana) as well as additional projects in Central and South America, Asia, and the United States.

BIBLIOGRAPHY

Babbel, Frederick W. *On Wings of Faith*. Salt Lake City, 1972.

Ballard, M. Russell. "Prepare to Serve." *Ensign* 15 (May 1985):41–43.

Benson, Ezra T. "Ministering to Needs through the Lord's Storehouse System." *Ensign* 7 (May 1977):82–84.

Ferguson, Isaac C. "Freely Given." *Ensign* 18 (Aug. 1988):10–15.

"Food for Destitute Greeks." *Deseret News* (Church Section), Feb. 20, 1954, pp. 8–9.

Hinckley, Gordon B. "The Victory over Death." *Ensign* 15 (May 1985):51–54, 59.

Pace, Glenn L. "Principles and Programs." *Ensign* 16 (May 1986):23–25.

Smith, Joseph F. "Our Duty to Humanity, to God and to Country." *IE* 20 (May 1917):645–56.

Times and Seasons 3 (Mar. 15, 1842):732.

ISAAC C. FERGUSON

HUMOR

Although LDS doctrines, practices, and experiences have in some circles evoked a measure of scoffing and laughter over the years, only since the 1970s has a body of published humor dealing with the Mormon experience appeared. Institutionalized LDS humor divides roughly into an early period when the Church was the object of outsiders' jokes and a modern period when members have become able to laugh at themselves.

As with many minority groups, the first humor that dealt with the Church was created by antagonists to turn people away from it. Much of this humor took the form of cartoons in the popular press, and verses and parodies of popular or folk songs (Bunker and Bitton, 1983). These attacks were prevalent in nineteenth-century periodicals, and such noted writers as Mark Twain and Artemus Ward took aim at available targets like Brigham Young and polygamy.

From this early period, almost no pro-Mormon humor or humor regarding the Church created by the members of the Church themselves survives. While it is certain that members enjoyed humor, as evidenced in numerous JOURNALS and letters, little of it was apparently directed at their own experiences and cultural practices. This was particularly true of published material. Latter-day Saints were too involved with building a new way of life to indulge in frivolity or of anything that might appear to question their commitment. Humor, therefore, was incidental.

Around 1900 this attitude began to change, expressly in the talks of Elder J. Golden Kimball, of the Seventy. During his long tenure as a General Authority, his iconoclastic wit and biting sense of humor not only made the Saints love and quote him, but also helped them to see a lighter side of their often difficult existence.

Still, little in-group humor appeared in print before 1948, when Samuel W. Taylor's novel *Heaven Knows Why!* was published. Playing on the cultural patterns of typical small-town western Mormonism, the book gained limited success and recognition as an alternative selection of the Literary Guild, but it also caused a stir of discontent in the LDS community, hitting too close to home and seeming to ridicule not only lifestyle but also sacred doctrines. Because of its limited acceptance, it quickly dropped out of print.

A turning point seems to have come as a result of World War II, which brought outsiders into the almost exclusively LDS Rocky Mountain communities and spread members of the Church throughout the world. The resulting interchange showed both groups that in many ways they were not as different from each other as they had assumed, and allowed them to laugh at their common foibles and presumptions.

As the Church became better known as an American lifestyle, its members felt freer to find humor in their own cultural patterns and practices. Concurrently, its rapid growth created a larger audience for specifically LDS materials as well as an audience educated, sophisticated, and affluent enough to understand, enjoy, and buy them.

Taylor's book, reissued in 1979, now has enthusiastic readers, as have the works of cartoonists Calvin Grondahl and Pat Bagley. Jack Weyland's *A New Dawn* and Alma Yates's *The Miracle of Miss Willie* are among recent novels that depict LDS cultural idiosyncrasies. Parodies and spoofs aimed at the LDS audience include Orson Scott Card's *Saintspeak*, Carol Lynn Pearson's "notebooks," and numerous articles by Chris Crowe.

However, this growing acceptance of culturally bound humor has limitations. LDS doctrines, ordinances, and temple ceremonies are not usually the objects of humor, although unexpected or unorthodox responses to specific doctrines, particularly those by nonmembers or of small children may be. Scandal or notoriety that might reflect on all members is not considered funny, but the everyday problems of family life, Church and missionary service, as well as the need to reconcile principles and practices, lend themselves well to humor. Latter-day Saints generally seem willing to laugh at themselves and their LIFESTYLE, but not at sacred things (*see* LIGHT-MINDEDNESS).

BIBLIOGRAPHY

Bunker, Gary L. and Davis Bitton. *The Mormon Graphic Image, 1834–1914.* Salt Lake City, 1983.

Cracroft, Richard H. "The Humor of Mormon Seriousness." *Sunstone* (Jan. 1985):14–17.

Wilson, William A. "The Seriousness of Mormon Humor." *Sunstone* (Jan. 1985):8–13.

MARGARET P. BAKER

HYMNS AND HYMNODY

Hymns have been central to the LDS tradition of worship from the earliest days of the Church. Latter-day Saints revere their hymnbook almost as scripture because of their belief that the first LDS hymnal had its origins in divine commandment. In July of 1830, only three months after the Church was organized, Joseph Smith's wife Emma Smith was instructed to "make a selection of sacred hymns . . . to be had in my church" (D&C 25:11). The resulting 1835 volume, *A Collection of Sacred Hymns, for the Church of the Latter Day Saints*, included among its ninety hymns a number of original, distinctively LDS texts. For example, two by the book's co-editor William W. Phelps, "The Spirit of God Like a Fire Is Burning" (*Hymns* 1985, No. 2) and "Now Let Us Rejoice" (*Hymns* 1985, No. 3) celebrate the restoration of the latter-day Church. These and other original hymns were printed alongside well-known Protestant texts by such authors as Isaac Watts and Reginald Heber. A second hymnal, expanded to 304 hymns, was printed in Nauvoo in 1841.

Under the direction of Brigham Young, Parley Pratt, and John Taylor, a volume familiarly known as the *Manchester Hymnal* was printed in Manchester, England, in 1840. Formally titled *A Collection of Sacred Hymns for the Church of Jesus Christ of Latter-day Saints in Europe*, this book served as the principal hymnbook of the English-speaking Saints for many decades. Converts from the British Isles brought it with them when they traveled to join the main body of the Saints in Utah. New hymns, most of them American in origin, were added to each later edition, but the *Manchester Hymnal* continued to be published in England until 1890. By 1912 it had gone through twenty-five editions. Like Emma Smith's hymnal and most others of the time, it printed the texts but not the music.

Emma Smith had looked forward to the day when the Saints would be "blessed with a copious variety of the songs of Zion," as she wrote in the preface to the first hymnbook. Her hopes were fulfilled; early LDS hymn writers continued to add important original hymns on such distinctive doctrines as the premortal life (Eliza R. Snow, "O My Father," *Hymns* 1985, No. 292), the latter-day restoration (Parley P. Pratt, "An Angel from on High," *Hymns* 1985, No. 13), and the gathering of the Saints to Utah (William G. Mills, "Arise, O Glorious Zion," *Hymns* 1985, No. 40).

In 1886 President John Taylor called together a committee to provide a musical supplement to the *Manchester Hymnal*. The result was the *Latter-day Saints' Psalmody*, which was published in Salt Lake City in 1889 and went through six more editions. The *Psalmody* emphasized home composition, that is, new music that was written by such LDS composers as George Careless and Ebenezer Beesley to accompany the old texts in the *Manchester Hymnal*. For some of the longer texts in the *Psalmody*, only the first few verses were printed.

During the 1870s and 1880s the Sunday School and Primary organizations began to print hymns and songs, singly and in collections, for their own use. In 1873 the Sunday School began publishing Sunday School hymns in the *Juvenile Instructor* magazine, and in 1880, under the direction of Eliza R. Snow, the Primary published a volume of texts and a companion volume of tunes.

In earlier decades the line between official and unofficial hymnbooks was not clearly drawn, and some of the LDS hymnals were private undertakings. An unofficial hymnbook, *Songs of Zion*, compiled by German Ellsworth and published in Chicago, became extremely popular. It went through eleven editions between 1908 and 1925.

Deseret Sunday School Songs, published by the Sunday School in 1909, was intended as a Sunday School songbook rather than a general worship hymnal. However, because so many Latter-day Saints loved its gospel-song hymns, with their energetic rhythms and simple exhortative texts, several of its hymns have found a secure place among the Mormons. "Master, the Tempest Is Raging" (*Hymns* 1985, No. 105) and "Put Your Shoulder to the Wheel" (*Hymns* 1985, No. 252) are two examples. The 1927 *Latter-day Saint Hymns*, a volume of more dignified and traditional hymns, was intended to supplement *Deseret Sunday School Songs* as the hymnal for sacrament meetings.

Hymns: Church of Jesus Christ of Latter-day Saints, printed in 1948, replaced both the 1927 hymnbook and *Deseret Sunday School Songs*. Many Church members were disappointed, however, to find that the 1948 hymnal omitted some favorites from among those in the *Deseret Sunday School Songs* and other sources. Responding to popular preference, the Church printed a new edition in 1950, restoring such well-established hymns as "A Poor Wayfaring Man of Grief" (*Hymns* 1985, No. 29) and "Have I Done Any Good?" (*Hymns* 1985, No. 223).

The 1950 hymnal retained official status until 1985, when it was replaced by *Hymns of The Church of Jesus Christ of Latter-day Saints*. This hymnal, published 150 years after Emma Smith's first one, retains almost one-third of the hymns she originally chose—a remarkable tribute to her judgment and to the well-defined and enduring nature of the LDS hymn tradition. There is little that is revolutionary about the new hymnal but much that is significant. Its publication provided an opportunity to omit outdated or little-used hymns in favor of new material of high quality. In all, seventy hymns that were part of the 1950 hymnal were dropped in 1985, and ninety-two new or newly borrowed hymns were added, of which forty-four are LDS contributions wholly or in part. Hymns by present-day LDS contributors continue to reflect Church thinking and concerns: fasting (Nos. 138, 139), home and family (Nos. 298, 300), missionary work (Nos. 253, 263), and so forth. Out of a total of 358 contributors, 168 are Latter-day Saints.

The 1985 hymnal shows that, as in the past, LDS hymnody embraces well-known material from other Christian traditions, for example, Martin Luther's "A Mighty Fortress" (No. 68) and Charles Wesley's "Rejoice, the Lord Is King!" (No. 66). Many of the hymns pair a Latter-day Saint text with a borrowed hymn tune, or an indigenous tune with a borrowed text. Tunes are again drawn from many sources: opera (Nos. 160, 196), popular songs of an earlier time (Nos. 34, 237), folk songs (Nos. 15, 284), and others. The selections overall, especially among the new hymns, reflect a strong denominational preference for traditional styles in both music and text. Because the custom of four-part congregational singing continues in most areas of the Church today, virtually all the hymns are printed with soprano, alto, tenor, and bass lines. Although a number of older gospel songs remain strong favorites, the ballad-type sacred song, important today in the congregational singing of some other denominations, has not found a place in Mormon hymnody.

A committee appointed by the General Authorities of the Church, and working under their guidance, recommended the hymns for the 1985 hymnbook. The goal was to include as many of superior artistic merit as possible while keeping in mind the preferences and needs of the general Church membership; a well-loved hymn ran little risk of being dropped, even if it did not meet high literary or musical standards. In the process of selecting and editing these hymns, certain issues that have become major points of discussion in other denominations presented far fewer difficulties. For example, male-oriented language with reference to God the Father and Jesus Christ was retained, consistent with the LDS concept of them as male. In addition, Latter-day Saints seem fairly comfortable with military metaphors in their hymn texts, though some language dating from times of actual physical conflict, particularly in "Up, Awake, Ye Defenders of Zion" (No. 284), was edited to make it less bellicose. Certain other texts that originally focused on North America were altered to reflect the Church's overall worldwide mission (Nos. 91, 290).

The present hymnbook is divided into eleven sections: Hymns about the Restoration, Praise and Thanksgiving, Prayer and Supplication, Sacrament, Easter, Christmas, Special Topics, Children's Songs, For Women, For Men, and Patriotic. The national anthems of the United States of America and the United Kingdom are included, and anthems for Canada, Australia, and New Zealand are available separately.

An eight-page appendix called "Using the Hymnbook" provides instructions for directors and organists. It is followed by seven indexes: Authors and Composers; Titles, Tunes, and Meters; Tune Names; Meters; Scriptures (an index correlating scriptural passages with hymn texts); Topics; and First Lines and Titles. Scripture references also appear with each hymn.

Subsequently, the Church Music Committee identified one hundred hymns from the 1985 hymnbook as the standard core of hymns to be published in other languages, with a list of fifty optional additional hymns. The remaining hymns in non-English hymnbooks reflect the choices and contributions of the members in the particular language areas. In this way the Church strives to preserve in its international hymnbooks a balance between Churchwide tradition and local preference.

The *Children's Songbook*, published in 1989, follows *The*

Children Sing (1951) and *Sing with Me* (1969) as the official music resource for the Primary organization. With its straightforward messages and attractive melodies, its simplified accompaniments, and its many color illustrations, the *Children's Songbook* is intended to appeal directly to children as well as to their parents and teachers.

BIBLIOGRAPHY

Cornwall, J. Spencer. *Stories of Our Mormon Hymns*. Salt Lake City, 1975.

Davidson, Karen Lynn. *Our Latter-day Hymns: The Stories and the Messages*. Salt Lake City, 1988.

Macare, Helen Hanks. "The Singing Saints: A Study of the Mormon Hymnal, 1835–1950." Ph.D. diss., UCLA, 1961.

Moody, Michael F. "Contemporary Hymnody in The Church of Jesus Christ of Latter-day Saints." Ph.D. diss., University of Southern California, 1972.

Pyper, George D. *Stories of Latter-day Saint Hymns*. Salt Lake City, 1939.

Weight, Newell B. "An Historical Study of the Origins and Character of the Indigenous Hymn Tunes of the Latter-day Saints." D.M.A. diss., University of Southern California, 1961.

KAREN LYNN DAVIDSON

I

IMMACULATE CONCEPTION

Immaculate conception is the belief of some Christians that from her conception in her mother's womb, Jesus' mother was free from original sin. Original sin holds that Adam's sinful choice in the Garden of Eden, made for all his descendants, led to a hereditary sin incurred at conception by every human being and removed only by the sacraments of the church. From this view arose the concept of Mary's immaculate conception. By a unique grace, Mary was preserved from the stain of original sin, inheriting human nature without taint in order that she be a suitable mother for Jesus. This teaching was defined as obligatory dogma by Pope Pius IX in 1854.

Latter-day Saints accept neither the above doctrine of original sin nor the need for Mary's immaculate conception (*MD*, p. 375). Instead, they "believe that men will be punished for their own sins, and not for Adam's transgression" (A of F 2), because Jesus' atonement redeems all, including Mary, from the responsibility for Adam's trespass (Moro. 8:8). "God having redeemed man from the fall, men became again, in their infant state, innocent before God" (D&C 93:38). For Latter-day Saints, Mary was a choice servant selected by God to be the mother of Jesus.

BIBLIOGRAPHY

"Immaculate Conception." *New Catholic Encyclopedia*, Vol. 7, pp. 378–82. New York, 1967.

Watlington, Amanda G. *Official Catholic Teachings: Christ Our Lord.* Wilmington, 1978.

CONNIE LAMB

INDIAN STUDENT PLACEMENT SERVICES

The Indian Student Placement Services was established among Native Americans by the LDS Church in part to fulfill the obligation felt by the Church to help care for the Indians in the Americas (2 Ne. 10:18–19). The program places Indian students in Latter-day Saint homes, where they live while attending the public school of the community during the academic year. Another goal of Indian Student Placement Services, in addition to giving Indian youth better opportunities for education, has been to develop leadership and to promote greater understanding between Indians and non-Indians.

The program started in 1947 in Richfield, Utah, when Helen John, a sixteen-year-old daughter of Navajo beet-field workers, requested permission to stay in Richfield to attend school. As an outgrowth of this request, Golden Buchanan of the Sevier Stake presidency and Miles Jensen, with Elder Spencer W. Kimball's support, organized an informal placement program that grew from three students in 1947 to sixty-eight in 1954, with foster homes in four western states.

In July 1954 the program was formalized under Church Social Services and the Southwest Indian Mission. For the next several years the program grew rapidly, peaking at 4,997 in 1972. The policy for participation was that the natural parents had to request the placement; then foster parents (recommended for the program by their bishop) provided free board, room, and clothing for the Indian children to help them have additional educational, spiritual, and sociocultural experiences. The Indian children had to be at least eight years of age, baptized members of the Church, and in good health. In 1972 the responsibility for recruiting and screening students for the program was given to local priesthood leaders, and the number of students leveled in the mid and late 1970s to around 2,500 a year.

In the early 1980s several of the Indian tribes from whom many of the placement students had come replaced their boarding schools with dramatically improved education on the reservations. In support of this move, the Church limited Indian Placement Student Services to high school students. New goals emphasized the development and strengthening of LDS family and religious values, with Church Social Services taking responsibility for establishing stronger ties and communication between natural families and foster families. The placement service would introduce young Native Americans to mainstream values and social roles without demanding the abandonment of the old for the new. In 1990 the program served about 500 high school students.

Supporters of the services believe that bicultural experiences have great value. Critics view intervention as an intrusion on the right to be fully Native American, a weakening of cultural pluralism, and a cause of psychological damage. However, empirical studies, even by critics, are ambivalent. One claims that the program has failed to raise achievement and IQ scores of placement students, but notes that placement students read more than their reservation counterparts. A second suggests that students suffer intercultural conflict within their foster families, but expresses surprise that these students function without major symptoms of psychological distress. Still another asserts that the placement experience interferes with the process of identity formation, but acknowledges that the program has done more for the Indian people than any other program to date.

Many theses, dissertations, formal reports, and published articles find that the program has been successful and valuable. Placement students usually come from rural families with stable but limited economic and cultural opportunities. Starting with limited language skills, the students in the placement program come out with less fear of failure, more confidence in their future, and higher academic skills and grades, and a better self-image than their reservation peers. Other studies indicate that placement services graduates are aware of a great variety of occupations open to them and are anxious to continue their education to prepare for them. They typically have come to believe in working hard for future rewards and feel that being Indian does not hold them down. They graduate from high school in larger numbers than non-placement Native Americans, and the college grades of rural placement students are on a par with the grades of urban Indian students.

Most placement students express more pride and interest in Indian culture than do students from Indian boarding schools. That they perceive themselves as truly bicultural, at ease in both societies, is confirmed by their rate of interaction with Indian students as well as with Anglo peers. They also become Church leaders. Most of them are active in the Church, go on missions, and agree with major Church beliefs; many marry in the temple.

Foster parents volunteer for religious reasons and remain in the program to see the child grow and develop emotionally and spiritually. They typically become very attached to their Indian children, maintaining a close relationship with them after graduation from school.

Accusations that the LDS Church used its influence to push children into joining the program prompted the U.S. government in 1977 to commission a study conducted under the auspices of the Interstate Compact Secretariat. Its findings rejected such accusations. In the resulting report, written by Robert E. Leach, Native American parents emphatically stated that they, not the children, decided to apply for placement. These parents typically stated that they were pleased that the program led their children to happiness and a better economic situation while the children still identified with their Indian heritage. This participation, they claimed, also helped the rest of the family to understand and deal more effectively with Anglos. They consistently expressed appreciation to the foster families for caring for their children. Some Indian leaders were intent on limiting the placement of Indian children among Anglos. However, after hearing testimony and examining current research, the committee agreed in 1977 to permit the LDS Indian Student Placement program to continue.

BIBLIOGRAPHY

Bishop, Clarence R. "An Evaluation of the Scholastic Achievement of Selected Indian Students Attending Elementary Public Schools of Utah." Master's thesis, Brigham Young University, 1960.

Chadwick, Bruce A., Stan L. Albrecht, and Howard M. Bahr. "Evaluation of an Indian Student Placement Program." *Social Casework* 67 (Nov. 1986):515–24.

The Church of Jesus Christ of Latter-day Saints Presiding Bishopric, Research and

Evaluation Services. *Indian Student Placement Service Evaluation Study*. Salt Lake City, May 1982.

Taylor, Grant H. "A Comparative Study of Former LDS Placement and Non-Placement Navajo Students at Brigham Young University." Ph.D. diss., Brigham Young University, 1981.

GENEVIEVE DE HOYOS

INSTITUTES OF RELIGION

Institutes of religion in The Church of Jesus Christ of Latter-day Saints refer to weekday religious instruction for students attending colleges, universities, and other postsecondary institutions where sufficient LDS students are enrolled. Together with the seminaries for high school students, institutes provide those students an opportunity for organized religious study in connection with their secular studies. The Church funds and administers the institutes of religion as part of its comprehensive CHURCH EDUCATIONAL SYSTEM (CES).

The institute program offers courses in the scriptures and related religious topics such as marriage, Church history, and world religions. Institutes also provide opportunities for students to associate socially, spiritually, and culturally with others who have similar ideals through the Latter-day Saint Student Association (LDSSA), which provides LDS student activities on and off campus.

The Church has established a general regulation that all full-time institute instructors should hold at least a master's degree. A majority hold a doctorate degree. Such degrees are generally not in religion, but in related fields such as education, counseling, or history. The Church expects institute faculty to possess scholarly competence in religion and related fields comparable to that of teachers at adjacent academic institutions, and to be exemplary in all aspects of their lives.

In 1989–1990, there were 317 full-time and several hundred part-time and volunteer instructors in LDS institutes throughout the world, with many full-time instructors serving more than one institute. In the same year, 125,534 students were enrolled in 1,273 institutes serving 1,711 non-LDS college and university campuses internationally.

Historically the rise of public higher education in the United

States led to the elimination of religious education from most university and college curriculums. Beginning in 1894, in response to the need for religious education on these campuses, various student organizations were established, including the Roman Catholic Newman Club, full-time Baptist ministries by campus chaplains, the Jewish B'nai B'rith Hillel, and others. LDS leaders addressed the need for weekday religious education for their college students as early as 1912. As the Church's junior colleges closed (*see* ACADEMIES; SCHOOLS), requests came to establish weekday religious education for LDS students on non-LDS college campuses.

To meet this need, in 1926 the Church initiated a program for LDS students attending the University of Idaho at Moscow, Idaho. University officials welcomed the institute adjacent to the campus. Initially called a college "seminary," the program was renamed the "institute of religion," which established a precedent for subsequent institutes.

In 1935, John A. Widtsoe of the Quorum of the Twelve Apostles outlined the purposes of the institutes of religion:

> During University years students meeting much new knowledge frequently have difficulty, unaided, in reconciling their religious beliefs . . . with their academic studies. . . . LDS Institutes have been established to meet this situation. They offer studies in religion on the college level, in college terms, dealing with the profound questions which every thinking individual has a right to ask. At the Institute students discuss these questions freely and frankly with the Institute Directors, either in classes or in private consultation ["Why Institutes," *Announcement of the LDS Institutes: 1935–1936, Department of Education, Church of Jesus Christ of Latter-day Saints*].

The Church soon constructed a building adjacent to the University of Idaho that became the headquarters for LDS students at the university. The principle of separation of church and state guided the development of the project and the direction of institute activities. The institute developed a cultural and social activities program providing fellowship for LDS students in the area. This fellowship extended beyond LDS students to faculty and other students on campus.

Institutes in Logan, Utah, at Utah State Agricultural College and in Salt Lake City at the University of Utah soon followed the Moscow institute. Shortly thereafter, the Church established institutes at other universities and colleges in Utah, Arizona, and Washington.

Before there were enough students to establish full-time institute programs on southern California campuses, Deseret Clubs were organized. These became the prototype for small LDS student organizations. These clubs continued until 1971, when the Church formally established the LDSSA as the official LDS student group on university and college campuses.

The first international LDS institute program was established in 1969 in Australia and was soon duplicated in New Zealand and Great Britain. The Church has since established institutes in sixty additional countries. These have become a source of support and training for new Church leadership in those areas.

BIBLIOGRAPHY

Anderson, A. Gary. "A Historical Survey of the Full-Time Institutes of Religion of the Church of Jesus Christ of Latter-day Saints, 1926–1966." Ph.D. diss., Brigham Young University, 1968.

Arrington, Leonard J. "The Founding of the LDS Institutes of Religion." *Dialogue* 2 (Summer 1967):137–47.

Berrett, William E. *A Miracle in Weekday Religious Education.* Salt Lake City, 1988.

STANLEY A. PETERSON

INTERFAITH RELATIONSHIPS

[*This entry has three articles:*

Christian
Jewish
Other Faiths

The articles focus on the efforts of the Church to relate, assist, understand, and cooperate with other faiths in common social, ethical, and religious quests.]

CHRISTIAN

The Church has never existed in isolation or insulation from other Christian faiths. Its roots and its nurture are in, and remain in, the

Christian heritage. But its claim that the heavens have opened anew, that a restoration of the lost radiance and power of the full gospel of Jesus Christ is under way at divine initiative, and its rejection of many long-standing traditions have generated misunderstanding and ill will. In the first generation in the United States, the solidarity of the Latter-day Saints was thought to be inimical to pluralism and at the same time aroused the ire of sectarians. Missionary efforts through personal contact more than through mass media and image making sometimes compounded the problem. In certain times and circumstances, there has been no will, or at least no lasting resolve by either side, for outreach and cooperation.

In three ways these tensions are being reduced:

1. Institutionally. Church officers now participate with leaders of other faiths in Christian interchange. LDS leaders in many countries are welcomed to interfaith devotionals with their Protestant, Catholic, and Orthodox counterparts. This has been in keeping with the precept and example of early Church authorities (*see* TOLERANCE). For mutual support, they likewise meet and organize, across varied lines and programs, for example, the chaplaincies of many nations of the free world, the Boy Scout movement, the National Council of Christians and Jews, and local and international service clubs concerned with social, ethical, and moral issues.

2. Educationally. The Church fosters the largest adult education curriculum in the world. Many of the courses are Bible-related, and some focus on Christian history and institutions. For high school and college-age students, who now exceed half a million, the Church provides similar courses in its seminaries and institutes adjacent to high schools and major universities. Teachers in the CHURCH EDUCATIONAL SYSTEM are given financial supplements to visit the Holy Land, to study the origins of the three great monotheistic religions, to become familiar with the vocabularies and worldviews of alternative Christian institutions, and to understand and recognize common ground in the lives of the youth they teach. LDS scholars of many disciplines are increasingly involved in the religious studies programs of academic and professional organizations.

The Church has opened its extensive broadcasting facilities to representative programming across the spectrum of Christian groups (*see* BONNEVILLE INTERNATIONAL CORPORATION; KSL RADIO). It has also been a major participant in religious broadcasts in the VISN Religious Interfaith Cable Television Network, which represents most major denominations in the United States.

To establish two-way interchange, the Richard L. Evans Chair of Christian Understanding was established at BRIGHAM YOUNG UNIVERSITY. Funded and advised by a variety of Christian groups (the initial commitment came from a Presbyterian), this endowment fosters religious studies symposia, lectures, forums, exchange programs, and visiting professorships. It also sponsors interfaith meetings where common as well as controversial theological issues are presented by representatives of each tradition, and where workshops help resolve tensions in an atmosphere of goodwill.

The Religious Studies Center at Brigham Young University produces distinguished volumes utilizing scholars of many faiths who represent interdisciplinary and comparative expertise. Although a literature of disparagement continues both from the left and from the right (*see* ANTI-MORMON PUBLICATIONS), Church leaders continually remind the membership that whatever may be said of those who make a religion of anti-Mormonism, a retaliatory response is neither wise nor Christian.

3. Practically in Christian Humanitarianism. At its best the pattern of LDS life, institutionally and individually, has not been to demand rights but to merit them, not to clamor for fellowship and goodwill but to manifest them and to give energy and time beyond rhetoric. In a major address to regional Church leaders, former President Spencer W. Kimball set the tone:

> We urge members to do their civic duty and to assume their responsibilities as individual citizens in seeking solutions to the problems which beset our cities and communities.
>
> With our wide ranging mission, so far as mankind is concerned, Church members cannot ignore the many practical problems that require solution if our families are to live in an environment conducive to spirituality.
>
> Where solutions to these practical problems require cooperative

action with those not of our faith, members should not be reticent in doing their part in joining and leading in those efforts where they can make an individual contribution to those causes which are consistent with the standards of the Church [Kimball, *Ensign* 8 (May 1978):100].

Examples of recent Church-encouraged projects that reach across different affiliations include cooperative emergency assistance, support for homeless shelters in many cities, and linkage with the work of the Salvation Army. At BYU, students of other faiths are often elected to student offices, and various service clubs strive against intolerance and clannishness. In the same spirit, the Church was among the first to give aid, with other Christian bodies, to disaster areas in such places as China, El Salvador, Nicaragua, Los Angeles, Peru, Armenia, Japan, Iran, Chile, and Greece. Through two special fasts, the Church raised $11 million for the hungry in Africa and Ethiopia, and utilized Catholic services as a delivery system (*see* HUMANITARIAN SERVICE).

Because so much in contemporary society is dissonant, centrifugal, and divisive, interfaith understanding and mutuality seem indispensable. LDS history suggests that what appear to be intractable political, social, and economic clashes are often, at root, religious. To overcome needless divisions and to heal the wounds of modern life, including the religious life, are not just the commission of Latter-day Saints but of all who take seriously the message and ministry of Jesus Christ. Unless in some there is Christlike concern for all, there is little hope for any.

BIBLIOGRAPHY
Arrington, Leonard. "Historical Development of International Mormonism." University of Alberta, *Religious Studies and Theology* 7 (1) Jan. 1987.
Keller, Roger R. *Reformed Christians and Mormon Christians: Let's Talk.* Ann Arbor, Mich., 1986.
Madsen, Truman G. "Are Christians Mormon?" *BYU Studies* 15 (Autumn 1974):73–94.

RICHARD P. LINDSAY

JEWISH

The chief nexus for interfaith relationships between Jews and Latter-day Saints has been Salt Lake City, Utah. A certain amount of contact has also occurred in the State of Israel as well as in cities in the United States with large Jewish populations, such as Los Angeles and

New York. Generally, relations between members of the two groups have been characterized by mutual respect and goodwill. Exceptions include sharp differences between Mormons and some Jews on the issue of the purpose of the Brigham Young University Center for Near Eastern Studies in Jerusalem (dedicated 1989; *see* BRIGHAM YOUNG UNIVERSITY: JERUSALEM CENTER FOR NEAR EASTERN STUDIES). However, a workable relationship prevails.

One of the earliest direct contacts between communities was initiated by Orson Hyde, an LDS apostle, who in 1841 traveled through Europe to reach the Holy Land. With rare exceptions, instead of seeking audience with European Jewish leaders to proselytize them, he warned them of difficulties that they would experience, and urged them to emigrate to Palestine. Orson Hyde continued on to the Holy Land, where, on October 24, 1841, he prayed on the Mount of Olives to "dedicate and consecrate this land . . . for the gathering together of Judah's scattered remnants" (*HC* 4:456–59).

Broader contacts began after 1853 with the arrival of the first Jewish family in Utah. While Jews tended to align themselves politically with non-Mormons, they enjoyed the goodwill of their LDS neighbors. Although some Jewish immigrants into Utah—particularly from eastern Europe and Russia—were ridiculed because of their language and their lack of acquaintance with frontier life, they found no cruelty, no restrictions of movement, and no ugly intolerance. While there were no handouts, charity, or dole, they discovered no restrictions on opportunity among the Latter-day Saints.

In 1900, when Utah Jewish leader Nathan Rosenblatt and his associates decided to build a synagogue for a second congregation, the principal help came from the LDS Church's First Presidency. When the building opened in 1903, Rosenblatt proclaimed his gratitude for the blessing and privilege of living in Utah with the tolerant, understanding men and women of the Mormon faith. He and his associates had always found them to be a people devoted to their own faith, yet a people who respected the Jewish Torah and knew what the noted teacher Hillel meant when he taught, "Do not do to your neighbor what you would not do to yourself."

Brigham Young University in Provo, Utah, regularly offers courses that focus on the religion and history of Jews and Judaism. In addition, Jewish scholars have lectured and taught courses at the university, particularly in recent years. In 1921 President Heber J. Grant offered clear counsel to Latter-day Saints against anti-Semitism: "There should be no ill-will . . . in the heart of any true Latter-day Saint, toward the Jewish people" (in *Gospel Standards*, Salt Lake City, 1941, p. 147).

An indicator of the reciprocal respect that has existed between Utah Jews and Mormons is the number of Jewish public officials elected to serve the state. These include the state's fourth governor (Simon Bamberger, 1917–1921), a district judge (Herbert M. Schiller, 1933–1939), a mayor of Salt Lake City (Louis Marcus, 1931–1935), and several legislators.

[*See also* World Religions (Non-Christian) and Mormonism: Judaism.]

BIBLIOGRAPHY
Brooks, Juanita. *History of the Jews in Utah and Idaho*. Salt Lake City, 1973.
Zucker, Louis C. *Mormon and Jew: A Meeting on the American Frontier*. Provo, Utah, 1961.
———. "Utah." *Encyclopaedia Judaica*, Vol. 16, pp. 33–34. Jerusalem, 1972.
———. "A Jew in Zion." *Sunstone* 6 (Sept.–Oct. 1981):35–44.

JOSEPH ROSENBLATT

OTHER FAITHS

In August 1852, while the Church was still struggling to establish itself in the western United States, President Brigham Young issued a bold call for missionaries to go to China, India, Siam (Thailand), and Ceylon (Sri Lanka). The seventeen missionaries who were sent formed some of the earliest contacts that LDS members had with non-Christians. Because of civil wars, rejection, and language and cultural difficulties, the work in most countries lasted only months; however, work in India continued until 1856. Although some attempts were made in the early twentieth century, the Church did not undertake further significant efforts to establish itself in non-Christian nations, including Asia, until after World War II.

Stimulated by experiences of LDS servicemen in Asia during and after the war, the Church established missions in East Asia at the end of the 1940s. Since then, wards and stakes led by local members have been established in Japan, South Korea, Hong Kong, Taiwan, and the Philippines; temples have been built in all these places except Hong Kong.

In the 1970s and 1980s, the Church expanded into such Southeast Asian nations as Singapore, Thailand, Indonesia, and Malaysia, and in the South Asian nations of India and Sri Lanka. Although small beginnings have been made in some Muslim countries, Church growth in such countries has been limited.

LDS health services programs in the Philippines and refugee assistance in Thailand have been favorably received. High-level contacts with government officials in many countries have elicited a positive response to the values of the Church and its members. Overall, the Church has made consistent efforts to remain sensitive to and abide by local laws and customs, including regulations based on religious sentiment.

Church growth in Africa has principally taken place in the last quarter of the twentieth century, particularly following the 1978 revelation allowing all worthy males to hold the priesthood. Congregations have been established in several countries, and Church membership is growing rapidly. In recent years, the Church has joined various charitable organizations in sending famine relief to stricken nations on the African continent (*see* ECONOMIC AID).

In an educational vein, Missionary Training Centers teach many foreign languages and courses on the religions and cultures of non-Western countries, and for educational purposes "culturegrams" have been developed that are now used by U.S. government agencies. In addition, courses on world religions are regularly taught in institutions of higher learning. Moreover, symposia on Islam and on the religions of Africa have been hosted at Brigham Young University, with a number of distinguished religious leaders and scholars participating.

In many countries, The Church of Jesus Christ of Latter-day Saints is viewed as an American church. However, Church leaders have strongly emphasized that it is universal, a church for all people everywhere (*see* WORLD RELIGIONS [NON-CHRISTIAN] AND MORMONISM). A powerful presentation by President Spencer W. Kimball in 1974 stressed the responsibility of the Church to share the gospel with all of God's children (*Ensign* 4 [Oct. 1974]:2–14). Consequently, in the last half of the twentieth century the Church has made its most significant efforts to establish itself throughout the world.

Generally the LDS outreach to non-Christians has had a positive, invigorating effect on members of the Church, has strengthened

Church membership significantly, and has brought about increased awareness of cultural differences as well as a willingness to work within those differences.

BIBLIOGRAPHY

Palmer, Spencer J. *The Expanding Church*. Salt Lake City, 1978.

———, ed. *Mormons and Muslims*. Provo, Utah, 1983.

SOREN F. COX

INTERNATIONAL GENEALOGICAL INDEX™ (IGI)

The International Genealogical Index™ (IGI) is a vital records index, which at the beginning of 1990 contained more than 147 million names of deceased persons from the 1500s to about 1875. The IGI lists individuals alphabetically according to place of birth/christening or marriage, and clusters similarly spelled surnames under a standard spelling.

The Church publishes the IGI to assist genealogical research and help members determine whether temple ordinances have been performed for deceased ancestors. Countries such as England (47,155,000 entries), Mexico 24,205,000, Germany (18,675,000), the United States (18,660,000), Scotland (10,745,000), and Finland (5,045,000), as well as more than ninety other nations are included.

Available on 9,200 microfiches and on compact disc, the IGI can be searched at the FAMILY HISTORY LIBRARY, Salt Lake City, or at any of the nearly 1,400 LDS FAMILY HISTORY CENTERS located in various parts of the world. Patrons can purchase copies of the microfiche in sets by region, state, or country from the Family History Department, LDS Church Headquarters, Salt Lake City, UT 84150, or copy up to 500 entries to a holding file that can be printed or copied to diskettes for home use.

BIBLIOGRAPHY

Family History Library. *Research Outline: International Genealogical Index* (on microfiche). 1st ed., Aug. 1988, Series IGI, no. 1, 2nd ed., Mar. 1989, Series IGI, no. 5 (compact disc).

GERALD M. HASLAM

J

JOURNALS

Journal writing among the early Latter-day Saints took impetus from a divine charge to the Prophet Joseph Smith on the day the Church was organized: "There shall be a record kept among you" (D&C 21:1). Although that was an official charge to the Church, individual members took it as a personal charge and began keeping journals. Joseph Smith himself worked regularly with scribes until his death, directing the recording of his daily activities. Much of what is known about the early events of the Church comes from the many personal journals kept by leaders and members.

Careful and complete records served as a protection against opponents of the Church. In instructions to the Quorum of the Twelve in 1835, Joseph Smith urged them to note down the procedures of meetings held, for "the time will come, when, if you neglect to do this thing, you will fall by the hands of unrighteous men. . . . If you will be careful to keep minutes of these things . . . it will be one of the most important records ever seen" (*HC* 2:198–99). Joseph Smith stated that the Saints had been somewhat delinquent in this charge.

In addition to Joseph Smith's comprehensive journal, which he kept with the aid of personal scribes, several early converts began to keep personal diaries, most of them sketchy but some very ambitious. It has been a common practice of missionaries to keep journals of their activities, though most of these early journals tended to be factual rather than reflective, and followed a quite standard format: the call, travel particulars, names of companions and Church members, lists of letters from home, sightseeing, release, and the return home. A frequent topic of Latter-day Saint journals is the writer's conversion to the Church.

Early journals usually are also quite reportorial, matter-of-fact in tone, sparing in detail, and often repetitive; yet they are valuable for historical reference, if not engaging in content or style, though some passages are eloquent in their plainness. Feelings and introspection are more characteristic of twentieth-century journals. Yet all journals are important resources for FAMILY HISTORY information.

Most Presidents of the Church have kept a journal of some type—either historical or personal, with or without the assistance of a secretary. From the founding of the Church, there was a steady flow of journal writing, the quantity increasing during times of reformation, as in 1856–1857, or when leaders urged the practice of journal keeping. Perhaps best known of the early diarists was Wilford Woodruff, who kept a meticulous personal record (including many drawings)—fifteen volumes covering the years 1833–1898. His record is rich in detail and personal insight on many important events in the early Church.

In 1977, in his *Guide to Mormon Diaries & Autobiographies*, Davis Bitton identified and cataloged some 3,000 pieces of LDS autobiographical writing, consisting largely of journals, mostly by men, in repositories throughout the United States, though mainly in the state of Utah. Many more uncataloged journals remain in the possession of individuals and families, and Bitton suggested that his bibliography be updated from time to time.

Twentieth-century LDS journals tend to be longer and more numerous, reflecting increased literacy, more time to write, and greater openness. Both Joseph F. Smith and Heber J. Grant, Church presidents from 1901 to 1918 and 1918 to 1945, respectively, left multivolume journal records. LDS journal writing received special stimulus during the presidency of Spencer W. Kimball (1973–1985), who himself kept an extensive journal of about eighty volumes. Typical of his many admonitions to Church members is a short remark in the 1977 October general conference: "A word about personal journals and records: We urge every person in the Church to keep a diary or a journal from youth up, all through his life" ("The Foundations of Righteousness." *Ensign* 7 [Nov. 1977]:4).

Also in recent years, a new reason for journal writing has been voiced: the value of journals as a gift to descendants—a linking of the generations. President Kimball said: "I promise you that if you will keep your journals and records, they will indeed be a source of great inspiration to your families, to your children, your grandchildren, and others, on through the generations. . . . Rich passages . . . will be quoted by your posterity" (p. 61).

Because of the admonitions of scripture and leaders, journal writing, especially in recent decades, has become an integral part of the religious experience of many Latter-day Saints. Parents have been encouraged to write their own personal journals and to help their children begin writing theirs, to make the experience pleasant. President Kimball said in 1980: "Those who keep a personal journal are more likely to keep the Lord in remembrance in their daily lives" (p. 61).

BIBLIOGRAPHY

Bitton, Davis. *Guide to Mormon Diaries & Autobiographies.* Provo, Utah, 1977.

Forbis, Dianne Dibb. "It's Child's Play: How to Help Your Child Begin a Journal." *Ensign* 7 (Jan. 1977):29.

Kimball, Spencer W. "President Kimball Speaks out on Personal Journals." *Ensign* 10 (Dec. 1980):60–61.

DON E. NORTON
JOANNE LINNABARY

K

KSL RADIO

KSL is a clear-channel Salt Lake City radio station, 1160 on the dial. Originally an independent KZN, it went on the air May 6, 1922. The Church bought controlling interest in the station on April 21, 1925.

Earl J. Glade, pioneer broadcaster, was general manager of the station for its first twenty years. He set standards and policies that continue to the present: a strong local and international news service, community and cultural interdependence, and sponsorship of quality-of-life improvements.

In 1932 KSL changed affiliation from NBC to CBS and, in the same year, increased its power to 50,000 watts. The station reaches into all the United States west of the Mississippi and, by occasional "skips," is heard as far away as New Zealand and Norway.

On December 26, 1946, KSL began broadcasting the first FM radio signal in Utah under the call letters of KSL-FM, and on June 1, 1949, KSL Television went on the air. The FM station was sold in 1978. KSL-TV has a survey area that includes seven western states.

In 1961, BONNEVILLE CORPORATION was created to give unified leadership to KSL and other BROADCASTING entities acquired and developed by the Church.

ARCH L. MADSEN

L

LAWSUITS

Church members are usually inclined to avoid litigation and to find less contentious ways of resolving differences that may arise. This inclination is based primarily upon teachings in the New Testament and the Doctrine and Covenants. The early experience of the Church added powerful reinforcements to scriptural condemnations of litigation. In the 1840s the Prophet Joseph Smith and other early leaders were obliged to defend themselves repeatedly against false charges. So oppressive were those charges that the Prophet at one time even said that he looked forward to the next life, where people would be reunited with their loved ones and where there "will be no fear of mobs, persecutions, or malicious lawsuits" (*TPJS*, p. 360).

The disparaging view of litigation begins with the Sermon on the Mount. Jesus taught his followers to settle disputes quickly and avoid court proceedings, to "turn the other cheek," and, if an adversary should obtain judgment against them in court to "let him have thy cloak also" (Matt. 5:25–26, 39–40). The apostle Paul condemned the practice that "brother goeth to law with brother, and that before the unbelievers" (1 Cor. 6:6). He counseled the Corinthian Saints to find a wise person from among them to judge the matter and, failing that, to suffer the wrong rather than to take it to legal authorities for a decision (verses 5–7).

More detailed instructions for dealing with offenses are contained in the Doctrine and Covenants, which counsels members to resolve their differences. But it also recognizes that some offenses are violations of criminal law that should be reported to civil authorities, while other categories of offenders should be dealt with by the Church (D&C 42:79–92). Instructions for Church disciplinary procedures are detailed (D&C 102:13–23).

When the main body of the Church was established in Utah in the mid-1800s, there was no civil authority, so Church courts exercised jurisdiction over secular as well as religious matters for the next several decades. However, following the establishment of civil courts, the need for Church courts diminished. They were formally discontinued in 1989 in favor of disciplinary councils.

Church courts never were intended to absolve members from the duty of resolving their disputes by reconciliation and mutual understanding whenever possible. Even when Church courts were available, members were regularly admonished to settle their conflicts by informal means and to avoid litigation. A typical example: "Be reconciled to each other. Do not go to the courts of the Church nor to the courts of the land for litigation. Settle your own troubles and difficulties" (J. F. Smith, *GD*, p. 257).

The preference for forbearance, forgiveness, and informal means of resolution of disputes, both among Church members and with people outside the Church, continues today, as shown by counsel given in a 1988 general conference of the Church: "We live in an environment . . . of litigation and conflict, of suing and countersuing. Even here the powers of healing may be invoked" (G. B. Hinckley, *Ensign* 18 [Nov. 1988]:54).

BIBLIOGRAPHY

Firmage, Edwin B., and Richard C. Mangrum. *Zion in the Courts: A Legal History of the Church of Jesus Christ of Latter-day Saints, 1830–1900.* Urbana, Ill., 1988.

GERALD R. WILLIAMS

LDS BUSINESS COLLEGE

The LDS Business College, located in Salt Lake City, Utah, is a fully-accredited, two-year institution of higher learning owned by the

Church, and operated and partially funded through the CHURCH EDU-CATIONAL SYSTEM (CES). The 800-plus students receive training for careers in business and industry.

Its forerunner, the Salt Lake Stake Academy, was founded in 1886 under the direction of Karl G. Maeser. Church leaders originally intended to establish the Academy as the Church's leading institution of higher learning, and the name of the school was changed to LDS College in 1889. When Young University (later the Church University) replaced LDS College as the "flagship" of the educational system of the Church, LDS College declined in significance. However, the Church University was closed in 1894, contributing to the subsequent growth of both LDS College and Brigham Young Academy in Provo, later BRIGHAM YOUNG UNIVERSITY (1903). An early emphasis on busi-ness courses at LDS College led to the creation of a department of business in 1895. When LDS College closed in 1931, the departments of business and music continued to function separately as the LDS Business College and the McCune School of Music.

After a long period in which Church policy required the college to be financially self-sufficient, CES resumed partial funding in 1986. At that time, a project to upgrade programs and facilities was begun. LDS Business College currently offers one- and two-year programs plus short courses and professional seminars in account-ing, marketing/management, computer information systems, office administration, health services, fashion merchandising, and interior design. In all courses of study along with imparting information and developing skills, a major emphasis is placed on the importance of morality and ethics in the business profession.

BIBLIOGRAPHY

Quinn, D. Michael. "The Brief Career of Young University at Salt Lake City." *Utah Historical Quarterly* 41 (1973):69–89.

KENNETH H. BEESLEY

LDS FOUNDATION

The LDS Foundation is the department of The Church of Jesus Christ of Latter-day Saints that encourages and facilitates voluntary charitable contributions to the CHURCH EDUCATIONAL SYSTEM and other charities of the Church.

Although it originated in the BRIGHAM YOUNG UNIVERSITY development office, it now operates under the direction of the Presiding Bishopric in serving a fuller Churchwide mission. Since 1972 the Foundation has assisted thousands of donors to contribute to the students and programs of Church institutions.

Support is received both from Church members and from individuals who are not members but who recognize the ability of Church institutions to assist humanity. Funding sources include corporations, private foundations, alumni of Church institutions of higher education, and private individuals.

The Foundation employs full-time professionals who help donors prepare contributions in the form of trusts, estates, planned gifts, and cash donations and accounts for all charitable donations to the Church other than the tithes and offerings of members. Main offices are in Salt Lake City and Provo, Utah.

BIBLIOGRAPHY

Wilkinson, Ernest L., and Leonard J. Arrington, eds. *Brigham Young University: The First One Hundred Years*, Vol. 3, pp. 537–93. Provo, 1976.

DAVID A. WANAMAKER

LDS STUDENT ASSOCIATION

The LDS Student Association (LDSSA) is an organization which sponsors social, religious, and recreational activities for LDS college students and their friends. The organization provides a framework wherein students have access to all phases of the Church that affect their lives during the week.

The purposes of LDSSA are to help college and university students stay closely affiliated with the Church, succeed in their studies, and achieve a balanced educational-social life while on campus; to motivate LDS students to become a powerful influence for good on the campus; to provide meaningful activities that are consistent with Church standards; and to coordinate Church-related activities for college students. These purposes are accomplished under the direction of the priesthood and in cooperation with the institutes of the CHURCH EDUCATIONAL SYSTEM. These student associations create a sense of belonging, an opportunity for leadership, and an expanded circle of friends who share similar values. For some students, LDSSA is the center of their school experience.

LDSSA was established in 1960, and has expanded to every college campus where there is an LDS institute of religion. In 1990, some 290 LDSSA organizations existed within the United States and Canada in post-secondary institutions, including community colleges, universities, and trade and technical schools. Each campus organization operates under the direction of an assigned local stake president who is also the priesthood leader for all LDS affairs on campus. He presides over an executive committee consisting of a student president, vice president(s), a secretary, and an education adviser, who is usually the director of the institute associated with the campus. The student leaders are called, set apart, and serve under the direction of the priesthood leader. The executive committee is the policymaking body for the local student association.

A student president presides over the chapter LDSSA council. The membership includes representatives of all LDS organizations that function on, or are influenced by, the school. These may include Lambda Delta Sigma sorority and Sigma Gamma Chi fraternity, young single adults, married students, campus stakes or wards, and other interest groups. While each of these groups operates as an independent agency, their activities are correlated through the LDSSA council, which strives to meet needs without undue overlap. The type of institution, geographic location, number of LDS students, and the social, cultural, and academic traditions influence how LDSSA is organized and how it functions to meet local and individual student needs.

At the general level of the Church, a governing board is made up of an executive director, presidents of Sigma Gamma Chi and Lambda Delta Sigma, and representatives of the General Authorities, seminaries, and institutes.

ELAINE ANDERSON CANNON

LIBRARIES AND ARCHIVES

Latter-day Saints believe that people should document God's dealings with them. Without sacred records, people are destined to "dwindle and perish in unbelief" (1 Ne. 3:13). In one of the first revelations received after the Church was formally organized, the Prophet Joseph Smith was instructed that "there shall be a record kept among you" (D&C 21:1). This directive, followed a few years later by instruction "to gather up the libelous publications that are afloat" (D&C 123:4), led to the appointment of a succession of Church historians, each charged with keeping an account of the activities of Joseph Smith, his successors, and the Church in general. Many of these ongoing chronicles, together with the accumulation of day-to-day records of Church enterprises and the papers of Church members, became the foundation of the modern Church Archives in Salt Lake City. The establishment of such archives was accomplished when there were few historical societies and no national or state archives in the United States.

Andrew Jenson, who served as an Assistant Church Historian for fifty years (1891–1941), tirelessly combed LDS communities and foreign missions for records. He wrote histories of hundreds of local wards, branches, missions, and settlements, and established a system for having local leaders produce manuscript histories (quarterly records of Church events and activities). His efforts greatly enriched the Church Archives, and the records have continued to expand with the donations of papers and diaries of many Church members throughout the years. Because of the growth of the Church, minutes of meetings of local congregations are no longer sent to the Archives, and the Manuscript Histories have been replaced by brief annual historical reports.

In the early days of the Church, leaders sought after texts that demonstrated a broad-based learning and cultural understanding. A library was established in Nauvoo in the Seventies Hall that contained many books, including those brought by missionaries who had served abroad. Although the disposition of the Nauvoo library is not known, the Latter-day Saints continued to maintain libraries after they moved west.

Today the main historical library of the Church is maintained and supervised by the Historical Department of the Church in Salt Lake City. It strives to maintain as complete a collection as possible on the Mormon experience throughout the world. It holds a copy of each edition, in each language, of all official Church publications. It attempts to collect all publications in which the Church or the Latter-day Saints are mentioned. It also holds a significant collection of works published by and about schismatic groups that follow teachings of Joseph Smith or the Book of Mormon.

Perhaps best known of all the LDS libraries is the FAMILY HISTORY LIBRARY. With approximately 1.6 million reels of microfilm, containing raw genealogical data and copies of published books, as well as a collection of some 200,000 hard-copy volumes, the Family History Library is used by genealogists throughout the world. Its resources are available through a network of over 1,500 local LDS FAMILY HISTORY CENTERS, each staffed by volunteers. Each library has a catalog of the main library's holdings and may order microfilm copies of most of the collection. In addition, the Church operates libraries/media centers in each of its meetinghouses to support the curriculum of the Church's teaching organizations.

Many college and university libraries, as well as other research institutions, hold significant collections on the Mormons and the Church. BRIGHAM YOUNG UNIVERSITY, Utah State University, and the University of Utah all have important Mormon collections. The other colleges and universities in Utah also hold notable materials, as do the Utah State Historical Society, the Daughters of Utah Pioneers Museum, and the Utah State Archives. Outside of Utah, the Library of Congress in Washington, D.C., has collected much published material on the Latter-day Saints. The National Archives has many records documenting the federal government's involvement with the Mormons and the Utah Territory. Research collections at Yale University, the New York Public Library, Princeton University, the University of Michigan, the Historical Office of the Reorganized Church of Jesus Christ of Latter Day Saints, the University of California at Berkeley, and the Huntington Library (San Marino, California), as well as many other libraries throughout the West, can be resources for scholars searching for LDS materials. Indeed, Mormon-related records may be found in any of the hundreds of archives and manuscript libraries throughout the United States.

BIBLIOGRAPHY
Evans, Max J. "A History of the Public Library Movement in Utah." Master's thesis, Utah State University, 1971.
———, and Ronald G. Watt. "Sources for Western History at the Church of Jesus Christ of Latter-day Saints." *Western Historical Quarterly* 8 (July 1977):303–312.

MAX J. EVANS

LIFESTYLE

Early Latter-day Saints, who typically gathered into their own communities and shared cultural and religious concepts and experiences, developed a distinctive lifestyle that helped overcome differences in social class or a variety of geographic and religious backgrounds among members of the fledgling Church. The members, mostly former Protestants from New England, New York, Ohio, eastern Canada, the British Isles, and Scandinavia, had compatible Christian and social values, and a shared purpose in building Zion and in creating the culture of their communities. A century and a half later, with more than seven million Latter-day Saints living throughout the world in a multitude of nations and in varied circumstances, the LDS lifestyle continues to be focused on shared personal beliefs and the desires to progress toward exaltation and to build up the kingdom of God on earth.

In the 1940s, more than a century after the Church was established, its one million members were concentrated largely in the western United States. Converts had tended to migrate to join the main body of the Church, and many Utah Church members and leaders were descended from early pioneers. In these circumstances, a concept of LDS lifestyle became clearly defined. Religious observance and participation in Church programs became almost inseparable from other aspects of life in communities comprised largely of Church members. The people with whom one worshiped at Church were also one's neighbors, schoolmates, and associates at work.

This lifestyle, especially in the LDS towns of the rural Intermountain West, was family-oriented and home- and Church-centered. Self-sufficiency through gardening, canning, sewing, and bread-making, and also commitment to hard work, service, duty, thrift, and education were shared cultural patterns and values. The lifestyle, based upon practical considerations, cultural heritage, and family traditions as well as Church teachings, reflected the influence of pioneer agrarian values, the independence and vigor of western frontiersmanship, and New England Puritanism. This lifestyle pervaded LDS society in North America, and even beyond as the Church began to expand rapidly throughout the world in the decades following World War II.

Today, Latter-day Saints make up groups ranging from entire small towns in Utah and surrounding states to small congregations of only a few individuals or families in other areas and countries. Latter-day Saints are now encouraged to build up the Church in their home areas rather than migrate to Utah. Converts retain national and family traditions while adopting the religion and moral teachings and activities of the Church.

While Latter-day Saints throughout the world feel a common spiritual heritage and devotion to their faith, their daily lives may vary considerably. Nevertheless, there are certain shared patterns of LDS lifestyle practiced throughout the world by faithful members regardless of language or cultural differences. These practices identify the members and families as Latter-day Saints and constitute a bond and similarity of values among members—even where there is significant cultural diversity.

A typical day begins and ends with individual and family prayer, and includes scripture study. The WORD OF WISDOM affects a Latter-day Saint's choices in food and drink. Clothing choices are influenced by teachings on modesty. Gospel teachings influence somewhat the choice of an occupation and affect one's conduct while at work, school, and home. Active Church members feel they should be good examples of Jesus Christ's message to their families and all other associates. Members' commitment to tithing and to making other contributions to the Church affects financial decisions. Latter-day Saints who live their religion avoid profanity and entertainment that advocates or encourages immorality. Many members have callings requiring significant weekly or even daily commitments of time and energy.

Church members are taught that they should establish valuative priorities in order to avoid becoming overwhelmed by the many demands on their time and energies. Important decisions are often made in consultation with one's spouse, parents, or perhaps the entire family, and with the Lord through prayer (cf. D&C 9:8–9). Since there are more opportunities and obligations available than one person can possibly fulfill, Latter-day Saints try to direct their energies by wise individual choices through thought, prayer, consultation with Church leaders, and personal inspiration through the guidance of the Holy Ghost. Such resources help them decide what is most important at any given time. The influence of Church culture, especially in the United States, is sufficiently strong that even those who become disaffected and no longer participate in LDS religious activities often continue to describe themselves as "cultural Mormons."

Each close-knit community of Saints may have distinctive characteristics, depending upon the area where such Church members live. Ideally, a Church meetinghouse, whether in a large or small ward, or involving a scattered few members, becomes a second home, a place where one is accepted, loved, helped, and given the opportunity to participate. A sense of belonging, both to the local ward or branch and to the worldwide community of those who have accepted the name of Christ through baptism and are bound to him by covenant, is the foundation of the spiritual and emotional life, as well as the practical daily life, of the Latter-day Saint.

[*See also* Civic Duties; Community; Family Life; Self-sufficiency.]

JAROLDEEN EDWARDS

LIGHT-MINDEDNESS

Modern scripture deals with "light-mindedness" as trivializing the sacred or making light of sacred things. Latter-day Saints were admonished early in the history of the Church to "trifle not with sacred things" (D&C 6:12; 8:10). At its worst, light-mindedness may become ridicule and then sacrilege and blasphemy—a deliberate irreverence for the things of God.

Divine personages and their names, temple ceremonies, the priesthood and its ordinances, and the saintly life, for example, are intrinsically holy. Other things are holy by association. The Lord has said, "That which cometh from above is sacred, and must be spoken with care, and by constraint of the Spirit" (D&C 63:64). The Saints were warned against "excess of laughter," "light speeches," and "light-mindedness," yet were taught to worship "with a glad heart and a cheerful countenance" (D&C 59:15; 88:121).

In practice, Latter-day Saints distinguish light-mindedness from lightheartedness; the latter is a triumph of the zestful, joyful spirit of the gospel over life's trials. Such cheerfulness and good humor do not preclude, but rather can complement, spirituality. While imprisoned in Liberty Jail, Joseph Smith wrote that the things of God are only made known to those who exercise "careful and ponderous and solemn thoughts" (*HC* 3:295); yet he later spoke of himself as "playful and cheerful" (*TPJS*, p. 307). The Church counsels against a light-minded attitude toward sacred matters but encourages joyfulness in worship and wholesome pleasure in recreation.

BIBLIOGRAPHY
Kimball, Spencer W. *We Should Be a Reverent People* (pamphlet), pp. 1–5. Salt Lake City, 1976.

WILLIAM L. FILLMORE

LITERATURE, MORMON WRITERS OF

[*This entry is made up of five essays:*

Drama
Novels
Personal Essays
Poetry
Short Stories

They discuss the development of Mormon literature after Orson F. Whitney's plea for members of the Church to write wholesome, instructive "Home Literature" (1888) to counter the intrusion of the "faithless" literature of the world that was coming into LDS homes. This charge initiated a creative and didactic impulse which continues as one vein of LDS literature to the present. The resulting stories, plays, and poems on Mormon themes, promoting LDS values and ideals helped build testimony among the youth of the Church.]

DRAMA

Theater has enjoyed a prominent position in the Church from its earliest days in Nauvoo. Thomas A. Lyne, a prominent Philadelphia actor-manager, joined the Church in Nauvoo, and was encouraged by the Prophet Joseph Smith to produce several popular plays. One such was *Pizarro*, in which Brigham Young played the role of the High Priest. Lyne lifted Nauvoo theater above the amateur level and entertained the Saints with such plays as Shakespeare's *Richard III*.

While the Church is justifiably proud of its overall support of the arts, the output of drama by LDS writers has been limited and rather late. The first major attempt at an LDS play written and produced by Latter-day Saints was Orestes Utah Bean's dramatic adaptation of B. H. Roberts' 1889 novel, *Corianton: A Nephite Story*, as *Corianton—An Aztec Romance or The Siren and the Prophet*. Between 1902 and 1912, it played from San Francisco to New York.

Other playwrights from Utah have achieved national prominence. Harold Orlob wrote musical comedies such as *Listen Lester*. Otto Harbach wrote many popular plays, including *Madam Sherry*; *Katinka*; *No No Nanette*; *High Jinks*; *The Silent Witness*; and *Up in Mable's Room*. Edwin Milton Royle achieved a national reputation with *Friends*; *The Squaw Man*; *The Struggle Everlasting*; and *These Are My People*. Despite the prominence of these playwrights, virtually no Latter-day Saints wrote plays with LDS characters or themes until late in the twentieth century.

The 1960s saw something of a flowering of LDS drama by Latter-day Saints about LDS subjects. Clinton F. Larson published a number of serious poetic dramas, several of which were produced, such as *Moroni*; *Mantle of the Prophet*; and *Mary of Nazareth*. Keith Engar's work includes *Right Honorable Saint* and *Montrose Crossing*, a thoughtful look at the exodus from Nauvoo. Doug Stewart and Lex de Azevedo's popular musical *Saturday's Warrior* and its sequel *Starchild* proved that LDS audiences would support overtly LDS theater with high production values. Predictably, a spate of musicals followed, including Carol Lynn Pearson's *My Turn on Earth*. Pearson also wrote *The Order Is Love*; *The Dance*; and a one-person show, *Mother Wove the Morning*.

James Arrington is an actor/playwright/producer who has become known among Latter-day Saints through touring his one-person production of *Here's Brother Brigham*. He also wrote and produced *Golden*, a one-person portrayal of the wit and wisdom of J. Golden Kimball (1853–1938), of the Seventy. In his *Farley Family Reunion*, Arrington plays all the characters, both male and female. He also collaborated with Tim Slover to produce another one-person show, *Wilford Woodruff: God's Fisherman*, a portrayal of the early years of an apostle and later President of the Church.

For decades Nathan and Ruth Hale wrote and produced plays in southern California, many of LDS theme and for LDS audiences. Since the mid-1980s they have done their work in Utah. Thomas F. Rogers has written a number of dramatic adaptations of nineteenth-century Russian novels, as well as works he describes as "plays of mitigated conscience," some overtly LDS, including *Huebner*; *Fire in the Bones*; *Reunion*; and *Journey to Golgotha*.

Promising younger LDS playwrights include Orson Scott Card (*Stone Tables*, and *Father, Mother, Mother, and Mom*); Robert Elliot (*Fires of the Mind*); Susan Howe (*Burdens of Earth*); Martin Kelly (*And They Shall Be Gathered*); Reed McColm (*Together Again for the First Time*, and *Holding Patterns*); and Tim Slover (*Dreambuilder* and *Scales*).

BIBLIOGRAPHY
Cracroft, Richard H., and Neal E. Lambert, eds. "Drama." In *A Believing People: Literature of the Latter-day Saints*, pp. 403–488. Provo, Utah, 1974.

ROBERT A. NELSON

NOVELS

Until recently, novels written by Latter-day Saints have tended to fall into two disparate categories: "faithful fiction" of the Home Literature tradition, a didactic and cautionary fiction intended primarily to instruct and inspire the youth of the Church; and "faithless fiction" of the Lost Generation tradition, generally a more sophisticated fiction in which dissenting or expatriate Latter-day Saints examine Church members' lives from a position critical of LDS history and tradition, teachings, leadership, and culture. In recent years, an increasing number of LDS writers have crafted novels that affirm their history and tradition and assert an LDS worldview while achieving artistic sophistication and literary craftsmanship.

HOME LITERATURE TRADITION. From the beginnings of the Church (1830) until after 1888, the Latter-day Saints, like many other nineteenth-century literal-minded American religious groups, manifested a deep distrust of fiction. Church leaders considered fiction simply not true, and counseled the Saints to avoid reading it. During the late 1870s and the 1880s, however, young Latter-day Saints, aware of their provincialism and isolation in the Utah Territory, were attracted by the allure of eastern education, sophistication, and lifestyles, and some began to show impatience, indifference, and even rebellion. To counter this tendency, Orson F. Whitney (1855–1931, ordained an apostle in 1906) delivered a landmark sermon, "Home Literature" (*Contributor* 9 [June 1888]:297–302; reprinted in Cracroft and Lambert, pp. 203–207), calling on Latter-day Saints to produce a pure and powerful literature on LDS themes and to promote LDS values among the youth.

Latter-day Saints began writing "faith promoting stories," a didactic literary impulse which continues today. The most important responses to Whitney, himself the author of an epic poem, *Elias* (1904), came from the prolific writing and editing of Susa Young Gates (1856–1933), young women's leader, daughter and confidante of Brigham Young, and founding mother of the Home Literature movement. She published more than thirty poems, forty-five short stories, and three novels, including *John Stevens' Courtship: A Story of the Echo Canyon War* (serialized in *Contributor*, 16–17 [1895–1896]). B. H. Roberts (1857–1933, set apart as one of the presidents of the Seventy in 1888) published the novel *Corianton: A Nephite Story* (serialized in *Contributor* 10 [1889]), based on Book of Mormon characters and events, and later redacted into a drama that played to large audiences in Utah, Chicago, and New York.

The most important author in this tradition is Nephi Anderson (1865–1923), a son of Norwegian converts to the Church, who published ten novels. The most famous and enduring is *Added Upon* (1898, fifty reprintings). Despite its heavy doctrine, light plot, and wooden characters, the book has inspired spinoffs in such late twentieth-century musicals as *Saturday's Warrior* and *My Turn on Earth*.

Anderson demonstrated better than any other LDS novelist to date the possibilities for fiction in Mormon experience, theology, and worldview. His primary purpose was to teach the restored gospel and promote, through telling an exciting story, "the good, pure, and the elevating" in LDS life and beliefs (*IE* 1 [Jan. 1898]:186–88).

LOST GENERATION.   Though Home Literature fell into a tedious pattern until taking on a new life in the 1960s, the rise of "Mormondom's Lost Generation" expatriate writers of "faithless fiction" in the 1930s and 1940s set in motion the second important literary impulse in Mormon literature. Five writers of varying accomplishment best illustrate this direction: Paul Drayton Bailey (b. 1906), Samuel Woolley Taylor (b. 1907), Maurine Whipple (b. 1910), Virginia Sorensen (b. 1912), and Vardis Fisher (1895–1968).

Paul Bailey's *For Time and All Eternity* (1964), though flawed, is his finest novel. Samuel Taylor, a son of an apostle and grandson of a President of the Church, is a noted film scenarist. His *Heaven Knows Why* (1948; 1979) is one of the funniest Mormon novels to date. His histories and biographies *Family Kingdom* (1951), *Nightfall at Nauvoo* (1971), and *The Kingdom or Nothing* (1976) are written with such imaginative license that they must be considered quasifictional. Maurine Whipple's *The Giant Joshua* (1941) is considered by many to be the finest Mormon novel. Though a "flawed masterpiece," it is, according to Eugene England, "the *truest* fiction about the pioneer experience" (p. 148). Another Lost Generation novelist, Virginia Sorensen, grew up in Utah, left the Church, married the novelist Alec Waugh (brother of Evelyn), and established herself as a Newbery Award writer of children's books. She is one of the best novelists produced by the LDS culture, and her finest novel, *The Evening and the Morning*, was published in 1949. An earlier novel, *A Little Lower Than the Angels* (1942), was her most popular.

A major novelist among the Lost Generation writers is Vardis Fisher (1895–1968), whose saga, *Children of God: An American Epic* (1939), won the Harper Prize. Fisher grew up in Annis, Idaho, in a devout LDS family, but became disaffected with the Church in his youth. In *Children of God* he returns to his roots and sweeps across LDS history from the first vision of Joseph Smith of 1820 through the Manifesto of 1890 (after which he feels the Church lost its vitality). While he claims this was his only Mormon novel, several other works have strong autobiographical threads.

The Lost Generation impulse continues to assert itself in such works as Levi S. Peterson's *The Backslider* (1986), Linda Sillitoe's *Sideways To The Sun* (1987), and Judith Freeman's *The Chinchilla Farm* (1989).

CONTEMPORARY HOME LITERATURE.   Writers in the revived Home Literature vein borrow from the popular sentimental and genteel tradition to write "faithful" novels teaching Mormon values and beliefs, but often oversimplify human problems and responses to those problems. Aimed primarily at LDS teenagers and young adults, the formula romance is a major literary tool for teaching them how to cope faithfully in a secularized world. Such works include Shirley Sealy's *Beyond This Moment* (1977), Susan Evans McCloud's *Where the Heart Leads* (1979), and Lee Nelson's multi-volume *The Storm Testament* (1982–1990). To date, the most successful and prolific writers for modern Mormon youth have been Jack Weyland and Blaine and Brenton Yorgason. Blaine Yorgason's *Charlie's Monument* (1976), *The Windwalker*, and *Massacre at Salt Creek* (1979) have been regional best sellers, as has their jointly written *The Bishop's Horse Race* (1979). Jack Weyland's *Charly* (1980) and *Sam* (1981) tell faith-promoting stories replete with hope, optimism, and happy endings.

FAITHFUL REALISM.   Many late-twentieth-century Mormon writers are both faithful Latter-day Saints and skilled writers. Foremost among these novelists is Orson Scott Card (b. 1951). A native of Orem, Utah, Card has won the Hugo and the Nebula awards, and has established himself as one of America's foremost science fiction and fantasy writers. His science fiction and fantasy have strong LDS undertones, especially his Alvin Maker series *Seventh Son* (1987), *Red Prophet* (1988), and *Prentice Alvin* (1989). His novel *Saints* (1984) is considered by many to be the best Mormon historical novel written since *The Giant Joshua.*

In the same spirit of faithful realism, a number of well-written novels examining the lives of Latter-day Saints have appeared in the last quarter of the twentieth century: Emma Lou Thayne's *Never Past the Gate* (1975), Robert H. Moss's *Nephite Chronicles* (seven novels to date); Douglas H. Thayer's *Summer Fire* (1983); Donald R. Marshall's *Zinnie Stokes, Zinnie Stokes* (1984); Randall Hall's *Cory Davidson* (1984); Larry E. Morris's *The Edge of the Reservoir* (1988); Chris

Heimerdinger's *Tennis Shoes Among the Nephites* (1989); and Gerald Lund's *The Alliance* (1983) and *The Work and the Glory: A Pillar of Light* (1990). These works are encouraging examples of truthful and faithful fictional treatment of the Latter-day Saints.

BIBLIOGRAPHY
Cracroft, Richard H., and Neal E. Lambert, eds. *A Believing People: Literature of the Latter-day Saints.* Salt Lake City, 1974.
England, G. Eugene. "The Dawning of a Brighter Day: Mormon Literature After 150 Years." *BYU Studies* 22 (Spring 1982):131–60.
Geary, Edward A. "Mormondom's Lost Generation: The Novelists of the 1940s." *BYU Studies* 18 (Fall 1977):89–98.
Hunsaker, Kenneth B. "Mormon Novels." In *A Literary History of the American West*, ed. Thomas J. Lyon et al., pp. 849–61. Fort Worth, Texas, 1987.

RICHARD H. CRACROFT

PERSONAL ESSAYS

Growing out of the LDS sermon and partaking of the honest reflection and responsible self-revelation often characteristic of "personal witness" or "testimony," the personal essay has become an important literary form for LDS writers. As essay writers explore personal experiences, draw lessons from them, and apply these lessons to the concerns of the community, they may describe, analyze, and frequently mitigate criticism, pain, and doubt. The result is often a satisfying piece of literature that can serve to entertain and enlighten, and to influence religious and moral conviction.

The personal essay was not a significant literary vehicle among the early Latter-day Saints. While they did keep diaries and write sermons and personal reminiscences, their group struggle for existence left them little time for interest in examining in writing their Church, their beliefs, or their individual differences. By the middle of the twentieth century, however, the Church was essentially at peace with its external surroundings, and a few LDS writers opened the era of the Mormon personal essay. In 1948, BYU English professor P. A. Christensen published his collection *All in a Teacher's Day*; his second collection, *Of a Number of Things*, appeared in 1962. Virginia Sorensen's landmark work, *Where Nothing Is Long Ago: Memories of a Mormon Childhood*, appeared in 1955. This work, usually thought of as fiction, has the point of view and effect on the reader of a personal essay, and it has influenced many recent LDS writers.

Since 1966, when the first issue of *Dialogue: A Journal of Mormon Thought* appeared, LDS personal essays have been published with increasing regularity, in its columns "From the Pulpit" and (since 1971) "Personal Voices," and in such publications as *Ensign, Sunstone, BYU Studies, Exponent II, Utah Holiday, BYU Today, This People*, and *Network*.

By the late 1970s, the Mormon personal essay was in full flower, with, for example, Lowell Bennion's collection *The Things That Matter Most* (1978); President Spencer W. Kimball's sermon-essays "The False Gods We Worship" (*Ensign*, June 1976) and "Fundamental Principles to Ponder and Live," popularly known as "Don't Kill the Little Birds" (1978), published in *Ensign*; and Hugh Nibley's distinctive, scholarly-personal essays, *Nibley on the Timely and the Timeless* (1978). In the 1980s, three writers directly influenced by Virginia Sorensen published collections that marked the blossoming of the LDS personal essay as a distinct literary genre: Eugene England (*Dialogues with Myself: Personal Essays on Mormon Experience*, 1984, and *Why the Church Is as True as the Gospel*, 1988), Edward Geary (*Goodbye to Poplarhaven: Recollections of a Utah Boyhood*, 1985), and Mary Lythgoe Bradford (*Leaving Home: Personal Essays*, 1987).

The essays of many others writing during this time were collected by Mary Bradford in *Mormon Women Speak: A Collection of Essays* (1982) and *Personal Voices: A Celebration of Dialogue* (1987). Most recently Don Norton has edited *Approaching Zion*, Volume 9 of *The Collected Works of Hugh Nibley* (1989), and Elouise Bell has published *Only When I Laugh* (1990), a collection growing out of her *Network* columns.

BIBLIOGRAPHY
For important evaluations of the Mormon personal essay, see Clifton Jolley, "Mormons and the Beast: In Defense of the Personal Essay," *Dialogue* 11 (Autumn 1978):137–39; Eugene England, "The Dawning of a Brighter Day: Mormon Literature After 150 Years," *BYU Studies* 22 (Spring 1982):131–60; and Mary Lythgoe Bradford, "I, Eye, Aye: A Personal Essay on Personal Essays," *Dialogue* 11 (Summer 1978):81–89, reprinted in her *Personal Voices: A Celebration of Dialogue* (Salt Lake City, 1987).

DONLU DEWITT THAYER

POETRY

Poetry may well be the most essential art. Its uses are numerous. It is most needed in times of urgency and danger, if one may take the quality and amount of poetry written, for example, in times of war as an indication. At such a time the need for poetry is social and communal; it is needed to exhort, to encourage, to unite, to comfort, to state once more those qualities and beliefs which are fundamental to the community from which it springs.

Such benefits were needed from the poems written by early Latter-day Saints. Their community was endangered, its beliefs were called into question, and its leaders were martyred; all this was material for poetry that was confirmatory and, in a sense, repetitive. It repeated, mostly in the form of hymns, and as simply and directly as possible, the truths accepted by the faithful. Such poetry is so much the result of the known situation that it is almost anonymous, ballad-like.

Later, when some permanence seemed probable to the community, Mormon poetry became didactic. Its use was still communal, as distinct from the personal use of poetry today—largely a matter between poet and reader—and its purpose was to instruct and to retell, in narrative form, those stories which were peculiar to the traditions of the Church.

There was little room for experiment in such work, nor was there much opportunity for individual lyric poetry in what Orson F. Whitney called Home Literature. It was produced for the promotion and continuation of faith, and necessarily designed for an LDS audience. This is a restriction which contemporary poets have felt increasingly less necessary. As Latter-day Saints have moved away from Utah in larger numbers, established viable communities in many places, and taken more and more positions of authority and importance in the world at large, they have seen more clearly the place they may assume in the general community. This has been at once a liberation and a source of individual concern to poets. That concern is often seen in contemporary poetry. The men and women who write that poetry are very much aware of what is happening in their art, are sophisticated and adventurous in technique, and completely modern in outlook, yet still need to hold to the clear values and confident virtues of the Church, a complex undertaking in a world and time as doubting as today's.

This has meant that, like the poetry of the English-speaking world in general, a great deal of contemporary LDS poetry is personal, lyric poetry, even if the subject matter is often purely Mormon, or at least clearly composed from an LDS point of view. At the same time, the range of such poetry is much wider. An LDS poet—indeed, an artist in any medium—feels little need now to teach, to speak to an entirely LDS audience, or to use the traditional LDS environments of farm and home.

All this may be clearly recognized in *Harvest*, an anthology of contemporary LDS poetry edited by Eugene England and Dennis Clark. Both men, themselves poets, had realized the importance of changes taking place in LDS poetry as they read the contributions of men and women to such journals as *BYU Studies*, *Dialogue*, *Literature and Belief*, and *Sunstone*.

Naturally, the poets themselves were the first to realize the direction in which their work was heading. Perhaps the first of them to devote his life to poetry, to dedicate serious and full-time effort to his craft, was Clinton F. Larson. Versatile, prolific, and skillful, and with a curious and searching mind, he shows a range of form and material that is unusually wide. Larson is a poet with a distinctive voice, and his influence is less specific than general; he may well have demonstrated to younger writers that the boundaries of their meditations extend farther than they thought, and that their images can be drawn from all aspects of life.

This is not to say that the great subjects of LDS poetry have vanished, but they have changed subtly. *Harvest* contains a surprising number of poems in which an idealized version of the old, simple, pastoral life of earlier years is celebrated. Generally, until the very youngest generation of poets, those who may live in New York or Los Angeles, who have traveled in Peru or China, the imagery is largely drawn from Utah, Idaho or Wyoming. And many poems continue to deal with parents and children, with homes and families. *Harvest* even contains a short section called "Hymns and Songs," which suggests that the very earliest strain of Mormon poetry still exists, old-fashioned as it seems, to call the community to share belief and sing together.

There are, of course, exotic exceptions to this general statement. Arthur Henry King, who came late and from England to the Church, offers quite other traditional virtues in his verse; R. A. Christmas speaks in a wry and memorably different voice. Loretta Randall Sharp has written some stanzas so beautiful and personal ("At Utah Lake" is such a gem) that they transcend such blanket generalizations as this article necessarily contains. The few poems of Bruce Jorgensen are of so steely a delicacy that one could wish from him a more fruitful dedication to his craft.

This last is a concern that might be examined seriously. Of all Utah poets, it may be that May Swenson is best known, and there is little doubt that she has spent her life as a serious poet. It may be time for other Latter-day Saints who write poetry to become poets in effect. It may even be happening. Donnell Hunter, whose verse carries the benign influence of William Stafford, publishes his work and that of others from his little Honeybrook Press in Rexburg, Idaho. Michael R. Collings, a poet represented in *Sunstone* and elsewhere, is about to start *Zarahemla: A Magazine of Poetry*, which should be a most helpful addition to those LDS journals which already publish poetry. But perhaps most hopeful of all, the very youngest LDS poets are beginning to see their work in national periodicals. In their twenties, most of them pursuing degrees in universities outside Utah or employed in various professions in many states and cities, these LDS poets are putting their poems alongside those of other young writers. Mormon poetry is finding a wider audience.

BIBLIOGRAPHY

Cracroft, Richard H., and Neal E. Lambert, eds. *A Believing People: Literature of the Latter-day Saints.* Salt Lake City, 1974.

England, G. Eugene, and Dennis M. Clark, eds. *Harvest: Contemporary Mormon Poems.* Salt Lake City, 1989.

Lambert, Neal E., and Richard H. Cracroft, eds. *Twenty-two Young Mormon Writers.* Provo, Utah, 1975.

LESLIE NORRIS

SHORT STORIES

The history of the Mormon short story begins with the quasi-official encouragement of all forms of LDS literary expression signaled in Orson F. Whitney's 1888 address "Home Literature." The first generation of "Home Literature" story writers included Susa Young

Gates, Augusta Joyce Crocheron, B. H. Roberts, and, most prominently, Josephine Spencer and Nephi Anderson. In "A Plea for
Fiction" and "Purpose in Fiction" (1898), Anderson urged the didactic value of "the good, pure, elevating kind" of fiction with "a message to deliver." Anderson's work displays some traits of good
"regional" or "local color" fiction, yet none of it is generally read or
remembered today. Spencer's stories, also moralistic, are less heavy-
handed than Anderson's (characters, not the author, deliver the "message"), and show more skill and attention to craft; seven appeared in
her book *The Senator from Utah* (1895).

Into the 1940s, Mormon writers seem to have worked in isolation from the high artistry of Continental, English, and American
short-story writers from the 1890s through the 1920s. Despite a leav-
ening of entertainment and humor after 1920, LDS stories largely
remained parochial; didactic; thematically and experientially superficial, unreal, or idealized; prescriptive; and artistically weak. One
exception might be the stories of Ora Pate Stewart gathered in
Buttermilk and Bran (1964) but written earlier.

In the 1940s and 1950s there emerged a generation of Mormon
"expatriate" writers, born between 1900 and 1930, well read in the
Continental and Anglo-American traditions, sometimes trained in literary criticism, and unable to subscribe to the didacticism of "Home
Literature." Their stories, though often nourished on the experience
and values of growing up in Mormon country, were largely "lost" to
an LDS audience. Ray B. West's "The Last of the Grizzly Bears"
(1950), Richard Young Thurman's "Not Another Word" (1957), and
Jarvis Thurston's "The Cross" (1959) show varying tensions between
rejection and nostalgia. Wayne Carver's "With Voice of Joy and
Praise" (1965) displays a rich sense of Utah folk culture, especially
its humor and its speech. The youngest expatriate, David L. Wright,
died before his promise could come to full fruition, but he did publish five stories in literary quarterlies in 1960 and 1961 and saw successful productions of plays based on two of the best, "Speak Ye
Tenderly of Kings" (1960) and "A Summer in the Country" (1960,
1976). The oldest expatriate, the novelist Virginia Sorensen, published *Where Nothing Is Long Ago* (1963), likely to remain one of the
best collections of Mormon short stories. Finely written, richly nos-
talgic, yet self-questioning, Sorensen's stories offer insights into the

"complex fate" of a Mormon writer removed from, yet deeply attached to, the LDS home place and the community that settled and still inhabits it.

The mid-1960s brought a major expansion in the Mormon short story with the inception of *Dialogue* (1966–) and the revitalization of *BYU Studies* (1967–), which opened outlets to LDS writers in both the "unsponsored" sector and the sponsored. Encouraged by anthologies such as *A Believing People* (1974, 1979), *22 Young Mormon Writers* (1975), the *LDSF* series (1982–), and *Greening Wheat* (1983); by awards and readings offered by the Association for Mormon Letters and other groups; by periodicals such as *Exponent II* (1974–), *Mountainwest* (1975–1981), and *Sunstone* (1975–), and by self-published books and the establishment of independent presses such as Signature Books, the expansion continued exponentially through the 1970s and 1980s. A new generation of writers, most born between 1930 and 1950, is still writing mainly, but not exclusively, for and about Latter-day Saints; yet they are no longer limited by didactic aesthetics, and are thoroughly committed to high standards of literary craft, complexity, and seriousness.

Donald R. Marshall's *The Rummage Sale* (1972, 1985) and *Frost in the Orchard* (1977, 1985) include some of the most various, experimental, multivoiced, and comical Mormon short fiction. "The Sound of Drums" (1972) and "The Wheelbarrow" (1977) examine the "good Mormon" as a sensitive, conscious, committed person who must find a way to love and live in a world that is often obtuse and vulgar.

Douglas H. Thayer's protagonists in *Under the Cottonwoods* (1977, 1983) are driven into perplexity by "perfection"; his craft is severe, his tone seldom humorous, his style deliberate, chiseled, almost mannered. Earlier stories draw on Romantic lyric form in their meditative strategies, and reveal a tense subsurface engagement between Romantic poetics and LDS theology. Thayer's later-published stories in *Mr. Wahlquist in Yellowstone* (1989) explore the seductive American myths of "wilderness" from a perspective implicit in LDS theology.

Gladys Clark Farmer's *Elders and Sisters* (1977) and Bela Petsco's *Nothing Very Important and Other Stories* (1979), both integrated collections, almost novels, deal with the special world of

Mormon missionaries in France and in southern California and Arizona. Petsco's book was the first entirely non–Utah-Idaho Mormon fiction.

Eileen Gibbons Kump's *Bread and Milk and Other Stories* (1979) employs a chronological sequence to portray the life of one woman, Amy Taylor Gordon, from age eight (the time of the Edmunds-Tucker Act) to her death many years later, in what may be the finest LDS historical stories yet written. Treating isolation and grace in a peculiarly Mormon way, her stories also suggest that though women submit to masculine will in ways that divide men from women and children from fathers ("Four and Twenty Blackbirds"), they are often humorously resilient ("Sayso or Sense").

Lewis Horne, in Saskatchewan, is geographically expatriated from Utah Mormondom but remains in touch with Latter-day Saint community and family life, as is shown in "Thor Thorsen's Book of Days" (1970). His sometimes "open-ended" stories have appeared widely in American and Canadian literary quarterlies since 1968, have been often cited, and have twice been included in the annual *Best American Short Stories*.

Karen Rosenbaum also experiments with "openness." Her agile, comic voice sounds in "The Joys of Mormonish" (1977) and "Hit the Frolicking, Rippling Brooks" (1978), but she also examines the erosion of simple faith in more somber tones in "The Mustard Seed" (1964) and "Low Tide" (1980).

Stories like those of the older "Home Literature" continue to flourish, represented by Shirley Sealy's professedly didactic *Beauty in Being* (1980) and Jack Weyland's witty teenage and young-adult situation- or problem-comedy stories in the Church youth magazine, *New Era*, collected in *First Day of Forever* (1980), *Punch and Cookies Forever* (1981), and *A Small Light in the Darkness* (1987). Lynne Larson's half-dozen Wyoming stories in *Mountainwest* (1976–1978), straddle the categories of "popular" and "literary"; her best may be "Original Sin" (1978; reprinted in *Greening Wheat*).

Harold K. Moon's collection *Possible Dreams* (1982) is literarily playful, a fact underscored in an introduction and a preface by the author and by the Bivilswiltz, the fantastic protagonist of several fables in the book.

Levi Peterson's *Canyons of Grace* (1982) was the first book of Mormon short stories since Sorensen's to be published outside the LDS circuit; and, in the title story and "The Confessions of Augustine" and "Road to Damascus," the first to deal overtly, in dramatic action, with significant tensions in Mormon theology, especially that between the "obduracy" of "inchoate matter" and the order imposed by divine will. His second collection, *Night Soil* (1990), gives wider play to the rambunctiously comic, folkloric, and tenderly humane elements in Peterson's imagination.

Marden J. Clark's *Morgan Triumphs* (1984) and Sharon M. Hawkinson's *Only Strangers Travel* (1984) are both linked series of stories in the Mormon tradition of "personal history"; like Sorensen, both mix memoir, personal essay, and short story.

Darrell Spencer's *A Woman Packing a Pistol* (1987) shows few overt signs of being the work of a Mormon writer; yet his mostly secular characters "live with the acts of God." Spencer writes postmodern, "open" stories to explore a moral universe that is radically open to personal agency and decision, full of possibility and surprise.

Judith Freeman's well-received *Family Attractions* (1988) includes four Mormon stories: "The Death of a Mormon Elder," "Pretend We're French," "Going Out to Sea," and "Clearfield."

In 1989 and 1990, several excellent collections of Mormon short stories were published: Douglas Thayer's *Mr. Wahlquist in Yellowstone* (1989), Neal Chandler's *Benediction* (1989), Linda Sillitoe's *Windows on the Sea* (1989), Pauline Mortensen's *Back Before the World Turned Nasty* (1989), Phyllis Barber's *The School of Love* (1990), Orson Scott Card's *The Folk of the Fringe* (1990), Levi Peterson's *Night Soil* (1990), and Michael Fillerup's *Visions* (1990).

Including many other writers who have not yet published collections, the Mormon expansion of the short story parallels and is part of a larger American and international renaissance of the genre, though so far it derives more from that renaissance than it contributes to it. Younger LDS writers seem simultaneously critical and loyal in their criticism; they find in Mormonism a sufficiently spacious world, and they locate the conflicts of their stories within that world, even within the parameters of their theology. This source of strength in their fiction makes them valuable, if sometimes disquieting, to the community within which they have chosen to remain.

BIBLIOGRAPHY
Cracroft, Richard H., and Neal E. Lambert. "Fiction." In *A Believing People: Literature of the Latter-day Saints*, pp. 255–306. Provo, Utah, 1974, 1979.

BRUCE W. JORGENSEN

M

MAGIC

"Magic" anciently implied something akin to sorcery, and modern definitions retain this sense as well as a host of other meanings that have accrued around the term over many years and from many cultures. On one point there is general agreement: "Magic" suggests the supernatural. Pretending to use the occult when so-called magic tricks are displayed is simply part of the entertainment. When it implies *governing* the forces of nature through supernatural means, however, magic takes on a markedly different character.

Latter-day Saints reject magic as a serious manipulation of nature and are advised to avoid any practice that claims supernatural power apart from the priesthood and spiritual gifts of the Church (*see* SATANISM). They are also counseled against using any fortune-telling devices. Both so-called white and black magic can be Satanic.

True miracles are done by the power of Jesus Christ. Devils may be cast out, but only in humility and by fasting, faith, and prayer, and the power of the true priesthood, with no fanfare or public acclaim (cf. Matt. 17:21; D&C 84:66–73). Regarding the discernment of true spirits from evil ones, the Prophet Joseph Smith taught that without the priesthood and "a knowledge of the laws by which spirits are governed," it is impossible to discover the difference between the miracles of Moses and the magicians of the pharaoh or between those of the apostles and Simon the sorcerer (*TPJS*, pp. 202–206). A test of a

godly spirit is to discern whether there is "any intelligence communicated" or "the purposes of God developed" (*TPJS*, p. 204).

Ultimately, it is irrelevant to the determination of its sources to
note that a so-called miracle is for the good of mankind. The Savior
recognized that miracles may come from an evil source: "Many will
say to me in that day, Lord, Lord, have we not prophesied in thy
name, and in thy name have cast out devils, and in thy name done
many wonderful works? And then will I profess unto them, I never
knew you: depart from me, ye that work iniquity" (Matt. 7:22–23).

The Lord gave instruction to Israel that the righteous were to call
upon him for revelation and to avoid magical devices and incanta-
tions that were prevalent among the other ancient nations (Isa.
8:19–20; Ex. 22:18). One danger of preoccupation with forms of
magic based on the power of Satan is that it draws people away from
the true source of inspiration and makes the worker of magic a servant of the adversary.

The Church holds that no person need unduly fear magic or
those who claim magical powers, for magic can have no power over
anyone unless the person believes that it can.

BIBLIOGRAPHY

Hinckley, Gordon B. "Lord, Increase Our Faith." *Ensign* 17 (Nov. 1987):52.

McConkie, Bruce R. "Magic." *MD*, pp. 462–63.

Smith, Joseph F. *GD*, pp. 375–77.

JANET THOMAS

MARRIAGE

[*This entry consists of two articles: The first article*, Social and
Behavioral Perspectives, *is an overview of the concept of marriage
patterns in LDS society; the second article*, Eternal Marriage, *focuses
on distinctive marriage beliefs practiced by members of the LDS
Church in their temples. One of the highest religious goals for Latter-
day Saints, both male and female, is to be married eternally in an
LDS temple and to strive continually to strengthen the bonds of love
and righteousness in marriage. Civil marriages are recognized as lawful and beneficial, but they do not continue after death.*]

SOCIAL AND BEHAVIORAL PERSPECTIVES

Marriage is more than a matter of social convention or individual need fulfillment in Latter-day Saint society and lifestyle; it is central to the exaltation of the individual person: "If a man marry a wife by my word, which is my law, and by the new and everlasting covenant, and it is sealed unto them by the Holy Spirit of promise, by him who is anointed, unto whom I have appointed this power and the keys of this priesthood, and . . . [they] abide in my covenant . . . [that marriage] shall be of full force when they are out of the world; . . . then shall they be gods, because they have no end; therefore shall they be from everlasting to everlasting" (D&C 132:19–20). Thus, Latter-day Saints consider it of utmost importance, "1. To marry the right person, in the right place, by the right authority; and 2. To keep the covenant made in connection with this holy and perfect order of matrimony" (*MD*, p. 118).

Central to LDS theology is the belief that men and women existed as spirit offspring of heavenly parents in a premortal life. Latter-day Saints view life on earth as a time to prepare to meet God (Alma 12:24) and strive toward becoming like him (Matt. 5:48; 3 Ne. 12:48). Becoming like God is dependent to a large extent on entering into "celestial marriage" for "time and all eternity," for eventually all exalted beings shall have entered into this highest patriarchal order of the priesthood. Latter-day Saints believe that the marital and family bond can continue in the post-earth life, and indeed is necessary for eternal life, or life in the celestial kingdom with God the Father; Mother in Heaven; Jesus Christ, and other glorified beings.

Given these doctrines, LDS marriages are distinct and different in several aspects from marriages in other denominations, and marriages of faithful Latter-day Saints differ from those of less observant Church members. Research on LDS marriages shows distinctions in four areas: sexual attitudes and behavior, marriage formation, divorce, and gender roles within the marriage.

SEXUAL ATTITUDES AND BEHAVIOR. Because of the importance of the marital bond and family relationships in both this life and the life to come, premarital or extramarital sexual relations are viewed as totally unacceptable. The power of procreation is vital to the entire plan of salvation. It is held sacred, to be used "only as the Lord has directed"; as such it is viewed as the "very key" to happiness

(Packer, "Why Stay Morally Clean," *Ensign* [July 1972]:113). Studies conducted through the 1970s and 1980s consistently showed that Latter-day Saints have more restrictive attitudes about and are less likely to have participated in premarital sexual intercourse than members of other religious denominations. Active Latter-day Saints also have more conservative attitudes about and are less likely to have engaged in premarital sexual intercourse than those who are less active in the Church (*see* SEXUALITY).

A recent sampling of U.S. households showed Mormons to be significantly less approving of teenagers having sex or of premarital cohabitation than non-Mormons (Heaton et al., 1989). Another study, of over 2,000 adolescents in public high schools in the western United States, showed that 17 percent of the Latter-day Saints had had premarital intercourse, compared to 48 percent of the Catholics, 51 percent of those with no religious affiliation, and 67 percent of the Protestants (Heaton, 1988). The difference continues when Church activity is taken into account and active Latter-day Saints are compared to inactive ones. The attitudes and behavior of inactive Mormons are more similar to those of other faiths (religiously active or inactive) than to active Latter-day Saints (Heaton, 1988).

Latter-day Saint attitudes about sex in marriage and frequency of sexual intercourse in marriage are similar to those in other faiths. Although no data exist on the frequency of extramarital sexuality, Latter-day Saints in general are less approving of extramarital sex than other American populations (Heaton et al., 1989).

MARITAL FORMATION. Members of the Church in the United States and Canada are more likely to marry and remarry than Catholics, conservative Protestants, liberal Protestants, or those with no religious affiliation (Heaton and Goodman, 1985). One study of Canadians indicates that Canadian Catholics are three times as likely, Protestants twice as likely, and those without a religious affiliation four times as likely as Latter-day Saints not to have married by age thirty (Heaton, 1988). The most recent national U.S. data show LDS more likely to be currently married and less likely to have never married than other similarly situated Americans (Heaton et al., 1989). Furthermore, the same data show that LDS men marry about one and one-half years earlier than their non-Mormon counterparts, but LDS females marry at about the same age as other females.

Although the findings are not conclusive, it appears that less active Mormons (those not marrying in a temple) marry at younger ages than those marrying in a temple (Thomas, 1983). Some of this difference may be accounted for by the number of active Latter-day Saint males serving missions during these early years. Most unmarried young LDS men who go on missions serve from about age nineteen until twenty-one.

Given the necessity of marrying another Latter-day Saint in a temple to achieve the greatest happiness in this life and exaltation in the highest level of the celestial kingdom hereafter, one would expect that Mormons in general, and active Latter-day Saints in particular, would have lower rates of interfaith marriages than members of other faiths or those with no affiliation. What little research has been done on LDS interfaith marriages tends to be based on small, localized samples. It appears, however, that in general (1) Mormon females are more likely to marry outside the Church than are Mormon males; (2) active Mormons are less likely to marry non-Mormons than are less active Mormons; and (3) non-Mormon spouses (especially non-Mormon husbands) are more likely to convert to the Church than Mormons are to convert to a non-Mormon spouse's faith (Barlow, 1977).

DIVORCE.   Based on research done in the 1970s and early 1980s, it has been concluded that Latter-day Saints are less likely to divorce than Catholics and Protestants and are far less likely than those with no religious affiliation. A study comparing Mormons in the United States and Canada with Protestants, Catholics, and those with no religious affiliation found that 14 percent of the Mormon men and 19 percent of the women had divorced. Comparable figures among the other groups were 20 percent and 23 percent for Catholic males and females; 24 percent and 31 percent for liberal Protestant males and females; 28 percent and 31 percent for conservative Protestant males and females; and 39 percent for males and 45 percent for females with no religious affiliation (Heaton and Goodman, 1985).

Latter-day Saints married in a temple ceremony are considerably less likely to divorce than those married outside the temple (Thomas, 1983). Among men and women who were married in the temple, 6 percent of the men and 7 percent of the women have been divorced, while among men and women not married in the temple the figures were 28 percent and 33 percent, respectively (Heaton, 1988).

GENDER ROLES. "God established that fathers are to preside in the home. Fathers are to provide, to love, to teach, and to direct. But a mother's role is also God-ordained. Mothers are to conceive, to bear, to nourish, to love, and to train. So declare the revelations" (Benson, p. 2). This statement, made by Church President Ezra Taft Benson, exemplifies the LDS teaching that men and women have different— but closely intertwined and mutually supporting—roles in the marital and family setting. Research bears out this distinctive emphasis. Mormon males and females tend to be more conservative and traditional in their gender role attitudes and behavior than members of other faiths (Brinkerhoff and MacKie, 1988; Heaton, 1988; Heaton et al., 1989). LDS males spend about the same amount of time performing household tasks as non-Mormon males, but Mormon females spend significantly more time at such tasks than non-Mormon females. LDS females spend more time performing not only traditional female tasks, but also traditional male tasks (e.g., outdoor tasks, paying bills, and auto maintenance) than do female non-Mormons. These differences in both attitudes and behavior are not viewed negatively by either LDS men or women. They are as likely to be satisfied with their marriages and their roles in marriage as their non-Mormon counterparts (Heaton et al., 1989).

BIBLIOGRAPHY
Bahr, Howard M., and Renata Tonks Forste. "Toward a Social Science of Contemporary Mormondom." *BYU Studies* 26 (1986):73–121.
Barlow, Brent A. "Notes on Mormon Interfaith Marriages." *Family Coordinator* 26 (1977):143–50.
Benson, Ezra Taft. *To the Mothers in Zion.* Salt Lake City, 1987.
Brinkerhoff, Merlin B., and Marlene MacKie. "Religious Sources of Gender Traditionalism." In *The Religion and Family Connection*, ed. D. Thomas. Provo, Utah, 1988.
Heaton, Tim B. "Four C's of the Mormon Family: Chastity, Conjugality, Children, and Chauvinism." In *The Religion and Family Connection*, ed. D. Thomas. Provo, Utah, 1988.
Heaton, Tim B., and Kristin L. Goodman. "Religion and Family Formation." *Review of Religious Research* 26 (1985):343–59.
Heaton, Tim B.; Darwin L. Thomas; and Kristin L. Goodman. "In Search of a Peculiar People: Are Mormon Families Really Different?" Society for the Scientific Study of Religion, Oct. 1989.

Thomas, Darwin L. "Family in the Mormon Experience." In *Families and Religion*, ed. W. D'Antonio and J. Aldous. Beverly Hills, Calif., 1983.

THOMAS B. HOLMAN

ETERNAL MARRIAGE

The principle of eternal marriage and the ordinances implementing it constitute a very distinctive and valuable part of the Church. It involves a ceremony performed in a holy temple by an officiator endowed with the priesthood authority to invoke covenants intended to be efficacious for time and eternity. This is a sacred and simple ceremony to unite husband and wife in the bonds of everlasting love and in the hopes of eternity. President Joseph Fielding Smith taught that such a marriage involves "an eternal principle ordained before the foundation of the world and instituted on this earth before death came into it" (Smith, p. 251), for Adam and Eve were given in marriage to each other by God in the Garden of Eden before the Fall (Gen. 2:22–25; Moses 3:22–25). This sacred act of marriage was the crowning act of all creation: "In the day that God created man, in the likeness of God made he him: Male and Female created he them; and blessed them" (Gen. 5:1–2). With his blessing they truly could set the pattern for their descendants thereafter who two by two, a man and a woman, could leave father and mother, cleave to each other, and "be one flesh" (Gen. 2:24). Thus began the great plan of God for the happiness of all his children.

Latter-day Saints believe that life is more secure and more joyous when it is experienced in the sacred relationships of the eternal family. Those who maintain such worthy relationships on earth will live as families in the celestial kingdom following the resurrection. Thus, a person who lives a righteous life in mortality and who has entered into an eternal marriage may look forward to an association in the postmortal world with a worthy spouse, and with those who were earthly children, fathers, mothers, brothers, and sisters. Bruce R. McConkie, an apostle, explained that an eternal family starts with "a husband and a wife, united in a family unit. It then goes out to our children—the spirits that God gives us to be members of our family—to our grandchildren and so on, to the latest generation. It also reaches back to our parents and our grandparents to the earliest generation" (p. 82). President Brigham Young said that eternal marriage "is the thread which runs from the beginning to the end of the holy Gospel of Salvation—of the Gospel of the Son of God; it is from eternity to eternity" (*Discourses of Brigham Young*, John A. Widtsoe, ed., Salt Lake City, 1971, p. 195).

Even as marriage marks an apex in God's creative processes, so, too, it is for each person the sacred culmination of the covenants and ordinances of the priesthood of God and, indeed, is truly a new and everlasting covenant (D&C 131:2). Eternal marriage is a covenant, a sacred promise that a wife and a husband make with each other and with God, attested to by both mortal witnesses and heavenly angels. Under proper conditions such marriages are sealed by the Holy Spirit of Promise, and the couple, through their faithfulness, can eventually inherit exaltation and glory in the celestial kingdom of God (D&C 132:19). The scriptures confirm that eternal marriage, performed by the authority of the priesthood, sealed or affirmed by the Holy Ghost, and sustained by a righteous life, "shall be of full force" after death (D&C 132:19; cf. 1 Cor. 11:11). The phrase "until death do you part" is regarded as a tragic one that predicts the ultimate dissolution of the marriage, and this phrase is not stated in the temple marriage ceremony.

The sacred ceremony of temple marriage is conducted in reverence and simplicity, and the occasion is a beautiful and joyous one for Latter-day Saints. The bride and the groom meet with family and friends in a designated sealing room of the temple. The officiator typically greets the couple with a few words of welcome, counsel, and fatherly commendations. He may admonish the couple to treat each other throughout life with the same love and kindness that they feel at this moment, and may add other words of encouragement, with his blessing upon their righteous undertaking. The couple is invited to come forward and kneel facing each other across an altar in the middle of the room. The sealer sometimes directs the attention of all present to the mirrors on opposite walls, reflecting endlessly the images of the couple at the altar, and he may comment on the symbolism. Then the sealer pronounces the simple words of the ceremony, which promise, on condition of obedience, lasting bonds with the potential for eternal joy between these two sealed for eternity. President Ezra Taft Benson said, "Faithfulness to the marriage covenant brings the fullest joy here and glorious rewards hereafter" (pp. 533–34). At the conclusion of the ceremony, the couple kiss over the altar and may then arise and leave the altar to exchange rings.

Through this ordinance of eternal marriage, men and women commit themselves in pure love to remain true to each other and to God through all eternity. Divorce is discouraged, and couples are taught to confine their intimate affections and sexuality solely to each other. To undertake and honor the covenants of temple marriage require living in ways that contribute to happy and successful family life. A couple's future may include conflicts and even divorce, which when it occurs is often a result of violating temple covenants; but the divorce rate among couples who have been sealed in a temple is very low (*see* DIVORCE; VITAL STATISTICS).

Eternal marriage is, of course, not just for the blessing, happiness, or benefit of the spouses. It is an act of service, commitment, and love that blesses the next generation. God commanded Adam and Eve to "be fruitful, and multiply, and replenish the earth" (Gen. 1:28). A primary purpose of temple marriage in this life is to grow and mature in sharing God's creative work in raising a family in righteousness. Parents enter into a partnership with God by participating in the PROCREATION of mortal bodies, which house the spirit children of God. At some future time all the worthy sons and daughters of God will be reunited with their Heavenly Parents as one eternal extended family in a state of resurrected glory.

People who live a worthy life but do not marry in the temples, for various reasons beyond their control, which might include not marrying, not having heard the gospel, or not having a temple available so that the marriage could be sealed for eternity, will at some time be given this opportunity. Latter-day Saints believe it is their privilege and duty to perform these sacred ordinances vicariously for deceased progenitors, and for others insofar as possible. Most of the sealing ordinances (temple marriage ceremonies) performed for the deceased are for couples who were married by civil authority in mortality but died without hearing the fulness of the gospel. In this program of vicarious service, men and women meet by appointment in the temple where they stand as proxies for parents, grandparents, or others who have passed into the next world and make the solemn covenants that will reach fruition for all who accept them in the spirit world, to culminate in the day of resurrection.

All leaders of the Church encourage couples to initiate their marriage vows in a holy temple. For those who do not, whether converts to the Church, LDS couples coming to devotion to the Church in later life, or young LDS couples who have married outside the temple and then felt the desire for eternal covenants, temple marriage is a renewal of vows first spoken in a civil marriage ceremony. For those commitments to be honored through eternity, couples must be married by an officiator having the power to bind on earth and in heaven (Matt. 16:19; D&C 124:93). Thus, they must go to a temple, where there are those ordained and appointed to the power to seal covenants for time *and* eternity.

For Latter-day Saints, eternal marriage is an avenue to everlasting joy. Matthew Cowley, an apostle, expressed his conviction that it is "a wonderful thing . . . to kneel at an altar in the temple of God, clasping the hand of one who is to be your companion not only for time, but also for all eternity, and then to have born into that sacred and eternal covenant children for eternity. God is love. Love is eternal. Marriage is the sweetest and most sacred expression of love, therefore, marriage is eternal" (Cowley, p. 444).

BIBLIOGRAPHY

Benson, Ezra Taft. *The Teachings of Ezra Taft Benson.* Salt Lake City, 1988.
Brown, Hugh B. *You and Your Marriage.* Salt Lake City, 1960.
Burton, Theodore M. *God's Greatest Gift.* Salt Lake City, 1976.
Cowley, Matthew. *Matthew Cowley Speaks.* Salt Lake City, 1954.
McConkie, Bruce R. "The Eternal Family Concept." In *Genealogical Devotional Addresses,* pp. 81–93. Second Annual Priesthood Genealogical Research Seminar, Brigham Young University. Provo, Utah, 1967.
Smith, Joseph Fielding. *The Way to Perfection.* Salt Lake City, 1931.

JAMES T. DUKE

MATERIAL CULTURE

The artifacts of a society are known as its material culture. Latter-day Saints, like all other cultural groups, have altered their physical surroundings to reflect their own worldview. Every object created or modified by members of a group is part of that group's material culture. LDS material culture encompasses a particular constellation of objects, only a few of which are unique. But, taken together, they create what can be identified as a Mormon environment.

In parts of the American West settled heavily by Latter-day Saints in the nineteenth century, the landscape reflects their peculiar approach to town building (*see* COMMUNITY). One of the top priorities for early settlers was the establishment of extensive irrigation systems that brought mountain water to every farm. Ditches were dug, and dams of a variety of designs were and still are used to divert water onto a plot of land in a rotating calendar of "water turns." The influence of irrigation can be seen to this day in Mormon-settled areas where green fields, shady, flower-filled yards, and rows of Lombardy poplars mark the landscape, even in the driest desert areas (*see* AGRICULTURE).

A settlement pattern used frequently by Mormon pioneers has become known as the Mormon village, with homes and businesses situated closely around the central square, streets oriented toward the cardinal directions, and farm lands extending out around this settlement. Farmers left the village to work fields allotted to them by their ecclesiastical leaders. Designs of outbuildings and houses were based on settlers' previous experience or on knowledge gained from neighbors through a process of oral tradition and example (*see* FOLKLORE). Hay was stacked with a "Mormon derrick," a device that can still be seen in several variations although no longer used, in the Mormon-settled West.

The most distinctive Mormon architecture has been in religious buildings: temples, tithing houses, and meetinghouses, for instance. Important LDS symbols, such as the beehive; the sun, moon, and stars; and the all-seeing eye, appear on many of these structures.

Most material objects found in early LDS homes were similar to those found in other American homes. Ethnic origins of the makers often influenced furniture design. Some furniture built by Mormon craftspeople bore cultural symbols similar to those found on buildings. Prior to the coming of the railroad, locally made furniture was distinctive, mostly because it had to be built out of local softwoods rather than eastern hardwoods. Thus, spindles, legs, and other parts had to be thicker than normal to support the same weight. One item of furniture, a lounge with a section that pulled out to accommodate two sleepers, became known as the "Mormon couch" because of its popularity in Utah.

Today, Latter-day Saints continue to surround themselves with objects typical of their home countries. In addition, an LDS home may contain elements that identify its occupants as practicing Saints. Often, there is a picture of a temple—usually the one where the residents received their endowments or were married. The temple motif may be carried out in other objects, such as quilts and embroidery (see FOLK ART). Photos of family members are often found in profusion, reflecting the cultural and personal emphasis on family.

The Church's emphasis on emergency preparedness, especially home food storage, has caused members to devise methods for creating storage space in homes of limited size. What appears to be a round table covered by a long tablecloth may actually be a large cylindrical container of wheat, beans, or rice. Food practices of the Latter-day Saints, also a part of material culture, often focus on the rotating use of storage foods.

LDS women contribute to their material culture through monthly Relief Society homemaking meetings, where they share recipes, craft ideas, and work methods. Particularly popular are inexpensive projects that transform utilitarian objects into decorative ones, such as a small kitchen strainer becoming a Christmas reindeer decoration through the application of colored felt shapes. A craft that becomes popular can sweep through homemaking meetings throughout the Church, and eventually may be seen in a majority of LDS homes for a time.

Even after death, material reminders of Latter-day Saints' religious values can be found in their gravestones. Symbols such as clasped hands and doves, while not unique to Mormon culture, evoke images of eternity for Latter-day Saints that are reflective of their beliefs. Modern gravestones often have an image of a temple on one side, with a list of the couple's children on the other, emphasizing again the idea that a good marriage and family are the best measures of a life well lived.

The Church itself contributes to the material culture of its members. It produces or has produced books of scripture, pictures, journals, lesson manuals, videotapes, sacrament trays, Primary bandalos, commemorative jewelry, and other items used by members in practicing their religion. Some, such as printed programs for ward sacrament meetings, are ephemeral, but they are no less part of the material culture.

Today, as the Church spreads throughout the world, it is more difficult to identify specifically LDS objects. The Salt Lake Temple is one symbol that is frequently represented in crafts from many cultures, including Tongan tapa cloth and Native American beadwork. Some symbols and objects may be universal to all Church members, while others will be localized. A bottle of home-preserved peaches is not unique in itself, but the sense of religious obligation to "put up fruit" and the implications of righteousness attached to the preserver are unique to this culture. All objects identifiable as "Mormon" are expressive of the values of their makers. Latter-day Saints will continue to manipulate their physical environment, mixing their religious values with influences from their ethnic or national cultures to create a landscape that is uniquely their own.

BIBLIOGRAPHY

Brunvand, Jan Harold. *A Guide for Collectors of Folklore in Utah*. Salt Lake City, 1971.

Cannon, Hal. *The Grand Beehive*. Salt Lake City, 1980.

———. *Utah Folk Art: A Catalog of Material Culture*. Provo, Utah, 1980.

Edison, Carol. "Mormon Gravestones: A Folk Expression of Identity and Belief." *Dialogue* 22 (Winter 1989):89–94. Also photos of folk art throughout the issue.

Fife, Austin E., and James M. Fife. "Hay Derricks of the Great Basin and Upper Snake River Valley." *Western Folklore* 10 (1951):320–22; and *Idaho Folklife: Homesteads to Headstones*, ed. Louie Attebery. Salt Lake City, 1985.

"The Tangible Past." *Utah Historical Quarterly* 56 (Fall 1988), special issue edited by Tom Carter.

ELAINE THATCHER

MATTER

By the end of the eighteenth century, modern scientific methods had begun to provide new insights into the fundamental nature of matter, and these negated the Greek philosophical position of form over matter. This change in scientific thinking was contemporary with the teachings of the Prophet Joseph Smith in the theological realm. His teachings returned theology to the intimate relationship between God and mankind of early Judeo-Christian writings. These concepts were in contrast to the position that deity is an embodiment of principles and philosophical ideals that transcend in importance the physical realities of matter. Furthermore, the view that matter was created from nothing (ex nihilo), a concept dominating theological and scientific thought for many centuries and still widespread in nineteenth-century thought, lost the support of modern science and was opposed by the gospel restored by Joseph Smith. Modern scientific theories of matter, from Antoine Lavoisier's (1743–1794) to Erwin Schrödinger's (1887–1961), maintain the permanence of matter.

In the twentieth century, atomic theory has embodied a number of fundamental nuclear particles and powerful mathematical theories. Some, falling outside human intuition, account for properties of matter newly discovered in this century. Concepts have led to the development of unified quantum mechanical and quantum dynamic theories for both matter and light. The conservation law of Lavoisier has been extended to include all equivalent forms of matter and energy and still constitutes one of the primary pillars of modern science.

It is significant that the teachings of the restored gospel on the eternal nature of physical matter, along with a parallel in the spiritual realm, embody these conservation principles. These are key statements: "The elements are eternal" (D&C 93:33). "The spirit of man is not a created being; it existed from eternity, and will exist to eternity. Anything created cannot be eternal; and earth, water, etc., had their existence in an elementary state, from eternity" (Joseph Smith, in *HC* 3:387).

Addressing the issue of creation ex nihilo, Joseph Smith asserted in one of his final sermons: "Now, the word create . . . does not mean to create out of nothing; it means to organize; the same as a man would organize materials and build a ship. Hence, we infer that God had materials to organize the world out of chaos—chaotic matter, which is element. . . . Element had an existence from the time [God] had. The pure principles of element are principles which can never be destroyed; they may be organized and reorganized, but not destroyed. They had no beginning and can have no end" (*HC* 6:308–309).

Extending the concept of the eternal nature of matter to the substance of spirit, Joseph Smith revealed, "There is no such thing as immaterial matter. All spirit is matter, but it is more fine or pure, and can only be discerned by purer eyes; we cannot see it; but when our bodies are purified we shall see that it is all matter" (D&C 131:7–8).

Parley P. Pratt, an apostle and close associate of Joseph Smith, wrote, "Matter and spirit are the two great principles of all existence. Everything animate and inanimate is composed of one or the other, or both of these eternal principles. . . . Matter and spirit are of equal duration; both are self-existent, they never began to exist, and they never can be annihilated. . . . Matter as well as spirit is eternal, uncreated, self existing. However infinite the variety of its changes, forms and shapes; . . . eternity is inscribed in indelible characters on every particle" (*HC* 4:55).

In strict analogy to principles governing physical matter, the revelations to Joseph Smith stress that eternity for spirits also derives from the eternal existence of spiritual matter or elements. The preeminent manifestation of the eternal nature of both physical and spiritual matter is found in the eternal existence of God and ultimately his human children as discrete, indestructible entities. In this unique LDS doctrine, matter in all of its many forms, instead of occupying a subordinate role relative to philosophical paradigms, assumes a sovereign position, along with the principles and laws governing its properties and characteristics.

BIBLIOGRAPHY

Pratt, Parley P. "Eternal Duration of Matter." *HC* 4:55.

DAVID M. GRANT

MENTAL HEALTH

Recognizing the need for mental health services, The Church of Jesus Christ of Latter-day Saints, like other religious organizations, supports a network of agencies through LDS Social Services that provides short-term care as needed and offers referral services when more extensive treatment is required. The Church endorses the work of licensed mental health practitioners provided that the suggestions and treatment offered are consistent with Church moral and lifestyle expectations.

Historically some critics have ascribed various mental afflictions of members to the influence of the Church. Today the assertion is sometimes made that as a result of their religion Latter-day Saints have high rates of divorce, drug abuse, depression, and suicide. This is not surprising, since stereotypes are frequently applied to new and different leaders and their followers. Virtually identical defects have been attributed to Jews, Native Americans, Roman Catholics, the Irish, and other groups (Bunker and Bitton; Bromley and Shupe). Research findings, however, show no evidence of unusual mental or social problems among Latter-day Saints.

National statistics show that the state of Utah, which is 70 percent LDS, has lower rates of mental and addictive disorders than U.S. averages. A National Institute of Mental Health report for 1986 ranked Utah as the second-lowest U.S. state in new inpatient admissions to state mental hospitals as a proportion of population. The National Association of State Mental Health Program Directors report for 1986 showed Utah's rate of outpatient mental cases per million population to be lower than that of thirty-six other states. These reports also show lower-than-average rates for alcohol and drug abuse, a finding confirmed in *Utah in Demographic Perspective* (1986). This report indicates that Utah ranks lowest of all the states in per capita alcohol consumption, and thirty-fifth in alcoholics per 100,000 population. Drug use among adolescents is low compared with national statistics. The overall mortality rate for suicide is slightly above the national average, but slightly below the average for the Rocky Mountain states.

Comparisons of LDS students at Brigham Young University with students at other schools on standard psychological measures, such as the Minnesota Multiphasic Personality Inventory, show more similarities than differences. On accepted indices of mental health, BYU students rank normal. Studies of divorce rates in Utah show that those counties with the highest proportions of LDS have the lowest divorce rates and are significantly below national averages. Studies of depression among BYU students and returned missionaries reveal average or lower levels.

Studies of depression among women in three Utah urban areas

show LDS women to be no more or less depressed than their non-Mormon counterparts. For example, using the Beck Depression Inventory, a study of women in the Salt Lake Valley found no differences between LDS women and others (Spendlove, West, and Stanish). Women who were more active in the LDS Church were found to be less depressed than those who were less active, but causal connections to Church activity were inconclusive. Educational level appeared a better predictor of depression scores than religious affiliation: The more educated were less depressed. Responses to a national questionnaire indicated LDS women to be in the middle range on depression when compared with other groups. LDS men had the lowest depression scores of any group (Bergin and Cornwall).

Overall, on average, Latter-day Saints as a group are psychologically normal. They do not manifest unusual rates or kinds of mental disorders, and they do not differ much from national normative samples. In some studies they show less illness, but results may be questioned because of the nature of the population sampled. Statistics for the state of Utah often look better than the national average because of the state's lack of large minority and poverty populations. Other states with similar demographics, such as Wyoming, Idaho, and the Dakotas, manifest similar statistical advantages.

For mainstream, middle class people, denominational affiliation is less relevant to variations in mental health than are such factors as family background, educational level, economic class, marital status, and intrinsic versus extrinsic religious orientation. General findings obscure considerable individual variation because there are diverse ways of being religious. "Intrinsically" religious persons, who hold to personal convictions and do not depend on religion as a crutch, manifest better mental health than the "extrinsically" religious, those who focus on the external trappings of a religious or "righteous" social image. Such variation occurs among Latter-day Saints, as it does among other groups. Thus, the relation between religiosity and pathology is complex. How specific denominations enhance or undermine mental functioning is currently a matter of speculation and controversy.

The LDS culture and lifestyle manifest an interesting combination of possible positive and negative influences for mental functioning. These may cancel each other and create a normal average profile. Some possible negatives include tendencies toward perfectionism and the self-negation that inevitably accompany failure to match unreasonably high expectations. Negative emotions are not readily expressed, and thus conflicts are often difficult to resolve. LDS subcultures are very "group-oriented." Numerous organizations and activities define and reinforce the lifestyle. People "out of step" are easily recognized, and conformity is valued. Individuality and personal self-expression may be inhibited to a degree, while obedience to authority is encouraged.

In theory, these negatives may be balanced by the warmth and social support provided by a cohesive and caring social network, marked by high emphasis on family commitment and active participation in a diverse system of social, religious, athletic, and cultural activities. While members may despair over having "too much to do," they can always find sympathetic peers. Hope is engendered by a positive philosophy of human nature and the eternal potential of human beings.

LDS philosophy is growth-oriented, so there is constant encouragement toward self-improvement. Problems occur when there is not enough tolerance for human imperfection in the process. When virtues like self-sacrifice, self-control, and hard work are overdone, they can take a toll, but when balanced with honest self-reflection and mutual support, they can be a stimulus for growth.

In establishing itself as an institutional partner in human civilization, the Church has manifested some growth pains. Insecurities that have accompanied being part of a new group are slowly giving way to the securities associated with having arrived as an established entity in the joint enterprise of cultural evolution. As this process has continued, these stresses have given way to a balanced subculture comparable to other mainstream groups.

BIBLIOGRAPHY

Bergin, Allen E., and Marie Cornwall. "Religion and Mental Health: Mormons and Other Groups." Annual Meeting of the Society for the Scientific Study of Religion. Salt Lake City, 1989.

Bromley, David G., and Anson Shupe. "Public Reaction Against New Religious Groups." In Cults and New Religious Movements, ed. M. Galanter. Washington, D.C., 1989.

Bunker, Gary L., and Davis Bitton. The Mormon Graphic Image, 1834-1914. Salt Lake City, 1983.

Martin, Thomas K.; Tim B. Heaton; and Stephen J. Bahr, eds. *Utah in Demographic Perspective.* Salt Lake City, 1986.

National Institute of Mental Health. *Additions and Resident Patients at End of Year 1986.* Rockville, Md., 1988.

Spendlove, David; Dee West; and William Stanish. "Risk Factors and the Prevalence of Depression in Mormon Women." *Social Science and Medicine* 18 (1984):491–95.

State Mental Health Program Indicators—1986. Alexandria, Va., 1989.

ALLEN E. BERGIN

METAPHYSICS

Metaphysics is the branch of PHILOSOPHY concerned with the ultimate nature of reality, including those aspects of it, if any, that are unavailable to empirical inquiry. The historical development of metaphysics in Western philosophical thought has been carried out largely by those philosophers and theologians who have aspired more to develop a unified system of ideas than to dwell upon diverse arrays of facts. Especially important to the theologians was the task of bringing abstract philosophical concepts into harmony with the concrete teachings of scripture. Their systems differed, but their common goal was to combine philosophy and scripture into a single coherent account of the ultimate nature of things.

TENTATIVENESS. LDS metaphysics stands apart, because the Church has not developed a traditional metaphysical theology and does not aspire to one. It has not been much influenced by philosophical thinking. LDS faith springs from two sources, scripture and ongoing RELIGIOUS EXPERIENCE. The absence of any systematic metaphysics of the Church follows from the belief that scripture, as the record of divine revelation, may be supplemented by new revelation at any time. A metaphysical system, to be true, must be all-inclusive. But faith in continuing revelation precludes the certainty that such a system exists. Thus, LDS metaphysics remains incomplete, tentative, and unsystematic, subject to revision in the light of things yet to be revealed by God. This tentativeness about metaphysical ideas has saved the Church from the crises that can arise when a religion's beliefs are tied to philosophical ideas which are later abandoned or discredited. The Church's lack of a systematic metaphysical theology has prompted some students of its doctrines who are used to such theology to assert that it has no theology at all, but it would be more accurate to say that its metaphysics and theology are not systematically formulated.

MATTER AND SPIRIT. In the absence of a metaphysical system, the LDS faith still displays some characteristic metaphysical ideas. Latter-day Saints regard MATTER as a fundamental principle of reality and as the primary basis for distinguishing particular beings. The import of this view reveals itself most strikingly in the doctrine concerning the material embodiment of God: "The Father has a body of flesh and bones as tangible as man's; the Son also" (D&C 130:22). This is not to be understood crassly; the matter of exalted bodies is purified, transfigured, and glorified. LDS teachings draw no ultimate contrast between spirit and matter. Indeed, "all spirit is matter, but it is more fine or pure" (D&C 131:7). This position avoids traditional difficulties in explaining the interaction of spirit and body.

The reality of matter implies the reality of space and time. Scripture speaks of the place where God dwells and of "the reckoning of the Lord's time" (Abr. 3:9). So God himself exists within a spatial and temporal environment. In accepting space, time, and matter as constitutive of reality, Latter-day Saints take the everyday world of human experience as a fairly reliable guide to the nature of things. But this acceptance is no dogma, and their belief remains open to the possibility that these three ideas, as presently understood, may be auxiliaries to more fundamental ideas not yet known.

PLURALISM. LDS thought clearly emphasizes the importance of the fundamental plurality of the world, with its continuing novelties, changes, conflicts, and agreements: "For it must needs be, that there is an opposition in all things" (2 Ne. 2:11). The world is not static but dynamic, not completed but still unfolding. This unfinished and future-oriented aspect of things provides the basis for growth and improvement. A monistic world or universe in which all differences are finally absorbed in a higher unity is viewed as impossible. The LDS Church has been less inclined than some other religions to regard the world of common experience as an inferior order of that which must be distinguished from a higher and altogether different realm. Heaven itself is regarded as offering the hope of endless progression rather than the ease of final satisfaction.

NATURAL AND SUPERNATURAL.   Latter-day Saints see a continuity between the traditional categories of natural and supernatural. They do not deny the distinction, but view it as one of degree, not of kind. God's creative act, for example, is not, as traditionally conceived, a creation ex nihilo, but an act of organizing material that already exists (Abr. 3:24). And creation is not a single, unique event, but an ongoing process that continues through the course of time: "And as one earth shall pass away . . . so shall another come" (Moses 1:38). God acts upon matter within the context of space and time. In comparison with human attributes, God's attributes are supreme and perfect. But the difference between God and mankind remains one of degree. God seeks to provide the guidance and the necessary help for human beings to overcome the differences and become like him. The injunction to be perfect "even as your Father which is in heaven is perfect" (Matt. 5:48) is taken to mean that mankind may indeed become like God by faithfully following his commandments. The principles or laws of goodness that underlie these commandments have their own abiding reality. God exemplifies them but does not arbitrarily create them.

FREEDOM AND PERFECTIBILITY.   Nothing is more central to LDS metaphysics than the principle of freedom. The weaknesses of humanity that lead to error and sin are acknowledged. But the claim that human nature is totally depraved is denied. The LDS Church affirms that ideally "men are instructed sufficiently that they know good from evil" and that "men are free according to the flesh, . . . free to choose liberty and eternal life . . . or to choose captivity and death" (2 Ne. 2:5, 27). Human experience has as its final goal the development of virtue and holiness in a world that is not totally the product of God's will. Reality itself poses the challenge to overcome obstacles and achieve greater good. Everyone's life is a response to this challenge.

BIBLIOGRAPHY
Roberts, B. H. *Joseph Smith—Prophet Teacher*. Salt Lake City, 1908.
———. *Comprehensive History of the Church*, 6 vols. Salt Lake City, 1930.

DENNIS RASMUSSEN

MILITARY AND THE CHURCH

Although the Church is opposed to war and recognizes that going to war is a very poor alternative in resolving conflicts, tens of thousands of Latter-day Saints have served their countries' armed forces, sometimes even fighting in opposing forces, especially in World War II. The Church considers being loyal citizens to be a duty of its members, irrespective of nationality. Responding to a call for military service is one appropriate manner of fulfilling this duty of citizenship. Latter-day Saints who choose military careers have no restrictions on either their fellowship or their callings in the Church. While any member is free to object to military service because of conscience, Church membership in and of itself is not a justification, and Church leaders have discouraged conscientious objection in every conflict of the twentieth century.

The moral question for Church members is much more one of the spirit than of the uniform. It echoes John the Baptist's counsel to soldiers to avoid violence and extortion, and to be content with their wages (Luke 3:14). The Book of Mormon repeatedly counsels soldiers to abhor the shedding of blood (Alma 44:1–7; 48:14–16, 23; Morm. 4:11–12). However, it also contains principles as to when war may be justified. Concerning the action of the Nephites when they were attacked by the Lamanites, the record states:

> Nevertheless, the Nephites were inspired by a better cause, for they were not fighting for monarchy nor power but they were fighting for their homes and their liberties, their wives and their children, and their all, yea, for their rites of worship and their church.
>
> And they were doing that which they felt was the duty which they owed to their God; for the Lord had said unto them, and also unto their fathers, that: Inasmuch as ye are not guilty of the first offense, neither the second, ye shall not suffer yourselves to be slain by the hands of your enemies.
>
> And again, the Lord has said that: Ye shall defend your families even unto bloodshed. Therefore for this cause were the Nephites contending with the Lamanites, to defend themselves, and their families, and their lands, their country, and their rights, and their religion [Alma 43:45–47].

One of the Church's first significant involvements with a national military was the organization and the march of the Mormon Battalion. In 1846, as the Latter-day Saints were beginning their westward migration, they responded to the U.S. Army's request for five hundred volunteers to serve in the conflict with Mexico. The battalion marched from Fort Leavenworth, Kansas, through New Mexico and Arizona into Mexico, and then on to California, without combat. Most of its men then journeyed to join their families in Utah. The relative isolation in Utah provided for very little involvement in the Civil War. The Spanish-American War saw two artillery units mobilized from Utah, with the first LDS chaplain and the first LDS servicemen's worship group organized. Involvement in World War I was similarly based in the activity of Utah soldiers but was far more extensive than in any previous military engagement.

In the period before World War II, President J. Reuben Clark, Jr., counselor in the First Presidency, vigorously advocated U.S. neutrality, and opposed the maintenance of a standing army with equal vigor when hostilities ceased. However, he was the Church spokesman when it made official declarations encouraging LDS men to respond to their governments' call for military service, despite the fact that these decisions were contrary to his personal viewpoint. In October 1940, he said, "We shall confidently expect that no young man member of the Church will seek to evade his full responsibility" (*CR* [Oct. 1940]:16). A 1942 First Presidency statement counseled Church members worldwide to be ready to respond to their government's call to military duty and exonerated the members' acts of war: "God . . . will not hold the innocent instrumentalities of the war, our brethren in arms, responsible for the conflict" (*MFP* 6:159). This statement has been reiterated during each subsequent period of military action.

The Church has always made significant efforts to help its members in the armed forces live by the same moral standards they would uphold at home. The General Servicemen's Committee was organized in 1941 with Elder Harold B. Lee as chairman. Members of the committee had geographical responsibilities, visited military installations, and appointed more than three thousand servicemen as group leaders and assistants. These priesthood leaders facilitated fellowship and organized opportunities for military people who could not meet with ordinary wards and branches to partake of the sacrament of the Lord's Supper. The principle of servicemen's group leadership as a special case of Church organization continues in force. LDS chaplains coordinate their activities with stakes and missions and are authorized to organize groups and call group leaders any time small numbers of LDS service people are put in circumstances that might restrict their access to worship.

The activities of the General Servicemen's Committee (in 1969 it became the Military Relations Committee) ebbed and flowed with the intensity of military conflict. This committee began providing publications specifically for service personnel during World War II. It distributed pocket-sized copies of the Book of Mormon, a hymnal, and a doctrinal compendium, *Principles of the Gospel*, and prepared brochures on military life, sexual morality, missionary opportunities, and the Word of Wisdom. These resources formed the basis of a preservice orientation program instituted during the Vietnam era by the Military Relations Committee. Every stake was provided literature, audiovisual resources, and a curricular outline to help people entering the military prepare for that challenge.

The missionary opportunities in the stresses of military life have proven to be significant, both on a personal and on a national basis. Many military people join the Church, and missionary success in countries such as Japan and Korea has gained momentum from the work of servicemen and women. The membership of the Church commonly prays for service people as a group, much as it does for the missionaries.

Servicemen's conferences are held frequently in Europe and the Far East. An English-speaking servicemen's stake was organized in Europe in 1968, providing members living there the full program of the Church in their native tongue.

BIBLIOGRAPHY

Boone, Joseph F. "The Roles of The Church of Jesus Christ of Latter-day Saints in Relation to the United States Military, 1900–1975." Ph.D. diss., Brigham Young University, 1975.

ROBERT C. OAKS

MINORITIES

[*In the Book of Mormon, God invites "all to come unto him and partake of his goodness; and he denieth none that come unto him, black and white, bond and free, male and female; and he remembereth the heathen; and all are alike unto God" (2 Ne. 26:33). As LDS missionaries have preached the gospel of Jesus Christ to "every nation, kindred, tongue, and people," people from many ethnic groups from all over the world have accepted baptism and become members of the Church. See* Vital Statistics.

Emphasis has been placed on taking the gospel to the American Indians and to the other peoples of the Americas. See Indian Student Placement Services.

Substantial LDS populations also exist in the Pacific Islands. See Polynesians.

In 1978 a revelation extended the priesthood to all worthy males. This allowed the priesthood to be held by blacks. See Blacks.]

MODESTY

[*A quality of mind, heart, and body, modesty is an attitude of humility, decency, and propriety that may be evidenced in thought, language, dress, and behavior. Modesty or immodesty is reflected in almost every aspect of human life. It will be manifest in the "example of the believers, in word, in conversation, in charity, in spirit, in faith, in purity" (1 Tim. 4:12). Articles pertaining to this topic are* Lifestyle; Modesty in Dress; Profanity.]

MODESTY IN DRESS

Latter-day Saints believe that modest dress reflects commitment to a Christlike life and shows respect for self, for fellow beings, and for God. In their homes and in the Church, they are taught that modest dress has a positive effect on both self-esteem and behavior.

According to LDS theology, the body is more than a biological entity; it is a temple that houses an eternal spirit (cf. 1 Cor. 3:16–17).

Physical intimacy is reserved for marriage. Modest dress serves as a physical and spiritual guard against immoral behavior and its inherent physical, emotional, and spiritual harm. Because modesty in dress cannot be reduced to a matter of particular styles, individuals are encouraged to use discretion to determine appropriate dress in varying situations.

Emphasizing the importance of modest dress, President Spencer W. Kimball stated, "I am positive that personal grooming and cleanliness, as well as the clothes we wear, can be tremendous factors in the standards we set and follow on the pathway to immortality and eternal life" (1979, p. 3).

BIBLIOGRAPHY
Kimball, Spencer W. *Faith Precedes the Miracle*, pp. 161–68. Salt Lake City, 1972.
———. "On My Honor." *Ensign* 9 (Apr. 1979):3.

MICHELE THOMPSON-HOLBROOK

MORMON HANDICRAFT

Mormon Handicraft, a consignment store for handwork, including quilts, rugs, dolls, baby clothes, and other handmade items, was founded in 1937 by Louise Y. Robison, then general president of the Relief Society. The store was organized as a means of allowing women to supplement their family income during the depression of the 1930s (*History of Relief Society*, p. 115). Mormon Handicraft followed the pattern of earlier women's co-op stores operated by Relief Societies from the mid-1870s to 1912 (*A Centenary of Relief Society*, pp. 83–84).

Operated as a nonprofit organization, the store was originally administered by the Relief Society leaders, who desired "to preserve the skills of our pioneer ancestors and the skills and crafts of the various countries" (*History of Relief Society*, p. 115). General Board member Nellie O. Parker declared, "For the world to beat a path to the door of Mormon Handicraft Shop is our aim; and if Emerson is right, we are confident it will be so when people know of the fineness and skill of the workmanship to be found here" (Parker, p. 417).

An advertising brochure proclaimed, "Rare skill in handicraft from every country has been perpetuated in Utah. . . . This cosmopolitan background, unique for thrift and versatility, has produced a handicraft guild not to be found in any other place in the world. . . . There is quality only hands can produce" (Parker, p. 417). The brochure was distributed in dining and lounge cars of trains coming into Salt Lake City and was placed in a display case in the Hotel Utah lobby. The campaign was successful: On one occasion, Parker reported, after a visit to the store, a buyer for the Altman Company ordered "up-to-the-minute luncheon sets, copper work and oxen-yoke lamps" (Parker, p. 417).

Beginning in 1960, its scope was broadened and Mormon Handicraft became a distribution point for materials and ideas for the Relief Society's homemaking meetings, particularly quilting and other handwork supplies. Through the Homemaking Department of the Relief Society, women learned and practiced homemaking arts. The monthly compassionate service instruction given in Relief Society, where members were taught ways to assist less fortunate Church members, often included the production and distribution of quilts, clothing, and other necessities for the home. Availability of materials and classes was, therefore, welcomed by local Relief Society leaders. The sale of materials also helped maintain the economic viability of Mormon Handicraft.

As the Church grew, the need for a centralized distribution and education point diminished, and the shop as a separate unit was closed in January 1986 (*Church News*, Jan. 26, 1986, p. 12). The store then became a division of DESERET BOOK COMPANY in June 1986. At the time of transfer, Ronald A. Millett, Deseret Book president, affirmed the company's goal of preserving Mormon Handicraft's reputation in both consignment and retail supply operations (*Church News*, June 8, 1986, p. 14).

In 1987, Mormon Handicraft accepted over 9,000 different items made by 1,900 contributors, ages fourteen to ninety-two. Contributors varied from the widow in Salt Lake City who for forty-eight years produced dish towels, stuffed animals, aprons, bibs, and almost ten thousand crocheted heart sachets, to the women in the Philippines who sold elaborate lace-edged handkerchiefs as their sole income source (*Church News*, Mar. 28, 1987, p. 10; *Mormon Handicraft: A Brief History*, p. 5).

BIBLIOGRAPHY

A Centenary of Relief Society, 1842–1942. Salt Lake City, 1942.
History of Relief Society, 1842–1966. Salt Lake City, 1966.
Mormon Handicraft: A Brief History (pamphlet). Salt Lake City, 1987.
Parker, Nellie O. "Mormon Handicraft." *Relief Society Magazine* 26 (June 1939):417.

CAROL L. CLARK

MORMONISM, AN INDEPENDENT INTERPRETATION

One may take two basic approaches to the study of Mormonism as a religion. The first, which involves examination and careful consideration of the claims of Mormonism to be the truth, is a predominantly religious undertaking. Investigators search for answers to the fundamental question of whether The Church of Jesus Christ of Latter-day Saints (or the Reorganized Church of Jesus Christ of Latter Day Saints, as the case may be) is, or is not, the only true Christian church and whether, in fact, the Saints have the only legitimate priesthoods of Jesus Christ (Melchizedek and Aaronic).

The other approach to the study of the Latter-day Saints has as its goal not truth so much as understanding. Scholars—both in and outside the academy—study LDS theology, doctrine, ritual, ecclesiology, organizational structure, and the Mormon experience across time in an effort to determine what sort of movement Mormonism is and where and how it fits into the grand mosaic of world religions.

In addition to all the individuals who became Mormon converts, large numbers of journalists and Gentile clerics mounted explorations of the first sort during the nineteenth and the early part of the twentieth century. Many of the journalists decided that Mormonism was not a religion at all, while most clerics concluded that it was a Christian heresy. As for academic approaches to the topic before the middle of the twentieth century, only a small number of scholars made serious efforts to comprehend where the Latter-day Saints stood among the world's religions.

Some scholarly studies of Mormonism were completed before that time. In an appendix to an article on "Scholarly Studies of Mormonism," Leonard J. Arrington listed thirty-two doctoral dissertations on Mormon history and culture that were completed by 1950 (p. 30). Additionally, almost as soon as professional associations of scholars started to publish articles and proceedings in journal form, articles about the Saints started to appear in professional journals. But despite the serious and systematic study represented in these dissertations and professional articles, only a small number of authors pulled back from their material to attempt a classification of Mormonism within a broad religious context.

This situation changed after World War II when Mormon and non-Mormon scholars alike went beyond intensive studies of such discrete aspects of Mormonism as land settlement patterns, migration, or church-state relations. The results of this new work generally emerged as analyses of Mormonism from the secular perspectives of sociology, and social, cultural, political, and economic history. Then in the 1950s, scholarly taxonomists, working from the viewpoint of the history and sociology of religion, proposed schemes of classification other than the old one of whether or not Mormonism was a Christian heresy.

There were precedents for this study, too. The Scottish historian Robert Baird, who published *Religion in America* (1844), the first systematic description of American Christianity, divided the nation's churches into evangelical and liturgical camps, and included Mormonism in the latter. While essentially correct as far as it went, this obviously superficial analysis reflected the author's concentration on worship forms and ecclesiastical organization and his neglect of essential doctrines. Other students of American religion pictured the LDS movement as an illegitimate hybrid, combining elements of Puritanism, congregationalism, evangelicalism, and the antidenominational Christians (Campbellites) into a deviant variety of Protestantism. In one or another form, this characterization of Mormonism as irregular or aberrant was the standard interpretation that found its way into surveys well past the 1960s (see Handy).

After World War II, religious history—or church history as it was then known—started to change. An increasing number of its practitioners began to approach the study of American religion outside a denominational context and without privileging Protestantism. Disparaging portrayals of Mormonism started to give way among students of American religion. At the same time, with the rise to prominence of social science on the academic scene and a virtual explosion in the number of graduate students pursuing degrees in history, a substantial new contingent of scholars turned their attention to the Latter-day Saints. Rather than debunking Mormonism, they treated the Latter-day Saint movement as a case study from which to generalize about religion and culture—or politics or economics.

Although sharing a similar basic attitude toward Mormonism, the new generation of scholars did not arrive at similar conclusions. The disciplinary approaches and research agendas of the historians and social scientists who worked on Mormonism were so different that their results were not only dissimilar but contradictory. Instead of clarification, they brought confusion. When the distinguished historian Sydney Ahlstrom prepared the text for his *Religious History of the American People* (New Haven, Conn., 1972), he was unable to decide how Mormonism ought to be categorized. "One cannot even be sure," he said, "whether [Mormonism] is a sect, a mystery cult, a new religion, a church, a people, a nation, or an American subculture; indeed, at different times and places it is all of these" (p. 508).

By the time Ahlstrom wrote, a general lack of agreement about Mormonism had replaced the earlier non-Mormon consensus that it was a Christian aberration. In attempting a synthesis, he had to confront a wide array of interpretations and classifications of the movement. Available to him were the works of the scholars who, concentrating on the relationships between the Mormon prophet, his successors, and the Mormon people, tended to argue that the Latter-day Saints are, finally, just one more group over whom a charismatic leader exercised undue control. However carefully written, scholarly treatments in this vein presented conclusions that ultimately coincided with Anthony Hoekema's definition of Mormonism as a cult.

By contrast, the work of those who primarily concerned themselves with LDS beliefs came to agree with William A. Clebsch's classification. Clebsch did not accept the cultic designation. He held that belief in the Church of Jesus Christ as the only true church and in the "restored" LDS Aaronic and Melchizedek priesthoods as the only legitimate priesthoods turned Mormonism into one more "sect to end all sects." Timothy L. Smith described the movement as an idiosyncratic form of primitive Christianity, hence, sectarian.

Taking another tack, Mario De Pillis found in early LDS history

a "Search for Authority," and from that reached a much broader conclusion. In 1956, sociologist Will Herberg, in the influential
Protestant-Catholic-Jew, argued that these three forms of organized
religion were the most satisfactory vehicles in America for establishing one's identity within the national culture. De Pillis added
Mormonism to Herberg's triad, making it the "fourth major religion
. . . generally accepted in American society."

Study of the movement's beginnings in New England and western New York, the celebrated Mormon trek, and the establishment of
an LDS kingdom in the Intermountain West confused the issue further, for geographical circumstance generated the idea that
Mormonism is an "American religion" (Thomas J. Yates, "Count
Tolstoi and 'The American Religion,'" *IE* 42 [Jan. 1939]:94). This
oft-repeated phrase, said to be Count Leo Tolstoi's, was a main idea
behind Thomas F. O'Dea's influential sociological study of the
Mormons (1957). It was also woven into Klaus Hansen's study of
Mormonism and the American Experience (1981), and reappeared in
R. Laurence Moore's study of *Religious Outsiders and the Making of
Americans* (1986).

In the same quarter-century that saw the appearance of enormous numbers of historical and sociological studies of the LDS
movement, a new discipline, religious studies, made its way into the
American academy. Combining insights from history and sociology
as well as anthropology, psychology, theology, and studies of comparative religion, religious studies methodology enabled scholars to
study religions without asking about their truthfulness. Significantly,
although religionists (the designation increasingly given to scholars
in religious studies) address the question of how religion provides an
avenue for accomplishing cultural tasks, they do not universally
define religion as a product of culture. Central also to this method of
studying religion is the distinction between the sacred and the profane (the ordinary, that which is not sacred) and separation of religion into its various dimensions: the mythological, doctrinal,
ritual/liturgical, ethical, social/institutional, and experiential.

This new discipline provided students of Mormonism with an
additional set of conceptual tools. Approaching Mormonism from this
perspective made it possible to see, for instance, that R. Laurence
Moore may be correct in his argument that the Mormons were reli-

gious outsiders who have moved a long way toward acceptance as insiders in America without concluding that Mormonism is an American religion. Geographical and social locations no more made Mormonism an American religion than the location of Christianity's beginnings in Palestine, Greece, and Rome made Christianity a Palestinian or Graeco-Roman religion.

American culture surely influenced Mormonism. But Fawn McKay Brodie, a biographer of the Prophet Joseph Smith who argued this way, said Mormonism was not simply an American cult or some sort of new subdivision of Christianity. Brodie understood Mormonism to be related to Christianity in much the same way that Christianity is related to Judaism. That insight foreshadowed a religious studies approach. She also saw Mormonism as a product of the creative genius of Joseph Smith, which, in sociological terms, placed Mormonism in the cultic category, one of the older ways of understanding the religion.

A religious studies approach permits an analysis that treats Mormonism as more than the sum of its parts. From this comprehensive viewpoint, any characterization of the movement as the creation of one or two powerful, charismatic figures is seen, at the very least, to be incomplete. The numerous definitions that label the movement as "a sect, a mystery cult, a new religion, a church, a people, a nation, or an American subculture" are also partial. All in all, Mormonism, from the religious studies perspective, is best understood as a new religious tradition. The movement rests on a foundational tripod composed of a prophetic figure, scripture, and experience—Joseph Smith, the Book of Mormon, and the corporate life of the early Saints. By grasping the interaction of these three, one can firmly place Mormonism in the overall sweep of religious history.

Although Smith's role as prophet was established among his first followers before the publication of the Book of Mormon, this mysterious work, claiming to be of ancient origin, supported his prophetic position. It contains statements showing that Joseph Smith's movement would fulfill Old Testament prophecy, making modern Mormonism an extension of ancient Israel. Following on this association, Joseph Smith's own revelations proclaimed the opening of a new dispensation of the fulness of times and the restoration of both the true Church of Jesus Christ and the Aaronic and Melchizedek priesthoods. Together the Book of Mormon and Smith's revelations provided a means for his followers to connect with Christianity's apostolic era and with ancient Israel, while at the same time stirring within them such intense millennial expectations that they came to believe that they were living on the edge of time, in the "winding-up scene."

The revelation for the Saints to gather heightened the power of Smith's message and his place at the head of the movement. It brought his followers together in a place where the Saints could hear the prophet's message with their own ears, see the construction of the House of the Lord, with their own eyes, and participate in the daily activities of a community entirely composed of Saints of the latter days. Whether in New York, Ohio, Missouri, or Illinois, the Mormons' association with their "living prophet" and the routine interaction that occurred among the company of Saints lent such transcendental significance to the events of their everyday lives that Smith and his adherents were collectively ushered into "sacred time." This experience, this conscious living-out of sacred history, was as crucial to the creation of this new tradition as was the initial appearance of the Book of Mormon and the revelations of the Prophet Joseph.

The importance of the revelations should not be underestimated. It was by means of revelation that the Saints came to perceive of their ecclesiastical institution as the Church of Jesus Christ, formed again in a new age, and their community as a communion of Christian Saints called together in a new dispensation. Revelation likewise added to the idea of reformation the much more radical conception of the "restoration of all things." Not only church, priesthood, and primitive *ecclesia* were restored, but also Hebrew patriarchy, a political kingdom developed on a Solomonic model, and "ancient ordinances" (the endowment, baptism for the dead, and marriage for time and eternity). These truly set the Saints apart. The incorporation of these ideas into the movement, first in the political organization of the kingdom of God and afterward in additions to Mormonism's temple ritual and cultural life (through plural marriage) forever separated Mormonism from Catholic and Protestant forms of Christianity.

From that point forward, Mormonism was not merely related to Christianity as Christianity had been related to Judaism, that is, as reformation and consummation; now there was a direct relationship with the Hebrew tradition. Gradually the Christian view of being connected to Israel through adoption, being grafted in, was replaced with a new understanding of the relationship between the Saints and Israel. Acceptance of the LDS gospel came to be regarded as evidence that the blood of Abraham flowed through Mormon veins—evidence that was confirmed through the ritual of the patriarchal blessing in which Saints are informed of their membership of adoption into the family of one of Jacob's sons. Although this belief is, ultimately, a rhetorical construction of blood descent, it gave the Saints an identity as a "chosen people" that had a powerful impact on their understanding of themselves.

Magnifying as it did the difference between the members of their re-formed Church of Jesus Christ and other Christians, the idea of the restoration of all things was not universally welcomed within the Mormon fellowship. Initially attracted to Mormonism by the emphasis on primitive Christianity, many of Smith's earliest followers felt ambivalent about innovations connecting the movement to ancient times. In Missouri and Illinois there was resistance by some to the creation of a Mormon political kingdom that involved physical as well as psychic separation from non-Mormons.

Growing out of this ambivalence, a rupture divided the movement into two branches after the murder of Joseph Smith in 1844. While the history of The Church of Jesus Christ of Latter-day Saints, headquartered in Salt Lake City, Utah, can be fully comprehended only through the lens of LDS belief in the "restoration of all things," the same is not true of the Reorganized Church of Jesus Christ of Latter Day Saints, headquartered in Independence, Missouri. Organized again (reorganized) in 1860 when Joseph Smith III, the Mormon prophet's eldest son, accepted the position of president and prophet to the church, this division of Smith's followers rejected the political kingdom of God and many, if not all, the innovations that the first Mormon prophet had introduced under the rubric of the "restoration of all things." Emphasizing the reformation character of the movement, they placed themselves and their church in a much closer relationship to traditional forms of Christianity than did the Saints who followed Brigham Young to the Intermountain West.

In the history of The Church of Jesus Christ of Latter-day Saints and in the distinctive temple beliefs and practices that separate it from the Saints who did not go west, Mormonism is found as a new religious tradition in its purest, most undiluted form. The Utah Latter-day Saints experienced a trek through "the wilderness" and an extended period of residence sequestered in a "land of promise" whose internal political organization and social system were dominated by restoration doctrines. Seclusion within their mountain fastness and a sense of being under siege accelerated the systematizing of their distinctive doctrines as well as the development of a temple-centered culture. These heightened and preserved the Saints' sense of separation and chosenness long after political, social, and economic isolation came to an end.

An advantage of considering Mormonism as a new tradition rather than a church, denomination, sect, or cult is that it clarifies the divisions within the movement. The break following the prophet's death between the Saints who went to the Intermountain West and those who remained in the Midwest cannot really be understood as an ordinary sectarian schism any more than the separation of Christianity into Eastern Orthodoxy and Roman Catholicism or the division of Islam into Sunni and Shi'ite Muslims were sectarian schisms. Within the Mormon tradition, then, there are two divisions, two churches. Because schisms have occurred in both of these divisions, Mormon sects also exist. Mormon fundamentalists, Saints who maintain the practice of plural marriage, are the most visible of such sectarian groups.

Latter-day Saints of all varieties are as certain of their identity as Christians as any Roman Catholic or Evangelical Protestant. But they live in a dispensation all their own. Their particular history, their singular doctrines and ritual practices, and their perception of themselves as a peculiar people do not simply set them apart from other Christians as one more subdivision of that tradition. Mormonism will remain separate and be best understood as a new religious tradition as long as the Saints maintain their belief that their church organization is the original Church of Jesus Christ, restored to them alone in 1830, *and* as long as they maintain the complementary position that in Mormonism is found the restoration of all things.

BIBLIOGRAPHY

Arrington, Leonard J. "Scholarly Studies of Mormonism." *Dialogue* 1 (Spring 1966):15–32.

Clebsch, William A. "Each Sect the Sect to End All Sects." *Dialogue* 1 (Summer 1966):84–89.

De Pillis, Mario. "The Development of Mormon Communitarianism, 1826–1846." Ph.D. diss., Yale University, 1961.

Handy, Robert T. *A History of the Churches in the United States and Canada*, pp. 224–27. New York, 1976.

Hoekema, Anthony A. *Four Major Cults*. Grand Rapids, Mich., 1963. The section on Mormonism was "extensively updated" and published separately by the same press in 1974.

Shipps, Jan. *Mormonism: The Story of a New Religious Tradition*. Urbana, Ill., 1985.

Smith, Timothy L. "The Book of Mormon in a Biblical Culture." *Journal of Mormon History* 7 (1980):3–21.

JAN SHIPPS

MORMONISM, MORMONS

"Mormonism" is an unofficial but common term for The Church of Jesus Christ of Latter-day Saints and the doctrinal, institutional, cultural, and other elements forming its distinctive worldview and independent Christian tradition. "Mormons" is the equivalent term for members of the Church, with "Mormon" being both the singular noun and the adjective.

Over the years these terms and other, less common variants have been widely used (such as "Mormonite" in early decades of the Church), but members prefer the official name revealed by the Savior to the Prophet Joseph Smith—The Church of Jesus Christ of Latter-day Saints—in order to emphasize the central role of Jesus Christ in their doctrine and worship (D&C 115:3–4). The shortened name that most contemporary members use instead of "Mormonism" is "LDS Church," with "LDS" used in place of "Mormon" and "Latter-day Saints" or "Saints" used instead of "Mormons."

The term "Mormon" derives from the Book of Mormon, published in 1830 and recently subtitled *Another Testament of Jesus Christ*. This book is accepted by the Church as scripture along with the Bible.

Mormonism refers to the divinely inspired doctrine taught by Joseph Smith and the succeeding leaders of the Church. It views human life as a stage in the eternal progression of intelligent beings who, as God's spirit children, must choose, in thought and deed, whether to accept or reject Christ's gospel, teachings, and covenants. Latter-day Saints see the Church's teachings as true Christianity, restored to earth in its original purity by Christ himself, and thus they frequently refer to the Church, its doctrines, and its priesthood as "restored." Basic Church doctrines include belief in a personal God vitally concerned with his children, the divinity of the Savior Jesus Christ and his infinite Atonement, the universal need for repentance and baptism by proper authority, continuing revelation through living prophets, the brotherhood and sisterhood of all human beings, the eternal sanctity of marriage and family, and the responsibility to be self-reliant and to help others. Many of the basic beliefs of the LDS Church are succinctly summarized in the thirteen Articles of Faith, which serve, among other things, as an outline of the basic doctrines for members of the Church.

A salient characteristic of Church practice is the delegation of specific ecclesiastical responsibilities to every active member of the Church. This results in a high level of voluntary member activity, commitment, and sense of community. Only men belong to the priesthood; but both women and men share priesthood blessings, and both hold significant leadership and teaching positions, perform missionary and temple work, and participate prominently in most Church meetings. Other notable Church practices include the encouragement of education, thrift, community service, missionary work, genealogical record keeping, and temple worship.

While the Church is clearly conservative on many issues, its central reliance on continuing revelation provides a divinely guided flexibility, especially in areas of practice. Through the living Prophet, changes are effected as revelation is sought and received. Two main practices discontinued over the years are polygamy, officially ended in 1890, and gathering to a central geographical location, largely ended in the 1920s (Allen and Leonard, p. 496–97). At the same time, other practices have been introduced: Tithing, revealed in the 1830s, has been normative since the 1890s; and the complete avoidance of drugs such as tobacco, alcohol, tea, and coffee has been formally required of all active members since the 1920s, nearly a century after first having been revealed (see WORD OF WISDOM). FAMILY HOME EVENINGS, introduced in 1915, were widely instituted as a weekly practice in the mid 1960s. Extension of priesthood authority to all worthy male members, regardless of race, was granted in 1978.

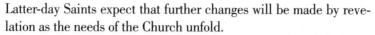

Latter-day Saints expect that further changes will be made by revelation as the needs of the Church unfold.

Mormonism is not a political ideology. The Church's policy regarding governments allows it to thrive in a wide variety of political contexts around the world. It supports separation of CHURCH AND STATE, respect for duly established law and government, and members' active participation in civic and charitable affairs (D&C 134; *see* POLITICS: POLITICAL TEACHINGS). War is generally condemned, but military service is not forbidden. Well before the 1950s, the Church frequently took positions on political issues, especially some affecting Utah. Since that time, Church leaders have increasingly urged members to decide such questions for themselves and have implemented a policy of Church neutrality toward government, except in instances where political developments clearly impinge on important moral issues or severely restrict members' freedom to practice their religion.

In common speech, the terms "Mormonism" and "Mormon" are not limited to the official teachings or practices of the Church, but often also refer to particular lifestyles, cultural viewpoints, historical events, philosophical outlooks, and artifacts that are characteristic of the broader Latter-day Saint tradition or culture. In most formal settings, however, the Church prefers to avoid the use of these substitute terms wherever possible, to direct attention to the true name of the Church.

BIBLIOGRAPHY
Allen, James B., and Glen M. Leonard. *The Story of the Latter-day Saints*. Salt Lake City, 1976.
Arrington, Leonard J., and Davis Bitton. *The Mormon Experience*. New York, 1979.
The Church of Jesus Christ of Latter-day Saints. *Gospel Principles*. Salt Lake City, 1981.
Richards, LeGrand. *A Marvelous Work and a Wonder*. Salt Lake City, 1988.
Talmage, James E. *AF*. Salt Lake City, 1988.

DONALD K. JARVIS

MORMONS, IMAGE OF

[*This entry consists of three articles giving a survey of the Mormon image as it has been and is reflected in* The Visual Arts, *in* Film, *and in* Fiction *from the earliest days of the Church to the present.*]

THE VISUAL ARTS

The early history of the Church, especially the uniqueness of its beliefs and practices, influenced the creation of an LDS, or Mormon, image in art. Caricature and cartoon were particularly well suited to the mass market, and Latter-day Saints were a favorite subject. Although some early works conveyed the complexities of the LDS experience, most people developed their image of members of the Church from portrayals that were selective and caricatured. While stereotypical images linger, current depictions of Latter-day Saints, frequently employing works by LDS artists, more accurately reflect the diversity and richness of Mormon life.

By 1860, media depictions had firmly established national stereotypes of Mormonism. During the next decades, negative, stereotyped images of Latter-day Saints appeared regularly in newspapers and magazines such as *Harper's Weekly, Vanity Fair, Cosmopolitan,* and *Collier's Weekly.* Although some images were humorous, the effect was essentially harmful. Bunker and Bitton explain: "The simple fact is that most of the illustrations treating the Mormons were not low-key or objective; they were cartoons and caricatures with an obvious point of view. And that point of view was, with almost monotonous regularity, negative" (Bunker and Bitton, p. 148).

This negative image developed when the social climate in the United States allowed open hostility toward unpopular religious and ethnic groups. Major themes about Latter-day Saints focused on the public disapproval of the practice of polygamy, the Utah War of 1857–1858, and clashes between U.S. officials and LDS leaders. Although artists created some fresh interpretations as new events transpired, they were usually only variations on established themes.

However, a few artists ignored the stereotypical image of the Latter-day Saints and produced work that conveyed the complexity of the religion and its people. Arthur Boyd Houghton, an artist for the *Graphic,* a British weekly pictorial journal, visited Salt Lake City in 1870 and created a series of drawings featuring the Saints. His scenes of LDS life are rendered with respect and dignity, and reveal his compassion for humble people. Two paintings attributed to Albert Bierstadt and one by Maynard Dixon show thriving LDS settlements, the result of Mormon cultivation of the desert. Enoch Wood Perry, Jr., painted excellent likenesses of Brigham Young and each member of the Quorum of the Twelve Apostles. Photographer William Henry Jackson's pictures and sketches of the West include images of Salt Lake City, Mormon wagon trains, and farm life.

The Latter-day Saints have never lacked for artists and illustrators of their own to tell their story. While graphic artists in the East were generally creating negative, stereotyped images, LDS artists in the West were producing a rich and authentic pictorial record of their experience. The early Mormon experience, including the migration west and pioneer life in Utah, was chronicled by British artist Frederick Piercy and Danish artist C. C. A. Christensen, both converts to the Church (*see* ARTISTS, VISUAL).

In recent years, interest in the portrayal of Mormons as Mormons has diminished in non-LDS media and among non-LDS artists. At the same time, the number of LDS artists, the diversity of their styles, and their interest in conveying LDS themes have all increased. Like the early artists who saw beyond the stereotypical images of their day, these modern artists have succeeded in conveying, at least in some measure, the complexities and richness of the LDS experience, made even more diverse as the Church has grown to include a worldwide membership.

[*See also* Art in Mormonism.]

BIBLIOGRAPHY
Bunker, Gary L., and Davis Bitton. *The Mormon Graphic Image, 1834–1914: Cartoons, Caricatures, and Illustrations.* Salt Lake City, 1983.
Gerdts, William H. "Utah." In *Art Across America: Two Centuries of Regional Painting,* Vol. 3, pp. 128–45. New York, 1990.

VIRGIE D. DAY

FILM

From the beginning of the twentieth century until the mid-1930s, the film portrayals of Latter-day Saints were generally negative. First publicly exhibited in the 1890s, commercial motion pictures continued the sensational characterizations depicted in the novels of the period. One of the earliest treatments was Thomas Edison's nickelodeon film *A Trip to Salt Lake City* (1905). More humorous than sinister, the film satirized the problems of a polygamous Mormon husband trying to give his many children a drink of water on a Pullman car bound for the city of the Saints.

More common were films such as *A Mormon Maid* (Lasky-Paramount, 1917), which portrayed the Danites, stereotyped in earlier fiction as a posse of Missouri Mormon firebrands, as night-riding henchmen costumed like the Ku Klux Klan in D. W. Griffith's *The Birth of A Nation* (1915). Inspired by anti-Mormon novelist Winifred Graham's *The Love Story of a Mormon* (London, 1911), *Trapped by the Mormons* (Pyramid, 1922) brought to the screen a portrayal of a marauding LDS missionary in England preying vampirelike on unwary women. This film capitalized on the unfounded fear that LDS missionaries exploited women left widowed by World War I. A film version of Zane Grey's *Riders of the Purple Sage* (Fox) was released in 1918 and rereleased in 1921 despite protests that its negative depictions of Latter-day Saints and Utah would hinder the state's business development. A sympathetic treatment of the Church was the feature-length historical drama *One Hundred Years of Mormonism* (Utah Moving Pictures Co., 1913).

From 1918 to 1945, approximately thirty anti-Mormon films were released worldwide. In the 1930s, however, the motion picture industry drafted a production code, which, among other things, forbade negative portrayals of religious organizations and their beliefs. In 1938, Twentieth Century Fox informed President Heber J. Grant that it planned to produce a motion picture based on Vardis Fisher's historical novel *Children of God.* While he privately expressed fears of another negative screen image, partly because Fisher's novel was not fully understanding of the Church and its early leaders, President Grant nevertheless cooperated fully with the studio. The resulting film, *Brigham Young*, released in 1940, although not totally pleasing to Church leaders, was in most respects very positive and reversed almost four decades of negative stereotypes. Met with critical praise, it vividly portrayed the persecutions of Latter-day Saints in Nauvoo during the 1840s, the murder of Joseph Smith, the trek west to the Great Basin, and the "miracle of the gulls" in 1848. The film showed Latter-day Saints not as the stereotyped wife stealers of earlier films but as industrious pioneers. In a fictional courtroom scene in which Brigham Young defends Joseph Smith, the dialogue depicts the LDS cause as inextricably linked with that of America's founders seeking religious freedom. Produced at a time when Americans watched with concern the rising persecution of Jews in Hitler's Germany, the film defended the right of Latter-day Saints, or any other minority, to exist in a pluralist nation.

Since the 1940 release of *Brigham Young*, portrayals of Mormon history and culture in Hollywood films and television generally have been limited to humorous episodes dealing with polygamy as in *Wagon Master* (RKO, 1950), *Paint Your Wagon* (Paramount, 1969), *They Call Me Trinity* (West Film, 1971) and *Trinity Is Still My Name* (West Film, 1972), and *The Duchess and the Dirtwater Fox* (Fox, 1976). The only commercial feature-length treatment of Mormons between 1940 and 1990 was *Brigham* (Sunset Films, 1977), a low-budget film covering approximately the same period as *Brigham Young* but lacking the dramatic value of the earlier film.

BIBLIOGRAPHY

D'Arc, James V. "Darryl F. Zanuck's *Brigham Young*: A Film in Context." *BYU Studies* 29 (Winter 1989):5–33.

Nelson, Richard Alan. "A History of Latter-day Saint Screen Portrayals in the Anti-Mormon Film Era, 1905–1936." Master's thesis, Brigham Young University, 1975.

———. "From Antagonism to Acceptance: Mormons and the Silver Screen." *Dialogue* 10 (Spring 1977):58–69.

JAMES V. D'ARC

FICTION

For the first hundred years of LDS history, interest in Latter-day Saints as a subject for popular fiction was remarkably high. Taking its stereotypes from the pseudo-histories and travel narratives that circulated widely, fiction about Mormons emphasized melodramatic characters and fantastic plots full of violence and mystery. Similar patterns continued into the mid-twentieth century, but since then, Latter-day Saints have appeared less frequently and usually only casually in non-Mormon fiction.

Themes of violence and melodrama appeared as early as the 1840s. Typically a beautiful young heroine was said to have escaped or to have been rescued by a heroic "Gentile" and carried from the Mormons and the drunken and lecherous clutches of a polygamous elder or bishop. Frequently the fleeing protagonists were pursued across the continent, sometimes even around the world, by secretive "Danites" or "avenging angels." In these pieces LDS leaders were characterized as scheming, rough, and tyrannical, and the culture as crude and repressive at best, violent and destructive at worst.

By the 1850s, fiction about the Latter-day Saints was almost a genre in itself. Often written by women (especially the wives of ministers) and following the pattern of the more famous *Uncle Tom's Cabin*, these novels and short stories exploited popular ideas, fears, and societal concerns, as in Orvilla S. Belisle's *The Prophets; or, Mormonism Unveiled* (1855) and Metta Victoria Fuller's, *Mormon Wives* (1856; published again in 1860 as *Lives of Female Mormons* and republished many times in Europe and translated into several languages).

Each succeeding decade added to the tide of new authors and titles. In the 1880s, for example, more than a score of book-length best sellers came from British and American presses. Even some of the best known writers of the nineteenth century found the topic of Mormonism appealing: Robert Louis Stevenson (*The Dynamiter*, 1885) and Arthur Conan Doyle (*A Study in Scarlet*, 1887) held Mormons up as objects of fear, and Charles Farrer Browne ("Artemus Ward Among the Mormons," 1866) and Mark Twain (*Roughing It*, 1872) treated them as objects of satire and laughter.

In the early twentieth century the same patterns generally continued. Zane Grey (*The Heritage of the Desert*, 1910, and *Riders of the Purple Sage*, 1912) used Latter-day Saints as central figures, and Jack London wrote of the Mountain Meadows Massacre in his novel *The Star Rover* (1915). How firmly entrenched the pattern remained even beyond mid-century is illustrated by the images in Irving Wallace's *The Twenty-seventh Wife* (1961) and J. C. Furnas's *The Devil's Rainbow* (1962), which paint Joseph Smith in terms of popular psychosis and caricature Mormon leaders in general. Even the works of more weighty novelists—Vardis Fisher's *Children of God* (1939), for example—follow the old patterns, with a sympathetic protagonist outside the Church struggling against unfavorable, repressive antagonists from within.

Latter-day Saints are not now as popular a subject as they once were for non-Mormon authors, and writers' interest in modern Mormons as Mormons is vastly different from what it was a hundred years ago. While Latter-day Saints may appear occasionally or casually in fiction (e.g., Alan Drury's *Advise and Consent*, 1959), they have become both too conventional and too well-known as individuals to be placed easily into alien molds (*see* STEREOTYPING OF LATTER-

DAY SAINTS). While some differences between LDS and non-Mormon culture still persist, these differences now seem to be less exotic or threatening and hence less accessible for exploitation.

BIBLIOGRAPHY

Arrington, Leonard J., and Jon Haupt. "Intolerable Zion: The Image of Mormonism in Nineteenth-Century American Literature." *Western Humanities Review* 22 (Summer 1968):243–60.

————. "The Missouri and Illinois Mormons in Anti-Bellum [*sic*] Fiction." *Dialogue* 5 (Spring 1970):37–50.

Lambert, Neal E. "Saints, Sinners and Scribes: A Look at the Mormons in Fiction." *Utah Historical Quarterly* 36 (Winter 1968):63–76.

NEAL E. LAMBERT

MORMON TABERNACLE CHOIR

The Mormon Tabernacle Choir originated in mid-nineteenth-century Salt Lake City. It consists of 300-plus voices carefully selected from many volunteers. Its members give of their time and talents freely in practices and performances, serving without pay. Probably best known for its weekly radio and TV program of inspirational music and messages, "Music and the Spoken Word," the choir has performed and recorded extensively. It performs regularly in the tabernacle on Temple Square and provides music at all general conferences of the Church.

The origins of the Mormon Tabernacle Choir may be found in the desire and commitment of early converts to include appropriate music in both sacred and secular events (*see* MUSIC). The process of collecting hymns for instruction and worship began only four months after the Church was organized in 1830 (*see* HYMNS AND HYMNODY), and a choir was organized as early as 1836 for the dedication of the Kirtland Temple.

As the Latter-day Saints moved west, President Brigham Young included musicians among members even of the advance parties. Consequently, a small choir first sang for a conference in the Salt Lake Valley on August 22, 1847, twenty-nine days after the first party arrived.

Early choirs in the Old Tabernacle (built in 1851) and in the present Tabernacle (completed in 1867) were small and undisciplined by later standards. With the appointment of George Careless as conductor in 1869, the Tabernacle Choir began to flourish. Careless assembled the first large choir, a total of 304 singers, by adding smaller groups from other areas to the eighty-five singers in the Salt Lake Tabernacle Choir for a general conference performance on October 8, 1873. The vision of a choral ensemble to match the size of the Tabernacle was thus born. Early conductors who had prepared the way for Careless included John Parry (1849–1854), Stephen Goddard (1854–1856), James Smithies (1856–1862), Charles John Thomas (1862–1865), and Robert Sands (1865–1869).

Careless was followed by Ebenezer Beesley (1880–1889), with Thomas C. Griggs, assistant; Evan Stephens (1889–1916), with Horace S. Ensign, assistant; Anthony C. Lund (1916–1935), with B. Cecil Gates and Albert J. Southwick, assistants; J. Spencer Cornwall (1935–1957), with Albert J. Southwick, D. Sterling Wheelwright, John R. Halliday, and Richard P. Condie, assistants; Richard P. Condie (1957–1974), with Jay E. Welch, assistant; Jay E. Welch (1974), with Jerold D. Ottley, assistant; and Jerold D. Ottley (from 1975 onward), with Donald H. Ripplinger, associate conductor.

During his tenure, Evan Stephens increased the size of the choir from about 125 to more than 300, making it the leading musical organization of Salt Lake City. To accommodate this larger size, the choir area of the Tabernacle was redesigned to create the present semicircular tiered seating. Stephens also took the choir to Chicago in 1893 on its first tour out of the state, beginning its now traditional role of emissary for the Church and the region.

Anthony C. Lund brought solid vocal training and a European choral sound to the choir. He excelled in music that required control and subtlety. J. Spencer Cornwall labored to raise the standards of the choir, to improve its sound as an ensemble, and to increase its repertoire from little more than one hundred pieces to almost a thousand. Under his direction the choir was active as a concert organization and released its first long-playing recording, in 1949. Richard P. Condie accelerated the recording activities of the choir and greatly increased its touring schedule. He produced what has been described as "the Tabernacle Choir sound," a large, romantic choral tone, heavy with feeling. Jerold D. Ottley has refined and shaped the traditional tone of the choir into a more flexible, precise, and energetic sound, one capable of expressing the subtleties of the finest choral literature.

Beginning with the installation of the first pipe organ in the Tabernacle in 1867, organists have been appointed to assist the choir. Among the finest musicians in the Church, they have also performed recitals, played for church and civic meetings, and composed music (*see* MUSICIANS).

The choir has profoundly affected music throughout the Church. Its consistently high artistic standard, frequent use of hymns and hymn arrangements, and exemplary service through music continue to inspire, instruct, and encourage Church musicians and the members they serve.

The choir rehearses for two hours every Thursday evening in preparation for its weekly broadcasts and uses Tuesday evenings as needed to prepare for recording sessions, concerts, tours, and general conferences of the Church. A number of choir members have university degrees in music, and many others are professionally trained. All are competent musicians. They include men and women from many walks of life.

The choir has released more than 130 recordings and several films and videotapes. Five of its recordings have achieved "gold record" status. Most popular has been a 1959 release of "The Battle Hymn of the Republic" with the Philadelphia Orchestra, for which the choir received a Grammy Award.

Many notable personalities, soloists, and conductors have appeared with the choir, including Eugene Ormandy, Jerome Hines, Sherrill Milnes, Marilyn Horne, and Maurice Abravanel.

The choir's first major concert tour culminated in a performance at the World's Columbian Exposition in Chicago in 1893. Subsequent domestic tours have included performances in thirty-two states and the District of Columbia. Tours outside the United States have included Canada, Australia, and sixteen nations in Europe, Asia, South and Central America, the South Pacific, and Scandinavia. The choir has appeared at thirteen world's fairs and expositions, performed at the inauguration of four U.S. presidents, and sung for numerous worldwide telecasts and special events. In his remarks during a broadcast marking the completion of sixty years of weekly broadcasts, U.S. President George Bush called the choir "one of America's greatest treasures." It has become an American institution.

[*See also* Mormon Tabernacle Choir Broadcast ("The Spoken Word").]

BIBLIOGRAPHY

Calman, Charles Jeffrey, and William I. Kaufman. *The Mormon Tabernacle Choir.* New York, 1979.

Petersen, Gerald A. *More Than Music: The Mormon Tabernacle Choir.* Provo, Utah, 1979.

K. NEWELL DAYLEY

MORMON TABERNACLE CHOIR BROADCAST ("THE SPOKEN WORD")

The Mormon Tabernacle Choir Broadcast is the traditional Sunday broadcast of the MORMON TABERNACLE CHOIR. It originates in the Salt Lake Tabernacle and is open to the public. Begun in 1929, this weekly performance has become the longest continuously presented nationwide network broadcast in American radio history.

During World War II, the choir broadcasts were aired extensively over Armed Forces Radio Network in Europe and the Far East. Thereafter, local stations extended the broadcast into the Pacific Islands, Australia, and South America. The choir made its television debut in 1962, and the weekly broadcast was relayed to over eight hundred radio and television stations worldwide.

With the sacred hymns and choral works, backed by the tabernacle organ, a brief message, the "Spoken Word," is given each Sunday. For forty-one years the voice and the message were those of Richard L. Evans, who during that period was called to be a Seventy, then a member of the Quorum of the Twelve Apostles. His messages and delivery attempted to capsulize—usually in less than two minutes—universal principles related to character, human relationships, and the conduct of life. In the spirit of bridge-building, he aimed at both timely and timeless insights. His undergirding message was that the differences that separate people are not nearly as great as the factors that unite them. Selected Spoken Word messages ran in a weekly syndicated newspaper column circulated nationally and were later published in a series of books. Over two thousand such messages were given before his death in 1971.

Through thousands of broadcasts the opening hymn has remained "Gently Raise the Sacred Strain," and the closing one, "As the Dew from Heaven Distilling," and the signoff phrase is "may peace be with you, this day and always."

[*See also* Mormon Tabernacle Choir.]

PAUL H. EVANS

MORMON YOUTH SYMPHONY AND CHORUS

The Mormon Youth Symphony and Chorus (often abbreviated MYSC) is an officially sponsored musical organization of the Church. It was organized in 1969 with a primary commission to promote a "greater understanding between all peoples and cultures."

The group is composed of young musicians ages 18 to 33 who have participated in school or community orchestras and choruses. These musicians come from various communities in Utah and rehearse two hours each week.

The MYSC performs approximately thirty times each year, including formal concerts in the Tabernacle, conference appearances, firesides, tours, broadcasts, and recordings. The programming was changed to the "Boston Pops" format when Conductor Robert C. Bowden received the baton in 1974. Bowden conducts and also composes and arranges much of the music for the groups. Tours have covered the United States. During the Bicentennial celebration of the Constitution in Washington, D.C., the symphony and chorus performed in the Kennedy Center. Many nationally prominent visiting artists have performed with them.

The Mormon Youth Symphony and Chorus has won fourteen national awards for television specials, including two Emmys, two George Washington Awards from the Freedom Foundation, and the Angel Award from Religion in Media. It has also performed for several national and international groups; such presentations have

included a television special for the Norwegian Broadcasting
Company as well as specials for American Veterans of World War II,
Korea, and Vietnam, and for the National League of American Pen
Women. The MYSC has eighteen commercial recordings to its credit.

MERRILL BRADSHAW

MOTHERHOOD

In an address on the blessings and responsibilities of motherhood,
President Ezra Taft Benson stated: "No more sacred word exists in
secular or holy writ than that of mother" (Benson, p. 1). Latter-day
Saints revere and respect motherhood, in part because of the mother's
role in shaping the FAMILY unit and the individuals within it.
President David O. McKay taught:

> Motherhood is the greatest potential influence either for good or ill in
> human life. The mother's image is the first that stamps itself on the
> unwritten page of the young child's mind. It is her caress that first awak-
> ens a sense of security; her kiss, the first realization of affection; her
> sympathy and tenderness, the first assurance that there is love in the
> world. . . . This ability and willingness properly to rear children . . .
> make motherhood the noblest office or calling in the world. . . . She who
> rears successfully a family of healthy, beautiful sons and daughters . . .
> deserves the highest honor that man can give, and the choicest bless-
> ings of God [McKay, pp. 452–54].

Obviously, the sociological significance of the mother's role is
immense: Her relationship with her children and her guidance in
their growing years influence the formation of values and attitudes
they will carry throughout their lives. But for Latter-day Saints, motherhood has meaning well beyond such sociological significance.

Church doctrine recognizes both a mothering and a fathering role
in the spiritual birth and premortal development of each person. In a
document issued in 1909, the First Presidency of the Church wrote
that "man, as a spirit, was begotten and born of heavenly parents,
and reared to maturity in the eternal mansions of the Father," and
that "all men and women are in the similitude of the universal Father

and Mother, and are literally the sons and daughters of Deity" (Smith, p. 884).

Following development in the premortal existence, each of God's spirit children has the opportunity to come to earth and acquire a mortal body that, when resurrected, will be bound with the spirit to form an inseparable, eternal soul. Providing mortal bodies for God's spirit children is a work given to mortal beings, with the greater measure of responsibility falling to mothers, who conceive, sustain, carry, and give birth to children. President Spencer W. Kimball said, "Mothers have a sacred role. They are partners with God. . . . [He] has placed women at the very headwaters of the human stream" (pp. 326–27).

The significance of motherhood continues undiminished following the birth of a child. The long-term stability, security, and peace of a human soul are built in large measure upon the foundation of love, and any individual's ability to give and receive love is rooted strongly in that person's earliest relationships. For most people, that earliest influence is the mother.

She who gives the child life is first and foremost the one to give it a way of life, teaching the child what it should or should not do. She encourages strong character formation as she teaches the child to impose limitations on some of its natural instincts. By her words and actions she teaches her child the regard that should be shown other individuals if that child wishes to be included and loved as a member of the family circle, later as a member of society, and finally as a participating member of the kingdom of God.

The ultimate responsibility of a mother, then, is to lead her child lovingly through its personal development and toward its divine destiny. Latter-day Saints believe that if a mother is prayerful and totally committed to such a weighty responsibility, she will receive divine intuitions and spiritual whisperings to aid her in her mothering. Living as a conduit for divine instruction to her child, a mother can greatly enhance its opportunity for joy and exaltation. The child who has been mothered in this profound way usually develops a moral conscience, a respect for society, a desire to contribute to the well-being of humankind, and, most important, a love of God and a love for self that will bring everlasting joy and inner peace.

Perhaps the most distinctive Latter-day Saint doctrine regarding motherhood emphasizes the role of a mother after death. The eternal nature of the family unit, when that unit is bound together by priesthood ordinances and temple covenants, guarantees to a faithful LDS mother the privileges, opportunities, and joys of motherhood with her children in a relationship that lasts eternally.

[*See also* Women, Roles of.]

BIBLIOGRAPHY
Benson, Ezra Taft. "To the Mothers in Zion." Salt Lake City, 1987.
Kimball, Spencer W. *The Teachings of Spencer W. Kimball*, pp. 324–51. Salt Lake City, 1982.
McKay, David O. *Gospel Ideals*, pp. 452–57. Salt Lake City, 1953.
Smith, Joseph Fielding. "Mothers in Israel." *The Relief Society Magazine* 57 (Dec. 1970):883–87.

PATRICIA TERRY HOLLAND

MOTION PICTURES, LDS PRODUCTIONS

As early as 1913, when the motion picture industry was in its early stages, leaders of The Church of Jesus Christ of Latter-day Saints expressed an interest in using the film medium: "The moving picture together with all the other modern inventions is to help us carry the Mission of Christ to all the world, and to bring humanity home to the true principles of salvation" (Young, p. 80). With the sanction of President Joseph F. Smith, Shirley "Shirl" Young Clawson and his brother Chester filmed many Church events and leaders from 1916 to 1929 in black and white and without sound. This era of film production for the Church ended tragically, however, when a fire killed Shirl Clawson and destroyed the studio and many of the films. The Church's next major move into film production began in the 1950s and has resulted in many award-winning items among the programs produced for home, classroom, and missionary use.

In 1946 Wetzel O. "Judge" Whitaker, chief of animation for Walt Disney Studios, invited three members of the Quorum of the Twelve Apostles—Elders Harold B. Lee, Mark E. Petersen, and Matthew Cowley—to tour the Disney Studios in Burbank, California. They were impressed with the potential of motion pictures to teach principles of the gospel. In that same year, wards, stakes, and missions began to be provided with motion picture projectors. Whitaker produced the first two films for the Church on a volunteer basis: *Church Welfare in Action* and *The Lord's Way*.

In January 1953 BRIGHAM YOUNG UNIVERSITY in Provo, Utah, created a department of motion picture production to produce films to be used by the Church and appointed Judge Whitaker as its founding director. The department produced poignant and appealing films such as *Come Back My Son* based on a story from the *Improvement Era* about reactivating an adult member of the Aaronic Priesthood. *How Near to the Angels*, the most ambitious LDS film project at that time, was a significant milestone because of its dramatic nature though it was only fifty minutes long. The film had as its theme temple marriage. *A Time for Sowing* showed the effect parents have on the behavior of their children. *Time Pulls the Trigger* looked at the connection between smoking and premature death. *With All Your Heart* showed a relationship between a spiritually sensitive bishop and reverence in Church meetings. *My Brother's Keeper* and *Shannon* dramatized the reclaiming of less active members of the Church. *The Search for Truth* presented the rational observations and testimonies of scientists on the reconciliation of science and religion. *Worth Waiting For* taught that happy marriages are worth preparing for. The most challenging film produced in this first decade of Church film production, and an enduring favorite, was *Windows of Heaven*, a film on blessings through the law of tithing.

MAN'S SEARCH FOR HAPPINESS, the first film written for a non-Mormon audience about the purpose of life, premiered at the 1964 World's Fair in New York City, where it was viewed by five million people. This film was subsequently translated into more languages than any previous Church film, including Afrikaans, Cantonese, Creole, Czech, Danish, Dutch, Esperanto, Finnish, French, French-Canadian, German, Hmong, Italian, Japanese, Korean, Mandarin, Navajo, Norwegian, Portuguese, Quechua, Quiche, Samoan, Serbo-Croatian, Spanish, Swedish, Tagalog, Taiwanese, Thai, Tongan, and Vietnamese. A Japanese version was filmed in Japan and premiered at the 1970 World's Fair Expo there.

No More a Stranger demonstrated the importance of fellowshipping new members in a ward. *And Should We Die* taught the principle of fasting and prayer. *The Three Witnesses*, a dramatic reenactment of the story of the Three Witnesses to the Book of Mormon, was used widely throughout the Church in teaching this aspect of early Church history. *Meet the Mormons* featured many on-camera, spontaneous interviews and testimonies, and showed the international nature of the Church. It was also translated into many languages. *Where Jesus Walked* is about the life of Christ and was filmed in the Holy Land.

In addition to the BYU motion picture studio, KSL television has preserved on film many speeches by General Authorities and selected specials, such as *Nauvoo*, and *Cumorah, Hill of History*. In 1967 Bonneville Media Communications was organized as a broadcast production facility to help develop a positive media image for the Church and to convey its doctrines and beliefs. Bonneville's direct gospel messages have included *Our Heavenly Father's Plan; Together Forever; What is Real;* and *Labor of Love.* Seasonal gospel films included *Mr. Krueger's Christmas, Nora's Christmas Gift;* an animated version of Henry Van Dyke's *The Other Wise Man;* O. Henry's Easter story *The Last Leaf;* and *Easter Dream.* Radio and television public service announcements broadcast regularly by over 14,000 stations worldwide, called the Homefront Series, are intended to promote family solidarity and to raise awareness of some basic teachings of the Church.

On September 1, 1974, Jesse E. Stay replaced Whitaker as head of the BYU motion picture studio. During Stay's tenure, *Go Ye Into All the World; The First Vision; Restoration of the Priesthood;* and *Morality for Youth* were completed.

On September 1, 1983, Peter N. Johnson replaced Stay and oversaw the production of *Teaching, A Renewed Dedication; Five-Year Retrospective of the Church in Action; Cameos on General Authorities; Teacher, Do You Love Me?; Lamp Unto My Feet; Things of My Soul,* a remake of *Man's Search for Happiness; How Rare a Possession: The Book of Mormon;* and *Called to Serve*—the major Church productions of the 1980s.

In 1991, control of the motion picture studio was transferred from BYU to the Audiovisual Department of the Church.

BIBLIOGRAPHY

Jacobs, David Kent. "The History of Motion Pictures Produced by the Church of Jesus Christ of Latter-day Saints." Master's thesis, Brigham Young University, 1967.

Whitaker, Wetzel O. *Pioneering with Film: A Brief History of Church and Brigham Young University Films.* Provo, Utah, n.d.
Young, Levi Edgar. "'Mormonism' in Picture." *Young Woman's Journal* 24 (Feb. 1913):80.

PETER N. JOHNSON

MURDER

Murder is condemned in latter-day scripture just as it is in the Ten Commandments and numerous other passages in both the Old and the New Testament. The Doctrine and Covenants declares that "thou shalt not kill" (D&C 42:18). The murderer "shall not have forgiveness in this world, nor in the world to come" (D&C 42:18).

In LDS doctrine, murder is second in seriousness only to the unpardonable sin of blasphemy against the Holy Ghost. And even that sin involves a kind of murderous treachery in that one who previously had obtained an absolute witness of Jesus' divinity (*TPJS*, p. 358) in effect "crucifies [Christ]" afresh or "assent[s] unto [his] death" (D&C 76:35; 132:27). Thus, murder can be thought of as the archetypal sin, as in the sin of Cain (Gen. 4:6–11, and esp. Moses 5:18–26, 31).

Murder violates the sanctity of life and cuts off the ability of its victims to "work out their destiny" (Benson, p. 355). Moreover, because "man cannot restore life," and restoration or restitution is a necessary step for repentance, obtaining forgiveness for murder is impossible (Kimball, 1969, p. 129; D&C 42:18–19). Murder wrenches all lives connected to the victim, and ultimately the perpetrator of this crime suffers even more than the victims. "For Cain suffered far more than did Abel, and murder is far more serious to him who commits it than to him who suffers from it" (Kimball, 1982, p. 188).

Secular punishment for killing is to be proved and "dealt with according to the laws of the land" (D&C 42:79). Those who have been convicted of, or have confessed to, homicide cannot be baptized without clearance from the First Presidency, and excommunication of members guilty of murder is mandatory. Joseph Fielding Smith, as an apostle, indicated that vicarious temple work should not be done for deceased murderers (*DS* 2:192).

The Church defines "murder" as the deliberate and unjustified taking of human life. If death is caused by carelessness or by defense of self or others, or if overriding mitigating circumstances prevail (such as deficient mental capacity or state of war), the taking of a human life may be regarded as something other than murder. In making the assessment of a member's guilt or innocence of murder, Church leaders are encouraged to be responsive to inspiration and to submit the facts of the case to the office of the First Presidency for review. In the final analysis, only God, who can discern the thoughts of the heart, can judge whether a particular killing is an unforgivable murder or not.

The Church's concern about murder is both more fundamental and broader than that found in legal definitions. Legal categories of homicide, such as manslaughter or negligent homicide (which typically involve carelessness or mitigating factors), are not necessarily murder, whereas killings involving extremely reckless conduct or "felony murder" may be.

The Church also leaves open the possibility that under some unusual circumstances, standard justifications for killing that would normally relieve the individual from responsibility for murder, such as self-defense or defense of others, may not apply automatically. Wartime military service is considered a mitigating factor, not a justification for indiscriminate killing, thus suggesting that even in warfare one's conduct is measured and weighed by God and is not a matter of license (*MFP* 6:157–61). Only the Lord has the power to give life or to authorize it to be taken. Both the Bible and the Book of Mormon depict situations in which God has commanded the taking of life to accomplish his purposes. Goliath (1 Sam. 17:46–51), the king of Bashan (Deut. 3:3), and Laban (1 Ne. 4:10–18) were slain by servants of God after having been delivered into their hands by the Lord.

A person convicted of murder by a lawful government may be subject to the death penalty. The Church generally has not objected to CAPITAL PUNISHMENT legally and justly administered. Indeed, scriptural records both ancient and modern condone such punishment (Gen. 9:5–6; Ex. 21:12, 23; 2 Ne. 9:35; Alma 1:13–14; D&C 42:19).

With respect to related offenses, the Church distinguishes ABOR-TION from murder but holds it an extremely grave action, not to be done except in extremely limited circumstances that might include incest or rape, perils to the life or health of the mother, or severe birth defects. As far as has currently been revealed, a person may repent and be forgiven for the sin of abortion.

SUICIDE is regarded as self-murder and a grievous sin if commit-ted by someone in full possession of his or her mental faculties. Because it is possible that a person who takes his or her own life may not be responsible for that action, only God can judge such a matter.

A person who participates in euthanasia—the deliberate, inten-tional putting to death of a person suffering from incurable conditions or diseases—violates the commandments of God. There is a differ-ence between *allowing* a terminally ill person to die of natural causes and the *initiating* of action that causes someone's death. The appli-cation or denial of life-support systems must be decided reverently, usually by competent and responsible family members through prayer and the consultation of competent medical authorities. It is not wrong to ask the Lord, if it be his will, to shorten the physical suf-fering of a person whose afflictions are terminal and irreversible.

BIBLIOGRAPHY

Benson, Ezra Taft. *Teachings of Ezra Taft Benson*. Salt Lake City, 1988.

Gardiner, Martin R. "Mormonism and Capital Punishment: A Doctrinal Perspective, Past and Present." *Dialogue* 12 (Spring 1979):9–25.

Kimball, Spencer W. *The Miracle of Forgiveness*. Salt Lake City, 1969.

———. *Teachings of Spencer W. Kimball*, ed. Edward L. Kimball. Salt Lake City, 1982.

W. COLE DURHAM, JR.

MUSEUMS, LDS

On April 4, 1984, the Museum of Church History and Art in Salt Lake City, Utah, was dedicated, culminating over 140 years of effort to erect a building specifically to house LDS Church museum exhibits. Collections of art, artifacts, sculpture, photographs, docu-ments, furniture, tools, clothing, handwork, architectural elements, and portraits represent past and present LDS cultures from around the world unified by a common theology.

One of the first museum references in Church history is from Addison Pratt, who on May 24, 1843, donated "the tooth of a whale, coral, and other curiosities" he had obtained in Polynesia as a young sailor, "as the beginning for a museum in Nauvoo" (*HC* 5:406). On April 7, 1848, paintings by Philo Dibble depicting the martyrdom of Joseph and Hyrum Smith and Joseph's last address to the Nauvoo Legion were exhibited to the Brethren in the log tabernacle, Pottawattamie County, Iowa. Dibble was asked to paint scenes from this time in the History of the Church and display them in "a gallery in Zion" (Wilford Woodruff Journal, 3:340).

A letter from Dibble pleaded for immigrating Saints to bring "glass, nails, oils, paints, etc., to the valley . . . that a museum may be established . . . of the works of nature and art" (*MS* 11 [1849]:11–12). A general epistle to the Church signed by Brigham Young and Willard Richards stated, "We also want all kinds of . . . rare specimens of natural curiosities and works of art that can be gathered and brought to the valley . . . from which, the rising generation can receive instruction; and if the Saints will be diligent . . . we will soon have the best, the most useful and attractive museum on earth" (*MS* 10 [1848]:85).

The first museum in the Salt Lake Valley, established in 1869, was owned by John W. Young, son of Brigham Young. It displayed a variety of curiosities, including geological and live natural specimens indigenous to the region. This Salt Lake City Museum and Menagerie was located in a two-room adobe house behind the west wall of the Lion House. The curator was Guglielmo Giosue Rossetti Sangiovanni, a native of London called "Sangio." In 1871 the Deseret Telegraph needed the property, and, shorn of its "zoo" character, the museum was moved to a top floor of a building opposite the south gate of the temple block. On September 18, 1878, ownership was transferred to the Church.

Joseph Barfoot, a devoted naturalist, became the second curator, and under his supervision the museum matured scientifically until his death in 1882. Under temporary caretakers and suffering from a lack of funds, the museum then went into decline. To save it, citizens formed the Salt Lake Literary and Scientific Association in 1885 and acquired the property from the Church, renaming it the "Deseret Museum." The association sold the building in which the artifacts were housed in 1890 and moved the collection to the Templeton Building with a new curator, James E. Talmage, appointed in 1891. Twelve years later the association built a three-story building, and again in 1903 the Deseret Museum was moved. J. Reuben Clark, Jr., assisted Dr. Talmage with the exhibits from 1891 to 1903.

In 1903, again being discommoded, the collection was boxed and stored and supervision again transferred to the LDS Church. In 1910 the collection was installed in the new Vermont Building opposite the temple block. William Forsberg assisted Dr. Talmage in creating a number of well-known displays, including the famous selenite crystals taken from a colossal geode found in southern Utah. Specimens taken from these crystals are now found in many prominent museums in the United States and Europe. Due to these far-sighted gifts of Dr. Talmage, the Deseret Museum gained membership in the prestigious Museum Association, headquartered in London.

The collection grew as a result of museum exchanges and gifts from missionaries returning from many lands. Over fourteen thousand items were exhibited; one section brought together by the Daughters of the Utah Pioneers (DUP) told the story of the struggle, survival, and unique life of the LDS colonization past and present. The DUP established a unit in every community to collect, preserve, and display historical memorabilia to acquaint posterity with the past. A library of two thousand volumes, some rare, was housed in the museum. *The Deseret Evening News*, July 22, 1911, stated: "This museum is one of the most valuable assets the state has among educational institutions." When Dr. Talmage was called to the Quorum of the Twelve Apostles, December 8, 1911, his son, Sterling B. Talmage, was appointed museum curator. To provide a more convenient location for visitors, the Church enlarged the Bureau of Information on Temple Square to hold several exhibits. At this time the collections were divided into categories. Some were transferred to the LDS University Museum and later to BRIGHAM YOUNG UNIVERSITY. The DUP collection was returned to that organization and is now housed in a museum near the state capitol. Many specimens were transferred to the Museum of Natural History at the University of

Utah. Items of interest to LDS Church members and visitors were placed on exhibit in the Bureau of Information on Temple Square. In 1976 the museum collection on Temple Square was again boxed and stored, making way for a new VISITORS CENTER and in preparation for the new Church Museum of History and Art.

Many of the original exhibits from the early museums form the nucleus of collections in several prestigious museums. The Museum of Church History and Art, opposite the west gates of Temple Square, maintains exhibits of LDS history and art, from the bas-relief over the entrance of the granite building to the restored 1847 log home of the Duel brothers. The galleries cover 160 years of Church history, spiritual events, art, and artifacts of a people who came west under difficult circumstances and successfully achieved their goal of preserving and promoting their theology in the beautiful, educational, and cultural environment of the Church.

BIBLIOGRAPHY

Johnson, B. F. "Philo Dibble Narrative." In *Faith Promoting Classics*. Salt Lake City, 1880; reprinted, 1968.

Rollins, Kerril Sue. "LDS Artifacts and Art Portray Church History: The New Church Museum." *Ensign* 14 (Apr. 1984):44–53.

Talmage, James E. "The Deseret Museum." *IE* 14 (Sept. 1911):953–82.

Wells, Junius F. "Joseph L. Barfoot." *Contributor* 3 (May 1882):250–52.

FLORENCE SMITH JACOBSEN

MUSIC

Throughout the Church's history, music has permeated the assemblies of the Saints and has energized their pursuit of spiritual and cultural betterment. The diversity of styles in the Church is echoed in the diversity of roles that music plays in LDS life.

As in many churches, congregational hymns open and close most ecclesiastical gatherings. In many LDS meetings instrumental music (most often organ) provides preludes, interludes, and postludes. Choral music is produced by many ward and stake choirs, and the Church's well-known MORMON TABERNACLE CHOIR is heard internationally on the weekly "Music and the Spoken Word" broadcast. Music also brightens most ward and stake social activities, such as cultural nights, parties, pageants, roadshows, dances and dance festivals, as well as family reunions and FAMILY HOME EVENINGS. Music of various styles regularly enhances Church productions designed to educate and proselytize through mass media, including audio and video tapes, films, filmstrips, commercials and programs for radio and television. Amid this diversity of musical endeavors, composers and performers usually follow the cooperative principles of early Mormonism, giving of their talents in anticipation of spiritual rewards—and also for their own enjoyment.

Although American Christian churches historically have held conflicting views on music, a revelation to the Prophet Joseph Smith in July 1830 (D&C 25) likened "the song of the righteous" to prayer, confirming the propriety of vocal music for worship. With this foundation, the Prophet formed a Church "singing department" in 1835 to teach note reading and vocal technique. In Nauvoo, and later in Utah, musical standards rose as several well-trained British musicians were converted to the Church and immigrated to the United States. These converts helped establish the propriety of instrumental music for worship, a matter not addressed in the 1830 revelation. Although congregational and choral singing clearly prevailed in the Church, instrumental music soon came to accompany it. Wind, brass, and string bands also proliferated in LDS culture, accompanying the military, recreational, and civic exercises of the Saints.

In pioneer Utah several relatively short-lived associations, including the Deseret Musical Association and the Deseret Philharmonic Society, collected musical scores, created a territorial roster of musicians, and disseminated new pedagogical techniques. At the same time, the Saints founded a number of musical businesses that imported instruments and sheet music into the Great Basin in Utah. Meanwhile, Brigham Young sent some of the Church's most skilled musicians, notably C. J. Thomas, on colonizing missions in the 1860s to ensure that the art would flourish even in outlying LDS settlements. From the 1870s through 1920, the Sunday School and other Church auxiliaries gradually assumed leadership in musical training, providing singing lessons and band memberships for young Latter-day Saints as well as publishing a large amount of newly composed music.

Little attempt was made to correlate or standardize LDS musical affairs until 1920, when President Heber J. Grant appointed a

General Music Committee for the Church. Primarily consisting of musicians connected with the Salt Lake Tabernacle, the committee assumed the tasks of evaluating styles of music appropriate to worship, recommending what types of instruments (predominantly the organ) should be played in Church meetings, overseeing the production of hymnals, and fostering musical education. In this last regard, the committee endeavored to train Church musicians in several ways, including hiring professionals to teach in wards and stakes, publishing manuals of choral conducting and organ technique, and issuing music newsletters. Throughout its history, much of the committee's effort went into directing the work of stake and ward music committees. In the 1970s the committee was succeeded by the Music Department (later Music Division) of the Church.

President Brigham Young set the tone for official LDS statements on music, defining it as a "magic power" that could "fill the air with harmony, and cheer and comfort the hearts of men, and so wonderfully affect the brute creation" (*JD* 1:48). Since his time, General Authorities of the Church have continued to praise music as a soothing influence, a purifier of thought, and a uniter of hearts. The type of music most consistently endorsed has been sacred vocal music prepared especially for LDS worship. LDS composers have written hundreds of hymns and anthems and have created many large-scale, sometimes modernistic sacred works, such as Evan Stephens's "dramatic cantatas" of the 1920s and the numerous oratorios composed since, which usually treat specifically LDS themes, for example, the *Restoration* oratorios of B. Cecil Gates and Merrill Bradshaw, Gates's *Salvation for the Dead*, and Leroy Robertson's *Oratorio from the Book of Mormon*. Moreover, beginning in Brigham Young's day, a strong tradition of theater music has developed among the Saints, one that has fostered the composition of musical scores both for commemorative pageants (e.g., those at Palmyra, New York; Nauvoo, Illinois; and Manti, Utah) and lighter stage works such as the pioneer centennial production *Promised Valley*, and also a host of youth-oriented musicals in the 1970s and 1980s.

A few stylistic issues have surfaced in the twentieth century. Some Church authorities have advised against certain popular styles of music, citing their loudness, their rhythmic intensity, and the indecency of some of their lyrics; members are counseled to be wise in selecting their recreational music. Questions also have been raised over the propriety of using styles of music found outside the hymnal in worship services. Nevertheless, in nonliturgical settings, ethnic religious music thrives and some LDS songwriters have adapted soft rock music for informal religious use. Much of this music has found its way into Church-sponsored songbooks and cassettes and into privately produced recordings for young Latter-day Saints.

The enduring value of much music indigenous to the Church is difficult to predict. On the one hand, the vernacular music often echoes the more ephemeral styles of denominational Christian music. On the other hand, some impressive settings have emerged from the hymnody of the Church, and some of the larger works manifest a continuing increase in sophistication. Furthermore, the extensive use of worship music borrowed from other Christian traditions unites the Saints to a larger fellowship of believers. Above all, the sheer abundance of music in the Church reveals how untiring are the aesthetic impulses of its members. Whether or not a distinctively LDS style emerges, music of many styles undoubtedly will continue to inspire the Saints.

BIBLIOGRAPHY

Hicks, Michael. *Mormonism and Music: A History*. Urbana, Ill., 1989.

Purdy, William Earl. "Music in Mormon Culture, 1830–1876." Ph.D. diss., Northwestern University, 1960.

Slaughter, Jay L. "The Role of Music in the Mormon Church, School, and Life." Ph.D. diss., Indiana University, 1964.

Some General Recommendations Concerning Music in The Church of Jesus Christ of Latter-day Saints. Salt Lake City, 1950; 2nd ed., 1962.

MICHAEL D. HICKS

MUSICIANS

From the early decades of The Church of Jesus Christ of Latter-day Saints, LDS composers, conductors, vocalists, and instrumentalists have helped to shape the Church's distinctive musical heritage. Some of these musicians have made their mark on the larger musical scene, while numerous others have focused their talents for the direct benefit of the Church.

Volunteer musicians—music chairmen, organists, pianists,

music directors, choir directors, and Primary music leaders—serve in the Church's weekly worship services. These musicians are called by priesthood leaders and serve without pay in the particular ward or stake in which they live. Contributing time and talents is an expected and rewarding part of Church membership, and both the highly trained musician and the beginner offer their talents as called upon. Wards require from fifteen to twenty-three musicians to fill outlined music positions, with twelve to twenty-four or more needed to sing in the ward choir.

Each ward and stake is responsible for providing the needed training for its own musicians with regard to their Church callings. In addition, since 1978 Brigham Young University has presented an annual Church Music Workshop, where many receive training in music skills.

Converts from the British Isles had a strong influence on MUSIC in the early Church. John Tullidge, an accomplished church musician from Weymouth, England, arrived in Salt Lake Valley in 1863. A singer, composer, arranger, teacher, and music critic, he edited the first Latter-day Saint hymnbook that included both words and music. Other musically trained English converts included C. J. Thomas, David Calder, Ebenezer Beesley, and George Careless. John Parry, born in North Wales, led a choir in Salt Lake City that was the precursor of the MORMON TABERNACLE CHOIR. Evan Stephens, from South Wales, brought the latter choir to wide recognition during his twenty-seven years as conductor (1889–1916).

Many influential Church musicians have been associated with the Tabernacle Choir. Almost half of the musical settings of the hymns in the 1889 Psalmody were composed by directors George Careless, Ebenezer Beesley, and Evan Stephens, or by Joseph J. Daynes, the first Tabernacle organist (from 1867 to 1900). Alexander Schreiner, who served for fifty-three years (1924–1977) as Tabernacle organist, was highly involved with musical affairs of the Church and endeared himself to audiences throughout the world. Other Tabernacle organists to 1989 have included John J. McClellan, Edward P. Kimball, Tracy Y. Cannon, Frank Asper, Wade N. Stephens, Roy M. Darley, Robert Cundick, John Longhurst, Clay Christiansen, and Richard Elliott, with Bonnie Goodliffe and Linda Margetts as associate organists.

During the late nineteenth century many musical performing groups and societies were organized among the Saints (*see* MUSIC). Behind every such effort was at least one motivated musician and often a supportive Church leader. President Brigham Young often sent such a musician to a particular settlement to promote the instruction and performance of music to enhance pioneer life.

Through the years, many Latter-day Saints have excelled in musical creativity and performance. For example, Emma Lucy Gates Bowen, a coloratura soprano, performed widely throughout the United States and Europe. Her brother, B. Cecil Gates, organized the McCune School of Music and Art in Salt Lake City in 1919. Together they formed the Emma Lucy Gates Opera Company in the 1920s.

Currently many accomplished Latter-day Saint musicians are affiliated with institutions of higher learning as composers, conductors, performers, historians, and theorists. Historically these have been concentrated in the music faculties at the University of Utah and, more recently, at Brigham Young University.

BIBLIOGRAPHY

Davidson, Karen Lynn. *Our Latter-day Hymns: The Stories and the Messages.* Salt Lake City, 1988.

Durham, Lowell M. "On Mormon Music and Musicians." *Dialogue* 3 (Summer 1968):19–40.

MICHAEL F. MOODY

N

NAME EXTRACTION PROGRAM

Name extraction programs sponsored by the LDS Church are based upon the doctrine of salvation of the dead. Names, dates, and places are the key elements in precisely identifying individual ancestors. Name extraction consists of systematically transcribing this information from original vital records. Church members perform temple ordinances for those whose names have been thus identified.

The Family History Department of the Church (formerly the Genealogy Department) initiated the first name extraction program, called Records Tabulation, in 1961. Department employees extracted data primarily from filmed copies of English parish registers. In 1978 the Church deployed name extraction to stake centers, the new program being called Stake Record Extraction. Since that date, name extraction is done by local Church members. Besides records of England, those of Mexico, Germany, Scotland, Finland, Sweden, Norway, and Denmark have been heavily extracted. From 1961 to 1989, over 100 million names were thus copied.

The department begins the extraction process by sending a microfilm to a stake. Extractors transcribe the desired information onto cards. Data entry workers at regional centers input information onto computer diskettes. To ensure accuracy, two transcriptions of each entry are made and compared to find and resolve discrepancies.

Names derived from the name extraction program are listed in the Church's INTERNATIONAL GENEALOGICAL INDEX. The sources from which the names have been extracted are listed by locality in the Parish and Vital Records Listing. Alphabetized printouts of the names extracted from each source are also prepared and made available for research through the Church's main FAMILY HISTORY LIBRARY in Salt Lake City and branch family history centers around the world.

The department increased its name extraction efforts in 1986 with the introduction of the Family Record Extraction Program. This differs from the older program in that a paper photocopy of the original record is given to extractors and they transcribe the information in their homes at their convenience. The extracted information is "data entered" at the stake center by means of a personal computer and submitted on diskettes to a central data base in Salt Lake City.

KAHLILE MEHR

NON-MORMONS, SOCIAL RELATIONS WITH

The social milieu of the Church in modern times may be compared to that of the New Testament Church. In each situation, a peculiar people amid multiple religious traditions and structures engendered hostility.

In and around Palmyra, New York, prior to the organization of the Church, the Smith family was welcomed in the community. But the announcements of new revelation, new scripture, and direct communication with God engendered a negative social reaction. Within a year, the family and all other members of the Church moved from that area. None returned for nearly eighty-five years. Similar hostilities developed in other areas. The missionary outreach of the fledgling Church extended into England, Scandinavia, and western Europe, where churches were mostly state-controlled, and alternative faiths were oppressed. To listen to, sympathize with, or join the Latter-day Saints often meant that one would be disowned by parents and relatives, socially ostracized, fined, jailed, or even in some instances threatened with death. The resulting stream of LDS emigrants to Church settlements in Ohio, Missouri, and Illinois was so extensive that even in the melting-pot atmosphere of America, they were often confronted immediately with suspicion and opposition.

Following its withdrawal from New York, the Church established its headquarters in Kirtland, Ohio. There the vigorous missionary thrust continued to bring into the Church many people with commitment and dedication, leaving little time in their lives for social relationships with those outside the Church, who often shunned friendly overtures when they were made. The reaction of many churches was strongly negative to the LDS influence, and the typical responses of Latter-day Saints was to draw closer to each other for mutual protection and support. Communication was sporadic and fleeting at best. Misunderstandings grew.

Under divine command, the Church relocated in northern Missouri, where rapid growth multiplied tensions and frictions. The specter of growing LDS economic and political power in five counties amplified the social stress. There was also the complication of "apostates," or dissidents, who often joined anti-Mormon coalitions. The "old settlers" and the new LDS ones were polarized. The Church's social and political difficulties in Missouri culminated in Governor Lilburn Boggs' infamous Extermination Order and resulted in some 1,500 LDS families being forced to abandon their farms, homes, and other possessions and flee for their lives into Illinois. There, a new LDS gathering place called Nauvoo was founded.

For a time Nauvoo was a community almost unto itself. Its singular status, the inclusive character of its life patterns, and the extension of the religious vision into all aspects of culture were stabilized by a strong self-sufficient charter and even a militia, the Nauvoo Legion. Many visitors came to view the new city, and efforts to promote cultural and intellectual exchange increased. Joseph Smith and about 1,500 other Church members joined the Masonic lodges in Nauvoo and nearby Keokuk and Montrose to promote fraternal relations (*see* FREEMASONRY IN NAUVOO). However, once again the old settlers outside the Church clashed with the LDS settlers, and hostilities grew.

Driven westward, the Saints settled in the Great Basin, where comparative freedom and peace enabled them to pursue their social, intellectual, and spiritual goals. For several decades social exchange and the development of intercultural relations with those outside the group were limited. The Church was the leading influence—social, political, economical, and educational. Relative calm and cooperation prevailed until tensions mounted, primarily over the practice of plural marriage. A half century passed before this issue was resolved, and in 1896, Utah Territory in the Great Basin became a state.

In the twentieth century, congenial relations have developed between the Church and other groups and institutions throughout the United States and the world. Church membership has become increasingly diverse and widespread, and new motivations for communication, goodwill, and cooperation have arisen. The needs of modern society have cried out for improved relations among faiths and people worldwide. The critical need for efforts and participation that unite churches and social organizations has become more apparent. Problems relating to the hungry and homeless, the illiterate and underprivileged, the drug-addicted and abused, and the victims of disintegrating family life have increased on a worldwide scale. The relative stability of LDS society is attractive to many who seek leadership and example. Latter-day Saints and their neighbors have increasingly recognized common ground and common causes. They participate extensively in such groups as Boy Scouts, chambers of commerce, service clubs, the YMCA, the United Fund, local school systems, and a variety of professional and benevolent civic organizations (*see* CIVIC DUTIES).

Although social relations of Church members with others are generally much more congenial in the late twentieth century than earlier, some sources of friction persist. Some negative responses continue to arise in other church communities because of LDS missionary efforts, with Latter-day Saints sometimes accused of being aggressive in both religious and nonreligious contexts.

[*See also* Interfaith Relationships; Social and Cultural History.]

DARL ANDERSON
DAVID K. UDALL
ELEANOR PARK JONES

O

OCCUPATIONAL STATUS

Occupational and employment data collected in the United States, Canada, Britain, Japan, and Mexico from 1980 to 1983 indicate that members of the Church differ in some respects from the general populations in which they live, but are generally similar.

In the United States, LDS men tend to be about 7 percent more likely than the rest of the population to be in the labor force. LDS women have labor-force participation rates almost identical to U.S. women generally, but LDS women are about 4 percent more likely to work part-time rather than full-time. In single-parent families, LDS women are some 16 percent more likely to be employed than other single mothers. LDS mothers with children under six years of age are 9 percent less likely to be in the labor force than other U.S. mothers of preschoolers.

Among LDS men and women who are employed, occupational distributions are very similar to the United States generally. LDS men are slightly more likely to be professionals and a little less likely to be machine or equipment operators, but in all other occupational categories the percentages tend to be virtually the same.

In Canada the occupational and employment figures tend to be very similar to the United States. Canadian LDS men are 7 percent more likely to have employment than the general population, and about half of the LDS women are employed and 9 percent more likely than others to work part-time. The occupational breakdowns in Canada for LDS men and women tend to follow the national patterns within a few percentage points.

Church survey data from Britain, Mexico, and Japan for the years 1981–1983 show that British LDS men had 87 percent participation in the labor force, the highest of the countries examined. The employment rate for LDS men in Mexico was 67 percent; in Japan, 77 percent; and in the United States, 85 percent. Japanese LDS women active in the Church were generally in the labor force at a slightly higher rate (5 percent higher) than other women in Japan.

When Church populations are compared, greater concentrations of white-collar workers are usually found in areas where members are mainly urban. Their proportion in specific white-collar categories varies somewhat in each country. In 1981–1983, LDS men were found more in managerial, administrative, and production positions in the five countries that were examined. Men and women were in professions in about the same proportion in all countries except Mexico, where greater numbers of women are in the professions (especially teaching), while LDS women were overrepresented in clerical, sales, and service occupations.

WILLIAM G. DYER

ORGAN TRANSPLANTS AND DONATIONS

Because the transplanting of body parts raises some concerns regarding ethics and moral issues, the Church has issued the following statement: "Whether an individual chooses to will his own bodily organs or authorizes the transplant of organs from a deceased family member is a decision for the individual or the deceased member's family. The decision to receive a donated organ should be made with competent medical counsel and confirmation through prayer" (*General Handbook of Instructions*, 11-6).

The transplanting of certain organs is now being done with increasing success. For example, transplantation of the cornea has been done for many years, and now a better than 90 percent chance of vision restoration is expected in cases of blindness due to corneal disease. As successful replacements increasingly occur, more people become aware of the various diseases and disorders that can be treated and cured by transplantation, and more people want to become recipients. According to the American Council on Transplantation, more than 50,000 people benefited from organ transplants in 1989. And according to the Intermountain Transplant Program, "more than 100,000 could benefit if enough organs and tissue were available."

Organs and tissue that can now be transplanted include the cornea, kidney, pancreas, heart, liver, skin, bone, veins, tendons, lung, bone marrow, and blood. Heart and liver donations are immediate matters of life and death. Donated kidneys replace thrice-weekly dialysis treatments. A donated pancreas may "cure" someone's diabetes. Donated eyes provide not only corneas for sight-restoring corneal transplants but also vital eye tissue for other surgical procedures and for research into blinding eye disorders.

According to organizations handling organs for transplantation, only those who meet strict criteria are considered for donors. These criteria include careful testing for infectious diseases, including AIDS. Because of these procedures and advances in transplant techniques, donors and recipients do not face the risks faced a few years ago.

In some instances, as where a kidney is needed, a close relative can serve as a donor. (A healthy person can continue a normal life with one kidney.) In the case of some organs, such as the cornea of the eye, the donated organ usually comes from one who signs a statement indicating a desire to donate organs upon death. In the event of an accident or untimely death, the donor's eyes may then be used with the consent of the family.

BIBLIOGRAPHY
General Handbook of Instructions, 11-6. Salt Lake City, 1989.

WAYNE A. MINEER

P

PAGEANTS

In the Church, pageants are outdoor theatrical productions that celebrate a place, person, or event in religious history. Some pageants depict the earthly mission of the Savior and his dealings with covenant peoples in Jerusalem and the New World, both before and after his resurrection. Other pageants dramatize some historical aspect of how the Church in this dispensation fulfills its mission of taking the gospel of Jesus Christ to every nation, kindred, tongue, and people (cf. Rev. 14:6).

Most pageants are initiated and sponsored by local Church leaders and carried out by Church members who reside in the area where the pageant is performed. They are usually presented out-of-doors on temporary stages on the site of the event or on or near the grounds of LDS temples. Typically they present a sequence of short but elaborate scenes that unseen speakers narrate over an audio system. The pageants often feature original music prerecorded by a professional orchestra and delivered through an audio system powerful enough to be heard for several hundred meters. Pageant casts consist of businessmen, homemakers, teenagers, children, college students, grandparents, craftsmen, and professional actors whose involvement is voluntary and without remuneration. Each pageant is typically presented for about seven performances to as many as 20,000 people at a single performance. No admission fee is charged.

LDS pageants often feature appropriately costumed casts of as many as 600 performers, and may include live orchestras, choirs, and dancers. Each pageant is different in form as well as content. The "City of Joseph" pageant in Nauvoo, Illinois, is a conventional musical play. The Calgary (Canada) Nativity Pageant in December portrays how the Savior's birth is a blessing to all peoples. "The Man Who Knew," in Clarkston, Utah, is a narrative drama about the life of Martin Harris.

The CUMORAH PAGEANT, near Rochester, New York, has been presented at the hill Cumorah since 1937. It depicts how Joseph Smith learned about and acquired the plates of gold from which the Book of Mormon was translated and it presents a dramatized sampling of some of the epic events and prophecies described in them. Cast members include young adults called from other areas of the Church to participate in the July–August productions. Other pageants, such as at the Manti, Utah, or Oakland, California, temples, depict the restoration of the gospel. The Mesa, Arizona, pageant presents the story of the Savior's life. Other pageants are performed in Independence, Missouri; Castle Valley, Utah; and Auckland, New Zealand.

LAEL J. WOODBURY

PERSONAL ANCESTRAL FILE®

Personal Ancestral File® is a genealogical software package produced by the Church for IBM-compatible, Macintosh, and Apple personal computers that enables users to organize, store, and search genealogical information; contribute genealogies to ANCESTRAL FILE™; and match and merge information from other genealogical data bases with their own files.

The package consists of three major programs: Family Records, Research Data Filer, and Genealogical Information Exchange. The Family Records program enables users to assemble pedigrees; group families together, showing relationships between family members for each generation; search pedigree lines; add, modify, and delete information about individuals; and display information on the screen and print it on genealogical forms. Research Data Filer helps users manage original research, including searching, sorting, and printing information by event, place, date, name of person, or relationship to others. Genealogical Information Exchange enables users to send Family Records data to another Personal Ancestral File user, prepare diskette submissions of names for LDS temple ordinance processing or contribution to Ancestral File, and copy data from one diskette to another.

BIBLIOGRAPHY

Long, Jack. "Personal Ancestral File 2.1." *MacWorld* (Sept. 1989):242–44.

Trivette, Donald B. "Personal Ancestral File Helps Organize Facts of Family History." *PC Magazine* (June 13, 1989):452.

DAVID M. MAYFIELD

PHILOSOPHY

Philosophy (the "love of wisdom") originated in the Western world in ancient Greece. The attempt to find wisdom by ancient thinkers such as Socrates, Plato, and Aristotle led them also to investigate the world (nature), the unseen world (METAPHYSICS), and how we know (EPISTE-MOLOGY). Wonder about nature through progressively refined epistemological procedures led through the centuries to modern scientific methods. As philosophers developed standards for accurate description and generalization, new sciences were born and detached themselves from philosophy: the first was physics, and the latest is linguistics. But the basic problems of epistemology, metaphysics, and ethics (including aesthetics and the philosophy of religion) dominate present philosophy as much as they did in ancient times. Although the solutions are more varied now, the basic issues remain the same.

Latter-day scriptures do not present a philosophical system, but they do contain answers to many classic philosophical issues. These scriptures preclude ex nihilo creation, idealism (immaterialism), a chance theory of causation, and absolute determinism. They affirm the eternality and agency of the individual person, the necessary existence of evil apart from God, a nonrelativistic good (righteousness), and the doctrine that all mortals are the offspring and heirs of God. God is affirmed as a perfected physical being who governs all things in pure love and who continues to communicate with his children on earth by personal revelation.

Observers of the LDS position have ascribed philosophical labels and tendencies to it, but that position usually will not fit neatly into the stock answers. It is empirical, yet rational; pragmatic, yet idealistic; oriented toward eternity, yet emphasizing the importance of the here and now. Affinities are found with the Cartesian certainty of personal existence, the positivist insistence on sensory evidence, the Enlightenment emphasis on elimination of paradox, and the postmodern respect for the "other." The ultimate standard for all being, truth, and good is Christ himself.

Contemporary analytic and existential movements in philosophy have had little impact on LDS thought, not because it is not aware of them, but because it has different answers to the questions they pose. The knowledge of God is established through careful experimentation with God's promises, which results in tangible consequences, culminating in the possibility of seeing God face to face. Existential angst is recognized and met by personal guidance from God to establish a path to righteousness and fulfillment, the general features of which each person must follow, but with individual parameters. The relativism of situational ethics is answered in spiritual assurance and power to do those things that are eternally worthwhile. Mind-body dualism is answered by the material nature of spirit (more refined matter) (D&C 131:7).

Answers to the questions How may I know? What is the seen world? What is the unseen world? and How shall I be wise? are all found personally by every fully participating Latter-day Saint. The equivalent of epistemology in an LDS frame is the ordinances, focusing on the ordinance of prayer. Through the ordinances and in connection with other epistemologies come all of the light and knowledge sufficient to live a spiritually successful life. Questions about the natural world are answered by one's culture as corrected by personal revelation. One must have some guidance on questions of metaphysics, and such is found in holy scripture and confirmed to each individual through personal revelation. The ultimate question as to how to be wise is answered both in general and in particular. The general answer is that to be wise is to love God with all of one's heart, might, mind, and strength, and to love our neighbor as God loves us (D&C 59:5). The particular answer is to repent of sinning and to live by the whisperings of the Holy Spirit and the counsels of the living prophet (Isa. 50:10–11).

While LDS culture does not encourage philosophizing directly, every LDS person is encouraged to become a profound theologian. Becoming such necessitates a heavy commitment to active study "in theory, in principle, in doctrine" to search out the weighty matters of time and eternity (D&C 97:14), which include the basic questions of the philosophers. The imperative "study it out in your mind" (D&C 9:7–8) is a standard for all LDS persons, not just for academics. "Time, and experience and careful and ponderous and solemn thought" (*TPJS*, p. 37) are not inimical to but are the preface to and foundation for personal revelation.

BIBLIOGRAPHY

Madsen, Truman G. "Joseph Smith and the Ways of Knowing," pp. 25–63. BYU Extension Publications, Seminar on the Prophet Joseph Smith, 1962.

Oaks, Dallin H. "Ethics, Morality, and Professional Responsibility." In *Perspectives in Mormon Ethics*, ed. Donald G. Hill, Jr., pp. 193–200. Salt Lake City, 1983.

Yarn, David H., Jr. "Some Metaphysical Reflections on the Gospel of John." *BYU Studies* 3 (Autumn 1960):3–10.

CHAUNCEY C. RIDDLE

PHYSICAL FITNESS AND RECREATION

The Church has always endorsed recreation and fitness as desirable and worthy of promotion. Recreational activities can strengthen social connections and a sense of community. Proper physical activities are any that are "clean, beneficial to health, conducive to true happiness and in harmony with the highest moral standards" ("Wholesome Recreation," p. 430). A latter-day apostle stated, "Recreation—good Latter-day Saint recreation—is one of the devices by which we may help the young people of this Church to learn and love the gospel of the Lord, Jesus Christ, and thereby learn to live righteously" (Petersen, p. 554).

During the nineteenth century, when most religions were condemning play as sinful (T.D., p. 178), Joseph Smith and Brigham Young advocated recreation as part of their religious teaching. Both men participated in recreational activities and sanctioned wholesome amusements. Moreover, it was noted of Brigham Young that "he not only enjoyed recreational pursuits himself, but some of his august religious speeches were on this subject" (Skidmore, p. 25). In the early days of the Church, recreation also provided respite from work, drudgery, hardship, and persecution. It is likely that the large number of converts from many nationalities and cultures, although they were drawn together by a testimony of Christ and the restoration of the gospel, were more easily assimilated into the new community of Saints when recreational activities were a common denominator (Skidmore, p. 9). According to one researcher on recreation, the Church was the first religious organization to construct halls adjacent to, or adjoining, chapels for the formal promotion of such activities as games and sports, music, drama, speech, and dance (Brinley, pp. 43, 104–105).

The physical body is viewed as a temple of God that the individual has stewardship from God to care for properly: "I speak of the religious doctrine which teaches that the human body is sacred, the veritable tabernacle of the divine spirit which inhabits it, and that it is a solemn duty of mankind to protect and preserve it from pollutions and unnecessary wastage and weakness" (Richards, p. 208). Isaiah recorded a promise to those who are willing to "wait upon the Lord" that they would "run and not be weary; and . . . walk, and not faint" (40:31). This promise is affirmed in the revelation to Joseph Smith known as the WORD OF WISDOM (D&C 89:20). Physical and spiritual health is promised as a consequence of obedience to spiritual law and observance of specific dietary and health habits.

BIBLIOGRAPHY

Brinley, Eldon D. "The Recreational Life of the Mormon People." Ph.D. diss., New York University, 1943.

Evans, Richard L. "Great Miracle: Housing for Body and Mind." *Church News* (Aug. 26, 1967):16.

McKay, David O. "The Whole Man." *IE* 55 (Apr. 1952):221–22.

Petersen, Mark E. "Building Spirituality Through Recreation." *IE* 51 (Sept. 1948):554–55, 598.

Richards, Stephen L. *Where Is Wisdom.* Salt Lake City, 1955.

Skidmore, Rex A. *Mormon Recreation In Theory and Practice: A Study of Social Change.* Philadelphia, 1941.

T.D. "Repose." *Nation* 2 (Feb. 1866):178.

"Wholesome Recreation: Ward Teacher's Message for August, 1939." *IE* 42 (July 1939):430.

CLARK T. THORSTENSON

POLITICS

[*Included in this entry are four articles:*

Political History
Political Teachings
Political Culture
Contemporary American Politics

The first article traces the history of the political issues in which The Church of Jesus Christ of Latter-day Saints has been involved since the restoration of the gospel. The second article examines the official teachings of LDS scriptures and prophets on political questions. The third article examines the perception of a political subculture in the membership of the Church. The last article examines the participation of the Church and its members in contemporary politics throughout the world.

The extent to which the Constitution of the United States of America *will protect distinctive religious practices is a question brought in many forms to American courts. The efforts of the Church to gain recognition and religious freedoms through direct negotiations with governments throughout the world are described in* Diplomatic Relations. *The attitudes and teachings of the Church derived from its scriptures and these experiences in law and politics are described in articles on* Church and State; Civil Rights; Constitutional Law; Politics: Political Teachings; *and* War and Peace.]

POLITICAL HISTORY

LDS involvement in American politics began with the conflicts between Mormons and non-Mormons in the 1830s and 1840s that led to the founding of a religious and political community in the Great Basin, organized by the U.S. Congress as Utah Territory. Mormonism emerged as a national political issue in the presidential election of 1856 with the Republican platform's condemnation of the "twin relics of barbarism"—southern slavery and Mormon polygamy. Political involvement continued in the social and political order of the state of Utah where, because of the high number of Latter-day Saints, there is identification between the political community and the dominant religion.

From its inception in western New York in 1830, the LDS

Church was politically controversial. The deepest cause of conflict directly or indirectly affecting political relationships between Latter-day Saints and others was the belief in continuing revelation. Non-Mormons viewed the claim of continuing revelation and the social and political forms built on that claim as threats to democratic self-government. While the Book of Mormon was being printed, a mass meeting of Palmyra residents pledged to boycott it. The Prophet Joseph Smith was arrested several times on charges brought, according to his accusers, "to open the eyes and understanding of those who blindly follow" him. When the Church was hardly large enough to "man a farm, or meet a woman with a milk-pail," recalled Sidney Rigdon, non-Mormons were already accusing them of wanting "to upset the Government" (*HC* 6:289).

The turmoil of the New York period was only a harbinger of intense conflicts to follow. As the practical implications of belief in new revelation and obedience to a new prophet became clear, anti-Mormon opposition intensified. For the Prophet and his followers, divine calling made possible—indeed, morally incumbent—the effort to create a just society, which the revelations called Zion. For non-Mormon neighbors, these efforts constituted challenges that they determined to resist.

Belief in continuing revelation had profound implications for the organization of political society among the Latter-day Saints. The establishment of Zion required the unity of the LDS community in righteousness. The effort brought social, economic, and political innovations, including the gathering of the Saints, consecration and stewardship, the United Order, and plural marriage. In all matters relevant to building Zion, the LDS community looked to the Prophet for guidance, concentrating power, even against his own inclinations, in his hands.

Efforts to establish Zion excited fear and animosity. Made uneasy by ever-increasing numbers of Latter-day Saints and shocked or bemused by their economic and social experiments, many non-Mormons viewed the Saints as alien and hostile, even as a threat to their freedoms as Americans. Because the Church seemed to erase the distinction between CHURCH AND STATE—in American liberal political thought an important pillar of liberty—some felt that it portended the rise of religious despotism. The result was recurring political conflict, which time and again threatened the LDS community.

The efforts to build a New Jerusalem in America began in 1831 with the gathering to Ohio and the designation of Zion in Jackson County, Missouri. As Church members built these new communities, differences with neighbors, and resulting tensions, were immediately evident. In Ohio, Joseph Smith and Sidney Rigdon were tarred and feathered by a mob. Random acts of violence threatened the young LDS community.

Matters were still worse in Missouri, where, in 1833, citizens of Jackson County banded together to remove the Latter-day Saints from the county, "peaceably if we can, forcibly if we must" (*HC* 1:374). They were justified, they claimed, because Mormonism was an evil for which the laws made no provision. Missourians saw these newcomers as "deluded fanatics" or "designing knaves" who claimed "to hold personal communication and converse face to face with the Most High God" and who threatened to take political control of the county (*HC* 1:375).

By late fall of 1833, the Latter-day Saints had been driven from Jackson County. Most found temporary refuge in Clay County, where they were at first kindly received. Eventually, however, antagonisms developed there as well when it became apparent that Saints would not be going back to their homes and lands in Jackson County. Before violence erupted, Church members abandoned Clay County in 1836 for the newly organized Caldwell County, created by the legislature specifically as a home for Mormons.

By the summer of 1838, trouble had erupted again. In Kirtland, economic failure associated with the Panic of 1837 contributed to dissent. Some criticized Joseph Smith's exercise of authority and charged him with "Popery," or the combining of spiritual authority and temporal power. As tensions escalated, Joseph Smith and most of the faithful left Ohio for Missouri. In Caldwell County, critics within the Church also soon took up the cry, creating such profound consternation that the community forced them out. Dissenters then stirred up non-Mormons who were already fearful of growing LDS strength. In this situation of rising tensions, Sidney Rigdon defiantly declared independence from mob depredations and vowed that the

Saints would meet future force with force. All that was required for a violent conflagration was a tiny spark.

Not surprisingly, political rivalry provided the spark. On August 6, 1838, non-Mormons in Daviess County, into which the rapidly increasing LDS population had spilled, attempted to prevent Latter-day Saints from voting at Gallatin, Missouri. A brawl resulted, and exaggerated accounts of the incident soon mobilized armed bands on both sides. After several skirmishes, a pitched battle occurred, with both sides suffering casualties. Following exaggerated reports of this battle, Governor Lilburn Boggs ordered the state militia to treat the Mormons as enemies to be exterminated or driven from the state. After Joseph Smith and other leaders were imprisoned, the Latter-day Saints were disarmed and then were forced from Missouri. After months of imprisonment, jailed Church leaders eventually escaped or were released.

Moving to Illinois, the Latter-day Saints built a new city, Nauvoo, along the banks of the Mississippi River. Apparently convinced that there would be no peace as long as Church members were politically at the mercy of non-Mormons, Joseph Smith sought and obtained political power for the new city. In the Nauvoo Charter, the Illinois legislature empowered the city to make any ordinances not prohibited by the CONSTITUTION OF THE UNITED STATES or that of Illinois and to organize a militia with power to execute said laws.

While Nauvoo flourished under the protection of the new city government and its own militia, the Nauvoo Legion, trouble soon developed. Non-Mormons resented Nauvoo's political power, which was based on increasing LDS numbers and on their willingness to vote as a bloc to reward political friends and punish political enemies. Bloc voting was both a reflection of the social unity of the LDS community and a defensive reaction to the abuses suffered in Missouri. Yet critics condemned the Saints for "yielding implicit obedience" to a "pretended prophet of the Lord" who, they charged, was a dangerous character entertaining "the most absolute contempt for the laws of man" (HC 6:4–5).

Even within the Church there was again restiveness, for the private introduction of plural marriage and Joseph Smith's increasing political power contributed to dissent. Dissidents established a newspaper, the *Nauvoo Expositor,* and attacked Joseph Smith for supposed moral imperfections and poor leadership. Declaring the *Expositor* a public nuisance, the Nauvoo City Council authorized Mayor Joseph Smith to order city police to destroy its press. In the resulting furor, the anti-Mormon *Warsaw Signal* called on the citizens of Illinois to take direct military action against the Prophet. Others spoke of extermination. With violence clearly a possibility, Joseph Smith allowed himself to be arrested on charges stemming from the *Expositor* incident and was imprisoned in Carthage, the county seat, where on June 27, 1844, he was murdered by a mob.

The Prophet's death brought a lull in hostilities, which provided time to complete the Nauvoo Temple and to make preparations to move to a new home in the West. When conflict broke out again in September 1845, Church leaders announced their intention to leave Illinois in the spring. By the summer of 1846, most Latter-day Saints had departed. Those remaining were forced out by an anti-Mormon attack on the city in September 1846.

The Missouri and Illinois cataclysms convinced Brigham Young and other Church leaders that the Latter-day Saints needed not just political power but political autonomy. According to the prevailing constitutional interpretation of states' rights, the federal government was largely prohibited from interfering with a state's domestic institutions (slavery, for example). To obtain such autonomy, Latter-day Saints did not necessarily have to remove themselves from the boundaries of the United States but only from existing states and territories. As the first settlers in a new area, they could possibly obtain the political autonomy necessary for protection within the federal Union.

As the Latter-day Saints embarked on their westward migration, some dreamed of an independent LDS nation, while others envisioned the establishment of a territory or state within the United States. When Church leaders selected the Great Basin as their probable destination, it was legally a remote part of Mexico. The Mormon Battalion contributed, at least marginally, to the effort by which the United States obtained title to the Southwest, including the Great Basin.

The first LDS pioneers entered the valley of the Great Salt Lake in July 1847. Until late 1848, when the Quorum of the Twelve Apostles established themselves in the valley, the settlement was governed by the Salt Lake Stake presidency and high council. President Brigham Young charged these local officials to "observe those principles which have been instituted in the Stakes of Zion for the government of the Church, and to pass such laws and ordinances as shall be necessary for the peace and prosperity of the city for the time being" (Morgan, p. 69). In December 1848, Church leaders petitioned Congress for a territorial organization. Later, they drafted a constitution for a proposed state of Deseret, with a bill of rights containing a strongly worded guarantee of religious liberty, and applied for admission to the Union. Brigham Young was elected governor of the would-be state.

In Congress, this hoped-for admission became enmeshed in the political maelstrom over slavery in U.S. territories raised by the Treaty of Guadalupe Hidalgo. In the Compromise of 1850, Congress organized the Latter-day Saints as the Territory of Utah. The compromise, adopting the principle of popular sovereignty, allowed settlers in the newly acquired territories to decide whether they would have slavery. Utah, attempting to remain aloof from the dispute over slavery, offended both anti- and proslavery congressmen by ignoring the matter in its constitution.

From the beginning of Utah's territorial period, relations between the LDS community and the federal government were tense. The first non-Mormon territorial officials became embroiled in controversy within days of their arrival and soon returned to the East, spreading inflammatory reports that deeply influenced congressional and public opinion. Later federal appointees were also critical. And the Church deeply agitated public opinion when it officially avowed plural marriage in 1852.

In the presidential election of 1856, the Republican party used public antipolygamy feeling to attack the Democratic party for its stand on slavery in the territories. Democrats in Congress had passed the 1854 Kansas-Nebraska Act, which, by repealing the Missouri Compromise, removed the last legal restraints on the spread of slavery to U.S. territories and established popular sovereignty as the political principle governing slavery in the territories. The Republican party, intent on restoring the Missouri Compromise by repudiating popular sovereignty, inserted the "twin relics" plank in the 1856 Republican platform in an effort to tar the Democratic party with Mormon polygamy. The point was that if the Democrats truly believed that the citizens of the territories alone had the power to legislate on slavery, logically they must also accept that the citizens of the territories should have the sole power to legislate on matrimony. Polygamy and slavery, according to the author of the "twin relics" plank, "rested precisely on the same Constitutional basis," and so "to make war upon polygamy, and at the same time strengthen the case against slavery as much as possible," he linked them together (Poll, p. 127).

The Republican strategy succeeded. Democratic party leaders concluded that to protect popular sovereignty as it related to slavery, they had to take a firm stand against polygamy. Senator Stephen Douglas, popular sovereignty's chief patron, attacked the Mormons as subversive aliens who recognized the authority of Brigham Young "and the government of which he is the head" above that of the United States. He accused Latter-day Saints of prosecuting "a system of robbery and murders upon American citizens" and called for the application of "the knife" to "this pestiferous, disgusting cancer" of Mormonism, "which is gnawing at the very vitals of the body politic" (*CHC* 4:221–22). It is possible that embarrassment over the linkage of polygamy and popular sovereignty contributed to U.S. President James Buchanan's decision, on the basis of vague and unsubstantiated reports, to take the extraordinary step of sending an army to Utah in 1857 to enforce federal law. The ostensible purpose of the army was to ensure that the territory accepted the replacement of Brigham Young as governor, but it had also been suggested to Buchanan that he might be able to upstage the commotion over slavery in the territories with the excitement of an anti-Mormon crusade.

A Republican-controlled Congress passed the first antipolygamy legislation in 1862. The Morrill Act outlawed polygamy and overturned certain acts of the Utah legislature, including one incorporating the Church, which shielded the practice of polygamy. The Civil War delayed enforcement, and when the federal government returned to the Utah situation after the war, it found that the act was unenforceable because territorial courts were in LDS hands. To remedy this situation, Congress passed the Poland Act of 1874, transferring control over criminal proceedings—including cases involving polygamy—from local courts to federally appointed officials. This act marked the transformation of the confrontation over plural marriage into a struggle over political power in Utah. The 1882 Edmunds Act prohibited polygamists (including virtually all Church leaders) from voting or holding office. It also established a federally appointed commission to control territorial elections, including voter registration. Utah women were among the first in the nation to vote, and WOMAN SUFFRAGE was now also under attack. The most sweeping legislation, the 1887 Edmunds-Tucker Act, required an antipolygamy test oath for voting and holding office, disfranchised women, disbanded the territorial militia, took control of public schools, abolished the Church's Perpetual Emigrating Fund, dissolved the Church as a legal entity, and seized much of its property. In the late 1880s, demands were made in Congress for even more stringent measures.

Latter-day Saints vigorously protested that this legislation violated their constitutionally protected right of the free exercise of religion, and in a series of cases, they challenged the antipolygamy legislation in the courts. *Reynolds v. United States* was decided by the U.S. Supreme Court in 1879. The appeal attacked the Morrill Act for failing to acknowledge the religious motivation behind plural marriage. A unanimous Court held, however, that to allow Latter-day Saints' religious beliefs to excuse them from obeying the law would be to "make the professed doctrines of religious belief superior to the law of the land, and in effect to permit every citizen to become a law unto himself" (98 U.S. [1879]). The *Reynolds* decision distinguished between religious opinions and religious practices, leaving the former free while allowing for government regulation of the latter (*see* CIVIL RIGHTS).

Decisions in later polygamy cases undermined that distinction, allowing for the direct or indirect regulation of religious opinion. The Court upheld the disfranchisement provisions of the Edmunds Act in *Murphy v. Ramsey*. Congress, according to the Court, was responsible for preparing the territories for statehood and self-government. In Utah this required curbing the political power of polygamists because nothing was more important in the founding of a self-governing commonwealth than "the idea of family, as consisting in and springing from the union for life of one man and one woman in the holy estate of matrimony" (114 U.S. 15 [1885]). The Court in *Davis v. Beason* upheld an Idaho test oath that disfranchised any member of any organization that taught its members "to commit the crime" of polygamy. According to the Court, the free exercise clause of the First Amendment did not protect individuals in advocating "any form of worship" and "any tenets, however destructive of society," merely by asserting them to be a part of their religious beliefs (133 U.S. 333 [1890]). In *The Late Corporation of the Church of Jesus Christ of Latter-day Saints v. United States*, the Supreme Court sustained the disincorporation and escheat provisions of the Edmunds-Tucker Act. The opinion described the Church corporation as a contumacious organization that, in defiance of the authority of the government, continued to encourage polygamy, "a crime against the laws, and abhorrent to the sentiments and feelings of the civilized world" (136 U.S. 1 [1890]). With plenary authority over the political affairs of territories, Congress had the power to abolish the Church corporation and the government could dispose of its property.

The Poland, Edmunds, and Edmunds-Tucker laws curtailed LDS political power. An all-out attack on plural marriage came in the late 1880s, in what Latter-day Saints called "the Raid." The thrust against the Church struck deeper than the practice of polygamy, however: it struck at the heart of the LDS community and threatened its survival in a world that, since the 1830s, had shown itself hostile. The deeper threat was reflected in the massive economic, social, and political dislocations occasioned by the Raid. Finally, facing even the loss of its temples, in 1890 Church President Wilford Woodruff concluded that "for the temporal salvation of the church" it was necessary to end the practice of plural marriage. In his Manifesto of 1890, he announced his intention to submit to the antipolygamy laws and to use his influence to induce Church members to do the same.

The Manifesto was only the beginning of the changes introduced by Church leaders in the 1890s to accommodate the Latter-day Saint community to the social, economic, and political forms of the larger society. They dissolved the local People's party, which had dominated electoral politics in Utah from its organization in the early 1870s, and encouraged members to affiliate with the Republican and Democratic national parties. They supported the development of a public school system. Finally, leaders reduced direct Church involvement in the economic life of the territory by selling off most business interests. The reward for their willingness to accommodate themselves to the forms of American liberalism came in 1896 with Utah statehood. Latter-day Saints relinquished important elements of the social, economic, and political order that they had established in the Great Basin in exchange for a measure of the political power and autonomy that decades of confrontation and conflict had demonstrated were necessary for their survival as a community.

The modus vivendi that Church leaders worked out with the American political community as the prerequisite for statehood reduced, but by no means ended, direct Church involvement in politics. In the first years after statehood, Church leaders quietly supported and participated in a system of power sharing between Mormons and non-Mormons, Democrats and Republicans. For example, the state's two seats in the U.S. Senate were divided between Latter-day Saints and non-Mormons until the election of 1916, when the Seventeenth Amendment (ratified 1913), providing for direct popular election of senators, removed the matter from the control of party or Church leaders.

Church leaders signaled their intention to curb their own political activity in the so-called Political Manifesto of 1896, which emphasized the importance of the religious duties of Church officers and required them to obtain approval of ecclesiastical superiors before seeking public office. This rule was applied more stringently for Democratic- than Republican-inclined Church officials. Church authorities in the 1890s encouraged the development of the Republican party among Church members, many of whom had avoided the party because of its harsh opposition to plural marriage.

Church leaders since 1896, with only a few exceptions, have avoided taking stands that by either identifying the Church with, or casting the Church in opposition to, either major political party would encourage a religious polarization of the parties. But they have been willing to take an official stand on such issues as public welfare and the repeal of PROHIBITION in the 1930s, Sunday closing laws in the 1950s, right-to-work laws and liquor by the drink in the 1960s, the Equal Rights Amendment (ERA) in the 1970s, and ABORTION in the 1970s, 1980s, and 1990s. While the Church by no means inevitably has its way in Utah politics, it is a pervasive influence in the state. Latter-day Saints help shape the political agenda of Utah, in large part determining the issues that are or are not live, and dictating the terms in which issues accepted as live are debated. Generally, the overwhelming majority of all officeholders, both Republican and Democratic, are LDS.

What the Latter-day Saints relinquished in order to secure statehood for Utah indicates what was really at stake in the nineteenth-century political conflicts. Both sides were well aware that the struggle was over more than a "peculiar institution." For Latter-day Saints, plural marriage symbolized obedience to the will of God revealed through latter-day prophets. For anti-Mormons, polygamy symbolized the potential for theocratic control, rooted in the religion's belief in continuing revelation. Territorial governor Caleb West told the Mormons in 1888 that the cause of their woes was their belief that "God governs them immediately, not alone in faith and morals, but in all affairs and relations of life, and that the counsel of the priesthood is the Supreme Voice of God and must be obeyed" (governor to Territorial Assembly, Jan. 9, 1888). The tenet of continuing revelation, an issue since the beginning, largely accounted for the struggles between the Latter-day Saints and the federal government over political power in early Utah. It generated continuing tensions in the politics of Utah, and containing them required the exercise of prudent statesmanship by leaders of both church and state. At the same time, the vitality of Utah as a democratic political community in the early twentieth century was the foundation for the relative peace that Latter-day Saints have enjoyed since then. That such peace remained somewhat precarious was evident when well-organized LDS lobbying efforts in several states against the ERA in the 1970s threatened to reawaken major apprehensions of priesthood influence on LDS voters.

Outside the United States, LDS efforts for legal recognition and freedom of operation under restrictive regimes were remarkably successful by 1990, precisely because Church leaders convinced government leaders that priesthood directives would not promote political activity that confronted constituted authority—would not, in fact, promote political activity in any particular direction. The fact that LDS political behavior both in Utah and in U.S. government service was observably stable and responsible was thus significant for the functioning and expansion of the Church in an international setting.

BIBLIOGRAPHY

Alexander, Thomas G. *Mormonism in Transition: A History of the Latter-day Saints, 1890–1930.* Urbana and Chicago, 1986.

Firmage, Edwin Brown, and Richard Collin Mangrum. *Zion in the Courts: A Legal History of the Church of Jesus Christ of Latter-day Saints, 1830–1900.* Urbana and Chicago, 1988.

Hill, Marvin S. *Quest for Refuge: The Mormon Flight from American Pluralism.* Salt Lake City, 1989.

Lyman, Edward Leo. *Political Deliverance: The Mormon Quest for Utah Statehood.* Urbana and Chicago, 1986.

Morgan, Dale L. "The State of Deseret." *Utah Historical Quarterly* 8 (Apr., July, Oct. 1940):65–239.

Poll, Richard D. "The Mormon Question Enters National Politics, 1850–1856." *Utah Historical Quarterly* 25 (1957):117–31.

ROGER M. BARRUS

POLITICAL TEACHINGS

Concerning the general duties of government and citizen, latter-day scriptures and the prophets of The Church of Jesus Christ of Latter-day Saints teach that governments should protect freedoms and provide for the public interest and that citizens should honor and uphold laws and governments. LDS theology endorses aspects of both individualism and communitarianism, and harmonizes these conflicting ideas by teaching that community members can share and promote ideals and principles but should never use force to achieve such conditions. Church leaders encourage members to be participants in public affairs even as they emphasize the separation of the management of CHURCH AND STATE. The Church rarely gives official counsel to its members regarding political issues. As with other religions, various opinions exist among Latter-day Saints as to how political teachings and principles should be applied.

Section 134 of the Doctrine and Covenants is a useful starting point for examining the major beliefs of members of the LDS Church concerning politics and government. In an 1835 meeting to discuss plans for publishing the Doctrine and Covenants, Church leaders prepared a declaration to the world concerning "earthly governments and law." Some members of the Church had been accused of being opposed to law and order, and were subsequently victimized by mobbings and violence. The declaration provided guidelines for the Saints in rebutting the charges of their enemies. Penned by Oliver Cowdery, with the possible participation of W. W. Phelps, this is one of the few sections of the Doctrine and Covenants not given by revelation to Joseph Smith.

Two central themes run throughout this section and related passages. First, the duty of government is to provide for the public interest in general and to protect freedom of conscience and religious belief in particular. Governments "were instituted of God for the benefit of man." Laws are to be enacted "for the good and safety of society" and to "secure to each individual the free exercise of conscience, the right and control of property, and the protection of life." Government officials are to make laws that are "best calculated to secure the public interest; at the same time, however, holding sacred the freedom of conscience" (D&C 134:1–2, 5). The separation of church and state is imperative: it is not "just to mingle religious influence with civil government, whereby one religious society is fostered and another proscribed in its spiritual privileges" (D&C 134:9). Governments do not have the right "to interfere in prescribing rules of worship, to bind the consciences of men, nor dictate forms for public or private devotion." They "should restrain crime, but never control conscience; should punish guilt, but never suppress the freedom of the soul." Governments have an affirmative duty to protect citizens "in the free exercise of their religious belief," but they do not have the right to "deprive citizens of this privilege, or proscribe them in their opinions," as long as such citizens do not promote sedition (D&C 134:4–7).

Second, the duty of citizens is to honor and sustain laws and governments. All people are "bound to sustain and uphold the respective governments in which they reside, while protected in their inherent and inalienable rights." Governments are responsible "for the protection of the innocent and the punishment of the guilty"; citizens are to "step forward and use their ability in bringing offenders against good laws to punishment" (D&C 134:5–6, 8).

Other passages in LDS scripture reflect these themes of governmental and citizenship duties. Members of the Church are to befriend the "constitutional law of the land" that supports the "principle of freedom in maintaining rights and privileges" (D&C 98:5–6). Church leaders have regularly indicated their belief that the CONSTITUTION OF THE UNITED STATES OF AMERICA is an inspired document. Citizens are to seek and uphold honest, wise, and good government leaders (D&C

98:10). Book of Mormon writers emphasize that every person is to enjoy "rights and privileges alike" and that political decisions are to be made "by the voice of the people" (Mosiah 29:25–27, 32).

New Testament admonitions to "render therefore unto Caesar the things which are Caesar's" (Matt. 22:21), to "be subject to principalities and powers, to obey magistrates" (Titus 3:1), and to "submit yourselves to every ordinance of man" (1 Pet. 2:13) also provide guidance to members of the Church concerning their obligations as citizens. In all nations, Latter-day Saints are encouraged to support their lawful governments; to participate actively in politics, civic affairs, and public service; and to support and promote just and righteous causes.

Because of its emphasis on free agency, individual accountability, and freedom of belief and conscience, LDS theology is quite compatible with Western traditions of liberal democracy that champion individual and minority rights, personal freedom, and religious pluralism. Laws are to ensure "the rights and protection of all" so that every person "may act in doctrine and principle pertaining to futurity, according to the moral agency which [God has] given unto him, that every man may be accountable for his own sins in the day of judgment" (D&C 101:77–78).

From a broader view of politics, however, Latter-day Saints have much greater expectations for collective action. Their theology includes a strong commitment to achieve a unified, cooperative society, characterized by spiritual convictions, strong social bonds, collective responsibilities, and material EQUALITY. Joseph Smith taught that "the greatest temporal and spiritual blessings which always come from faithfulness and concerted effort, never attended individual exertion or enterprise" (*TPJS*, p. 183). Unity and cooperation in temporal affairs are preconditions for spiritual progress: "If ye are not one ye are not mine" (D&C 38:27); "If ye are not equal in earthly things ye cannot be equal in obtaining heavenly things" (D&C 78:6).

Respect for individual rights and a strong commitment to collective action come together in the belief that communities can be built on shared principles and ideals, but force can never be employed to achieve those ends. Unity and cooperation cannot be attained by coercion, but only through love: power is to be exercised by "persuasion, by long-suffering, by gentleness and meekness, and

by love unfeigned" (D&C 121:41). The goals of individual righteousness and COMMUNITY are well captured in this description of the
city of Enoch from the Pearl of Great Price: "And the Lord called his
people ZION, because they were of one heart and one mind, and dwelt
in righteousness; and there was no poor among them" (Moses 7:18).

While Latter-day Saints aspire to such a community of the faithful, they have been encouraged throughout their history to participate in public affairs even under other conditions. "It is our
duty," said Joseph Smith, "to concentrate all our influence to make
popular that which is sound and good, and unpopular that which is
unsound. 'Tis right, politically, for a man who has influence to use it"
(*HC* 5:286). Brigham Young charged members of the Church, "Let
every man and woman be industrious, prudent, and economical in
their acts and feelings, and while gathering to themselves, let each
one strive to identify his or her interests with the interests of this
community, with those of their neighbor and neighborhood, let them
seek their happiness and welfare in that of all" (*JD* 3:330).

In 1903 the First Presidency of the Church issued a statement
emphasizing the separation of religious and political activity:

> The Church . . . instructs in things temporal as well as things spiritual.
> . . . But it does not infringe upon . . . the domain of the state. . . . Every
> member of the organization in every place is absolutely free as a citi-
> zen. . . . In proclaiming "the kingdom of heaven's at hand," we have the
> most intense and fervent conviction of our mission and calling. . . . But
> we do not and will not attempt to force them upon others, or to control or
> dominate any of their affairs, individual or national [*MFP* 4:79, 82].

In 1968, the First Presidency issued a statement concerning the
obligations of citizenship:

> We urge our members to do their civic duty and to assume their respon-
> sibilities as individual citizens in seeking solutions to the problems
> which beset our cities and communities.
>
> With our wide ranging mission, so far as mankind is concerned,
> Church members cannot ignore the many practical problems that
> require solution if our families are to live in an environment conducive
> to spirituality. . . .
>
> Individual Church members cannot, of course, represent or commit
> the Church, but should, nevertheless, be "anxiously engaged" in good

causes, using the principles of the Gospel of Jesus Christ as their constant guide.

There are differing views among Church members concerning how to put these principles into practice. From one view, government intervention ought to be minimal in order to encourage volunteerism, freedom of choice, and individual responsibility. Others believe governments should pursue a wide range of collective purposes and promote shared values. There are also differences concerning the role of religious ideas in political discourse. Some believe, much like those in other churches who have not hesitated to mix politics and religion in issues such as CIVIL RIGHTS, ABORTION, and environmental pollution (see EARTH), that religious principles having corresponding secular purposes should be part of public debate and be enacted into law if they can gain sufficient support in the political system. Others favor a more distinct separation between religious belief and public discourse, where public debate is limited to issues and values that can be defended on "rational" grounds, so that religious beliefs do not influence the making of laws (see POLITICS: POLITICAL CULTURE).

Brigham Young stated clearly the LDS commitment to a broad conception of collective effort in working toward a vision of a celestial community, while expressing ambivalence about earthly politics: "As for politics, we care nothing about them one way or the other, although we are a political people. . . . It is the Kingdom of God or nothing with us" (*Millennial Star* 31 [1869]:573).

BIBLIOGRAPHY

Cannon, Donald Q. "Church and State." In *Insights into the Doctrine and Covenants: The Capstone of our Religion*, ed. R. Millet and L. Dahl, pp. 183–96. Salt Lake City, 1989.

Firmage, Edwin Brown. "Eternal Principles of Government: A Theological Approach." *Ensign* 6 (June 1976):11–16.

Nibley, Hugh. "Beyond Politics." In *Nibley on the Timely and the Timeless: Classic Essays of Hugh W. Nibley*, ed. T. Madsen, pp. 279–305. Provo, Utah, 1978.

GARY C. BRYNER

POLITICAL CULTURE

Contrary to some popular characterizations, Latter-day Saints do not all think or vote alike on political matters and do not share a distinctive political subculture. American Latter-day Saints tend to be slightly more pragmatic, less cynical, more optimistic, and less alienated than the average American citizen, but only in minor variations from the broad national political culture. The earliest Latter-day Saints were Americans before they became Latter-day Saints. If Latter-day Saints as a group were markedly less or more optimistic or less or more cynical than the average U.S. citizen, that might indicate the presence of a distinctive political subculture, but there is no evidence for this.

A political culture is generally understood to be a patterned set of ways of thinking about how politics and governing ought to be carried out, and a subculture is a somewhat differing view peculiar to a smaller area or group. During the nineteenth century, when Latter-day Saints "gathered" together in well-structured communities throughout the Intermountain West, there was a distinctive Mormon political subculture. It was based on a model of consensus politics and a deference to ecclesiastical authority, which set it apart from the dominant American political culture of the time. This subculture slowly dissipated as the intermountain LDS commonwealth was integrated into the larger political and economic patterns of the United States, despite the continued majority status of Latter-day Saints in many communities.

In a strict sense, there is no such thing today as "a Mormon political culture." The mark of such a subculture is the frequency and likelihood of certain political behaviors observable over time and in well-defined situations, not the source of the ideas that it expresses. While various tenets of their faith may predispose many Latter-day Saints to one side of some political disputes in the United States, such a predisposition is not sufficient to indicate the presence of a unique political subculture.

In the late twentieth century, Latter-day Saints are found in many different countries, living under many different political systems. That which ties them together is a set of religious beliefs, not an identifiable set of habits of thinking or acting about politics. Were a cross-polity survey to be taken, the empirical beliefs, likes and dislikes, values, and priorities of Latter-day Saints in political matters would be polity-specific. German Latter-day Saints, for example, would resemble other Germans more than they would Mexican, French, or Samoan Latter-day Saints.

Some maintain, nonetheless, that there is an identifiable LDS political subculture in America, or at least in Utah. This perspective may confuse a regional pattern of attitudes and behaviors with a religious one. It also reflects the ubiquitous disagreements between minorities and the majority in any population. Latter-day Saints in Utah (the only state where they constitute a majority of the population) are no more sensitive to the feelings of alienation and oppression perceived by members of other denominations than are other religious or cultural majorities in other parts of the world.

Since statehood in 1896, Utah has been in the mainstream of American politics. In the twenty-two presidential elections between 1904 and 1988, Utah gave its electoral (and majority) votes to the national winner all but three times. The partisan preferences of Utah voters are essentially the same as those of other intermountain and western voters in presidential and congressional elections. Divisions between voters are essentially partisan, not ecclesiastical, even in strongly LDS areas.

Belief in the LDS worldview does not produce predictable or demonstrable similarities in political habits of thought and expectations, regardless of geographical, economic, or social differences. The often fervent divisions among LDS voters over political issues and candidates cast serious doubt on the existence of any unifying, religiously determined political behaviors.

Latter-day Saints' attitudinal orientations are generally intensifications of typically American attitudes. For example, the idea of political efficacy—the feeling citizens have that they can influence what the government does and the belief that government listens to what ordinary citizens say—is a key indicator of the type of political culture a country has. In all cross-polity surveys, U.S. citizens demonstrate significantly higher levels of political efficacy than citizens of any other country. Perhaps because of the stress in LDS theology on the value of individual effort and the right of individual agency, Latter-day Saints demonstrate higher levels of efficacy than most other groups in American political life. How directly related to religious beliefs such attitudes may be is difficult to establish empirically. However, there may be some overlap or holdover from earlier times.

Latter-day Saints also ascribe a higher level of legitimacy to political leaders, possibly a holdover from the mingling of ecclesiastical and political authority in nineteenth-century Utah. Finally, voting participation statistics indicate that the growing political alienation in America has made few inroads in strongly LDS areas.

A crucial determinant of a community's or a nation's political stability and governmental effectiveness is the extent to which its citizens give their primary political loyalties to it rather than to a particular region, tribe, or religion. Although Latter-day Saints are deeply attached to their religion, for this attachment to affect their political behavior has been the exception rather than the rule. For example, during the 1930s and 1940s the President of the Church and at least one of his counselors were implacably opposed to the policies of President Franklin D. Roosevelt and expressed their views publicly and privately. Nevertheless, Utah voters joined decisively with national majorities voting for the Democratic candidates from 1932 through 1948. In the ten presidential elections since 1952, only in 1964 did Utah vote Democratic, again joining an overwhelming national majority. This Republican hegemony is found not only in LDS areas but also nearly all the western states.

There is no detectable pattern or set of political behaviors common to Latter-day Saints. Appearances of a unique LDS political homogeneity disappear when regional and national trends are taken into account. No institutional or doctrinal mechanism exists for passing on a political culture, especially in light of the high percentage of converts. The growing international character of the Church and its membership will no doubt produce even greater political heterogeneity among Latter-day Saints in the future.

BIBLIOGRAPHY
Poll, Richard D., et al. *Utah's History*, pp. 97–112, 153–73, 243–74, 387–404, 409–428, 481–96, 515–30, 669–80. Provo, Utah, 1978.

WM. CLAYTON KIMBALL

CONTEMPORARY AMERICAN POLITICS
Latter-day Saints are an integral part of the politics of the Intermountain West of the United States. They play important roles in U.S. politics and government, and members have held high positions in all three branches of the federal government and in many state and local governments. The Church encourages its members throughout the world to be involved in government and civic affairs (*see* CIVIC

DUTIES). Official Church statements on such matters as the Equal Rights Amendment (ERA) and the MX missile have been important in the politics of these issues.

On most issues and in most elections, the Church has remained neutral, admonishing its members to study the issues and vote according to their conscience. A member of the First Presidency said in 1951:

> The Church, while reserving the right to advocate principles of good government underlying equity, justice, and liberty, the political integrity of officials, and the active participation of its members, and the fulfillment of their obligations in civic affairs, exercises no constraint on the freedom of individuals to make their own choices and affiliations. . . . Any man who makes representation to the contrary does so without authority and justification in fact [Richards, p. 878].

The Church encourages individual choice in elections, although through the 1960 election Church leaders often publicly endorsed or indicated their personal preference for U.S. presidential candidates (Jonas, p. 335). Despite any corporate interest it may have in Utah (*see* BUSINESS: CHURCH PARTICIPATION IN), the Church has not become directly involved in elections in those jurisdictions for many years.

While many non-LDS candidates have been elected to public office in Utah, Church membership and affiliation do appear to be important to political success in Utah, as well as in some surrounding areas of the Intermountain West with large LDS populations. Candidates for office sometimes advertise their Church affiliation, Church leadership positions, and family size as part of their political campaigns. Local Church officials sometimes become involved in politics either as candidates or as supporters of candidates. Some voters incorrectly infer an implicit Church endorsement of candidates or issues in these situations.

While the Church rarely takes an official stand on candidates or issues, it does possess substantial political power. Its membership constitutes an overwhelming majority (70 percent) in the state of Utah and significant portions of the population in Idaho, Arizona, and Nevada. It also exercises political influence through its corporate and business interests. The Church's business interests and its print and broadcast media (BONNEVILLE INTERNATIONAL) give it a means to participate in politics. Editorials from these media are often considered to reflect the views of the Church.

Church members in the late twentieth century are generally Republicans, often strong Republicans, though in earlier generations Democratic influence prevailed. Data on Utah indicate that 69 percent of the Latter-day Saints are Republicans, a figure higher than the 57 percent of Utahans who are Republicans and the 47 percent of western Americans who are Republicans. Increased Church activity is even more strongly correlated to Republican partisan identification. This relationship between Church activity and attachment to the Republican party is also related to age; younger, very active Latter-day Saints are most likely to classify themselves Republicans. Party identification among members of the Church has the same behavioral consequences as it does among non-Mormons nationwide. Most members of the Church are politically conservative, both by self-classification and in attitudes toward economic, social, and lifestyle issues. The conservatism of many Church members reinforces their partisan preferences, especially with regard to the national political parties. Little is known about the partisan or ideological predispositions of LDS members outside the United States.

Recent nationally prominent LDS political figures also tend to be disproportionately Republican, although for all of U.S. history, LDS congressmen and senators have been only about 50 percent Republican. LDS congressmen tend to come from Utah and surrounding states, but include several California members of the U.S. House of Representatives. Utah, Idaho, Michigan, and Arizona have all had LDS governors. LDS-elected gubernatorial officials and national legislators represent an even partisan balance.

Several Latter-day Saints have played key roles in recent Republican administrations. President Eisenhower's cabinet included apostle and later President of the Church Ezra Taft Benson as secretary of agriculture. President Nixon's cabinet included David M. Kennedy as secretary of the treasury, and George Romney as secretary of housing and urban development. The Ford, Reagan, and Bush administrations also had several members of the Church as key staff. Church members played a generally less visible role in the Democratic administrations of Kennedy, Johnson, and Carter.

Church members have been important participants in the judicial branch as well. While no member of the Church has been appointed to the U.S. Supreme Court, several Latter-day Saints have served as court of appeals, district court, and state supreme court judges.

The Church has been most visible politically in discussion of moral issues. In 1976, after years of silence on political issues, the Church issued a statement opposing the ERA: "We recognize men and women as equally important before the Lord, but with differences biologically, emotionally, and in other ways. ERA, we believe, does not recognize these differences. There are better means for giving women, and men, the rights they deserve" ("First Presidency Issues Statement Opposing Equal Rights Amendment," *Ensign* 6 [Dec. 1976]:79). This formal institutional opposition sparked significant local organizing by private Church members acting on their own accord against the amendment in Florida, Illinois, Maryland, Nevada, and Virginia. Not all Church members opposed the amendment. Some had spoken publicly in support of the amendment before the Church position was announced.

During the early 1980s the Church took a position on the MX missile controversy. Many Church leaders had long been critical of war and armaments. But others were in favor of preparations for defense. Thus, elected officials could find Church authorities either favoring or opposing defense spending, new weapons systems, and foreign military activities. Utah representatives in Washington tend to promote defense spending, and Utah has a large defense industry.

In 1981, Church President Spencer W. Kimball and his counselors issued a strongly worded letter opposing the deployment of the MX missile in the desert of western Utah and neighboring eastern Nevada. The statement criticized not only the MX missile but also the form of warfare it exemplified: "With the most serious concern over the pressing moral question of possible nuclear conflict, we plead with our national leaders to marshal the genius of the nation to find viable alternatives which will secure at an earlier date and with fewer hazards the protection from possible enemy aggression, which is our common concern" ("First Presidency Statement on Basing of MX Missile," *Ensign* 11 [June 1981]:76).

The Church has also opposed legalized GAMBLING, including

state-run lotteries ("Church Opposes Government-Sponsored Gambling," *Ensign* 16 [Nov. 1986]:104–105), and has made moral arguments against liberalizing access to alcoholic beverages.

BIBLIOGRAPHY
Arrington, Leonard J., and Davis Bitton. *The Mormon Experience: A History of the Latter-day Saints*, pp. 243–307. New York, 1979.
Jonas, Frank. "Utah: The Different State." In *Politics in the American West*, ed. F. Jonas. Salt Lake City, 1969.
Richards, Stephen L. "Awake, Ye Defenders of Zion." *IE* 54 (Dec. 1951):877–80.

DAVID B. MAGLEBY

POLYNESIAN CULTURAL CENTER

The Polynesian Cultural Center is located in Laie, Hawaii, on the north shore of the island of Oahu. It is a 42-acre visitor attraction owned and operated by The Church of Jesus Christ of Latter-day Saints for the purpose of preserving and sharing the heritage of Pacific island cultures while providing employment, scholarships, and grants to students at the adjacent BRIGHAM YOUNG UNIVERSITY—HAWAII.

In seven authentically recreated villages, representative dwellings, furniture, and artifacts from Fiji, old Hawaii, Samoa, Tonga, Tahiti, Maori New Zealand, and the Marquesas Islands are featured in a landscape of island foliage and lagoons. Visitors may observe or participate in demonstrations of arts, crafts, dances, music, games, and food preparation presented by villagers and performers, many of whom come from the cultures they portray. Various kinds of island cuisine are available in restaurants and snack bars. Daytime and evening shows and concerts are held on the grounds and in the 2,773-seat amphitheater. An IMAX theater with an ultra-large screen shows cultural and educational films shot on locations in the South Pacific.

Precursors to the present production consisted mainly of a *hukilau*—a fishing festival with luau and entertainment. That production was begun by Church members in the 1940s and continued for several years in Laie. In 1959 students and faculty at the Church College of Hawaii (now Brigham Young University—Hawaii) organized "Polynesian Panorama," a production of songs and dances that played regularly to audiences in Waikiki.

In 1962 Church President David O. McKay authorized construction of the present center. Special "labor missionaries" donated their skills, using building materials from Hawaii and the other islands represented. The original 12-acre center opened on October 12, 1963. Hugh B. Brown, a counselor to President McKay in the Church's First Presidency, presided at the opening ceremonies. In 1975–1976 the center was redesigned and greatly enlarged.

The labor missionaries helped realize the dream of Matthew Cowley, an apostle who worked for years with the Latter-day Saints in New Zealand, when he said, "I hope to see the day when my Maori people will have a little village at Laie with a beautiful carved house. . . . The Tongans will have a little village out there, and the Tahitians and Samoans—all those islanders of the sea!" (O'Brien, p. 73).

The center is a nonprofit organization that attracts almost a million visitors a year. It is administered locally by a president and governed by a board of directors chaired by a member of the Church's Quorum of the Twelve Apostles.

BIBLIOGRAPHY

O'Brien, Robert. *Hands Across the Water: The Story of the Polynesian Cultural Center.* Laie, Hawaii, 1983.

CHARLES JAY FOX

POLYNESIANS

Polynesia is most frequently identified as those Pacific islands lying within an enormous triangle extending from New Zealand in the south to Hawaii in the north and the Easter Islands in the extreme east. The major Polynesian ethnic groups include Hawaiians, New Zealand Maoris, Samoans, Tongans, and Tahitians.

A basic view held in the Church is that Polynesians have ancestral connections with the Book of Mormon people who were descendants of Abraham and that among them are heirs to the blessings promised Abraham's descendants. Since 1843, the Church has undertaken extensive missionary efforts in the Pacific islands, and large numbers of Polynesians have joined the Church.

The belief that Polynesian ancestry includes Book of Mormon people can be traced back at least to 1851, when George Q. Cannon taught it as a missionary in Hawaii (he was later a counselor in the First Presidency). President Brigham Young detailed the belief in a letter to King Kamehameha V in 1865. Other Church leaders have since affirmed the belief, some indicating that among Polynesian ancestors were the people of Hagoth, who set sail from Nephite lands in approximately 54 B.C. (cf. Alma 63:5–8). In a statement to the Maoris of New Zealand, for instance, President Joseph F. Smith said, "I would like to say to you brethren and sisters . . . you *are* some of Hagoth's people, and there is NO PERHAPS about it!" (Cole and Jensen, p. 388.) In the prayer offered at the dedication of the Hawaii Temple, President Heber J. Grant referred to the "descendants of Lehi" in Hawaii (*IE* 23 [Feb. 1920]:283).

Among scholars, the exact ancestry of the Polynesian peoples is a matter of debate. While some non-LDS scientists have insisted on their Western Hemisphere origins, the prevailing scientific opinion from anthropological, archaeological, and linguistic evidence argues a west-to-east migratory movement from Southeast Asia that began as early as 1200 B.C.

What seems clear from the long-standing debate is that considerable interaction was maintained over the centuries from many directions. The island peoples had both the vessels and the skill to sail with or against ocean currents. It would be as difficult to say that no group could have migrated from east to west as to argue the opposite in absolute terms. Church leaders, who have attested to Polynesian roots in the Nephite peoples, have not elaborated on the likelihood of other migrating groups in the Pacific or of social mixing and intermarriage.

Throughout the Church's history in the islands, Polynesian members have demonstrated spiritual receptivity, maturity, and leadership. In 1990, more than 100,000 Polynesians, including approximately 30 percent of the Tongans and 20 percent of the Samoans, were members of the Church. In all areas of Polynesia, local leaders preside over organized stakes and wards. Missionary work continues, much of it under the direction of local mission presidents and missionaries. In Tonga and Samoa, for example, almost the entire force of missionaries is made up of local youth, and hundreds of others have been called to serve missions elsewhere in the world.

Some Polynesian Latter-day Saints have left their homelands and established communities abroad. Honolulu, Auckland, and Los Angeles have extensive LDS Polynesian populations. Thousands of LDS Polynesians have also migrated to Utah's Wasatch Front area and to Missouri, California, and Texas.

BIBLIOGRAPHY
Britsch, R. Lanier. *Moramona*. Laie, Hawaii, 1989.
———. *Unto the Islands of the Sea*. Salt Lake City, 1989.
Clement, Russell T. "Polynesian Origins: More Word on the Mormon Perspective." *Dialogue* 13 (Winter 1980):88–89.
Cole, W. A., and E. W. Jensen. *Israel in the Pacific*. Salt Lake City, 1961.
Loveland, Jerry. "Hagoth and the Polynesian Tradition." *BYU Studies* 17 (Autumn 1976):59–73.

ERIC B. SHUMWAY

PORNOGRAPHY

Pornography refers to explicit depictions of sexual activity in written or pictorial form in an exploitive style. The purpose of these presentations is erotic arousal for commercial gain. Most of it presents highly inaccurate, unscientific, and distorted information about human SEXUALITY. It is, in a sense, sex miseducation marketed for financial gain in a variety of formats, including books, magazines, motion pictures, television, videotapes, and even telephone. The Church of Jesus Christ of Latter-day Saints condemns all forms of pornography.

The Church views sexuality positively—as a sacred gift from God with the primary purposes of reproducing life upon the earth and bonding the husband and wife together in an eternal, affectionate, committed relationship. High standards of personal morality and sexual conduct, including chastity before marriage and fidelity in marriage, are taught as norms for Church members. These standards are perceived as reflecting God's will and counsel for his earthly children.

Pornography is seen as degrading sex and creating an unhealthy extramarital sexual interest in individuals, thereby contributing to a weakening of the marital relationship. Much of this filmed, photographed, or written "prostitution" is actually antisexual because it gives a great deal of false information about human sexuality. Also, since much pornography depicts violence and aggression against females, it raises risks of conditioning viewers to sanction these as acceptable behavior. The best evidence suggests that all sexual deviations are learned, and pornography appears to be a major facilitator in the acquisition of these deviations.

Introducing immoral or inappropriate sexual stimuli into the mind of those who view it can create fantasies that may never be erased. It has the potential for corrupting the values of, and degrading, those who indulge. It suggests behaviors that could negatively affect or even destroy one's marriage and family. Pornography, in a sense, is an attack on the family and the marriage covenant as well as on the bonds of affection or trust that hold a marriage and family together.

Additionally, involvement in pornography promotes a voyeuristic interest in sex, one form of sexual illness. This is a regressive fantasy approach to sexuality with major health risks. These various hazards have been documented at length by the U.S. Pornography Commission, convened under the sponsorship of the U.S. Department of Justice.

The experience of many men and adolescent males who repeatedly experiment with, or voluntarily expose themselves to, pornography suggests four possible consequences. First, there is a risk of addiction. Once involved with it, many get "hooked," as with a highly addictive drug, and keep coming back in a compulsive fashion for more. Second, they desire increasingly deviant material. In time, they need rougher and more explicit material to get the same kicks, arousal, and excitement as initially. Third, they become desensitized to the inappropriateness or abnormality of the behavior portrayed, eventually accepting and embracing what at first had shocked and offended them. Fourth, with appetite whetted and conscience anesthetized, they tend to act out sexually what they have witnessed. This almost always disturbs the most intimate aspects of marital and family relationships and attacks the participants' spiritual nature. As an individual acts out his desires and appetites, there is a significant risk of venereal infections, some of which are incurable and life-threatening. When this occurs, the health and life of the marital partner is also jeopardized.

The Church strongly counsels its members to avoid involvement with pornography for the many reasons cited above. An important additional reason is that involvement with it is also perceived as leading to a loss of contact with, and consciousness of, God and the Holy Spirit. It can lead to a psychological, sexual, and spiritual regression. Becoming addicted to pornography can lead to a loss of control and eventually to the loss of moral agency.

The Church counsels its members to be responsible citizens in the communities where they live, to join organizations that attempt to improve community values, to let their voices be heard, and to work for, in legal ways, limits being placed on the dissemination, broadcast, sale, and rental of illegal pornographic materials.

BIBLIOGRAPHY

"Church Leaders Suggest Ways to Fight Pornography." *Ensign* 14 (Apr. 1984):37–39.

Cline, Victor B. "Obscenity: How It Affects Us, How We Can Deal with It." *Ensign* 14 (Apr. 1984):32–37.

———, ed. *Where Do You Draw the Line?* Provo, Utah, 1974.

Monson, Thomas S. "Pornography—The Deadly Carrier." *Ensign* 9 (Nov. 1979):66–67.

Shapiro, Gary R. "Leave the Obscene Unseen." *Ensign* 19 (Aug. 1989):27–29.

VICTOR B. CLINE

POVERTY, ATTITUDES TOWARD

For Latter-day Saints, as for all Christians, attending to the needs of the poor is service to God (Matt. 25:31–40; Mosiah 2:17; D&C 42:38) and an expression of the greatest spiritual gift, the attitude of charity (1 Cor. 13:13). King Benjamin explained in the Book of Mormon that, as a result of true repentance, people are filled with the love of God and the desire to administer to those in need (Mosiah 4:16). It is no excuse that "the man has brought upon himself his misery," for all are beggars dependent upon God, who gives generously (Mosiah 4:17–23). Benjamin required that the poor also carry this attitude and covet not—those who cannot give are to say in their hearts, "I give not because I have not, but if I had I would give" (Mosiah 4:24–25). Giving to the poor is essential to retaining a remission of one's sins and walking guiltless before God (Mosiah 4:26). Anyone who cries unto God sends up a petition in vain without giving "to those who stand in need" (Alma 34:28).

In 1935 the Church established an extensive Welfare Services program to assist those in need. In addition, all members of the Church are encouraged to give their time and resources wherever possible. Efforts to help the poor are designed to relieve suffering by supplying immediate needs (cf. Luke 10:29–42; 16:19–39), to build self-sufficiency through employment, and to teach people to give willingly (D. McKay, *CR* [Oct. 1941]:54). Widows or orphans are to be provided for (James 1:27; D&C 83:6), especially those destitute because of persecution (D&C 42:30, 39; 52:40; 104:14–18). Indolence on the part of those who are able to work is condemned (Prov. 20:4; 1 Tim. 5:8, 13; D&C 42:42); the poor are to contribute their own labor, whenever possible (Deut. 15:7–11; 24:19; 2 Thes. 3:10). Through the efforts of all living the gospel law in an ideal society worthy of the presence of the Lord, there are "no poor among them" (Moses 7:18; Acts 4:32–35; 4 Ne. 1:2–3; D&C 42:30–33).

Those who willingly give to the poor are promised many blessings, including eternal life (Luke 18:18–23; Matt. 25:31–40), deliverance (Ps. 41:1), forgiveness (Alma 4:13–14), happiness (Prov. 14:21), material rewards (Prov. 19:17; 28:27; Jacob 2:17–19; Deut. 24:19), and answers to prayers (Alma 34:28). Strong condemnations are repeated against those who refuse to share with the poor (2 Ne. 9:30; D&C 56:16). Caring for the poor is a significant moral challenge and obligation (Deut. 15:11; *CWHN* 9:193).

Under the law of Moses, the poor were to be treated generously (Epsztein, pp. 108–134). The corners of fields were left for them to reap (Lev. 19:9–10; Deut. 24:19–21); the produce of the land every seventh year was given first to the poor and the stranger (Ex. 23:10–11; Lev. 25:3–7); loans to the poor were interest free (Lev. 25:35–37; Ex. 22:25–27); Hebrews sold into bondage to other Hebrews were emancipated and generously supplied after six years of service (Ex. 21:2–6; Deut. 15:12–15); and the tithes not used by the Levites were given to the poor (Deut. 14:28–29; 26:12–13). Still, this did not absolve the responsibility to do more if another remained in need (Deut. 15:11).

The law of consecration, revealed to Joseph Smith in 1831 (D&C 42), invited the members to give all they possessed to the Church, receive back what they needed (their stewardships), use what they received to provide for themselves, and give their surplus to the Church. These surpluses and the residues of their inheritances were held in the bishop's storehouse and used first to help the poor (Cook, 1985). Latter-day scriptures speak warnings equally to the rich and to the poor: "Wo unto you rich men, that will not give your substance to the poor, for your riches will canker your souls. . . . Wo unto you poor men, whose hearts are not broken, whose spirits are not contrite, and whose bellies are not satisfied, and whose hands are not stayed from laying hold upon other men's goods, whose eyes are full of greediness, and who will not labor with your own hands!" (D&C 56:16–17).

Most fundamental, however, is the generosity of individuals. As a minimum, most Latter-day Saints believe they should fast for two meals (twenty-four hours) each month and give the equivalent of these two meals, or more, as a fast offering. In addition, many believe they are expected to do more, to contribute to organized charities and to give personal assistance in the form of money, training, and encouragement (*see* ECONOMIC AID; HUMANITARIAN SERVICE).

[*See also* Wealth, Attitudes Toward.]

BIBLIOGRAPHY

Cook, L. W. *Joseph Smith and the Law of Consecration*. Provo, Utah, 1985.

Epsztein, Leon. *Social Justice in the Ancient Near East and the People of the Bible*. London, 1986.

Nibley, Hugh W. *Approaching Zion*. Salt Lake City, 1990.

DAVID J. CHERRINGTON

PREMARITAL SEX

Throughout the centuries, the Lord has declared very clearly that sexual relations outside of marriage are sin (cf. Ex. 20:14; Deut. 5:18; 22:13–30; 2 Sam. 13:12; Matt. 5:27–30; 19:18; Acts 15:20; 21:25; 1

Cor. 5:1; 6:18–20; Alma 39:3–6; D&C 42:22–26). In like manner, The Church of Jesus Christ of Latter-day Saints teaches that premarital sex is sin and counsels its members to abstain from it. Recognizing that the "new morality," which advocates that consenting partners may do whatever their appetites urge them to do, is nothing more than the "old immorality," the Church rejects the popular view that sex before marriage is not sinful and is justifiable as "normal and natural." Rather, the Church teaches that sex should be a sacred expression of love between a husband and wife and that both men and women should abstain from sexual activity until their marriage. It teaches that sex before marriage is an expression of lust, not love, and admonishes its members not to participate in it or in any other kinds of activities that excite sexual desires. The Church teaches that those who have participated in premarital sex may repent of their sin, reminding them that true repentance requires that they abstain from sexual relations except with their legal spouse.

[*See also* Marriage.]

BIBLIOGRAPHY
Kimball, Spencer W. *The Miracle of Forgiveness*, pp. 213–32. Salt Lake City, 1969.

H. REESE HANSEN

PRESS, NEWS MEDIA, AND THE CHURCH

Early press coverage of The Church of Jesus Christ of Latter-day Saints was shaped by the traditions of the partisan press. Some journalists treated the Latter-day Saints with a degree of fairness, but the more common approach was ridicule and hostility. Outside media took a rather dim view of the Church, and when the LDS media were confrontational, non-Mormon media responded with a hostility that increased as the nineteenth century continued. Joseph Smith's arrest and martyrdom grew partly out of the Nauvoo City Council's suppression of the *Nauvoo Expositor*, an opposition press. In the latter part of the century, developing technology and urbanization fostered unprecedented big-city newspaper circulation battles and the rise of yellow journalism. Among those vilified were the Latter-day Saints, particularly their practice of plural marriage.

The press's perception of the Church began to change slowly after the practice of polygamy was officially suspended in 1890 and Utah was granted statehood in 1896. Then in the early twentieth century press coverage continued to improve as the Church began to be recognized as an influential American institution, and the public began listening to MORMON TABERNACLE CHOIR BROADCASTS. Still later, Latter-day Saints in government and business such as George Romney, governor of Michigan; Ezra Taft Benson, secretary of agriculture in the Eisenhower cabinet; and J. Willard Marriott, president of the Marriott Corporation, also helped the press view the Church with an air of greater approval and commendation. The creation of the Church's PUBLIC COMMUNICATIONS office in 1970 has further helped with media relations throughout the world. Although there are still occasional flare-ups of sensational news about the Church and individual members, the general view of Mormons provided by the mainstream media in the last decades of the twentieth century has been more accurate and better balanced.

BIBLIOGRAPHY

Mulder, William, and A. Russell Mortensen, eds. *Among the Mormons: Historic Accounts by Contemporary Observers*. New York, 1969.

Lythgoe, Dennis Leo. "The Changing Image of Mormonism in Periodical Literature." Ph.D. diss., University of Utah, 1969.

PAUL ALFRED PRATTE

PROCREATION

Latter-day Saints have an exceptionally positive view of procreation. After God commanded Adam and Eve to "multiply and replenish the earth" (Gen. 1:28), he pronounced all of his creation, including the power of procreation, "very good" (Gen. 1:31). President Joseph F. Smith noted, "The lawful association of the sexes is ordained of God, not only as the sole means of race perpetuation, but for the development of the higher faculties and nobler traits of human nature, which the love-inspired companionship of man and woman alone can insure" (*IE* 20:739).

Mankind existed in a premortal life as spirit children of God. This earth was created to provide physical life and experience in a second estate. The divine plan of procreation provides physical bodies for premortal spirits. Thus, "children are an heritage of the Lord" (Ps. 127:3). To beget and bear children is central to God's plan for the development of his children on earth. The powers of procreation therefore are of divine origin. An early LDS apostle, Parley P. Pratt, noted that the desires and feelings associated with procreation are not evil, but are ordained of God for sacred purposes:

> The fact is, God made man, male and female; he planted in their bosoms those affections which are calculated to promote their happiness and union. That by that union they might fulfill the first and great commandment . . . "To multiply and replenish the earth, and subdue it." From this union of affection, springs all the other relationships, social joys and affections diffused through every branch of human existence. And were it not for this, earth would be a desert wild, an uncultivated wilderness [Pratt, pp. 52–54].

Procreation is a divine partnership with God, and Church leaders counsel husbands and wives to seek his inspiration as they use their agency to bring children into the world even in difficult situations and circumstances (*see* BIRTH CONTROL). The responsibilities of procreation include providing for the child's temporal well-being (1 Tim. 5:8), as "children have claim upon their parents for their maintenance until they are of age" (D&C 83:4). By seeking spiritual guidance and by following other divine laws, such as tithing and making fast offerings, parents are blessed of the Lord to provide the daily necessities for their children (cf. Mal. 3:3–10).

The abuse of the divine privilege and power of procreation in licentious indulgence has serious consequences. First is the loss of the Spirit to direct one's life (cf. Ex. 20:14; Prov. 6:32; D&C 42:22–24; 63:14–16). In addition, when the creative powers are prostituted, they become a detriment to one's emotional, physical, social, and spiritual well-being (*see* ABORTION; ABUSE, SPOUSE AND CHILD; ADULTERY).

Using the power of procreation does not alienate one from God. Rather, properly used, it enables mortals to become cocreators with him in the divine plan of salvation, which stretches across the eternities and includes the opportunity for the faithful to participate in family life and eternal increase.

BIBLIOGRAPHY

Barlow, Brent A. "They Twain Shall Be One: Thoughts on Intimacy in Marriage." *Ensign* 16 (Sept. 1986):49–53.

Packer, Boyd K. "Why Stay Morally Clean." *Ensign* 2 (July 1972):111–13.

Pratt, Parley P. *The Writings of Parley P. Pratt,* ed. Parker P. Robison. Salt Lake City, 1952.

BRENT A. BARLOW

PROFANITY

General Authorities of the Church have defined profanity to include the following: (1) blasphemy (irreverent use of the Lord's name); (2) swearing; (3) vulgarity (coarse jokes, foul stories, lewd words); (4) use of the Lord's name without proper authority; and (5) any type of filthiness in speech that is degrading and soul-destroying.

Profanity has become a common practice among both young and old, both male and female, in today's society. Some may be inclined to say that the commandment "Thou shalt not take the name of the Lord thy God in vain" (Ex. 20:7) is outdated. However, the wide use of profanity in contemporary society does not excuse Latter-day Saints from using any form of profanity or other blasphemous speech: "The Lord will not hold him guiltless that taketh his [God's] name in vain" (Ex. 20:7). President Spencer W. Kimball told the Church, "We, as good Latter-day Saints . . . do not use foul language. We do not curse or defame. We do not use the Lord's name in vain" (1981, p. 5).

To strip profanity and vulgarity from one's vocabulary not only is commendable and a mark of refinement but it is also a commandment from God. Early members of the Church were told in a general epistle that "the habit . . . of using vulgarity and profanity . . . is not only offensive to all well-bred persons, but is a gross sin in the sight of God, and should not exist among the children of the Latter-day Saints" (*MFP* 3:112–13). Profanity makes the holy profane, the sacred commonplace, the serious flippant, and the precious cheap.

To refrain from profane and vulgar speech also shows self-control. H. Burke Peterson, of the Seventy and former First Counselor in the Presiding Bishopric, said, "We might consider vulgarity in a couple of ways: first, *as an expression* of personal weakness, and second, *as a contribution to* personal weakness" (Peterson, p. 38). Similarly, President Kimball described profanity as "the effort of a feeble brain to express itself forcibly" (1974, p. 7).

Instead of using profane speech, Latter-day Saints should "enlighten, edify, lift, motivate, elevate, build and uplift" others through their words (Brewerton, p. 73). By doing so, they will not forfeit the multitude of blessings promised them if they "bridle [their] tongues" (James 1:26).

BIBLIOGRAPHY

Brewerton, Ted E. "Profanity and Swearing." *Ensign* 13 (May 1983):72–74.

Kimball, Spencer W. "God Will Not Be Mocked." *Ensign* 4 (Nov. 1974):4–9.

———. "President Kimball Speaks Out on Profanity." *Ensign* 11 (Feb. 1981):5.

Peterson, H. Burke. "Purify Our Minds and Spirits." *Ensign* 10 (Nov. 1980):37–39.

GRANT VON HARRISON

PROHIBITION

Partly because belief in the WORD OF WISDOM supported abstinence from alcoholic beverages, Prohibition was an important political and moral issue for LDS leaders and members in the early twentieth century. Although LDS voters were naturally inclined to support legislation that limited the consumption of liquor, Utah, the state most affected by LDS votes, differed little from other western states in its position on Prohibition, with a variety of moral, political, and social issues influencing the position.

In 1908, when four states had already passed statewide prohibition laws, 600 saloons were operating in Utah. That year the national Anti-Saloon League began to recruit Prohibition supporters among the Protestant clergy and LDS General Authorities in the state. Heber J. Grant, then an apostle, became the leader among Latter-day Saints in lobbying for Prohibition. Utah Republican leader Senator Reed Smoot, also an apostle, was concerned that support for Prohibition might alienate non-Mormon Republican supporters. President Joseph F. Smith was also torn between his desire for Prohibition and his desire for defeat of the American Party, an anti-Mormon third party in the state. With many views affecting its vote, the 1909 state legislature narrowly defeated a statewide prohibition bill, and Governor William Spry later vetoed a local option bill that would have given cities authority to ban alcoholic beverage sales.

In 1910 President Smith instructed the Quorum of the Twelve to ignore statewide prohibition and work for local option. After a local option bill passed the state legislature in March 1911, Church leaders encouraged members to vote their communities "dry" in statewide elections. Most communities did so, but Salt Lake City, Ogden, and other cities with large non-LDS populations continued to allow the sale of alcohol.

Statewide prohibition again became a major political issue in 1915, with Elder Grant leading the supporters. Although Senator Smoot was no longer opposed to Prohibition, Governor Spry was. A prohibition bill easily passed the Utah legislature, but not in time to avoid the governor's pocket veto. During 1916 many LDS leaders were chagrined that Utah had not yet voted for Prohibition, particularly since Idaho, Colorado, Arizona, Washington, and Oregon had already done so.

Utah joined the ranks of the "dry" states on February 8, 1917, when newly elected Governor Simon Bamberger signed a law making Utah the twenty-third state to adopt statewide prohibition. In 1919 Utah joined other states in ratifying the Eighteenth Amendment to the federal Constitution, making Prohibition national in scope.

After the depression began in 1929, anti-Prohibition forces gained strength in Utah and the rest of the country. Nevertheless, led by Grant, who had become President of the Church in 1918, LDS leaders continued to support national Prohibition. Despite this support, the citizens of Utah voted in November 1933 for both national and state repeal. One month later Prohibition ended in Utah and the rest of the nation.

BIBLIOGRAPHY

Thompson, Brent G. "Standing Between Two Fires: Mormons and Prohibition, 1908–1917." *Journal of Mormon History* 10 (1983):35–52.

BRENT G. THOMPSON

PROLONGING LIFE

Medical science has made it possible to sustain physical life by artificial support systems under circumstances where functional and productive life may be no longer feasible. Prolonging life in these situations presents a moral and ethical dilemma for the medical profession and the family of the afflicted individual. On the one hand is the emotion of hope for recovery of useful function in a situation where the science of prognosis is imperfect and based to a certain extent on probability analysis, while on the other hand is the reality that physical death is imminent without life-support measures. Members of the medical profession deal with this dilemma by calculated evaluation of the data presented in the clinical situation and may present recommendations to the family and other concerned individuals as regards prognosis and what should be done. The family must analyze these recommendations in a situation clouded by the intense emotion of anticipated separation from a loved one.

Latter-day Saints are sustained during these trying times by their faith in Jesus Christ, whose teachings provide the strength, reason, and hope to guide one in making difficult decisions regarding life and death. "He that heareth my word, and believeth on him that sent me, hath everlasting life, and shall not come into condemnation; but is passed from death unto life" (John 5:24).

Jesus Christ presented himself as the Savior of mankind through the atonement and the resurrection: "I am the resurrection, and the life: he that believeth in me, though he were dead, yet shall he live: And he that liveth and believeth in me shall never die" (John 11:25–26).

Belief in everlasting life after mortal death should allow faithful Latter-day Saints to make wise and rational decisions regarding artificially prolonging life when medical means to restore useful and functional existence have been exhausted. This is reflected in Church policy regarding prolonging life:

> When severe illness strikes, Church members should exercise faith in the Lord and seek competent medical assistance. However, when dying becomes inevitable, death should be looked upon as a blessing and a purposeful part of an eternal existence. Members should not feel obligated to extend mortal life by means that are unreasonable. These judg-

ments are best made by family members after receiving wise and competent medical advice and seeking divine guidance through fasting and prayer [*General Handbook of Instruction*, 11-6].

BIBLIOGRAPHY

General Handbook of Instructions. Salt Lake City, 1989.

DONALD B. DOTY

PROTESTANTISM

Christian Protestantism may be viewed as the product of late medieval "protests" against various elements of the Roman Catholic church. Though there were always persons within Catholicism pressing for reforms, the beginning of the Protestant Reformation is usually dated to 1517 when Martin Luther (1483–1546), an Augustinian monk in Wittenberg, Germany, published his ninety-five theses against papal indulgences. The theses challenged the authority of the pope and by extension of the Roman Catholic church. Protestants since that time are generally considered to be those Christians who are neither Roman Catholics nor Eastern (or Russian) Orthodox.

Although Protestant theology is varied today, it can be characterized by four basic beliefs: (1) the Bible is the Word of God and all authority resides within its pages as it bears witness to Jesus Christ; (2) the Bible should be in the language of the people, who, by the power of the Holy Ghost, can gain their own understanding of God's Word; (3) all church members hold the priesthood and should be involved in the total life of the church, meaning that no mediatorial priesthood is necessary; and (4) people are saved by their faith, through the grace of God, and not by any works they may do apart from or in addition to faith.

While Latter-day Saints share with Protestants a conviction of the importance of the scriptures, an extensive lay priesthood (but given only by the laying on of hands by those having proper priesthood authority), and the primacy of faith in Jesus Christ as Lord and Savior as the first principle of the gospel, they differ from them by affirming a centralized authority headed by a latter-day prophet and by a number of other doctrines unique to the Church, i.e. temple ordinances for the living and the dead, and the eternal nature of the marriage covenant. Despite some important differences, Latter-day Saints actually share much in doctrine, heritage, and aspiration with Roman Catholics, Eastern Orthodox, and Protestants. Even so, they view themselves as embodying an independent Christian tradition standing on its own apart from these other traditions. The Church of Jesus Christ of Latter-day Saints is not a *reformation* of a previously existing ecclesiastical body but is instead a *restoration* through heavenly ministrations of authority and of truths, structures, and scriptures that God returned to the earth through the Prophet Joseph Smith and his successors.

BIBLIOGRAPHY
Dillenberger, John, and Claude Welch. *Protestant Christianity.* New York, 1954.

JOHN DILLENBERGER
ROGER KELLER

PROTESTANT REFORMATION

The sixteenth-century Reformation was a major religious upheaval that has had repercussions to the present day. When Martin Luther challenged the Catholic doctrine of the sacraments, boldly declaring that salvation comes not by human works but by the grace of God alone through faith in Jesus Christ, he set in motion a complex series of events that not only broke the religious stronghold of the Catholic church but also had a profound impact on political, social, and cultural events as well.

LDS perspective regards the Protestant Reformation as a preparation for the more complete restoration of the gospel that commenced with Joseph Smith. Thus, the Protestant Reformation initiated a return to pure Christianity, a work that could not be completed without divine revelation and restoration. The leaders of the Reformation are honored as inspired men who made important progress, but without direct revelation they could not recover the true gospel or the priesthood authority to act in God's name. That was the mission of the Prophet Joseph Smith.

Perhaps the greatest legacy of the Reformation was the

increased attention to freedom, one's own freedom more than that of others. This concern eventually grew into religious toleration and the desire for greater political self-determination. The ending of the single, "universal" church and the proliferation of new churches and sects had echoes in the political arena, most notably in the independence of the United States of America. A great many factors contributed to the establishment of the United States, but the political and religious heritage of the Protestant reformers was certainly among them.

The restoration of the gospel through Joseph Smith took place within the context of this post-Reformation world. Yet Joseph Smith is not considered a successor to the reformers in the sense of building on their teachings. He claimed to receive his knowledge and priesthood authority directly by revelation, not by the study of other writers, thus initiating a new dispensation of the gospel rather than a continuation of the Reformation.

The religious environment of early-nineteenth-century America was predominantly Protestant. That environment encouraged religious differences and resulted in many rival churches. Among the characteristics of that religious revivalism was an emphasis on the Bible and Bible reading, a feature that was first promoted by the sixteenth-century humanists and reformers. The Bible used by Joseph Smith and others of his day was the English King James Version of 1611. It was his own reading of the Bible (in particular James 1:5–6) that led Joseph Smith to his first personal encounter with God.

The Reformation legacy is also seen in the frontier emphasis on congregational religion, emphasizing the right and ability of individual congregations to organize themselves as autonomous religious bodies, conducting their own worship services and generally governing their own affairs. Congregationalism grew out of the sixteenth- and seventeenth-century English Calvinist tradition in particular, but it was also practiced by other groups.

Especially important in relation to the Restoration was the concept that religion is personal, a one-on-one relationship between God and the individual worshiper. This was a key feature of the Reformation Anabaptists, who believed, much as Latter-day Saints do, in personal revelation and individual responsibility. The

Anabaptists rejected infant baptism, teaching instead that baptism was a cleansing covenant with God, entered into only after the exercise of faith and repentance. Many other Anabaptist doctrines are remarkably similar to Latter-day Saints beliefs, including the concept of restoration itself, which the Anabaptists called Restitution—meaning the restitution of the apostolic Church of the New Testament.

Not as many specific doctrines are shared with mainline Protestants, but Latter-day Saints do have in common a devoted faith in Jesus Christ as Redeemer of the world and as personal Savior. This faith was the moving force in the actions of Martin Luther and other early reformers, and was central to the life and work of the Prophet Joseph Smith. It remains today a central tenet of the Church.

BIBLIOGRAPHY

Grimm, Harold J. *The Reformation Era, 1500–1650,* 2nd ed. New York, 1965.
Jensen, De Lamar. *Reformation Europe: Age of Reform and Revolution,* 2nd ed. Lexington, Mass., 1981.
Spitz, Lewis W. *The Protestant Reformation, 1517–1559.* New York, 1985.

DE LAMAR JENSEN

PUBLIC COMMUNICATIONS

The Public Affairs Department of The Church of Jesus Christ of Latter-day Saints was organized in 1972 in response to a long-felt need for channeling and coordinating information about the growing Church throughout the world. The department handles news-media relations, hosts visiting dignitaries, and maintains liaison with volunteer public communications representatives called to serve in stakes and missions. Originally, the department also produced radio and television public service announcements and exhibits for Temple Square and other VISITORS CENTERS, but these functions were later transferred to the Missionary Department of the Church. In 1983 the department's name was expanded to Public Communications/Special Affairs after the original department merged with Special Affairs, the Church's government and community relations office.

Forerunners to the department were the Church Radio, Publicity, and Mission Literature Committee, organized in 1935 with recently returned missionary Gordon B. Hinckley (later an apostle and counselor in the First Presidency) as its director, and the Church Information Service, organized in 1957 with Theodore Cannon as director. Wendell J. Ashton was the first managing director of the Public Communications Department. Subsequent managing directors have been Heber G. Wolsey (1978–1983), Richard P. Lindsay (1983–1989), and Bruce L. Olsen (1989–).

Divisions in the department include Media Relations; National News Placement; Community Relations; Field Publications Liaison; Hosting; and Administration. Area offices with full-time directors are situated in Washington, D.C.; Los Angeles; Toronto; London; Paris; Frankfurt; São Paulo; and Sydney. The headquarters staff in Salt Lake City coordinates the efforts of local public communications directors, designated to serve in the stakes, regions, and areas.

The department is responsible to, and counsels with, the Church's Special Affairs Committee, comprised of members of the Quorum of the Twelve Apostles and the Presidency of the Quorums of the Seventy. It maintains ongoing contacts with news media at local, national, and international levels. The staff prepares and distributes both print and electronic news and feature releases about the Church, its programs, events, and activities. Public-affairs radio and television programs are produced and distributed for the use of the media and community organizations; queries from the media and the public are answered; and news media representatives are hosted. Designated spokespersons convey Church policy statements on pertinent issues to the public via the media. Designated staff members monitor legislative issues affecting the Church, its operations, and its members, and keep the leaders of the Church apprised of such developments. In addition, designated members of the staff join with representatives of other Churches and national organizations committed to combat such things as pornography, alcohol abuse, gambling, and various other social problems.

ARCH L. MADSEN

PUBLIC RELATIONS

Many public relations programs, activities, and services exist in The Church of Jesus Christ of Latter-day Saints to support its public ministry. These efforts are coordinated by the Church Public Affairs Department and are grounded in Christ's instruction to his disciples, "Go ye therefore, and teach all nations" (Matt. 28:19). This instruction was repeated in revelations to the Prophet Joseph Smith (D&C 1:4–5; 49:11–14; 71:1–2; 84:62).

Making Christ's gospel known throughout the world has been central to the Church's purpose from the beginning. Sharing the gospel requires Church members to reach out to others (*see* TOLERANCE). Various approaches have been used over the years to attract interest and to introduce and explain the Church, its people, and their beliefs. Now, as at first, personal communication and distribution of printed materials, especially the Book of Mormon, are the principal methods of sharing the gospel. Joseph Smith's brother Samuel undertook the first formal missionary journey shortly after the Church was organized in April 1830. Soon, other missionaries went to the eastern United States, to Canada, and to England, taking with them the Book of Mormon as their primary teaching tool and preaching to local congregations and in homes and at street meetings. In 1831 the Church purchased a printing press and by 1832 had begun producing newspapers, books, and broadsides.

Organized missionary work is a major part of Church public relations. Since 1830, more than half a million members of the Church have served as full-time missionaries. As of 1990, they were serving in eighty-eight countries and twenty-two territories, teaching in sixty-seven languages and providing printed materials in more than fifty languages. In addition to scriptures, tracts, and other reading material, missionaries have added videotapes and other modern visual aids to their presentations.

The Church fosters cultural and social relationships with the general public through concerts, theatrical performances, and making Church buildings available for civic and educational events. For example, before its own facility was built, the Utah Symphony used the Salt Lake Tabernacle for its performances free of charge for thirty-two years. Church buildings also have been used as polling places and for town meetings and other noncommercial gatherings.

The MORMON TABERNACLE CHOIR is prominent in the Church's public relations image. In early recognition of its appeal, the choir was invited to perform at the World's Columbian Exposition in 1893 (*see* EXHIBITIONS AND WORLD FAIRS). The choir's radio broadcast, presented weekly since 1929, is the longest-running network program in broadcasting history (*see* BROADCASTING). The choir has made more than 150 recordings, has performed at U.S. presidential inaugurations and world fairs, and has gone on many concert tours.

In 1935 the Church formed a Radio, Publicity, and Mission Literature Committee to develop ways to use the latest communications media in missionary work. The committee produced film strips, pamphlets, tracts, books, recordings, radio programs, and exhibits and supervised translations of the Book of Mormon. Under President David O. McKay, the Church began to use professional public relations consultants, who recommended that the Tabernacle Choir make recordings with the Philadelphia Symphony Orchestra and worked to obtain press coverage of the CUMORAH PAGEANT in New York. In 1957 the Church Information Service was begun, with a primary purpose to distribute accurate information about Church activities of interest to the general public.

In 1972 the Church formed a Department of Public Communications. In 1974 President Spencer W. Kimball stated: "When we have used the satellite and related discoveries to their greatest potential, and all the media—papers, magazines, television, radio— . . . to their greatest power, . . . then and not until then shall we approach the insistence of our Lord and Savior to go into all the world and preach the Gospel to every creature" ("When the World Will Be Converted," Regional Representatives' seminar, Apr. 4, 1974). Accordingly, the Public Affairs Department, headquartered in Salt Lake City (with smaller offices in twelve other cities), and staffed by full-time public-relations professionals, focuses on serving the media and effectively using modern communications technology.

The Church makes regular use of network and cable television, radio, telephones, print, and electronic exhibits for programming and public-service advertising in many countries.

Services to the media include recorded newscasts; radio, television, and print releases; features and interviews; magazine pieces; and broadcast-quality public affairs programs. Church news regarding doctrines and activities is available through official releases. Also, Church positions on public issues such as pornography, drugs, and parenting are announced.

The Public Affairs Department coordinates the volunteer service of 3,500 local public communications directors in the stakes and missions of the Church. These individuals, many of them business and professional leaders, interact with local media and arrange coverage of Church events of local interest. They report to the Church on public reactions in their local areas and, as directed, respond to commendations and criticism.

When the Church is criticized (see ANTI-MORMON PUBLICATIONS) or involved in controversy, the Public Affairs Department may provide responses and position statements. The standard Church response to criticism is to deal respectfully but not to debate with critics. When controversy arises, the Church strives to keep its comments within the scope of its activities, so as not to interfere with the jurisdiction of other entities.

Under the direction of the Missionary Department, the Church maintains some thirty-seven volunteer-staffed VISITORS CENTERS and historical sites. Volunteers also conduct tours of new and remodeled temples before they are dedicated. About ten million people annually tour Church places of interest. Distinguished visitors to Church headquarters in Salt Lake City are hosted by volunteers who arrange tours, visits to members' homes, interviews with Church leaders or directors of Welfare Square, and visits to the FAMILY HISTORY LIBRARY, the Museum of Church History and Art (see MUSEUMS), and other sites.

In 1988 the Church became a charter member of the Vision Interfaith Satellite Network, a project of twenty-two faith groups. A milestone in interdenominational cooperation, VISN provides people of faith with original, value-based cable television programs. The Church's programs appear in the schedule fourteen or more times weekly.

BIBLIOGRAPHY

For a general overview, see Leonard Arrington and Davis Bitton, *The Mormon Experience: A History of the Latter-day Saints* (New York, 1979). The symposium on the Church and the public media in *Dialogue* 10 (Spring 1977) includes an interview with Wendell Ashton (then managing director of public communications) and articles on history, journalism, and the challenges of presenting a clear and appealing, but not misleading, image of the Church to a wide variety of public audiences.

ELIZABETH M. HAGLUND

R

RACE, RACISM

The Church of Jesus Christ of Latter-day Saints teaches that all humans are literally the spirit offspring of the eternal Heavenly Father (Acts 17:26, 29). The concept of race refers to populations identifiable by the frequency with which a selected number of genetically determined traits appear in that population. While all human groups belong to the same species (*Homo sapiens*), they may be differentiated into various races by such traits as skin pigmentation, hair color, head shape, and nose form. A negative concept of racism implies that one set of racial characteristics is superior to others. The Church denounces this viewpoint.

In 1775, Johann Friedrich Blumenbach established five human races differentiated by skin color. Later anthropologists used other characteristics of the human body and arrived at a different number of racial subdivisions, from a minimum of two to a maximum of several dozen. By limiting criteria, most anthropologists now agree on the existence of three distinct groups: the Caucasoid, the Mongoloid, and the Negroid.

The apostle Paul taught in the New Testament that God "hath made of one blood all nations of men for to dwell on all the face of the earth" (Acts 17:26). In the sight of God, race, color, and nationality make no difference, an idea stressed in the Book of Mormon: "He inviteth them all to come unto him and partake of his goodness;

421

and he denieth none that come unto him, black and white, bond and free, male and female; and he remembereth the heathen; and all are alike unto God, both Jew and Gentile" (2 Ne. 26:33).

Spencer W. Kimball, in speaking of race and racism as President of the Church, said: "We do wish that there would be no racial prejudice. . . . Racial prejudice is of the devil. . . . There is no place for it in the gospel of Jesus Christ" (pp. 236–37).

Latter-day Saints believe that Jesus Christ came to earth to die for all mankind and to teach them how to live. He taught two great commandments: first, to love God with all one's heart, might, mind, and strength; second, to love one's fellow men as one loves oneself (Matt. 22:36–39). Throughout his life, Jesus showed how to obey these two commandments.

Prior to June 1978, priesthood denial to blacks within the Church aroused both concern about, and accusations of, racism in the Church, especially during the civil rights movement of the 1960s in the United States. For more than a century Presidents of the Church had taught that blacks were not yet to receive the priesthood, for reasons known only to God, but would someday receive it. As made clear in Official Declaration—2 (appended to the Doctrine and Covenants in September 1978), there had long been an anticipation that the priesthood would be made available to all worthy men—an anticipation realized and announced June 9, 1978.

In the October 1978 Semiannual general conference of the Church, President Spencer W. Kimball restated to the world that he had received a revelation making all worthy male members of the Church eligible for the priesthood without regard for race or color.

BIBLIOGRAPHY
Bush, Lester E., Jr., and Armand L. Mauss, eds. *Neither White Nor Black*. Midvale, Utah, 1984.
Hunter, Howard W. "All Are Alike Unto God." *Ensign* 9 (June 1979):72–74.
Kimball, Spencer W. *The Teachings of Spencer W. Kimball*, ed. Edward L. Kimball. Salt Lake City, 1982.
LeBaron, Dale E. *All Are Alike Unto God*. Salt Lake City, 1990.

RITA DE CASSIA FLORES
ENOC Q. FLORES

RELIGIOUS EXPERIENCE

In the gospel of Jesus Christ, personal religious experience is the foundation, vitality, and culmination of religious life. As in the biblical book of Acts, LDS religious experience is varied and owes as much to firsthand experience as to texts and traditions. Latter-day Saints may recognize as a religious experience feelings or impressions that build faith in Christ, show that God hears and answers prayer, manifest what is good and right, enhance personal conviction of truth, or confirm that one's life is approved of God. The sum of one's religious experiences is sometimes called a "testimony." Interpretations of these experiences are derived from cumulative personal experience, which language is often inadequate to describe. The frequency, intelligibility, coherence, and shareability of these phenomena among Latter-day Saints are relatively unique.

Regardless of individual differences in age, culture, and language, such experiences enhance the underlying unity of the members of the Church, enabling them to feel one with each other and with the prophets. They recognize familiar religious experiences in one another's words and actions and in the scriptures. While the transmission of these experiences is often oral (as in testimony meetings, classes, conversations), many are also preserved in diaries, journals, and family histories. Some of these have become widely familiar and almost normative.

At the core of a Latter-day Saint's life is conversion to the gospel. First impressions are often crucial. Converts frequently testify to feeling a divine assurance, unexpected and unheralded, that truth is to be found in the Book of Mormon and in the teachings of the Church. They also commonly speak of feeling clean, of being washed of their sins, and of being spiritually reborn with an infusion of new life, peace, joy, light, warmth, and fire. The experience of finding oneself, though a sinner, accepted by the Lord, often becomes the foundation of a lifetime commitment to God, because maintaining this feeling is desired above all else. Classic examples of this are found in the conversions of Alma$_2$ (Mosiah 27; Alma 36) and Joseph Smith (*PJS* 1:5–8).

Latter-day Saints believe that the divine love they receive in individual religious experience should be reflected to others as charity (Mosiah 2:17–21; 5:2; Moro. 7:46). Rendering service to others in the name of Christ produces feelings of joy and happiness that Latter-day Saints treasure as religious experiences.

Baptized members are given the gift of the Holy Ghost by the laying on of hands, entitling them to the companionship of the Holy Ghost. President Lorenzo Snow described his reception of this gift as "a tangible immersion in the heavenly principle or element, the Holy Ghost" (*Biography and Family Record of Lorenzo Snow* p. 8, Salt Lake City, 1884), saying that he "tasted the joys of eternity in the midst of the power of God" (Journal, p. 3, Church Archives, Salt Lake City). Alfred D. Young said it was "as if warm water was poured over me coming on my head first. I was filled with light, peace and joy" [*Autobiography (1808-1842)*, BYU Special Collections].

Individual Latter-day Saints speak of being shown righteous courses of action by the Holy Ghost, being warned of dangers and evils, and being otherwise inspired and guided. One sister, reflecting on her life, wrote that the Holy Ghost "warns, counsels, reproves, commends, instructs, and when necessary commands" (*YWJ* 27 [Nov. 1916]:691–92). Motivational changes are chronicled, as are infusions of energy, compassion, insight, healing power, and beauty, and also refinement of talents, faculties of communication, and Christlike love.

Impressions of the Holy Ghost often come after much preparation in fasting, prayer, service, and study. At other times they come unbidden and arrive at unexpected moments as a "still, small voice" (1 Kgs. 19:12). The Prophet Joseph Smith observed that the word of the Lord "has such an influence over the human mind—the logical mind—that it is convincing without other testimony" (*HC* 5:526). Joseph Smith further remarked, "sudden strokes of ideas" from the Holy Ghost attend a flow of pure intelligence (*TPJS*, p. 151); "the answer comes into my mind with such a logical sequence of thought and ideas, and accompanied by such a burning feeling within, that I know it is of God" (cited in W. Berrett, "Revelation," address to seminary and institute faculty, Brigham Young University, June 27, 1956, p. 9).

Such influences and impressions of the Holy Ghost may come as inspiration amid duties in the home, at work, or in Church callings, as well as self-knowledge in the most menial of everyday tasks. Typical reported examples include a glimpse of celestial origins and destiny (Heber C. Kimball); impressions of impending events (Wilford Woodruff); guidance and reassurance in emotional crises such as the death of a loved one (Zina D. H. Young); or insight and strength in pressing practical needs or predicaments (Amanda Smith). Many members of the Church attest to receiving inspiration in creative processes, such as when writing religious poetry, drama, music, or scriptural commentary, or when seeking a solution to a scientific or genealogical research problem. Personal revelation is probably the most widely shared and unifying form of religious experience among Latter-day Saints. It also helps explain the confidence with which many Latter-day Saints make religious decisions.

Latter-day Saints may receive individual blessings from a priesthood bearer in which they seek the guidance of the Holy Spirit (*see* FATHERS' BLESSINGS). Through such personal experiences most Latter-day Saints have received needed direction, restoration of spiritual and physical health, or other divine aid. One Church leader describes the giving and receiving of blessings as vitalizing and enlightening, through "an essence of force or power" inherent in the holy priesthood. Diaries commonly report experiences such as this: "He blessed me. I felt the influence and power of the Lord upon him and upon me. I have never forgotten that blessing from that day to this and I never shall" (Ezra T. Clark).

A wide range of manifestations of the Spirit—visions, dreams, visitations, contact with the dead, miraculous aid in answer to prayer—is known in every LDS community, though not generally publicly heralded. For example, Karl G. Maeser reported experiencing the gift of interpretation where all language and cultural barriers were removed; Franklin D. Richards received the gift of prophetic dreams; James G. Marsh, the gift of visions; and Lucy Mack Smith, the gift of faith.

LDS religious experience also includes pentecostal outpourings, dramatic and overwhelming spiritual manifestations, witnessed simultaneously by many people and recorded privately. Of the foundation experiences of the Restoration the most crucial were shared, witnessed, and recorded. Each conferral of divine priesthood authority was shared by at least two persons and included visitations analogous to the appearance of Moses and Elijah on the Mount of Transfiguration (Matt. 17:2–4). Here the experience was no less objective than the deliverances of sense-experience. Several hundred experienced the outpouring of spiritual gifts in the Kirtland Temple dedication (see Backman, pp. 284–309). Several thousand, including many children, witnessed the experience in Nauvoo when the "mantle" fell upon Brigham Young and he was providentially portrayed in Joseph Smith's likeness. Approximately 63,000 participated in the dedicatory sessions of the Salt Lake Temple, and many reported seeing visions and hearing heavenly music.

LDS journals are replete with testimonies that the Spirit of the Lord enlivens all of the senses—seeing, hearing, smelling, tasting, and touching—and that one is more physically alive and aware when spiritually quickened. This illumination is more than an aid to physical perception; it is a medium of comprehension. Latter-day Saints sometimes speak of a "sixth sense," interrelated with the other senses, that apprehends spiritual things. All things "are revealed to our spirits precisely as though we had no bodies at all" (*TPJS*, p. 355). One may be lighted up "with the glory of [his] former home" (J. F. Smith, *GD*, p. 14) and be led to say with Eliza R. Snow, "I felt that I had wandered from a more exalted sphere" ("O My Father," *Hymns of The Church of Jesus Christ of Latter-day Saints*, no. 292, Salt Lake City, 1985).

Many Latter-day Saints record such experiences in the setting of temple ordinances, sensing a oneness with departed friends and relatives—"they are not far from us, and know and understand our thoughts, feelings, and motions, and are often pained therewith" (*TPJS*, p. 326)—and "seeming to see" and "seeming to hear" the realms of the spirit world (J. Grant, *JD* 4:134–36).

LDS spiritual experiences are often related to scripture study. One convert had mastered the entire Bible in Hebrew, German, and English. After receiving the gift of the Holy Ghost, he found new meaning in familiar verses (O. Hyde, *JD* 8:23–24). Another who had memorized New Testament books found, after receiving the Holy Ghost, that "new light dawned upon" him in "bold relief," which the Book of Mormon clarified and confirmed: "Truths were manifested to me that I had never heard of or read of, but which I afterwards heard preached by the servants of the Lord" (C. Penrose, *JD* 23:351). Still another, praying through his youth for some great manifestation, learned slowly and for a lifetime, "line upon line, precept upon precept," until he felt his whole being was a testimony of the truth (J. F. Smith, *GD*, pp. 501–550).

Today, psychological, positivistic, and existential thought raises questions about religious awareness. There is much preoccupation with criteria of meaning and with the logic of religious discourse. The sum of LDS religious experience, however, suggests that anyone may appeal to the way of the prophets: Look and see.

BIBLIOGRAPHY
Backman, Milton V., Jr. *The Heavens Resound*, pp. 284–309. Salt Lake City, 1983.
Madsen, Truman G. "Joseph Smith and the Ways of Knowing." BYU Extension Publications, Provo, Utah, 1962.

TRUMAN G. MADSEN

RELIGIOUS FREEDOM

[*Latter-day Saints have always been vigorous defenders of religious liberty and have frequently been the victims of religious persecution. For accounts of LDS beliefs concerning religious freedom see* Church and State; Constitution of the United States; *and* Politics: Political Teachings. *The history of the LDS struggle for freedom is summarized in* Politics: Political History. *The efforts of the Church to be recognized and to enjoy religious liberty in new countries are explained in* Diplomatic Relations.]

RESTORATIONISM, PROTESTANT

Beginning about 1800, a religious movement known as the Second Great Awakening swept across the American frontier. The Church of Jesus Christ of Latter-day Saints emerged in this setting.

Many people in this period were seeking the original vitality of the New Testament Church, and those who espoused this point of view were called "restorationists." Protestant restorationism, as manifested in the early nineteenth century, followed the lead of the early reformers Martin Luther and John Calvin, who believed that the church should be firmly rooted in the scriptures. But even their theologies contained complexities that to the nineteenth century restorationists seemed far removed from day-to-day life. Men of differing persuasions, often unlettered, emerged to sound the cry for the restoration of biblical Christianity.

In New England, Elias Smith and Abner Jones, both Baptists, organized a "Christian church" in Portsmouth, New Hampshire. They sought the New Testament Church in its simple, nondenominational form and thus called themselves Christians. In Virginia and North Carolina, a similar movement developed under the leadership of James O'Kelly and Rice Haggard, both dissatisfied Methodist ministers. Their group was also to be known as Christians, and the Bible was to be their only creed. In 1811, the two groups united. William Kincaid, an illiterate frontiersman, converted at a revival meeting, led another group of Christians in Kentucky.

Barton W. Stone, a Presbyterian minister from Virginia and North Carolina, sought the experience of religion that he saw in the New Testament. He finally left the Presbyterian church in Kentucky to found a "Christian church." Thomas Campbell, a Presbyterian educated in Glasgow, Scotland, believed the church should be founded upon the Bible only, and his followers coined the slogan, "Where scripture speaks, we speak, and where scripture is silent, we are silent." In Pennsylvania he founded the Christian Association of Washington for the cultivation of piety. His son, Alexander, who influenced Sidney Rigdon, was the restorationist who founded the church known today as the Disciples of Christ.

Virtually all restorationists believed that the New Testament Church was to be restored, that there should be no CREEDS, that baptism should be by immersion, that salvation was through faith and repentance, and that there were a remission of sins and a gift of the Holy Ghost. They differed, however, in other points: whether the remission of sins and the gift of the Holy Ghost were a result of baptism, simply a product of faith, or conferred by the laying on of hands; whether there had been a loss of authority; whether all things were to be restored, including New Testament miracles and gifts of the

Spirit, or whether only some things would be restored; and whether religious experience was necessary.

Latter-day Saints were more comprehensively restorationist than any other group. The principal LDS beliefs that created the most discussion were that the authority of the priesthood was restored to Joseph Smith by heavenly messengers; that remission of sins follows baptism, which is essential to salvation; that all things (including miracles) are to be restored; that revelation is as requisite today as in the past; and that, as in the New Testament Church, the scriptural canon is not closed. The acceptance of these beliefs led Sidney Rigdon to break with Alexander Campbell and embrace the restored gospel as taught by Latter-day Saint missionaries.

BIBLIOGRAPHY

Bushman, Richard L. *Joseph Smith and the Beginnings of Mormonism*. Urbana and Chicago, 1988.

Garrison, Winfred Ernest. *Religion Follows the Frontier: A History of the Disciples of Christ*. New York, 1931.

JOHN DILLENBERGER
ROGER R. KELLER

RICKS COLLEGE

Ricks College is a private, two-year accredited college owned and operated by The Church of Jesus Christ of Latter-day Saints in Rexburg, Idaho, an agricultural community in the heart of the Upper Snake River Valley (less than 100 miles south of the Yellowstone/Grand Teton National Parks). With approximately 7,500 students and 300 faculty, Ricks is one of the largest private two-year colleges in the United States. It is a liberal arts college with a broad curriculum in the arts and sciences, and it is also noted for its career programs in technology, agriculture, nursing, and other disciplines.

Ricks College grants the associate degree in arts and sciences, emphasizing general education to students who plan to pursue bachelor's degrees at four-year colleges or universities, as well as degrees in specialized programs.

HISTORY.   LDS settlers in the Rexburg area were faced with sending their children to public schools where sentiment was strong against them. In November 1888 the settlers established the Bannock Stake Academy, an elementary school with eighty-two students and three teachers, with Thomas E. Ricks, the president of the Bannock Stake, as Chairman of the Bannock Stake Academy Board of Education. In 1898 it was renamed the Fremont Stake Academy and high school courses were added. On October 1, 1903, the school was named Ricks Academy after Thomas E. Ricks. In 1915 college courses were first taught. During the Great Depression it was rumored that the school would be closed. The Church offered to give the college to the state of Idaho, but that offer was rejected, and the Church continued its operation. Under John L. Clarke, president of Ricks from 1944 to 1971, the college expanded from a student body of 200 to 5,150. In the late 1940s the Church Board of Education approved third and fourth college years, and for six years the college graduated students with four-year degrees. However, in 1956 Ricks discontinued its junior and senior years. Since 1984 the college has again experienced rapid growth, and in 1989 the Board of Trustees set the 7,500 enrollment ceiling.

MISSION. The mission of Ricks College is officially declared to (1) build testimonies of the restored gospel of Jesus Christ and encourage living its principles; (2) provide a high-quality education for students of diverse interests and abilities; (3) prepare students for further education and employment, and for their roles as citizens and parents; and (4) maintain a wholesome academic, cultural, social, and spiritual environment.

GENERAL EDUCATION. The Ricks College General Education program is designed to help students develop the ability to think and write clearly, maintain lifelong patterns of effective living, appreciate aesthetic and creative expressions of humanity, gain knowledge of the social and natural world, understand themselves and their relationship to God, and cultivate sensitivity to personal relationships, moral responsibilities, and service to society. Students seeking associate degrees study religion, English literature and composition, natural and physical science, social science, and health and physical fitness, and they must demonstrate proficiency in mathematics.

PHYSICAL PLANT, MATERIALS, AND EQUIPMENT.   The Ricks College main campus is located on 255 acres at the south edge of Rexburg. In 1990, the main campus had forty-six buildings with about 1.6 million square feet of space and a replacement value of nearly $110 million. These buildings contained equipment valued at over $21 million.

The library, a building of 98,000 square feet, includes a serials collection of 750 titles and contains nearly 141,000 volumes, excluding bound periodicals and government publications.

The college owns a livestock center as part of its agricultural program on 140 acres, including 21 buildings, a few miles west of Rexburg. The college also owns a 160-acre outdoor learning facility on Badger Creek in Teton Valley.

RELATIONSHIP TO THE CHURCH.   The Ricks College Board of Trustees is composed of Church leaders and is chaired by the President of the Church. The Church provides approximately 70 percent of the operating funds for the college. Student tuition and fees, campus auxiliary income, and gifts to the college provide the remainder of college operating funds.

Currently (1990) thirty-six student wards in four stakes function at Ricks College. Students are required to take religion courses every semester. Graduates of Ricks consistently remark on the unique spirit of the college, the commitment of faculty to the progress of students, and the overall sense of community and caring they experienced there.

STUDENTS.   Ricks College has an open admission policy. Selectivity is used only as it applies to the Code of Honor, which each student must promise, in an ecclesiastical interview, to observe. Since Ricks has academic programs spanning a wide range of ability levels, the goal has been to admit any student who could benefit from the Ricks College experience.

Currently the Admissions Office admits 95 percent of those who apply. Of those admitted, approximately 80 percent actually enroll. Students from all fifty states and thirty foreign countries attend Ricks.

The attrition rate at Ricks is higher than at most two-year colleges because many Latter-day Saint students attend Ricks for one year and then serve a Church mission. Once they complete the mission, many desire to move to a university. In 1989–1990, Ricks College graduated 1,557 students.

BIBLIOGRAPHY
Jolley, JoAnn. "Rexburg and Ricks College." *Ensign* 14 (Jan. 1984):21–27.

SCOTT SAMUELSON

S

SAINTS

The revealed name of the Church is The Church of Jesus Christ of Latter-day Saints (D&C 115:4), wherein the term "saints" is synonymous with "members." The Church has no "patron saints" and does not canonize or venerate the dead. The usage of the term follows biblical precedents in which "saints" refers to Israelites as the chosen people of God—that is, as a community of believers set apart from nonbelievers (cf. "the congregation of the saints," Ps. 89:5). The Hebrew and Aramaic usage of the term in the Old Testament and in the writings of the Essene community is *qadosh* and *qaddish*, respectively, meaning "separate, set apart, holy."

Paul used the term "saint" (Greek *hagios* also denotes "set apart, separate, holy") in referring to baptized members of the Church of his day (e.g., Phil. 1:1). The Book of Mormon also designates "saints of God" as all those who belong to the "church of the Lamb" (1 Ne. 14:12).

Used this way, the term today denotes all members of Christ's Church, who, through baptism, have expressed a desire to follow the Savior's counsel to become more Godlike, toward the ideal to be "even as your Father which is in heaven is perfect" (Matt. 5:48), and who, though imperfect, strive to live in a manner that will lead them toward that goal.

BIBLIOGRAPHY
Nelson, Russell M. "Thus Shall My Church Be Called." *Ensign* 20 (May 1990):16–18.

JAMES K. LYON

SATANISM

The cult of Satanism has evolved over many years. At the present time, symbols related to Satan have become so prevalent that the warning voices of leaders in the Church have again been raised concerning some people's fascination with the power of evil. Latter-day Saints are admonished to avoid any contact with Satanism, even with the good intention of learning about it in order to warn others of its dangers.

The answer that Jesus Christ gave when Satan offered him the glories of the world if he would fall down and worship him could be a guide to Church members when confronted with similar temptations: "Get thee hence, Satan: for it is written, Thou shalt worship the Lord thy God, and him only shalt thou serve" (Matt. 4:10).

Bruce R. McConkie, an apostle, warned, "One of Satan's greatest aims, as he works his nefarious schemes among men, is to get them 'to worship him'" (*MD*, p. 193). From earliest times, many evil things have been done in the name of Satan worship (Moses 6:49). Satanism may claim to offer powers beyond those available to humans through righteous sources, but the worship of Satan leads only to destruction.

The forces of evil cannot overcome a person without some willingness on the part of the individual (1 Cor. 10:13). President Brigham Young said, "You are aware that many think that the Devil has rule and power over both body and spirit. Now, I want to tell you that he does not hold any power over man, only so far as the body overcomes the spirit that is in a man, through yielding to the spirit of evil" (pp. 69–70).

BIBLIOGRAPHY
Cannon, George Q. *Gospel Truth*, ed. Jerreld L. Newquist. Salt Lake City, 1987.
Young, Brigham. *Discourses of Brigham Young*, ed. John A. Widtsoe. Salt Lake City, 1946.

JANET THOMAS

SATELLITE COMMUNICATIONS SYSTEM

Communications satellites, as here referred to, are small radio transmitters orbiting the earth. Typical geosynchronous orbits are 22,300 miles above the equator. These tiny man-made moons make possible transmission of voice, data, radio, and television signals to every point on the globe. The introduction of The Church of Jesus Christ of Latter-day Saints to satellite broadcasting came during the first satellite exchange between North America and Europe, which included a performance by the MORMON TABERNACLE CHOIR in front of Mount Rushmore, South Dakota. Since that time the Church has developed its own private satellite distribution system. In 1982 it purchased transponder capacity on Westar IV from the Public Broadcasting Service. Transmitting, or "uplink," facilities were built in City Creek Canyon near Salt Lake City from which signals from the tabernacle and elsewhere could be beamed into space. Receiving, or "downlink," antennas were installed at many stake centers across North America. The Church has global communication capabilities, enabling signals to reach cable operators, stake centers, and other satellite receiving facilities.

Programming sent by Church satellite includes conferences, educational and professional training, firesides and special religious programs, entertainment, and BRIGHAM YOUNG UNIVERSITY sports. Most important, this system brings the General Authorities closer to the Saints throughout the world.

Satellite communications systems allow for open as well as encoded transmissions. This flexibility permits Church use of the system for public as well as private communications. The private use holds the promise expressed by President Gordon B. Hinckley in a general conference address: "We are now expanding the miracle of satellite transmission . . . to develop the means whereby the membership of the Church, wherever they may be, can be counselled in an intimate and personal way by [the Lord's] chosen prophet. Communication is the sinew that binds the Church as one great family" (p. 5).

BIBLIOGRAPHY
Hinckley, Gordon B. "Faith: The Essence of True Religion." *Ensign* 11 (Nov. 1981):5.

Pace, Geoffrey L. "The Emergence of Bonneville Satellite Corporation: A Study of Conception and Development of a New Telecommunications Service." Master's thesis, Brigham Young University, 1983, pp. 12–79.

BRUCE L. CHRISTENSEN

SCHOOLS

LDS theology places great importance on the acquiring of knowledge. This knowledge includes not only religious truth but truth in the sciences, arts, and humanities as well (*TPJS*, p. 217; D&C 131:6). Congruent with that value and throughout its history, the Church has established and operated numerous schools and universities to provide educational opportunities for its members.

Comprehensive higher education is offered at Brigham Young University (campuses at Provo, Utah; Laie, Hawaii; and Jerusalem, Israel) and Ricks College in Rexburg, Idaho. Correspondence study is also available at the secondary, college, and adult education levels through Brigham Young University. The LDS Business College in Salt Lake City offers postsecondary instruction in business and related fields. Full-time primary and secondary schools currently are owned and administered by the Church in the South Pacific and Mexico, providing education to approximately 10,000 students.

In the Pacific islands, two high schools, one large elementary school, and four meetinghouse elementary schools are operated in Samoa, two high schools in Tonga, one technical college and one elementary school in Fiji, one high school in Kiribati, and the Church College of New Zealand in Hamilton. Initially established to provide an educational opportunity for the Maori people, the college in New Zealand presently is a high school with college preparatory courses. Local teachers are hired on a full-time basis, and in a few cases full-time missionary couples with educational experience also provide instruction.

In Mexico City, the Benemerito campus offers secondary education (the last two years are college preparatory) and is the largest of all primary and secondary schools in the Church (2,300 students). The Juárez Academy in Juárez, Mexico, provides a high school education, and is the only remaining academy of those established between 1875 and 1911 (*see* ACADEMIES).

The Church's schooling enterprises arose in response to concerns over the secularization of the schools, the need for trained teachers for public schools and trained leadership in the Church, LDS youth's participation in other denominational schools, and youth leaving home for their schooling. The establishment of schools, and subsequently an educational system, drew the Church into a relationship with state public school systems in the United States. This relationship divides into five periods:

ORIGINS (1830–1846). Educational efforts were hampered by frequent and difficult moves from New York to Kirtland, Ohio, to Missouri, to Nauvoo, Illinois, and finally, to the Great Basin. As was customary in the frontier, most education was provided at home by parents teaching their children the basic skills of literacy and a general understanding of the scriptures and religious values. As early as 1831 efforts were made to collect and write books for schools (D&C 55:4); subsequently, some formal schools were established. Most prominent among these was the School of the Prophets, established first in Kirtland, Ohio, in 1833, involving fewer than twenty-five adults in instruction intended to prepare them for religious missions and other assignments. Subjects taught included geography, English grammar, Hebrew, literature, philosophy, politics, and theology. Later, in Illinois in 1841, a system of LDS common schools and the University of the City of Nauvoo were established under the direction of the University of Nauvoo Board of Regents. Tuitions and a basic child and adult curriculum were established, but the program's objectives were largely unrealized as persecution forced the families to move to the West.

EARLY UTAH PERIOD (1847–1869). The first schools in Utah were conducted in tents and log huts. At the outset, schools were taught by private teachers who advertised, charged fees, and gathered a few students around them. The UNIVERSITY OF DESERET was established in 1850 in Salt Lake City to train teachers for schools; however, it survived only two years because few could afford to pay tuition. For the next twenty years, schools throughout the state were held primarily in Church meetinghouses, loosely organized on ecclesiastical lines, sparsely financed by member tuition, and sometimes by Church supplements, or local tax funds in the late 1860s. Church leaders encouraged parents to send their children to school and pay the tuition, usually a few cents per week. The children, however, often worked with their families on farms and ranches and could attend classes only intermittently. Church–state relationships were not an issue because no government-sponsored territorial school system existed at the time. The curriculum reflected Church belief. Most materials, however, had to be imported from the East, and teachers generally lacked formal credentials. Often they were only slightly more knowledgeable than their students.

PROTESTANT–MORMON RIVALRY (1869–1890). The period was initiated with the establishment of St. Mark's Episcopal School in Salt Lake City in 1867. Catholics, Presbyterians, Methodists, Baptists, Lutherans, and Congregationalists soon followed with their own schools, especially after the completion of the railroad in 1869. Their object was not only to serve their own people but also to convert the Latter-day Saint children attending their schools, although few were converted. Many LDS students did attend, however, because the quality of education they offered was often superior to what Latter-day Saint residents could provide in their own schools. The establishment by non-LDS territorial school officials of a tax-supported public school system in 1890 with its prohibition of sectarian religious teaching and administration initiated the demise of de facto Church influence in most of the schooling. For a time afterwards, the Church sought to maintain its own school system by establishing secondary school academies modeled after the Brigham Young Academy. Eventually, however, other sources of education became available, the expense of providing education became prohibitive, and the Church relinquished its efforts to provide a comprehensive system of education for all its members.

ESTABLISHMENT OF SUPPLEMENTAL RELIGIOUS EDUCATION CLASSES (1890–1953). The Church initiated a policy of providing released time religious instruction concurrent with the regular offerings of the state public education system. Beginning in the 1920s, Church academies, or high schools, were either discontinued or turned over to the state. Some academies that had achieved junior college status were sold to the state in the 1930s.

GROWTH AND EXPANSION (1953–1990). During this period, seminaries and institutes were established in all fifty states and many foreign countries. Much of this growth was realized because of decisions not to build additional universities or junior colleges, and to endeavor to establish schools where educational opportunities could not be provided by the local government. Currently owned schools were maintained only until the time that local government could assume responsibility. Schools in Indonesia, Chile, Tahiti, American Samoa, and Mexico were closed as improved public school programs became more available to members of the Church in those countries. In 1965, the Church schools outside the United States administratively became part of the Unified Church School System. Presently, the schools are administered separately from the institutions of higher education.

BIBLIOGRAPHY
Arrington, Leonard J. "The Latter-Day Saints and Public Education." *Southwestern Journal of Social Education* 7 (1977):9–25.
Bennion, Milton Lynn. *Mormonism and Education.* Salt Lake City, 1939.
Clark, James R. "Church and State Relationships in Education in Utah." Ph.D. diss., Utah State University, 1958.
Moffit, John C. *The History of Public Education in Utah.* Salt Lake City, 1946.
Palmer, Spencer J. "Educating the Saints." In *The Expanding Church.* Salt Lake City, 1978.

A. GARR CRANNEY

SCIENCE AND RELIGION

Because of belief in the ultimate compatibility of all truth and in the eternal character of human knowledge, Latter-day Saints tend to take a more positive approach to science than do some people in other religious traditions who also claim a strong foundation in scripture. The LDS experience includes encounters between religious belief and the natural sciences in three broad areas. For the most part, LDS responses to discoveries in American antiquities and New World archaeology have been enthusiastic, but sometimes cautious, as these findings are thought to have some potential for expanding contemporary understanding of the ancient Book of Mormon peoples and Book of Mormon geography. Latter-day Saints have often been defensive toward, though they have not necessarily rejected, developments in geology and the biological sciences that bear on the nature of the Creation and the age of the earth (*see* EVOLUTION). The revelations to Joseph Smith of an Abrahamic astronomy and three creation accounts, having some variation, have also stimulated positive interest in astronomical and cosmological issues. In particular, these revelations affirmed the plurality of worlds and heliocentrism in the scriptural writings of ancient prophets. Historical, scientific, philosophical, and theological factors have tempered discussions of science and religion in the LDS context.

Conceptions of scientific knowledge have changed many times since Greek antiquity. Thus, for example, modern understanding of the nature of the cosmos has changed radically from Aristotle in early Greece; to Galileo, Descartes, and Newton in the seventeenth century; to Lyell and Darwin in the nineteenth century; and in the twentieth century to Einstein, Hubble, and Hawking. Science itself continues in a state of constant flux, so that the total collection of scientific ideas at any point in time could never be considered final truth. Consequently, scientific theories are forever tentative and are not likely to be fully compatible with revealed religion at any particular time.

Realizing this, scholars today recognize that older descriptions of "conflict" or open "warfare" between science and Christianity are often mistaken. Nor could LDS thinking about science be described in this way. The Church is distinguished by its acceptance of ongoing revelation and the view that divine revelation underlies its scriptures and teachings. Consequently, Latter-day Saints assume that ultimate truths about religious matters and about God's creations can never be in conflict, as God is the author of both. They look forward to a time when more complete knowledge in both areas will transcend all present perceptions of conflict.

As early revelations to Joseph Smith seemed to invite reflections on the nature of the universe and the place of human beings in it, Latter-day Saints came to reflect the kind of optimism about a future reconciliation of science and religion that characterized many of their contemporaries. As positive ideas and attitudes about the compatibility of science and religion emerged with growing confidence among Latter-day Saints, many began to use the theories and observations of science to support their religious beliefs. Two main reasons for this appear to be that (1) LDS theology is philosophically committed to a positive conception of "true" science, and (2) Latter-day Saints could invoke science in partial support of the revealed world of the restoration (true religion).

These LDS appeals to science are distinct from the traditional Christian efforts in natural theology, which assumed that science can lead to a theology of nature in which science and Christianity are compatible. While individual Latter-day Saints freely invoke philosophical arguments and scientific evidences to affirm religious claims, these have never been considered official or conclusive. Latter-day Saints tend to be dubious of natural theology because the existence and nature of God can be known only through revelation, not through speculative theology.

Several basic Church teachings combine to provide additional support for a positive attitude toward science. Because God governs his creations through the laws of nature, of which he is the author, science is perceived as one important means of gaining understanding of his governance. Furthermore, LDS scriptures teach that "the glory of God is intelligence, or, in other words, light and truth" (D&C 93:36) and that the knowledge and intelligence gained in this life will be an advantage in the next (D&C 130:18–19). Finally, Latter-day Saints also use pragmatic and empiricological methods as legitimate means of gaining knowledge. They believe God expects them to use all forms of knowledge, including the revelatory and the scientific. Yet, revelation is always primary, and there is little sympathy among Latter-day Saints for the emphasis on science that leads to a rejection of scripturally based understanding.

While LDS publications from 1832 to the Nauvoo exodus in 1846 occasionally examined scientific ideas, extensive use and discussion of scientific themes did not emerge until the 1850s. Early Latter-day Saint speculations on science were set forth occasionally in conference addresses and published in the *Journal of Discourses*, the *Millennial Star*, and in the writings of apostles Parley P. Pratt and Orson Pratt. For example, Orson Pratt, the first LDS science-philosopher, wrote in 1873 that "the great temple of science must be erected upon the solid foundations of everlasting truth; its towering spires must mount upward, reaching higher and still higher, until crowned with the glory and presence of Him, who is Eternal" (*Deseret News* 22 [1873]:586).

Beginning in the 1890s, positive LDS speculations on science generally, and specifically in such fields as astronomy, cosmology, evolution, geology, and paleontology, while not always harmonious, drew on the ideas of the first academically trained LDS scientists (and later General Authorities) James E. Talmage, John A. Widtsoe, Joseph F. Merrill, and Richard R. Lyman. All four of these highly influential apostles used their scientific expertise to further the view that "correct" science and revealed religion are in close harmony because the author of both is God. Thus, Talmage asked rhetorically, "What is the field of science?" His answer: "Everything. Science is the discourse of nature and nature is the visible declaration of Divine Will. . . . There is naught so small, so vast that science takes no cognizance thereof. . . . Nature is the scientist's copy and truth his chief aim" (c. 1895). "Among our young people," Talmage wrote elsewhere, "I consider scientific knowledge as second in importance only to that knowledge that pertains to the Church and Kingdom of God. . . . Nature, as we study it, is but the temple of the Almighty" (c. 1900).

In 1930, Widtsoe wrote:

> Science . . . is the recognition by the mind through human senses of the realities of existence. The mind of man is a noble instrument, a preeminent possession, by which he becomes conscious, not only of his own existence, but of the conditions of external nature. . . . The glory of physical conquests, of the sea and earth and air, have often dazzled men to such a degree that they have forgotten that back of all discovery and progress is the power of observation and thought. Without mind, there is no science, no progress, only extinction [*In Search of Truth* (Salt Lake City, 1930), pp. 36–37].

Later, in *Evidences and Reconciliations*, one of Widtsoe's most widely known books, he wrote, "The Church supports and welcomes the growth of science. . . . The religion of the Latter-day Saints is not hostile to any truth, nor to scientific search for truth" (Vol. 1, p. 129).

Other (non-scientist) Church authorities, principally Joseph

Fielding Smith, writing in the first half of the twentieth century, and later Bruce R. McConkie, vigorously criticized the ideas of some that the scriptures could be reconciled with scientific theories, in particular, evolutionary accounts of the origin of man.

Talmage, Widtsoe, and B. H. Roberts, writing in the first half of the twentieth century, probably have contributed more than any other LDS authorities with the possible exception of the Pratt brothers after the initial years of Church growth to scientific topics and their assumed general harmony with the gospel. That this attitude continues and is presently sustained within the larger Latter-day Saint culture, particularly among LDS scientists, is also supported by recent studies that suggest that the LDS community has produced more scientists per capita than most religious groups in twentieth-century America (*see* SCIENCE AND SCIENTISTS).

BIBLIOGRAPHY

The finest scholarly examination of the complex relation between the natural sciences and religion from the Middle Ages to the twentieth century can be found in David Lindberg and Ronald Numbers, eds., *God and Nature: Historical Essays on the Encounter Between Christianity and Science* (Berkeley, Calif., 1986). For a discussion of numerous issues dealing with science and the LDS Church by prominent LDS scientists and authorities, including Henry Eyring, Carl J. Christensen, Harvey Fletcher, Franklin S. Harris, Joseph F. Merrill, Frederick J. Pack, and John A. Widtsoe, see Henry Eyring et al., *Science and Your Faith in God* (Salt Lake City, 1958). For a discussion by LDS scientists affirming the compatibility of their faith and their fields of specialty, see Wilford M. Hess, Raymond T. Matheny, and Donlu D. Thayer, eds., *Science and Religion: Toward a More Useful Dialogue*, 2 vols. (Geneva, Ill., 1979). On the issue of American antiquities, see John Sorenson, *An Ancient American Setting for the Book of Mormon* (Salt Lake City, 1985). For a review of issues dealing with evolution and geology, respectively, see Duane E. Jeffery, "Seers, Savants and Evolution: The Uncomfortable Interface," *Dialogue* 8 (Autumn–Winter 1973):41–75, and Morris S. Petersen, "[Fossils and Scriptures]," *Ensign* 17 (Sept. 1987):28–29. For an extensive examination of science and cosmology and their relationship to LDS theology, see Erich Robert Paul, *Science, Religion, and Mormon Cosmology* (Champaign, Ill., 1991).

ERICH ROBERT PAUL

SCIENCE AND SCIENTISTS

In a world where science and religion have sometimes been at odds, Latter-day Saints stand out for their positive attitudes toward science and their high proportion of involvement in scientific careers. Active scientists are often called to positions of Church leadership, and a number of LDS scientists have been internationally recognized for scientific work. With Church sponsorship, BRIGHAM YOUNG UNIVERSITY maintains sizable programs in most scientific fields of study and supports significant research in many of these. The positive attitude toward science is often attributed to distinctive theological beliefs.

In the nineteenth century, some Latter-day Saints showed great interest in science, but none were broadly known as practicing scientists. Their experience in those early decades included constantly moving from place to place, struggling with persecution and economic loss, carrying the message of the restored gospel to the nations of the earth, and establishing new communities on the American frontier. While this life afforded little opportunity to become professional scientists, several pursued their scientific interests as they were able, including Orson Pratt's early establishment of an observatory in Salt Lake City. Distinctive cultural factors present from the earliest years eventually led Latter-day Saints to pursue careers in science in large numbers.

The commitment to education and the pursuit of truth was reinforced by teachings of early Church leaders and specifically by revelations received by Joseph Smith. One statement based on revelation explains that "whatever principle of intelligence we attain unto in this life, it will rise with us in the resurrection" (D&C 130:18). Another scripture asserts that "all things are created and made to bear record of me, . . . things which are in the heavens above, and things which are on the earth, and things which are in the earth: . . . all things bear record of me" (Moses 6:63). Thus, for many Latter-day Saints, the pursuit of scientific knowledge is a religious quest.

Latter-day Saints also teach that God created all things using laws natural to his environment; that the natural world is a world of pattern, law, order, and meaning; and that men and women possess the ability to discover truth and to use that knowledge to improve the world in which they live. Because they believe that God works by law, the study of the world can also be seen as a study of the divine. From this perspective they see themselves as coworkers with God in improving the human condition. These same ambitions are reinforced by the instillation of the value of hard work and the idea that all men and women are responsible to the larger society as well as to their immediate families. Further support for scientific activity can be found in repeated encouragement to young people to work for long-term goals and to leave the world a better place than they found it. These indirect sources of encouragement for scientific endeavor are often supplements by LDS leaders teaching that God reveals certain truths through scientific research and not alone through prophets. President Brigham Young claimed that "God has revealed all the truth that is now in the possession of the world, whether it be scientific or religious. The whole world [is] under obligation to him for what they know and enjoy; they are indebted to him for it all" (*JD* 8:162).

As the LDS community stabilized and became part of mainstream America in the twentieth century, these attitudes began to bear fruit in scientific endeavor. A 1940 study established that Utah led all other states in the number of scientific men born there in proportion to the population (Thorndike, pp. 138–39). A thorough analysis of state-by-state contributions to science from 1920 to 1960 found that Utah led all other states by a wide margin in the proportion of its university graduates who eventually received doctoral degrees in science (Hardy, p. 499). Unpublished research indicates that this high productivity continued through the 1970s, though Utah dropped to second place among the fifty. It is generally recognized that the high percentage of Latter-day Saints in Utah largely accounts for Utah's distinctiveness in these studies. Researchers find that the LDS beliefs described above correlate strongly with positive attitudes toward science, as they also distinguish Latter-day Saints in this regard from most other Christian groups.

A number of LDS apostles and other General Authorities have been scientists. Even in the earliest decades, Orson Pratt demonstrated exceptional interest and competence in his scientific avocations; his contributions were highly valued by the Mormon people. Later, in the frontier period, individual Latter-day Saints began to pursue formal scientific studies, first by correspondence courses, and later by traveling out of the state for enrollment in scientific institutions. James E. Talmage graduated from Lehigh University and studied at Johns Hopkins University before completing a Ph.D. through correspondence work at Illinois Wesleyan University. He undertook pioneering geological studies on the Great Salt Lake before his call to the apostleship in 1911. John A. Widtsoe studied biochemistry at Harvard University and in 1899 received a Ph.D. in chemistry from Göttingen University in Germany. Joseph F. Merrill received his Ph.D. in physics from Johns Hopkins University in 1899. These three succeeded one another in the European mission presidency and contributed a great deal to the enthusiasm for scientific thinking among Latter-day Saints in the first half of the twentieth century. The rise of European ideologies that embraced science and technology while rejecting Christian values led them to a more cautious endorsement of scientific realism in later years.

Examples of prominent LDS scientists in the mid-twentieth century include chemist Henry Eyring and physicists Harvey Fletcher and Willard Gardner. Eyring pioneered the application of quantum mechanics to chemistry and developed the Absolute Rate Theory of chemical reactions, for which he received the National Medal of Science. He was elected president of the American Chemical Society (1963) and of the American Association for the Advancement of Science (1965). Fletcher directed research at Bell Labs, where he played a central role in the development of stereophonic reproduction. He was elected president of the American Physical Society (1945). The American Society of Agronomy cited Gardner as "the father of soil physics" for his descriptions of the movement of water through unsaturated soils by reference to capillary potential. The number of Latter-day Saints significantly involved in scientific pursuits continued to grow throughout the twentieth century.

Two apostles were called in the 1980s from careers in medicine and engineering. Russell M. Nelson, a prominent heart surgeon, received a Ph.D. in surgery from the University of Minnesota for his research on gram negative bacterial toxinemia. Richard G. Scott used his degree in mechanical engineering as a base for advanced studies at the Oak Ridge laboratory in Tennessee and a career in nuclear engineering.

Like people in other religious traditions, the Latter-day Saints have also discovered scriptural reasons for some ambivalence toward modern science. In some instances, prominent Church leaders have voiced strong skepticism about science in general and about certain

theories of psychology, evolutionary biology, and astronomy in particular. Some have suggested that a number of these scientific ideas
are incompatible with the scriptures and the basic doctrines of the
Church. Others have proposed ways to reconcile these and have
emphasized the ultimate compatibility of all truth, whether revealed
to prophets or discovered by scientists.

The Church's governing councils have consistently refrained
from being drawn into official discussions of such matters. Early-
twentieth-century controversies over biological EVOLUTION did stim-
ulate formal statements from the First Presidency. But these were
carefully drawn to avoid dampening legitimate scientific activity
while clearly articulating and defending basic doctrinal positions of
the Church. Church leaders and scientists have repeatedly noted the
essentially tentative character of scientific theorizing and experimentation and have emphasized the necessity of divine revelation for
sure guidance in their lives. Similarly, scriptures have been frequently invoked to indicate that religious understanding also is
incomplete and that additional revelation is both expected and necessary (D&C 101:32–34; A of F 9). Such statements have reminded
Latter-day Saints that both science and revealed religion are continually building toward greater understanding of truth.

[*See also* Matter; Metaphysics.]

BIBLIOGRAPHY
Eyring, Henry. *The Faith of a Scientist*. Salt Lake City, 1967.
Hardy, Kenneth R. "Social Origins of American Scientists and Scholars." *Science*
185 (Aug. 9, 1974):497–506.
Hess, Wilford M., and Raymond T. Matheny, eds. *Science and Religion: Toward a
More Useful Dialogue*. Geneva, Ill., 1979.
Green, Paul R., comp. *Science and Your Faith in God*. Essays by Henry Eyring,
Harvey Fletcher, and others. Salt Lake City, 1958.
Merrill, Joseph E. *The Truth-Seeker and Mormonism: A Series of Radio Addresses*.
Independence, Mo., 1946.
Pack, Frederick J. *Science and Belief in God*. Salt Lake City, 1924.
Paul, Erich Robert. *Science, Religion, and Mormon Cosmology*. Champaign, Ill.,
1991.
Rich, Wendell O. *Distinctive Teachings of the Restoration*. Salt Lake City, 1962.
Talmage, James E. "The Earth and Man." Speech printed in *Deseret News*, Nov. 21,
1931, pp. 7–8. Reprinted in *Instructor* 100 (Dec. 1965):474–77 and 101 (Jan.
1966):9–11, 15.
Thorndike, E. L. "The Production, Retention and Attraction of American Men of
Science." *Science* 92 (Aug. 16, 1940):137–41.

Widtsoe, John A. *Joseph Smith as Scientist: A Contribution to "Mormon" Philosophy*, 2nd ed. Salt Lake City, 1920.

———. *In Search of Truth: Comments on the Gospel and Modern Thought*. Salt Lake City, 1930.

———. *Evidences and Reconciliations*, arr. by G. H. Durham, 3 vols. Salt Lake City, 1960.

ROBERT L. MILLER

SCOUTING

The Boy Scout movement began in England under the guidance of Lord Robert Baden-Powell in 1909. It appeared in the United States early in 1910 as the Boy Scouts of America (BSA), where a variety of churches used its programs as a part of their ministries to youth and families. After investigating the new scouting movement, the Young Men's Mutual Improvement Association (YMMIA) of The Church of Jesus Christ of Latter-day Saints organized the MIA Scouts on November 29, 1911, with the intent to provide worthwhile leisure time and athletic activities for its young men. On May 21, 1913, the MIA Scouts, upon invitation from the National Council, became part of the BSA.

Under YMMIA direction, this program moved rapidly forward in the Church. In 1928 Church leaders designated scouting as the activity program for the deacons and teachers of the Aaronic Priesthood and transferred its administration to the Presiding Bishopric.

In that same year the Vanguard program was developed by the Church for young men older than Boy Scout age. In 1949 Cub Scouting was officially adopted by the Church, and the primary organization was asked to administer scouting for boys under twelve years of age, with boys eight to eleven as Cub Scouts and eleven-year-old boys as Boy Scouts of the Blazer Patrol. In 1959 the Vanguard program was replaced by the Explorer Scout program, designed by the Church for older boys and later adopted by BSA for use throughout the United States.

Over time the Church's scouting program for older boys was divided into the Explorer program, for young men age sixteen through eighteen, and the Venturer program, for those fourteen and fifteen.

The Venturer program was eventually replaced with the nationwide BSA "Varsity Scout" program.

In 1977 responsibility within the Church for the scouting program was transferred from the Presiding Bishopric to the newly organized Young Men Presidency, which has operated since that time under the direction of the Quorum of the Twelve Apostles.

As scouting evolved, the Church adopted scouting programs in the United States that correspond with specific age groups and Aaronic Priesthood quorums. Currently those programs include Boy Scouts for deacons quorum members, Varsity Scouts for teachers quorum members, and Explorer Scouts for priests quorum members. In each case, the scouting program serves as a part of the activity program for the Aaronic Priesthood quorum.

Although scouting has become an integral part of the Church's activity program for young men in the United States, it is less prominent in Church units in other countries. Many scouting organizations throughout the world follow principles and policies incompatible with Church standards. As a result, the Church authorizes wards and branches to associate only with scouting programs affiliated with the World Scouting Organization. In countries where this organization operates, Church units are urged to affiliate with, and develop, full scouting programs. Because scouting institutions are rare in Western Europe, the Church there has developed its own scouting organization, known as Aaronic Priesthood Scouting, as part of the activity program for the Aaronic Priesthood.

Wards and branches in the United States sponsor scouting units as part of their Aaronic Priesthood program. As a result, the Church has for years led all other organizations, religious and otherwise, in the total number of scouting units sponsored by any one chartered organization. In 1990 the Church registered 24,560 scouting units with BSA. During that same year, the public schools sponsored 16,543 units; the United Methodist Church, 11,179 units; and the Roman Catholic Church and affiliations, 9,530. The public schools enrolled 1,096,914 scouts; the Roman Catholic Church, 298,997; and the United Methodist Church, 333,086. The Latter-day Saints enrolled 342,156 scouts and 139,557 adult leaders that year.

Church leaders have taken an active role in BSA affairs at the national level as well as in Church scouting. Most of the Presidents of the Church since the time scouting was organized have been honored by the BSA, including George Albert Smith, Heber J. Grant, David O. McKay, Harold B. Lee, Spencer W. Kimball, and Ezra Taft Benson, all of whom have received significant honors for their contribution to scouting on a national level. Most recently, President Ezra Taft Benson received the Bronze Wolf Award, given by the World Scouting Organization for distinguished service to scouting around the world. He also received the Silver Beaver and Silver Antelope awards from BSA in recognition of many years of service on a local and national level.

In addition to Church presidents, Thomas S. Monson, Vaughn J. Featherstone, Robert L. Backman, Marion D. Hanks, and others among the General Authorities, have also served in positions of distinction and leadership at the national level of the Boy Scouts and have been recognized for their contribution on behalf of the Church.

Both the program and the support service system of the BSA have been influenced by LDS volunteers, and many of the values, objectives, and goals of the Church for its young men are reflected in the expanding program of BSA.

When the BSA was first organized, certain religious principles were defined as the keystone of the organization, including (1) belief in God, (2) reverence for God, (3) fulfillment of religious duties, and (4) respect for beliefs of others. Because these principles have remained at the heart of scouting, the Church has embraced and promoted scouting as a major part of its program for young men.

The BSA and the Church have forged a close working relationship. In partnership with the Church, the BSA provides its programs, facilities, support, and training. The Church, in turn, provides youth, youth leaders, financial support, and promotion of its implicit values. This relationship has flourished because scouting continues to support wholesome leisure-time activities, to provide a spiritual view of life that is compatible with the Church's teachings, and to encourage boys and leaders to be loyal to the Church.

BIBLIOGRAPHY

Boy Scout Handbook. Irving, Tex., 1990.

Hillcourt, William. *Baden-Powell: The Two Lives of a Hero.* Irving, Tex., 1985.

Scouting, A handbook on relationships between The Church of Jesus Christ of Latter-day Saints and the Boy Scouts of America, published by the Church. Salt Lake City, 1985.

Strong, Leon M. "A History of the Young Men's Mutual Improvement Association, 1875–1938." Master's thesis, Brigham Young University, 1939.

Williams, John Kent. "A History of the Young Men's Mutual Improvement Association 1939 to 1974." Master's thesis, Brigham Young University, 1976.

LOWELL M. SNOW

SCULPTORS

The earliest LDS sculptors were English emigrant craftsmen who provided ornamentation for the Nauvoo and pioneer temples. A temple sunstone, one of the most distinctive surviving artifacts from Nauvoo, is part of the collection of the Smithsonian Institution.

A tradition of creating public monuments that celebrate the history of the Latter-day Saints is now a century old. Contributors include Cyrus Dallin (1861–1944), who studied in Paris. He sculpted the angel Moroni that caps the tallest tower of the Salt Lake Temple. This beaux arts sculpture has become the most recognized and copied piece in the LDS tradition. Most of Dallin's career was spent in Boston, where he sculpted John Winthrop, Paul Revere, and Massasoit. His life-sized bronze equestrian figures also grace Chicago, Kansas City, Philadelphia, and Vienna.

A grandson of Brigham Young, Mahonri Young (1877–1957), also studied in Paris, where he was strongly influenced by Rodin. "This is the place" monument, which marks the entry of the pioneers into the Salt Lake Valley, is one of his major religious works, the largest sculptured monument in Utah.

Avard Fairbanks (1897–1987), who created the Department of Fine Arts at the University of Utah, is well known in the Church for his elaborate frieze around the Hawaii Temple, his statue of the restoration of the Aaronic Priesthood, and the Winter Quarters Cemetery Monument. He was knighted by King Paul of Greece after sculpting "Lycurgus the Lawgiver."

On Temple Square (Salt Lake City) stands a monument to the dramatic epic of the pioneer trek, the Mormon Handcart Companies, sculpted by Torlief Knaphus (1881–1965), a convert from Norway.

The Mormon Arts Festival, held at Brigham Young University since the early 1970s, has displayed religious pieces produced by

Franz Johansen (1929–) and Trevor Southey (1940–) that are now in the Museum of Church History and Art. The Monument to Women sculpture garden in Nauvoo displays life-sized bronze statues of women. Most of the pieces are done by Dennis Smith (1942–), but the sculpture of Joseph and Emma Smith was created by Florence Hansen (1920–).

The last quarter of the twentieth century has produced many LDS sculptors, including some with roots in cultures that reflect the international presence of the Church. Representative sculptors are Epanaia Christy (1921–) and Mataumu Alisa (1942–) from Polynesia; Native Americans Lowell Talishoma (1950–), Oreland Joe (1958–), and Harrison Begay (1961–); Victor de la Torres (c. 1935–) of Venezuela; and Mae Cameron (n.d.) from Australia.

[*See also* Architecture; Museums, Latter-day Saint; Symbols, Cultural and Artistic.]

BIBLIOGRAPHY

Gibbs, Linda Jones. *Masterworks*. Salt Lake City, 1984.

Olpin, Robert S. *Dictionary of Utah Art*. Salt Lake City, 1980.

Oman, Richard G. "Sculpting: An LDS Tradition." *Ensign* 20 (Oct. 1990):38–43.

Swanson, Vern G. *Sculptors of Utah*. Springville, Utah, n.d.

RICHARD G. OMAN

SECT

In ordinary usage the word "sect" refers to any body of followers or adherents, ranging from the main religions of the world to small groups of heretics. "Sect" derives from the Latin *sequi*, to follow. In sociological terminology, a sect is a separately organized religious group that meets specified criteria. Technically, this term does not adequately describe The Church of Jesus Christ of Latter-day Saints.

As defined by social scientists, three criteria are central in determining whether a religious group is a sect: (1) a sect is organizationally simple; (2) it stands in high tension with the dominant society (typically because sect members view themselves as a "faithful remnant" of the pure religion that has been rejected by society); and (3) it views itself as uniquely legitimate, the sole source of salvation.

Applying these criteria to The Church of Jesus Christ of Latter-day Saints is not always easy. With respect to these factors, the organizational structure of the LDS Church is obviously complex and international in scope. While the nineteenth-century commitment to building a literal political and economic kingdom and the practice of plural marriage placed the LDS Church in tension with its host societies, neither of these practices sociologically characterize the twentieth-century Church. In fact, the Church has always embraced many values central to the dominant value systems of the United States and other host countries, including an emphasis on family, hard work, and national loyalty. Nevertheless, moderate tension remains, partly because of the Church's claim of unique legitimacy.

"Churches" and "denominations" in sociological terminology differ from sects in that both of the former are organizationally complex and have positive relationships with society. Denominations accept the legitimacy claims of other religious groups, while churches do not (Roberts, pp. 181–202). There are several problems in classifying The Church of Jesus Christ of Latter-day Saints according to this typology. Its claim to unique legitimacy makes it something other than a denomination, while its lack of societal dominance makes it something other than a church (except in Utah and certain other locations).

To explain unclear cases like this, sociologists developed an additional classification—the "established sect" (Yinger, pp. 266–73). An established sect is organizationally complex while retaining moderate tension with society and the claim to unique legitimacy. While the LDS Church meets these criteria, social scientists increasingly argue that it deviates sufficiently from conventional religious traditions to warrant even further classification outside of the church-denomination-sect typology. They argue that the term "new religion" is perhaps the most accurate and that modern-day Mormonism is on the verge of becoming a major new world religion (Stark, pp. 11–12).

[*See also* Cult.]

BIBLIOGRAPHY

Roberts, Keith A. *Religion in Sociological Perspective*, 2nd ed. Belmont, Calif., 1990.
Stark, Rodney. "How New Religions Succeed: A Theoretical Model." In *The Future*

of New Religious Movements, ed. D. Bromley and P. Hammond, pp. 11–29. Macon, Ga., 1987.

Yinger, J. Milton. *The Scientific Study of Religion*. New York, 1970.

LAWRENCE A. YOUNG

SELF-SUFFICIENCY (SELF-RELIANCE)

The term "self-sufficiency" refers to a principle underlying the LDS program of Welfare Services, and to an ideal of social experience. Self-sufficiency is the ability to maintain one's self and relates to women and men being agents for themselves. Independence and self-sufficiency are critical keys to spiritual and temporal growth. A situation that threatens one's ability to be self-sufficient also threatens one's confidence, self-esteem, and freedom. As dependence is increased, the freedom to act is decreased.

Church writings often use the terms self-sufficiency and "self-reliance" interchangeably. Teachings pertaining to Welfare Services emphasize and place considerable importance on both individual and family independence. Six principles form the foundation of the infrastructure of the welfare program. Three of these principles emphasize responsibility to care for one's own needs: work, self-reliance, and stewardship; the other three focus on responsibility to others: love, service, and consecration (Faust, p. 91).

President Spencer W. Kimball defined Welfare Services as the "essence of the Gospel . . . the Gospel in action" (Kimball, p. 77). Within the context of welfare, the term self-sufficiency also includes an emphasis on prevention, temporary assistance, and rehabilitation. Self-sufficiency is helping oneself to the point of reliance. Welfare, a program based on self-sufficiency, helps individuals to help themselves. Home industry, gardening, food storage, emergency preparedness, and avoidance of debt reflect the applications of self-sufficiency (*Welfare Services Resource Handbook*, p. 21).

Since the inauguration of Welfare Services in 1936 by President Heber J. Grant, self-sufficiency has continued to be refined and clarified by Church leaders. This focus has remained as the Church has expanded to countries outside the United States and Canada, and most recently to developing countries of the world. While the Church responds to crises and natural disasters abroad, it is still in a planning stage regarding the tremendous cross-cultural challenges pertaining to the principle of self-sufficiency (*International Welfare Services*, p. 1).

As a social ideal, self-sufficiency includes spiritual, intellectual, and emotional dimensions. Just as the world is economically interdependent, agricultural communities and enterprises have been interdependent; families, farms, and other units have specialized in a product or service with the intent to engage in trade for the additional necessities of life. Self-sufficiency is central to such interdependence and is necessary for one to be in a position to assist others, beginning with one's own family, neighbors, and ward. A universal concern of individuals can be personal integrity and identity within the larger social systems. A responsible, productive, and integrated life in a varied and changing world is desirable and exemplified by Christ and others of integrity discussed in the scriptures.

New Testament teachings conceive of liberty as a person's relationship to God and others (Buttrick, p. 121). Christ gave his followers sacred charge and opportunity to serve the poor, needy, sick, and afflicted. Rather than looking on God as the only one able to provide, individuals as self-sufficient beings work together in mutual responsibility, compassion, gentleness, and love.

Perspective on the balance between an individual person's being totally self-sufficient and also needing assistance comes from the understanding that everyone is self-reliant in some areas and dependent in others. Latter-day Saints accept the observation that everyone is flawed and imperfect; everyone experiences human limitation or poverty. Scriptures recognize that poverty resides in both temporal or spiritual matters. In fact, all are "beggars" for a remission of sins (Mosiah 4:20). Nevertheless, a certain equality emerges from human interdependence, noted in the counsel to be equal in both heavenly and earthly things: "For if ye are not equal in earthly things ye cannot be equal in obtaining heavenly things" (D&C 78:6). From one's strengths, each should endeavor to help another; on the other hand, one should accept the help of another. "If a man be overtaken in a fault, ye which are spiritual, restore such an one in the spirit of meekness; . . . bear ye one another's burdens, and so fulfill the law of Christ" (Gal. 6:1–2). Interdependence, then, creates the opportunity to participate in the sanctifying experience of giving and receiving (Romney, p. 91).

In a gospel sense, there exists an interdependence between those who have and those who have not. The process of sharing lifts the poor, humbles the rich, and sanctifies both. The poor are released from bondage and limitations of poverty and are able to rise to their full potential, both temporally and spiritually. The rich, by imparting of their surplus, participate in the eternal principle of sharing. A person who is whole or self-sufficient can reach out to others, and the cycle of equality and giving repeats itself.

Without self-sufficiency it is difficult to exercise these innate desires to serve. Food for the hungry cannot come from empty shelves; money to assist the needy cannot come from an empty purse; support and understanding cannot come from the emotionally starved; teaching cannot come from the unlearned. Most important of all, spiritual guidance only comes from the spiritually strong. Indeed, self-sufficiency forms the basis to bear one another's burdens and to live interdependently.

BIBLIOGRAPHY

Buttrick, George A., ed. "Liberty." In *The Interpreter's Dictionary of the Bible*, Vol. 3, pp. 122–23. New York, 1962.

Faust, James E. "Establishing the Church: Welfare Services Missionaries Are an Important Resource." *Ensign* 12 (Nov. 1982):91–93.

International Welfare Services. Salt Lake City, 1981.

Kimball, Spencer W. "Welfare Services: The Gospel in Action." *Ensign* 7 (Nov. 1977):76–79.

Romney, Marion G. "The Celestial Nature of Self-Reliance." *Ensign* 12 (Nov. 1982):91–93.

Welfare Services Resource Handbook. Salt Lake City, 1980.

VAL DAN MACMURRAY

SEMINARIES

Seminaries are that part of the CHURCH EDUCATIONAL SYSTEM which provides weekday religious instruction for youth, usually from the ages of fourteen to eighteen, to balance their secular secondary education with study in the scriptures, religious teachings, and moral values of their faith. To accomplish this objective, four year-long courses are offered: Old Testament, New Testament, Doctrine and Covenants/Church history, and the Book of Mormon. These courses are designed in three basic formats: released-time, early-morning, and home-study.

Released-time seminaries operate during the regular school day in Church-owned facilities near junior and senior high schools. The courses are taught by professionally trained teachers. At the request of parents, students are "released" by the school district to attend one class period a day in a seminary course. This allows the students to receive the moral, character, and scriptural education available through Church-related instruction along with regular public school education in a nearby facility. The constitutionality of released-time religious education has been tested and upheld in the courts in cases involving Catholic and Protestant programs (with some LDS participation as *amicus curiae*). The legality of the LDS approach has also been resolved in various western U.S. states to allow released-time classes, but not to permit transfer of high school credit for those classes. It is common for enrollments in released-time seminaries to exceed 80 percent of the total number of LDS youth attending the high school.

Early-morning seminaries provide weekday religious instruction in areas where local public school laws do not grant released-time or where the LDS population does not warrant the establishment of a released-time seminary program. These classes generally meet before the regular school day begins, usually in an LDS meetinghouse convenient to the high school. The instructors are generally local members appointed on a part-time or volunteer basis. Typically, between 50 to 70 percent of eligible LDS youth are enrolled where early-morning seminary classes function.

Home-study seminaries are provided to meet the needs of LDS youth living where distance or other problems make participation in a daily class impossible or inadvisable. Curriculum materials based on the four regular courses have been developed for students to study daily at home. Home-study students generally meet once each week in a class taught by an appointed teacher. Average enrollment levels in home-study seminary programs are usually a lower percentage of the LDS youth of an area than that of the early-morning and released-time seminaries.

ADMINISTRATION. Seminaries are directly administered by the office of Religious Education and Elementary and Secondary Schools of the Church Educational System, which is governed by the Church Board of Education. The First Presidency of the Church presides over this board, with board members appointed from among the Quorum of Twelve Apostles and other general church officers, including the presidents of the women's Relief Society and the Young Women organization. Professional educational administrators responsible to the central administrator of Religious Education in the Salt Lake office are appointed to supervise the day-to-day operation of the high school seminary program throughout the world. Stake presidents also assist in local administration, especially in encouraging registration of the youth of their stakes.

HISTORICAL BACKGROUND. Shortly after the LDS pioneers arrived in the Salt Lake Valley in 1847, the leaders of the Church directed the establishment of SCHOOLS to provide education for its members. In the last quarter of the nineteenth century, each stake was encouraged to establish an ACADEMY to offer secondary educational instruction. Classes in religion were an essential component of this Church-sponsored school system.

In the early 1900s, when Utah public high schools became more fully established, Church leaders decided to close their academies and to support the public high schools, thus eliminating the need for Church members to fund both Church-owned and public schools.

To supplement secular public education with religious instruction, the first Latter-day Saint seminary was established in 1912 adjacent to Granite High School in Salt Lake City. When this released-time seminary program proved to be effective, it was quickly adopted in other communities with a high ratio of LDS youth. In 1990 released-time seminaries were operating in Utah, Idaho, Wyoming, Arizona, Oregon, and some parts of Colorado. From 1950 to 1970, early-morning seminaries had been established throughout California and other western states. With the home-study adaptation, the Church has essentially established seminary programs of one variety or another in all fifty states. Graduation from seminary is accomplished by students completing all four courses and living lives which reflect the moral teachings of their faith.

In the fall of 1970, when the Church Board of Education deter-

mined that the seminary program should reach the membership of
the Church throughout the world, the seminary program was interna-
tionalized, with course materials translated into sixteen languages.
In 1990, the seminary program was operating in more than ninety
countries and territories with more than 300,000 students enrolled.

BIBLIOGRAPHY
Berrett, William E. *A Miracle in Weekday Religious Education.* Salt Lake City, 1988.
Quinn, D. Michael. "Utah's Educational Innovation: LDS Religion Classes,
1890–1929." *Utah Historical Quarterly* 43 (Fall 1975):379–89.
Widtsoe, John A. "The Church School System." *IE* 26 (1923):863–69.

JOE J. CHRISTENSEN

SENIOR CITIZENS

The Church of Jesus Christ of Latter-day Saints has always had concern for the well-being of its older members. "Mormon attitudes
toward old age were influenced by Joseph Smith and other Church
leaders, and by scriptural injunctions to honor the elderly" (Reeves,
p. 150). Latter-day Saints view aging as an important part of God's
plan and believe that completing one's mortal probation and enduring
to the end are essential in the plan of salvation.

While programs for the youth of the Church currently are better
known than programs for the elderly, the reverse was true during the
nineteenth century. The best example is the Old Folks movement,
founded as a private initiative by Charles R. Savage, which began
with annual excursions to various Utah locations in 1875 and continued until the turn of the century, when stake presidencies and
ward bishoprics were instructed by the First Presidency to organize
stake and ward Old Folks committees. They were to entertain the
elderly in their wards and stakes twice a year, a function which continued in some wards and stakes through the 1960s.

The elderly in the Church have often immersed themselves in
genealogical and temple work. As early as 1951, Church leaders
urged older people also to become more involved in missionary work.
Today, many of them serve effectively as full-time missionaries.

Conference addresses of General Authorities are replete with
advice to, and about, the elderly. Two dominant themes in the first

half of this century were that children should care for their aging parents and that old people should avoid government doles. More recently, Church President Ezra Taft Benson identified eight areas in which he urged the elderly of the Church to be involved: (1) to serve often in the temple; (2) to collect and write FAMILY HISTORIES; (3) to render missionary service or give support to the missionaries; (4) to provide leadership by building family togetherness (*see* FAMILY ORGANIZATION); (5) to accept and fulfill Church callings; (6) to plan for a sound financial future; (7) to render Christlike service; and (8) to stay physically fit, healthy, and active (*Ensign* 19 [Nov. 1989]:4–6).

Research comparing older Mormons with other senior citizens is limited. One study (Peterson) found that older Mormons are more family-oriented, more active in their religion, and more conservative in religious beliefs; however, it also concluded that older Mormons are like the general population in matters of health-consciousness and contentedness. Perhaps the most comprehensive study of aging Mormons within a family context is the *LDS Family Longitudinal Study*, sponsored by Brigham Young University. This projected twenty-year study was initiated in 1983 with approximately 1,200 individuals from 133 three-generation families. It suggests that most older Church members are doing rather well; however, individual conditions and challenges vary considerably.

BIBLIOGRAPHY

Peterson, Evan T. "A Comparative Analysis of Elderly Mormons and Non-Mormons." Annual Meeting of the Association for the Sociology of Religion, Chicago, Aug. 14–16, 1987.

Reeves, Brian D. "Hoary-headed Saints: The Aged in Nineteenth-Century Mormon Culture." Master's thesis, Brigham Young University, 1987.

EVAN T. PETERSON

SEX EDUCATION

Latter-day Saints are instructed that parents have the divinely appointed responsibility and privilege of teaching their children moral and eternal values associated with human SEXUALITY and reproduction. Except in unusual cases, they cannot ignore or shift the ultimate responsibility for educating their children about sex to any other person or entity.

The scriptures define the union of the spirit and the body as the soul of man (D&C 88:15) and declare that MARRIAGE and FAMILY in the highest degree of heavenly glory are eternal (D&C 131:2; 132:19). Therefore, LDS discussion about sex respects the physical body, life, marriage, family, the intentions of God the Creator, and the shared creative powers he has entrusted to a heterosexual husband and wife (*see* PROCREATION). The spirit of the Lord's law of love and righteousness requires one to keep sacred and appropriate all sexual desires and all related behaviors. All people are admonished to remain chaste before marriage and totally faithful in marriage (*see* ADULTERY).

At an early age, children begin to recognize sexual differences. The Church encourages parents to establish open communication by providing their children correct information and by being aware of each individual child's readiness for specific instruction so that children will feel free to talk with their parents about sex differences and functions.

Parents are counseled to help their adolescent and older children understand the need to stay in control of their emotions and behaviors relative to physical desire and to teach them how to make personal decisions about sexual behavior based on moral awareness, with the realization that virtue and moral cleanliness lead to strength of character, peace of mind, lifelong happiness, and a fulness of love. LDS scriptures counsel, "See that ye bridle all your passions, that ye may be filled with love" (Alma 38:12).

A Parent's Guide was developed by the Church to provide information and suggest teaching methods to parents. It helps parents teach children in the home about sacred and personal matters appropriate to each age through all the stages of childhood, adolescence (*see* DATING AND COURTSHIP), and marriage. President David O. McKay taught, "The home is the best place in the world to teach the child self-restraint, to give him [or her] happiness in self-control, and respect for the rights of others" (*IE* 62 [Aug. 1959]:583). Latter-day Saints view the home as the proper place for teaching children about care for the body, gender roles, sexuality, changing physical and emotional needs, prevention of sexual abuse, and enjoyment of proper and virtuous intimacies.

Where schools have undertaken sex education courses and programs, the Church believes the materials used should advocate abstinence from sex before marriage and should teach correct principles that will produce long-term happiness. Thus, the Church believes that public education should in no way promote or encourage sexual promiscuity, a lifestyle that is unhealthy, immoral, and fraught with potentially serious consequences. The Church takes the position that when sex education is taught in the schools, the teacher and the course materials should encourage parental involvement in sex-educational discussions to foster respect for the family, human life, and natural differences between the sexes. When educators teach about human sexuality, they should feel that they have been entrusted by the parents of their students with the privilege of discussing and teaching a subject that has eternal significance to the family and family members.

BIBLIOGRAPHY

"Sex Education." *General Handbook of Instruction*, 11-5. Salt Lake City, 1989.

A Parent's Guide. Salt Lake City, 1985.

DARLENE CHIDESTER HUTCHISON

SEXUALITY

In LDS life and thought, sexuality consists of attitudes, feelings, and desires that are God-given and central to God's plan for his children, but they are not the central motivating force in human action. Sexual feelings are to be governed by each individual within boundaries the Lord has set. Sexuality is not characterized as a need, or a deprivation that must be satisfied, but as a desire that should be fulfilled only within marriage, with sensitive attention given to the well-being of one's heterosexual marriage partner. As the offspring of God, humans carry the divine Light of Christ, which is the means whereby the appropriate expression of sexual desires can be measured. Depending on whether men and women are true or false to this light, they will be the masters or the victims of sexual feelings. Such desires are to be fulfilled only within legal heterosexual marriage, wherein sexual involvement is to be an expression of unity, compassion, commitment, and love. Mutuality and equality are to be the hallmark of a married couple's physical intimacy.

The purposes of appropriate sexual relations in marriage include the expression and building of joy, unity, love, and oneness. To be "one flesh" is to experience an emotional and spiritual unity. This oneness is as fundamental a purpose of marital relations as is procreation. President Spencer W. Kimball stated:

> The union of the sexes, husband and wife (and only husband and wife), was for the principal purpose of bringing children into the world. Sexual experiences were never intended by the Lord to be a mere plaything or merely to satisfy passions and lusts. We know of no directive from the Lord that proper sexual experience between husbands and wives need be limited totally to the procreation of children, but we find much evidence from Adam until now that no provision was ever made by the Lord for indiscriminate sex [1975, p. 4].

Furthermore, as Paul noted, "Let the husband render unto the wife due benevolence: and likewise also the wife unto the husband. The wife hath not power of her own body, but the husband: and likewise also the husband hath not power of his own body, but the wife" (1 Cor. 7:3–4). Thus, physical intimacy is a blessing to married couples when it is an expression of their mutual benevolence and commitment to each other's well-being, an affirmation of their striving to be emotionally and spiritually one. The key in sexual matters is unselfishness. Self-centered pursuit of physical desire is destructive of the unity and love that characterize healthy marital relations. Such love or charity is long-suffering, kind, not envious, does "not behave itself unseemly, seeketh not [one's] own, is not easily provoked, thinketh no evil" (1 Cor. 13:4–5), and is compatible with the Light of Christ, which directs all in the ways of righteousness.

Bringing children into a loving home is considered a sacred privilege and responsibility of husbands and wives. Given that context, BIRTH CONTROL is a matter left to the prayerful, mutual decisions of a righteous couple, with the counsel that husbands must be considerate of their wives, who experience the greater physical and emotional demands in bearing children. A woman's health and strength are to be preserved in childbearing; thus, wisdom should govern how a husband and wife carry out the responsibility to become parents and to care for their offspring.

Sexual feelings in the mature man or woman are relatively strong and constant, and they are not evil. An early apostle of this dispensation, Parley P. Pratt, noted:

> Some persons have supposed that our natural affections were the results of a fallen and corrupt nature, and that they are "carnal, sensual, and devilish," and therefore ought to be resisted, subdued, or overcome as so many evils which prevent our perfection, or progress in the spiritual life. . . . Our natural affections are planted in us by the Spirit of God, for a wise purpose; and they are the very main-springs of life and happiness—they are the cement of all virtuous and heavenly society—they are the essence of charity, or love. . . . There is not a more pure and holy principle in existence than the affection which glows in the bosom of a virtuous man for his companion [p. 52].

As with any appetite or passion, physical desire can be distorted, overindulged, or misused. Spencer W. Kimball observed that, as in all other aspects of marriage, there are virtues to be observed in sexual matters: "There are some people who have said that behind the bedroom doors anything goes. That is not true and the Lord would not condone it" (Kimball, 1982, p. 312).

The Church prohibits sexual involvement except between a man and woman who are lawfully married to each other. Latter-day Saints are expected to abstain from sexual intercourse prior to marriage and to honor the marriage covenant by confining sexual relations to the spouse only (*see* PREMARITAL SEX). Sexual morality also requires abstention from activities that arouse desires not expressible until marriage. Sexual abstinence prior to marriage is considered not only right and possible but also beneficial. Abstinence is not viewed as repression, nor are there any particular negative consequences to so living.

Parents have the obligation to teach their children both the goodness—the sacredness—of the power to create life (*see* PROCREATION) and the principles of maturation and sexual development. Church leaders encourage parents to discuss sexuality openly with their children, answering their questions straightforwardly and contrasting the

Lord's plan for his children—which includes their eventual ability to produce children themselves—with the ways this power to create life can be profaned or abused. Children are to be prepared while young and, according to appropriate stages of development, are to be taught regarding human reproduction and the emotional and spiritual meanings of the procreative power and sexual desires that will grow within them (*see* SEX EDUCATION). Parents are expected to teach correct principles and to be examples of what they teach, treating each other with compassion and charity and living in a relationship of absolute fidelity.

Fundamental to all parental instruction is a parent-child relationship of love and trust. Youth are vulnerable to sexual enticements both because of the strength of their developing desires and because they are still growing in understanding and responsibility. Full comprehension of the consequences—to themselves and to succeeding generations—of the failure to abstain sexually may not come simultaneously with their sexual interests. Trust and respect for parents can help insulate adolescents from temptation while their capacity to exercise full rights and responsibilities matures.

Parents' responsibility to educate children sensitively and directly should not be delegated to the public schools or other agencies outside the home. When public sex-education programs are offered, LDS parents are counseled to assure that such programs adequately acknowledge the sanctity of marriage and promote family-oriented values and standards. When such agencies undertake sex education, LDS parents should have prepared and taught their children in such a way that school programs will at best be a supplement to the foundations of understanding established in the family circle.

The standard of sexual morality endorsed by the Church applies equally to men and women. Given that the power to create life is central to God's plan for his children, sexual transgression is most serious (*see* ADULTERY). Those who violate the law of chastity may be subject to Church disciplinary procedures, designed to help them cease their transgressions and restore them to full fellowship. Whether it is adultery, fornication, sexual abuse, incest, rape, perversion, or any other unholy practices, such behavior is to be addressed vigorously by local Church authorities, who seek the repentance of perpetrators and the protection of any victims.

Homosexual relationships are prohibited (*see* HOMOSEXUALITY). In such cases, the Church affirms that such distortions in sexual feelings or behavior can, with the Lord's help, be overcome. A compassionate interest in the well-being of transgressors and the healing of relationships should motivate Church interest and action. Sexual wrongdoing is not to be condoned, ignored, or addressed casually. Transgressors themselves can be forgiven, but only by repenting and coming unto Christ and, through his atonement, turning away from their destructive beliefs and practices.

Victims of rape or incest often experience trauma and feelings of guilt, but they are not responsible for the evil done by others, and they deserve and need to be restored to their sense of innocence through the love and counsel of Church leaders.

Practically speaking, the benefits of living a chaste life prior to marriage and of observing a relationship of fidelity after marriage apply to every dimension of marriage and family relationships. By remaining chaste before marriage and totally faithful to one's spouse in a heterosexual marriage, one can avoid some physically debilitating diseases, extramarital pregnancies, and venereal infections passed on to offspring. The sense of trust, loyalty, love, and commitment essential to the ideal of oneness in marriage and family life is not damaged or strained. Furthermore, one's relationship to and confidence in God are strengthened. By governing the power to create life, one sets the stage for the exercise of these desires, not whimsically, but with a reverence for the sacredness of the divine powers of creation.

BIBLIOGRAPHY

Foster, Lawrence. *Religion and Sexuality: Three American Communal Experiments of the Nineteenth Century.* New York, 1981.

Kimball, Spencer W. "The Lord's Plan for Men and Women." *Ensign* 5 (Oct. 1975):2–5.

———. *The Teachings of Spencer W. Kimball,* ed. Edward L. Kimball. Salt Lake City, 1982.

Pratt, Parley P. *Writings of Parley Parker Pratt,* ed. Parker P. Robison. Salt Lake City, 1952.

Rytting, Marvin. "On Sexuality." *Dialogue* 7 (Winter 1972): 102–104.

"Sexuality and Mormon Culture." *Dialogue* 10 (Autumn 1976):9–93. Entire issue on sexuality.

TERRANCE D. OLSON

SISTERHOOD

Sisterhood, like brotherhood, is rooted in the gospel of Jesus Christ that views God as the actual father of the immortal and eternal spirits of earthly women and men. President Barbara B. Smith of the Relief Society, said in 1976, "We look upon ourselves as being part of the family of the Lord, and so our sisterhood is one that has a deep understanding of this relationship" (Smith, pp. 7–8). Sisterhood in this broad sense includes all women in the world.

The title "Sister" also has a more special meaning in reference to the women of the Church. Every Latter-day Saint woman is appropriately called "sister." The term does not relate to a woman's profession or ecclesiastical calling, as it does in some religious and professional groups. Members of The Church of Jesus Christ of Latter-day Saints often refer to women members collectively as "the sisterhood of the Church," "sisters in the gospel," or simply as "the sisters."

"The sisterhood of the Church" may refer specifically to members of the Relief Society, organized by the Prophet Joseph Smith in 1842, which includes all adult women of the Church—over two million in 1990. Lucy Mack Smith, the Prophet's mother, expressed the sisterly quality of the society in a classic statement: "This institution is a good one," she told the women assembled in their second meeting. "We must cherish one another, watch over one another, comfort one another, and gain instruction, that we may all sit down in heaven together" (Relief Society Minutes of Nauvoo, Mar. 24, 1842, LDS Church Archives). A later prophet would speak of "a society of sisters," and refer to "the loving fellowship" of the Relief Society visiting teaching program, which from the beginning has been a channel for sisterly concern (Kimball, p. 2).

The organizational network of the Church promotes sisterhood by providing women opportunities to work and study together, to share religious convictions, and to serve others in charitable ways. Like Dorcas in the early Christian church (Acts 9:36), LDS sisters have traditionally sewn clothing for the needy. In the late nineteenth century they worked together in producing silk, saving grain, and managing retail stores. Later they held nurse training classes and sponsored maternal and child health clinics. They have also extended their service through cooperation with the Red Cross and other community agencies. The nature of the tasks has changed with time, but the sisterhood itself continues.

Several publications have helped to expand this network of concern. The sisters published *Woman's Exponent* from 1872 to 1914, *Relief Society Bulletin* in 1914, and *Relief Society Magazine* from 1915 to 1970. Currently, the *Ensign,* the Church's monthly magazine for adults, carries articles by and about women, messages from women leaders, and reports of women's conferences. The international magazines carry much of the same material in translation, keeping the sisters of the Church in touch worldwide.

Contributions from sisters in many nations financed two major projects in the 1950s and 1970s: the Relief Society headquarters building in Salt Lake City and the Monument to Women statuary gardens in Nauvoo, Illinois. At the dedication of the latter in 1978, some twenty thousand women celebrated their sisterhood at the place where their society had begun. In 1984, the Relief Society Building also became the headquarters of the primary (for children) and of the young women (girls twelve to eighteen), enabling the general women leaders of the Church to work closely together in their mutual concern for nurturing the young.

Since the early days of the Church, women's service in the temples of the Church has contributed a profound religious dimension to their sisterhood. By participating in temple ordinances, in which they minister by divine commission to their "sisters in the gospel," worthy LDS women can help ensure the eternal nature of family ties and create friendships in the process.

The sisters also sustain each other in personal ways. Like Ruth and Naomi, the women of the early LDS Church who left homes and friends to live in a strange land found comfort in each other's loving support. Women who join the Church today often need the same kind of support as do those who are uprooted in an increasingly mobile society. To an elderly woman living alone, sisterhood may mean the assurance that she is not forgotten but has friends and significant work to do with them, perhaps in a nearby temple. To a young mother it can mean practical help in her home and empathetic sharing of problems in a Relief Society class.

Although LDS sisterhood includes a rich diversity of cultures, and occasional disagreements over local issues, its most important aspect is still the bonding relationship of a common faith. As one sister said of that faith, "It is a bond that connects women with women and with the Savior across generations" (Peterson, p. 79).

BIBLIOGRAPHY

Mulvay Derr, Jill. "'Strength in Our Union': The Making of Mormon Sisterhood." In *Sisters in Spirit*, ed. M. Beecher and L. Anderson. Urbana, Ill., 1987.

Kimball, Spencer W. "Relief Society: Its Promise and Potential." *Ensign* 6 (Mar. 1976):2–5.

Peterson, Grethe B. "BYU Women's Conference Draws Thousands." *Ensign* 10 (Apr. 1980):79.

Smith, Barbara B. "A Conversation with Sister Barbara B. Smith, Relief Society General President." *Ensign* 6 (Mar. 1976):7–8.

JANATH RUSSELL CANNON
JILL MULVAY DERR

SOCIAL CHARACTERISTICS

The major social characteristics and attitudes of Latter-day Saints in the United States, along with the challenges and problems they face, can be compared to those of other religious groups. Comparisons can be based on information that has been gathered about Latter-day Saints in the United States regarding their family characteristics, such as marriage, divorce, fertility, and sexual attitudes, as well as their social class, gender roles, substance use and health, political affiliation, attitudes toward social issues, religiosity, and migration.

SOURCES. Each year a random sampling of about 1,500 U.S. adults is interviewed in the National Opinion Research Center's Cumulative General Social Survey (NORC). From 1972 to 1988 this yielded a sample of 23,356, of whom 288 (1.2%) were LDS, a very small sample of the total Church population.

A supplemental source is the annual national survey of high school seniors conducted by Johnston, O'Malley, and Bachman (1988) for the National Institute on Drug Abuse (NIDA). They survey approximately 16,000 U.S. high school seniors each year regarding their lifestyles and substance use (62,570 students from 1984 to 1987). Beginning in 1984 they included "LDS" as one of the

TABLE 1. MARITAL CHARACTERISTICS BY RELIGIOUS
AFFILIATION

| | | Religious Affiliation | | | | | |
		Protestant	Catholic	Jew	Other	None	Mormon
Percent ever married		87	81	83	74	66	89
Percent married							
by 19	Female	49	37	24	34	40	45
	Male	18	12	3	13	18	23
Percent married							
by 21	Female	70	61	50	56	65	74
	Male	42	33	17	32	40	49
Percent "very happy"							
in marriage	Female	63	62	69	70	60	72
	Male	67	68	65	63	55	62
Percent ever							
divorced or separated		18	11	10	20	23	18
SAMPLE SIZE		14,678	5,809	515	368	1,626	288

Source: NORC pooled surveys for 1972–1988.

responses to the religion question (1.6% chose that response). These proportions of Latter-day Saints are similar to Stark's (1989) estimate that 1.6 percent of the population of the United States is LDS.

In addition, data on Church members have been published in various professional journals. Heaton and Goodman (1985) report information from a national, random sample of 1,500 Latter-day Saints and make comparisons with NORC data.

For comparisons in this article between Latter-day Saints and other religious groups, percentage differences larger than 5 percent are statistically significant.

MARRIAGE. Heaton and Goodman (1985) reported that 97 percent of Latter-day Saints over age thirty have married, which is higher than the marriage rate in the same category for Catholics, Protestants, or those with no religious affiliation. According to NORC data, a higher percentage of LDS Church members have been married than any other religious group. Eighty-nine percent of LDS adults have been married, compared to 87 percent of Protestants, 81 percent of Catholics, and 83 percent of Jews (Table 1).

AGE AT MARRIAGE.   Latter-day Saints also tend to marry early. Forty-five percent of LDS women and 23 percent of LDS men have married by age nineteen. By age twenty-one 74 percent of LDS women and 49 percent of LDS men have married. This is considerably higher than for any other religious group (Table 1).

MARITAL HAPPINESS.   Sixty-six percent of married Latter-day Saints say they are "very happy" in their marriages, compared with 65 percent of Protestants and Catholics and 57 percent of those with no religion. LDS women tend to report more marital happiness than other women, particularly Protestant and Catholic women. On the other hand, LDS men report lower levels of marital satisfaction than all other men except those with no religion (Table 1).

DIVORCE AND REMARRIAGE.   The divorce rate is lower among Latter-day Saints than among Protestants, "other," and "none," but higher than among Catholics or Jews, as shown in Table 1. Eighteen percent of Mormons report that they have been separated or divorced, compared with only 11 percent of Catholics and 10 percent of Jews. In the survey of Latter-day Saints by Heaton and Goodman (1985), they reported that 17 percent had been divorced. NORC data for 1978, 1980, 1982, and 1983 showed considerably higher rates of divorce for the non-LDS or "other" religious groups than those shown in Table 1 (additional research is needed to resolve this discrepancy). After divorce, Latter-day Saints are more likely to remarry than persons from other religious groups (Heaton and Goodman, 1985).

FERTILITY.   Thornton (1979) found that Latter-day Saints in the United States and Canada have a high fertility rate. Although LDS fertility has decreased substantially during the twentieth century, it remains considerably higher than that of other religious groups. Heaton and Goodman (1985) found that LDS women average about one child more than women in other religious groups.

NORC data illustrate the relatively high rate of childbearing among Church members. More than 50 percent of Latter-day Saints have three or more children, compared with 36 percent of Catholics and 37 percent of Protestants. About one in five Church members has five or more children, compared with only one in ten among Protestants and Catholics. Only about 2 percent of Jews have five or more children.

TABLE 2. RELIGION AND FERTILITY

| | Religious Affiliation | | | | | |
	Protestant	Catholic	Jew	Other	None	Mormon
Children ever born						
Percent with 3 or more children	37	36	21	25	20	52
Percent with 5 or more children	11	11	2	5	5	22
Ideal number of children						
Percent who say ideal number of children is . . .						
2	50	43	49	54	56	23
3	22	26	29	20	16	18
4	14	15	7	8	12	26
4 or more	22	26	16	19	17	54
SAMPLE SIZE	14,678	5,809	515	368	1,626	288

Source: NORC pooled surveys for 1972–1988.

Among all religious groups except Latter-day Saints, the ideal number of children is two. Forty-three percent of Catholics said that two is the ideal number of children, compared with only 23 percent of Latter-day Saints. More than 50 percent of Latter-day Saints said that the ideal number of children is four or more, compared with 26 percent of Catholics and 22 percent of Protestants (Table 2).

SEXUAL ATTITUDES. A greater percentage of Latter-day Saints dis-

TABLE 3. SEXUAL ATTITUDES AND RELIGION

| | Religious Affiliation | | | | | |
	Protestant	Catholic	Jew	Other	None	Mormon
Percent who said that . . .						
Premarital sex is always wrong	34	25	13	22	7	58
Extramarital sex is always wrong	76	71	46	43	58	90
Homosexuality is always wrong	77	67	33	55	40	90
SAMPLE SIZE	14,678	5,809	515	368	1,626	288

Source: NORC pooled surveys for 1972–1988.

TABLE 4. EDUCATION BY RELIGION (IN PERCENT)

| | Religious Affiliation | | | | | |
	Protestant	Catholic	Jew	Other	None	Mormon
Women						
College graduate	12	11	35	17	25	18
Postgraduate	4	4	14	11	9	8
Men						
College graduate	17	19	52	37	27	22
Postgraduate	8	8	31	13	17	14

Source: NORC pooled surveys for 1972–1988.

approve of premarital sex, extramarital sex, and homosexuality than any other religious group. As shown in Table 3, 58 percent of the Latter-day Saints said that premarital sex is always wrong, compared with 34 percent of Protestants and 25 percent of Catholics. About three-fourths of Protestants and more than two-thirds of Catholics said that extramarital sex and homosexuality are always wrong, compared to 90 percent of Latter-day Saints.

SOCIAL CLASS. LDS Church members tend to be middle class in terms of education, occupation, and income. They tend to have somewhat fewer people in high-status occupations than Jews or those with no religion, but somewhat more than Protestants and Catholics.

EDUCATION. Eighteen percent of LDS women and 22 percent of LDS men in the NORC survey have graduated from college. This is significantly higher than the comparable percentages among Protestants and Catholics, but lower than among Jews and those with no religious affiliation. Fourteen percent of LDS men and 8 percent of LDS women have received graduate education. Jews and those with no religion have higher percentages, while Catholics and Protestants have lower percentages (Table 4).

OCCUPATION. The data on occupations are similar to the data on education. Among both men and women, Latter-day Saints have more professionals and managers than Catholics or Protestants but fewer than Jews or "others." They have fewer operative workers than any other religious group except Jews. LDS women are overrepresented among service occupations, with 25 percent in service occupations,

TABLE 5. PERCENT IN SELECTED OCCUPATIONS BY RELIGION

| | *Religious Affiliation* | | | | | |
	Protestant	*Catholic*	*Jew*	*Other*	*None*	*Mormon*
Women						
Professional	15	15	25	19	23	23
Manager	7	7	16	8	12	8
Clerical	29	37	37	27	30	30
Operative	14	13	6	21	9	6
Service	19	16	5	15	15	25
Men						
Professional	14	16	35	26	21	17
Manager	14	14	26	19	11	16
Clerical	5	8	10	5	7	8
Operative	18	15	3	10	16	10
Service	8	8	3	10	8	7
SAMPLE SIZE	14,678	5,809	515	368	1,626	288

Source: NORC pooled surveys for 1972–1988.

compared with only 19 percent of Catholic women, the religion with the next highest percentage (Table 5).

INCOME. Table 6 gives a distribution of family income by religious affiliation. About one in five LDS families has an income less than $10,000 per year, while 15 percent earn more than $50,000 per year. The only religious group dramatically different from Latter-day Saints in income distribution is the Jewish: Almost half of Jewish families earn $50,000 or more, while less than 10 percent have incomes

TABLE 6. FAMILY INCOME BY RELIGION (IN PERCENT)

| | | *Religious Affiliation* | | | | | |
		Protestant	*Catholic*	*Jew*	*Other*	*None*	*Mormon*
Income level							
$0–9,999		26	15	10	29	18	22
10,000–24,999		33	34	17	23	33	24
25,000–49,999		30	36	24	34	34	39
50,000 or more		12	15	49	14	15	15
	TOTAL	101	100	100	100	100	100
SAMPLE SIZE		14,678	5,809	515	368	1,626	288

Source: NORC pooled surveys for 1972–1988.

TABLE 7. PERCENT WHO STRONGLY AGREE THAT A PRESCHOOL
CHILD IS LIKELY TO SUFFER IF HIS/HER MOTHER WORKS

| | *Religious Affiliation* | | | | | |
	Protestant	*Catholic*	*Jew*	*Other*	*None*	*Mormon*
Percent who strongly agree	13	16	14	8	15	22
SAMPLE SIZE	14,678	5,809	515	368	1,626	288

Source: NORC pooled surveys for 1972–1988.

below $10,000. Although the differences are not large, Latter-day
Saints have a few more middle-income families than the other religions. Thirty-nine percent of LDS families have incomes between
$25,000 and $50,000, which is higher than for any of the other religious groups.

GENDER ROLES.   Brinkerhoff and Mackie (1985) studied how religion is related to gender role attitudes among college students. They
found that the more religious students tend to have more traditional
attitudes. Those with no religion were the most egalitarian, followed
by Catholics, Protestants, and Latter-day Saints.

As shown earlier in Table 4, LDS women are more likely to graduate from college than Catholic or Protestant women, but less likely
than Jewish or nonaffiliated women. For graduate education the pattern was similar—a higher percentage of LDS than Catholic or
Protestant women have received graduate education.

As shown in Table 5, LDS women are more likely to be employed
in professional occupations than Catholic or Protestant women.
Twenty-three percent of LDS women are employed in professional
occupations, which is similar to Jewish women and women with no
religious affiliation.

Respondents to the NORC survey were asked if they agreed or
disagreed with the following statement: "A preschool child is likely to
suffer if his or her mother works." Agreement with this statement is
higher among Latter-day Saints than among any other religious
group. As shown in Table 7, 22 percent of LDS strongly agree with
the statement, compared with only 16 percent of Catholics and 13
percent of Protestants.

SUBSTANCE USE.   LDS doctrine prohibits the use of alcohol, tobacco,
and other addictive drugs. Among adults and adolescents, usage

TABLE 8. SUBSTANCE USE BY RELIGIOUS AFFILIATION

| | Religious Affiliation | | | | | |
	Protestant	Catholic	Jew	Other	None	Mormon
Adults						
Percent who drink alcohol	65	85	86	66	87	28
Percent who smoke	36	38	28	34	49	14
SAMPLE SIZE	14,678	5,809	515	368	1,626	288
High school seniors*						
Percent who drink alcohol	62	75	79	51	70	33
Percent who smoke	28	32	30	25	32	14
Percent who use marijuana	22	25	28	18	32	14
Percent who use cocaine	5	7	8	5	9	5
SAMPLE SIZE	29,949	18,704	914	3,642	7,046	972

*Percent who used during the past 30 days.
Source: Adults: NORC pooled surveys for 1972–1988.
Seniors: NIDA pooled surveys for 1984–1987.

rates are considerably lower among Latter-day Saints than among other religious groups (Table 8). Only 28 percent of adult Latter-day Saints say they drink alcohol, compared with 65 percent of Protestants, 85 percent of Catholics, and 86 percent of Jews. Fourteen percent say they smoke tobacco, compared with 36 percent of Protestants, 38 percent of Catholics, and 28 percent of Jews.

The NIDA survey of substance use among high school seniors reveals substantial differences between Latter-day Saints and other religious groups (Table 8). About 33 percent of LDS high school seniors said they had used alcohol within the previous thirty days, compared to 62 percent of Protestants and 75 percent of Catholics. The percentage of LDS seniors who smoke is half as large as among the other religious groups—14 percent among LDS, 28 percent among Protestants, and 32 percent among Catholics. The differences for marijuana are not as large, but are still lower for LDS students. For example, 14 percent of LDS seniors had used marijuana during the past month, compared to 22 percent among Protestants and 25 percent among Catholics. LDS students also have low rates of cocaine use. Five percent had used cocaine during the past month, compared to 5 percent among Protestants, 7 percent among Catholics, and 8 percent among Jews.

TABLE 9. PERCEIVED HEALTH BY RELIGIOUS AFFILIATION (IN PERCENT)

		Religious Affiliation				
		Protestant	Catholic	Jew	Other	None	Mormon
Health						
Good or excellent		72	77	78	81	79	85
Fair		21	18	17	16	17	12
Poor		7	5	6	4	3	3
	TOTAL	100	100	101	101	99	100
SAMPLE SIZE		14,678	5,809	515	368	1,626	288

Source: NORC pooled surveys for 1972–1988.

HEALTH.   Jarvis and Northcott (1986) observed that Latter-day Saints have longer life expectancy than non-LDS because of lower than average rates of cancer, heart disease, and infant deaths. Self-reported health of NORC respondents (Table 9) shows 85 percent of Latter-day Saints report that their health is good or excellent, which is higher than any other religious group. Only 3 percent of LDS rate their health as poor.

POLITICAL AFFILIATION.   Stark (1989) reported that Utah is the most Republican state in the nation, judging from the fact that a higher percentage of people voted for Reagan there in 1984 than in any other state. Data on religion and political party affiliation confirm that Latter-day Saints strongly favor Republicans. Almost half of Church members are Republicans, compared with only 27 percent of Protestants, 18 percent of Catholics, and 11 percent of Jews. Nineteen percent of Latter-day Saints say they are "strongly Republican" compared to only 10 percent of Protestants and 6 percent of Catholics. The percentage of people who are Democrats is smaller among LDS members than among any other religious group (Table 10). In 1984, 85 percent of Mormons voted for Reagan compared to 57 percent of Protestants, 57 percent of Catholics, and 41 percent of Jews.

ABORTION.   Jews are the most accepting of abortion, while Latter-day Saints are the least accepting. Less than one-fourth of Latter-day Saints favor abortion if the reasons are lack of money, being unmarried, or not desiring the child. The next-closest group is the

TABLE 10. POLITICAL PARTY BY RELIGION (IN PERCENT)

| | Religious Affiliation | | | | | |
	Protestant	Catholic	Jew	Other	None	Mormon
Democrat	41	46	55	34	30	26
Independent	30	35	32	48	54	26
Republican	27	18	11	14	13	46
Other	2	1	2	4	3	1
Strongly Democrat	18	18	20	10	16	6
Strongly Republican	10	6	2	4	7	19
SAMPLE SIZE	14,678	5,809	515	368	1,626	288

Source: NORC pooled surveys for 1971–1988.

Catholics, and more than one-third of them favor abortion in the above-stated circumstances. Sixty-seven percent of Latter-day Saints favor abortion if the fetus is deformed, compared with 74 percent of Catholics and 96 percent of Jews. Almost 90 percent of Latter-day Saints favor abortion if the health of the mother is endangered by the pregnancy. This percentage is similar to most other religious groups, although Jews and those with no religion have percentages of 97 and 95, respectively (Table 11).

DEATH PENALTY. A majority of Americans approve of the death penalty for murderers. Of the six religious groups shown in Table 11,

TABLE 11. PERCENT FAVORING ABORTION, DEATH PENALTY, AND LEGALIZATION OF MARIJUANA BY RELIGION

| | Religious Affiliation | | | | | |
	Protestant	Catholic	Jew	Other	None	Mormon
Abortion if . . .						
Endangered health	88	83	97	88	95	88
Rape	79	75	96	81	91	71
Defective fetus	79	74	96	80	91	67
Poor	45	40	85	61	74	24
Unmarried	41	37	85	53	71	24
Do not desire child	40	36	81	71	53	22
Death penalty	67	71	68	60	62	89
Legalization of marijuana	18	22	41	28	50	10
SAMPLE SIZE	14,678	5,809	515	368	1,626	288

Source: NORC pooled surveys for 1972–1988.

TABLE 12. MIGRATION SINCE AGE 16 BY RELIGION

	Religious Affiliation					
	Protestant	Catholic	Jew	Other	None	Mormon
Current residence compared to residence at age 16						
Same city	43	46	38	30	41	31
Same state	26	25	20	21	23	28
Different state	32	29	42	50	36	41
TOTAL	14,678	5,809	515	368	1,626	288

Source: NORC pooled surveys for 1972–1988.

Latter-day Saints show the greatest support for the death penalty while "others" give the least support. Eighty-nine percent of Latter-day Saints favor the death penalty compared to 67 percent of Protestants, 71 percent of Catholics, and 60 percent of "others."

LEGALIZATION OF MARIJUANA. Only one in ten Latter-day Saints supports the legalization of marijuana, compared with about two in ten among Protestants and Catholics. Forty-one percent of Jews and half of those with no religion favor legalization of marijuana.

RESIDENCE AND MIGRATION. Latter-day Saints are less likely than individuals from other religious groups to have grown up in a large city and somewhat more likely to have lived in "open country but not on a farm." Only 9 percent of Mormons were living in a large city at the age of sixteen, compared to 11 percent of Protestants, 22 percent of Catholics and 51 percent of Jews. Twenty percent of Mormons were living on a farm at sixteen, compared to 27 percent of Protestants, 10 percent of Catholics, and 11 percent of Jews.

Do certain religious groups tend to grow up and live in the same city or state? When Latter-day Saints become adults, do they tend to stay in the area where they were raised, or migrate elsewhere? NORC respondents were asked if they lived in the same city, same state, or a different state than they lived in at age sixteen (Table 12). Forty-one percent of Latter-day Saints lived in a state different from the one where they lived at age sixteen, while 31 percent lived in the same city as they did at age sixteen. In this, Latter-day Saints are not dramatically different from members of other religious groups. They appear somewhat more mobile than Catholics and Protestants in that a higher percentage live in a different state than they did at age sixteen.

When one compares various selected social characteristics of Latter-day Saints with other religious groups in the United States, one finds both similarities and differences. Latter-day Saints as a whole have higher rates than other religious groups with respect to marriage rates, rates of marital satisfaction, fertility, and life expectancy, as well as higher disapproval rates on sexual relations outside of marriage, abortion, and the legalization of marijuana. Latter-day Saints have fewer divorces than most Protestant groups, but more than Catholics and Jews; they tend to have higher rates of education, income, and occupational status than Protestants and Catholics, but typically lower rates in these respects than Jews.

BIBLIOGRAPHY

Brinkerhoff, Merlin B., and Marlene MacKie. "Religion and Gender: A Comparison of Canadian and American Student Attitudes." *Journal of Marriage and the Family* 47 (1985):415–29.

Heaton, Tim B., and Kristen L. Goodman. "Religion and Family Formation." *Review of Religious Research* 26 (1985):343–59.

Jarvis, George K., and Herbert C. Northcott. "Religion and Differences in Mortality." Mimeographed, Department of Sociology, University of Alberta, Edmonton, Alta., 1986.

Johnston, Lloyd D.; Patrick M. O'Malley; and Herald G. Bachman. *Illicit Drug Use, Smoking, and Drinking by America's High School Students, College Students, and Young Adults: 1975-1987.* Rockville, Md., 1988.

Stark, Rodney. *Sociology*, 3rd ed. Belmont, Calif., 1989.

Thornton, Arland. "Religion and Fertility: The Case of Mormonism." *Journal of Marriage and the Family* 41 (1979):131–42.

STEPHEN J. BAHR

SOCIAL AND CULTURAL HISTORY

As a people, members of The Church of Jesus Christ of Latter-day Saints have over time taken on distinctive qualities as their beliefs and historical experience have given shape and force to their society. Indeed, geographers speak frequently of a "Mormon Culture Region" covering all of Utah and extending into neighboring states, with identifiable traits that set it apart. Observers have long seen LDS social organization as more coherent and tightly knit than most societies in the United States.

Several forces have shaped LDS cultural and social life. Belief in the gathering motivated most early converts to migrate to areas where they could live with other Saints. Joseph Smith urged them, once gathered, to build homes in towns rather than on their farms, thus minimizing the physical distance between households and enhancing opportunities for social interaction. Joseph Smith founded programs to help build a more cohesive society and taught that cooperation was superior to individual enterprise. Priesthood power was extended to all the faithful, thus breaking down traditional class-based social hierarchies. The LDS belief that God inspired those acting in Church callings invested both local and general leaders with legitimacy at a time when authority in general was questioned widely among Americans. Priesthood office and Church position became a fluid alternative hierarchy, providing an effective mechanism for directing social and cultural change.

Other elements have combined with these to shape the distinctive aspects of LDS society. The Church did not, as did many rapidly growing Christian movements of the early nineteenth century, reject popular public entertainments. Indeed, excelling in fine arts, music, dance, drama, and other forms of cultural expression could be seen as a sacred obligation. Individual creative works were recognized and appreciated, but the more robust Mormon cultural expressions were those requiring unified action and cooperation. Moreover, the influx of immigrants—beginning in the 1840s from Great Britain and in the 1850s from Scandinavia—brought directly to Utah pioneer settlements institutions not as readily accessible to many other agrarian societies in the western United States.

Distinctive elements of social and cultural life in the first LDS areas—Kirtland, Ohio, and the various Missouri settlements—were related principally to religious activities. They included the designing and constructing of the Kirtland Temple (1836), with Aaronic and Melchizedek pulpits that corresponded to priesthood organization; the writing of HYMNS expressing distinctive beliefs; the forming of a choir to sing LDS hymns at the dedication of the Kirtland Temple; and the founding of the School of the Prophets to encourage both secular and religious learning. Popular amusements, vernacular architecture, and crafts were similar to those in other rural American districts, with the exception that horseracing and cardplaying were avoided. In the mid-1830s, the movement was as yet too young and the number of Latter-day Saints too few for either new doctrines or historical experience to have made them markedly different culturally from other Americans.

By the mid-1840s, however, some distinctive elements were becoming evident. Because earlier persecutions had reinforced a natural group solidarity, members looked inward and limited association with those not of their faith, whom they came to call gentiles. Resulting isolation focused the process of selecting and adapting cultural and social forms from the greater society, making them more distinctive. Nauvoo, Illinois, a temporary respite from persecution, saw the largest group "gathered" yet, further favoring the development of distinctive social and cultural institutions. The division of Nauvoo into political "wards" led eventually to a practice of dividing Church membership into geographically defined congregations called wards. The ward was to become a social institution of first importance—perhaps the most powerful single instrument of LDS social organization.

Nauvoo also saw the introduction of temple-related teachings and practices that had important implications for social and cultural life. Baptism for the dead permitted Church members to be baptized as proxies for deceased ancestors; sealings united husbands and wives through eternity; and the endowment, another ordinance with eternal implications, also strengthened group commitment to building together the kingdom of God. Celestial and plural marriage, popularly called polygamy, was taught privately (publicly in 1852); with the Law of Adoption, plural marriage extended the concept of family to incorporate all of society.

Some left the Church over Nauvoo innovations. Those who embraced the restoration of these additional doctrines and ordinances found themselves farther from a Protestant Christianity that came to seem increasingly hostile. The result was even stronger identity and solidarity among those who accepted the teachings and endured the opprobrium they engendered.

Folk amusements in Nauvoo were those commonly found elsewhere in the United States. The city had bowling alleys and billiard halls. Men engaged in horsemanship and in personal contests, such as foot races and wrestling matches. Swimming, an early version of baseball called "Old Cat," and fencing were popular recreations.

Intellectual life was encouraged by lyceums, a debating society, a lending library, and art exhibits. The Nauvoo charters provided for a university, which administered the public school system and kept salient the hope of developing an LDS-controlled intellectual center for the Saints—a hope not realized until the founding in Utah of the UNIVERSITY OF DESERET (1850), BRIGHAM YOUNG UNIVERSITY (1875), and numerous ACADEMIES. The *Times and Seasons* (1839–1846) continued a tradition of LDS journalism that had begun in 1832 with the publication of the *Evening and the Morning Star* in Missouri (1832) and in Ohio (1832–1834), and would culminate in founding the *Deseret News* in 1850, which remains a Church-owned Salt Lake City daily newspaper.

Recent convert Gustavus Hills organized the Nauvoo Musical Lyceum in 1841. Partly through his efforts, choral music became so popular that in 1842 the women's Relief Society organized its own choir, as did several outlying settlements. These choirs continued throughout the Nauvoo period to sing a varied repertoire of religious, popular and even comedic songs, at both religious services and civic events. The first band to become an enduring institution was a twenty-piece ensemble, mostly percussion instruments and fifes. The band or other musicians provided music for the most popular entertainment in the city, dancing. Dances were held on every possible occasion and became an enduring feature of LDS social life. So important was music to the city's cultural life that in 1845 the Saints completed a Music Hall that would seat more than seven hundred persons.

In 1846 the Saints left Nauvoo for the West. That winter as many as 16,000 (by some estimates) gathered into settlements across Iowa and, especially, on both banks of the Missouri River. Band and choral music, and dancing, continued even in these severe circumstances. Though advance parties reached Utah the next year, the settlements on the river's east bank, centered in Kanesville, remained heavily LDS until 1852. This Iowa interlude (1846–1852) was of great importance in shaping LDS social and cultural institutions. Wards clearly became, for the first time, ecclesiastical jurisdictions with their own leaders and meeting schedules. Dancing, singing societies, and schools proliferated. The women, meeting frequently and informally, blessed and comforted one another and ministered to those needing assistance. Efforts were made to work the Law of Adoption and plural marriage into viable institutions that would enhance the cohesiveness of the larger COMMUNITY. Perhaps most important, the First Presidency was reorganized in December 1847, with Brigham Young, just returned from the Salt Lake Valley, being sustained in place of the martyred prophet. In Utah Brigham Young would take the lead in elaborating developments already begun in Nauvoo.

The earliest years of pioneering in Utah left little time for cultural and social activities beyond the perennial dancing, singing, and band music. But by 1852 the population was again sufficiently concentrated, this time in Salt Lake City, to recommence the ambitious agenda begun in Nauvoo. That winter Church leader Lorenzo Snow and his sister Eliza R. Snow organized the Polysophical Society, an informal discussion and debating society for men and women; comparable societies founded in many wards continued their activities throughout the decade. In 1853 a public lending library opened in the city. In 1852 Sicilian-born convert Domenico Ballo came to Salt Lake City with a band he had organized in St. Louis. The Ballo and the older William Pitt bands played, in addition to favorite hymns, such popular songs as "Auld Lang Syne," an occasional patriotic rendering of "Yankee Doodle" or "La Marseillaise," and selections from Mozart, Meyerbeer, and Rossini.

Choral music remained widespread and popular. In 1852 members revived the old Nauvoo choir. Because they performed first in the just-completed old adobe tabernacle and, after 1867, in a new tabernacle (which still graces Temple Square), it became known as the Tabernacle Choir. Eventually the "MORMON TABERNACLE CHOIR" became one of the two or three most widely recognized symbols of the Latter-day Saints. Its several hundred members from different backgrounds express themselves as a unified, harmonious whole— the epitome of LDS cultural expression. In 1929 the choir began regular weekly network radio broadcasts, which continue.

Cultural life in early Salt Lake City was not limited to music. The Deseret Dramatic Association, organized in 1852, first performed in the old Social Hall. The Social Hall housed musical performances, balls, and receptions as well as theatrical productions. It was super-seded in 1862 by the Salt Lake Theatre, a lavish building seating 1,500 and constructed at some sacrifice, one of the important cultural institutions of the early west. The Deseret Dramatic Association maintained an ambitious repertory schedule, in some seasons performing three times a week. A typical program began with prayer, featured a long, serious play, and ended with a short comedy or farce.

Dancing was popular throughout the territory, and every community prized its fiddlers. Most holidays ended with a grand ball that might last until two or three in the morning. "Square dances," ordered in prescribed patterns like the Virginia Reel, were the usual fare. An occasional risqué round dance such as the waltz was permitted as the century wore on. In Salt Lake City the Social Hall routinely hosted dances; larger affairs could be held at the Salt Lake Theatre, whose orchestra seats could be covered by a spring floor.

Architecture in Salt Lake City was for the most part spare, practical, and derivative. Greek Revival style, ordered and simple, was as popular in Utah as elsewhere in the United States. The Gothic Revival style can be seen in the Salt Lake Temple, and in other buildings, notably, Brigham Young's residence, the Lion House. The Federal-style architecture of public buildings the Saints had used in the Midwest was replicated in the city hall and other early civic structures. Homes were generally simple adobe or brick, built in traditional or pattern-book styles and sometimes reflecting the ethnic background of the owner. Such homes were commonly symmetrical, ornamented according to the combined tastes of owner and builder, and designed to look complete while awaiting the addition of a second story or wing as family needs and means permitted.

The considerable variety seen in houses was contained by a rigid city plan, an adaptation of principles Joseph Smith recommended in his 1833 "plat of the city of Zion." The plan called for homes of adobe, rock, or brick on large city lots uniformly set back from the broad, square-surveyed streets. A central square was set aside for the temple, and streets were named for their direction and distance from it. In outlying towns the central square contained churches, schools, and other civic structures. Farm land was outside the town proper. Early visitors were invariably impressed with the neatness and order of Mormon towns, always noting, in addition to the street pattern, the gardens, and the clear, mountain water that ran in small ditches along the streets.

This general pattern was followed in remote villages as well as in Salt Lake City. The compactness of the village system made it possible to sustain, even in towns with as few as two hundred or three hundred citizens, a full complement of bands and choirs, theater groups, and the ubiquitous community dances. Church leaders were acutely conscious of the social consequences of such a settlement pattern, pointing out in an 1882 letter the "many advantages of a social and civic character which might be lost . . . by spreading out so thinly that intercommunication is difficult, dangerous, inconvenient and expensive."

Despite the stress on group activities, there were several fine ARTISTS in early Utah. These included William W. Major, an accomplished painter, and C. C. A. Christensen, trained at the Royal Academy in Denmark, who painted faith-promoting scenes from LDS history. Norwegian convert Danquart A. Weggeland also did excellent work, mainly in painting sets for the Salt Lake Theatre and scenes in LDS temples and meetinghouses. George M. Ottinger worked extensively with historical representations, portraits, and landscapes.

Landscape painting played a lesser role in Utah ART until, in the 1890s, John Hafen, Lorus Pratt, Edwin Evans, and John Fairbanks studied in Paris under Church sponsorship. They returned to devote their considerable talents to painting Church scenes adorning interiors of LDS temples. Alfred Lambourne and H. L. A. Culmer, also prominent landscape artists of this later period, emphasized the romantic qualities of Utah landscapes in a style worthy of the famous Rocky Mountain painters Albert Bierstadt and Thomas Moran. Since Latter-day Saints did not commonly use statuary in adorning church interiors, there was relatively little public demand for sculpture. Two early pieces are well known: the lion that dominated the entryway to Brigham Young's Lion House, and the eagle carved in 1859 by Ralph Ramsey for the entrance to Brigham Young's estate.

Early photographers Marsena Cannon, Charles W. Carter, Charles Savage, George Anderson, and Elfie Huntington did excellent work, often recording important events as well as everyday scenes in Utah folk life. The notable writers included Parley P. Pratt,

Eliza R. Snow, Hannah Tapfield King, and Sarah Elizabeth Carmichael. Most of their work was devotional poetry, often set to music to become part of the rich repertoire of LDS hymnody. Newspapers and magazines were published wherever opportunity permitted, including manuscript newspapers laboriously copied by hand and circulated from house to house in smaller towns. For a time the *Peep O'Day* (1864) served the literary set in the capital. Thousands of diaries and journals kept by individuals, recording the routine of their lives and their interpretation of the world about them, provide an often eloquent literary legacy.

There have been several distinct periods in LDS social and cultural life, each influenced by a different relationship between the Saints and the society around them. From 1847 to 1857 the LDS community was relatively small and undisturbed. Ward organizations played a secondary role to the central community, and since almost all in Mormon communities were Church members, community endeavor was LDS endeavor. This began to change in 1857–1858 when the Utah Expedition brought a large non-Mormon military and freighting population to Utah Territory. During the 1860s, the Civil War and gold and silver strikes in Utah and the surrounding territories brought a continuous stream of new settlers. That decade culminated in the completion of the transcontinental railroad, forever ending earlier autonomy and isolation.

As a more secular Utah sprang up, the Latter-day Saints, also growing in numbers, found themselves for the first time unable to dominate all the central public institutions. They responded by changing the center of community life from the Salt Lake downtown area to the dozens of individual wards. Each ward began to foster a full range of religious, educational, social, economic, recreational, and cultural activities designed to keep the growing numbers of young within the fold. Ward grammar schools, for example, avoided the secularization of public education, as did the later academies for secondary education.

Many wards founded cooperative stores as local outlets for the central Zion's Cooperative Mercantile Institution (ZCMI). In 1874 President Young took a dramatic step in founding the United Order of Enoch, a regionwide economic plan aimed at placing production and distribution under community-owned cooperatives. Though almost every ward organized an order, the plan had an important economic effect in only a few localities. Nonetheless the effort indelibly impressed upon Latter-day Saints the understanding that they would one day live and work under a celestial economic order based on cooperation and sharing.

Beginning in 1849, individual wards founded Sunday Schools for children, their activities first coordinated on a Churchwide basis in 1872. The Retrenchment Association for young women was begun in 1869—its name changing in 1875 to the Young Women's Mutual Improvement Association (YWMIA), a complement to the Young Men's Mutual Improvement Association (YMMIA), also founded that year. Both societies aimed to provide a full complement of cultural and recreational activities for LDS youth, thus shielding them from the influences of the outside world. Even younger children were brought into this net of concern with the founding of the Primary organization in 1878, which held weekly recreational and instructional programs for children between the ages of three and eight (later raised to eleven). Beginning in 1867, Relief Societies were reinstituted throughout the Church. They provided women an organization for mutual assistance that was concerned with maternal and child health matters, administering to the needs of the poor, socializing, and adult education. Their leaders also published the *Woman's Exponent*, which was discontinued in 1914 and replaced by the *Relief Society Magazine* (1915–1970).

As these organizations proliferated, the Latter-day Saints were moving toward their ultimate confrontation with the federal government over plural marriage. By the end of the 1880s, the U.S. Congress had passed laws disincorporating the Church, taking over most of its properties, and disfranchising its women. Faced with the destruction of the Church as an institution, in 1890 Church President Wilford Woodruff issued the Manifesto and began the process of better integrating the Saints into American society. Whereas in the 1860s Latter-day Saints had responded to the broader society by creating complete ward-centered societies, they now involved themselves in secular workplaces and civil governance, and sent their children to public schools. Ward schools fell into disuse, between 1913 and 1924 many Church-sponsored academies were closed, and ward stores were sold to private entrepreneurs.

Still, the Church remained committed to institutional responses that helped meet the needs of members in a changing world. Though they could not duplicate tax-supported public schools, they began in 1912 to build SEMINARY buildings near high schools, where Church-supported religious instruction (and social and recreational activities) could be offered to LDS youth. In the 1920s, they extended the same concept to higher education with the institute program (*see* CHURCH EDUCATIONAL SYSTEM). Leaders stressed as never before the importance of attending Church services regularly. They gave new emphasis to observance of the WORD OF WISDOM, a health code revealed in 1833, as a principal index of faithfulness and group identity. Determined to co-opt entertainments popular in the outside world, they sponsored parallel activities—they were always opened with prayer, were alcohol and tobacco free, and were carefully chaperoned. If in the secular world competition in SPORTS became popular, the Latter-day Saints would found their own leagues. If public dances were tempting youth, they would have more and better dances.

Through Mutual Improvement Associations (MIA), Relief Societies, Primary, and the various priesthood quorums, ward bishops administered a remarkable array of social and cultural activities, involving youth and adults in choirs, dancing, speech, drama, and sports. In 1895 the MIAs founded the "Mutual Improvement League," opening gymnasiums that sponsored athletic and fitness programs for men and women. After this league's demise, the YMMIA and the University of Utah built Deseret Gymnasium in 1910 to foster physical fitness in a wholesome environment.

As team sports became more popular in the broader society, the Church began to sponsor these activities within the wards as well. Beginning in 1901, Church leaders held a special "June conference" annually for the Mutual Improvement Associations. Leaders sponsored an athletic field day in connection with the 1904 conference, an event that continued for some years. By 1906 baseball, basketball, and track and field competitions were being held among the various wards, and in 1910 the General Board of the MIA set up a standing "Committee on Athletics and Field Sports."

One consequence of this Church sponsorship of athletics was the development of Churchwide tournaments and competitions. Young men of 17–24 years ("M-Men") held their first Churchwide basketball tournament in 1922 and added a softball tournament in 1934. Boys were at first not deemed physically capable of the strenuous sport of basketball, so a new sport, "Vanball," was invented, combining elements of basketball and volleyball; it was played in competition until the end of World War II. From World War II until the 1960s the Church held competitions at both senior and junior levels in basketball, softball, volleyball, and golf, with more than a thousand teams from the United States, Canada, and Mexico competing for the chance to play in all-Church tournaments. Tennis tournaments also were held in the 1950s, but were dropped partly because, as an individual sport, tennis was not the kind of "mass participation" activity the Church had generally favored.

Beginning with the exercise and fitness movement at the turn of the century, sports activities for young women somewhat paralleled those for young men but lagged behind a little. Young women participated fully in annual sports field days. Later came camping programs that, by 1950, saw as many as 20,000 girls certifying annually. Because wards and stakes had flexibility to meet local needs and interests, compared with young men's athletics, the girls' team program varied widely. A swimming achievement program and all-Church golf and tennis tournaments accommodated individual young women who wished to participate. Eventually young women competed in volleyball, softball, and basketball, and by the 1970s sports opportunities for young men and women were generally comparable.

In addition to social dances in ward meetinghouses, dance festivals with colorful pageantry became a common feature of June Conference. Beginning in the 1930s, "Road Show" competitions were held at stake and higher levels, the youth of each ward (with leaders) preparing an original fifteen-minute musical that could quickly be moved from meetinghouse to meetinghouse, so that members of each congregation could enjoy an evening of theatricals in their own neighborhood. Youth also competed for local, stake, and general awards in speech.

The primary site for all of these activities was the local ward meetinghouse. In one sense the home became a place from which the Saints commuted to their main center of socializing and worship— the ward meetinghouse. Ward activities occupied at least some family members part of virtually every day of the week, much of

Saturday, and most of Sunday. Because Latter-day Saints learned to see the meetinghouse as the primary place for socializing, it was difficult for those not part of the ward to become part of their world.

Though the ward still remains the center of social and cultural life for committed Latter-day Saints, since the 1960s Church leaders have initiated changes that have diminished its role as the focal point of LDS neighborhoods and communities. A consolidated meeting schedule greatly reduced the amount of time spent at the meetinghouse. A more restricted definition of Church purposes, "to spread the gospel, perfect the Saints, and redeem the dead," called into question the relevance of Church-sponsored cultural and social activities not contributing to these aims. Reallocating tithing funds to pay ward expenses reduced the need to cooperate in fundraising events to pay for socials and other activities. With both construction and maintenance of buildings managed by centrally funded contract, meetinghouses were no longer a product of community labor and sacrifice. At the same time, Churchwide competitions in speech, drama, and athletics were discontinued, leaving strong regional competition in some areas and perhaps less incentive for good local programs in others.

Church leaders saw gains in these new initiatives that would outweigh the losses. The great sacrifices members had made to sustain the many ward and Church programs would be reduced. There would also be a better distribution of Church resources, with more equality across geographical and class lines. Though the Saints in heavily LDS Utah might have a leaner program, members in developing areas could have more.

Latter-day Saints have proudly borne the stamp of being "a peculiar people," an identity that helped maintain the energy and commitment that characterized the classic, close-knit ward community. Some observers feel that this cohesive sense of community is the genius of LDS society. Latter-day Saints face the challenge of maintaining that cohesiveness and their sense of special identity and mission in a complex, changing world. Bereft of many occasions when the Saints traditionally were brought together to worship, work, and play, LDS society must continue to adjust or it could lose its focus. Drawn out of the broader society by faith in the Restoration, early Latter-day Saints learned to select and adapt cultural and social forms upon which they put a distinctive and compelling stamp. As the Church expands internationally, that process must continue. The challenge facing the Church in the twenty-first century is to find ways to maintain that energy and develop that sense of identity among peoples of diverse cultures throughout the world.

BIBLIOGRAPHY
No comprehensive study exists of the social and cultural history of the Latter-day Saints. Much useful material can be gleaned from studies of particular periods of LDS history. See also bibliographies for articles on Education, Music, Dance, Sports, Art, Artists, Sculpture, and Drama. Also helpful is Davis Bitton, "Early Mormon Lifestyles; or the Saints as Human Beings," in *The Restoration Movement: Essays in Mormon History*, ed. F. Mark McKiernan et al. Lawrence, Kans., 1973.

DEAN L. MAY

SOCIALIZATION

In general, socialization refers to the processes used to internalize the ways of a particular group in order to function therein (Elkin and Handel, p. 4). In this light, LDS socialization faces a number of challenges in the contemporary world, notably in aiding its members to observe a health code (*see* WORD OF WISDOM); to oppose all forms of premarital and extramarital sexual behavior; to spend two years at their own expense in missionary work; and in the face of social pressures to the contrary, to have large families—generally two more children than the national average (Heaton; Thomas, 1983).

Many processes that lead to effective socialization within the LDS culture are similar to those found in American culture generally. Mormon parents are similar in many respects to other American parents, including the love and support they express to their children and the nurturing and disciplinary controls they exercise within the family (Kunz; Thomas, 1983). Nevertheless, some researchers contend that Latter-day Saints are more effective than some other groups in socializing their members to accept specific group values and behavior (Christensen; Smith). Some hints at possible reasons may be found in the degree to which LDS families participate in home religious observance (FAMILY PRAYER, scripture study, and FAMILY HOME EVENING).

The influence of home religious observance is perhaps best understood through research conducted by the Church on young men between the ages of twelve and eighteen. It found that home religious observance is a reliable predictor of what an adolescent's private religious observance (individual prayer, study of the scriptures, etc.) will be. Home religious observance also somewhat predicts public religious observance, but only half as accurately as does private religious observance. In turn, private religious observance is the single best predictor of a young man's internalizing religious goals and values specific to the LDS lifestyle, such as serving a mission for the Church, temple marriage, premarital chastity, and Church activity (Thomas, Olsen, and Weed). Having these as part of one's future plans is the best predictor of both private and public religious behaviors during the young adult years, ages twenty to twenty-eight (Roghaar).

This research also indicates that LDS male adolescents decide at a relatively young age on a general lifestyle that either includes or excludes plans to serve a mission or marry in the temple. In interviews, many said they could not remember when they made their mission decision but that it was a long time ago. Some said it was made before baptism (eight years of age). Thus, many adolescents at an early time form a general view of themselves that either includes or does not include a mission, and then they construct a lifestyle consonant with that orientation.

Research shows that other dimensions of the young person's religious world are important to understanding LDS socialization. While Church programs such as participation or nonparticipation in Aaronic Priesthood activity, SCOUTING, and daily religious education (*see* SEMINARY) during the school year has limited direct effect on socialization outcome, independent of family influences, research shows that these programs can reinforce basic orientations and internalization of values begun in the family. Cornwall shows that religiously committed LDS families usually channel their children into seminary, which in turn influences their peer associations, who then reinforce the religious values held by the parents. Roghaar further shows the positive influence of seminary education by pointing out that children from Latter-day Saint families who do not participate extensively in Church-sponsored activities will more likely remain active as young adults if they do complete four years of religious education during their adolescent years.

During the expanding social world of the late adolescent years, the family influences tend to weaken, whereas the influence of an adult adviser who represents the religious organization increases. Indeed, the influence of these adult representatives of the Church often exceeds that of the family for late adolescents between the ages of sixteen and eighteen. The crucial dimension of this relationship between the adolescent and the adult seems to center on the degree to which the adolescent has association with an adult whom he or she respects, admires, wishes to emulate, and finds easy to talk to.

[*See also* Values, Transmission of.]

BIBLIOGRAPHY

Christensen, Harold T. "Mormon Sexuality in Cross-Cultural Perspective." *Dialogue* 10 (Autumn 1976):62–75.

Cornwall, Marie. "The Influence of Three Agents of Religious Socialization: Family, Church, and Peers." In *The Religion and Family Connection: Social Science Perspectives*, ed. D. Thomas, pp. 207–31. Provo, Utah, 1988.

Elkin, F., and G. Handel. *The Child and Society: The Process of Socialization*, 3rd ed. New York, 1978.

Heaton, Tim B. "Four C's of the Mormon Family: Chastity, Conjugality, Children, and Chauvinism." In *The Religion and Family Connection: Social Science Perspectives*, ed. D. Thomas, pp. 107–24. Provo, Utah, 1988.

Kunz, Phillip R. "Religious Influences on Parental Discipline and Achievement Demands." *Marriage and Family Living* 25 (1963):224–25.

Roghaar, Bruce. "Young Men of Sound Understanding." Paper presented at Church Education System Symposium, Brigham Young University, Provo, Utah, Aug. 15, 1990.

Smith, Wilford E. "Mormon Sex Standards on College Campuses, or Deal Us Out of the Sexual Revolution!" *Dialogue* 10 (Autumn 1976):76–81.

Thomas, Darwin L., ed. "Family in the Mormon Experience." In *Families and Religions: Conflict and Change in Modern Society*, ed. William V. D'Antonio and Joan Aldous, pp. 267–88. Beverly Hills, Calif., 1983.

———, and Joseph Olsen. "Young Men Study Revisited: A Five-Year Follow-up of Priest Age Young Men's Mission Decisions." Unpublished report, Research and Evaluation Division, The Church of Jesus Christ of Latter-day Saints, Nov. 1986.

———. *The Religion and Family Connection: Social Science Perspectives*. Provo, Utah, 1988.

———; Joseph Olsen; and Stan E. Weed. "Missionary Service of L.D.S. Young Men: A Longitudinal Analysis." Paper presented at the Society for the Scientific Study of Religion, Salt Lake City, Oct. 1989.

Weed, Stan E., and Joseph Olsen. "Policy and Program Considerations for Teenage Pregnancy Prevention: A Summary for Policymakers." *Family Perspective* 22 (1988):235–52.

DARWIN L. THOMAS

SOCIETY

[*Mormon life is inseparably involved with people. See, generally,*
Community; Family; Lifestyle; Marriage; Social and Cultural History;
Social Characteristics; Socialization; Values, Transmission of; Vital
Statistics; Women, Roles of; *and* Youth.

*Belonging to the Church is the basis of many aspects of Latter-
day Saint societal values and concepts. See* Senior Citizens *and*
Sisterhood.

On the single individual in LDS society, see Dating and Courtship
and Divorce.

For discussions of specific social topics, see various entries under
Business; Education; Family; Fine Arts; Folk Art; Folklore; Humor;
Literature; Material Culture; Mental Health; Minorities; Music;
Politics; Science; Sports; *and* Symbolism.

*Social relations with members of other religious groups are treated
under* Interfaith Relationships; Non-Mormons, Social Relations with;
and Tolerance.]

SPORTS

The LDS Church was a pioneer among religious faiths in promoting
physical activity, sports, and recreation for members (Parkin, p. 67).
Joseph Smith, the first Prophet of the Church, enjoyed and excelled
in running, wrestling, jumping, and playing ball. Brigham Young, his
successor, taught that recreation (including sports) is a spiritual
activity that develops not only the body but also the mind and the
spirit. He encouraged the building of recreation halls in conjunction
with chapels for worship (Parkin, p. 15). These halls, later called cultural halls, are still part of a meetinghouse and are used extensively
for sports, recreational, and cultural activities.

During the early years of the Church, participation in sports was
informal. But gradually programs became well structured. In 1904 in
Salt Lake City, one of the earliest leagues for "outdoor activities and
friendly competition" was organized (Strong, p. 101–102). In 1904
and for a few years thereafter, an annual field day that included a
variety of athletic activities was held in the Salt Lake Valley. The first

formal basketball league for boys was started in Salt Lake City in 1908. During the decade 1910–1920, competition in baseball and basketball spread from the Salt Lake Valley to many other LDS settlements.

The completion of the Deseret Gymnasium in 1910, near the Salt Lake Temple, made it apparent that Church leaders continued to encourage physical activity and sports. The facility included a gymnasium, a swimming pool, bowling lanes, tennis courts, and dressing rooms. It accommodated sports and exercise activities for both men and women (*Deseret Evening News*, Sept. 20, 1910, p. 5). By 1922, gym membership exceeded four thousand.

The 1911 June conference sessions for activity leaders of individual wards (congregations) focused on volleyball, wrestling, fencing, swimming, gymnastics, running, jumping, vaulting, and baseball (*IE* 14 [June 1911]:751–52). In 1922 Church leaders issued formal guidelines for recreation and sports. "The recreation program under the direction of the MIA [a Church program that served youth and young adults] must do more than provide amusement. Through it we must emphasize the fundamental ideals and standards of the Church. Ours is the opportunity to enrich leisure, to spiritualize recreation" (*M.I.A. Activity Manual*, p. 5).

By 1926 team sports such as baseball, basketball, and soccer, and lifelong activities such as walking, hiking, camping, tennis, swimming, skating, and dancing, were being encouraged. At this time the need for emphasis on sportsmanship came into focus. Quoting Walter Camp, one leader counseled, "Play fair, but play hard, win if you can, lose if you must, but take a whipping without whimpering" (*Recreation Organization and Leadership*, pp. 50–51). Leaders taught that the desire to win should not be so intense that participants could not enjoy the game.

For two decades following World War II, "all-Church" tournaments flourished in sports such as basketball, softball, and volleyball, and to a lesser degree in tennis, golf, and horseshoes. By 1962 more than 3,500 basketball teams and 50,000 players were involved. Teams came to Salt Lake City not only from neighboring states but also from as far away as Washington, D.C., Canada, and Mexico (*Church News*, Feb. 24, 1962, p. 9).

In 1963 Elder Ezra Taft Benson, later to become the thirteenth

President of the Church, spoke to more than 1,400 participants attending the all-Church softball tournament banquet. "This is the greatest softball tournament in the world. Its purpose is to build men, men of character, men of strength, and faith, to build testimonies, to build men who love the Lord" (*Church News*, Aug. 31, 1963, p. 4). So popular was all-Church tournament competition in the major sports involved that it grew to include three divisions of play: juniors (ages 16–17), seniors (ages 18–19), and college students. Televised finals, devotional meetings, banquets, and other features of highly organized competitive sports became the custom for all-Church tournaments. Sportsmanship trophies, superior in importance and appearance to championship trophies, became a highlight of the tournaments.

Worldwide Church growth in the 1960s made it impractical to continue these popular tournaments. In 1971 Church leaders announced that sports would henceforth be emphasized on a local basis and teams would no longer travel to Salt Lake City. Where practical, tournaments were to be held in various regions of the Church (*New Era* 1 [Sept. 1971]:44–45). This change accommodated larger numbers of new members with differing interests in sports appropriate to their cultures.

Today LDS meetinghouses continue to have large cultural halls that accommodate sports and recreation. With more than 15,000 wards in the Church in 1990, combined male and female sports participation in three selected team sports is estimated to be as follows: basketball, 552,000; softball, 690,000; volleyball, 207,000.

Since the first printed guidelines in 1922, Church authorities have continued to provide local leaders with instructions that give purpose and direction to Church sports: "Sports programs should provide year-round opportunity for involvement and should include a wide variety of individual and team sports. All who have a desire to participate should have the opportunity" (*Physical Fitness, Sports, and Recreation Manual*, p. 17). President David O. McKay aptly summarized the position of the Church on sports and play when he taught that practicing Mormons work, worship, pray, and play (*Family Home Evening Manual*, p. iii).

Since 1977 the coordination and leadership of Church sports have been the responsibility of activities committees at the ward and stake levels. These committees give local leadership to cultural arts, socials, service projects, and sports. Regional (three to six stakes), multiregional (fifteen to thirty stakes), and area sports directors are called as needed to organize and supervise tournaments in the eighteen designated geographical areas of the worldwide Church.

The Church also supports a full intercollegiate athletic program at Brigham Young University and BYU—Hawaii. But beyond intercollegiate athletics, both schools have large intramural programs that serve thousands of students.

The Church promotes both physical and spiritual fitness for all members. Sports for females have somewhat paralleled sports for males through the years, except that all-Church tournaments for women in team sports have never been held. Characteristic of the Church sports program from the beginning is that there is no practice or play on Sunday.

[See also Physical Fitness and Recreation.]

BIBLIOGRAPHY
Family Home Evening Manual. Salt Lake City, 1968.
M.I.A. Activity Manual. Salt Lake City, 1933.
Parkin, Darrell Lloyd. "The Athletic Program of the Mormon Church: Its Growth and Development." Master's thesis, University of Illinois, 1964.
Physical Fitness, Sports, and Recreation Manual. Salt Lake City, 1984.
Recreation Organization and Leadership. Salt Lake City, 1926.
Strong, Leon M. "A History of the Young Men's Mutual Improvement Association, 1875–1938." Master's thesis, Brigham Young University, 1939.

CLAYNE R. JENSEN

STEREOTYPING OF LATTER-DAY SAINTS

From the time Joseph Smith's visions became public knowledge, many stereotypes—pejorative and nonpejorative generalized impressions—have shaped the public image of the Church and its members. In general, stereotypes travel by word of mouth or through the media of popular culture and tend to exaggerate or to distort selected characteristics.

The Church's first century produced media stereotypes that were largely pejorative and relatively uniform. In the early years, Joseph

Smith and the fundamental claims of the Church were the principal targets. The dominant images questioned prophetic credibility and impugned the validity of the Book of Mormon. Although some sympathy was evoked by the persecutions in Missouri, the martyrdom of Joseph and Hyrum Smith, and the expulsion of Mormons from Illinois, negative stereotypes predominated.

When the practice of plural marriage was publicly announced in 1852, the stereotypes changed. From then on the dominant images in Europe as well as in the United States were of treacherous, cruel, lustful males; degraded and gullible females; and neglected, unmanageable children. Brigham Young became the major target of denunciation. He was depicted as wily and unscrupulous, and his followers as credulous and victimized.

Pejorative stereotypes peaked in conjunction with the antipolygamy legislation of the 1880s. They declined for a few years after the Church discontinued plural marriage in 1890, but reappeared in the early twentieth century. While occasional nonpejorative images were generated by travelers' accounts or other sympathetic sources, images of Latter-day Saints in the media between 1830 and 1930 were, for the most part, derogatory.

By the 1930s, however, the prevailing stereotype of Latter-day Saints had become positive. The next few decades consolidated that image, portraying the Saints as loyal citizens with a circumspect lifestyle and a communal ethic that "took care of their own." Factors supporting this stereotype included more exposure to Latter-day Saints and their lifestyle, more favorable media coverage, increasing stature as a worldwide Church, and gradual, if sometimes reluctant, acceptance into the sociopolitical, economic, and religious establishment of America. Still, pejorative images continued to compete with the more favorable versions, and most people outside the intermountain region knew little about the Church beyond the abandoned practice of polygamy, the exodus west to Utah under Brigham Young, and the weekly broadcasts of the MORMON TABERNACLE CHOIR.

Since 1960, the substantial growth of the Church in Latin America and other parts of the world has supported the overall view that international impressions were improving. Yet Church growth was sometimes a mixed blessing, for LDS missionaries and members became stereotyped targets for those who mistakenly associated the

Church with the politics of the United States. In the United States, both positive and negative views provided the public with information, true and false, about the Church and piqued their curiosities. Church positions on social issues such as ABORTION and the Equal Rights Amendment evoked both favor and opposition. The Church's own PUBLIC RELATIONS efforts, intended to educate the public about Church doctrines and the importance of the family, have offered alternative stereotypes of the Mormons as wholesome people and good citizens.

As others become more acquainted with Latter-day Saints, they realize that Church members include the normal variety of human beings with differing personalities and interests. Given the vagaries of public opinion and private belief, however, stereotypes of Latter-day Saints will continue to exist, although they are becoming more positive.

BIBLIOGRAPHY
Bunker, Gary L., and Davis Bitton. *The Mormon Graphic Image, 1834-1914.* Salt Lake City, 1983.
"Imagemakers: Mormons and the Media." *Dialogue* 10 (Spring 1977):12–113.

GARY L. BUNKER

STERILIZATION

Sterilization, including voluntary vasectomies, tied fallopian tubes, or premature hysterectomies, are serious matters with moral, spiritual, and physiological ramifications. God's primordial instruction to mankind is to "be fruitful, and multiply and replenish the earth" (Gen. 1:28). The privilege and power to procreate may be God's greatest gift to mankind and, within the sacred marriage covenant, is an obligation for which God will hold men and women fully accountable. Latter-day Saints affirm that life's most lofty and ennobling values are found in marriage, procreation, parenthood, and family life. Any impediment or interference with this sacred opportunity may warrant God's judgment:

> Surgical sterilization should only be considered (1) where medical conditions seriously jeopardize life or health, or (2) where birth defects or

serious trauma have rendered a person mentally incompetent and not responsible for his or her actions. Such conditions must be determined by competent medical judgment and in accordance with law. Even then, the person or persons responsible for this decision should consult with each other and with their bishop . . . and receive divine confirmation through prayer [*General Handbook of Instructions*, 11-15].

Consistent with Church policies concerning BIRTH CONTROL and ABORTION, leaders have advised its married members not to resort to any practices that destroy the power of having children. The First Presidency has declared, "We seriously deplore the fact that members of the Church would voluntarily take measures to render themselves incapable of further procreation" (p. 11-5).

BIBLIOGRAPHY
General Handbook of Instructions. Salt Lake City, 1989.

LORRY E. RYTTING

STILLBORN CHILDREN

Medically, a stillborn child is a dead fetus developed to a point at which it normally would have been viable. Religiously, one major question is whether a stillborn child ever was "a living soul" (Moses 3:7) that can be resurrected and be part of its parents' eternal family. Because "there is no information given by revelation" (*DS* 2:280), the Church has made no official statement on the matter. President Brigham Young once stated as his opinion that "when the mother feels life come to her infant it is the spirit entering the body" (*JD* 17:143). Others have speculated that the spirit might not enter the fetus until just before birth, and still others have suggested that three elements constitute a living soul—body, spirit, and "breath of life" (Moses 3:7).

Because Church policy permits temple sealings to be performed for children who die after birth, but not for those who die before birth, some have concluded that stillborn children will not be resurrected. However, the current *General Handbook of Instructions* (1989) states that the policy of not sealing stillborn children to their parents implies "no loss of eternal blessings or family unity" (6-8). Latter-day Saints trust God's loving kindness to accord to each of his spirit children the eternal state which is proper, through judgment which is both just and merciful.

BIBLIOGRAPHY

Greenwood, Val D. "I Have a Question." *Ensign* 17 (Sept. 1987):27–28.

JEANNE B. INOUYE

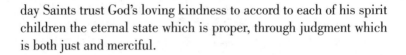

SUFFERING IN THE WORLD

Suffering is inherent in mortality. Physical bodies are subject to pain and discomfort from hunger, disease, trauma, violence, and exposure. As a social being, man is vulnerable to emotional suffering that often rivals physical pain—anxiety, rejection, loneliness, despair. Among the sensitive there are also other levels of profound suffering. They may relate, for example, to the awareness of the effects of sin or the anguish of the abuse or indifference of one's loved ones. And there is vicarious suffering in response to the pain around one and the sense of the withdrawal of the Spirit. For Latter-day Saints, Jesus' words on the cross "My God, my God, why hast thou forsaken me?" is a measure of the depth of his suffering (Matt. 27:46).

Mankind's attempts to explain the necessity of suffering are varied: (1) it is an essential element in testing and building moral character; (2) it is the unavoidable side effect of agency; (3) it is illusory or utterly mysterious. Whatever partial consolations these attempts provide, suffering remains.

LDS doctrine provides two explanations that are uncommon in the Judeo-Christian tradition. First, all mankind chose to enter mortality with full knowledge of the great price that would be required of the Christ and of discipleship in his name. Second, one's suffering is to be in the image of that of the Lord, whose suffering was requisite "that his bowels [might] be filled with mercy . . . that he [might] know according to the flesh how to succor his people according to their infirmities" (Alma 7:12). In no other way could the redemption of the universe and the unleashing of authentic love and compassion be achieved. Jesus described his own mission almost entirely in terms of healing: "to bind up the brokenhearted, to proclaim liberty to the captives, and the opening of the prison to them that are bound; . . . to comfort all that mourn; to appoint unto them that mourn in Zion, to give unto them beauty for ashes, the oil of joy for mourning, the garment of praise for the spirit of heaviness" (Isa. 61:1–3; Luke 4:18–19).

Only in the life to come amid the glories of the New Jerusalem will the full effect of Christ's mission "wipe away all tears from their eyes; and there shall be no more death, neither sorrow, nor crying, neither shall there be any more pain" (Rev. 21:4). Even so, for Latter-day Saints the embrace of his messiahship and the proclamation of his gospel were intended to relieve needless pain and suffering. They do so in many ways. First, they provide a foundation for hope that through the atonement of Jesus Christ one may find reunion with God. Second, they offer continuous access to the Holy Ghost, the Comforter, and, through this, to an inner peace that "passeth all understanding" (Philip. 4:7). Third, they teach the law of the harvest, that many blessings follow naturally from obedience to the laws that govern them and that much unhappiness can be avoided, including sin and its accompanying pain, shame, and spiritual bruising. And finally, they establish a community built on kinship, a society of mutually supportive and protective fellow believers whose charge is to "bear one another's burdens, that they may be light; yea, and are willing to mourn with those that mourn; yea, and comfort those that stand in need of comfort" (Mosiah 18:8–9).

Latter-day Saints do not believe that pain is intrinsically good. In their teaching there is little of asceticism, mortification, or negative spirituality. But when suffering is unavoidable in the fulfillment of life's missions, one's challenge is to draw upon all the resources of one's soul and endure faithfully and well. If benefit comes from pain, it is not because there is anything inherently cleansing in pain itself. Suffering can wound and embitter and darken a soul as surely as it can purify and refine and illumine. Everything depends on how one responds. At a time of terrible desolation and imprisonment, the Prophet Joseph Smith was told, "My son, peace be unto thy soul; thine adversity and thine afflictions shall be but a small moment; and then, if thou endure it well, God shall exalt thee on high. . . . Know thou, my son, that all these things shall give thee experience, and shall be for thy good. The Son of Man hath descended below them all. Art thou greater than he? Therefore, hold on thy way, . . . fear not what man can do, for God shall be with you forever and ever" (D&C 121:7–8; 122:7–9).

BIBLIOGRAPHY

Kimball, Spencer W. "Thy Son Liveth." *IE* 48 (May 1945):253, 294.

———. "Tragedy or Destiny." *IE* 69 (Mar. 1966):178–80, 210–12, 214, 216–17.

Madsen, Truman G. "Evil and Suffering." *Instructor* 99 (Nov. 1964):450–53.

CARLFRED BRODERICK

SUICIDE

From an LDS perspective, suicide is a moral issue and is to be handled with particular sensitivity and human caring. The *General Handbook of Instructions* (1989) says, "A person who takes his own life may not be responsible for his acts. Only God can judge such a matter. A person who has considered suicide seriously or has attempted suicide should be counseled by his bishop and may be encouraged to seek professional help" (11-5). Such contacts need to be personalized and enduring. The inclination to commit suicide represents a crisis in a person's life and should not be taken lightly. Underlying causes should be identified and treated.

The body of a person who has committed suicide is not dishonored. If the person has been endowed and otherwise is in good standing with the Church, the body may be buried in temple clothes. Normal funeral procedures are followed (*see* BURIAL).

Suicide and attempted suicide are painful and dramatic aspects of human behavior, but this does not mean that they should not be dealt with in terms of the same basic principles as those applicable in understanding and managing any other aspect of human behavior. Thus, principles associated with concepts of agency, accountability, Atonement, eternal life, immortality, resurrection, and family establish the frame of reference Latter-day Saints use to guide their responses to such behaviors as they occur.

Despite traditions and beliefs that recognize and honor the ways in which value decisions led to the death and martyrdom of Jesus Christ and of Joseph Smith, there is no support in LDS doctrine for anyone intentionally seeking death.

The ancient commandment "Thou shalt not kill" is interpreted in most traditions to include a prohibition against killing oneself. In LDS doctrine, "Thou shalt not kill" has been extended to "nor do anything like unto it" (D&C 59:6). This extension is relevant in considering a variety of life-threatening behaviors that suicidologists identify as suicide equivalents (e.g., death as a result of deliberate reckless driving) or "slow suicide" (e.g., drug and alcohol abuse).

Suicide prevention sometimes is criticized by people who claim that individuals have an innate right to do whatever they want with their lives, including a right to kill themselves if they want to. Suicide, however, is never fully an individual matter. Even when difficult physical and biological factors are present, suicide is a social act, with interpersonal, family, and social systems ramifications.

A social milieu organized to help people find adequate housing and life goals of learning, loving, and working provides genuine choices between life and death. It is the position of the Church that when there are such choices, the majority of people, including those who are suicidal, will choose life. This is not to deny inequity, unfairness, conflict, instability, evil, aging, and illness of loved ones, but to provide a basis for behavior so that when crises occur, they will be seen as resolvable.

BIBLIOGRAPHY
Ballard, M. Russell. "Suicide: Some Things We Know, and Some We Do Not." *Ensign* 17 (Oct. 1987):6–9.
General Handbook of Instructions. Salt Lake City, 1989.

CLYDE E. SULLIVAN

SYMBOLS, CULTURAL AND ARTISTIC

LDS cultural and artistic symbols express a distinctive view of the universe and the purpose of life, and tie the present to the historical past. These symbols derive principally from four basic sources: religious ordinances, scriptures, historical experience, and adaptations of other traditions. In the Church today, symbols can be seen in a variety of contexts, including in the continuation of ordinances; in presentations of music, poetry, literature, and drama; in visual arts, sermons, and architecture; and even in settlement patterns of pioneer towns.

The scriptures revealed through the Prophet Joseph Smith give perspective to the symbolism of the ordinances of the gospel and to the creation of the earth. A key passage contains the word of God to Adam, which revealed that everything in the universe has an important and unique role in the plan of salvation:

> And behold, all things have their likeness, and all things are created and made to bear record of me, both things which are temporal, and things which are spiritual; things which are in the heavens above, and things which are on the earth, and things which are in the earth, and things which are under the earth, both above and beneath: all things bear record of me [Moses 6:63].

The focal point of "all things" and of symbolism relating thereto is Jesus Christ. Baptism by immersion is symbolic of the death, burial, and resurrection of Christ (Rom. 6:3–5; D&C 76:51–52). Adam was given instruction regarding the symbolism of baptism: "Inasmuch as ye were born into the world by water, and blood, and the spirit, which I have made, . . . even so ye must be born again into the kingdom of heaven, of water, and of the Spirit, and be cleansed by blood, even the blood of mine Only Begotten" (Moses 6:59). This ordinance also symbolizes the atonement of Christ, which makes the cleansing of mankind possible and makes of the repentant new creatures.

Symbols are associated extensively with sacred gospel ordinances performed in the temple. The temple is a house of order. The orderliness is symbolized in the endowment ceremony, which portrays the journey of individuals from the premortal existence through mortal life and death to life after death. The temple, or House of the Lord, is also symbolic of the Lord's dwelling place, where one can go to learn godliness. For some, the temple symbolizes the conjunction of heaven and earth, where those who seek heaven come out of the world for instruction and receive symbolic reminders of God's plan for his children. Symbols in the temple are linked to the biblical events of the Creation and the fall of Adam, and to the need for redemption. Dramatic presentations, special clothing, and symbolic instruction during the temple ceremonies represent various stages in an individual's eternal progression. The temple clothing is white, suggesting purity and the equality of all mankind before God.

Various levels or ways of living are reflected in the architecture of the temple, including the sun, moon, and stars as representative of kingdoms in the hereafter, and the "all-seeing eye" as suggesting the total knowledge, love, and concern that God has for his children. Entry into God's kingdom requires prescribed ordinances, including baptism. Baptismal work is conducted in some temples on a level below ground, to symbolize the eventual burial and resurrection of all from the grave (D&C 128:12–13). The baptismal font rests on the backs of twelve oxen, representing the twelve tribes of Israel.

Latter-day scriptures also contain striking symbols that depict the passage through mortal life. In the dream of Lehi in the Book of Mormon (1 Ne. 8:5–34), a desolate waste represents an individual's position in this world, where one is blinded by "mists of darkness" (the temptations of the devil). Many are in a "great and spacious building," which stands for the pride and vanities of the world that must be abandoned. An iron rod represents the word of God, leading one to the Tree of Life. The universal symbolism of the cosmic tree is described by an angel as a representation of the love of God (cf. 1 Ne. 11:8–25, 35–36).

Latter-day scriptures are thus teleological in tone and theme, reflecting that all things and happenings in the universe have a purpose and are under God's ultimate direction. The motion of earth and the planets "denote there is a God" (Alma 30:44), as do other orbs of light, which "roll upon their wings in their glory, in the midst of the power of God, . . . and any man who hath seen any or the least of these hath seen God moving in his majesty and power" (D&C 88:45, 47).

Church history has been a fountainhead of symbols that reflect similar patterns of the spiritual quest for a better world. The Sacred Grove in which Joseph Smith in his first vision beheld the Father and the Son may symbolize for some the human potential for contact with God and the enlightenment that comes through personal revelation; Carthage Jail (where Joseph and Hyrum Smith were murdered), the cost of discipleship; the expulsion from Missouri and exodus from Nauvoo, the adversity that the Church must overcome; and the establishment of the Church in the West, the fulfillment of God's promises.

The beehive has become the symbol of the industry and cooperative behavior necessary to achieve an ideal society. The symbolism of pilgrimage and pioneering also depicts the path of personal commitment and perseverance that a person must pursue through mortality in order to partake of the fruit of the tree of life and inherit the kingdom whose glory is that of the sun. The sacrifices required to participate in both temporal and spiritual journeys convey that the events of one's life are imbued with eternal significance, and that God is working in and through history.

LDS theology and symbolism have both correspondence with and independence from Judeo-Christian roots. Indeed, the fresh combinations of rich religious symbols are to Latter-day Saints a part of God's continuous revelations to man.

[*See also* Architecture; Folk Art; Sculptors.]

BIBLIOGRAPHY

Andrews, Laurel B. *The Early Temples of the Mormons*. Albany, N.Y., 1978.
Cooper, Rex E. *Promises Made to the Fathers*. Salt Lake City, 1990.
Eliade, Mircea. *The Sacred and the Profane*. New York, 1959.
Hamilton, C. Mark. "The Salt Lake Temple: A Symbolic Statement of Mormon Doctrine." In *The Mormon People: Their Character and Traditions*, ed. Thomas G. Alexander, pp. 103–127. Provo, Utah, 1980.
Heiss, Matthew K. *The Salt Lake Temple and the Metaphors of Transformation*. Master's thesis, University of Virginia, 1986.
Olsen, Steven L. *The Mormon Ideology of Place: Cosmic Symbolism of the City of Zion, 1830-1846*. Ph.D. diss., University of Chicago, 1985.

REX E. COOPER

T

TEA

Devout Latter-day Saints do not drink teas containing caffeine. This practice derives from an 1833 revelation known as the WORD OF WISDOM, which states that "hot drinks are not for the body or the belly" (D&C 89:9). Hyrum Smith, Assistant President of the Church, later defined "hot drinks" as COFFEE and tea (*T&S* 3 [June 1, 1842]:800), thereby establishing the official interpretation for later generations. Caffeine, a cerebral and cardiovascular stimulant, has caused health concerns in recent years. The revelation has not been interpreted as proscribing herbal teas, for it states that "all wholesome herbs God hath ordained for the constitution, nature, and use of man" (D&C 89:10).

BIBLIOGRAPHY
Stratton, Clifford J. "The Xanthines: Coffee, Cola, Cocoa, and Tea." *BYU Studies* 20 (Summer 1980):371–88.

JOSEPH LYNN LYON

THEODICY

Theodicy is the attempt to explain God's goodness and power and reconcile these with the evident evil in the created world. Since most theologians and religious philosophers in the West have assumed both God's unconditional power and his absolute goodness, the existence and persistence of evil are often held to be inexplicable. In recent centuries the absence of a convincing theodicy and the frequent theological resort to mystery as an explanation have led many to atheism.

Latter-day Saint scriptural sources have reshaped certain dimensions of the problem and its resolution.

SELF-EXISTENCE AND OMNIPOTENCE. Traditionally, the affirmation of God's sovereign power is expressed philosophically by the concept of "omnipotence," which means that God can do absolutely anything at all, or at least anything "logically possible." This often accompanies the dogma that all that is was created ex nihilo (from nothing) by God. The conclusion follows that all forms of evil, even the "demonic dimension," must be directly or indirectly God-made.

In Latter-day Saint sources, God is not the only self-existent reality. The creation accounts and other texts teach that God is not a fiat creator but an organizer and life-giver, that the "pure principles of element" can be neither created nor destroyed (D&C 93; *TPJS*, p. 351), and that the undergirdings of eternal law, with certain "bounds and conditions," are coexistent with him (cf. D&C 88:34–45). "Omnipotence," then, means God has all the power it is possible to have in a universe—actually a pluriverse—of these givens. He did not create evil.

APPEARANCE AND REALITY. Often omnipotence is taken to mean that God is able to overrule or overcome whatever lesser powers interfere with his sovereign will. This view still leaves God responsible for everything that occurs, just as it occurs. It follows that if God is truly good, then, despite appearances, all that happens must be good, however horrible the "good" may seem for human beings. "Evil" then is held to be privative (an absence), simply in the human mind, or a matter of perspective. The conclusion follows that this is the best of all possible worlds. But the problem then arises all over again, for why does not God exercise his power to remove the pain that arises from mortal misunderstanding?

Latter-day Saint scripture teaches unmistakably that such things as sin and sinfulness, ignorance, deformity, disease, and death are real. As they and their effects continue to increase and prevail, then even from the perspective of God, this is a less than perfect world. Another realm is conceivable where these evils in individual and community life have been overcome.

INVIOLATE FREEDOM.   Traditional thought has often held that God limits his own power for the greater good. Usually this view is associated with insistence on the importance of human freedom. Character and personality, it is argued, can develop only if human beings are genuinely free. Likewise, God's love, if authentic, must be voluntary. These goods are held to outweigh the evil introduced by free agents into the world, even when the consequences are terribly destructive. Mormon thought concurs. Creation is indeed a "vale of soul making." Experiences of contrast are indispensable to knowledge and growth (2 Ne. 2; D&C 122). God's self-limitation is essential to the attainment of his purpose. Moreover, God not only will not but cannot ultimately coerce men to choose life over death. "All intelligence . . . is free to act for itself in that sphere in which God has placed it. . . . Behold, here is the agency of man and here is the condemnation of man" (D&C 93:30–31). God can bring good out of the experience of evil to the degree that his creatures harmonize their will with his and continue to seek, affirm, and embrace him. In that cooperative mode, he can, and will, enable all his creatures to become what they have it in them to become (D&C 88:14–40).

NATURAL EVIL AND THE NATURE OF POWER.   It is commonly observed that not all evil is caused by human beings. Earthquakes, epidemics, plagues, volcanic eruptions, and other natural disasters occur. Furthermore, these and some evils caused by human aberration are of such magnitude as to call for divine intervention. The Holocaust is a glaring modern instance. Such considerations underscore the scriptural teaching that although God has power over the elements, and though there is divine intervention, divine influence over human beings is never "controlling" or "manipulating"; it is liberating, empowering, and persuading. This is the power continuously exercised by God, even in the midst of tragedy and affliction. It is the power most to be sought and most to be emulated.

"No power or influence," says the Doctrine and Covenants of the uses of authority, "can or ought to be maintained . . . [except] by persuasion, by long-suffering, by gentleness and meekness, and by love unfeigned" (D&C 121:41). Indeed, in the exercise of power "without compulsory means," it is not enough to say that man needs God. It is also the case, and eternally, that God needs man.

CREATIVE COMPLICITY.   Some contemporary movements affirm either that human beings emerged from a long and mindless process of evolution or that they have been "thrown" or thrust into the world. Either way, creatures exist without their permission in a predicament not of their own making. Latter-day Saint thought returns to the oft-forgotten scriptural thesis that all mankind participated in the original plan of life and prepared for the hazards and traumas waiting in this world. In an act of faith and foresight, the entire human family elected to enter mortality. For Latter-day Saints the cumulative witness of sacred texts, ancient and modern, is that, with rare exceptions, every person who ever lived will have benefited from the mortal sojourn and from embodiment.

JOHN COBB, JR.
TRUMAN G. MADSEN

THEOGONY

Theogony refers to the origin of God and has been a subject of religious inquiry throughout the ages. Ancient peoples, notably Sumerians, Egyptians, Greeks, and Romans, developed elaborate genealogies for their various gods, rationalizing and mythologizing the birth and characteristics of each. This is in contrast to the monotheistic, Judeo-Christian view that God is eternal, uncaused, and without origin. The traditional argument states that if every effect has a cause, there must be a first cause that has always existed, and that is God.

The LDS theogonic view is unlike all others. It is based on a doctrine of eternal existence of all intelligent beings (D&C 93:29) coupled with a belief in their eternal progression (see D&C 93:13–14). By embracing truth and light, uncreated intelligence is capable of growing in knowledge, power, and organization until it arrives at the glorified state of godhood, being one with God (*see*

DEIFICATION). This process known as eternal progression is succinctly expressed in the LDS aphorism, "As man is, God once was. As God is, man may become" (Lorenzo Snow). Adam was told by God, "Thou art after the order of him who was without beginning of days or end of years, from all eternity to all eternity. Behold, thou art one in me, a son of God; and thus may all become my sons" (Moses 6:67–68).

CHARLES R. HARRELL

TOBACCO

Devout Latter-day Saints do not use tobacco in any of its forms. They abstain because of an 1833 revelation known as the WORD OF WISDOM, which states that tobacco is "not for the body, neither for the belly, and is not good for man," except as a poultice for bruises and treating "all sick cattle" (D&C 89:8).

The Word of Wisdom was originally given to show the will of God, but not as a commandment. Abstinence from tobacco was expected of all fully participating Church members by the early twentieth century.

Tobacco contains nicotine, which is a cerebral and vascular stimulant. The burning of the tobacco leaf also releases and produces a large number of chemicals, many of which are absorbed by the body and are known to cause cancer and other serious diseases.

BIBLIOGRAPHY
U.S. Department of Health and Human Services, Public Health Service, Centers for Disease Control, Center for Chronic Disease Prevention and Health Promotion, Office on Smoking and Health. *Reducing the Health Consequences of Smoking: 25 Years of Progress. A Report of the Surgeon General.* DHHS Publication No. (CDC) 89-8411. Rockville, Md., 1989.
Wilson, J. D., et al., eds. *Harrison's Principles of Internal Medicine*, 12th ed., pp. 2158–61. New York, 1991.

JOSEPH LYNN LYON

TOLERANCE

The LDS principles of tolerance are rooted in the teaching that all who have lived, now live, and will yet live on this earth are spirit children of God and are responsible only to God for their religious beliefs and practices. "We claim the privilege of worshipping Almighty God according to the dictates of our own conscience," says Article of Faith 11, "and allow all men the same privilege, let them worship, how, where or what they may."

A corollary of this statement is a declaration of belief regarding governments and law, adopted by the Church in 1835. It affirms that governments have no power to prescribe rules of worship to bind the consciences of men or to dictate forms for public or private devotion. In matters of religion, the declaration asserts, "men are amenable to God and to Him only for the exercise of their religious beliefs, unless their religious opinions prompt them to infringe upon the rights and liberties of others" (D&C 134). The Church has maintained these principles while accommodating to secular authority: "We believe in being subject to kings, presidents, rulers, and magistrates, in obeying, honoring and sustaining the law" (A of F 12; cf. D&C 134:1–12).

Related to this is a doctrine of primordial individual freedom. For Latter-day Saints agency is indestructible. All truth is "independent in that sphere in which God has placed it, to act for itself, as all intelligence also" (D&C 93:30). The individual's freedom to search for this truth should not be contravened, and in the last analysis it cannot be. Even God cannot coerce belief. The only power justified on earth or in heaven is loving persuasion (D&C 121:41).

Intolerance often arises from sectarian conviction. But contrary to stereotypes, The Church of Jesus Christ of Latter-day Saints is neither a SECT nor a CULT. It has an extensive scriptural foundation, but no formalized CREEDS and no closed canon. As the Prophet Joseph Smith said to Stephen A. Douglas, Latter-day Saints are "ready to believe all true principles that exist, as they are manifest from time to time" (*HC* 5:215). They are taught to "gather all the good and true principles in the world and treasure them up" (*TPJS* p. 316). Commitment to truth in this inclusive sense is commitment to the view that all philosophies, religions, and ethical systems have elements of truth and that all persons have a portion of light. This is a buttress for tolerance, goodwill, and fellowship on a worldwide scale (*see* WORLD RELIGIONS [NON-CHRISTIAN] AND MORMONISM). "If ye will not embrace our religion," Joseph Smith said, "embrace our hospitalities" (*WJS* 162).

The crucial need for tolerance has been impressed upon Latter-day Saints by the buffetings, persecutions, and drivings of their own history. In various places in the world they have sometimes been denied civil and even survival rights.

The Church itself has a long history of forbearance. The Prophet Joseph Smith taught that "the same principle that would trample upon the rights of the Latter-day Saints would trample upon the rights of the Roman Catholics, or of any other denomination. . . . If it has been demonstrated that I have been willing to die for a Mormon I am bold to declare before heaven that I am just as ready to die for a presbyterian, a baptist or any other denomination. It is a love of liberty which inspires my soul, civil and religious liberty. . . . " He added, "If I esteem mankind to be in error shall I bear them down? No. I will lift them up and in their own way, too, if I cannot persuade them my way is better" (*TPJS*, p. 313).

Within the Church two principles taught by Joseph Smith have prevailed: "I teach the people correct principles and they govern themselves" (*JD* 10:57–58), and, "It does not prove that a man is not a good man because he errs in doctrine" (*HC* 5:340).

Latter-day Saints today face the challenge of being a religious majority in some areas of the world and a minority in others. Tolerance is reinforced by its converts, who come from diverse religious and cultural backgrounds and by its hundreds of thousands of returned missionaries, who have, early in their lives, learned the languages, customs, and religious concerns of multiple cultures and peoples. Today as the Church grows in Latin America, Asia, and Africa, it faces new challenges to its commitment to tolerance and goodwill.

BIBLIOGRAPHY
Hunter, Howard W. "All Are Alike Unto God." In *Devotional Speeches of the Year, 1989*, pp. 32–36. Provo, Utah.

GEORGE ROMNEY

U

UNITED STATES OF AMERICA

The Church of Jesus Christ of Latter-day Saints was first organized in the United States. It is now known worldwide as one of the most distinctive and successful religions organized in America. Its members acknowledge that its American origins made possible much of its contemporary success. They also believe that the United States of America is a divinely blessed land of promise and that it will continue to play a pivotal role in important events of the Restoration and the last days.

ROLE IN THE RESTORATION OF THE GOSPEL. Latter-day Saints believe that the United States was divinely prepared as a suitable place for the prophesied restoration of the gospel of Jesus Christ. Their scriptures teach that God kept the Americas hidden from the rest of the world until the time had come when he could accomplish his purpose and prepare the way for the American Republic (2 Ne. 1:8–9), that COLUMBUS was inspired in his discovery of the Western Hemisphere (1 Ne. 13:12), and that the Lord governed and controlled the settling of the continent (1 Ne. 13:13–19). The War of Independence, the ultimate victory of the colonies, the establishment of representative political institutions, and the peace and prosperity that prevailed in early nineteenth-century America were all divinely inspired and guided.

By 1820, at the time the Restoration commenced, political domination of the American continents by European nations had ceased. The established state religions that had prevailed in the majority of the English colonies had been replaced by constitutional guarantees of the separation of CHURCH AND STATE. Representative political institutions and a commitment to individual liberty, freedom of speech and religion, and freedom of assembly sustained unprecedented religious toleration and a spirit of inquiry. Economic arrangements largely free of the direction of governments or guilds contributed to a sense of freedom and a cascade of innovations. A vast, sparsely inhabited continent encouraged mobility and attracted the restless and those seeking a new life. This combination of conditions provided fertile ground for establishing a new church and enabling it to grow and flourish.

A PROMISED LAND WITH RESPONSIBILITIES.   Latter-day Saints view the American continent as a land "choice above all other lands" (1 Ne. 13:30). It is the land in which the New Jerusalem will be established (3 Ne. 20:22). It is also a land whose security, prosperity, potential, and stature are conditioned by the actions of its inhabitants. Further, the land of America was designated to be a land of liberty for the Gentiles. It has been a land of liberty for the righteous. The Book of Mormon teaches that no king shall be raised up here and that those who seek to establish a king in this land shall perish (2 Ne. 10:11).

Latter-day Saints believe that the United States is guaranteed protection against all other nations only on the condition of righteousness. It is a blessed land for all the inhabitants of the earth who will act righteously, but it is, and will be, cursed to those who will not act righteously (2 Ne. 1:7; Ether 2:9–12).

Not only is the United States a land of great promises, it is also a land with special responsibilities. It serves as a standard of liberty to the world, as a warning to oppressors, and as a star of hope to the oppressed (cf. O. Hyde, *JD* 6:368). The United States has a mission to be a benefactor to all nations. Moreover, it is to provide an example of righteousness and good government to all people. It has a mission to teach the principles of freedom and religious liberty (Benson, pp. 588, 655).

REVERENCE FOR THE U.S. CONSTITUTION.   Latter-day Saints respect and revere the Declaration of Independence and the CONSTITUTION OF

THE UNITED STATES as documents framed by the hands of wise men who were raised up and inspired by God (D&C 101:80). They recognize that the Constitution and the law of the land are the foundation of the people's freedom (D&C 98:8; *see also* CONSTITUTIONAL LAW) and that its principle of freedom, which maintains "rights and privileges, belongs to all mankind, and is justifiable before" God (D&C 98:5). As a matter of loyalty to the message of God and in the service of their fellow citizens, Latter-day Saints are taught to uphold, defend, and cherish the Constitution.

Speaking in the Doctrine and Covenants, the Lord instructs the Saints to observe the constitutional laws of the land, to uphold them by their votes, and to sustain good, wise, and honest officials to administer them. In this sense, the Saints carry on much of an older American civil religion (*see* POLITICS: POLITICAL TEACHINGS).

ATTITUDE TOWARD THE UNITED STATES.   During the first two decades following the organization of the Church in 1830, the Latter-day Saints suffered much persecution within the boundaries of the United States. They were driven from Ohio to Missouri, to Illinois, and finally to the Rocky Mountains, which were not a part of the United States at that time (*see* POLITICS: POLITICAL HISTORY).

When expelled from the state of Missouri under an Extermination Order of its governor, they held that the federal government, by virtue of the Constitution, had the responsibility and power to protect and reinstate them in their rights. President Martin Van Buren, when confronted with this request, replied, "Your cause is just, but I can do nothing for you" (*HC* 4:40, 80).

In 1845, following the martyrdom of Joseph Smith, Brigham Young addressed letters to all the governors of the states and territories in the Union, asking for asylum within their borders for the Latter-day Saints. All either were silent or flatly refused. Three members of Congress negotiated with the Saints to have them leave the confines of the United States. Ultimately, the main body of the Church left Nauvoo, the city they had founded and then the second-largest city in the state of Illinois, and, beginning in 1847, settled in the Great Basin in an area then governed by Mexico.

This pattern of persecution did not weaken the Latter-day Saints' attachment to the principles of free government. Upon arriving in the valley of the Great Salt Lake, they raised the American flag and announced their determination to live under the U.S. Constitution.

Notwithstanding the martyrdom of the Prophet Joseph Smith and the sustained persecution suffered by the Saints as a whole, they were able to differentiate the Constitution and the laws of the United States consistent with it from the cruel and illegal deeds committed against Church members in various states of the Union. The Church and its members have continued to see the Constitution and laws of the United States as a potential and real source of protection for their worship, as is reflected in a number of court cases involving these issues.

LATTER-DAY SAINTS IN THE UNITED STATES.   During the early period of the Church's history, the United States was a place of gathering. Tens of thousands of converts, principally from England and Europe, journeyed across the Atlantic Ocean and the American continent to the headquarters of the Church, first in Nauvoo and then in Salt Lake City.

The economic opportunity and relative prosperity enjoyed by members of the Church in the United States helped provide a strong financial base that has sustained a growing global missionary effort, the establishment and support of congregations in developing countries, and humanitarian relief programs. By the middle of the twentieth century, the Church had become virtually a worldwide faith, a trend that accelerated sharply during the last half of the century.

LDS wards and branches exist in all fifty states, with a heavy Latter-day Saint population in several Rocky Mountain and western states. By 1990, Church membership in the United States had grown to more than 4 million, making it the sixth-largest religious denomination in the nation.

BIBLIOGRAPHY
Allen, James B., and Glen M. Leonard. *The Story of the Latter-day Saints*. Salt Lake City, 1976.
Benson, Ezra Taft. *The Teachings of Ezra Taft Benson*, pp. 569–705. Salt Lake City, 1988.
Cowan, Richard O. *The Church in the Twentieth Century*. Salt Lake City, 1985.

ROGER B. PORTER

UNIVERSITY OF DESERET

On February 28, 1850, two and a half years after the pioneers entered Great Salt Lake Valley, the General Assembly of the State of Deseret chartered the University of Deseret, which eventually became the University of Utah. The founding of the university in the early years of Utah settlement, the first such institution west of the Mississippi, indicates the value Latter-day Saints placed on education.

Although chartered as a university, the school had a humble beginning and slow and interrupted development in its early years. Its first term opened for men on November 11, 1850, in a private home in Salt Lake City. The second term opened in 1851 for both women and men and was held in the State House, known later as the Council House. After the third term, held in 1852, lack of funds closed the school.

In 1867 the University of Deseret reopened, primarily as a business school, and in 1884 its first building was constructed on the site now occupied by West High School. The first commencement exercises, in 1886, conferred ten normal (teaching) and two bachelor degrees. By the 1890s 400 students were enrolled, and B.A. and B.S. degrees were offered in classical, scientific, and normal programs.

In 1892, four years before statehood, an amendment to the University of Deseret charter changed the name to the University of Utah. In 1894, Congress granted sixty acres of land from Fort Douglas on the east bench of Salt Lake Valley to the university, which established its campus there.

In the 1890s, a nationwide financial crisis and the competition of other institutions for students and funds threatened the fledgling state university. Responding to the crisis, the LDS Church discontinued its support of its own recently founded university in Salt Lake City and urged Latter-day Saints to "faithfully devote their influence and energy . . . to the University of Utah."

BIBLIOGRAPHY

Chamberlin, Ralph V. *The University of Utah: A History of Its First Hundred Years, 1850–1950.* Salt Lake City, 1960.

GRETHE BALLIF PETERSON

V

VALUES, TRANSMISSION OF

Like other religious organizations, The Church of Jesus Christ of
Latter-day Saints is concerned about transmitting its values to its
young people. Its youth are viewed as future leaders, teachers, and
parents who will one day influence the growth and success of other
Church members, including their own children. Of central interest
to the Church is helping young people gain a foundation of basic values that will have vital influence on later behavior and future religious development.

The process of transmitting these values is neither simple nor
easy. It focuses on the conditions and experiences of home and family. Domestic factors have the greatest potential for positive or negative influence in a child's life. In addition, the Church provides a
multi-faceted support program in the form of the second-strongest
influences—leaders, teachers, and advisers seen by youth as credi-
ble, respected, and approachable adults.

The Lord has commanded parents, first and foremost, to teach
their children the gospel (D&C 68:25–28; cf. Deut. 6:7; 2 Ne.
25:23–27; Jacob 3:10; 4:2–5). This obligation cannot be delegated.
President David O. McKay taught, "The home is the first and most
effective place for children to learn the lessons of life. . . . No other
success can compensate for failure in the home" (*Family Home
Evening Manual*, p. iii; also quoting J. E. McCulloch, *Home: The*

Savior of Civilization [Washington, D.C., 1924], p. 24). Church leaders continue to stress the need for parents to teach values in the home.

Church support for parental duties was apparent as early as President Brigham Young: "Let the keynote of your work be the establishment in the youth of an individual testimony of the truth and magnitude of the great Latter-day work, and the development of the gifts within them" (*GD*, p. 391).

Well-documented trends throughout the world give ample reason for concern about young people. Although the level and intensity of problematic social behaviors are lower among active, involved LDS youth (*see* SOCIAL CHARACTERISTICS), there are so many negative influences that the reinforcement of traditional Christian values has become a persistent concern of the Church.

Prevention is the preferred mode of addressing potential problems among the youth of the Church, and the best preventative efforts are those that do indeed inculcate values. Such efforts take several approaches: formal and informal, and systematic, localized, and individualized.

The Church regularly provides its youth with educational instruction, service opportunities, social activities, role models, leadership experiences, speaking opportunities, teaching assignments, and frequent personal interviews with ecclesiastical leaders. The settings for these efforts are Primary for children, Young Women for girls twelve to eighteen, Aaronic Priesthood quorums and Young Men for boys twelve to eighteen. Church-sponsored sports programs, Sunday School classes, summer camps, youth conferences, firesides, Scouting, and seminary also supplement the efforts of parents through family home evening and other interaction. The Church also publishes the *Friend* and the *New Era*, monthly magazines for young children and for youth to age eighteen. Lessons, speeches, and magazine articles designed for the youth of the Church are usually based on personal experiences, scriptural models, or values stressed by the Presidents of the Church.

Youth growing up in the Church advance through a series of stages in their maturation that give some structure to their formation of religious values. At the age of eight, girls and boys are prepared by their parents and teachers for baptism and are interviewed by their bishop before they are baptized and confirmed. Baptism and confirmation are occasions for individual attention, as well as family participation and celebration. From a young age children are encouraged to bear their testimony in Church meetings and in the home, and are asked to memorize the Articles of Faith in order to graduate from Primary. Young men typically are ordained deacons, teachers, and priests in the Aaronic Priesthood at the ages of twelve, fourteen, and sixteen, respectively. They are inducted into service and leadership experiences in these ordinations. They also advance through the ranks of the Scouting program, where the values of the Scout Law are taught. Young women from twelve to eighteen similarly advance through a program of study and activity that involve the setting and achieving of many value-shaping goals. In addition, most young people in the Church receive a patriarchal blessing during their teenage years. This may serve as an influential personal guide to the values and goals they will adopt for the rest of their lives.

In the late 1970s and early 1980s, the Church conducted studies of the process of value acquisition and program effectiveness, first within the Young Women organization and later within a U.S. sample of young men (Weed, Condie, Hafen, and Warner; "Key to Strong Young Men"). These studies validated the Church's placing emphasis on the family as the most important agent for the transmission of values. Home religious observance was the strongest predictor of positive outcomes and explained more of the difference between young men's religious intention and behavior than all other factors combined. Home religious observance included the examples set by parents, experiences, and activities such as FAMILY PRAYER, family home evening, scripture study, and informal discussions about religion. Indicators of value acquisition included one's intention to be active in the Church, to be morally clean, and to serve as a full-time missionary.

A second important factor noted in transmitting values was the nature and quality of interpersonal relationships between the youth and their adult Church leaders. This factor became more significant as boys grew older, with sixteen- to eighteen-year-old boys strongly influenced by Church leaders whom they trusted, respected, and admired, as people in whom they felt they could confide. Having trusted leaders can be especially important to young LDS converts in combining the basic values taught in their homes with Church doctrines and principles.

Home and family, combined with high-quality relationships with Church leaders, were more influential than any particular programs or activities. These results comprised not just a simple tabulation of expression by youth of important influences in their lives but empirical data confirming the relationship between what youth valued and what they actually did.

The implications of the study are both reassuring and disconcerting. It is reassuring to the Church to know that its emphasis on parental responsibility contributes directly and significantly to the goals of the Church for its young people; that its young people, even in the challenging teenage years, are influenced by caring adult leaders; and that value acquisition and religious SOCIALIZATION do not require great expense and elaborate facilities. Less reassuring is the knowledge that many of the programs, activities, and lessons are not as productive by themselves as had been hoped. For the youth, a particular lesson's content may not be as important as who presents it and the mutual relationships of trust, confidence, respect, and admiration that are built between the youth and the presenter. The leader's personality and example of faith apparently carry more weight than the carefully planned curriculum prepared at Church headquarters.

Peers and the CHURCH EDUCATIONAL SYSTEM are also strong value-transmission factors as young people mature. These factors build on the relationships and activities experienced by teenagers, but as these young people leave home, institutes of religion near college campuses, wards composed of students and singles, and Church institutions of higher learning, such as BRIGHAM YOUNG UNIVERSITY, provide young adults with additional opportunities to develop relationships with dedicated leaders and teachers and with peers who have similar values.

For many young men and women, service as a full-time missionary is a powerful experience in the transmission of spiritual values from the Church to the individual. Working as a full-time missionary for eighteen months (for women) or two years (for men) becomes for many a rite of passage from a culturally based religious identity to one that is spiritually based, or internalized. During this time, many benefits of gospel instruction, the baptismal covenant, priesthood ordinations and blessings, and the temple endowment are realized and become securely embedded as one's ideals for life.

This religious identity gives the young adult an image of what it means to be a religious person, a son or daughter of God, a disciple of Jesus Christ, a member of the Church. Seeing oneself as wanting and striving to be consistent with those images gives much of the meaning and purpose to LDS life. Church members often describe the experience of receiving a witness or testimony from the Holy Ghost as a sacred moment, which contributes to, or further solidifies, their commitment to the gospel of Christ and their personal identity within the community of Saints.

BIBLIOGRAPHY

Family Home Evening Manual. Salt Lake City, 1968.

Fife, Austin E. "Folk Elements in the Formation of the Mormon Personality." *BYU Studies* 1 (Autumn 1959):1–17.

"Key to Strong Young Men: Gospel Commitment in the Home." *Ensign* 14 (Dec. 1984):66–68.

Kimball, Spencer W. "Therefore I Was Taught." *Ensign* 12 (Jan. 1982):3–5.

Oaks, Dallin H. "Parental Leadership in the Family." *Ensign* 15 (June 1985):7–11.

Smith, Joseph F. "Auxiliary Organizations." In *GD*, p. 391.

Weed, Stan; Spencer Condie; Bruce Hafen; and Keith Warner. *Young Women Study. A Technical Report.* Research and Evaluation Division, The Church of Jesus Christ of Latter-day Saints. Salt Lake City, 1977.

STAN E. WEED

VISITORS CENTERS

The Church maintains and staffs several historical sites and visitors centers. Their main functions are to introduce visitors to the history and doctrine of the Church, to help them understand the blessings of the restored gospel, and to strengthen the members and provide them with missionary opportunities.

Most tour guides at visitors centers and historic sites are volunteers, called to serve from six months to two years. They are taught specific information to present to visitors individually or in guided tours, and they are encouraged to meet the needs of their guests, answer questions, and have friendly personal interaction with them. Visitors are taught that the Church is a Christian religion and that Jesus is the Christ. An atmosphere of goodwill and positive public relations is sought for and fostered by the attendants and tour guides.

Visitors centers typically feature visual displays, films, photographs or paintings, replicas, and artifacts regarding the local site, as well as presentations about the Savior Jesus Christ, the Prophet Joseph Smith, the Bible and the Book of Mormon, and the purpose of life on earth. Books and pamphlets are also made available.

As of 1990, ten visitors centers were located near Church temples. These centers are open to the public and explain the purposes of temples, but the temples themselves are not open to the public once they have been dedicated to sacred services. Visitors centers are located near the temples in Mesa, Arizona; Laie, Hawaii; Idaho Falls, Idaho; Los Angeles and Oakland, California; Mexico City, Mexico; Hamilton, New Zealand; St. George and Salt Lake City, Utah; and Washington, D.C.

As of 1990, seven other visitors centers were also maintained by the Church. They are located in New York City; at the hill Cumorah, near Palmyra, New York; in Nauvoo, Illinois; in Independence, Missouri; in San Diego, California; at Welfare Square in Salt Lake City; and in Montevideo, Uruguay. Fifteen additional historical sites are likewise maintained and staffed by the Church, offering tours and historical information to all who are interested. Several other historical sites are owned and maintained by the Church but are not staffed.

GARETH W. SEASTRAND

VITAL STATISTICS

The membership of The Church of Jesus Christ of Latter-day Saints has undergone dramatic growth and increased geographic dispersion, and its composition is unusual in several respects. This discussion of LDS demographics will focus on (1) size, growth, and distribution of the population; (2) sources of growth and redistribution, including fertility, mortality, migration, conversion, and disaffiliation; and (3) composition of the membership in terms of age, gender, race, marital status, household structure, and socioeconomic status. Several of the statistics will be summarized for major geographical regions.

The Church implemented record-keeping procedures from its organization in 1830. Its records provide several sources of information. First, such vital events as the blessing of children (soon after birth) and baptism (after age eight) are recorded, and summary statistics are compiled. Second, a membership record is created and updated with information on marriages, ordinations to the lay priesthood, and geographic relocation. In the United States and an increasing number of other countries, membership records are computerized and some summary statistics are compiled. Third, every ward and branch is instructed to compile quarterly and annual reports that include information on the size of the congregation, numbers in attendance at church services, and group composition. Fourth, sample surveys of the membership have been conducted in the United States and some other countries by the Church's Research Division. These surveys provide up-to-date information comparable to demographic data available at the national level, and provide a basis for comparison between Latter-day Saints and the host societies in which they live. Fifth, Latter-day Saints are encouraged to compile information on their ancestors. These genealogies provide interesting historical information on LDS demographics. Finally, some sources of data for national populations in the United States and Canada include religion, and these populations contain a sufficient number of Latter-day Saints to allow separate analysis and comparison between them and other groups.

The accuracy of data is limited by several factors. Record keeping is often assigned to lay members with insufficient time, resources, and training to ensure a high level of accuracy. Changing procedures and personnel also create inconsistencies in collection procedures. Undercounts, missing reports, delays in recording change, and computational errors detract from data quality. Despite these problems, it is assumed that official data sources generally mirror demographic changes in actual Church membership.

Figure 1

GROWTH IN TOTAL MEMBERSHIP

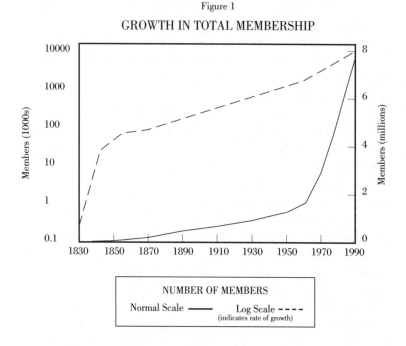

NUMBER OF MEMBERS

Normal Scale ———   Log Scale - - - -
(indicates rate of growth)

SIZE, GROWTH, AND DISTRIBUTION

SIZE AND GROWTH. From its inception, the Church has viewed missionary work as divinely mandated and thus has been committed to increasing its membership. Beginning with the six people who officially organized the Church in 1830, the membership exhibits a classic pattern of exponential growth (Fig. 1). Since 1860, the membership has grown at a relatively steady rate, doubling approximately every nineteen years. Growth was slower in the first half of the twentieth century, but picked up again after 1950. Membership stood at 7.76 million at the end of 1990.

In addition to the United States, with 4.27 million members, nine other countries had more than 100,000 members. Thirty-eight countries had at least 10,000 members. The ratio of Latter-day Saints per 1,000 in the national population varied widely, from a low of .1 in Nigeria to more than 300 in Tonga. Eight countries had at least 1 percent of their population belonging to the LDS Church. Recent growth rates also vary widely, from a low of 0.0 in Scotland to a high of .23 in Portugal. With some exceptions, growth rates are rel-

Figure 2

PROJECTIONS OF CHURCH MEMBERSHIP

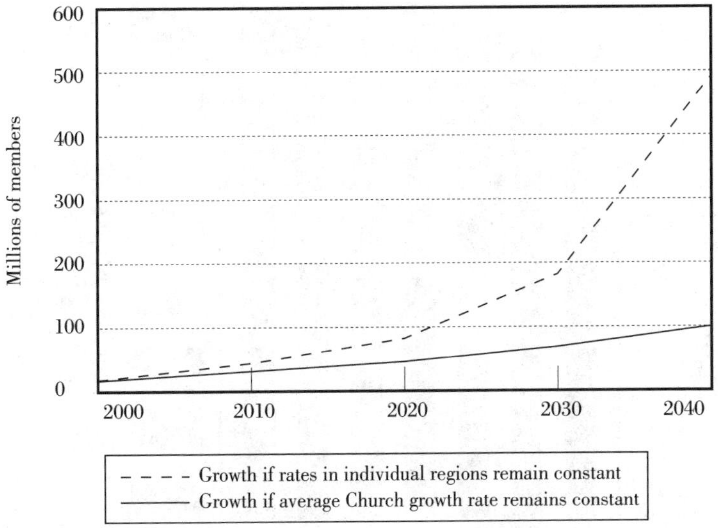

- - - - Growth if rates in individual regions remain constant
———— Growth if average Church growth rate remains constant

atively low in Europe and the South Pacific, while Latin America and some areas of Asia and Africa have relatively high rates of growth.

Although projections based on current growth rates are usually not precise predictions of the future, such projections do indicate future possibilities. Using past patterns of growth as a baseline, religious sociologist Rodney Stark has projected an LDS population of 265 million by the year 2080. Using this projection, Stark has predicted that the LDS Church will become the next major world religion. If growth rates for the total membership observed between 1980 and 1989 remain constant, the membership will increase to 12 million by the year 2000, to 35 million by 2020, and to 157 million by the mid-twenty-first century (Fig. 2). But some regions are growing faster than others. If regional rates of growth remain constant, growth will be even more dramatic in some areas.

GEOGRAPHIC DISTRIBUTION. Growth has been accompanied by shifting distribution of the population. The first few decades were marked by several relocations of a core LDS community and by a substantial

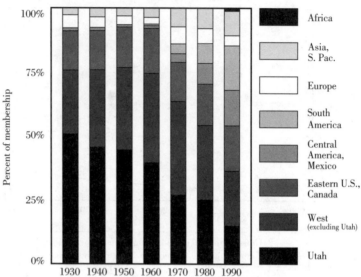

Figure 3
DISTRIBUTIONS OF CHURCH MEMBERS

infusion of new convert immigrants from Great Britain and northern Europe. By the turn of the century, the core of the Church was firmly established in Utah (Fig. 3). In 1930 one of every two Latter-day Saints resided in Utah, an additional 30 percent lived in the western United States, and another 11 percent lived in the rest of the United States or Canada. In short, the membership was largely in the United States (90 percent) and concentrated in the Great Basin.

By 1960, 90 percent of the membership still lived in the United States; but Utah's share had declined by 10 percent, and the other western states had gained 10 percent. After 1960, significant expansion of the international membership is evident. The share of members in South America increased from 1 percent in 1960 to 16 percent in 1989. In the same period, Mexico and Central America increased from 1 percent to 11 percent, and an Asian population appeared with 5 percent of the total. The share of the population has remained fairly stable for Europe (4–5 percent) and the South Pacific islands (3–4 percent). Although a majority of the membership still resides in the United States (57 percent), an increasingly international mix is evident. Rapid growth between 1980 and 1989 in countries such as the

Figure 4

GEOGRAPHIC DISTRIBUTION OF THE MILLION
NEW MEMBERS WHO JOINED, 1987–1989

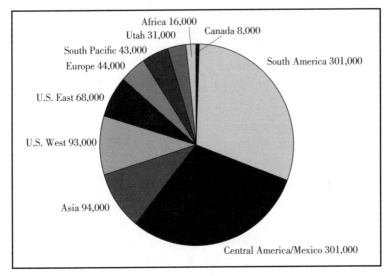

Africa 16,000
Utah 31,000   Canada 8,000
South Pacific 43,000
Europe 44,000
South America 301,000
U.S. East 68,000
U.S. West 93,000
Asia 94,000
Central America/Mexico 301,000

Philippines (from 57,000 to 213,000), Mexico (from 237,000 to 569,000), and Brazil (from 102,000 to 311,000), along with potential new sources of growth in Africa, East Europe, and Asia, implies dramatic shifts in the distribution of Church membership.

Another way to consider growth is to focus on the distribution of new members. Between 1987 and 1989, nearly a million new members were added. Figure 4 shows the geographic location of this growth. South America, Central America, and Mexico contain more than 60 percent of these new members. Another 9 percent comes from Asian countries. Three percent of new growth is occurring in Utah, and other western states continue to be a solid source of new adherents. The total contribution of the United States and Canada amounts to one-fifth of the growth. The remaining 10 percent comes from Europe, the South Pacific, and Africa.

Membership projections based on the assumption that each area will continue to grow at the same rate observed between 1980 and 1989 indicate that geographic shifts may become even more dramatic. The membership in the United States, Canada, and Europe is growing at a relatively slow pace, such that their percentage would drop to 40 percent in the year 2000, to 22 percent in 2010, and to about 11 percent by 2020. Although the African membership is growing at a high rate (14 percent annually), it has such a small base that it would constitute less than 3 percent by 2020. Asia would grow to more than 13 percent of the membership by 2020. But the biggest gains would be in Mexico and Central and South America. Collectively, these areas would increase their share to 46 percent in 2000, to 62 percent in 2010, and to 71 percent in 2020.

SOURCES OF POPULATION CHANGE

The basic demographic equation states that population change equals births minus deaths plus net migration. For religious institutions, conversion and disaffiliation must also be discussed.

FERTILITY. Fertility refers to actual childbearing rather than to the biological capacity to give birth. LDS theology supports attitudes and behaviors that directly influence fertility (Bean, Mineau, and Anderton; *see also* MARRIAGE). Consistent with a pronatalist doctrine, LDS fertility in the United States has been higher than the U.S. average, probably since the inception of the Church.

Genealogical records of persons living in Utah show a high average family size throughout the nineteenth century (Fig. 5). Family size is lower, however, for the earliest members of the Church (those born before 1830) than for those who reached the prime years of childbearing during the period of Utah settlement. This rise in fertility is consistent with the frontier hypothesis that low population density and easy access to new land promotes early marriage and larger families. As population growth and economic development led to a more urbanized, secularized society, family size declined. Family size also was larger for those who evidenced greater attachment to the LDS Church (lifetime-committed and converts) than for nonactive LDS and for non-LDS residents. This difference is consistent with LDS teachings favoring increased birthrate.

In the twentieth century, the LDS and Utah birthrates generally have been parallel with, but substantially higher than, birthrates in the United States (Fig. 6). After 1965, the United States birthrate continued to decline, but Utah experienced another baby boom while the total LDS birthrate leveled off at a relatively high level. Since 1980, both Utah and total LDS birthrates have declined precipitously, though

Figure 5

AVERAGE NUMBER OF CHILDREN BORN TO WOMEN
Utah Genealogies

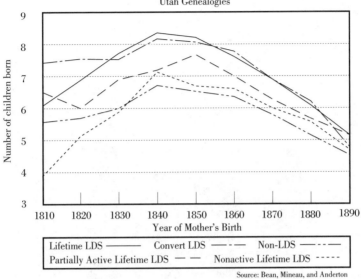

Source: Bean, Mineau, and Anderton

Figure 6

BIRTHRATES: LDS, UTAH, AND U.S., 1920–1985

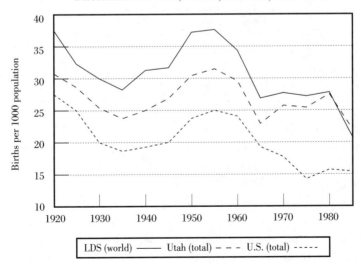

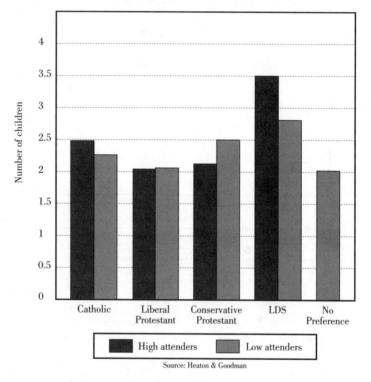

Figure 7

CHILDREN EVER BORN IN THE U.S.A.
By Religion and Church Attendance, 1981

Source: Heaton & Goodman

still remaining above total U.S. levels. As an increasingly larger share of the LDS population in the United States resides outside of Utah and the LDS population grows in other countries, neither the Utah nor the total LDS fertility rate provides an accurate measure of LDS fertility in the United States. Trends do, however, support the conclusion that Latter-day Saints respond to many of the same historical forces that affect family size of broader populations, and that LDS families have persistently been larger than the U.S. national average.

A comparison of LDS family size in the United States with family size in other major religious groups shows that LDS families are substantially larger, especially for Mormons who attend church regularly (Fig. 7). Latter-day Saints who regularly attend church average one child more per family than Catholics, and the difference is even greater in comparison with both liberal and conservative Protestants. Larger LDS family size is sustained by pronatalist religious beliefs, by contact with a reference group sharing similar values, and by socialization into the LDS subculture (Heaton). As the Church spreads into other cultural contexts, it remains to be seen how the interplay between religious pronatalism and broader societal trends will be resolved. LDS fertility appears to be above the national average in Britain and Japan but below average in Mexico (Heaton). Commitment to the LDS Church does not have uniform influence on family size in these three countries. These cross-cultural differences suggest that converts will be flexible in adapting to the pronatalist beliefs of their new religion.

High birthrates have been an important source of growth throughout LDS history. In the frontier era, high fertility was necessary to fuel population expansion. After 1900, conversion rates for several decades were relatively low, and fertility was the major source of growth. As LDS birthrates dropped in the United States in the late twentieth century, conversions in various countries became the major source of growth. Although LDS family size will most likely adjust to broader social trends, it seems that emphasis on childbearing will remain a distinctive feature of the religious tradition.

MORTALITY.   The LDS code of health, known as the WORD OF WISDOM, prohibits the use of alcoholic beverages, tobacco, coffee, and tea. Conformity to this code should reduce death rates. Utah death rates are below rates in the nation at large and in the mountain states for most major causes of death, including heart disease, cancer, cerebrovascular disease, accidents, pulmonary disease, pneumonia/flu, diabetes, liver disease, and atherosclerosis. Utah suicide rates are higher than the national average, but lower than in the mountain states as a whole (Smith). Unfortunately, the accuracy of such reports of death are difficult to verify. Deaths of nonparticipating members can go unrecorded on Church records for years, thus creating imprecise estimates of respective death rates.

Studies of specific LDS populations in California (Enstrom), Utah (Gardner and Lyon; Lyon, Gardner, and West), and Alberta, Canada (Jarvis) show that LDS men are about half as likely to die of cancer as other men. LDS women also have lower cancer mortality, but the difference is not as great as for men. Latter-day

Saints also have a lower risk of dying from cardiovascular and respiratory diseases. Death rates are lower for Latter-day Saints who have higher levels of religious participation. In short, adherence to the Mormon code of health appears to lower death rates from several diseases. But lower mortality is not as important as high fertility or conversion in creating high rates of growth in the LDS membership.

MIGRATION.   Migration was a common experience for early Latter-day Saints as the central settlement shifted from New England to Kirtland, Ohio; to Missouri; to Nauvoo, Illinois; and finally to Utah. During this early period, a major missionary effort was launched in Britain and western Europe. Converts were encouraged to gather to the center of Mormon activity, and the Church established a fund to support immigration from Europe. Indeed, the infusion of new members from Europe was crucial to expansion and possibly even survival of the Utah Church. In some years, the number of new baptisms reported by the British mission exceeded the total reported growth in LDS membership. Of the women in the Utah genealogical data base who were born between 1820 and 1849, more than 20 percent were born in Scandinavia, more than 40 percent in Great Britain, and an additional 2–4 percent in other European countries (Bean, Mineau, and Anderton). Although the LDS Church had its beginnings in the United States, there was a significant period when a majority of the membership was foreign-born. By the turn of the century, however, more than 90 percent of members were born in Utah. Immigration had virtually ceased as a source of growth.

Gathering to Utah is no longer encouraged; indeed, members have been encouraged to remain and build the Church wherever they reside. LDS migration trends in the United States between 1976 and 1981 suggest, however, some persistent attraction to Utah (Larson). Utah Mormons are somewhat less likely to move to another state, and those born in Utah are more likely to return to their state of birth in a subsequent move than are Mormons born elsewhere. Between 1976 and 1981, there was also a net flow of migrants into Utah. It appears that Utah, as the center of LDS culture, still has some power to draw migrants from other areas. There is virtually no information

Figure 8

GROWTH FROM CONVERT BAPTISMS, 1987–1990

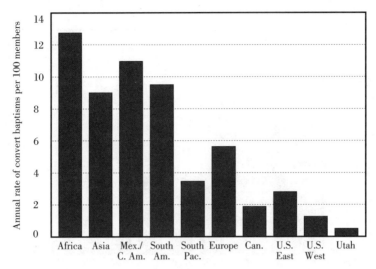

on migration patterns of Latter-day Saints outside of the United States.

CONVERSION. As a result of missionary efforts, 330,877 convert baptisms were reported in 1990, up from 210,777 in 1980. In 1987–1989, Church membership grew at approximately 4 percent per year because of convert baptisms (Fig. 8). Conversion rates tend to be higher in areas where the LDS presence is relatively recent than in areas with more extended contact. Growth due to conversion during this period varied from a high of 13 percent in Africa to a low of .5 percent in Utah. Latin America and Asia had rates a little under 10 percent, Europe was a little above 5 percent, the eastern United States and the South Pacific were around 3 percent, and Canada and the western United States were between 1 and 2 percent.

Reporting procedures render it impossible to get exact data on whether new members are children of members or new converts. An approximation can be made, however, by comparing the reported number of convert and eight-year-old baptisms. For the entire membership the ratio of convert baptisms to eight-year-old baptisms increased slightly from 2.59 for 1980–1984 to 2.72 for 1985–1989. The ratio

Figure 9

CONVERT BAPTISMS AND CHILD BAPTISMS
(AGE 8), 1980–1990

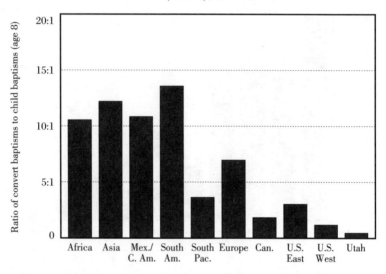

varies dramatically from region to region (Fig. 9). In Asia and South America there are roughly fifteen converts for every eight-year-old baptized. The figure for Mexico and Central America is somewhat lower, with about ten converts per eight-year-old. Europe, Africa, the eastern United States, and the South Pacific have values between two and ten converts per eight-year-old, while Canada falls between one and two converts per eight-year-old baptized. In the western United States, converts and children are about evenly numbered, but in Utah, children baptized outnumber converts by about five to one. In most parts of the world, a majority of Latter-day Saints join the Church through conversion rather than family socialization. This trend stands in contrast to the late nineteenth and early twentieth centuries, when a majority of Mormons had been raised in an LDS family.

DISAFFILIATION. Not all whose names are on the Church records as members would consider themselves to be so. In the 1981 Canadian census, for example, 82,000 people stated Mormon as their religious preference, yet LDS records reported 85,006 members. The difference implies that 3–4 percent of members on the records do not consider themselves to be Latter-day Saints. Official statistics on

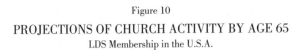

Figure 10
PROJECTIONS OF CHURCH ACTIVITY BY AGE 65
LDS Membership in the U.S.A.

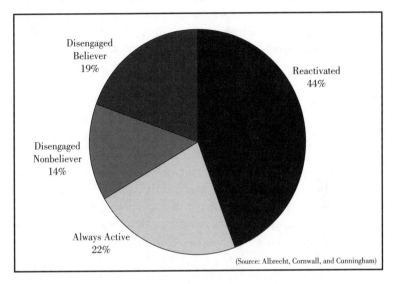

Disengaged
Believer
19%

Reactivated
44%

Disengaged
Nonbeliever
14%

Always Active
22%

(Source: Albrecht, Cornwall, and Cunningham)

excommunication are not published, but formal excommunication or removal of names from the records is rare, probably affecting less than 1 percent of the membership. More common is the experience of disaffiliation or disengagement. A recent study of LDS members in the United States indicates that 44 percent experience a period of inactivity at some time and then resume religious involvement (regularly attending meetings), while 22 percent remain active throughout their entire lives (Fig. 10). Eight out of 10 current members will become disengaged for a period of at least one year. About 1 of every 5 members retains his or her religious belief but does not attend meetings (disengaged believers); and only 14 percent remain disengaged nonbelievers.

Evidence of net change in membership comes from national social surveys of self-reported religious affiliation. One such survey reports a 36 percent net gain for Mormons among people who switch religions (Roof and Hadaway).

In areas outside the United States where the Church is less well established and where most growth is from recent conversion, retention of members may not be as high. Attendance at sacrament meeting varies substantially. Asia and Latin America have weekly attendance rates of about 25 percent, Europe averages about 35 percent, and Africa, Canada, the South Pacific, and the United States average between 40 percent and 50 percent. Integration of new members is more difficult in areas of high growth due to conversion because there are fewer established members to help converts become acculturated.

DEMOGRAPHIC CHARACTERISTICS

GENDER RATIOS. LDS gender ratios are similar to those of national populations, except they are also greatly influenced by the conversion process. In most populations, there are slightly more male than female births, but males experience a higher mortality rate, such that females predominate at older ages. It can be problematic within the Church if gender ratios in certain areas are substantially unequal, since Latter-day Saints are encouraged to marry within their own faith and because a majority of higher-level leadership positions are not available to women, who do not hold the priesthood required to fill these positions (see WOMEN, ROLES OF). The ratio of males to females for geographic areas is shown in Figure 11. Africa is unusual because there are substantially more men than women who are members of the Church. This indicates that African men are more likely to be converted than are African women. Latter-day Saints in Utah, other western states, and the South Pacific have gender ratios of approximately 95 males per 100 females, which is the value for the total U.S. population. Ratios in the Church are somewhat below the U.S. average in the eastern United States, Canada, and Asia, and females outnumber males by a large margin in Latin America and Europe.

Information from the 1981 Church Membership Survey of the United States and Canada indicates that gender ratios become smaller for older age groups, for singles, and for those who attend church regularly (Goodman and Heaton). For example, among singles over age 30 who attend church weekly, there are only 19 men for every 100 women.

AGE. Church membership statistics are reported separately for children under twelve, youth aged twelve to eighteen, and adults. The ratio of children to adults gives some indication of age structure (Fig. 12). This ratio ranges from more than sixty children per one hundred adults in the South Pacific to about thirty children per one hundred adults in

Figure 11

GENDER RATIOS BY REGION
Males per 100 Females, 1990

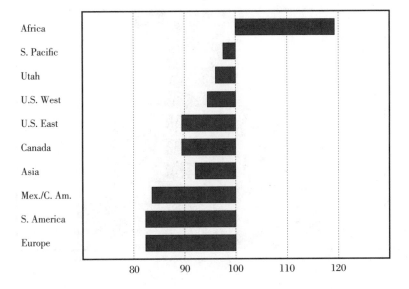

Figure 12

CHILD DEPENDENCY RATIOS
Children per 100 Adults, 1990

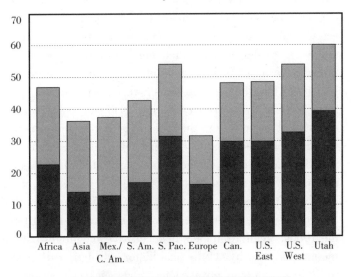

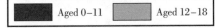

Figure 13

DISTRIBUTION BY AGE AND SEX
1000s of Members (U.S.), 1990

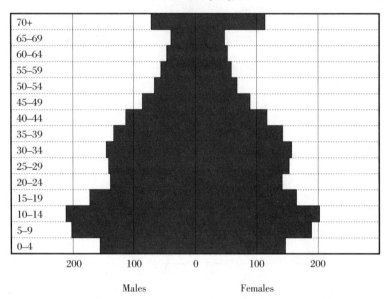

Males   Females

Europe. Ratios for young children (under twelve) are particularly high in Utah and the South Pacific, where fertility contributes a larger share of growth, but relatively low in areas where conversion rates are highest. On the other hand, ratios of children aged twelve to eighteen to adults are greater in areas where conversion rates are high. This is probably because a substantial number of converts join in late adolescence. Thus, the overall ratio is lowest in Europe because of relatively low fertility and conversion rates. Differences in ratios suggest substantial variability in the types of activities and programs that would be most beneficial to the membership in each locale.

More detailed age categorization is possible where membership records have been computerized. The age-sex structure of the U.S. membership reflects several trends (Fig. 13). Smaller numbers in the two youngest age groups are a consequence of declining fertility in the 1980s. Smaller numbers in successive age groups over age fifteen are created by (1) the past history of high birthrates, which result in greater numbers at each younger age; (2) new converts, who

Figure 14

YEARS OF EXPERIENCE AS
LDS CHURCH MEMBERS, 1990

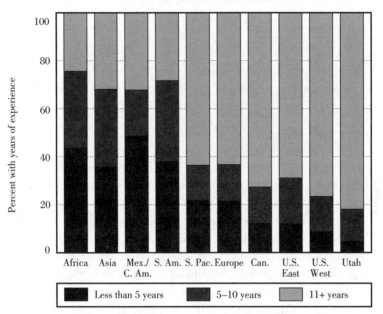

tend to join in the late teens and twenties; and (3) mortality, which creates declining numbers at older ages. The shape of the age pyramid also suggests that the near future will bring declining numbers of young children, temporarily growing numbers who may serve missions or want to enroll in Church universities, a larger number available for marriage, and possibly a high fertility "echo" when the large ten-to-fifteen age group reaches childbearing age.

At the youngest ages, males outnumber females by a slight margin in the U.S. membership. A higher percentage of females converting to the Church creates a more equal gender ratio in the twenties. Higher female conversion and higher male mortality rates shift the numbers in favor of females in the thirties. At older ages, females outnumber males by a substantial margin.

Another way to think of age from an organizational perspective is to focus on years of experience in the organization. Using membership totals for past years, one may estimate the percent of current members with various amounts of experience (Fig. 14). Consistent with patterns of growth, Africa, Asia, Mexico, and Central America have high percentages of members with limited experience as Latter-day Saints: Roughly two-thirds of the members have been LDS less than nine years, and between a third and a half have less than four years' experience. Between one-fifth and one-third of those in the South Pacific, Europe, Canada, and the United States (excluding Utah) have fewer than nine years' experience. In Utah, 84 percent of the membership has belonged for at least nine years. As one would expect, rapidly growing areas have only a small pool of well-seasoned Church members, while the opposite is the case for the membership of more established areas.

RACE-ETHNICITY. Ethnic MINORITIES are underrepresented in many LDS congregations. In the United States, where about 77 percent of the population were non-Hispanic whites in 1980, 95 percent of the LDS population were non-Hispanic whites. About 12 percent of the U.S. population and only 0.4 percent of the LDS population were black (*see* BLACKS). Hispanics and Asians constituted about 8 percent of the U.S. population and less than 3 percent of the LDS population. American Indians had a higher percentage in the LDS Church (1.1 percent) than in the U.S. population (0.6 percent).

The spread of the Church in Asia, the South Pacific, and Africa signals an increasingly diverse ethnic membership. Straight-line growth projections discussed above suggest the possibility of a Hispanic majority by 2010. In any event, international expansion implies a decline in the dominance of white North Americans.

MARRIAGE RATES AND HOUSEHOLD COMPOSITION. LDS teachings on marriage continue to be a distinguishing feature of belief and practice. In the early Church, plural marriage was one of the LDS family's most widely noticed features. After it was taught openly in Utah, this practice increased quite rapidly. Of the Utah women born between 1830 and 1840 who ever married (they would have reached the prime marriage ages in the 1860s, when plural marriage was at its peak), about 30 percent entered into such marriages (Bean, Mineau, and Anderton). The practice faded in the face of national pressures. Only about 12 percent of the women born between 1855 and 1859 entered polygynous marriages, and the practice was rare among women born after 1880.

Figure 15

PERCENT MARRIED AND TYPE OF MARRIAGE, 1990

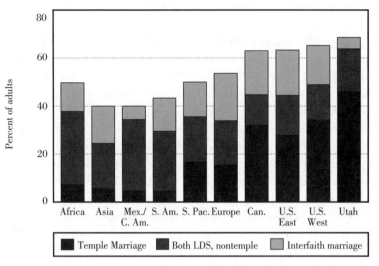

In the United States in the late twentieth century, LDS members have higher rates of marriage and lower rates of marital dissolution than the national population (*see* DIVORCE; MARRIAGE). Marriage patterns vary in different areas of the Church (Fig. 15). Marriages performed in LDS temples are the LDS ideal. The percentage of adults in a temple marriage varies from about 45 percent in Utah to less than 2 percent in Mexico and Central America. Temple marriage is relatively common among Latter-day Saints throughout the United States and Canada but is relatively rare in other areas of the world. Marriage outside the temple is about as frequent as temple marriage and is the most common form of marriage outside the United States and Canada. In some areas, a significant minority of marriages involve one partner who is LDS and another who is not. These interfaith marriages involve only about 5 percent of the membership in Utah, Mexico, and Central America, but reach nearly 20 percent in other parts of the United States and in Canada. There are more than twice as many LDS women as LDS men married to spouses of another faith.

The total percent married ranges from just over 40 percent in Asia to almost 70 percent in Utah. Differences in the percent married are attributable to (1) high conversion rates among young people who have not yet married; (2) regional variation in the age at which people marry; and (3) regional variation in divorce rates and in the propensity for divorced people to convert to Mormonism.

Less information is available on LDS household composition, but sample surveys show characteristics of the United States, Britain, Mexico, and Japan in the early 1980s. In Figure 16, three types of households are distinguished: (1) married couples with one or both being LDS; (2) households headed by LDS singles (never married, divorced, or widowed); and (3) households with LDS children but in which neither husband nor wife nor single head is LDS. Married-couple households are the majority in the United States and Britain and form a slight majority in Mexico. Single households constitute 20–30 percent. Japan and, to a lesser degree, Mexico are characterized by many households in which children are the only LDS Church members. Married-couple households are further divided into both-member and one-member couples. Both-member marriages predominate in the United States, Britain, and Mexico, but one-member marriages are more common in Japan. A significant portion of both-member marriages have not been solemnized in a temple, especially outside of the United States.

Regarding the presence of children (under age eighteen) in households, a majority of married-couple LDS households in each country have children, but the percent of married-couple households without children living at home is substantial (43 percent in the United States, 35 percent in Britain, 24 percent in Mexico, and 33 percent in Japan). In many of these cases, the children are grown and have left their parents' home. Although a majority of single-headed households do not have children, a proportion (ranging from 0.9 percent in Japan to 9.7 percent in Britain) are single-parent families.

The distribution of households does not fit any uniform pattern across countries. The idealized vision of a family with a husband and wife married in the temple and children present describes only one out of five LDS families in the United States and less than 3 percent of LDS families in Japan. Information for these four countries suggests that the household composition of the LDS membership is diverse.

SOCIOECONOMIC STATUS.   Membership records and statistical reports from local areas do not include information on socioeconomic status.

Figure 16

COMPOSITION OF HOUSEHOLDS
WITH AT LEAST ONE LDS MEMBER

United States

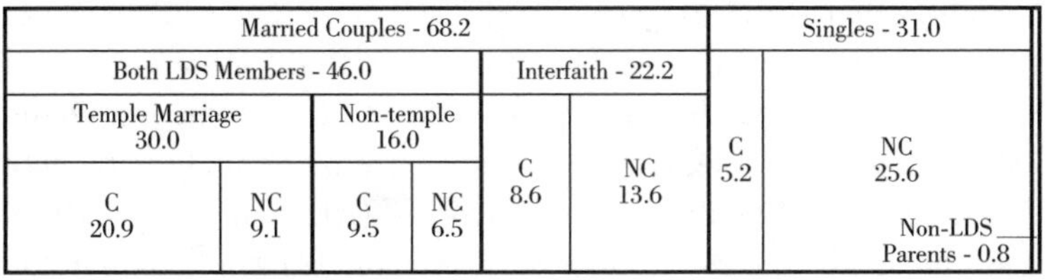

Married Couples - 68.2					Singles - 31.0	
Both LDS Members - 46.0				Interfaith - 22.2		
Temple Marriage 30.0		Non-temple 16.0		C 8.6	NC 13.6	C 5.2	NC 25.6
C 20.9	NC 9.1	C 9.5	NC 6.5				Non-LDS Parents - 0.8

United Kingdom

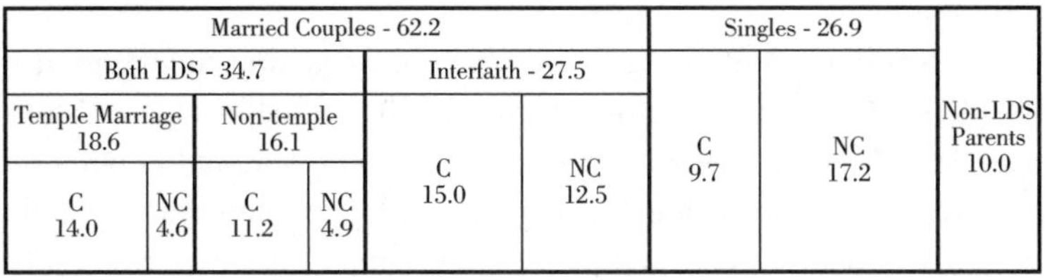

Married Couples - 62.2					Singles - 26.9		
Both LDS - 34.7				Interfaith - 27.5			Non-LDS Parents 10.0
Temple Marriage 18.6		Non-temple 16.1		C 15.0	NC 12.5	C 9.7	NC 17.2	
C 14.0	NC 4.6	C 11.2	NC 4.9				

Mexico

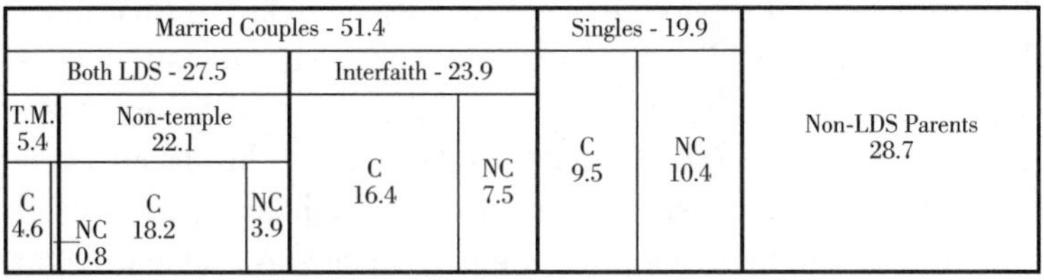

Married Couples - 51.4				Singles - 19.9		
Both LDS - 27.5			Interfaith - 23.9			
T.M. 5.4	Non-temple 22.1		C 16.4	NC 7.5	C 9.5	NC 10.4	Non-LDS Parents 28.7
C 4.6	NC 0.8 — C 18.2	NC 3.9				

Japan

Married Couples - 28.1			Singles - 29.3	Non-LDS Parents - 42.6
oth LDS - 7.4 / Interfaith - 20.7				
T-3.5 / N-3.9	C 13.0	NC 7.7	NC 28.4	
C-2.7 / C-3.2 — NC 0.7			C - 0.9	
NC 0.8				

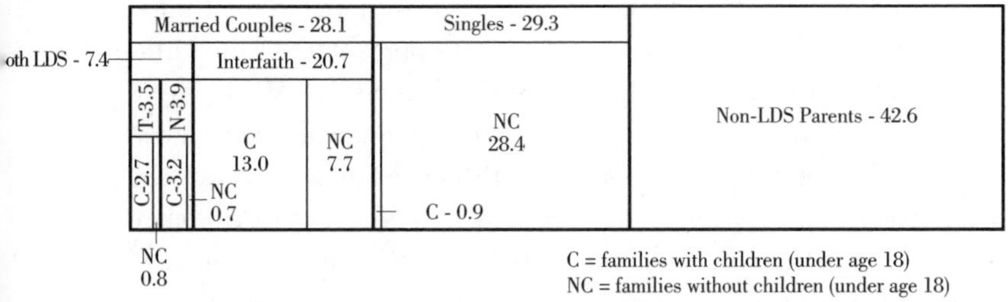

C = families with children (under age 18)
NC = families without children (under age 18)

Note: Numerals represent the percentage

Sample survey data are available from a few countries, but the data must be interpreted with caution because survey response rates favor those who participate in Church activities most frequently. Socioeconomic information may be more indicative of participating members than of all members.

Studies in the United States indicate that LDS educational attainment is above the national average and that, compared to the population as a whole, Latter-day Saints are more likely to be both highly educated and religiously involved (Albrecht and Heaton). Possible explanations for the positive role of EDUCATION are that the Church has emphasized the importance of gaining knowledge and that education facilitates participation in an organization staffed by lay volunteers.

A similar orientation toward educational achievement can also be observed in other countries. Figure 17 shows that in Japan, Latter-day Saints are more than twice as likely as the national population to have college experience. In Britain, Church members are only slightly above the national average in educational experience. In Mexico, where the comparison standard is postprimary rather than college experience, Church members exceed that national rate by a factor of two. The percentage with postsecondary education is higher among Canadian Saints than the national population. Less-representative samples also show above-average LDS educational attainment in some African countries (Heaton and Jacobson).

Adult male employment rates are quite high and relatively uniform throughout most countries of the world, and available evidence indicates that averages for LDS males are similar to national averages. Female employment is much more variable. In the early 1980s, about half of LDS adult women were in the labor force in the United States, Canada, and Britain (Fig. 18). These percentages were virtually identical to the national averages. LDS women in Mexico were less likely to be in the labor force when compared with LDS women in the United States, but were still slightly above the national average for Mexico. Japan presents a contrast, as 63 percent of LDS women are in the labor force. This is notably higher than the rate for LDS women in other countries or for Japanese women as a whole.

A comparison of the OCCUPATIONAL STATUS of Latter-day Saints with national populations shows that within each country Church

Figure 17
PERCENT OF ADULTS WITH COLLEGE EXPERIENCE
1981–1983

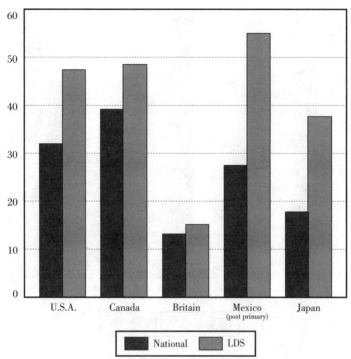

members are at least as likely to have professional occupations (Fig. 19). In Japan and Mexico the LDS percentages are substantially higher than those for the total population (the Mexico comparisons are based only on six cities where the LDS survey was conducted). African data also suggest that Church members have above-average occupational attainment (Heaton and Jacobson).

Although information on education, employment, and occupation is limited to a few countries, patterns suggest that Mormons have average or above-average socioeconomic attainment. In some Third World countries, joining an American-based church may be associated with upward mobility. Missionary efforts may also focus, either intentionally or unintentionally, on middle- or upper-level socioeconomic groups. Finally, an emphasis on achievement and

Figure 18

PERCENT OF WOMEN IN THE LABOR FORCE, 1981–1983

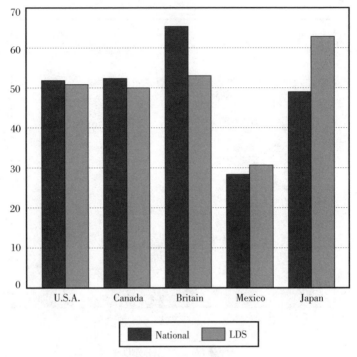

SELF-SUFFICIENCY may promote and develop higher socioeconomic attainment within the membership.

Information on income is more difficult to obtain than for education and employment because of national differences in reporting and individual reluctance to divulge income. Surveys conducted in the early 1980s indicate that LDS income is about the same as the national average in some countries. In the United States, reported average household income of Church members was $22,294, slightly above the national average of $21,063. In Britain, 33 percent of Latter-day Saints and 32 percent of the national population had incomes below £5,000, while 3 percent of Church members and 4 percent of the national population had incomes above £10,000. In the 1981 Canadian census, LDS men were a little above the national average ($17,222, compared to $16,918), but LDS women were a little below average ($7,243, compared to $8,414). In Mexico and

Figure 19

PERCENT OF LDS IN LABOR FORCE IN
PROFESSIONAL OCCUPATIONS, 1981–1983

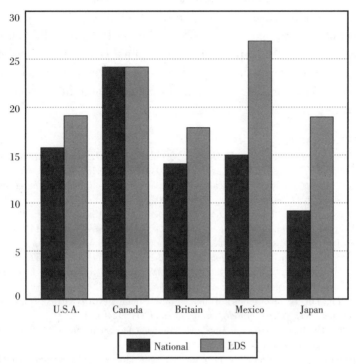

Japan the percentage of income going to the poorest and richest fifths of the population were approximately equal for Latter-day Saints and the national population. Although LDS family income may be slightly above the national average in the United States, LDS per-capita income is lower, due in part to larger family size.

Measures of poverty, which take into account household size, show that 13 percent of U.S. LDS households fell below the poverty level in 1981, compared to a national figure of 14 percent. As in the U.S. population as a whole, female-headed LDS households with children are especially prone to fall below the poverty level (Goodman and Heaton).

As the LDS Church expands in developing countries, the economic status of the membership will continue to change. A rough approximation of economic status of the membership can be computed by multiplying the per-capita gross national product (GNP) of each country by the proportion of all LDS membership in that country and summing the product across all countries. For 1974 this procedure yields a per-capita LDS GNP of $6,044, or 88 percent of the U.S. national per-capita GNP. By 1987, the LDS figure had become only 75 percent of the national GNP. Projections of Third World growth presented above suggest even greater decline in the average income of the total LDS membership in the coming years.

BIBLIOGRAPHY

Albrecht, Stan L., and Tim B. Heaton. "Secularization, Higher Education, and Religiosity." *Review of Religious Research* 20 (Sept. 1984):43–58.

Bean, Lee L.; Geraldine P. Mineau; and Douglas L. Anderton. *Fertility Change on the American Frontier*. Berkeley, Calif., 1990.

Enstrom, James E. "Health Practices and Cancer Mortality Among Active California Mormons." *Journal of the National Cancer Institute* 81 (1989):1807–1814.

Gardner, John W., and Joseph L. Lyon. "Cancer in Utah Mormon Men by Lay Priesthood Level." *American Journal of Epidemiology* 116 (1982):243–57.

Goodman, Kristen L., and Tim B. Heaton. "LDS Church Members in the U.S. and Canada: A Demographic Profile." *AMCAP Journal* 12 (1986):88–107.

Heaton, Tim B. "Religious Influences on Mormon Fertility: Cross-National Comparisons." *Review of Religious Research* 30 (1989):401–411.

Heaton, Tim B., and Kristen L. Goodman. "Religion and Family Formation." *Review of Religious Research* 26 (1985): 343–59.

Heaton, Tim B., and Cardell K. Jacobson. "The Globalizing of an American Church: Mormonism in the Third World." Unpublished paper, Aug. 1990.

Jarvis, George K. "Mormon Mortality Rates in Canada." *Social Biology* 24 (1977):294–302.

Larson, Don C. "A Descriptive Analysis of United States Mormon Migration Streams." Unpublished paper presented to the Western Social Science Association, Albuquerque, N.M., Apr. 1989.

Lyon, J. L.; J. W. Gardner; and D. W. West. "Cancer Incidence in Mormons and Non-Mormons in Utah During 1967–75." *Journal of the National Cancer Institute* 65 (1980):1055–61.

Roof, W. C., and C. K. Hadaway. "Review of the Polls: Shifts in Religious Preference: The Mid-Seventies." *Journal for the Scientific Study of Religion* 16 (1977):409–412.

Smith, James E. "Mortality." In *Utah in Demographic Perspective*, ed. Thomas K. Martin, Tim B. Heaton, and Stephen J. Bahr, pp. 59–69. Salt Lake City, 1986.

Stark, Rodney. "The Rise of a New World Faith." *Review of Religious Research* 26 (1984):18–27.

TIM B. HEATON

VOCABULARY, LATTER-DAY SAINT

Although Latter-day Saints share with other Christian faiths a general Judeo-Christian linguistic heritage, "Mormon language" includes many words and phrases that have distinctive meanings. Also, many words commonly used in other branches of Christianity are not common in LDS language.

From scripture and the religious vocabulary of the western world, LDS language inherits such words as "angel," "apostle," "atonement," "baptism," "covenant," "damnation," "deacon," "exaltation," "the Fall," "glory," "God," "heaven," "hell," "Israelite," "judgment," "Messiah," "oath," "patriarch," "priesthood," "prophet," "redemption," "repentance," "resurrection," "sacrament," "saint," "salvation," "sin," "soul," "tabernacle," "temple," "Urim and Thummim," and "Zion." Even though these words come from a common heritage, most of them have significantly different connotations in LDS vocabularies, as do many other words.

Conspicuously absent from LDS language, or used infrequently, are many terms of other Christian cultures, such as "abbot," "archbishop," "beatification," "cardinal," "catechism," "creed," "diocese," "eucharist," "host," "limbo," "outward sign," "inward grace," "minister," "parish," "pastor," "preacher," "purgatory," "radio or television evangelist," "rapture," "rectory," "sanctuary," and "Trinity."

LDS language is likewise distinctive in terms of address and titles. Members address one another as "Brother" and "Sister" in preference to "Mister" or "Mrs.," or a professional title such as "Professor" or "Doctor." Aaronic and Melchizedek Priesthood offices are almost never used as titles of address, with the notable exception of "Bishop" and "Elder," and the latter term may apply to any male Church leader (but is usually reserved for missionaries and members of presiding councils—the Twelve and the Seventy). The only other frequently used title is "President," a term widely used for both men and women in a presiding position in many of the units of the Church.

Unique names found in the Book of Mormon have been carried over into given names for places and persons, such as Abinadi, Ammon, Ether, Korihor, Laman, Lehi, Moroni, Nephi, and Zoram.

Alma, usually a woman's name in English and Spanish, is a man's name in the Book of Mormon and in many older LDS families. LDS colonizers honored settlements with Book of Mormon names such as Lehi, Moroni, and Nephi. Other unique or uniquely used LDS words include "Deseret," "Kolob," "Liahona," "disfellowship," and "telestial." Some terms also have specialized meanings in reference to LDS temples, such as "baptism by proxy," "celestial room," "temple recommend," "sealings," "endowment," and "garment."

Problems with the transfer of English connotations into other languages are extensive. Distinctions in LDS theology have led some LDS translators to avoid literal transliteration of commonly used terms in favor of coining a new word, borrowing the English word, or reviving an archaic term.

Because of the worldwide missionary program of the Church and the immigration of converts from many lands to the United States, there is a high level of language-consciousness among Church members. Brigham Young University has among its 27,000 students an unusually high percentage (up to one-third) who speak and read languages learned during missionary service. The "gift of tongues" is often spoken of in reference to missionaries' ability to learn languages rapidly, although the term is also used in reference to biblical modes of speaking in tongues and interpretation of tongues (cf. D&C 46:24–25).

Since its organization in 1973, the Deseret Language and Linguistics Society has solicited papers for its annual symposium on all aspects of LDS language, and a selection of these papers has been published annually since 1974.

BIBLIOGRAPHY

Harris, John B., and William A. Wilson. "And They Spake with a New Tongue (on Missionary Slang)." In *Conference on the Language of the Mormons*, ed. Harold S. Madsen and John L. Sorenson, pp. 46–48. Provo, Utah, 1974.

McNaughton, Patricia T. "Ordinary Language for Special Purposes." *DLLS Annual Symposium* (Brigham Young University). Provo, Utah, 1979.

Monson, Samuel C. "Some Observations on the Language of Hymns." *DLLS Annual Symposium* (Brigham Young University). Provo, Utah, 1979.

ROBERT W. BLAIR

W

WAR AND PEACE

LDS ideas about war and peace are complex. They synthesize a number of basic values. First are the ideals of finding peace in Christ (John 14:27), turning the other cheek and loving one's enemies (Matt. 5:39, 44), repeatedly forgiving one's enemies (D&C 64:10; 98:23–27, 39–43), and renouncing war and proclaiming peace (D&C 98:16). Next are the goals of establishing a perfect community of righteous, harmonious people and of welcoming the millennial reign of Jesus for a thousand years of peace. Third is a fundamental aversion to any use of force or violence that denies personal agency (D&C 121:41–44). Next is the recognition that war was the tactic Satan used in the premortal existence and that he continues to reign with violence on this earth (Moses 6:15). Then there is acknowledgment that it is appropriate and sometimes required to take up arms in defense of one's family, religion, and freedom (Alma 43:45–47; 46:12). Next are the ethical and legal distinctions between deliberate murder and the killing of opposing soldiers in the line of combat duty. There is an obligation of all citizens to honor and obey the constitutional law of their land (*see* CIVIC DUTIES), together with the belief that all political leaders are accountable to God for their governmental administrations (D&C 134:1). And finally, there is the role of the UNITED STATES OF AMERICA as a nation of divine destiny with a mission to lead the way in establishing international peace and individual freedom on earth. Under the extreme pressures and agonies that may arise from differing circumstances, an individual must have personal faith, hope, charity, and revelation to implement all these principles in righteousness.

Countries may define their interests differently and hence make reliance on force more or less salient, with various political and ethical consequences. For example, a group may adopt a radical pacifist position, but its survival then depends on the attitudes of others. Thus, in the Book of Mormon, the survival of the converted Lamanites who vowed never to shed blood was vouchsafed by the Nephites and by their own sons, who were not bound by their oath of pacifism (Alma 27:24; 56:5–9).

War also has some legal status in international law: "War is a fact recognized, and with regard to many points regulated, but not established by International Law" (L. Oppenheim, *International Law*, London, 1952, p. 202). In the exercise of their sovereignty, states may limit the initiation or conduct of war, but the present political system of self-help grants the right to make war as one's safety, vital interests, or sense of justice may dictate. Over time peaceful conditions may emerge, but as long as separate independent entities exist, the likelihood of resort to armed conflict remains, and in any sovereign state wherein LDS citizens reside they are pledged to "being subject to kings, presidents, rulers, and magistrates, in obeying, honoring, and sustaining the law" (A of F 12).

TEACHINGS OF THE BOOK OF MORMON AND THE DOCTRINE AND COVENANTS. The LDS response to the political realities of war is largely conditioned by the concept of the justification of defensive war provided in the Book of Mormon and in modern revelation. The main statements come from accounts of Moroni$_1$ (a Nephite commander, c. 72–56 B.C.), from the prophet Mormon (final commander of the Nephite armies, c. A.D. 326–385), and from guidance given to the Church in 1833, when persecutions were mounting in Missouri (see D&C 98).

Captain Moroni raised a banner on which he laid out the principal Nephite war aims: the defense of "our God, our religion, and freedom, and our peace, our wives, and our children" (Alma 46:12). Legitimate warfare is described here in defensive terms. Moroni established a forward defense perimeter, constructed protective fortifications for some cities, and deployed his main armies as mobile striking forces to retake captured towns. His purpose was "that they might live unto the Lord their God" (Alma 48:10), giving no support for war as an instrument to expand territorial or political control (Morm. 4:4–5). He taught the Nephites to defend themselves but "never to give an offense, yea, and never to raise the sword except it were against an enemy, except it were to preserve their lives. And this was their faith, that by so doing God would prosper them in the land" (Alma 48:14–15). They sought the guidance of prophets before going to battle (Alma 16:5; 43:23; 3 Ne. 3:19–20). Moroni "glor[ied]" in this position "not in the shedding of blood but in doing good, in preserving his people, yea, in keeping the commandments of God" (Alma 48:16). Even in the conduct of war itself, indiscriminate slaughter, plunder, and reprisal were prohibited (see *CWHN* 8:328–79).

Four centuries later, when the Nephite forces "began to boast in their own strength, and began to swear before the heavens that they would avenge themselves of the blood of their brethren who had been slain by their enemies" (Morm. 3:9), Mormon, their leader, withdrew from command. Vengeance belonged only to the Lord (Morm. 3:15). When Mormon's sense of duty caused him again to lead the armies, he knew that the Nephite turn to aggression and bloodthirsty reprisal betrayed a deeper corruption that ultimately spelled their doom. As his people drifted into barbaric acts of torture, rape, and enslavement, Mormon lamented the depravity of his people: "They are without order and without mercy" (Moro. 9:18); and they were destroyed.

Even if the sword is taken up in self-defense, it is a fearful choice. It should be undertaken only if God commands (D&C 98:33) and after "a standard of peace" has been offered three times (98:34–38). Great rewards are promised to those who warn their enemies in the name of the Lord, who patiently bear three attacks against themselves or their families, and who repeatedly forgive their enemies (98:23–27, 39–43). If an enemy "trespass against thee the fourth time, . . . thine enemy is in thine hands, and if thou rewardest him according to his works thou art justified"; but if forgiveness is again extended, "I, the Lord, will avenge thee of thine enemy an hundred-fold" (98:31, 44–45). Accordingly, in the Missouri persecutions and in Nauvoo at the time of the 1844 martyrdom of Joseph and Hyrum Smith, the posture of the Church was strictly defensive;

likewise, the 1857 military threat of the Utah Expedition was defused without the occurrence of bloodshed.

HISTORICAL PERSPECTIVES.   In several respects, the LDS response to the subsequent historical realities of war has paralleled the experience of Christianity in general. As long as the early Christians had no responsibility for government, they were obliged only "to obey magistrates, to be ready to every good work" (Titus 3:1), to render unto Caesar "the things which are Caesar's, and unto God the things that are God's" (Matt. 22:21). Paul saw the real battle as being one with evil spiritual forces (Eph. 6:12). Once it became clear in early Christianity that the second coming of Jesus was not at hand and that the Roman Empire had become Christian, responsibility for political order became a Christian duty. There then developed a theory of war culminating in the doctrine of "just war" formulated by theologians such as Thomas Aquinas.

Likewise, millennial enthusiasm initially focused Latter-day Saints more on the gathering of Israel than on accommodation to the world. An early and continuing LDS theme was that the hour was drawing near for the end of worldly states. With the collapse of "Babylon" would come intense conflicts and the wrath of God (D&C 63:32–33). Bloody war would arise at home and abroad (D&C 38:29). The Civil War prophecy in 1832 foretold increasing turmoil until the "full end of all nations" (D&C 87:6). War in this perspective is the harbinger of the apocalyptic end of the world, and the Church is to raise the voice of warning "for the last time" and gather the faithful together to "stand in holy places, and be not moved, until the day of the Lord come" (D&C 88:74–88; 87:8).

Animated by this vision, President Brigham Young counseled the Saints to "flee to Zion . . . that they may dwell in peace" (*MFP* 2:107). Little hope was given for the reclamation of the secular society. This tendency toward withdrawal, however, was counterbalanced by the LDS perspective on the divine inspiration undergirding the Constitution of the United States and the fact that the Church was inevitably drawn into national politics (*see* UNITED STATES OF AMERICA; CHURCH AND STATE). Although the attempt to establish Zion attracted the hostility of many politicians, Church leaders took an active role in national affairs, supporting the Mexican War, immediately responding to a request by President Lincoln to protect the mail and telegraph route east of Fort Bridger during the Civil War (1862), and proving their loyalty in the Spanish-American War (1898). After the Manifesto of 1890, the division between the Church and the larger society declined, leading to a reconciliation with the existing political order.

World Wars I and II impelled the Church to speak about the religious duties of citizens of warring states, balancing the condemnation of war with statements about civic duties and the relative justice of the causes and conduct of particular combatants. In 1939, the First Presidency asserted that the commandment "Thou shalt not kill" (Ex. 20:13) applies both to individuals and to political entities and condemned the notion of war as an instrument of state policy (*MFP* 6:88–93). Later in 1940 and 1942 they warned against the self-righteous justifications of the belligerents, which could cloak genocidal acts of mass destruction (*MFP* 6:115–17), putting distance between the Church and the state: "The Church itself, as such, has no responsibility for these policies, as to which it has no means of doing more than urging its members fully to render that loyalty to their country and to free institutions which the loftiest patriotism calls for" (*MFP* 6:156). The combatants are "the innocent instrumentalities of the war," who cannot be held responsible for their lawful participation (*MFP* 6:159). At the same time, reference to "free institutions" and the observation that "both sides cannot be wholly right; perhaps neither is without wrong" (*MFP* 6:159) point out that there are other grounds on which to evaluate one's participation in war, just cause and just conduct.

Echoing the concerns of the Book of Mormon for just war, the First Presidency warned people not to convert a legitimate war of self-defense into a bloody search for vengeance or the killing of innocent civilians. President J. Reuben Clark, Jr., held that "to be justified in going to war in self-defense, a nation must be foreclosed from all other alternatives" (Firmage and Blakesley, p. 314). President Joseph F. Smith identified wickedness in the whole system of states as the root of world war: "I presume there is not a nation in the world today that is not tainted with this evil more or less. It may be possible perhaps, to trace the cause of the evil, or the greatest part of it, to some particular nation of the earth; but I do not know" (*MFP* 5:71). At the same time, he also affirmed "that the hand of God is striving with certain of the nations of the earth to preserve and protect human liberty, freedom to worship him according to the dictates of conscience, freedom and the inalienable right of men to organize national governments in the earth" (*MFP* 5:71). Accordingly, the Church supported the war "to free the world from the domination of monarchical despotism" (*MFP* 5:71).

Although some used the global threat of nazism, fascism, and communism to justify war beyond a reaction to direct and immediate threat to American territorial integrity or political independence, others such as J. Reuben Clark in the 1940s continued to plead for a neutral, unarmed United States: "Moral force is far more potent than physical force in international relations. I believe that America should again turn to the promotion of peaceful adjustment of international disputes" (cited in Firmage and Blakesley, p. 298).

Since World War II, the LDS stance toward just cause and just conduct in war has provided guides by which to evaluate participation in specific conflicts without departing either from the obligation of civic obedience or the generalized condemnation of war. These attitudes accommodate the cross-cultural and millennial aspirations of a worldwide church and the demands placed on citizens in a world of competing secular states whose ultimate demise is inevitable.

[*See also* Military and the Church.]

BIBLIOGRAPHY

Berrett, William E. "The Book of Mormon Speaks on War." In *A Book of Mormon Treasury*, pp. 275–84. Salt Lake City, 1959.

Blais, Pierre. "The Enduring Paradox: Mormon Attitudes toward War and Peace." *Dialogue* 17 (Winter 1984):61–73.

Firmage, Edwin Brown. "Violence and the Gospel: The Teachings of the Old Testament, the New Testament, and the Book of Mormon." *BYU Studies* 25 (Winter 1985):31–53.

———, and Christopher L. Blakesley. "Clark, Law and International Order." *BYU Studies* 13 (Spring 1973):273–346.

Garrett, H. Dean. "The Book of Mormon on War." In *A Symposium on the Book of Mormon*, pp. 47–53. Salt Lake City, 1986.

Oaks, Dallin H. "World Peace." *Ensign* 20 (May 1990):71–73.

Packer, Boyd K. "The Member and the Military." *IE* 71 (June 1968):58, 60–61.

Roy, Denny; Grant P. Skabelund; and Ray C. Hillam, eds. *A Time to Kill: Reflections on War*. Salt Lake City, 1990.

Walker, Ronald W. "Sheaves, Bucklers, and the State: Mormon Leaders Respond to the Dilemmas of War." *Sunstone* 7 (July–Aug. 1982):43–56.

ROBERT S. WOOD

WEALTH, ATTITUDES TOWARD

[*For related articles, see* Business; Equality; Poverty, Attitudes Toward.]

Latter-day Saints view wealth as a blessing and also as a test. The Lord has repeatedly promised his people, "Inasmuch as ye shall keep the commandments of God ye shall prosper in the land" (Alma 36:30). But wealth can lead to pride and inequality: "Woe unto the rich, who are rich as to the things of the world. For because they are rich they despise the poor, and they persecute the meek, and their hearts are upon their treasures" (2 Ne. 9:30). Therefore, attitudes toward wealth and the use of material abundance reveal a person's priorities: "Before ye seek for riches, seek ye for the kingdom of God. And after ye have obtained a hope in Christ ye shall obtain riches, if ye seek them; and ye will seek them for the intent to do good" (Jacob 2:18–19). To those who will inherit the celestial kingdom, God has promised the riches of eternity.

LDS beliefs about the nature and purpose of life influence Church members' attitudes toward wealth. Thus, the concept of wealth has both materialistic and spiritual dimensions: wealth is an accumulation of worldly possessions; it is also an acquisition of knowledge or talents. Since MATTER and spirit are of the same order, material wealth can become refined and sanctified by the influence of God's spirit as it is consecrated to his purposes. Latter-day Saints are encouraged to increase in all honorable forms of wealth, knowledge, and obedience, which increase the "wealth" or worth of the human soul and to "lay up . . . treasures in heaven" (Matt. 6:20; D&C 18:10; 130:19; *see* EDUCATION: ATTITUDES TOWARD EDUCATION).

The world and its resources belong to the Creator. Material blessings may be delivered from heaven if the recipient conforms to the Christian ideals of integrity, honesty, and charity. All people are of divine origin and have come to earth to know good and evil and to be tested to see if they will choose the good. By the grace of God and by their diligent labors consistent with divine law, both the earth and mankind can be perfected and glorified.

If the earth's resources are not wisely and carefully husbanded, however, wealth can become a curse. It is the "love of money," not money itself, that is identified as the root of all evil (1 Tim. 6:10).

President Brigham Young warned that wealth and perishable things "are liable to decoy the minds of [the] saints" (*CWHN* 9:333). Wealth may result in misuse and un-Christian conduct, immoral exploitation, or dishonesty. Greed and harmful self-indulgence are sins, and the pursuit of materialistic goals at the expense of other Christian duties is to be avoided. People with materialistic wealth draw special warnings regarding responsibility toward the poor; riches can canker the soul and make entrance into heaven exceedingly difficult (Matt. 19:24; D&C 56:16).

Thus, the accumulation and utilization of wealth confront the human family with some of its major challenges in determining the righteousness of goals and the correctness of behavior. "In many respects the real test of a man is his attitude toward his earthly possessions" (F. Richards, p. 46). The prosperity that results from honest and intelligent work is not necessarily repugnant to the spiritual quality of life, but the Church consistently warns of the risks of "selfishness and personal aggrandizement" that lurk in accumulating wealth (S. Richards, *CR* [Apr. 1928]:31).

Personal reflection, prayer, and inspiration are needed in deciding how to use one's wealth. Fairness, justice, mercy, and social responsibility are individual requirements; improper behavior is not to be excused by the behavior of others, reflected in market forces or windfall accumulations. The responsibility of each human being is to think and act in ways that ennoble the divine nature. President N. Eldon Tanner outlined five principles that epitomize the Church's counsel on personal economic affairs: pay an honest tithing, live on less than you earn, distinguish between needs and wants, develop and live within a budget, and be honest in all financial affairs (*Ensign* 9 [Nov. 1979]:81–82).

While not taking vows of poverty, Latter-day Saints covenant to use their wealth, time, talents, and knowledge to build up the kingdom of God on earth (D&C 42:30; 105:5). Providing for a family is a sacred requirement (1 Tim. 5:8). The mission of the Church in many countries of the world requires considerable resources to sustain Church members in seeking the spiritual growth and perfection of themselves and others. Ignorance, disease, and poverty can be overcome only with the assistance of material assets that result from the wise use of human talent and the resources abundant in nature. Thus the Church and its members seek to obtain the material resources that are needed to build the kingdom of God.

The principles taught in the standard works concerning the accumulation and use of wealth are sufficiently broad to permit an ongoing dialogue among Church members about what is pleasing in the sight of the Lord. Some emphasize that man must work and that the fruits of his labor are his due and right (D&C 31:5). Others point out that although man must work, God makes life and its abundance possible, and thus everything rightly belongs to him (Mosiah 2:21–25) and comes to man "in the form of trust property" to be used for God's purposes (S. Richards, *CR* [Apr. 1923]:151). Some suggest that there are no limits on the profits one may gather provided the pursuit is legal and the ultimate utilization is appropriate. Others see business and legal standards of secular society as falling short: "Except your righteousness shall exceed the righteousness of the scribes and Pharisees, ye shall in no case enter into the kingdom of heaven. . . . Ye cannot serve God and mammon" (Matt. 5:20; 6:24). Having taught correct principles in the scriptures and through his priesthood leaders, the Lord leaves it to Church members to govern themselves through individual righteousness, with knowledge that all will be held personally accountable for the choices they make.

BIBLIOGRAPHY
Johnson, Richard E. "Socioeconomic Inequality: The Haves and the Have Nots." *BYU Today* 44 (Sept. 1990):46–58.
Nibley, Hugh W. *Approaching Zion*, Vol. 9 in *CWHN*. Salt Lake City, 1989.
Richards, Franklin D. "The Law of Abundance." *Ensign* 1 (June 1971):45–47.

R. THAYNE ROBSON

WOMAN SUFFRAGE

Though far removed from the centers of agitation for woman suffrage, LDS women were neither strangers to it nor indifferent about it. They were aware of efforts for a national suffrage act and of several unsuccessful congressional bills between 1867 and 1869 that urged adoption of woman suffrage in the territories. The first organized effort to secure woman suffrage in Utah occurred on January 6, 1870, when a group of LDS women met in the Salt Lake City Fifteenth Ward to protest a proposed congressional antipolygamy bill. Asserting their right to "rise up . . . and speak for ourselves," the women voted to demand of the territorial governor "the right of franchise" and voted also to send representatives to Washington with a memorial defending the free exercise of their religion (Fifteenth Ward Relief Society minutes, Jan. 6, 1870; *Deseret News*, Jan. 11, 1870). This preliminary meeting precipitated a mass rally of more than five thousand women in Salt Lake City a week later to protest publicly against proposed antipolygamy legislation. Spurred by congressional inaction on woman suffrage and no doubt impressed by this demonstration of female political acumen, the legislature of Utah Territory, with the approval of the acting non-Mormon governor, enfranchised Utah women a month later, on February 12, 1870.

The response of LDS women to their new political status varied. One comment expressed at a subsequent Fifteenth Ward Relief Society meeting was that women were already surfeited with rights. Another urged caution to avoid "abusing" their new political power. Sarah M. Kimball, president of the ward Relief Society, rejoiced in announcing that she had always been a "woman's rights woman" (Fifteenth Ward Relief Society minutes, Feb. 19, 1870; Tullidge, pp. 435–36). Immediately thereafter, the Relief Societies initiated programs of instruction to educate women in the political process. In reviewing these events some years later, Eliza R. Snow distinguished Latter-day Saint women from women activists elsewhere who "unbecomingly clamored for their rights." Asserting that Mormon women "had made no fuss about woman suffrage," she explained that they were given the vote only when God "put it in the hearts of the brethren to give us that right" (Senior and Junior Cooperative Retrenchment Association minutes, Aug. 8, 1874).

Mormon women did fuss in 1880, however, about extending their political rights to include holding public office, and they lobbied the legislature to amend the voting act accordingly. Though the legislature approved, the governor refused to sign the amendment. This action was followed by several attempts by local non-Mormons to disfranchise Utah women, whom they viewed as so oppressed by the Church patriarchy that they would vote as their husbands instructed. This, they argued, would further entrench Mormon political hegemony and perpetuate plural marriage. These efforts were similarly unsuccessful.

An alliance of LDS and eastern suffragists was forged in 1879 when Emmeline B. Wells and Zina Young Williams represented Mormon women at the national woman suffrage convention in Washington. From the time of the first congressional attempt in the 1860s to repeal woman suffrage in Utah as an antipolygamy measure, eastern suffragists had lobbied against each congressional effort to do so. Though strongly opposed to polygamy, eastern suffragists were equally opposed to linking suffrage with attempts to eradicate polygamy. With help from prosuffrage congressmen, their effort delayed federal antipolygamy legislation and earned them a measure of condemnation for their support of the unpopular Latter-day Saints.

The Edmunds Act of 1882 withdrew the vote from polygamists, and the Edmunds-Tucker Act of 1887 disfranchised all Utah women. The false logic and injustice of disfranchising all women in Utah Territory in order to attack polygamy were repeatedly asserted by the suffragists and other sympathizers. For Utah women, this withdrawal of rights after they had had them for seventeen years ignited their determination to regain the vote permanently with Utah statehood.

In 1889 Utah women for the first time initiated a campaign to obtain the ballot. Within four months of an organizational meeting in January 1889, the Woman Suffrage Association of Utah had fourteen branches. When President Wilford Woodruff officially ended plural marriage with the 1890 Manifesto, statehood was imminent, and Utah suffragists prepared to put woman suffrage into the law of the new state. By the time the constitutional convention convened in 1895, both political parties had agreed to support woman suffrage. Unexpected dissent in the convention, however, almost derailed passage of the measure, evoking high-flown rhetoric on both sides. B. H. Roberts, leader of the opposition, posed the traditional argument that women would defile themselves if they entered the "filthy stream of politics," while Orson F. Whitney countered that women would help refine the political process and bring their own special capabilities to the betterment of society (Official Report of the Proceedings and Debates of the Convention, Vol. 1, pp. 469, 473, 505–513). Utah suffragists immediately gathered petitions and lobbied to hold delegates to their original pledge. The measure finally passed, and in January

1896 Utah became the third state to join the Union with equal suffrage.

BIBLIOGRAPHY

Beeton, Beverly. "Woman Suffrage in Territorial Utah." *Utah Historical Quarterly* 46 (Spring 1978):100–120.

Carter, Kate B., comp. *Woman Suffrage in the West.* Salt Lake City, 1943.

Tullidge, Edward M. *The History of Salt Lake City.* Salt Lake City, 1886.

White, Jean Bickmore. "Woman's Place Is in the Constitution: The Struggle for Equal Rights in Utah in 1895." *Utah Historical Quarterly* 42 (Fall 1974):344–69.

CAROL CORNWALL MADSEN

WOMEN, ROLES OF

[*Two articles appear under this entry and reflect the evolving nature of women's roles in the context of Church doctrine and culture:*

Historical and Sociological Development
Gospel Principles and the Roles of Women

The first article discusses the roles of women as they emerged during significant periods of the Church. The second article describes the impact of gospel principles on the roles, and eventually, the lives of women in the Church.]

HISTORICAL AND SOCIOLOGICAL DEVELOPMENT

LDS beliefs create a unique feminine identity that encourages women to develop their abilities as potentially Godlike individuals, while at the same time asserting that the most important activities for both men and women center around the creation and maintenance of family relationships.

The eternal potential for women has always been based on doctrinal canon, which has remained essentially unaltered since the Church was organized. However, women's temporal roles have taken different forms depending on the situations confronting the Church at various times in its history. Across all the historical periods, the application of the LDS theological perspective on women to pragmatic circumstances has meant that the Church's female membership always played a central role in ensuring the success of Mormonism as a religion and as a society.

WOMEN'S ROLES IN THE CHURCH'S FORMATIVE PERIOD (1830–1847). Typical of most adherents to newly formed and struggling religions, the early Latter-day Saints reacted to stresses by emphasizing an intensely spiritual orientation to everyday living. Although the authority to administer most ordinances and preside over most gatherings was restricted to a male priesthood, the gifts of the Spirit were not considered to belong to men alone. Women received personal revelation, healed the sick, prophesied future events, and performed various other actions that required spiritual gifts. The faith of these women and their ability to develop spiritual qualities were essential for keeping the Church alive during its difficult first years. They voted on Church matters, assisted in temple ceremonies, and contributed to welfare activities. As a group, women obtained an ecclesiastical identity through the formation of the Relief Society, viewed by the Prophet Joseph Smith as an integral and essential part of the Church. Additionally, the women provided much of the physical labor, doctored the sick and injured, assisted in reestablishing a succession of new communities, and cared for the needs of members whose families had faced hardships.

WOMEN'S ROLES IN THE CONSOLIDATION PERIOD (1847–1920). The broad-scale migration of the Latter-day Saints from the Midwest of the United States to the sparsely populated Great Basin region of the West marked the beginning of the consolidation of the LDS religion. Separated from the larger Anglo-American civilization by hundreds of miles of forbidding and unsettled terrain, the Latter-day Saints were able to set up their community under guidelines dictated by their religion. Among the social practices that became prominent after the migration to the West, and that significantly influenced women's lives, were plural marriage and the assignment of adult men to extensive tours of duty as Church missionaries. A woman whose husband divided his time between multiple wives and/or missionary service was often obliged to provide single-handedly both material and emotional support for herself and her children.

The growth of the population and its socialization in the Church were important factors in consolidating and strengthening the LDS organization; and much of this responsibility fell to the women. Because of the absence of their husbands, women enlarged their role as "mothers in Zion" with aspects not generally associated with nineteenth-century feminine domesticity. President Brigham Young encouraged the education of both girls and boys in "the manners and customs of distant kingdoms and nations, with their laws, religions, geographical location, . . . their climate, natural productions, the extent of their commerce, and the nature of their political organization" (*JD* 9:188–89; Widtsoe, p. 211). He also suggested that women should "keep books and sell goods" (*JD* 12:374–75; Widtsoe, p. 218), and exhorted them to "vote . . . because women are the characters that rule the ballot box" (*JD* 1:218; Widtsoe, p. 367). Some LDS women participated in political action concerning their gender, as evidenced by their being the second female population, after that of Wyoming, to vote in a national election.

The admonitions of President Young reflect an image of female responsibility drawn both from the belief that women and men are eligible for the same "eternal progression" and from the dependency of the early Utah Church on maintaining a capable and resourceful female membership. The women's response to the necessity of developing broad practical abilities and to an intense devotion to family forged the image of LDS women that emerged from practical as well as religious factors during this period.

WOMEN'S ROLES IN THE EXPANSIONIST ERA (1920–PRESENT). Throughout the early 1900s, the ideal of LDS converts flocking to Utah from all corners of the globe to build up an isolated "Zion" was gradually transformed into one of establishing the Church in many different countries and cultures. This change, accompanied by the encroachment of non-LDS settlers into "Mormon country," confronted the Church with the social issues of integrating its membership into non-LDS societies. Delimiting and articulating the position of LDS women was one of those issues; however, the role of women was not a topic that aroused much controversy.

The centrality of the family in LDS culture and doctrine fit easily into the popular nineteenth-century Victorian ideal of a highly, not to say exclusively, domestic role for women. The necessity of consolidating the Church as a community and as an organization was replaced by the desire to form a stable population that could fit comfortably into ambient cultures, particularly the culture of the United States.

Until the latter half of the twentieth century, the traditional role of women presented few obstacles to achieving this goal. As industrialization pushed the sphere of American males progressively out of the home, and that of females increasingly into it, most Latter-day Saints simply followed the pattern of secular society. In accordance with its family-centered doctrines, the Church readily endorsed the ideal of women as homemakers, wives, and mothers. The popularization of feminism in the 1970s presented LDS women with a complex set of expectations and competing priorities. Secular analyses set the attainment of an individual's personal goals or advancement in opposition to dedication to the family; LDS belief defines the two as inextricably intertwined.

The divergence of LDS religious beliefs from the theoretical basis of secular society presents modern-day LDS women with a perplexing set of role dilemmas. In the first place, they are inculcated by LDS doctrine and the historical examples of other LDS women with the twin beliefs of developing their personal abilities and centering their lives in their families. On the other hand, like all women, they operate in the larger societal context of legal, political, and economic systems in which these two ideals are sometimes seen as mutually exclusive.

BIBLIOGRAPHY

Arrington, Leonard J., and Davis Bitton. "Marriage and Family Patterns." In *The Mormon Experience: A History of the Latter-day Saints*, pp. 185–205. New York, 1979.

Beecher, Maureen, and Lavina F. Anderson, eds. *Sisters in Spirit: Mormon Women in Historical and Cultural Perspective*. Chicago, 1987.

LeCheminant, Ileen Ann Waspe. "The Status of Women in the Philosophy of Mormonism, 1830–1845." Master's thesis, Brigham Young University, 1942.

Shipps, Jan. *Mormonism: The Story of a New Religious Tradition*. Chicago, 1985.

Young, Brigham. *The Discourses of Brigham Young*, ed. John A. Widtsoe, pp. 194–218. Salt Lake City, 1977.

MARTHA NIBLEY BECK

GOSPEL PRINCIPLES AND THE ROLES OF WOMEN

The present role of women in LDS society is singular to the degree that it reflects the teachings and doctrines of the Church. Among the most fundamental of these is individual agency, or the right to choose. Consistent with this doctrine, a woman's role varies with her circumstances and the choices that she makes within the context of LDS belief; she may fill many roles simultaneously.

One function of women is the consistent attention to the needs of others—not only family but all within reach of their help. Most render care personally in times of illness, death, or other life crises, but often they work in a coordinated effort with other members of the Relief Society. To "share one another's burdens, that they may be light" (Mosiah 18:8) is a principle and expectation associated with the very essence of a woman's membership in the Church (*see* SISTERHOOD).

Caring for those in need often leads women to develop better ways of handling problems and to acquire specialized skills. Early in the history of the Church, women became nurses, midwives, and doctors; some established hospitals and baby clinics, while others started schools for young people. They also developed home industries, carried out a thriving silk culture, and established a large grain-storage program.

The Latter-day Saint community in the mountain West, perhaps because of polygamy, perhaps because men were often away on missions, provided an unusual independence for women—and an interdependence among polygamous wives. These conditions offered both the impetus and the practicality for women to acquire education and training uncommon to many women of their day. No less typical, LDS women today continue to take part in helping to "bring forth and establish the cause of my Zion" (D&C 6:6). They care for the poor and sick; serve proselytizing, welfare, and humanitarian missions; and teach children and youth, realizing their contribution to the temporal and spiritual welfare of the Saints.

The companionship role is the one most often identified for women in the Church. Adam "began to till the earth," and "Eve, also, his wife, did labor with him" (Moses 5:1). President Spencer W. Kimball pointed out that women are "full partners" with men (Kimball, p. 42). This companionship is not limited to the husband and wife partnership but includes women serving cooperatively with men (e.g., Priesthood and Relief Society) to carry out the work of the Church. From the early days, "the women of the Church have voted side by side with the men on all questions submitted to the Church membership for vote, . . . an advanced concept in 1830 when no women and few men voted in any church and few women had political franchise" (*History of the Relief Society*, p. 102).

Underlying the companionship role is the inherent EQUALITY of men and women as suggested by the creation account: "In the image of his own body, male and female, created he them, and blessed them" (Moses 6:9). Spiritual gifts, promises, and blessings of the Lord are given to those who qualify, without regard to gender. The receipt of spiritual gifts is conditional on obedience, not gender (D&C 46:9–25).

Bruce R. McConkie of the Council of the Twelve emphasized the equality of men and women in things of the spirit:

> Where spiritual things are concerned, as pertaining to all of the gifts of the Spirit, with reference to the receipt of revelation, the gaining of testimonies, and the seeing of visions, in all matters that pertain to godliness and holiness and which are brought to pass as a result of personal righteousness—in all these things men and women stand in the position of . . . equality before the Lord [*Ensign* 9 (June 1979):61].

Temple ordinances are further evidence that "neither is the man without the woman, neither the woman without the man, in the Lord" (1 Cor. 11:11).

> It is to be noted that the highest blessings therein [the temple] available are only conferred upon a man and woman jointly. Neither can receive them alone. In the Church of Christ woman is not an adjunct to but an equal partner with man [Widtsoe, p. 373].

Women and men, although equal in status, fulfill some separate and different roles in the work of the Church. To men is given the responsibility of holding the priesthood, with many prescribed duties. The role for women is less precisely defined, though no less real. According to Neal A. Maxwell of the Quorum of the Twelve:

> We know so little about the reasons for the division of duties between womanhood and manhood as well as between motherhood and priesthood. These were divinely determined in another time and another place. We are accustomed to focusing on the men of God because theirs is the priesthood and leadership line. But paralleling that authority line is a stream of righteous influence reflecting the remarkable women of God who have existed in all ages and dispensations, including our own [Maxwell, p. 94].

Wielding an influence for good, women fill myriad assignments in the Church: They preside over, direct, and staff the organizations for women (Relief Society), young women (Young Women), and children (Primary) at ward, stake, and general levels; they teach doctrinal study classes for adults, youth, and children; they direct choirs and dramatic productions; they officiate in temple ceremonies; they serve as members of welfare committees at all levels of the Church; and they organize cultural and recreational events in which all members participate.

LDS women also fulfill societal roles such as physicians, lawyers, professors, homemakers, administrators, teachers, writers, secretaries, artists, and businesswomen. Additionally, many serve in community, political, and volunteer capacities. Consistent with the LDS belief that the greatest good that parents do is in their own home and that no other involvement ought to have precedence over their concern for family, members are encouraged to make pivotal decisions with regard to their effect on the family. This priority of family unavoidably influences the role expectations for women, including that of mother, wife, homemaker, and teacher. Latter-day Saint women are taught from their youth to prepare for marriage and homemaking, as well as for a vocation. Camilla Kimball, wife of President Spencer W. Kimball, counseled every girl and woman to: "qualify in two vocations—that of homemaking, and that of preparing a living outside the home, if and when the occasion requires. A married woman may become a widow without warning. . . . Thus a woman may be under the necessity of earning her own living and helping to support her dependent children" (*Ensign* 7 [Mar. 1977]:59).

Church leaders have long urged women, individually and as a group, to obtain all the education available to them, to "be given to writing, and to learning much" (D&C 25:8). Schooling for women has been encouraged not only for their own fulfillment and achievement but also for its value in helping them make the home a place of learning and refinement and for its importance in the lives of children. Even though training and education may open many career opportunities for women, the role of mother is dominant for those who have young children, and they are urged to use their training to benefit their children.

The Church does not oppose women working outside the home per se, and recognizes the contributions that they make in government, professions, business, and in creative fields. Marvin J. Ashton of the Quorum of the Twelve explained that "a woman should feel free to go into the marketplace and into community service on a paid or volunteer basis if she so desires when her home and family circumstances allow her to do so without impairment to them" (Ashton, p. 93). It is understood that some mothers are required to work for the support of their children, but it is hoped that whenever possible, mothers with children in the home will make home their priority career.

All women are daughters of "glorious mother Eve" (D&C 138:39) who, as the "mother of all living" (Moses 4:26), left a legacy that is the inheritance of every woman. This role transcends the care of an immediate family. It describes a nature and attitude that is basic for all women. President Harold B. Lee expressed this when he addressed the women of the Church assembled in the Tabernacle: "Now you mothers over the Church. . . ." Every woman, whatever her family status, calling, or occupation, is involved in the roles of one who nurtures, lifts, consoles; who tenders love; and who protects and preserves families.

BIBLIOGRAPHY

Ashton, Marvin J. "Woman's Role in the Community." In *Woman*. Salt Lake City, 1979.

History of the Relief Society, 1842–1966. Salt Lake City, 1966.

Kimball, Spencer W. "Privileges and Responsibilities of Sisters." *New Era* 9 (Jan. 1979):42.

Maxwell, Neal A. "The Women of God." In *Woman*. Salt Lake City, 1979.

Widtsoe, John A. "The 'Mormon' Women." *Relief Society Magazine* 30 (June–July 1943):372–75.

BARBARA B. SMITH
SHIRLEY W. THOMAS

WOMEN'S TOPICS

[*Women; their roles in the family, in The Church of Jesus Christ of Latter-day Saints, and in the community; and other issues of concern to them are the subjects of several articles in this volume of the encyclopedia.*

For a discussion of both doctrinal perspectives and historical influences on women's roles, see Feminism; Motherhood *(cf.* Fatherhood*);*

Sisterhood; *and* Women, Roles of. *Related articles include* Family *and* Marriage.

For issues related to sexuality and reproduction, see Abortion; Birth Control; Sex Education; *and* Sexuality.

Among Church auxiliary organizations, three are headed by women: Primary; Relief Society; *and* Young Women.

[*See also* Abuse, Spouse and Child; Divorce; *and* Woman Suffrage.]

WORD OF WISDOM

Word of Wisdom is the common title for a revelation that counsels Latter-day Saints on maintaining good health and is published as Doctrine and Covenants, section 89. The practice of abstaining from all forms of ALCOHOL, TOBACCO, COFFEE, and TEA, which may outwardly distinguish active Latter-day Saints more than any other practice, derives from this revelation.

Called "a Word of Wisdom" in the introduction, the revelation was given to Joseph Smith at Kirtland, Ohio, on February 27, 1833, when the School of the Prophets was meeting at his home in the Whitney Store. It came in response to the Prophet's inquiry about tobacco, which was being used by some of the men attending the school. The revelation states that it is specifically for the latter days because of "evils and designs which do and will exist in the hearts of conspiring men" (D&C 89:4). The Word of Wisdom limited alcohol use to wine for the sacrament and hard liquor for washing the body. It noted tobacco as useful only for treating bruises and sick cattle. Hot drinks (later defined as coffee and tea) were not for "the body or belly" (D&C 89:9). Additional advice was given permitting the use of meat, but suggesting that it be restricted to winter or times of famine (D&C 89:12–13). The revelation places strong emphasis on the use of grains, particularly wheat, as the staple of the human diet (D&C 89:14, 16–17), and upon fruits and vegetables ("herbs," verse 11; cf. 59:17–18) in season. The Word of Wisdom also states that some "herbs" are present on the earth for the healing of human ailments (D&C 89:8–11). Church members should not consume alcohol, tobacco, tea, or coffee and should use moderation in eating other foods.

Those who follow this counsel and keep the other commandments of God are promised that they will have "health in their navel and marrow to their bones," "shall run and not be weary, and shall walk and not faint," "shall find wisdom and great treasures of knowledge, even hidden treasures," and "the destroying angel shall pass by them . . . and not slay them" (D&C 89:18–21; cf. Dan. 1:3–20; 2:19–30).

The promises associated with the Word of Wisdom are considered both temporal and spiritual. The temporal promise has been interpreted as better health, and the spiritual promise as a closer relationship to God. These promises reflect the concern of the Church with both the temporal and spiritual welfare of its members. They also reflect God's concern with the condition of the physical body of every person, paralleling aspects of other religious health codes defining types of foods forbidden for health and spiritual reasons.

The introduction to the 1835 printing of the revelation in the Doctrine and Covenants indicated that it was given as counsel or advice rather than as a binding commandment, though the revelation states that it was "adapted to the capacity of the weak and the weakest of all saints" (D&C 89:3). Compliance with its teachings was sporadic from the late 1830s until the early years of the twentieth century. The Church encouraged leaders to be an example to the people in abstaining from alcohol, tobacco, tea, and coffee; but no binding Church policy was articulated during this time.

The PROHIBITION movement, spearheaded by the Protestant Evangelical churches in America, focused on alcohol consumption as a political rather than a moral issue. The movement intensified the Church's interest in the Word of Wisdom. There is evidence that Church Presidents John Taylor, Joseph F. Smith, and Heber J. Grant wanted to promote adherence to the Word of Wisdom as a precondition for entering LDS temples or holding office in any Church organization; and indeed, by 1930 abstinence from the use of alcohol, tobacco, coffee, and tea had become an official requirement for those seeking temple recommends. While abstinence from these substances is now required for temple attendance and for holding priesthood offices or other Church callings, no other ecclesiastical sanctions are imposed on those who do not comply with the Word of Wisdom.

Other dietary aspects of the Word of Wisdom have not received the stress that the abstinence portions have. While some leaders, such as John A. Widtsoe, have emphasized the benefits of eating whole grains, no distinctive dietary practices have emerged that distinguish Mormons from non-Mormons, though the use of whole-grain cereals is often assumed to be higher among Latter-day Saints than other people.

With the appearance of cola drinks in the early 1900s, the Church was confronted with cold beverages containing caffeine, a harmful substance believed to make coffee and tea unacceptable. While no official Church position has been stated, leaders have counseled members to avoid caffeine and other addictive chemicals.

Church leaders universally caution against any use of such DRUGS as marijuana and cocaine and the abuse of prescription drugs. While none of these substances are mentioned specifically in the Word of Wisdom, the concept of the sanctity of the body and the deleterious effects of chemical substances on it have been emphasized as an extension of the Word of Wisdom.

Many of the health benefits associated with abstinence from the substances mentioned in the Word of Wisdom did not become clear until the latter part of the twentieth century. During World War I use of cigarettes among men became widespread, and during World War II, among women. The association of cigarette smoking with lung cancer was documented in the early 1950s, but official statements by scientific bodies accepting this relationship as causal did not occur until the mid-1960s. Since that time, many other diseases have been associated with cigarette smoking, including cancers of the oral cavity, larynx, esophagus, kidney, bladder, and pancreas; peptic ulcers; coronary heart disease; chronic bronchitis; infant mortality; and chronic obstructive airway disease.

Studies have found that Latter-day Saints have substantially lower risk for all of these illnesses (30–80 percent below that of non-Mormons living in Utah or in other areas of the United States) and that people who abstain from these substances are at much lower risk of these diseases than those who do not. Few health risks have been clearly identified with the use of tea and coffee, though some evidence suggests that those who abstain from coffee may be at lower risk for peptic ulcers, cancer of the pancreas, and coronary heart disease. Some studies estimate that those complying with the Word of Wisdom increase their life expectancy up to seven years.

BIBLIOGRAPHY

Alexander, Thomas G. *Mormonism in Transition*, pp. 258–71. Urbana, Ill., 1986.

Arrington, Leonard J. "An Economic Interpretation of the 'Word of Wisdom.'" *BYU Studies* 1 (Winter 1959):37–49.

Backman, Milton V., Jr. *The Heavens Resound: A History of the Latter-day Saints in Ohio 1830–1838*, pp. 234–36, 257–61. Salt Lake City, 1983.

Bush, Lester E., Jr. "The Word of Wisdom in Early Nineteenth-Century Perspective." *Dialogue* 14 (Autumn 1981):47–65.

———. "The Mormon Tradition." In *Caring and Curing: Health and Medicine in the Western Religious Traditions*, ed. R. Numbers and D. Amundsen, pp. 397–419. New York, 1986.

Enstrom, James E. "Cancer Mortality Among Mormons." *Cancer* 36 (1975):825–41.

———. "Health Practices and Cancer Mortality Among Active California Mormons." *Journal of the National Cancer Institute* 81 (1989):1807–1814.

Gardner, John W., and Joseph L. Lyon. "Cancer in Utah Mormon Men by Lay Priesthood Level." *American Journal of Epidemiology* 116 (1982):243–57.

———. "Cancer in Utah Mormon Women by Church Activity Level." *American Journal of Epidemiology* 116 (1982):258–65.

Lyon, Joseph L., et al. "Cancer Incidence in Mormons and Non-Mormons in Utah, 1966–1970." *New England Journal of Medicine* 294 (1976):129–38.

———, and Steven Nelson. "Mormon Health." *Dialogue* 12 (Fall 1979):84–96.

———; John W. Gardner; and Dee W. West. "Cancer Incidence in Mormons and Non-Mormons in Utah during 1967–1975." *Journal of the National Cancer Institute* 65 (1980):1055–61.

Peterson, Paul H. "An Historical Analysis of the Word of Wisdom." Master's thesis, Brigham Young University, 1972.

Widtsoe, John A., and Leah D. Widtsoe. *The Word of Wisdom: A Modern Interpretation*. Salt Lake City, 1937.

Woolley, F. Ross; Katharina L. Schuman; and Joseph L. Lyon. "Neonatal Mortality in Utah." *American Journal of Epidemiology* 116 (1982):541–46.

JOSEPH LYNN LYON

WORK, ROLE OF

The role of work, as it has been consistently explained in the scriptures and taught by The Church of Jesus Christ of Latter-day Saints, involves four principles: Work is a universal obligation; work enhances the quality of life on earth; daily work has eternal consequences; and work will continue in the eternities.

A UNIVERSAL AND LIFELONG OBLIGATION.   In the Church no individual who is able to work is excused from working. This principle refers to more than paid employment; it also means worthwhile activities that provide useful products or services for one's family and others.

The obligation to work was stated when the Lord commanded Adam and Eve to dress the Garden of Eden (Gen. 2:15) and was reemphasized later, when they were driven out. The ground was cursed for their ultimate benefit (Gen. 3:17–19), and work is viewed as a blessing and an opportunity: "God has blessed us with the privilege of working. When he said, 'Earn thy bread by the sweat of thy brow,' he gave [us] a blessing. Men and women have so accepted it. Too much leisure is dangerous. Work is a divine gift" (McKay, p. 4).

The Ten Commandments instruct, "Six days shalt thou labour" (Ex. 20:9). Other scriptures explain that life is to be a rhythm of work and worship (Ex. 31:15; Neh. 13:15–22).

Latter-day Saints do not view work as drudgery, as though its only purpose is to sustain life. Although the use of technological equipment and labor-saving devices is encouraged, their value lies in making work more efficient, not in eliminating it. Work is the natural lot of all people, and they are enjoined to be diligent in their labors (Prov. 6:6–8; 1 Thes. 4:11; 2 Thes. 3:10–15).

THE QUALITY OF LIFE.   Work is necessary for personal development and represents a major source of happiness and fulfillment. "Our Heavenly Father loves us so completely that he has given us a commandment to work. This is one of the keys to eternal life. He knows that we will learn more, grow more, achieve more, serve more, and benefit more from a life of industry than from a life of ease" (Hunter, p. 122).

Individuals are encouraged to work with a happy, cheerful attitude. "Learn to like your work. Learn to say, 'This is my work, my glory, not my doom'" (McKay, p. 4). Enthusiasm for labor is especially extolled in such LDS hymns as "Today, While the Sun Shines," "Improve the Shining Moments," "Let Us All Press On," "I Have Work Enough to Do," and "Put Your Shoulder to the Wheel."

Work can also serve as a rehabilitative or therapeutic activity. The apostle Paul directed, "Let him that stole steal no more: but rather let him labour, working with his hands" (Eph. 4:28). This application of work is consistent with modern work-therapy programs that have helped ex-convicts return to society, mental patients function more effectively, students improve their academic performance, the disabled obtain greater self-esteem, and drug abusers conquer their chemical dependencies.

ETERNAL CONSEQUENCES.   Work has lasting implications beyond the temporary reimbursement received in this life. Dedicated work helps to develop attributes of godliness: self-discipline, perseverance, accountability, and integrity. Idleness is condemned in the scriptures: "Cease to be idle" (D&C 88:124; 1 Tim. 5:8, 13; D&C 42:42; 60:13). The curse of idleness is not an arbitrary penalty imposed on those who use their time unproductively but a natural consequence of acting contrary to humanity's divine nature (Maxwell, p. 26). The final judgment, we are assured and warned, will be unto every one according to his work (e.g., Rev. 22:12).

WORK IN THE HEREAFTER.   Work will not cease with death. "Work with faith is a cardinal point of our theological doctrine and our future state—our heaven, is envisioned in terms of eternal progression through constant labor" (Richards, pp. 10–11; cf. Rev. 13:14; D&C 59:2). Detailed information about the nature of work in the hereafter has not been revealed. However, "what little information we have of a tactical nature suggests that we will be intelligently involved doing specific things which are tied to the eternal purposes of our Father in heaven" (Maxwell, p. 26; cf. Sill, p. 7).

The Latter-day Saint work ethic is similar to the Protestant work ethic regarding the central role of work in a devout life; however, the Latter-day Saint view maintains a strict distinction between work and worship. Although dedicated work builds character and is a form of service to God, it alone is not sufficient to express worship for God. No matter how much service humans render, they still remain "unprofitable servants" overwhelmingly blessed by God (Mosiah 2:21). Other sacred activities such as prayer; attending meetings; making and renewing covenants through baptism, the sacrament, and temple ordinances; and serving the needy are more direct and explicit forms of worship and are a ritual dimension of the LDS pattern of life.

Some measures in the Church are taken to keep the commandment to work from being misconstrued to encourage "workaholism," or a frantic compulsion to be constantly busy. Church members are encouraged to use judgment in how much they undertake and are counseled not to run faster than they have the strength (Eccl. 9:11; Mosiah 4:27; D&C 10:4).

The importance of work is to be balanced with other worthwhile pursuits. Members are exhorted to be anxiously engaged in a good cause (D&C 58:26–28), including fine arts, music, dance, and literature (D&C 88:118; 136:28). Brigham Young taught the need for a balance between physical and mental labor: "Some think too much, and should labor more, others labor too much, and should think more, and thus maintain an equilibrium between the mental and physical members of the individual; then you will enjoy health and vigor, will be active, and ready to discern truly, and judge quickly" (*JD* 3:248).

The Latter-day Saint work ethic was clearly evident during the settlement of the western United States. After the Mormon pioneers entered the Salt Lake Valley, they immediately began turning the desert into fertile farms and thriving cities. Their motto became "Industry," and their symbol, the beehive. During the first decade there, the Mormons colonized approximately ninety-six communities, and before the end of the century at least 500 more. Opinion surveys indicate that Latter-day Saints continue to accept the moral importance of work and take pride in craftsmanship.

[*See also* Occupational Status.]

BIBLIOGRAPHY

Arrington, Leonard J. *Great Basin Kingdom.* Lincoln, Neb., 1958.

Cherrington, David J. *The Work Ethic: Working Values and Values That Work.* New York, 1980.

Hunter, Howard W. "Prepare for Honorable Employment." *Ensign* 5 (Nov. 1975): 122–24.

Maxwell, Neal A. "I Have a Question." *Ensign* 6 (Aug. 1976):26.

McKay, David O. "Man Is That He Might Have Joy." *Church News* (Aug. 8, 1951):2, 4.

Nibley, Hugh W. "Work We Must, But the Lunch Is Free." In *CWHN* 9:201–251.

Richards, Stephen L. "The Gospel of Work." *IE* 43 (Jan. 1940):10–11, 60–61, 63.

Sill, Sterling W. "In the Sweat of Thy Face." *Church News* (May 8, 1965):7.

DAVID J. CHERRINGTON

WORLDLY, WORLDLINESS

Latter-day Saints use the term "world" to refer to the planet Earth as well as to the social conditions created by those who live carnal, sensuous, and lustful lives (*MD*, p. 847). Worldly refers to people whose thoughts and interests are engrossed in fleeting, temporal pursuits of mortality such as power, success, gain, or pleasure.

Jesus said, "My kingdom is not of this world" (John 18:36), and "I have overcome the world" (John 16:33). In endeavoring to follow his example, Latter-day Saints seek to overcome the world as he did by valuing spiritual wealth and eternal treasures above earthly goods and attainments.

The apostle Paul defined worldly pursuits as "adultery, fornication, uncleanness, lasciviousness, idolatry, witchcraft, hatred, variance, emulations, wrath, strife, seditions, heresies, envyings, murders, drunkenness, revellings, and such like: . . . they which do such things shall not inherit the kingdom of God" (Gal. 5:19–21). In contrast, the things of God or the fruits of the Spirit are "love, joy, peace, longsuffering, gentleness, goodness, faith, meekness, temperance" (Gal. 5:22–23).

Just as the Father sent Jesus into the world, the Savior sent his disciples into the world (John 17:18). Latter-day Saints, therefore, do not believe in asceticism—a withdrawal from the world in an effort to avoid worldliness and to obtain spirituality. Their commission is to be in the world but not of the world, to improve the quality of life on earth by such things or activities as rearing good children, pursuing education, expanding their knowledge of all truth, contributing to the well-being of members of their communities, and sharing the gospel with others. Through example and precept, they seek to encourage all people to put off worldliness and become spiritually reborn by obedience to the laws and ordinances of the gospel. In summary, LDS doctrine cautions that "Men drink damnation to their own souls except they humble themselves and become as little children, . . . putteth off the natural man and becometh a saint through the atonement of Christ the Lord" (Mosiah 3:18–19).

BIBLIOGRAPHY
Nibley, Hugh W. *Approaching Zion*. In *CWHN* 9. Salt Lake City, 1989.

C. RICHARD CHIDESTER

WORLD CONFERENCES ON RECORDS

Two World Conferences on Records have been sponsored by The Church of Jesus Christ of Latter-day Saints in Salt Lake City, Utah. In celebration of the Diamond Jubilee of the FAMILY HISTORY LIBRARY and to exhibit the newly constructed GRANITE MOUNTAIN RECORD VAULT, the GENEALOGICAL SOCIETY OF UTAH hosted the first world conference, August 5–8, 1969. The theme, "Records Protection in an Uncertain World," emphasized that, since no one organization can preserve all the valuable records of the world, each nation or society must preserve its own records from wear, deterioration, neglect, and natural or man-created disasters.

Sessions combined two types of meetings: records preservation, usage, and accessibility; and genealogical research. For the first time on a world scale, a conference brought together genealogists, archivists, demographers, and technical experts on microfilming and other methods of preserving records. Two hundred and eighty specialists in these fields presented 180 seminars during the four days to an audience of both amateurs and professionals from national and governmental bodies, private institutions and societies, and individuals from every state in the United States and forty-five nations.

The second World Conference on Records was held August 12–15, 1980. The theme, "Preserving Our Heritage," was stimulated by Alex Haley's 1976 book *Roots*. Much of the conference focused on gathering, preparing, and preserving personal and individual family histories—writing "the history of the heart"—in addition to factual genealogical data. The featured speaker, Alex Haley, said: "In all of us there is a hunger . . . to know who we are and where we come from." Attendance of 11,500 more than doubled that of the previous conference, including representatives from each of the United States and from fifty nations. Printed copies of the sessions of the conferences were made available at the Genealogical Society headquarters in Salt Lake City.

BIBLIOGRAPHY

Jolley, Joann. "The World Conference on Records—Writing the History of the Heart." *Ensign* 10 (Oct. 1980):72–75.
"The World Conference on Records." *IE* 72 (Jan. 1969):22–24.

DORIS BAYLY BROWER

WORLD RELIGIONS (NON-CHRISTIAN) AND MORMONISM

[*This entry consists of seven articles:*

Overview
Buddhism
Confucianism
Hinduism
Islam
Judaism
Shinto

The articles gathered under this title generally explain the relationships between Latter-day Saints and persons of other faiths, and illustrate differences and similarities in belief between non-Christian religions and the LDS religion. On the former subject, see also Interfaith Relationships: Jewish *and* Interfaith Relationships: Other.]

OVERVIEW

Latter-day Saints believe that God has inspired not only people of the Bible and the Book of Mormon, but other people as well, to carry out his purposes. Today God inspires not only Latter-day Saints but also founders, teachers, philosophers, and reformers of other Christian and non-Christian religions. Since LDS belief is grounded in a theistic biblical faith, it has been relatively easy for scholars and believers to perceive parallels between it and traditional Christianity, Judaism, and Islam. Now that the Church has become a global movement extending into Asia, comparisons between the gospel of Jesus Christ and the principal religions of India, China, Korea, and Japan are increasingly significant.

The gospel does not hold an adversarial relationship with other religions. Leaders of the Church have said that intolerance is a sign of weakness (R. Lindsay, "A Mormon View of Religious Tolerance," Address to the Anti-defamation League of B'nai B'rith, San Francisco, February 6, 1984). The LDS perspective is that "we claim the privilege of worshiping Almighty God according to the dictates of our own conscience, and allow all men the same privilege, let them worship how, where, or what they may" (A of F 11). The Church teaches that members must not only be kind and loving toward others but also respect their right to believe and worship as they choose.

George Albert Smith, eighth President of the Church, publicly advocated the official Church policy of friendship and TOLERANCE: "We have come not to take away from you the truth and virtue you possess. We have come not to find fault with you nor to criticize you. . . . We have come here as your brethren. . . . Keep all the good that you have, and let us bring to you more good, in order that you may be happier and in order that you may be prepared to enter into the presence of our Heavenly Father" (pp. 12–13).

On February 15, 1978 the First Presidency of the Church issued the following declaration:

> The great religious leaders of the world such as Mohammed, Confucius, and the Reformers, as well as philosophers including Socrates, Plato, and others, received a portion of God's light. Moral truths were given to them by God to enlighten whole nations and to bring a higher level of understanding to individuals. . . . Our message therefore is one of special love and concern for the eternal welfare of all men and women, regardless of religious belief, race, or nationality, knowing that we are truly brothers and sisters because we are sons and daughters of the same Eternal Father [Palmer, 1978].

In the words of Orson F. Whitney, an apostle, the gospel "embraces all truth, whether known or unknown. It incorporates all intelligence, both past and prospective. No righteous principle will ever be revealed, no truth can possibly be discovered, either in time or in eternity, that does not in some manner, directly or indirectly, pertain to the Gospel of Jesus Christ" (*Elders' Journal* 4, no. 2 [Oct. 15, 1906]:26). "If there is anything virtuous, lovely, or of good report or praiseworthy, we seek after these things" (A of F 13).

BIBLIOGRAPHY

Palmer, Spencer J. *The Expanding Church.* Statement of the First Presidency, Feb. 15, 1978, frontispiece. Salt Lake City, 1978.

——, and Roger R. Keller. *Religions of the World: A Latter-day Saint View.* Provo, Utah, 1989.

Smith, George Albert. *Sharing the Gospel with Others,* ed. Preston Nibley. Salt Lake City, 1948.

SPENCER J. PALMER

BUDDHISM

"Buddhism has been the most important religious force in Asia for nearly two thousand years. No other religion has affected the thought, culture, and politics of so many people. In aesthetics, architecture, dance, drama, handicrafts, literary arts, and music Buddhism has also been the single most important civilizing influence in the Eastern world" (Palmer and Keller, p. 49).

Siddhartha Gautama (563–483 B.C.), the founder of Buddhism, acknowledged no God, no soul, and no future life; he taught of the bliss of nirvana, which involves the extinction of ego and lust. Caught in the legacy of karma, one's life is bequeathed to another who falls heir to it—a continuation that is sometimes called "stream of consciousness," the "aggregates of character," or the "skandas." Consequently, the historical Buddha did not advocate worship or prayer, but practiced introspective meditation as a form of spiritual discipline.

The philosophy of Gautama (Gotama, in Pali), sometimes called Theravada Buddhism, with its emphasis upon the worthlessness of the physical body, of individuality, of this phenomenal mortal life, of faith in God, and of judgment, disagrees with LDS doctrine. In the restored gospel, mankind is the literal, personal offspring of God. It is a privilege to be born into mortality to gain a physical body, so that one can become more like the Heavenly Father, who is a personal, tangible being (cf. D&C 130:22). Self-fulfillment, not self-negation, is the purpose of earth life. Latter-day Saints seek to emulate Christ and, through the power of his divine atonement, to be personally exalted into the presence of God after death, and to become like him.

This is not to say that the gospel and Buddhism contradict one another in every way. The LDS religion, like Buddhism, advocates meditation, reverence, inspiration, and moderation. Latter-day Saints embrace elements similar to those of the Eightfold Middle Path, which advocate freedom from ill will and cruelty, and abstinence from lying, talebearing, harsh and vain thought, violence, killing, stealing, and sexual immorality.

Other dimensions of Buddhist doctrine and practice, in the schools of Mahayana Buddhism in northern Asia, are similar to LDS doctrine and practice. Both LDS belief and Mahayana Buddhism are theistic. The Bodhisattva ideal of benevolence and compassionate service, of helping others who cannot by themselves reach the highest realms of spirituality, is not only largely consistent with the vicarious sacrifice and redeeming love of Jesus Christ, but also is expressed in wide-ranging, loving service on behalf of the living and the dead carried out within Latter-day Saint temples.

BIBLIOGRAPHY
Palmer, Spencer J., and Roger R. Keller. *Religions of the World: A Latter-day Saint View*. Provo, Utah, 1989.

SPENCER J. PALMER

CONFUCIANISM

The Confucian focus upon moral example as the basis of harmony in society, government, and the universe is consistent with LDS views. However, Confucius was not interested in METAPHYSICS or theology; he did not advocate belief in God, nor did he talk about life after death. He was concerned with humans in their social setting.

Arguments that Confucianism is not a religion have often been answered by references to its sacred text. One could also point to the lives of millions who have sought to practice its teachings by honoring parents and deceased ancestors through acts of affection and piety in the home or through performances at tombs, shrines, and temples that convey spiritual belief as well as moral affirmations (Palmer, p. 16). For Latter-day Saints, morality is based upon the individual's relationship with God as an expression of one's faith in God and upon obedience to his will.

Confucian morality is generally expressed in social and cultural ways. Values of loyalty, virtue, respect, courtesy, learning, and love are preserved primarily through outward courtesies and formalities, including traditional family ceremonies. Filial piety is the ultimate virtue. It includes honoring the spirits of one's ancestors not only by observances at graves and family tombs but also by striving to achieve acclaim in learning, in the mastery of sacred texts, and in aesthetic arts such as music, poetry, and painting.

The Confucian quest for sagehood, for refinement and cultivation of the ideal human, has its counterpart in the Latter-day Saint quest for eternal life. Both the sage and the true Latter-day Saint personify the transforming power of righteous behavior. In LDS scripture it is sometimes referred to as putting off "the natural man" and becoming a saint, one characterized as being "submissive, meek, humble, patient, full of love, willing to submit to all things which the Lord seeth fit to inflict" (Mosiah 3:19).

Latter-day Saints and Confucians share a mutual concern for the salvation of the extended family. Though the focus differs, both carry out devotional ceremonies in sacred places on behalf of departed ancestors. In this respect, both the LDS Church and Confucianism may be called family-centered religions. Both place importance upon genealogical research, the preservation of family records, and the performance of vicarious holy ordinances on behalf of their dead. In both instances, there exists a commitment to the idea that the living can serve the needs of departed loved ones.

Church members believe that Elijah, the Old Testament prophet, personally appeared to Joseph Smith in the Kirtland Temple in 1836 and conferred priesthood keys, or authority, by means of which the hearts of children could turn to their ancestors and to the promises of salvation made to the fathers and the hearts of forebears could turn to their children (D&C 110:13–16), with the result that families and generations can be joined together "for time and for all eternity." Joseph Smith's remark concerning the dead "that they without us cannot be made perfect—neither can we without our dead be made perfect" (D&C 128:15; cf. Heb. 11:40) also resonates in the Confucian world.

BIBLIOGRAPHY
Palmer, Spencer J. *Confucian Rituals in Korea*. Berkeley, Calif., 1984.
———, and Roger R. Keller. *Religions of the World: A Latter-day Saint View*. Provo, Utah, 1989.

SPENCER J. PALMER

HINDUISM
Unlike the LDS Church, Hinduism has no founder, no central authority, no hierarchy, no uniformly explicated or applied moral standards. However, Hindus and Latter-day Saints share at least two fundamental beliefs—the continuing operation of irreversible cosmic law and the importance of pursuing ultimate union with the divine—though these principles may be understood differently.

Hinduism and the gospel of Jesus Christ differ in their perceptions of deity. In Hinduism there exist many gods, of thunder, drink, fire, sky, mountains, and the like, who are variously playful, capricious, vindictive, loving, and law-abiding. During the period of classical Hinduism, Brahma, Vishnu, and Shiva emerged to represent, respectively, the three primary functions of creation, preservation, and destruction. However, among the gods there is no generally recognized order.

For Latter-day Saints, God the Father, his son Jesus Christ, and the Holy Ghost form a tritheistic group of individuals of unified purpose and power, always systematic and ethical. The Father and the Son have bodies of flesh and bones, and the Holy Ghost is a personage of spirit (D&C 130:22). The physical world was organized by the Father, through the instrumentality of the Son, who is the only Savior of the world, having willingly submitted to the suffering in Gethsemane and to crucifixion as an atoning sacrifice so that humankind could be delivered from death and sin. Several ordinances of the Church are similitudes of the life, death, and redemption of Christ.

LDS belief and Hinduism both subscribe to a belief in an antemortal existence. Hindus believe that premortal experiences determine inequalities of earthly life, including the caste system. In LDS cosmology, eternal laws of cause and effect were applicable in the premortal existence, as they are for inhabitants of the current temporal world: "There is a law, irrevocably decreed in heaven before the foundations of this world, upon which all blessings are predicated—and when we obtain any blessing from God, it is by obedience to that law upon which it is predicated" (D&C 130:20–21). Valiant souls from the pre-earth life may be ordained to be leaders here (Abr. 3:23; cf. Jer. 1:4).

In Hindu terminology, the cosmic law of justice is called "karma." Hindus believe that individual spirits are reincarnated repeatedly on earth in accordance with the effects of karma. Those who have not yet merited release from this wheel of rebirth are in a state of negative karma. If they improve their deeds during the next incarnation, they can improve their karmic condition and may even gain freedom to reach Nirvana.

To Latter-day Saints, mortality is considered an extension and continuation of premortal performance in proving and preparing persons for exaltation in life after death. Humans are born only once on earth, and all mortal beings at birth are candidates for exaltation in the celestial kingdom. Hindus believe that the accumulated prebirth experiences have more consequence in determining one's future state than the actions of mortality. For Church members, birth is not an indication of failure to achieve release from the wheel of birth but rather a positive step forward along the path from premortal life to mortal life to immortality and eternal progression. In this connection, the fall of Adam was no accident. It was an essential event in the plan of reunion with God (cf. 2 Ne. 2:25).

At the philosophical level, Hinduism sees the phenomenal world as an illusion, but within the manifold appearances there is Brahman, the World Soul. Individual life is an invisible aspect of Universal Life. The ultimate object of all works, devotion, and knowledge is to gain release from egotistical lustful attachments to this physical world so as to achieve a state of peace that comes from identity with the impersonal Universal Soul, or Nirvana.

Gaining a conscious union with God is also a prime objective of LDS belief, although it is perceived differently. Jesus not only declared that he and his Father were one but also prayed that his disciples would likewise become one with them (John 10:30; 17:11), both in mind and will, as well as in heightened states of celestial consciousness, that is, to develop thoroughly Christlike and godlike qualities (D&C 35:2; 76:58; 1 Cor. 6:17; Heb. 2:11; Rom. 12:2). In purpose, power, and personality, and even in the glorification of the body, humankind can become perfect (Matt. 5:48; 3 Ne. 12:48). Unlike Hinduism, the LDS faith does not seek the relinquishment of individuality. Free agency and personal responsibility are not impaired but ultimately honored and enhanced.

BIBLIOGRAPHY
Palmer, Spencer J., and Roger R. Keller. *Religions of the World: A Latter-day Saint View*. Provo, Utah, 1989.

SPENCER J. PALMER

ISLAM

Interest in the Church's associations with Islam has appeared in literary comparisons, within LDS teachings, and through historical contacts. The initial comparison was perhaps made in 1834, when the anti-Mormon Pastor E. D. Howe suggested that Joseph Smith matched Muhammad's "ignorance and stupidity," thereby coining an analogy that experienced polemical and "scientific" phases. The polemical phase entailed American Protestants vilifying the Church and its prophet by likening them to Islam and Muhammad, long presumed fraudulent by Christians. This disputative tactic had been used against Protestants during the Counter-Reformation, and emphasized such allegations as sensuality, violence, and deception. These polemics yielded a literary corpus—for example, "The Yankee Mahomet" and books by Joseph Willing and Bruce Kinney. The scientific phase began when the explorer and Arabist Richard Francis Burton visited Utah in 1860 and rephrased in academic discourse the analogy, subsequently elaborated by David Margoliouth, Eduard Meyer, Hans Thimme, and Georges Bousquet. These Orientalists and sociologists of religion apparently felt they could study fully documented Mormonism as a proxy for underdocumented Islam.

The Church's doctrinal posture toward Islam has also gone through phases. Islam is not mentioned in either the Book of Mormon or the Doctrine and Covenants. Yet articles in *Times and Seasons* suggest that some LDS spokesmen initially echoed medieval Christian views of Islam as fanatical heresy (Editorial, 3 [15 Apr. 1842]; "Last Hour of the False Prophet," 5 [Apr. 1, 1844]; "Mahometanism," 6 [Jan. 15, 1845]). But speeches by apostles George A. Smith and Parley P. Pratt in 1855 evoked more positive traditional interpretations: that Islam, fulfilling biblical promises made to Ishmael (Gen. 21), was divinely instigated to "scourge" apostate Christianity and to curb idolatry. Perhaps unknowingly paraphrasing Muhammad ibn Abd al-Wahhab (d. 1792), George A. Smith applied historical judgment to Islam's experience: "As they abode in the teachings which Mahomet gave them, . . . they were united and prospered; but when they ceased to do this, they lost their power and influence" (pp. 34–35). More recently, perhaps in the context of the Church's growth to global dimensions, Muslim cultures have figured prominently in dicta—such as those by President Spencer W. Kimball and Elders Howard W. Hunter, Bruce R. McConkie, and Carlos E. Asay—stressing that God is no respecter of persons on grounds of race or color. In the "Easter Message" of February 15, 1978, the LDS First Presidency wrote that Muhammad and other nonbiblical religious leaders and philosophers "received a portion of God's light.

Moral truths were given to them by God to enlighten whole nations." On balance, Mormon teachings thus seem to have cast Islam in a positive historical role.

Latter-day Saints' historical contacts with Islam include missions in countries with Muslim populations. Some LDS proselytizers have expressed sentiments articulated earlier by such Catholic and Protestant missionaries as Cardinal Lavigerie and Samuel Zwemer: that Islam's own doctrinal claims (e.g., God is one not three; Jesus was a prophet, not God's son; apostates from Islam merit death), Islamic society's holistic character, and the sad legacy of Muslim–Christian relations make difficult the converting of Muslims to Christianity. Since World War II many LDS professionals have lived in Muslim communities. Some have chronicled their experience in terms that are human (Marion Miller) or historical-theological (Arthur Wallace). At least one has engaged in radical syncretism (Ibn Yusuf/Lloyd Miller; see Green, 1983). Governments of Islamic countries, most of which ban proselytizing, such as Egypt and Saudi Arabia, have allowed discreet worship by LDS families. In 1989 Jordan permitted the establishment of an LDS cultural center in Amman.

BIBLIOGRAPHY
For general reviews of the literature, see A. H. Green, "Joseph Smith as an American Muhammad," *Dialogue* 6 (Spring 1971):46–58; and "The Muhammad-Joseph Smith Comparison: Subjective Metaphor or a Sociology of Prophethood," in *Mormons and Muslims*, ed. Spencer J. Palmer, Provo, Utah, 1983. This latter volume constitutes a collection of essays on the subject. For recent authoritative LDS statements, see Spencer W. Kimball, "The Uttermost Parts of the Earth," *Ensign* 9 (July 1979):2–9; and Howard W. Hunter, "All Are Alike Unto God," *BYU Devotional Speeches*, Provo, Utah, 1979, pp. 32–36.

ARNOLD H. GREEN

JUDAISM

The views of The Church of Jesus Christ of Latter-day Saints and its members toward Jews and Judaism have been shaped chiefly by LDS teachings and by historical contacts with Jewish communities. These teachings include regarding the Jews as an ancient covenant people with a prophesied role in the contemporary gathering of Israel and in events of the last days, and the contacts include educational activities in Israel and LDS proselytizing efforts outside of Israel.

Latter-day Saints share some traditional Christian positions toward Judaism, such as acknowledging debts for ethical foundations and religious terminology. Moreover, they have adopted stances expressed in Paul's mildly universalistic writings: Bible-era Judaism, based on the law of Moses and embodying the Old Testament or covenant, was essentially "fulfilled" in Jesus Christ (cf. 3 Ne. 15:4–8), so Christianity became the New Covenant and therefore spiritual "Israel." However, they have tended not to share the anti-Semitic postures of some Christian eras or groupings. Reflecting a more positive view, the Book of Mormon contains such passages as "Ye shall no longer hiss, nor spurn, nor make game of the Jews, . . . for behold, the Lord remembereth his covenant unto them" (3 Ne. 29:8), and President Heber J. Grant stated, "There should be no ill-will . . . in the heart of any true Latter-day Saint, toward the Jewish people" (*GS*, p. 147).

Mormons consider themselves a latter-day covenant people, the divinely restored New Testament Church. In this light, they have interpreted literally the Lord's mandate to them to regather Israel. While seeing historical judgment in Assyrian, Babylonian, and Roman treatment of biblical peoples, they have viewed the "scattering" as having beneficially diffused the "blood of Israel" worldwide. As a result, the Prophet Joseph Smith said that the Church believes in the "literal gathering of Israel" (A of F 10). This is done principally by missionary work searching for both biological and spiritual "Israelites" among the Gentile nations.

In LDS eschatology, the first Israelite tribe thus being gathered is Ephraim, with which most Latter-day Saints are identified through patriarchal blessings. To this "Semitic identification" has been attributed the substitution of Judeophilia for anti-Semitism among Mormons (Mauss). Indeed, LDS doctrine has envisaged a partnership both in promulgating scripture—in Ezekiel 37:16, Latter-day Saints find allusions to the Bible and Book of Mormon—and in erecting millennial capitals: Ephraim will build the New Jerusalem in an American Zion, Jews ("Judah") will gather in "the land of their fathers" (3 Ne. 20:29) to rebuild (old) Jerusalem, a prominent theme in the Book of Mormon (see 2 Ne. 6, 9–10, 29; Ether 13) and the Doctrine and Covenants (sections 39, 42, 45, 110, 133). Like several post-Reformation evangelical groups, Latter-day Saints have anticipated a return of Jews to Palestine as part of Israel's gathering. Indeed, the Prophet Joseph Smith sent Orson Hyde, an apostle, to Jerusalem, where in October 1841 he dedicated the land and prayed "for the gathering together of Judah's scattered remnants" (*HC* 4:456). On grounds that "the first shall be last," Brigham Young said that the conversion of the Jews would not occur before Christ's second coming (Green; cf. Ether 13:12). Yet Palestine was subsequently rededicated for the Jews' return by several apostles in the Church: George A. Smith (1873), Francis M. Lyman (1902), James E. Talmage (1921), David O. McKay (1930), and John A. Widtsoe (1933).

The creation by modern Zionism (secular Jewish nationalism) of a Jewish community and then a state in Palestine tested LDS doctrine's equating the Jews' "return" with Israel's "gathering" (i.e., conversion, but in different locations). While Rabbi Abraham Kook's disciples viewed Zionism's success from Jewish eschatalogical perspectives, some Latter-day Saints began regarding it from LDS perspectives: a secular preparatory stage for the messianic era. A latter-day apostle, LeGrand Richards, and some others in effect identified Zionism and the State of Israel as the expected "return," the physical prelude to the spiritual "gathering." Others, such as Elder Bruce R. McConkie, wrote that the Zionist ingathering was not that "of which the scriptures speak. . . . It does not fulfill the ancient promises." He saw it as a "gathering of the unconverted" but "nonetheless part of the divine plan" (*Millennial Messiah*, Salt Lake City, 1982, p. 229).

Pre–World War I contacts with Jewish communities were apparently influenced by Brigham Young's dictum. Jews immigrated into Utah after 1864, aligning politically with non-LDS "Gentiles." Yet they related well to the LDS majority, which did not proselytize them. Indeed, to the earliest Jewish settlers in Utah, the LDS Church provided meeting places for services and donated land for a cemetery. Utahans have also elected several Jews to public office, including a judge, state legislators, and a governor (see Brooks, 1973).

An LDS Near East mission (from 1884) was based temporarily at Haifa, where a cemetery contains graves of missionaries and German converts. Teaching mostly Armenians and German colonists, this mission ignored the longtime resident Jews of the Old Yishuv and had few contacts with new Zionist immigrants. After World War I some LDS leaders felt impressed to begin "gathering" Jews. New York Mission President (1922–1927) B. H. Roberts wrote pamphlets later consolidated into *Rasha The Jew*, Mormonism's first exposition directed at Jews. In this same vein, Elder LeGrand Richards composed *Israel! Do You Know?* and then received permission to launch experimental "Jewish missions," the largest being in Los Angeles. This and smaller Jewish missions (Salt Lake City; Ogden; San Francisco; Portland, Oreg.; New York; Washington, D.C.) were disbanded in 1959, when the First Presidency directed that Jewish communities not be singled out for proselytizing.

Noteworthy interaction has accompanied Brigham Young University's foreign study program in Jerusalem (begun 1968), based first at a hotel and then at a kibbutz. Seeking a permanent facility, BYU leaders were granted a location on Mount Scopus by Jerusalem's municipal authorities. Construction began in 1984 on the Jerusalem Center for Near Eastern Studies and, because it was such a prominent facility on such a choice site, drew opposition; ultra-Orthodox Jews, suspecting a "missionary center" under academic cover, warned of "spiritual holocaust." However, anti-Mormon campaigns failed to halt construction of the center, partly because U.S. congressmen and Jewish leaders, as well as Israeli liberals, defended it. The controversy reached Israel's Knesset, which obliged BYU to strengthen its nonproselytizing pledge. This contest was linked to the larger debate between Israel's secularists, who valued pluralism, and its militant Orthodox, who feared a new alien presence.

LDS contacts with Judaism have led to an exchange of converts. Salt Lake's synagogue Kol Ami has been attended by some ex-Mormons. Perhaps a few hundred Jews have become Latter-day Saints. Like Evangelical Jews, most have continued to emphasize their Jewishness, and fellow Mormons have welcomed them and considered them "of Judah." Convert memoirs have appeared; for honesty and literary quality probably none surpasses Herbert Rona's *Peace to a Jew*. Jewish Mormons formed B'nai Shalom in 1967 to function as a support group and to facilitate genealogical research.

BIBLIOGRAPHY
For Mormon activities in Palestine/Israel, see Steven W. Baldridge and Marilyn Rona, *Grafting In: A History of the Latter-day Saints in the Holy Land*, Salt Lake

City, 1989. On LDS attitudes and behavior toward Jews, see Herbert Rona, *Peace to a Jew*, New York, 1952; Armand L. Mauss, "Mormon Semitism and Anti-Semitism," *Sociological Analysis*, 29 (Spring 1968):11–27; Arnold H. Green, "A Survey of LDS Proselyting Efforts to the Jewish People," *BYU Studies* 8 (1968):427–43; and Juanita Brooks, *History of the Jews in Utah and Idaho*, Salt Lake City, 1973. For theological dimensions, see Truman G. Madsen, ed., *Reflections on Mormonism: Judeo-Christian Parallels*, Provo, Utah, 1978.

ARNOLD H. GREEN

SHINTO

Shinto, the earliest and largest native religion of Japan, has no known founder, no sacred scriptures, no systematized philosophy, no set of moral laws, no struggle between good and evil, no eschatology or life after death, no ecclesiastical organization. Shinto is "the way of the gods." It is folkways and spiritual feeling toward the awesomeness, the purity, the beauty of unspoiled nature.

In the Japanese view, the ever-present powers and spirits within nature are the *kami*, or gods, but they are neither transcendent nor omnipotent. Shinto has a rich mythology. Its luxuriant polytheism is dominated by Amaterasu, the goddess of the Sun, and by her brother Susano, who is most often frivolous and rude.

The LDS Church, on the other hand, has a founder, a set of sacred scriptures, a philosophical basis, a declared body of ethics and doctrine, and a structured church organization, and accepts a tritheistic Godhead through obedience to whom mankind can overcome the evils of this world. The Father, Son, and Holy Ghost are the supreme Godhead, perfect, tangible beings whose light and love emanate from their presence "to fill the immensity of space" (D&C 88:12; cf. 130:22).

Latter-day Saints believe that God's work and glory are to "bring to pass the immortality and eternal life of man" (Moses 1:39). But Shinto is concerned with the here and now. It expresses a "joyful acceptance of life and a feeling of closeness to nature" (Reischaur, in D.B. Picken, *Shinto: Japan's Spiritual Roots*, Tokyo, 1980, pp. 6–7).

No counterpart to the central tenet of LDS faith—the crucifixion and atonement of Christ—exists in Shinto. While the LDS Church and many other world religions concentrate on the theology of death and sin, the importance of holy writ, and the responsibilities of parenting and church service, Shinto values and attitudes are transmitted through festive celebrations of the powers within mountains, waterfalls, trees, and other aspects of nature.

BIBLIOGRAPHY
Palmer, Spencer J., and Roger R. Keller. *Religions of the World: A Latter-day Saint View*. Provo, Utah, 1989.

SPENCER J. PALMER

INDEX

72. *See also* Social Services,
LDS
LDS Student Association (LDSSA),
258, 260, 275–76
LDS University, 4
LDS University Museum, 355
Leach, Robert E., 257
Leadership abilities, curriculum on
development of, 135
Lee, Harold B.: on curriculum,
137; missionary policies of,
156; as chairman, 320; tours
studio, 348; as Scout, 450; on
nature of women, 573
Lee, Rex E., 52
"Let Us All Press On," 578
Libraries and archives, 137,
277–79, 431. *See also* Family
History Library
Life, prolonging, 411–12
Lifestyle, 279–81, 334–35. *See
also* Community
Light-mindedness, 281–82. *See
also* Humor
Lincoln, Abraham, 558–59
Lindsay, Richard P., 416
Linn, William, 18
Lion House, 30, 70, 354, 485–86.
See also Beehive House
Literature, Mormon writers of,
282–92; drama, 283–84; novels,
284–88; personal essays,
288–89; poetry, 290–92; short
stories, 292–97; the Pioneer
period, 486–87. *See also* Dead
Sea scrolls; Folklore
Litigation, 272–73
Lives of Female Mormons, 340
Logan High School, 48
Logan Temple, 29
London, Jack, 340
Longhurst, John, 360

Los Angeles Temple, 115
Lotteries. *See* Gambling
Love Story of a Mormon, 338
Lund, Anthony C., 342
Luther, Martin, 412–13, 415, 428
Lyceums, 483
Lyman, Francis M., 593
Lyman, Richard R., 48, 442
Lyne, Thomas A., 283

Madsen, Arch L., 46, 61
Maeser, Karl G.: as superintendent
of schools, 96; directs Brigham
Young Academy, 51–52,
178–79; directs Salt Lake Stake
Academy, 274; receives gift,
425
Magazines, Church, 45, 137
Magdalene, Mary, 171
Magic, 298–99. *See also* Satanism
Major, William W., 32, 486
Man, origin of, 191–92, 447, 512
Man's Search for Happiness, 193,
349
Management, Marriott School of,
56
Manchester Hymnal, 249
Manifesto of 1890: pacifies
government, 20–21, 93, 559;
political history of, 383; social
integration and, 488; woman
suffrage and, 565
Manti Temple, 29
Marcus, Louis, 265
Margetts, Linda, 360
Margoliouth, David, 590
Marijuana, 479
Marriage, 299–307; Catholic and
LDS view of, 76; effects of
dating and courtship on,
143–44; is ordained of God,
195; eternal, 195–96, 304–7;

Friendswood Public Library
416 So. Friendswood Drive
Friendswood, TX 77546-3952